The process of learning

The Process of Learning

Third edition

John B Biggs

Phillip J Moore

Prentice Hall

New York London Toronto Sydney Tokyo Singapore

Acquisitions Editor: Joy Whitton
Production Editors: Fiona Henderson & Fiona Marcar
Cover design: The Modern Art Production Group,
            Melbourne, VIC.
Typesetter: Kim Webber, Wyong, N.S.W
Printed in Australia by McPherson's Printing Group

    5 97
ISBN 0 7248 1003 X

National Library of Australia
Cataloguing-in-Publication Data

Biggs, J. B. (John Burville)
  The process of learning.

  3rd ed.
  Bibliography.
  Includes index.
  ISBN 0 7248 1003 X.

  1. Learning, Psychology of. 2. Educational psychology
  I. Moore, Phillip John. II. Title.

370.1523

Prentice Hall, Inc., *Englewood Cliffs, New Jersey*
Prentice Hall Canada, Inc., *Toronto*
Prentice Hall Hispanoamericana, SA, *Mexico*
Prentice Hall of India Private Ltd, *New Delhi*
Prentice Hall International, Inc., *London*
Prentice Hall of Japan, Inc., *Tokyo*
Prentice Hall of Southeast Asia Pty Ltd, *Singapore*
Editora Prentice Hall do Brasil Ltda, *Rio de Janeiro*

 PRENTICE HALL

A division of Simon & Schuster

CONTENTS

Preface   vii

Introduction   ix

PART 1: OVERVIEW   1

Chapter 1   Everyday and school learning   3

PART 2: THE DEVELOPING STUDENT   29

Chapter 2   Cognitive development over the years   31

Chapter 3   The development of understanding   65

Chapter 4   Moral and social development   89

Chapter 5   Culture, language and multiculturalism   115

Chapter 6   Intelligence and the IQ   147

Chapter 7   Exceptional children and their needs   173

PART 3: COGNITIVE AND MOTIVATIONAL PROCESSES   201

Chapter 8   Learning and memory   203

Chapter 9   Learning and personality   235

Chapter 10   Why students are motivated   255

Chapter 11   How students are motivated   279

PART 4: METACOGNITIVE PROCESSES   303

Chapter 12   How students approach their learning   305

Chapter 13   Learning and handling text   337

PART 5: THE OUTCOMES OF LEARNING   375

Chapter 14   Learning and its evaluation   377

Chapter 15   Techniques of assessing learning   405

PART 6: TEACHING AND LEARNING   443

Chapter 16   Teaching for better learning   445

Chapter 17   Learning about better teaching   483

Glossary   521

References   535

Author Index   569

Subject Index   577

PREFACE

Educational psychology is an essential part of teacher education. As a foundation discipline of education, it is important for teachers to understand in its own right. But more importantly educational psychology helps to provide a stabilising structure. The modern classroom is a busy place, requiring on average a non-trivial decision every two minutes (see Chapter 17). Teachers need a conceptual framework to make that complexity more manageable.

Unfortunately, the link between educational psychology and what happens in classrooms is not always clear to teacher education students. Psychology doesn't *prescribe* what classroom teachers do; events move too fast for that. What it does do is provide you with a way of thinking, an outlook, that brings consistency to your decisions, in line with the body of professional knowledge that validates teaching as a profession. Tradition and 'craft knowledge' are important in education, but we have moved from the position where these are the only bases on which teaching expertise is built.

This third edition is different from the first and second in several ways, the most obvious being that the original coauthor, Ross Telfer, has gone on to literally higher things; he is now Australia's first Professor of Aviation at the University of Newcastle. We wish him all the very best in this exciting new venture. His place has been taken by Phil Moore, Associate Professor of Education at the University of Newcastle. Despite these changes, the book is definitely a third edition of *Process of Learning* (first edition, 1981; second edition, 1987), not the first edition of a brand new text.

As in the previous editions, we have wherever possible used Australian sources and references. We believe it is important that teachers realise that there is a wealth of Australian research which can be drawn upon to improve the quality of education. Actually, we got a bit of stick for this in the last edition, with one colleague pointing out we shouldn't be 'parochial'; good research and quality ideas are universal and should not be compromised. You can't win them all. Let's just say we have used Australian research *without* compromising quality.

We should mention some differences to the second (1987) edition:

- The distinction between the basic principles being discussed (in Section A) and the applications to educational practice (in Section B) no longer applies. We still see the connection between theory and practice as extremely important but in the spirit of current thinking, we have wherever possible 'situated' the theory in the context as we discuss it.
- The 'learning activities' at the end of each chapter are meant to further 'situate' learning. The activities are designed for use in the educational psychology classroom (or in

individual study) and are based on assumptions about deep learning that permeate this edition: a sound knowledge base, interaction with others and active learner involvement. The activities vary, with some extensively using the text and others requiring research well beyond the material presented.

- The theoretical position is clearer. The 1987 edition introduced ideas from the ongoing research in metacognition, student learning and the qualitative/ethnographic strand. The 1993 edition takes this line much further. More than 200 new references have been incorporated and we have striven to build these into the text, sharpening and updating these important directions, which form three thrusts: students *construct* their knowledge, they do not absorb it; their learning takes place in a *context;* and student, teacher and context form a balanced *system.*

- But never fear! The thrust is intentionally practical and the overall structure is simpler.

     As the psychologist Kurt Lewin said many years ago: 'There's nothing so practical as a good theory'.

We have tried to use non-sexist and non-racist language throughout: 'she' and 'he' are used sparingly and then only for good communicative reason. Thus, too, we have used the terms 'Aboriginal' and 'aborigine' when referring to the 'indigenous people of Australia', the preferred term of the Office of Aboriginal Affairs, also in the interests of communication. (We are told the term 'Koori' refers to N.S.W. tribes only.)

We are grateful to many people for their assistance in producing this book. Formal acknowledgment of those firms and individuals for permission to reproduce previously published text and artwork is given in the text. Here we would like to express our sincere thanks to Patricia Aslen, Karen Allum and colleagues, Lorna Chan, John Kirby and Jill Scevak for their suggestions and insightful comments, Mary Stroud and Fanny Wong for their meticulous typing and assistance and Ken Scott for his photographic expertise.

Finally, we express our appreciation to the editorial staff of Prentice Hall of Australia, in particular Joy Whitton and Fiona Marcar.

John Biggs
Phil Moore

INTRODUCTION

The book is divided into six main parts.

Part 1: Everyday and school learning
Chapter 1 examines the reasons why schools exist and why they change the nature of learning from the spontaneous and (mostly) pleasant activity it is in everyday contexts to something that needs a complex superstructure, teachers, and educational psychology textbooks.

Part 2: The developing student
Chapters 2–7 each deal with aspects of the student as an individual and as a member of society. We start in Chapter 2 with cognitive development, focusing on the question: 'What develops with age?' We all know that kids change in their thinking from infancy to adolescence and here we try to convey the essential features of those changes, which appear to occur in stages.

We also know that kids become better at doing things, as outlined in Chapter 3. They not only go through stages in their thinking, but they learn particular things and become more expert at each stage. One area in which they show marked differences between what they learn spontaneously and what they are supposed to learn in school is how they explain natural phenomena.

Kids develop socially as well as cognitively. Chapter 4 shows how they develop progressively more sophisticated ideas of right and wrong, and how people should behave towards each other. Chapter 5 shifts the focus to society, dealing with minorities and such issues as gender, ethnicity and age.

Chapters 6 and 7 deal with students' abilities, once thought to be the most important contribution psychology had to make to educational practice. This is not how modern educators see their role, however. They aim to bring out the potential of all students, not just to educate towards the goal of academic success, which is the easy prerogative of the bright. Chapter 6 deals with theories of intelligence and intelligence measurement. Chapter 7 looks at provision for special needs at both ends of the abilities spectrum— creativity and giftedness on the one hand and children with learning difficulties on the other.

Part 3: Cognitive and motivational processes
Education involves engaging cognitive, motivational and metacognitive processes in students. Chapter 8 deals with handling or processing information from the environment: attending to important information, learning and memorising it, and recalling it on cue. Chapter 9 deals with a 'softer' side of information processing and how arousal and anxiety can influence our thinking.

Motivation is also a cognitive process in that our motives steer and give direction to our thinking. Chapters 10 and 11 deal with the reasons people have for learning. Having already established that teachers see motivation as their single biggest problem, we look at the common reasons people have for learning and how action is related to the probability of success.

Part 4: Metacognitive processes

'Metacognitive' processes, briefly discussed in the contexts of conditional knowledge and self-management, are dealt with in Chapters 12 and 13. Chapter 12 deals with metacognition in general. Systematic approaches to learning—the surface, deep and achieving approaches—are products of various levels of metacognitive processes and make the difference between handling a task well or badly. In this chapter the nature of conditional knowledge is expanded and we show how students use such knowledge in working out their strategies for handling particular tasks, except the basic tasks of reading and writing which deserve a chapter on their own and a fancy phrase to describe them. They get both in Chapter 13, 'text processing', which means not only learning to read and to write, but reading and writing to learn.

Part 5: Outcomes of learning and their assessment

Chapter 14 examines the conceptual basis for assessment: how we need to think about learning in order to think about assessing learning. Chapter 15 deals with some of the more important techniques for assessing learning and how they fit into the conceptual framework discussed in Chapter 14.

Part 6: Teaching and learning

The previous chapters are concerned with espoused theory. What remains is to put them together to show how espoused theory and theory-in-practice can be combined effectively to (a) enhance learning and (b) enhance teaching. In theory these should be the same thing, but in practice they are not. Chapter 16 deals with relationships between teaching, process and product, with particular emphasis on those situations that are 'learning-rich'.

Chapter 17 deals with you, the teacher, as the joint product of teacher education, espoused theory and theory-in-practice. What makes the expert teacher? We look at what the research says about this, with particular reference to the bane of new teachers: classroom management.

May your knowledge about expert teaching be declarative this year, procedural next year, and conditional the year after.

PART 1

OVERVIEW

EVERYDAY AND SCHOOL LEARNING

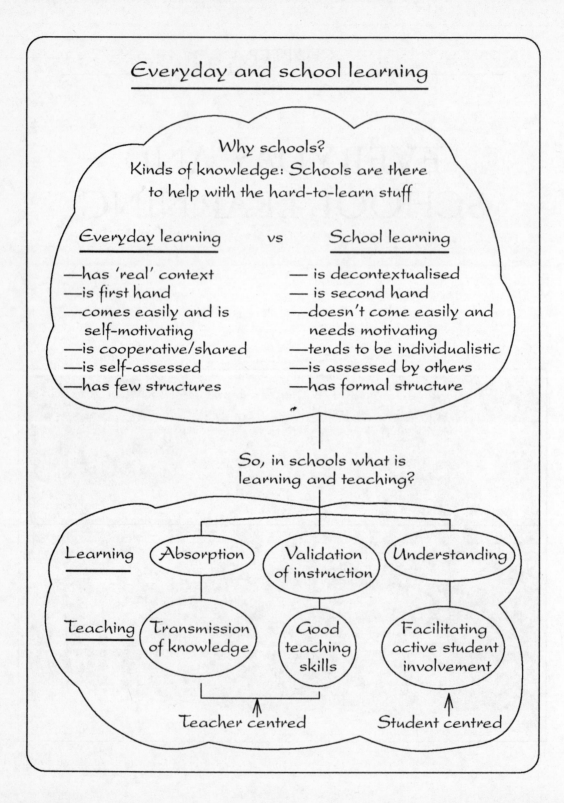

Everyday and school learning

Why schools?
Kinds of knowledge: Schools are there
to help with the hard-to-learn stuff

Everyday learning   vs   School learning

—has 'real' context   — is decontextualised
—is first hand   — is second hand
—comes easily and is   —doesn't come easily and
  self-motivating   needs motivating
—is cooperative/shared   —tends to be individualistic
—is self-assessed   —is assessed by others
—has few structures   —has formal structure

So, in schools what is
learning and teaching?

Learning   (Absorption)   (Validation   (Understanding)
                              of instruction)

Teaching (Transmission   (Good   (Facilitating
            of knowledge)   teaching   active student
                              skills)   involvement)

Teacher centred   Student centred

EVERYDAY AND SCHOOL LEARNING

In this chapter, you will find out:

- why we have schools;
- how learning in schools differs from everyday learning;
- why some kinds of knowledge are easier to learn than other kinds;
- what declarative, procedural, and conditional knowledge are;
- what common conceptions exist about learning and about teaching.

Why schools?

Bob was not a good student at school. His father, a noncommissioned officer in the armed services, was transferred from base to base so many times that, by the time Bob was 13, he had attended five primary schools and two high schools. He was reading at an age 9 level, when he read at all, which was as little as he possibly could.

When Bob turned 16, he'd had enough. He quit school and being semi-literate in Parramatta in 1985 meant the dole. His one dream, now remote, was to own a hot-rod. He hung around wreckers' yards, mainly out of his interest in cars, although he did earn a few dollars on the side by helping out now and then. He began to learn quite a bit about how cars were put together and the names of the parts.

One day a battered HT was towed in: motor OK, chassis OK, bodywork shot to bits. The yard manager saw him eyeing it. 'Two-fifty to you, Bob. As is. Cost ya a bit to get it on the road but.'

He not only had the $250, he had the time. And the local library had the right auto-motive manuals. In 6 months he rebuilt the car from scratch, with cheap but good parts from his mate the wrecker, teaching himself (at first with painful slowness) from the manual the finer points about polishing heads and ports and about high lift cams: the sort of stuff you don't learn in wreckers' yards. He took out subscriptions to half a dozen mag-azines and read them from cover to cover, skipping nothing, comprehending (almost) everything. He is, in 1992, a skilled mechanic, in great demand by the customers at the garage where he now works.

A simple little success story, but a true one. Bob was labelled by his teachers and himself as a slow learner. He had spent 10 years in school and had emerged barely able to use the most important skill the school is charged to teach, reading from text, which many others learn to do in a fraction of the time it took him. But he wasn't dumb. He had taught himself to do what those other fast readers would have taken years to do at the tech.

Now consider this. Seligman (1970) tells us that he once ate some sauce bearnaise in a restaurant and shortly afterwards was violently ill. He could not eat sauce bearnaise for some considerable time afterwards, despite the fact that he knew that the cause of the illness was gastro-enteritis. Seligman next pondered the 'Grandad' treatment for juvenile drinking, in vogue in the Appalachians. Gramps and grandson sit eyeball to eyeball across the kitchen table with a bottle of sour-mash whiskey between them. Sonny is to match Grandad, tumbler for tumbler. By the time the bottle is empty, Sonny will not drink again for many years. The ploy is universal. Aboriginal people in the north-west of New South Wales seem to have dealt with smoking in a similar manner (see Box 1.1).

Box 1.1   *Learning (the hard way)!*

… We used to go on our own and make our own little fire at night to play around. We were playing one night and all decided to have a smoke so got some brown paper and bark of the pine tree and sitting around talking never noticed Dad coming, nearly done a double take when he spoke behind us. 'Oh yous want to smoke' and goes over and gets his tin of Log Cabin. Makes me, Billy and Ethel and Archie a cigarette each and sat down with us and made us smoke it. I was sick, sweat was pouring off me, crying too but he wouldn't let us stop until we said we wouldn't smoke again and so I haven't either. Our eyes and noses were running and he just sat there with a big long switch in his hand, the old stinker.

Jean Hamilton (1989, 53).

Vomit was to Seligman's cerebrations what Newton's bruised skull was to his. Some physical unpleasantness sparked a new train of thought: in Newton's case it was about gravity, in Seligman's about why some things are learned rapidly and easily while others are not. And, as our story of Bob shows, some things are learned slowly and with much difficulty under some conditions, and the same things quite easily, under different conditions. Well, what things are learned rapidly? What are learned slowly? What conditions facilitate learning? What conditions inhibit learning?

And given Bob's experience, why schools?

Preparedness for learning

Seligman's reasoning followed the line that, as there is considerable survival value in instantly learning to avoid foods that make you ill, we learn things that do have survival value more easily than things that do not. How could that be? Because we are biologically prepared, probably through natural selection, to learn quickly and easily those things that are related to our survival. You can see this by looking at Table 1.1, which lists some of the things that are particularly easy to learn ('prepared' learnings, list A) and particularly difficult to learn ('unprepared' learnings, list B).

What else distinguishes the easy-to-learn list A from list B? The prepared learnings are *situated*; they are learned in a particular context and involve direct action by us. Knowledge is a 'co-production' of an activity and its situation (Brown, Collins & Duguid 1989); that is, you learn about something in its particular context and it is this context that gives your knowledge life. Knowledge out of context is much more difficult to learn. For example, learning to use words by studying their meanings from definitions in a dictionary is far harder than learning words in context, as young children do.

Table 1.1 *Learnings for which we are prepared and unprepared*

A Prepared learnings

Learning to avoid certain foods
Learning to walk
Learning to talk
Learning to read emotions from facial and bodily gestures: recognising friendliness, hostility, fear, love
Learning to imitate people who are significant to us
Learning how to do simple acts and skills

B Unprepared learnings

Learning by verbal instruction of how-to-do skills
Learning from strangers or from people we dislike, when they explain verbally rather than demonstrate
    by example
Learning to read and write
Learning how to use other symbol systems
Learning how to understand symbolic manipulations
Learning by rote things we do not understand
Learning to decide between several options when we cannot see the immediate consequences of each
Learning to change habitual behaviour by logical argument (e.g., giving up smoking when you know it
    is bad for you)
Learning complex problems in the abstract

    Learning to walk, to talk, to carry out simple skills, or to recognise the emotional states of others, are things that have been easily learned from ancient times. All these learnings are specific to a given *situation*. Verbal communication and mechanical tools were widely used by *Homo habilis* 3 million years ago. Such a learning context, where knowledgeable elders teach younger novices how to carry out culturally important skills on a one-to-one basis, is still centrally important today, as parents teach their children, or in the apprenticeship model of on-the-job training. It is a very natural and powerful learning situation, involving the kind of knowledge, 'knowing-how' (Ryle 1949), that enables us to engage the world directly.

    Ryle contrasts 'knowing-how' with 'knowing-that'. To know that something is the case is an indirect kind of knowing that does not necessarily lead to effective action. To find from the dictionary that a word means so-and-so does not mean we know how to use the word in context. Knowing-that is knowledge for which (if Seligman is right) we are not biologically prepared. Knowing-that is more abstract and involves working on propositions or statements *about* the world rather than immediate action upon objects. These statements are organised into bodies of knowledge called subjects or disciplines (e.g., mathematics, biology, history, fine arts, language, psychology). They constitute our cultural heritage, and are preserved in symbolic form so that they need not be learned afresh by each new generation.

Declarative, procedural and conditional knowledge

We now call knowing-that and knowing-how 'declarative' and 'procedural' knowledge respectively. In earlier editions of this book, a similar distinction was made between *content learning* and *process learning*.

Declarative knowledge refers to knowledge 'about facts and things' (Anderson 1985): knowledge that so-and-so is the case. Declarative knowledge is also called 'propositional' knowledge because it is expressed in statements in propositional form, or in other words, in sentences asserting that so-and-so is the case. Most of what is taught in school is of this kind; children are taught about the world. Declarative knowledge is necessarily about the experience of other people, which tends to make it boring for young children who are much more interested in what is happening to them than in being told about what has happened to other people, or what other people have seen and what they think about it. Thus, declarative knowledge is isolated from any personal context; it is expressed in formal written language strictly according to rules if it is to be clearly understood. It is 'disembedded' from its context, as Donaldson (1978) puts it. It has to be independent of body language or shared personal perspectives so that it may be accessible to different readers, with non-standard dialects, in different contexts and eras.

Children have to learn the formal language, as well as the second-hand knowledge it is conveying. Most find this learning pretty dull stuff, which isn't their fault, or that of the school although it is up to the school to try to make things as interesting as possible. That is probably the major challenge of teaching and one we deal with in several chapters. In fact, you are no doubt heartily agreeing right now that being told in propositional form about different forms of knowledge is dull stuff. Never mind; we're getting back to Bob in a moment.

Declarative knowledge is therefore quite abstract, ranging from descriptions of facts and things, to theoretical explanations of things, to formal grammar itself. Declarative knowledge addressed in the compulsory years of schooling is usually little more than descriptive, while in senior high school and at university, declarative knowledge is increasingly theoretical.

Procedural knowledge is knowledge leading to action. When such knowledge is not easy to put into words, it is called 'tacit'. A gymnast, for example, may be quite unable to express how she performs a particular feat, but she obviously 'knows' it because she can do it perfectly whenever she wants to. On a different level, a mathematician or scientist may have a hunch (which is a form of tacit knowledge) about the solution to a problem before they can prove it; an experienced teacher 'just knows' when it is time to switch the pace or direction of the lesson, or to revamp the example.

More explicit forms of procedural knowledge include knowing how to perform various cognitive activities (Anderson 1985), such as problem solving. Procedural knowledge at this level is concerned with quite explicit strategies for handling problems, and while this often may involve a considerable amount of declarative knowledge, the basis of procedural knowledge still requires first-hand engagement: knowhow. The marriage of declarative and procedural, with conditional as celebrant (see below), is required for engaging the world in an informed and competent way

Conditional knowledge is knowing when and why a procedure is appropriate (Paris, Lipson & Wixson 1983). It involves both the other two forms of knowledge, knowing about the situation (declarative), as well as what to do (procedural). It also involves *metacognitive* or self-knowledge; that is, knowing whether you have the requisite knowledge, whether you can apply it and whether you are applying it adequately or not. Quite simply, if you don't know when you are off the right track and don't check to find out, you'll probably not reach your destination. Knowing that you know, and knowing when you don't know, are aspects of conditional knowledge that are basic to virtually any complex performance. Chapter 12 expands this point and its relevance to students learning in the classroom.

Knowledge, survival and schools

What have the different forms of knowledge to do with schooling? Quite simply, they are learned with varying degrees of difficulty. Procedural knowledge is in general the easiest to acquire and declarative the hardest. Declarative knowledge is also unrelated to survival and that is probably the clue. Declarative knowledge comes much later in our evolutionary history; no one dies, or has fewer children, if they are unable to do mathematics or to read. The earliest known symbolic writing system was devised by the Ebla in the Middle East about 6000 years ago, a mere 300 generations. Universal education is only five generations old. Biology can therefore have had little to do with preparing the average individual to learn how to handle symbols. People show enormous variation in their aptitude for learning to read and write, possibly because the genetic factors involved are unevenly distributed and have yet to be ironed out by natural selection.

Thus, most people do not learn to use the symbol-handling tools of literacy and numeracy easily. Because these tools are necessary for living in modern society, and most people need help in acquiring skill in using those tools, they go to school for that help. Schools first came about in order to teach the tools for handling declarative knowledge. They have other functions too—to socialise, to acculturate, to teach self-management, to protect children from exploitation, to name but a few—and some of these functions will be addressed in due course. But their main job is to help us learn important things that we wouldn't otherwise learn: to acquire the tools necessary for accommodating ourselves to society and to obtain access to our store of declarative knowledge. There is no point in setting up schools to teach students things they would learn at home or in their immediate community. Consider Box 1.2.

Box 1.2   *Should schools teach unprepared learning?*

In the first two years of life, for example, the infant acquires a primitive concept of causality, of the nature of objects, of relations, of language and of many things, largely without the benefit of formal instruction or adult 'teaching' … an infant … is curious, interested in the world around him and eager to learn. It is quite evident that these are characteristics of older children as well … Consequently, it is quite safe to permit the child to structure his own learning. The danger arises precisely when the school attempts to perform the task for him. To understand this point, consider the absurd situation that would result if traditional schools were entrusted with teaching the infant what he spontaneously learns during the first years … One can speculate as to the outcome of such a program of training!

Ginsburg & Opper (1987: 224–5)

What do you think would be the outcome of such training? We speculate that if schools *did* provide such a program of training for the early developmental tasks, children would learn to walk and to talk just the same. These behaviours are biologically prepared and any program for instruction in them is simply unnecessary. But it *is* necessary for reading, because learning to decode an artificial symbol system is abstract and difficult, and needs special help. Whether that difficulty derives from a lack of biological preparation, or from a lack of parental or other 'scaffolding', or both reasons acting in interaction with each other, is beside the point.

Conditional knowledge comes of being streetwise. It is not specifically taught in school although, as formerly noted, it certainly helps in mastering complex tasks, whether school-based or not. Despite their overall aims, schools are generally too busy being managerial to foster self-management. But they should foster it, and good schools do.

The crucial fact is that there are certain kinds of learning that are important to our society, and if they are not provided for in special institutions dedicated to that purpose, most people will not otherwise learn them. Such learnings include learning the codes that enable one to read and write and the knowledge of disciplines that those codes unlock. The problem is that such knowledge is abstract, impersonal and not usually very interesting. But it is compulsory to learn it, or at least to go through the motions.

Differences between everyday and school learning: Bob's problem

Given that much (but maybe not all) of the content taught in school is dealt with out of context, and is in any case unlikely to be of interest or immediate use to most students, teachers and students seem to be labouring under a considerable handicap. Add to that the amazing logistics of compulsory education (education is the most extensive—and expensive—single industry in most countries). The organisation of curricula, providing teachers with knowledge about different teaching methods, establishing systems of assessment, setting up the resources and buildings where all this takes place (just to mention the important parts) mean bureaucracy in action, from state department, to school, even to classroom. These bureaucracies make learning more difficult and more remote.

If all this sounds discouraging so early in your program, hear us out. You will have to work in that paradoxical world of school; a world that children are legally compelled to enter in order to acquire the 'responsible self-direction' the New South Wales Department of Education says they should, in readiness for another world. Remarkably, the compulsion in one world is to provide the autonomy for the other. How then does the learning in those two worlds, inside and outside school, differ (Resnick 1987; Sternberg & Wagner 1986)?

Content

Everyday learning is mostly concerned with personally valued content which is experienced first-hand and is situated functionally in context. This 'situated' nature of everyday learning solves many other problems, particularly those of motivation and acquiring self-management skills. The content learned in school, however, is declarative knowledge; statements about what *other* people experienced first-hand and thought important. We have to learn about wheels if we are to avoid reinventing them.

Motivation

Much everyday learning springs from a felt need to learn. An Eskimo boy feels that it is important to learn how to fish, so he learns how to fish. Likewise, an Australian boy feels that it is important to learn how to drive, so he learns how to drive; he doesn't need to be prompted to do so. But he almost certainly *does* need to be motivated to learn mathematics. Declarative knowledge does not often provide its own motivation for learning, when it does it becomes a rather special case that we call *intrinsic* motivation (see Chapter 10).

Cognitive processes

As we have seen, everyday learning tends to be situated in a specific context; the operations learned on the job most often apply to that context only and support tools are provided (Scribner 1986). Thus, the processes involved in the two worlds are different. Calculating change in the outside world is an 'add on', using real money as a tool, but in school it is a 'take away' using symbols only. There are many such examples, where the school processes are more complex and harder to learn and to use, and children find that confusing. Scribner (1986) found that experienced dairy workers used job-specific techniques for estimating orders, while inexperienced workers used school-taught algorithms. The experienced workers were far more accurate.

You see, institutions aim to teach 'pure' mental operations that apply across a lot of specific instances. This is fair enough, but it is possible that the need to operate without tools has gone too far. It is only recently that calculators have been allowed into the mathematics lesson, and open-book exams are still the exception rather than the rule. While the intent of restricting students' access to tools is to ensure that students can 'really' handle a range of problems unaided and over a variety of contexts, the fact is that this restriction often emphasises lower order cognitive processes. Declarative knowledge is 'known' when it is memorised accurately; procedural knowledge becomes using the algorithm correctly rather than knowing when and why you use it in the first place.

Individual cognition

In everyday practice, other people provide a resource; you use them and they use you to help solve each other's problems. As Scribner notes with the dairy workers, roles are complementary. That is true of almost any job or organisation. Now look at what happened to Adam, a primary school child who was performing very well in an after-school cooking class (Cole & Traupman 1980). But hang on, his teachers have labelled him 'learning disabled': he can't read! In the cooking class Adam's role was to fetch ingredients; he was the official mixer, so that he could always legitimately ask what he was to do next and thereby avoid reading the recipes. But he got his job done. Goodnow (1991: 31) comments on this study:

> Adam is defined as 'disabled' only because school situations insist on the universal importance of working solo, denying the value of skill in using others as resources and ignoring the relevance of such skills to everyday life.

Shared problem solving is rarely encouraged in school. Mostly it is seen as cheating, a punishable offence.

Mentor relationships

A special case of the social nature of everyday life is the mentor relationship, where in a work environment an older, experienced colleague (mentor) and a beginner (protege) form a bond promoting the career development of both (Healy & Welchert 1990). It exists in tertiary institutions, particularly at postgraduate level, and in technical training, as apprenticeships. But secondary schools seem designed specifically to discourage mentor relationships, since they are organised by subject department, not by class, year, or any other basis that might foster constant teacher–student interaction. The contacts students do have with a teacher are made and broken several times a day; a pattern repeated with a new set of teachers the following year. Clearly, subject matter and the formal delivery system are considered all-important, not the formation of bonds between teacher and student that might facilitate learning in less structured and informal ways.

Accreditation and assessment

In everyday life, evaluation is ultimately up to the consumer, not the producer. You pay for what you get. Evaluation by the producer is a matter of quality control. Evaluation in schools is much much more than that. Bloom (1971) estimates that being assessed, publicly, in front of peers and with reports regularly being sent back to parents, is one of the most frequent, and potentially most damaging, things that schools do. In everyday life, assessment is a natural part of the game of learning; frequently, learning is self-assessed.

In school, learning is rarely self-assessed. It is done by others, using a range of artificially structured tests and instruments, testing competence in tasks that are school-based, not ones that have their validity outside school. Testing dominates the way students approach their learning: mostly adversely. We assess what is most easily assessable, inevitably accuracy of replay, rather than what constitutes good learning or competent handling of life tasks. The problem of the artificiality of most testing and examining, and how it may be minimised, is addressed in Chapters 14 and 15.

Formal structure

Schools have an elaborate superstructure involving the design, delivery and evaluation of course content: the length and timing of classes, the design of the curriculum, the allocation of human and material resources, the need for assessment, and the rules and regulations necessary (and unnecessary) for governing the operation of such a complex organisation (rules of behaviour and dress, routines for different occasions, assemblies and the like). This superstructure exists mainly for administrative, collegial and social reasons rather than for educational ones, which raises problems when we want to change existing practices for ones that are better educationally (Reid 1987). Everyday learning is largely free of this superstructure.

The paradox: Bob's problem

Let us return to Bob. It seemed that he did better outside school than inside. And so he did, but he couldn't have managed to follow those car manuals if he hadn't acquired the rudiments of reading in school, however painfully, reluctantly, and slowly. At least when he felt a genuine need to read, he did. He read because it was important to achieve his goals; he honed his rudimentary skills in a few months in a situated context. In school, his reading was 'desituated'; it was something someone else decided he had to do and on which he was publicly tested. Lying low and changing schools so often certainly helped him to maintain his low profile, and he became one of the large numbers of people who are barely literate after years of schooling. When his learning became 'situated', that is reading became an important tool in a meaningful context, he learned to read. Isn't this saying that Bob's schools had failed, where a wrecker's yard succeeded?

No, because the wrecker's yard didn't *teach* Bob how to read; the schools he attended managed that (just). What the yard did was to provide a *context* which was the stimulus for Bob to use his rudimentary skills and perfect them. But wouldn't schools make a better job of the thousands of Bobs around if the context of learning in school were a little more situated? Does learning in school *have* to be so different from learning in everyday life?

Much of the *content* of schooling does; a wrecker's yard is no place to teach the skill of reading. However, the *context* of schooling certainly need not be as learner-unfriendly as it typically is. Such features as:

- individual rather than social learning, either by mentor relationships or cooperatively with peers;
- doing things 'in the head' rather than using tools; and
- teaching what is assessable rather than what is useful

are not essential to school. They also generate huge motivational problems.

How then do you teach abstract declarative knowledge? Rather than not teaching it, as some suggest (Brown et al. 1989; Illich 1971), we should teach within contexts that we know do work in making learning easier. The content doesn't become situated, the context does. As we see in the next two chapters, declarative knowledge originally derives from quite concrete contexts involving acting upon the immediate environment. We can use these contexts, with peer activity by all means, to construct more abstract knowledge. And of course, schools are increasingly doing just that; the suggestion is not terribly radical. This book simply brings these suggestions together into a coherent conceptual framework.

To summarise, then, schools exist because there are socially and culturally important things to learn that would not be learned if left to chance or to everyday experience. Schools are needed to help facilitate the kinds of learning, particularly those involving symbolic representations of knowledge, that humans typically find difficult to learn. That difficulty is well summed up by Brown, Bransford, Ferrara and Campione (1983) when they say that for most students, most of the time, school learning is 'cold', whereas everyday learning is 'hot'. While true, it would be pointless if schools simply replicated everyday experience. However, we can certainly warm things up a little in school by using the methods of everyday life rather than of the institution.

What should be learned in school?

Historically, schools were designed to teach the procedural knowledge necessary to operate the alphanumeric symbol systems and the declarative knowledge that those systems could convey: that is, the traditional academic disciplines. In Chapter 2 we see that this is a quantum leap in terms of the abstract thinking required in comparison with everyday operations. Originally, education was only for an elite.

Since schooling became compulsory, these aims have broadened considerably. Box 1.3 tells us what two state systems gave as the goals of schooling.

Box 1.3 *The aims of education*

New South Wales
The central aim of education which, with home and community groups, the school pursues is to give individual development in the context of society through recognisable stages of development towards:

perceptive understanding,
mature judgement,
responsible self–direction and
moral autonomy.

(Vaughan, 1973, p.14)

Victoria
The central aim of education in Victoria is to provide educational experiences of the best possible quality, for children, youth and adults. Through these experiences they will have the fullest
opportunity to:

1. reach an understanding of themselves and society (educational opportunity);
2. develop to their highest level of intellectual, emotional and social competence
    (educational achievement);
3. achieve socially responsible self–direction (education and values); and
4. build an abiding sense of community throughout our society (education and
    community)

Victorian Education Gazette, 13 February, 1980)

and more recently, in the context of strategic and management planning;

New South Wales
'Our mission is to educate the public school students of New South Wales for the benefit of
each individual, the community and the nation.'
   The objectives below provide a focus for planning in the Department of School Education
by identifying the major areas of activity during the 1990s.

1. To develop in students the knowledge, skills and attitudes required in key learning
    areas, to enhance their quality of life and contribution to society.
2. To enable students to achieve high standards of learning and develop self-confidence,
    high self-esteem and a commitment to personal excellence based on a positive set of
    values.
3. To develop respect for others and an appreciation of Australia's multicultural
    heritage and to promote informed citizenship in our democracy and the world
    community.
4. To develop attitudes and competencies for life-long learning and provide a
    foundation for further education, training and employment.
5. To ensure equality of educational opportunities and to provide for groups with
    special teaching and learning requirements ...'

Education 2000, NSW Department of School Education, 1992, p. 17.

and Victoria
Purposes of schooling include:

Schools should—
•   enable students to participate in a broad general education;
•   develop in students an understanding of their world and of the wider society and an abil-
    ity to control their own affairs and participate in the management of their society;

- enable all students to develop the practice of constructive and reflective thinking on matters raised in the school curriculum;
- enable all students to learn to work with other members of the school community in sharing in and reflecting on experience together;
- enable all students to find learning both demanding and satisfying through the provision of learning situations in which they have continued opportunities for success;
- enable all students to engage in learning which integrates theoretical understandings with practical activities; and
- effectively assist students to overcome the effects of poverty, handicap or other disadvantage.

The School Curriculum and Organization Framework: P–12. Ministry of Education (Schools Division), Victoria, 1988, p. 9.

Statements of aims and purposes of education and schooling in other states are essentially similar, sometimes they are referred to as 'mission statements'. Schools might have come about to teach the basic cultural heritage and the tools for interacting with it, but these aims include more than that. They also include the values of education, interacting with other people and both emphasise 'self-direction'; the obvious point that schools should encourage students to become *autonomous* learners, in readiness for the world outside.

This generally 'liberal-progressive' view of the role of schools is in fact endorsed on a wide scale. Campbell (1980) surveyed a group of 1567 people in six states, including teachers, students, parents, business people and unionists, and concluded:

- The main function of schools is not to prepare children for the workforce, but for coping and contributing to society. Living, not earning a living, is the focus.
- The basic curriculum should be primarily concerned with literacy and numeracy skills, but not to the exclusion of discovering new knowledge and developing inquiry skills.
- Children may be motivated by structure and firm discipline, but more successful motivators are: teacher warmth, challenging learning tasks, cooperative participation.

These aims and expectations provide the guidelines for teaching. They assume a great deal of psychology: of learning, of motivation, of development, of human interaction, of what this book is about.

We now get back to the problem of the content of much—not all, as we now see—school learning. We can't do much about the abstractness of declarative and higher order procedural knowledge (such as occurs in mathematical problem solving, for example), but we can teach it in a learner-friendly *context*. We all seem agreed on that. Why don't we?

The institutionalisation of learning

As already noted, the education industry is huge. Each state has its own bureaucracy to manage thousands of schools, tens of thousands of teachers and hundreds of thousands of students. Until recently, this vast management exercise was controlled centrally, creating its own system, with its own life and momentum. But then, as we see in Chapter 16, the classroom forms its own system, a feature teachers can use positively.

In other words, the context of learning too easily becomes *institutionalised*. To young children, learning is fun. To young adults, learning gives power over the world. To school students learning is … well, what you do in schools. Learning means being taught and passing the test. The higher the mark, the better the learning.

If you asked a student, 'What do you know of the law of supply and demand?' and received the reply, 'Nothing. We haven't done that yet', what would you conclude about that student's ideas on learning? Probably that the student has been trapped in an institutional way of looking at learning; learning means going through a course and emerging with at least a pass mark. In fact, students have been 'doing' supply and demand, procedurally, most of their school lives: every time a trade is made between one Vegemite sanger for a bite of the new kid's salami blintz.

This 'learning' is what is taught in school and that often has little relationship to what is experienced in real life. Students use the same assumptions as did Aristotle 2000 years ago to find their way around the world, yet they pass exams in post-Newtonian physics (Viennot 1979). For instance, Gunstone and White (1981) describe several experimental demonstrations with Physics I students. In one, a majority of students predicted that of two balls held in front of them, one heavy and one light, on release the heavy will reach the ground first, because 'heavy things have a bigger force', or 'gravity is stronger nearer the earth' (!). The exam content for the matriculation physics exam had obviously been 'learned'—they'd all passed it—but it had not been taken on board. Not even the fact that the formula involved does not contain a term for the mass of the object dropped.

Good teaching in the institutional view is doing the right things in front of a class of students. Shavelson and Stern (1981) found that from a sample of United States high school teachers, most planned their teaching in terms of the activities they were themselves to carry out. They focused on their own teaching, not on the learner learning. This conception of teaching is based on the institutional and managerial aspects of student learning and important though they be, they are incidental to the real issue, which is the quality of the learning of the students.

This institutional conception of teaching and learning is inevitable and not necessarily bad, as long as it is seen as a means and not an end. One thing it does mean is that it professionalises teaching.

Is teaching a profession?

What is the difference between a witchdoctor and a medical practitioner? Both might note the appropriate symptoms in their patients; both might alleviate those symptoms by administering compounds containing quinine. In one case, the quinine is contained in chewed-up bark and, in the other, in a capsule.

The mode of administration is not the issue. The essential difference lies in the reasons *why* the treatment is given. While each practitioner would have an explanation, only one fits the comprehensive network of knowledge and procedures that we call *science*. It would not do even if the witchdoctor gives the perfectly logical and non-magical reason that chewing the bark of the cinchona tree has usually worked in the past. Such an answer is based on the inductive principle: if such-and-such works for this disorder, it is likely to do so again. But that is not the point.

The cure rate of folk medicine or witchdoctoring might not even differ from that of your friendly neighbourhood general practitioner. Yet in our culture the latter is regarded as a professional and the witchdoctor is not. What, then, is the difference between a profession and a craft or trade? It comes down to two interrelated issues (Telfer & Rees 1975):

- a protected licence to practise;
- an intensive education in the underlying theoretical knowledge that gives validity to the skills and expertise required to practise.

How does teaching shape up as a profession? All state education departments require evidence of credentials before teachers can be employed, and these credentials depend upon the satisfactory completion of approved tertiary studies, which must include some psychology as the scientific study of learning.

Does that make teaching a science? As long ago as 1899, William James said:

I say moreover that you make a great, a very great mistake, if you think that psychology, being the science of the mind's laws, is something from which you can deduce definite programs and schemes and methods of instruction for immediate schoolroom use. Psychology is a science and teaching is an art; and sciences never generate arts directly out of themselves. (James 1962:3)

But psychology is not irrelevant to education:

Teaching must *agree* with the psychology, but need not necessarily be the only kind of teaching that would so agree; for many diverse methods of teaching may equally well agree with psychological laws. (ibid)

So, although teaching may well be an art, it does appear that there is a theory behind the practice of that art. Teachers, of course, have to know their subject matter; they also need certain theoretical knowledge about the nature of learning. And as we shall see in detail in Chapter 17, *expertise* in teaching depends on two kinds of knowledge: 'craft knowledge' (Leinhardt 1990), gained from much experience and knowledge deriving from 'espoused' theory.

Espoused theory and theory-in-use

Espoused theory is the 'official' and explicit theory behind a particular professional practice; *theory-in-use* is the actual reason for the practice (Argyris 1976). All activities, even witchcraft, have a theory-in-use; only professions have an espoused theory. A professional decision is one where the theory-in-use is the espoused theory.

For example, teachers may use the technique of praising students for doing good work and ignoring their mistakes, because it was the way they were taught; thus was formed the personal theory-in-use that students do better when they feel good about things. If other teachers did the same because they had read the espoused theory relating to self-concept (Chapter 11) and to behaviour modification (Chapter 17), their espoused theory and theory-in-use would coincide. These second teachers would be more the 'professional' teachers (but not necessarily the 'better' ones).

Ideally, teachers educated in the declarative knowledge of espoused theory would act on that knowledge, so that it became procedural knowledge, the theory-in-use. To what extent do teachers do this?

One of the authors ran an in-service class in educational psychology and asked the group to think up incidents in which they or another teacher said or did something to a student in the expectation that the student would learn something, or change behaviour appropriately, as a result. Two such incidents are reported as follows

Example 1. A matter of damages

Ms X arrives at her GA classroom one morning to find two Year 7 boys brawling viciously. She breaks them up and discovers one is a 'foreigner' from another class, who was being forcibly removed by a boy from the home class. The boys suffered only minor damage, but a bicycle parked in the racks outside the classroom had been knocked in the scuffle and a lamp broken. The owner of the bike was not involved.

Having got the general picture, Ms X then asked them both what was to be done about the damage to the bike. They agreed spontaneously to pay for the damage.

'Very good,' she said, 'an excellent idea. I think the principal would be pleased to hear that you have settled the matter this way. Why don't you see him just after lunch and explain the matter and then we'll forget about it.'

Over lunch, Ms X described to the principal what had happened.

'Hmmmmm,' was the ominous and only, response.

'Oh dear,' thought Ms X. 'Have I blown it?'

She had. As soon as the two entered his office, the principal had a spasm:

'What's all this I hear? Were you fighting? And did you break the bicycle lamp?'

'Well, yes sir, but sir, we'll pay ...'

'QUIET! Now listen to me, you two young louts, I will not, do you understand, I will NOT, tolerate fighting in my school ...'

And so on. He did not comment on the fact that they had offered to pay restitution. In his eagerness to prove whatever he needed to prove, he had completely overlooked why they had been sent to him. Or maybe he had only one script to play when interacting with naughty boys. Either way, his theory-in-use had no relation to any known espoused theory. He was not a professional.

Ms X, on the other hand, was convinced that her decision to allow the boys time to decide what they thought they should do, and then let them relate their ideas to the principal, was a *professionally correct* one. Her natural, 'commonsense', theory-in-use would have dictated, she thought, a display of anger and the desire to punish. What she had overlooked, in the detachment of espoused theory, was that the principal might act less professionally than she (he, of course, had not had her advantage of a year's in-service course of educational psychology). Paradoxically, had she operated from her theory-in-use, the confrontation between the boys and the principal would not have taken place. On the other hand, her own personal relationship with the boys might well have suffered more than it did in the event. She in fact benefited greatly in the boys' relative estimations of her and the principal.

Example 2. Room to save face

Tom, a student in a Special School, was a sullen 15 year old, given to bouts of depression. During such a bout, he was requested by the teacher to answer a question.

Silence.

'Tom! I asked you a question!' Loudly, this time.

Silence.

Furious, the teacher strode to Tom's desk and, lowering his face to the level of the other's, repeated slowly, 'I—asked—you—a—question!'

Mumble—which sounded rather like 'F..k off'.

'What?? *What* did you say?'

'F..k off.' No mistake this time.

'*Apologise this instant,* or you'll go to the principal.'

'F..k off.'

'*Right!* Off we go!'

And so the feuding ended up in the principal's office. The principal was relatively young and a female. She remembered something from conventional wisdom which said, 'Always allow the other person room to save face'. What that says is sharpened up considerably in some exciting stuff (which is also in this book) about self-concept theory, arousal and its effect on working memory, and quality of decision-making. With this powerful conceptual brew under her belt, she knew she had to keep them in her office until they had cooled down to the point where each could give just a little. Otherwise, it was a complete impasse and she would have an increasingly unmanageable problem on her hands.

She talked her way through the '*Apologise*' / '*Make me*' volleys until they subsided. Both parties by now were beginning to sense the impossibility of the situation they had constructed. In a few minutes the boy apologised to the teacher, both returned to the classroom; the principal slumped on her desk with relief.

There is a striking contrast here (the reverse of Example 1) between the professionalism of teacher and principal. The teacher was operating only on an emotional level: all he could see was the affront to his authority and his concern to protect it pushed him into a corner from which there was no exit. The principal's professionalism found the exit. Had the principal relied on the traditional theory-in-use ('The authority of a teacher must always be upheld'), she would have sided with the teacher, at the boy's considerable personal expense. In Special Schools you're not supposed to do that. Are you in any schools?

The professionalisation of education involves increasing reliance on espoused theory, as far as possible, in everyday decision-making. We have seen in the above examples that espoused theory has the following characteristics:

- Decisions can be *justified* in terms of a public theory, the validity of which may be tested scientifically. Commonsense decisions are often hard to justify theoretically. How do you justify 'Well it's obvious, isn't it? You can't let 'em get away with that!'? or 'It's always worked for me. Take my advice!'? Unless you understand *why* it worked, the time will probably come when it does not.
- Decisions are *non-personal*, which does not mean impersonal or uncaring. You don't decide to do this or not do that because that little rat Smith is involved.
- Decisions are *value free*, if possible. In the two above examples, the commonsense theory-in-use involved value judgments, meaning the decision was on the basis of what is 'good', 'the thing to do', instead of what the most productive outcome would be. As we saw in Example 2 particularly, getting worked up emotionally is likely to diminish the chances of arriving at a good decision.

Well, where does all this leave the preservice student, about to embark on a career in teaching? Clearly, the development of professionalism takes time: it will not happen in a preservice course. The first few years will be problem-based learning with a vengeance.

There is more to great teaching than putting theory to work effectively, as we also see in Chapter 17, but that is certainly a positive step forward. In a word, that is the aim of this book; to provide good espoused theory, so that we may 'drastically reduce, if not eliminate, the need for wisdom' (Suppes 1974: 4).

Conceptions of learning and teaching

What do you mean when you say you 'learn' something? We have already looked at the institutional answer: 'When we have passed a test on it'. Two other broad forms of answer have been noted: quantitative and qualitative ones (Cole 1990; Marton & Saljo 1984). Beaty, Dall'Alba and Marton (in press) distinguish several levels of each type of conception, with *what* and *how* aspects to each level. The following conceptions were obtained from tertiary students, but similar ones, at the lower levels, have been found in children as young as 8 (Pramling 1983).

Quantitative conceptions

A: *Increasing one's knowledge*

What: 'Learning new things'. Precisely what is learned is unspecified, beyond 'bits of information'.

How: 'absorbing', 'storing'. The process is also unspecified, except increasing, or absorbing.

B: *Memorising and reproducing*

What: 'Facts'. Isolated but specified items of knowledge.

How: 'Rote learning', 'getting it right'. Repetition, memorising.

C: *Applying*

What: 'facts and procedures'. Similar to (B), but the facts are broader and include procedural knowledge of rules and algorithms

How: 'Make use of it in some way'. Facts do have a context in which they are used, which means they have to be adjusted to the applied context, not reproduced exactly.

Conceptions A to C are all concerned with isolated items, ranging from unspecified 'things' to facts and procedures; they are learned by restricted or lower order processes such as rote learning. Applying or using is the level in simple maths problems: applying an algorithm to a standard problem-type.

The quantitative tradition has in general dominated the psychology of learning and particularly of assessment (Cole 1990; see also Chapter 14). People holding this conception think that a good scholar is someone who knows *more* than other people. This view of knowing is hugely rewarded in TV quiz shows like *Sale of the Century* or *Mastermind*, both of which require the rapid retrieval of trivial and unrelated pieces of knowledge. The board game *Trivial Pursuit* is well named. Experts at such games make us lesser mortals gape in awe as these self-made scholars of the esoteric tell us on cue the name of the driver of the first steam locomotive to go from London to Edinburgh in under 6 hours. Speed and accuracy of memory, that is what good learning is.

This is also what many people think schools should be about: drill students in the basic skills and get them to learn lots of unrelated facts. If arithmetic is doing sums, then higher mathematics is doing very long and difficult sums. One of the present authors spent his first year 'out' in an industrial suburb. One Year 8 boy brought a note from an enthusiastic parent, thanking him for giving his son some homework, which was an unexpected event and 'please continue to stuff the gen into him'. Learning was having a head stuffed full of facts. Many teachers in fact use an 'absorption' conception of teaching (Tobin & Fraser 1988); they see their job to present the information, usually in an expository style, and for the students to absorb it.

Qualitative conceptions

D: Learning is understanding the meaning of content

What: 'ideas'. For the first time, meaning becomes paramount. It's not the words and sentences that need focusing on, but what they stand for; what the author is trying to say.

How: 'grasping', 'understanding', 'seeing'. The procedures of understanding are not always specifiable, but basically involve relating what is learned to other knowledge (discussing, finding analogies).

E: Seeing something in a different way

What: 'a view of things', 'principles'. Learning now produces a *change* in what is understood. The object of understanding is bigger than an idea. Once you understand several ideas, they feed each other, the world is perceived differently. Education 'broadens your outlook'.

How: 'by studying things become a pattern'. As we gain more knowledge about something, it will appear different to us.

F: Changing as a person

What: 'the meaning of experience'. A philosophy of life.

How: 'by deep involvement in learning', 'by coming to be in charge'.

Most 'official' statements about the aims of education refer to meaning and realisation of potential; that, by the end of school, students should be able to understand society, their place in it, be able to clarify and talk about their own values, to be able to direct themselves; in short, to reach Stage F by holding an explicit philosophy for their lives. On the other hand, many practices in school, from curriculum (teaching the basics), method (expository) and assessment (number right in a factual test), are clearly based on quantitative assumptions about learning and teaching.

The quantitative and the qualitative levels of conception are not antagonistic, but feed each other. You can't form a view of something until you know the facts. The problem occurs when you just stop at the facts; and teaching and assessing in a way that emphasises the facts is a good way of telling students to indeed stop at the facts. Rote learning then becomes an end, the purpose of learning, rather than a means towards acquiring understood and usable knowledge. It is necessary to rote learn scientific formulae, as part of learning to think like a scientist; the mistake is to conclude that that is the way scientists think. We talk of a 'scientist's way' of seeing things, or an 'historian's way'. Ideally, when students graduate from university they should see the world from the viewpoint of their discipline. What they have studied has shaped a 'paradigmatic' way of thinking (Bruner 1985).

The development of tertiary students from their first year to graduation has been traced by Perry (1970). First, they go through an Absolutist position. They see that there is a Right Answer to every problem and it is known to Authority. Knowledge is perceived as 'quantitative accretions of rightnesses to be collected by hard work and obedience (paradigm: a spelling test)' (Perry 1970: 9). This is a clear example of conception A. Then there is a phase of an intellectual free-for-all, where anyone's opinion is as good as anyone else's. Finally, there is a structuring along the lines of conception E, forming a different view, which hopefully develops into F, a consistent philosophy.

Constructivist view of learning

Underlying the shift from quantitative conceptions of learning (A to C) to qualitative (D to F) is a *constructivist* view of learning. Constructivism isn't a theory so much as a perspective on learning with the following emphases:

- people actively construct knowledge for themselves;
- knowledge is based on categories derived from social interaction not observation, it's the *way* you come to look at things as much as what you are looking at;
- people determine their own knowledge.

In the early stages of learning, the content learned is seen to be external to the learner; facts and procedures exist independently of who is learning them. At this level, 'absorption' models are appropriate; one needs to take the facts on board. Spellings, declarative statements of fact, using the four rules of number, are straightforward matters of right or wrong, independently of who is doing them. The teacher's view of what is 'correct' can be used to assess whether or not learning has occurred.

Meanings and points of view, however, cannot exist independently of the learner. Making sense of something is what the individual does (or doesn't). What you understand about something is not what I might understand. Say a bus travels from Sydney to Brisbane via the Pacific Highway, with a detour through Lismore and Nimbin, visiting an area of rainforest before coming back to the Gold Coast. The passengers include an Aborigine, the manager of a woodchipping firm, a member of the Wilderness Society, an ex-hippie, a Japanese tourist, a compulsive gambler, a geologist, a Liberal politician, a Labor politician, a 5 year old, a farmer and a geography teacher. When you ask each for details of what was seen on the trip and what was learned you will indeed discover that:

- learning is constructed;
- what is learned depends on the way you look at things; and
- learning is self-determined.

In these respects, learning in the classroom is no different.

Knowledge in the constructivist view is relativistic, not absolute; that is, it is not 'out there' waiting to be discovered (the woodchipper missed Leadbeater's possum; the Greenie missed the ideal layout for a golf course). People, like scientists, progressively construct their kind of knowledge, as the best guess yet for making sense of the evidence and existing knowledge. This process is never complete. A conceptual system is constructed and if it works, it is publicly accepted until disproved, or until the whole paradigm of which it is part is replaced (Kuhn 1962). This is also the way children learn. Each new 'hypothesis' is a code or 'schema' (see Chapter 8); each new 'paradigm shift' a developmental stage (see Chapters 2 and 3).

There are some important educational implications of this view (Candy 1991; Driver & Oldham 1986):

1. What is learned may not be what the teacher *intends* to be learned. The major determinants of learning are internal to the learner.
2. What is learned depends on what is already known. The most important determinant of learning is existing knowledge; you construct with the bricks and blueprints you already have. New knowledge obviously affects the outcome, but not as powerfully or directly as we may assume.

3. Learning is an ongoing process; it is continuous and active. One lesson is not going to contain the learning associated with a concept; as with supply and demand (see above) the child will have relevant experiences prior to and following formal instruction. It is better if formal instruction tries to encourage and make those links explicit rather than ignore them.

4. Learners have final responsibility for their learning. Adopting a constructivist view, then, one must *allow* learners to develop self-direction and not force 'correct' constructions onto them.

5. Constructed meanings share common characteristics. Through language and shared social experiences, people's constructions allow communication and acknowledgment of mutual validity.

The most important determinant of learning is existing knowledge. Learning is an on-going process: it is continuous and active.

6. Teachers who see their role as passing on established truths will be threatened if students question their utterances. Students have grounds for questioning from conception E onwards.

The last three points provide most difficulty for teachers. If a student's construction or understanding of a concept is incorrect, then isn't it unprofessional *not* to correct it? Yes, but the student is the one who must accept that it is incorrect and then reconstruct it correctly. Otherwise, like Gunstone and White's students, they'll say: 'Yes, yes, of course, weight doesn't matter' and continue to solve problems (correctly) using the formula for *g* (which doesn't contain a term for the mass of the object falling): and continue to believe that heavy objects fall faster. What confusion!

As Wittrock (1977: 180) says:

> ... methods of teaching should be designed to stimulate students actively to construct meaning from their own experience rather than stimulating them to reproduce the knowledge of others.

Facing students with their misconceptions is an important first step (Ramsden 1988), but this is only a conceptual slap on the wrist if it doesn't effect a reconstruction. Reconstruction is a complex matter, with many factors that may facilitate it, including direct learner activity, peer interaction and many other points, which will take most of this book to explain.

A teacher who holds a quantitative conception of learning based on absorbing the right stuff, so that students who give responses not matching the teacher's are marked 'wrong' and in need of correction, may be able to operate effectively when teaching 'the basics', but even then there is room for opinion. What do you do if a student adds-on to obtain the correct answer to a 'subtraction' problem? Do you give a cross or a tick? Even at this level of teaching the basics, then, good teaching requires a constructivist view. It is hoped that your teacher education courses will provide that. Because how you view the educational process, whether as teacher or student, and therefore how you teach or learn, will be guided in part by the conceptions of teaching and learning that you hold.

Three levels of learning and teaching

The levels we have been discussing, including the discussion of institutionalising learning, contain three major different conceptions of learning, with complementary conceptions of teaching:

Level 1 (Quantitative)

(a) *Learning:* Learning is a matter of how much is learned, incorporating conceptions A, B and C. As already noted, many people hold this view. It is not, however, peculiar to the unsophisticated. More sophisticated quantitative conceptions would include the 'back to basics' movement, which saw the curriculum as a collection of essential facts and skills, to be taught, assimilated and tested on cue; and currently, competence assessment in the form of performance indicators.

(b) *Teaching:* Teaching is the transmission of knowledge. Many teachers, especially beginning teachers, see their task as one of transmitting knowledge that emanates from an external source (Russell & Johnson 1988); the task of learners therefore is one of absorption. If learning is inadequate, in this view of teaching, it is the student's fault: a lack of ability, preparation, or motivation. The student either submits to remediation of some kind, or drops out, as 'unmanageable', or 'not the academic type'.

Level 2 (Institutional)

(a) *Learning:* Learning needs validating, by being taught and evaluated in an institution of learning. This conception follows from the idea of compulsory schooling and, to some extent holds schools accountable for what they do: parents, employers, higher educational institutions, all need some kind of reassurance as to standards at various points throughout schooling. Often, however, the institutional aspects of managing the process of learning dominate the intrinsic reasons why students are in school.

(b) *Teaching:* Teaching is the efficient orchestration of teaching skills. Here teachers are prepared to adapt their techniques to different students and are sensitive to different needs. They see good teaching as beginning and ending with effective management, both of teaching resources and of the students themselves. They are maestros, conducting the Classroom Symphony Orchestra. At the tertiary level they are 'inspirational' lecturers: witty, devastating, vastly entertaining. In each case, every class becomes an occasion for a solo performance to a student audience, whose role is to admire rather than to learn.

Level 3 (Qualitative)

(a) *Learning:* Learning involves meaning, understanding, and a way of interpreting the world: conceptions D, E, and F. Many tertiary teachers see their discipline as involving particular qualities of thinking and problem solving and want their students to acquire learning that way (Entwistle 1984). It exists at school level too: both New South Wales and Victorian Departments include 'responsible self-direction' in their aims (see also Chapter 7). It made its first official entry into Australian education in the Karmel Report (1973), where the realisation of individual potential become the first aim of education, rather than socialisation, or job preparation.

(b) *Teaching:* Teaching is the facilitation of learning, actively involving both teacher and student. The teacher interacts with the learner in line with the assumption that learning involves the active construction of meaning by the student and is not something that is imparted by the teacher. This conception of teaching is espoused in the present volume and is developed throughout. The teacher's role is thus to engage the student in effective learning activities.

Level 3 is a student-centred approach to teaching, whereas both Levels 1 and 2 are teacher-centred. Problems in learning are not seen as the 'fault' of any of the participants, but as lying in the interaction between both parties, although the teacher, as senior partner, must clearly take more responsibility for initiating and maintaining as fruitful an interaction as possible. In the end, though, as with horses: you can lead them to water but they're the ones whose tummies have to get wet on the inside.

The conceptions of teaching are hierarchical:

- *Level 1* assumes that the teacher possesses the appropriate content knowledge and the ability to present fluently in an expository context.
- *Level 2* assumes teacher content knowledge and teaching skills additional to expository skill.

- *Level 3* assumes all that Levels 1 and 2 assume, plus (in line with the constructivist model) some understanding of student learning processes, so that learning may be enhanced by orchestrating teaching appropriately.

An aim of this book is to help student teachers develop a Level 3 conception of their role. But it needn't be as dry as it may be sounding:

> Teaching can … be an exhilarating and joyful experience, expanding the teacher's life through skills, or human relations, or both. Teaching well is a thrill. (Connell 1985: 127)

Summary

Why schools?

Some things, like food aversions, are learned incredibly easily and rapidly. Other things, like learning to read, are learned with difficulty; sometimes, it seems, with more difficulty inside school than outside. What is it that makes things easy and difficult to learn? Knowledge takes different forms: procedural, declarative and conditional. Much procedural knowledge, knowing-how, directly engages the world and is related to survival; it is easily acquired. Declarative knowledge is abstract and related to using symbol systems; it is hard for most to acquire. We need the help of schools.

Differences between everyday and school learning: Bob's problem

Two main features determine school learning: its nature (primarily but not exclusively to deal with what's abstract and difficult to learn), and its logistic superstructure, necessary for organising the fact that at least 10 years of every citizen's life is to be programmed in detail. Together, these features make school learning different from everyday learning in several ways: its content is indirect and abstract, young students don't see the importance of schoolwork and need to be motivated, the cognitive processes employed are general rather than tuned to the particular context, individuals work solo rather than collaboratively, mentor relationships with senior colleagues are discouraged, the work of individuals is ruthlessly and publicly assessed, decisions as to curriculum, teaching method and rules of conduct are formalised and institutionalised. Schools could be a little more learner-friendly.

What should be learned in school?

Historically, the first responsibility of schools was to teach how to use symbol systems and the declarative knowledge they conveyed. Today, with compulsory education for all, the aims are broadened to include social and moral values, and self-management and autonomy of operation. The institutionalisation of schooling seems however to work in the opposite direction of these splendid aims, in that schooled knowledge is in danger of becoming separated from working knowledge of the world. It also introduces an institutionalised way of thinking about teaching and learning. Teaching is too complex and sophisticated a task now to be left to the wisdom of craft knowledge. Teaching is based on matching the theories one uses at the chalkface with the professional theories one espouses.

Conceptions of learning and teaching

A conception of learning is what you think learning is: what is learned and how it is learned. The way you go about learning, and about teaching yourself, will be guided by your conceptions. Two broad conceptions are commonly distinguished: quantitative and qualitative, with some hierarchically organised levels within each. Quantitative conceptions see the contents of learning as isolated items, the processes low level. Qualitative conceptions operate with meaning as the content, the processes as cognitively high level. Knowledge is constructed by the learner, not expounded from without and is necessarily relativistic, a feature some teachers find hard to live with. Constructivism is a broad view of learning that is founded on the qualitative conceptions. Corresponding conceptions of teaching can be found: Level 1 conceptions are quantitative, Level 2 institutional, and Level 3 qualitative.

Learning activities

1. Differences between everyday and school learning

In this chapter we spent some considerable space discussing the differences between everyday and school learning. This activity looks at similarities and differences between everyday and school learning and is designed to tease out those differences in a methodical manner by having you take each of the dimensions we presented (motivation, cognitive processes, individual cognition, through to formal structure) and then comparing them. One way of doing this would be to draw up a matrix with the dimensions down the side and 'Everyday' and 'School' along the top. In this way each of the 'cells' could show the nature of the learning in that context.

If done as a class activity, groups could be formed to prepare overhead transparencies for presentation to the class. Alternatively, groups could be assigned to dimensions and then asked to report back to the class with examples of everyday and school learning for their assigned dimension.

2. The aims of education

We presented the aims of education for two Australian states in Box 1.3. Are the aims of education explicitly spelled out in the state in which you reside? The purpose of this activity is twofold. First, we want you to examine the aims of education in the two states that we have mentioned and also in others if you can locate them. This is a compare and contrast activity and could be done as a class or small group discussion. What are the commonalities in the expressed aims, what are the differences? Can you identify what types of knowledge (declarative, procedural, conditional) are being focused upon?

Second, we want you to be introspective about your own schooling. Can you remember instances where such aims were pursued by the school? Take, for example, the notion of responsible self-direction from the New South Wales aims statement. Were you encouraged to be self-directed? If so, how, and if not, why do you think this may not have occurred? Again, discussion groups could be a way of conducting this activity.

3. Levels of learning and teaching

This activity is aimed at finding out people's views on learning and teaching in the context of the three basic conceptions we introduced in this chapter: Level 1 (quantitative), Level 2 (institutional) and Level 3 (qualitative). For this activity you are to 'interview' several people (say, in different age brackets) to get a feel for what they think school type learning and teaching are all about. As a class activity, a set of questions could be generated which could then be used in the interviews. Questions such as 'What is learning?', 'What should people learn at school?', 'How should people learn when they are at school?' and 'How should learning be assessed?' could be used. If you wanted, the focus could be more specific with questions such as 'What do you think of rote learning?', 'Should all learning be for understanding?' and 'Should teachers teach with a view to changing students' philosophies of life?'

With younger students you will need to make the questions less complex than our examples.

When you have gathered your data from the interview, attempt to categorise it in terms of the quantitative, institutional and qualitative dimensions. Do older people have different perspectives on what should be learned and how it should be taught? Finally, what are your own views? The results could be presented to the class using a poster format.

Further reading

On schools and everyday learning

Resnick, L. B. (1987). 'Learning in school and out', *Educational Researcher*, **16** (9), 13–20; Sternberg, R. J. & Wagner, R. (eds) (1986). *Practical Intelligence*. Cambridge: Cambridge University Press.

The first reference spells out in more detail the ways in which school learning differs from everyday learning and points out the nice paradox that the best learning that takes place in school is when the conditions of learning are *most* like everyday contexts, not least like. Sternberg and Wagner's concern relates to the next chapter, but is very relevant here: What has being clever in school got to do with being clever at ... stacking milk crates (Scribner), betting on horses (Ceci & Liker) or publishing academic papers (Wagner & Sternberg)? You've got it.

On autonomy and responsible self-direction

Candy, P. C. (1991) *Self-direction for Lifelong Learning*. San Francisco: Jossey-Bass.

This is 'the definitive text in the area of adult education', as the blurb so rightly says. If we mean what we say in this chapter (and in others), this text has definitive things to say to youth educators, as well as to adult educators, if students now in school are to operate with adult autonomy later. Chapter 8, 'Understanding the individual nature of learning', is relevant to the present chapter because it presents a thorough analysis of the constructivist position. Beyond that, the text addresses the general educational aim of *self-direction*, which is the espoused aim of many state educational systems. Part 4, 'Promoting self-direction in learning' (Chapters 11, 12 and 13) discusses what that means in practice.

On conceptions of learning and teaching

Marton, F., Hounsell, D. & Entwistle, N. (eds) (1984). *The Experience of Learning*. Edinburgh: Scottish Universities Press.

This book concentrates on how tertiary students experience the context of learning. The issues addressed parallel those which concern us with primary and secondary students for many chapters of the present book: conceptions of learning and approaches to learning (Marton & Saljo), changes in conception as a result of years of tertiary study (Morgan, Taylor & Gibbs), assessing qualitative outcomes of learning (Dahlgren), approaches to learning (Marton), effects of teaching context and assessment on learning (Ramsden), essay writing (Hounsell). Don't attempt to read the whole book at once; for now, the first couple of chapters (including Marton & Saljo on approaches), then use it to fill out other chapters as appropriate.

PART 2

THE DEVELOPING STUDENT

COGNITIVE DEVELOPMENT OVER THE YEARS

Cognitive development over the years

What develops?   How does it develop?

modes?

sensori-motor   physiologically

ikonic   knowledge in
                                  previous mode

concrete-symbolic   challenge

formal   support

post-formal

Do adult learners differ from younger learners?

COGNITIVE DEVELOPMENT OVER THE YEARS

In this chapter, you will find out:

- what it is about children's learning that typically changes with age;
- when the common stages in thinking emerge between birth and adulthood;
- what Piaget said happens during cognitive development and how that differs from what psychologists now say;
- that the level of abstraction of what is learned changes during development;
- how thinking changes during adulthood.

Ages and stages

Have you ever picked up an old family photograph album and seen photos of the same person taken at regular intervals: as a baby, a toddler, a preschooler, a primary school student, a pre-adolescent, an early adolescent, a young adult, a 40 year old, a retiree? No? Well if you do, you will get a very strong sense of individual continuity: this person progressing through life. Yet at each of those ages, that person is cognitively, physically and emotionally more like other people of the same age than like himself or herself 20 years past, or 20 years hence.

Teachers are more interested in how children of similar ages resemble each other than in individuals' biographies. They have to be. Working in an educational system that is organised around grouping children of like ages, teachers need to know some of the more important ways in which age peers resemble each other, at least in those areas that affect their decision-making with students. Is it an accident that children begin compulsory schooling at 5 or 6 years of age in most countries; that there is a change to a different system of schooling when they reach about 12 years; that children may leave school at about 15–16 years; and that they start university at 18 or 19 years? Probably not, for many psychologists believe that these are the ages at which the quality of children's thinking typically undergoes important changes.

Thinking develops in stages. At least in developed countries, there are key periods during which most children learn to do important things:

- In infancy, children learn to coordinate their movements in relation to their physical environment.
- At two years, all but the handicapped are learning to speak, to interact with others, to discover that one's own needs have to be accommodated to those of others and to enter the realms of imagination and fantasy.
- At 6 years, most children are on the way to learning how to read and then to write, and to use these and other symbol systems to find out about and control reality.

• At adolescence, most begin to theorise about their world: to think abstractly in terms of the possible and to wonder at how their world might otherwise be.

People also develop physically, emotionally, socially and morally, as well as cognitively, but here in this chapter we are concerned with cognitive development and in particular with the question of what it is that is doing the developing. We also review development throughout adulthood and the implications both for continuing education and for the school system.

The first question is deceptively simple:

What develops?

Piaget's contribution

The most influential theory of development, both in terms of its impact on psychology and on education, was put forward by the Swiss psychologist, Piaget (1950). His answer to the question 'what develops?' was 'logical structures'. He showed that the highest and most complex human thinking in adults can be described by an abstract system of symbolic logic, which he took to be the goal towards which cognitive development was directed. It worked like a master computer program: the logical structures being the software, we ourselves the hardware. All the information we take in through our senses is run through this program and our behaviour is the output (Piaget didn't put it this way, but it is a convenient metaphor for getting at what his theory says).

Each stage shift mentioned above (say at 5 years of age, or at adolescence) in our simplified Piagetian model is like adding a new, more powerful version of the program that handles more dimensions of a problem at each such shift. Piaget studied how children solved tight logical problems, starting with extremely simple ones (hiding objects), to very abstract logical and mathematical ones.

He proposed that thinking developed in stages and each stage had its own logical integrity (he called it a 'structured whole'). It was as if all cognitive processes were controlled throughout each stage by the master program for that stage. Thus, his theory predicted a similarity, or 'evenness', in the way students at a particular stage handled problems. This evenness was dictated by the kind of logical *operations* the child used to interact with the world. From birth to 18 months, operations are implicit in actions, or 'sensori-motor' connections. Actions then become internalised as mental images, but until the age of 5 or 6, these images do not conform to any logical operations, hence the stage between 18 months and around 6 years is called 'preoperational'. Then follows the stage of 'concrete operations' until early adolescence, which gives way to 'formal operations' from about 12 years of age. Operational thinking doesn't incorporate only interactions with the physical world. The social world, as well as moral judgment, would be subject to the same program (Kohlberg 1969).

These stages occurred due to an interaction between innate factors and attempts to cope with a demanding environment. Two processes were stipulated as governing cognitive behaviour within and across stages: assimilation and accommodation. The person would 'assimilate' the meaning of an environmental message much as we say we assimilate food; and 'accommodate' mental structures to the demands of the message if it couldn't be assimilated immediately, much as our bodies accommodate to too much food and too little exercise by getting fat. The biological tone of these metaphors arises from the fact that Piaget was once a biologist, a very clever little biologist, who was offered the job of curator of the natural science museum in Geneva on the basis of a paper he'd written on molluscs in Lake Geneva. However, he decided not to take it but to continue with his schooling instead: he had, at the tender age of 12, been exercising his emerging formal operations.

Many of these Piagetian concepts, revolutionary at the time, have become merged with modern cognitive psychology, while others are now seen to be mistaken. Some of his important contributions:

- Recognising that innate structures interacted with self-initiated operations upon the environment.
- Giving rise to *constructivism*, which stresses that people construct their own knowledge (see Chapter 1).
- Assimilation and accommodation are processes now recognised generally as encoding and recoding (see Chapter 8).
- Accommodation/recoding is strongly associated with intrinsic motivation, when the match between the pace and level of difficulty of the task and the learner's existing structures is appropriate (see Chapter 10).
- The context of learning should emphasise both self-regulation and interaction with others (see Chapter 12).

So you see that Piaget has quite a lot to say to us. For several years, the Piagetian model governed progressive educational thought (Furth 1970; Ginsburg & Opper 1979; Lovell 1961), but one aspect of his theory was particularly misleading, the question of stage evenness: that at any given stage, all tasks will be handled by the same 'master program'. Evenness would lead us to expect that a student would solve arithmetic problems in the same way as problems in social studies would be solved; and that tasks of a certain level cannot be learned, and should not therefore be taught, until the master program appropriate to that level was 'ready'. Neither of these expectations is supported by evidence.

Post-Piaget

Thus, subsequent research has shown that children do not consistently approach tasks in the way their developmental stage (or master program) says they 'should' (Fischer & Sylvern 1985). Particularly is this so in school tasks, where students appear to operate at different stage levels in different subject areas and even in the same subject from one day to the next (Biggs & Collis 1982a). Neither is adolescence the peak of cognitive development, as we shall see later.

Neo-Piagetian psychologists have taken several aspects of Piaget's theory, including the notions of constructivism and stages, and strongly modified other aspects, in particular those relating to the nature of what develops, the role of other aspects such as working memory (see Chapter 8), and the importance of the kind of task being handled at the time.

As to what develops, there are several suggestions: problem solving strategies (Case 1985; Siegler 1986), central conceptual structures comprising problem solving strategies generalisable over a domain (Case 1991; 1992), specialised structural systems for different content areas (Demetriou 1988), skills in increasingly complex structures (Fischer 1980), logical mappings (Halford 1982). It would only be confusing to review these here in detail, but some features are common to most modern theories (Biggs 1992):

- each stage is more abstract than its predecessor;
- each stage provides an upper limit to the level of abstraction of what may be learned;
- learning occurs within and across stages, so that it is possible to distinguish substages or levels within stages.

It is convenient to distinguish levels and stages in terms of *optimal level* and *skill acquisition* (Fischer & Pipp 1984). Optimal level refers to the fact that there are upper limits to the level of complexity that a person can handle, and that these upper limits are at least partially age-related; this is what cognitive development is about and is the subject of the present chapter. Skill acquisition refers to the way in which people become cleverer at doing particular tasks; this is what learning is about and is the subject of the next chapter.

Development thus refers to the kinds of things that people are able to do which are limited by their age rather than by their skill. Babies can learn to find things that are hidden from them, but they cannot use words to wonder about where they might have been hidden; 7 year olds can make marks on paper to say what they would like for Christmas, but they cannot use symbols to prove an argument is incorrect.

The Piagetian stages give a strong clue to what is happening: not because logical programs are masterminding how children perform during these stages, but because children become progressively more able to do different sorts of things. Precisely what they do that is different depends on the task being undertaken and theorists have different ideas about that. For instance, Fischer (1980) sees the changes that occur as being quite task-specific, whereas Case (1991) sees them as *central conceptual structures*, each structure relating to a whole domain of tasks: numerical, musical, social and so on. Further, Case (op. cit.) sees these structures as being directly teachable, a claim which if substantiated would have profound effects on education .

What all would agree with is that one of the major changes with age is that the contents of learning are represented in progressively more abstract terms. This progression in the abstract nature of what may be learned at different developmental stages forms the basis of our present discussion.

What is learned at each developmental stage?

While theorists tend to agree that thought progresses in four or sometimes five stages up to early adulthood, which in many ways correspond with Piaget's original stages, a confusing terminology for these stages has arisen. Case (1985) refers to sensorimotor, inter-relational, dimensional and vectorial stages, Halford (1982) to element, relational, system and multiple-system mappings. Such terms presuppose a detailed knowledge of each theory. Here, we use descriptive terms that are close to Piaget's but without his structural implications, and which simplify the key issue: what develops across stages is the level of abstraction, or *mode*, in which thought is represented (Bruner 1964a).

1. *Sensori-motor* (from birth; most people seem to agree about this name at least). The most concrete way of acting towards the world is by *doing something*, giving a motor response, to a sensory stimulus. For the first 18 months, learning becomes very complex, but the content is concerned with coordinating actions with each other in increasingly complex patterns, and with the environment. We learn motor skills continuously into adulthood, but during infancy it is the only mode available.
2. *Ikonic* (from 18 months). To make an action more abstract, it must be represented internally. Piaget (1950) defined thought as the internalisation of action; the simplest such representation of an action is to imagine it, to form an internal picture or *ikon*

(Bruner 1964a). The next mode of thinking after the sensori–motor mode is thus called *ikonic*, which begins to occur after the first year and which generalises, with the help of language, after 18 months.

3. *Concrete-symbolic* (from 6 years). The next mode deals in concepts and operations, which are linked directly to *concrete* experience by *symbols*. Number operations can be carried out symbolically, yet relate uniquely to real world happenings. There is logic and order between symbols and the world they directly refer to.

4. *Formal* (from 12 years). To understand that concepts can relate to other concepts is to talk literally 'in principle'. Principles are more abstract than concepts: concepts relate to concrete happenings, principles to hypothetical happenings. The order to be found in abstractions allows thinking about logical possibilities.

5. *Post-formal* (from 18 years). Principles may relate to other principles and thus form academic *disciplines*. To study and then to question and reshape these disciplines, as in research, is to operate more abstractly still.

Modes are the stuff of which learning is made and they define the developmental stages. Let us look at the sorts of things that typically go on at each stage.

The sensori–motor mode

The infant is born with a few basic reflexes, such as sucking and an extraordinary degree of plasticity; it is ready, waiting to learn. For the first two months nothing very much seems to be happening from the outside, then the first social reactions occur: reacting to a parent's face, to others, reaching out for objects, following movements with the eyes. The initial reflexes come from a purely biological phase of existence. The first smile of recognition, which is not just wind, is the first evidence of coordination between movements and an outside stimulus. Now is the time for mobiles to dangle enticingly, for rattles to shake, for Teddies to be clutched; those actions are what give the objects their meaning.

The development of object permanence.

Over several months following birth, babies show a consistent pattern in their reaction when objects with which they have been playing are hidden from them (Piaget 1950). Piaget used these data to infer that the infant had a conception of how *permanent* objects are. Do objects still exist when out of sight and out of mind? Eighteenth century philosophers—the pre-Thatcherite British empiricists—argued the toss over that one. It depends how old you are, Piaget concluded. He set up several little scenarios, which his subjects (his own children) must have found infuriating:

1. A toy is removed while the baby is playing with it. It is not missed (the toy that is). The baby shrugs and bangs its gums onto something else.

2. A toy is removed while an older baby is playing with it and it *is* missed. If the toy is placed under a cushion, the baby crawls over to retrieve it. However, if the toy is then transferred from one hiding place to another and the baby sees this happening, it nevertheless goes to find the toy under the *first* cushion, not to where it 'saw' the toy being placed. The 'thinking' going on here is in the muscles, so to speak, not the brain (Bruner 1966).

3. The toy is missed, whether or not it is being played with. The baby will now search the second cushion after unsuccessfully searching the first.

4. The toddler seeks to find the toy in the logical place: where it was seen to be *last* hidden.
5. Next, the fiendish Piaget hides the toy while the toddler is *not* watching. The first search is where it might be thought to be, but if it isn't there, other likely hiding places are investigated.

These relationships between the child's actions and the hidden object show an increasing ability to handle information. First, in (1), the child's actions do not relate to the object except in an immediate and transitory sense. Then, in (2), the act of playing (or sucking, or hitting) defines the object, so that the continuity of the action means that the object is missed and is actively searched for. Once the first action, based on the first perception of where it is hidden, has been run off, that's all there is: end of object search.

In (3), the child has to act on the first information about the hiding place, but can then put the perceptions of object removal into sequence and then acts upon that sequence. In (4), however, acting in sequence is no longer necessary. As long as the transfers are physically visible, the information is integrated, and action based on where the object was *last* hidden follows directly. There is no need to run through the previous sequence. This signifies the peak of the sensorimotor period, as action and perception are integrated.

The next level, however, signifies something qualitatively different. To find the object when its transfer has *not* been physically witnessed is to internalise and hypothesise: to imagine where it *might* be. That requires thinking in images, which belongs in the ikonic mode, not the sensori-motor mode. This kind of search takes place about 14–16 months of age, at the age when language proper develops. The coincidence is not accidental.

The coordination of movements with information from the senses thus proceeds with increasing structural complexity within the sensorimotor mode. Until about 18 months, this remains the major mode for learning, although there are flashes of ikonic thought months earlier than this. When a 1 year old recognises Grandpa in a black-and-white photograph, ikonic thought is involved. A small two-dimensional, static, monochrome picture is not at all like interacting with a big, three-dimensional, active, technicoloured, Grandpa. A different and more abstract level of processing is involved; this kid is working with images, not with immediate percepts.

So the toddler feels a new mode of operating coming on. Sensori-motor learning is not however *displaced* in favour of learning in the ikonic mode, as the Piagetian model suggests. Both co-exist and, rather than fading out, sensori-motor learning improves. Older children and adults are in fact much better at acquiring motor skills than are infants; they make better gymnasts, for instance. But that leaves a tricky question; does the performance of gymnasts involve *only* the sensorimotor mode? We return later to that one.

The ikonic mode

Piaget (1950) defined thought as the 'internalization of action'. The simplest way of doing that is to *imagine* the action, by forming what Bruner (1964a) referred to as an internal picture of it, or an 'ikon'. We can also internalise the feel of something that we have done. So another way to internalise an action is to *feel* it: to like it, or to hate it.

The stage following the sensori-motor one is thus called *ikonic*. This is a term used to describe sacred images, which captures both the visual and the affective aspects. Ikonic thought begins after the first year of life and generalises, with the help of language (for which it is a necessary prerequisite) after 18 months.

The ikon, as the first and simplest form of internal representation, may be regarded as an image or photocopy of reality that incorporates much feeling. The distinction between cognition and affect, what is thought and what is felt, is however unclear at this stage, as is the distinction between one emotion and another. As these distinctions become clearer (perhaps to help make them clearer), the child thinks in polarities of good/evil, nice/nasty, like-it/hate-it.

Naming

Internalisation makes language itself possible. Unless there is some form of inner representation of an object, it cannot be referred to in its absence; its name is attached to its inner representation, not to the object itself. The ikonic form of inner representation has its limitations; in particular, this global, holistic mix of affect and image is rigid and uni-dimensional. That mix is associated, unanalysed, with a name or label, to which it becomes attached in a powerful and special way. Naming an object somehow explains it. You greet someone in the street.

'Who dat?'
'That's Mr Twittingham Thumpwhacker.'
'Ah.'

No more questions. A non-ikonic mind might inquire more: about TT's antecedents, his relationship to one, his salary, his love life. But the name is, in this case unsurprisingly, enough.

Egocentricity

Piaget (1926) described ikonic thought as egocentric, which follows from the unidimensional aspect of ikonic thinking. There is only one way of seeing things: the way the child sees them. Piaget meant the literal, not the moral, meaning of 'egocentric'. Consider his mountain experiment.

4 and 5 year olds are presented with a papier mâché model of a mountain scene, a peak on the left and a tree on the right. The children were asked to draw (a) what *they* saw and then (b) what someone would see from the *opposite* side of the table. Children younger than 7 years drew exactly the same picture; their view of the scene was everyone's view. Older children reversed the peak and the tree. Likewise, if young children are asked who is standing to the left of someone in a photograph, they point to the person standing on the right (i.e., to their own left). These effects now seem to depend on context. When more familiar situations are used, even 3 year olds could see that their teddy bear might see something different from a different vantage point (Borke 1978; Donaldson 1978).

A verbal version of egocentricity (from a male 5 year old):

'Do you have any brothers or sisters?'
'A sister.'
'Any brothers?'
'No.'
'Does your sister have any brothers then?'
'No.' (I don't have any brothers so neither does my sister).

Flavell and his colleagues (1968) carried out several experiments on the ability of young children to take on roles and give information. In one, two children are separated by a screen, each having the same array of pictures in front of him. One child tells the other which picture he has chosen and his partner points to a picture in front of him:

'This one?'
'Yes' (but cannot see which one is referred to).

Piaget described 'egocentric speech' in children, where the speaker does not take into account the knowledge and perspective of the listener. When two 6 year old boys talked together, 40% of their conversation was entirely self-focused; their 'dialogue' was monologue-in-turn, each speaker referring back to where *he* left off, not where his partner did. This is not, alas, limited to children.

Emotion

Unidimensionality also applies to the emotions. Preschool children are incapable of seeing themselves as experiencing more than one emotion at a time (Fischer & Bullock 1984). Two examples.

- A little girl was both happy at receiving a bike for her birthday but sad that it was only a three-speed and not a 10-speed.

Preschoolers couldn't handle this, seeing her as either happy or sad.

- A girl was nasty and nice in turn to another girl.

When asked to retell the story afterwards, a 5 year old turned it into two separate stories: one about a girl who acted nastily and the other about the girl, in a different story, who acted nicely.

The mythic stage

Where only sensori-motor and ikonic modes are available, thought is egocentric and emotions are simple. Children structure reality by using what is best known and familiar to them: themselves. Not only do they assume that other people think and feel as they do, but so do animals, plants and inanimate features such as rocks. They believe (for a while) that animals speak to them, that Teddy is hurt when he is smacked, that trees get tired as they wave to make wind. Later, they know these are not *really* true, but it helps to make sense out of the world if they assume that they are. Even in primary school, children classify natural phenomena that move, such as clouds, as 'living', although they correctly classify plants and animals as living (Angus 1981). Features used to interpret the world before formal instruction commences are difficult to eradicate.

How does a child make best sense out of this world of chattering animals, tired trees, inexplicable happenings and simplistic emotions? The paradigmatic way of science is not yet available to them, so they resort to narrative: myths, fables, legends and fairy stories. These are what engage young children's minds most powerfully (Egan 1984). Fairy stories are powerful because they reflect so accurately the characteristics of the ikonic mode. The characters portray one or two outstanding characteristics (big and bad, poor but honest). Meaning is always clear, so is who is to be disapproved of and how it all ends (good will be rewarded). The context is remote ('once upon a time …') but the time-line is linear and inevitable ('… and they lived happily ever after').

Egan calls childhood the *mythic* stage, but the fascination of high fantasy continues way beyond primary school, and so he suggests that the emotional power of myths, and later of romances, should be used to help structure the curricula, for social science, science and mathematics. Children's minds are then engaged with what they understand best and react to with meaning (Egan 1988).

Miraculous happenings, the triumph of good over evil, and emotional simplicity have a hold over people's minds well into adulthood. These are precisely the ingredients of TV soapies, professional wrestling, and political and religious fundamentalism. Lower level modes are accessible to all people: the higher and more abstract modes only to a few. So, if you want to influence the maximum number of people, target those modes that are available to everybody. The ikonic mode is the target: lots of pictures, loud repetitive slogans, little written language, emotional appeal, and little analysis and criticism.

Adult ikonicising rises beyond myth-making. The intuitive knowledge displayed in aesthetics, and even by mathematicians (Hadamard 1954) and scientists, is essentially ikonic: pictorial, a high degree of affect, difficult to put into words. Gardner (1985) relates the story of how the chemist Kekule arrived at the structure of the organic benzene ring compounds; he had a hypnogogic dream of six snakes chasing each others' tails. They formed a ring. He woke up; he had discovered his metaphor. The truth thus revealed had then to be established to the satisfaction of the scientific community by evidence and argument.

Another of Gardner's stories (op. cit.: 225) tells of Isadora Duncan, the famous dancer. She got up from a dinner party one night and danced, stunningly. When asked to explain what the dance 'meant', she replied: 'If I could tell you what it is, I would not have danced it.' It was not available as declarative knowledge; her sensori-motor calisthenics weren't her point either; their ikonic software was.

The ikonic mode is thus not a presymbolic mode of information processing restricted to early childhood. Like the sensori-motor mode, it continues to grow in power and complexity well beyond childhood. Whether that increase occurs solely within the ikonic mode, or in interaction with other modes, is an important question considered later.

The concrete-symbolic mode

The most interesting and profound change occurring throughout the childhood years is that which permits the acquisition and use of the skills of text processing: reading and writing (Mason & Allen 1986). Using symbol systems for acting on the environment is a powerful thing to do. Such systems include writing, mathematical symbols, maps and musical notation.

The point of this stage is reflected in its name. It involves the ability to process symbols in a disembedded context, cold, with little paralinguistic support (Donaldson 1978). It is to communicate without having a warm or personal relationship to the sender; to attend to words and symbols and what they mean, not to use words as broad indicators of meaning, with body language such as a nudge and a wink to show what we really mean. It is to outgrow the warm fuzzies of ikonicism. Mastery of these systems, and of their application to real world problems, is the major task in primary and secondary schooling. Learning to read in order to read to learn, and learning to write in order to learn more effectively, may sound catchy things to do, but they capture the principal aims of schooling: to help the individual handle a world in which symbol systems are a major tool.

The most interesting and profound change occuring throughout the childhood years is that which permits the acquisition and use of the skills of text processing.

Stories and myths, the units in the ikonic mode, may become very rich, complex and emotionally compelling, but they do not underpin a culture based on science and technology. Trees do not talk back; evil does not always get its comeuppance. Time and space have inevitability, a cold prickly that defies wishful thinking.

Aspects, symbols and operations

To illustrate the difference between ikonic and concrete-symbolic units of thought, let us look yet again at one of Piaget's experiments. Three coloured marbles (R for red, Y for yellow, B for blue) are placed in one end of an opaque tube. The tube is tilted and the child is asked to predict the order in which the marbles will emerge the other end when the tube is rotated. The simplest case is no rotations. Children using the ikonic mode can predict that outcome easily; the ikon that went in (R–Y–B) is the same as that which comes out.

The tube is then rotated one half-turn, which reverses the order. A preschooler will still predict the original order, R–Y–B, and will be very surprised when B–Y-R emerges: so turning makes it backwards! Thus, when the trial is repeated the correct response is likely to be given, because it is still fairly easy to read an ikon backwards. But now we give *two* half-turns. Ikonic reasoning argues that as the tube is still being turned, it's still backwards. Or maybe an extra turn really messes up the order. So there could be two replies to this one: B–Y–R (backwards again) or Y–B–R or B–R–Y (really messed up). But its neither: R–Y–B again!

Ikons are clumsy and global; there is not all that much you can do with them and they do not predict a changing physical world very well at all. So to handle this problem effectively, we need to *abstract* or disembed the salient features and link them to some kind of symbol system. The salient features are:

- There are only two aspects of the colours to be considered, reverse order and same order.
- The number of turns determines whether the outcome is reverse or same.

These features are abstracted from the ikon and make it possible to operate in the concrete-symbolic mode, correctly shadowing the world with symbolic representations, appropriately linked.

The simplest concrete-symbolic response is to take these two abstractions and coordinate them mentally, trying to match the turn with whether it is reverse or same. This breaks down fairly quickly, but if a third element is brought in—*keep count*—the problem is manageable, if clumsy. Thus, a better way of handling the problem is:

(a) learn that one gives reverse, two gives same, three gives reverse, four gives same;
(b) keep count of the number of turns actually given.

But that is clumsy. Better still, code the number of turns as an *odd* or an *even* number. All you have to do is to count the number of turns and note if that is odd or even.

What we see developing through the concrete-symbolic mode, then, are the following aspects:

- use of *critical aspects* of the problem;
- *a symbol system* to represent them;
- a set of appropriate *operations* to perform on the symbols.

In other words, the individual is working at one step removed from reality, but still firmly linked with what is given and present in the situation. There are no hypotheticals, or what-ifs.

Conservation

The essence of the concrete-symbolic mode is finding a coordinating relationship that gives stability to the task in question, or what Piaget called conservation. Lemonade is poured into two identical glasses to the same height. The child agrees that both are the same. One glass is then poured into a tall thin glass so that the lemonade reaches a higher level. If the ikonic mode is used, as it typically is until around five years, the tall glass is chosen:

> 'Because there's more.'
> 'Why?'
> 'Because it's taller.'

When the tall glass is poured into a squat broad glass, the child now prefers the original, because:

> 'It's now taller and there's more in it.'

In the ikonic mode, judgments are based on appearance and total impressions. 'Conservation' demands that appearances be ignored in favour of the coordinating relationship: nothing has been added or taken away, so the result remains constant. This point applies whatever the context or however familiar the task; yet Piaget showed (rather against his own theory) that conservation in the lemonade-and-glass experiments was obtained a year or so earlier than conservation of weight. In the latter experiment, two identical balls of plasticine are placed one in each pan of a balance and the child agrees that they weigh the same. But if one ball is rolled into a long thin sausage, the child will now state that the sausage weighs more than the ball. Conservation of volume is obtained even later, nearer 11 or 12 years; the balls of plasticine are each placed into a graduated cylinder already half-filled with water. The water level rises equally in both cases. One of the balls is taken out of its cylinder and rolled into a long thin sausage: the child now predicts that it will displace more water than the ball.

The same logic explains all three cases of conservation, but the lemonade case is resolved much earlier and more readily than others. Again we see that context rather than a general structure determines behaviour. Logical structures are not the point, but other factors such as familiarity with the task, its complexity, and the number of unknowns.

Formal and post-formal modes

Somewhere after beginning high school, some students will show that they can operate in the formal mode, with many giving formal responses by Year 11 and onwards. These responses are *context-free,* which means that they often lack closure or a definite conclusion. Responses in the formal mode typically contain phrases like: 'Only if ... which is likely to be the case ... the effect is similar to ... all these effects assume ... if these changed, then ...' The undergraduate's way of winning arguments uses the formal mode: 'It depends what you mean by a screwed-up economy. If you look at it from the banks' point of view, they're making big profits for future investment; arguably for the long-term benefit of the country. Ah! But I did say "arguably". And I did say "long term". Let's take each separately. If, on the other hand, you look at it ... blah, blah, blah.'

Such arguments come from general principle, which can be applied to several sets of particulars, hence references to alternative meanings and circumstances determining different interpretations. This is in contrast to the concrete-symbolic position which uses language directly and focuses on the particular given case. The appreciation of general principle ushers in the world of the possible, of what *might* be the case.

Exhausting what might be the case: The pendulum problem

The pendulum problem (Piaget & Inhelder 1958) requires one to find the relationships between factors influencing the swing (or period) of a pendulum. The student is supplied with strings of different lengths, a ruler and a light and a heavy weight. A weight is attached to a string; the resulting pendulum is suspended and pushed. The student times the period of swing and reports the result. Ikonic children tend to have the firm idea that the strength of the push determines how fast the pendulum swings. They duly observe and note this finding; their preconceptions govern what they actually see. In fact, the amount of push has nothing to do with the period of the swing.

Children operating in the concrete-symbolic mode are not thus misled by their preconceptions; they are able to observe quite accurately. They then examine other factors.

Does the heaviness of the weight have an effect? Or the length of the string? To test these ideas, they might first tie a light weight to a short string and time that. The first one went faster; thus, the swing depends upon both weight and the length of the string, right? Wrong; the experiment was not properly controlled, as not all the possibilities were examined.

It is necessary to control for weight independently of length and for length independently of weight; logically, there are *four* possibilities, not two. The question is not heavy–long versus light–short; but heavy–long versus heavy–short versus light–long versus light–short. Thus, the following table can be set up and the results noted for each alternative:

Weight	Length	Result
Heavy	Long	Slow
Heavy	Short	Fast
Light	Long	Slow
Light	Short	Fast

Weight has no effect at all; the period may be slow or fast with a heavy or a light weight. But altering length affects periodicity every time: a short string produces a fast period, a long string a slow period, whatever the weight. This is an example of experimental control in scientific research; you work out all the possibilities and then rule them out, one by one.

To think in the formal mode is to conceive reality not only in terms of what is, but also in terms of what might possibly be within the given constraints; we look at all possibilities of length and weight. Formal thought is flexible; if one solution does not work, look at plausible alternatives and try them out.

Verbalising in the formal mode

Thought in the formal mode is not however limited to mathematical and scientific thinking. As we have seen when undergraduates argue, it-depends-what-you-mean-by can be used in contexts ranging from politics to deciding the best football team. Questioning-the-question is another example of formal flexibility, which can equally be used as an argument-winning strategy. You don't accept the given question, but generate one that should have been asked (and that you can answer): 'So what we *should* be addressing is not the question of balance of payments, but the big one. Who stands most to gain by selling off Tasmania to the private sector? ...'

But teachers and students need to be careful about 'doing a formal'. Some HSC examiners may not take kindly to a paper that begins: 'This question is misleading. What the examiner should be asking, if I read the intent correctly, is ...' On the other hand, other examiners might be delighted at some originality for a change. It is a high-risk strategy; examiners know it is easy to do a 'snow-job', using the trappings of the formal mode to conceal substantive ignorance.

The appreciation of political cartoons is essentially a formal task (Elkind 1968). The point of a good cartoon is the metaphor that is hidden in it, which may require the formal mode to decode it. Many cartoons involve the principle of the *reductio ad absurdum*, in which the logical implications of a situation are played out to a ludicrous end — but to get the joke, you have to abstract the implied principle.

For example, in an article 'How good is your sense of humor?' *(Weekend Magazine*, 10 July 1971), 10 jokes were listed, with four punch-lines given for each: one had to pick the best and funniest line and then match one's choice with the punch-line selected by the 'panel of experts'. As we hope you will see (Box 2.1), the 'best' punch-line is the formal one.

Box 2.1   *At what level of development is your sense of humour?*

A man with an unpronounceable European name changed it to McGillicuddy. Three months later he changed it once more, this time to MacDonald. When asked why he had done this, he replied:

1. I liked the MacDonald tartan better than the McGillicuddy one.
2. I decided I'd rather be a Mac than a Mick.
3. Every time I met someone, he would ask me what my name was before I changed it.
4. We Scots like to have change.

It's not difficult to see which is the superior choice: 1, 2 and 4 all involve a simple extension of the original joke, structured by fact or preference; whereas 3 involves an extension of the joke in terms of intrinsic logical structure. The latter is embedded abstractly in the joke, the rest are given fairly directly and obviously. Try it out on children of different ages and see what they say.

Source: Weekend Magazine, 10 July 1971.

Self-awareness in the formal mode

Adolescent thought, entering as it does the formal mode, deals with a world of *possibilities*. These possibilities are not only those generated by the laws and principles that govern social systems and the physical world, but also *oneself*. As we shall see in Chapter 12, metacognition is an important set of processes that involves awareness of oneself. The formal mode allows this kind of self-awareness to reach levels not available in childhood.

Such self-awareness often arrives as a moment of truth, dominating adolescent thinking to the point where they think and behave in what appears to be a very egocentric way. The egocentrism of adolescence is however quite different from that of early childhood (Elkind 1967). Thinkers in the ikonic mode, typically preschoolers, are unselfconscious in their egocentrism; there simply is no other perspective but their own. Adolescents, on the other hand, discriminate all too easily between their world and other people's and alternatively cringe and swagger at the comparison. Other people have a view too and it includes ... (ta dum) ... *me*! Hence both the pretension and the morbid self-examination of adolescence; my-view-of-me and their-view-of-me keep offering different, sometime incompatible, perspectives. The task of adulthood is, with experience, to reconcile those perspectives so that the 'real' Twittingham Thumpwhacker finally stands up. Unfortunately, this task is rarely concluded; the formal realisation of self would see that answer varying according to the period of life in question (see 'The course of cognitive growth in adulthood', below).

The awareness of self evolves in stages that Piaget described in his earlier work (Piaget 1932). He described *allocentric* (as opposed to egocentric) thought as enabling individuals to see others and themselves in the same light; as the Golden Rule says, 'Do unto others as you would have them do unto you'. Allocentrism is also involved in what professional writers call a sense of audience, that is, evaluating your own text from how the reader is likely to see it, not how you see it. Audience sense does not unequivocally appear in children's writing (under normal conditions) until middle to senior high school or Years 11 to 12, which is when essay writers can talk about what they were going to say from the point of view of the presumed reader, as opposed to their own point of view as the writer (Burtis, Bereiter, Scardamalia & Tetroe 1984).

Allocentrism, then, means thinking about ourselves in the formal mode, subjecting ourselves to the same critical scrutiny as we would others. When we can do this, we can weave many more possibilities and contexts into our plans about ourselves, and for the first time really begin to compare ourselves with others on standardised dimensions. This means too that the foundations are there for a realistic self-concept, not one based on wish-fulfilment or evaluations reflected from others.

All that, however, takes time; it certainly does not fall into place by the end of adolescence. In late adolescence, most individuals are still too impressed (one way or the other) with their self-discovery to allow their discovered self to occupy a realistic place in relation to the rest of the world and to meet the same standards they wish on everyone else. 'Oh, but *my* case is different', they say. Don't we all?

Formal thinking in the tertiary sector

In formal thought, principle is used to explain the world and to order the behaviour of people. It enables us to deduce what might happen in particular circumstances that we have not yet actually experienced, to conclude that the world is a stable and ordered place, to solve equations with two unknown variables, to apply the four rules of number meaningfully to indeterminate quantities, to vote for a political party whose policies are against our own personal interests, to define the formal characteristics of an Agatha Christie novel ...

When we take topics within a content area, we come with experience to be able to define more and more of these principles, and after a while we see them beginning to interrelate. When that happens we can say that we are beginning to appreciate an *academic discipline:* physics, biology, mathematics, literary criticism and so on. And that is the progress followed by students at university. They enter with a smattering of principles, which they continue to acquire systematically until the time comes when they have an overview, a grasp, of established knowledge in that discipline. Degree structures at tertiary level in the basic disciplines are thus hierarchical: a student reads the major subject in increasing depth from first through second to third year, and by the end of third year the student should be thinking like a physicist about physical science matters, or like a historian about history.

In many professionally oriented courses the structure is different. They are designed to give some competence in several relevant subjects, with a view to their application in the chosen field of professional practice. A teacher, for example, needs to know the content area, how to design curricula, how to teach different kinds of topics in appropriate ways to different levels of students, how to evaluate their learning, to understand the role of school in society, to understand how individuals learn and are motivated, something of the nature of human abilities, and so on and on. Thus it is not so much studying a discipline in increasing depth, but integrating a range of declarative and procedural knowledge to form an espoused theory that will guide theory-in-practice in the classroom. The integration, too, is a task calling for formal thought.

Post-formal thought

Let's 'do a formal' on the conventional wisdom and question its questions. What if the orthodoxy has assumed something that ought not to be assumed? What if parallel lines *do* meet? What if the 'Mahogany Ship' had grounded in Sydney Cove, not in the Bight; and what if its cargo comprised Portuguese convicts and its captain was searching for prison space? What if the dinosaurs had not been exterminated 63 million years ago: would not egg-laying *Saurus sapiens,* unfettered by the limitations the birth canal places on cranial capacity, be vastly more intelligent than *Homo sapiens*? These are *post-formal* questions. They give rise to research on the one hand, science fiction on the other: the paradigmatic way and the way of narrative, respectively (Bruner 1985).

Thus, formal thought isn't the end of the road, contrary to the impression given by Piaget. Post-formal thought may be seen in high-level innovations in many fields, such as the prodigious performances in music, mathematics, literature and the arts noted by Gardner (1985). Demetriou and Efklides (1985) tested post-formal thought by requiring the respondent to operate in novel systems and, in a metacognition test, to report on their processing while solving novel problems; few could do so (see also Commons, Richards & Kuhn 1982).

Such a deficit may explain the difficulty some hitherto high-achieving undergraduates have in coming to terms with the requirements of research, as opposed to coursework, higher degrees. Research requires that the established orthodoxy be questioned; existing theory does not explain this phenomenon; those results are inconsistent; there is a flaw in this experiment. A research student has to question established authority and to design a solution or a procedure to satisfy the problem. A bachelor graduate goes into the world to practise this or that profession with a reasonably clear idea of the state of the art in the relevant discipline. A researcher is more interested in what the discipline is not and what it might become.

Optimal level: The accumulation of modes

You will have noticed that Piaget's experiments have frequently been cited to illustrate functioning in these modes. What then are the differences between neo-Piaget and vintage Piaget? There are two major ones:

1. The mode is a *medium* in which learning and thinking take place. There is no necessary structural connection between learning one topic and learning another. Thus, the cognitive level at which one particular topic is learned is independent of the level at which a different topic is learned. There are no necessary structural links across topics; we do not expect 'evenness'.
2. With age, higher level modes of thinking and learning become possible, *in addition to* those already in use. The lower levels are not replaced by the higher levels; whereas stages replace each other, modes accumulate.

These differences are important, so different terminology is used. Thus 'mode' of thinking is used rather than 'stage' of thinking because stage implies an irreversible sequence, whereas mode implies simply that in the present case a particular medium for handling the problem in question has been used. Thus, at any given age, the highest emerging mode places an *optimal level* at which the child of that age can operate, but he or she can equally operate below that level. Piaget thought that operating below the given stage level was exceptional and pathological, calling it a '*decalage*'; it is however extremely common and often quite adaptive (Biggs & Collis 1982a; Fischer & Bullock 1984). Learning can in fact be 'multimodal', where more than one mode is used, as we see below. Another difference is that in Piagetian theory people are described as 'being at' or 'belonging to' a particular stage, which immediately tells a Piagetian how to expect a child to operate in most tasks. However, to say that a child can operate optimally in the concrete-symbolic mode in a task means only that the maximum level for that child is concrete-symbolic: that under the most favourable conditions the child is capable of operating at that level, but don't hold your breath. Under conditions of low motivation, or an unfamiliar task or context, a suboptimal performance is likely.

Thus, different terms are generally used to designate modes as opposed to stages.

- 'Sensorimotor' remains the same, although Bruner (1966) used the term 'enactive'. Sensorimotor implies the coordination of perceptual input with motor output, whereas enactive implies a more general learning-by-doing. Either term seems satisfactory: certainly coordination is important at the early stages of learning, while later, as the learning becomes more autonomous, enactive is an adequate description.
- Bruner's term 'ikonic' is preferred to 'preoperational' because the latter refers to subsequent stages based on logical operations. The crucial point is that it is the nature of the stuff of learning, not the logic used during learning, that is now the issue.
- 'Concrete operations' is referred to as 'concrete-symbolic' mode and 'formal operations' becomes simply 'formal' mode. Piaget did not refer to a 'post-formal' stage.

The modes and their general ages of acquisition, are depicted in Figure 2.1:

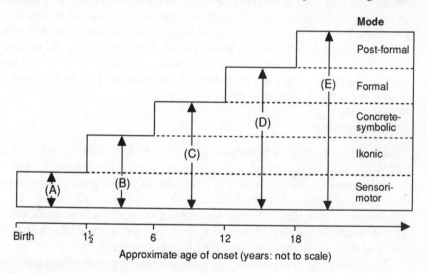

Fig. 2.1 *The accumulatiom of modes at typical ages*

As the figure shows, from birth until around 18 months only the sensorimotor mode is available to a child (A). A child of 5 years, say, has either ikonic or sensorimotor modes, with ikonic being the optimal level (B). A 10 year old child has three modes available, concrete-symbolic being optimal (C). A typical 16 year old has three modes, the formal mode being optimal (D), and in adulthood some people have post-formal as optimal (E). These optimal levels do not mean that most, or even much, of the time a person will be functioning in that mode. Optimal only means that given the right kind of demanding task and the motivation and the conditions such as available time and other resources, then the individual may handle the task within the optimal mode. It is inappropriate, then, to use modes as a means of describing people: an ikonic child, a formal adolescent.

It is important for teachers to realise this. Piagetian theory was once interpreted as saying that normally all tasks *should* be handled in the way dictated by the person's developmental stage, and that there was something wrong if they were not so handled. All adolescents should in this view be taught formally, that is, deductively, from first principles. They should not; we know that such teaching emphasises declarative at the expense of procedural knowledge, that it makes learning unnecessarily difficult and that it is extremely boring.

Readiness

Also according to this interpretation, you wouldn't teach content before children were 'ready' (e.g. Biggs 1959; Furth 1970; Lovell 1961). If, in the conservation experiments, the child saw the number of sweets in a line changing according to whether they were packed closely together or strung out, then evidently that child had not grasped the idea that quantity was constant unless something has been added or taken away, and was not yet be 'ready' for arithmetic. To add things up, you must assume that five objects are still five in number, whether they are packed closely together or spread out in a long line.

But that argument assumes that children use the logician's concept of number and they do not (Brainerd 1975). Children construct their own ways of handling particular tasks. Even when they have grasped the key point in conservation (that if nothing has been added or taken away the result is the same) for one task, it does not follow that they will see that same point in another context or with a different task. Sweets spread out are one thing, plasticine rolled out is another. You can't predict from a test result in one context to a different context, even if the test involves the same principle. Logicians look at number and counting with their formal and even post-formal modes, children with ikonic and sensori-motor modes.

Intermodal learning

Children (and adults) learn 'bottom up', that is they recode their understandings gained in lower modes to higher ones over time. As we saw in Chapter 1, children *already possess* at an everyday level (= ikonic in most cases) a working understanding of many of the concepts taught declaratively in school. We learn in an ascending cycle: even formal adults learn a new game of cards with sensorimotor practice hands, much ikonic support and then some declarative back up about the rules. They do not learn the rules first and then apply them perfectly with their first hand.

Thus, learning in one mode can facilitate learning in another; learning can be *intermodal*.

Figure 2.1 suggests that there are two ways of learning across modes: from higher to lower ('top-down') or from lower to higher ('bottom-up'). These describe how learning may proceed across modes, a fact that can be used to generate highly successful teaching strategies.

Top-down

The sensori-motor learning of adolescents and adults is vastly superior to that of infants. You may not find that at all surprising, but if learning proceeded only within and not across modes it would be. Of course, the brains and nervous systems of adults are more highly developed than those of infants, but more important than that, adults use higher order modes when they learn in a lower mode.

Imagine that you are practising your dart-throwing skill (don't move a muscle); you will find that your *actual* dart-throwing skill improves with your mental practice and of course sports coaches use that principle (Paivio 1986). Singing coaches require their students to imagine that their voice emerges from a mask about a foot above and away from their face ('singing into the mask'): the voice projects better as a result.

Let us consider the learning of motor skills a little further. Three stages in motor skill learning are usually postulated (Fitts 1962): *cognitive* analysis of the task and verbalisation of what is involved, so that the learner understands what to do; *fixative*, involving practice to the point of competent performance; and *autonomous*, involving further practice to the point of automaticity. Presumably the target in motor skill learning is sensori-motor, but the first of Fitts' stages does not require sensor-imotor involvement; the kind of knowledge aimed at here is declarative (to verbalise and to understand what is involved). The fixative stage focuses primarily on the sensori-motor (target) mode and the final goal of autonomous skill involves tacit, procedural knowledge.

Several modes are thus engaged in learning the skill, although its performance is realised in the sensori-motor mode. Individuals with different purposes, however, would variously use different modes in the service of skill learning. Performing artists will naturally focus on the skill itself; Olympic athletes want to get the skill tuned to the finest point. Others use the execution of a skill to make an ikonic point. The skill of a virtuoso violinist is not deployed merely to make us gape in admiration at the speed at which notes are played, but to move us by the interpretation of the music. Coaches would be more oriented towards the higher order modes, involving declarative knowledge of physiology, nutrition and mechanics, in order to derive better strategies for training and for performance.

Skill learning, then, with a lower mode as target, can be enhanced by the use of higher modes: formal, concrete-symbolic and ikonic. The same of course applies to learning in other 'lower' modes, such as dancing, fine arts and music performance. In teaching painting, you don't just teach skill in brushstrokes and copy from set models, such as the bowl of fruit in the Victorian art classes.

Bottom-up

Here the target is located in a high-level mode and lower levels are used in reaching it. In an oft-quoted and deeply misunderstood phrase, Bruner once said:

> Any subject can be taught in some intellectually honest form to any child in any stage of development. (1960: 33)

What that means is precisely that you can teach the sensori-motor and ikonic prototypes of concrete-symbolic or formal knowledge; and not only that you can, but *should* (Bruner 1964a). Even to learn at the symbolic level, Bruner (1964b) concluded that it was better to retrace through enactive (sensori-motor) and ikonic levels, an example being teaching mathematics by Dienes' multibase arithmetic blocks (Dienes 1963), as discussed further in Chapter 8.

Bottom-up learning has actually long been advocated in progressive educational circles. Inductive, experiential, workshop, constructivists and discovery classroom methods also assume the bottom-up principle. Egan (1988:2) describes an interesting attempt in the elementary school to 'use the power of the story form in order to teach any content more engagingly and meaningfully'. The story form has been well learned in the ikonic mode prior to school and Egan proposes that it can be used to draw students into any academic content, thus attacking a concrete-symbolic target from an ikonic baseline.

He uses a technique of abstracting conflicting concepts that are intrinsic to a topic and working through the conflict in such diverse areas as social science, mathematics, English and science. The technique does not cover the whole curriculum of each, but it provides a structure, motivation and imaginative challenge: a useful framework for the drier concrete-symbolic content to follow.

Resnick, Bill and Lesgold (1992) give a more focused account of linking primary (Years 1–3) student's ikonic ('protoquantitative', they call it) knowledge of number with the traditional requirements of arithmetic teaching: computation and problem solving. We cannot describe the program, except to note the six principles that guided them:

1. Draw children's informal knowledge, developed outside school, into the classroom.
2. Develop children's trust in their own knowledge.
3. Use formal notations (e.g., equations) as a public record of discussions and conclusions.
4. Introduce key mathematical structures as quickly as possible.
5. Encourage everyday problem finding.
6. Talk about mathematics, don't just do arithmetic.

In interaction, these principles in a sense do the obvious; they use students' present knowledge and understanding of number ideas, which is considerable but intuitive and not expressed in traditional paradigms, and *integrate* that with mathematical operations and the symbol system, rather than *fighting* them as 'incorrect' (see also, 'Dealing with alternative frameworks' in the next chapter). The results were dramatic, both in performance and in attitudes to arithmetic. In Chapter 8, we return to bottom-up methods of teaching when we look at information processing, learning and memory.

The processes of developmental growth

How does development occur? Why do new modes open out for our use? There are several possibilities:

- *Physiology,* the biological process of maturation, allows new ways of thinking to emerge as a result of changes in the brain and nervous system. Physiological changes may make shifts *possible,* but they do not guarantee them; other conditions are necessary.
- *Prior knowledge,* obtained by building up a number of related tasks to a high level of competence in the previous mode.
- *Confrontation or challenge,* which forces the realisation that the existing repertoire of lower level modes is inadequate to handle a new problem.
- *Social support,* which again has both cognitive and motivational aspects.

Let us look at each of these factors in turn.

The role of physiology

Precisely how physiology affects our ability to handle abstract tasks is a matter that has not been researched well (Fischer & Bullock 1984). At least it is clear that brain size, brain wave patterns and sleep cycles appear to undergo periodic and regular changes, which on average seem to parallel the ages at which modal changes typically occur. Epstein (1978) reports rapid growth in brain areas (measured by skull circumference) at the key ages, although Marsh (1985) reanalysed Epstein's own data and found that spurts did exist, but not in the regular intervals suggested.

Case (1985) refers to 'waves of myelinisation' occurring at the crucial age periods (which would not show up in skull circumference) and says that 'these waves take place in neurological systems which serve different psychological functions' (p.380). The myelin sheath is a fatty protective coating that improves the efficiency of neural transmission and these sheaths grow fairly suddenly in different brain areas throughout childhood, the last such wave of myelinisation occurring between 18 and 25 years, the age period in which post-formal thought develops. When these sheaths grow, they protect neurones from interfering with each other, resulting in more rapid and efficient operation. It could easily be the case that progressively higher order (more abstract) thinking becomes possible as more and more areas of the brain start interacting more efficiently. Whatever the actual mechanism, the idea is quite plausible.

A physiological explanation can, however, only be part of the story. To put it crudely, physiology may determine the 'stuff' with which we think, but the specific content, the thoughts themselves, can only come from experience. Thus, a person will reach the higher modes only with sufficient and appropriate experience in the relevant content and only with a great deal of experience (e.g., formal writing and schoolwork) will that mode become the preferred option. Early in our acquisition of a task, then, we prefer working in a more concrete mode, but later, with experience, we come to operate more efficiently in the most abstract modes.

A high level of competence or prior knowledge in the previous mode

Another prerequisite, then, is to build a knowledge base of related topics. Three processes are relevant here (Vosniadou & Brewer 1987):

1. *Accretion:* in which new factual information is gradually acquired within existing cognitive structures.
2. *Weak restructuring:* in which cognitive structures 'evolve' to better interpret the information and is a 'vertical' process, wherein the contents are organised under a relating or integrating concept. The essence of the relating concept is that it incorporates what may be construed as *common* to the aspects of the task, so that they are no longer disconnected.
3. *Radical restructuring:* in which different cognitive structures (different in terms of structure and the phenonema they explain) are used to reorganise the problem or topic. This is a shift in thinking extended into the next, more abstract, mode.

These three steps form a hierarchy. Radical restructuring is not accomplished until knowledge has been gained (1) and structured (2). One essential ingredient in operating at a higher modal level in a particular task or content area is likely to involve the growth of a high degree of competence in that specific task in the previous mode. This is another way of saying that developmental growth requires that we become cleverer at particular tasks. That provides the link between learning and development and is the subject of Chapter 3.

Confrontation and challenge

But why should the student try to radically restructure at a higher level? For the same reason as applies within modes; there is a mismatch between what is known and what is needed to be known. As we shall see in Chapter 10, such a mismatch may be very motivating. We are seekers after meaning; we have to interrelate things as much as possible in order to make sense out of a large, complex and changing environment. We are creatures that respond to a felt need to make sense. We are simply built that way.

In shifting from one mode to another, then, *prior knowledge* and *confrontation with a problem* requiring reorganising that knowledge are both necessary. Do we then call these new principles out of thin air? Hardly. We get them from other people, which is where the next condition comes in.

Social support

Several writers refer to social support as a factor in hastening development (Bidell & Fischer 1992; Valsiner 1992; Vygotsky 1978). Vygotsky referred to 'zones of proximal development', within which children become increasingly ready to shift into a more abstract mode and, with appropriate social support from parent or teacher, they may operate at that higher level.

Interaction with other people hastens development in two ways: by providing the *content* (what to go for) and by providing provisional *support* in getting there.

Scaffolding

Scaffolding, or embedded teaching (Fischer & Bullock 1984) is a common form of support. Scaffolding in language learning is when parents (in particular) provide supportive structures in a close one-to-one (dyadic) interaction with their child. In embedded teaching, as opposed to the formal teaching dealt with in schools, the flow of information is tuned to the child's ongoing and self-initiated activity and is continually adjusted to suit, in nature and rate of flow, the child's immediate behaviour:

> 'What's this?'
> 'That's macaroni, darling.'
> 'Macagroni?'
> 'Macaroni.'
> 'Macaroni.'
> 'That's right, darling, macaroni.'

Formal teaching does not involve such closely interwoven interaction:

> 'That's macaroni on your plate.'
> 'Nxtgz.'

In formal instruction, unlike in embedded teaching, the initiative for volunteering the information is the teacher's and the child's response is not the baseline, let alone the cue, for the teacher's response. Formal instruction is non–interactive; like the macaroni, you take it or leave it. Formally instructed knowledge is thus less likely to be deeply integrated with existing knowledge, but is accumulated on the side, in isolation from what the child perceives as important knowledge.

Modelling

Another important social support for cognitive change is modelling, both by peers and by teachers. Other people provide both examples of what can be done and the push to do them: to be as good as others, to be like someone who is admired by doing the same things, to be better than others (see Chapter 10). Peers also play an important role in developing metacognitive processes, so that self-awareness, planning for realistic goals, are likely to encourage cognitive growth (see Chapter 12).

Providing content

Both peers and teachers play the important role of providing the *content* that will help the child structure experience vertically. Where do we obtain most of those integrating, superordinate concepts that create weak and radical restructuring? From other people, wiser than us! We do not reinvent the wheel all the time: we try to understand what others are saying and use that as best we may.

Thinking in a higher mode may thus be promoted in the following ways, once the biological hardware is in place:

- establishing well-structured prior knowledge;
- providing challenging problems;
- providing social support both of peers and of adults to scaffold thinking, to provide helpful content, and to motivate.

The school may contribute to all three, possibly more so than it does already. The school has three main processes to foster:

1. the *accretion* of relevant knowledge (a horizontal process) and familiarisation with it;
2. the task of *interpreting* knowledge (a weak restructuring);
3. the task of *generalising* knowledge (a radical restructuring, across modes).

Enhancing each of these processes raises different issues for curriculum, teaching method and assessment. Processes (1) and (2) involve becoming cleverer, a large issue dealt with in the next chapter.

The course of cognitive growth in adulthood

Piaget (among others) gave the distinct impression that the peak of cognitive performance was in adolescence and it's downhill from there. It's not. A great deal of research shows change for the better in adult thinking, long after adolescence: in emotional development and in our relationships with other people (e.g., Erikson 1959; Levinson et al. 1978), in cognitive processes (Knox 1977; Schaie 1979), and in metacognitive aspects of thinking (Volet, Lawrence & Dodds 1986; Demetriou & Efklides 1985). There is a balance of gains and losses (Baltes 1987).

Tested intelligence and brain deterioration

So, whence this myth of adolescent perfection? Data used to derive norms for intelligence tests seemed to show that intelligence reached a peak in the early twenties, then slowly declined thereafter, with increasing rapidity from age 60 or so (e.g., Wechsler 1955). IQ data are, however, obtained cross-sectionally; they are group *averages* of people, aged 20, 30, 40, 50, etc., who have received different amounts of schooling, so that the older the group generally the less the schooling. As many of Wechsler's items reflected the effects of schooling, and as IQ is related to schooling (see Chapter 6), older people obtained lower IQs.

When people are followed *longitudinally* (their own performance is compared to what they themselves did earlier), the decline is evident in some, disappears in others and reverses in still others (Knox 1977; Schaie 1979). *Lifestyle* determines whether or not there is a decline from early childhood. People who leave school early, and get jobs that do not require the sorts of things sampled in IQ tests, start dropping in performance in their twenties, but those in professions in which they have to 'use their brains' do not decline until much later. People may deteriorate rapidly in retirement, but that is often due to their software ('I've been chucked on the rubbish heap'), not to their hardware.

Nevertheless, it is true that the brain changes that occur after the early twenties *are* detrimental. Brain cells die at an increasing rate and are not replaced, a process which is markedly hastened by drugs (alcohol being the most significant in our society), chemicals (such as aluminium), and factors affecting oxygen supply (smoking and snoring being a bad combination). Such factors, with heredity, bring about enormous differences in the rate at which the brain deteriorates and when manifest signs of senility occur. *Consistent* deterioration in test scores after early adulthood occurs only in speeded or timed items involving sensori-motor coordination. Unlike the standard industrial practice of hiring and firing—last on first off—with cognitive deterioration, it's the first mode to develop that is the first to decline.

The upside is that in everyday life we value 'maturity of judgment', 'experience', and other cognitive improvements with experience. What improves? Older people *know* more; they are more worldly-wise. They score higher on test items measuring what Cattell (1971) calls 'crystallised intelligence', that is, test items involving world knowledge, formal reasoning, vocabulary, and the use of language generally (Knox 1977). Experience also helps people handle conditional knowledge more effectively: to discriminate better, to learn to plan ahead, to watch themselves so that they do not make the same mistake again; in general, to be more *metacognitive* (see Chapter 12).

Thus, it should come as no surprise, although it will to highly intelligent adolescents, that Volet, Lawrence and Dodds (1986) showed that adults of average intelligence were far superior to highly intelligent scholarship girls in solving problems that required planning and coordinating one's activities. The subjects were given a map of Perth City Centre and a bus timetable; their task was to plan a Saturday morning in town (when some shops closed at 1 p.m.) to include some specified shopping, to visit a friend in hospital, and to be back home on a certain bus. Almost all adults accomplished all tasks; almost none of the bright girls did.

Likewise, mature age tertiary students are better at planning academic study than regular students of the same academic year; the older the student, the clearer they tend to be about their motives for studying, the relevance of their learning to their own lives, and the need for planning and organisation (Biggs 1987a). Paradoxically, it is the mature age student who *feels* insecure: 'I've forgotten how to study!' The evidence is however that they are far better at it than their younger classmates.

Stages through the lifespan

The notion of stages and processes in adulthood came first from post-Freudian psycho-analysts in treating adult patients. The two most influential today are Erikson (1959), with his eight stages covering the entire lifespan, and Jung (1956), who concentrated on problems associated with the middle adult years (the so-called 'midlife crisis').

Levinson et al. (1978) used a Jungian framework to study 40 adult males in depth (the restriction to males, Levinson says, was due to logistics not choice; he claims the same principles apply to women). They found stage-like 'seasons', during which subjects confronted typical problems or *choices* that must be faced. An incorrect choice now exacted a high price at a later choice period. These periods of self-evaluation, choice, and commitment occur at three key seasons: in the early twenties, at 40, and at 60 years of age.

After leaving school or university, young males have to show competence in the two areas in which Freud (1905) said mature adults have to do well: love and work. They form a 'dream' of the kind of life they want as adults; all depends on how realistic the dream is, both in real-world terms and in the sense of being true to oneself. Next, a mentor appears, usually a teacher or older colleague, who forms a special guiding relationship towards realising the dream. An occupation is 'formed' rather than chosen: likewise marriage and family. Love balances work; but if the balance is wrong, it hangs out in the mid-stage review around age 30, a divorce prime time. A more major review occurs at the end of the thirties, ushering in the midlife transition, a time of moderate to severe crisis.

Age 40 is what Jung called the 'noonhour of life'. Before then, all has gone into realising the dream, at the expense of other important aspects of the self, which now need to be expressed. Usually by 40, a person will either have achieved the dream, or will know that it never will be. The individual now turns inwards, to the hitherto neglected aspects of self: women tend to become more aggressive and 'masculine', men more nurturant and 'feminine'. Some really cut loose; Paul Gauguin, once a timid bank clerk in Paris, raged his way to Tahiti, there to paint and to make love on a generous front. Others may dwell on death and impermanence and then embrace their antidotes; jogging, dieting, and giving up substances.

Towards the end of the forties, or later, the lucky ones achieve a kind of equilibrium Jung referred to as *individuation,* a state of integration that has religious overtones. On reaching that state, one dreams of the mandala, a symbol of integration, comprising outward-reaching lines surrounded by a circle, the whole signifying completion. A cross surrounded by a halo is one example. Another is a swastika, which adorns Chinese Taoist temples on the one hand, the tailfins of Messerschmitts on the other.

The world has changed rather critically since the mid-seventies when Levinson's work was undertaken. Nevertheless, it is important that teachers recognise that thinking develops progressively after leaving school and to be aware of some of the tasks that young people face on entering adult life. Studies are urgently needed for Australia; particularly those that apply to both sexes and that take into account the difficulties many young people have, not only in forming an occupation, but in coping with the prospect of being denied the opportunity of even making the attempt.

Do adult learners differ from younger learners?

Knowles (1978) thought so. He called the adult learner a 'neglected species' and proposed *androgogy* as the science of instruction suited to the adult, as *pedagogy* is that suited to the child. Some of the more important features of the adult learner are :

1. Adults are motivated to learn particular topics because their life situation has defined a need to know, or because they have developed an interest in a topic. They rarely study something because they have been told it will be important to them one day: it already is important, now.
2. What adults learn is thus based in current experience. Genuine problems define what is important to learn, not the fact that the topic belongs in a particular subject area.

3. Adults come to a topic with a background of experience in the area, often considerable, and often a high degree of success.
4. Adults are strongly oriented towards *self-direction* in their learning, whereas younger students react to a learning situation directed by others (teachers).
5. Individual differences between learners, in their knowledge, styles and competencies, increase with age, so that older students are more diverse than younger students.

Adults are frequently highly self-directed, defining for themselves what they want to know, where to go to find out and when their requirements for that learning have been met (Candy 1991; Tough 1971). On the other hand, they believe in the need for formal qualifications. As adults, they have a higher personal stake, both financial and in their self-esteem; success and failure are much more important to them. When institutional learning is structured too heavily, adults can go overboard in struggling for high grades and in being competitive. As noted, mature age learners often incorrectly feel unfairly disadvantaged when in the same class as younger through-the-system students: but not always (see Box 2.2).

Box 2.2   *Reflections of a MAS*

Mr Ted Miller's reason for coming to university was an awareness of impending early retirement. He says his first days as a MAS (mature-age student) were horrific.

'When one walked towards the first lecture or tutorial after half a lifetime spent out in the marketplace, humility was the dominant mood! In this new and strange environment, you were unsure of what responses were expected of you, wondering what that turbulent sea of young students thought of you, but more importantly what your tutor thought of this strange, too well-dressed, middle-aged creature who was trying too visibly hard to blend into the group. You had to learn a new jargon', Mr Miller says, 'new parking regulations and most importantly you had to learn all over again how to listen and analyse what was being said. One had to mimic the proverbial duck: serene on the surface but paddling like hell underneath!'

Experience urged Mr Miller to be a 'joiner'—joining in with literary clubs, extracurricular societies, lunch-time seminars, philosophy lectures and even creative writing. This is the only arena where students can meet and mingle socially without any unspoken competitive pressure inhibiting conversation. Here is where the aged MAS eventually finds out that his or her paranoid generation gap exists only in the imagination; that he or she is simply accepted for personality and intellect.

The remainder of their undergraduate years completes the metamorphosis of the mature student, Mr Miller says. 'We learn that the library is the sanctum sanctorum and the very nerve centre of the University and that spending many hours there, reading and writing, does pay off in higher grades. We probably have less distractions. We place a great deal of emphasis on organising our time and our study material, and we gradually, but inexorably, are being made aware of our own intellectual limitations. Perhaps this latter self-knowledge is the single most important step.'

'However coming to university is not a denial of our mortality; but like the noted writer, who, when in his seventies, took up his first piano lessons, it is an affirmation of how much we value life.'

(Mr Miller, aged 58, is an Arts Honours student who is working on Classical Renaissance Epic Poetry. He had a long successful working life as a manager in Philips Industries Ltd. He presented his 'reflections of a mature age graduate' at a conference of Arts Deans at the University of Newcastle.)

Source: The Gazette, University of Newcastle, 17 December 1985.

As we have seen, their advantages more than outweigh their disadvantages. Records of mature age students' progress invariably show that while drop-out rates are higher, those who stay in the system achieve considerably better results than younger students. Ultra-competitiveness and feelings of insecurity are the dark side of adult learning. They arise because the institution takes over directing matters, whereas adults have been doing this for themselves during their non-school lives. Table 2.1 contrasts institutional with mature adult learning decisions.

Table 2.1   *Decisions about learning and who makes them*

Decision	Institutional response	Mature adult response
What to learn	As set out in the official syllabus, usually defined in self-contained subject areas.	As suggested by the experience of the problem situation, but help often needed to know where to go.
How to go about learning	As directed by the teacher who plans activities and exercises.	By reading, asking others, being metacognitively resourceful.
What resources to use	What the institution makes available; what teacher says to use.	What the situation turns up.
How will learning be evaluated; when to stop	As laid down, by exam, test, by institution; fail, or continue if successful.	When personally satisfied or when problem is solved; topic 'learned' because it works. No formal testing.

But it does not follow that the institutional mode of learning is better for younger students and the self-directed mode better for older ones. The problem of reconciling self-direction, institutional direction, and effects on the quality of learning exists at all ages. So we disagree with Knowles that the difference between adults and younger learners is so great that they are different species. On the contrary, the psychology of adult learning provides a good basis for designing instruction for schools in general (Candy 1991). This point is developed in later chapters, especially 12, 16 and 17.

Summary

Ages and stages

In our society, children learn to do typical things during sucessive age periods. These things are very physical and concrete in infancy, becoming quite abstract in young adulthood. There is a period in between, from around 6 years of age to 16, which in most Western countries spans the years of compulsory schooling. That is no accident; it is when children learn how to handle symbol systems.

What develops?

What develops, what might account for the ages and stages, is a matter of more controversy than that something develops. Piaget, the great pioneer in cognitive developmental research, thought that logical structures developed. He neatly demonstrated what children can typically do at various ages and described some important characteristics of these stages, but he was wrong in nominating successively complex logical systems as the key issue. The essence, it now seems, is that the 'stuff', rather than the structure, of the optimal performance at each age is what becomes progressively more abstract; that is a matter of development. The growth of complexity of the performance is a matter of learning.

The sensori-motor mode

From birth to 18 months or so, sensori-motor connections form the main basis of infant learning. These connections grow in complexity to the point where children can observe and put together information about their world, using objects as tools in dealing with the world. From about one year onwards, a different and more abstract form of handling the world appears: imagination.

The ikonic mode

Internalised images and their affective counterparts, feelings, create a whole new ball park, in which language is a major player. The next four to five years see the development of fluent oral language and its use in creating myths and stories: the fusion of language, feeling and structure. The major characteristic of this mode is unidimensionality: the stories have a single theme, affect is unmixed, some things are very good and others are very bad.

The concrete-symbolic mode

The ikonic world is simple and direct. The concrete-symbolic world is multidimensional and indirect. Written symbols form texts which refer to the experienced world; they talk about the rain without getting wet. Texts make declarative knowledge feasible. The creation of text and learning to crack its code, are dealt with in a later chapter; here the prerequisites of text, handling are described. These are the operations that help us disembed symbols from their referents. A typical one is reversibility, another is conservation. These allow us to preserve our concepts of the world while doing things to the world; we rotate a tube and maintain the order of its emerging contents, or tip a glass of wine into a tall flute glass and know we'll drink the same amount. Or read about such things and understand the world better for having done so. Thus are text, and mathematics and science possible.

Formal and post-formal modes

Concrete-symbolic reasoning is not however very theoretical, it being focused on representations of the actual rather than of the possible. Formal reasoning moves into that next stage of abstraction, which provides theories binding our concepts together in plausible ways. Text now is a tool for exploring what might conceivably confront us; the systematic application of theorising over particular content domains provides us with academic disciplines. One such content domain is oneself, about which the systematic application of theorising can bring much of both pleasure and pain to oneself and considerable irritation to others.

Post-formal thinking seems comparatively rare and is associated with highly competent performance in quite specialised areas.

Optimal level: The accumulation of modes

The present account differs from Piaget's in two main ways. First, modes are not like stages in that they replace each other, but rather they accumulate on top of each other. Second, modes are the stuff of learning, not its structure; we learn in the *medium* of motor responses, ikons, or semantic meanings. Thus, as we grow older we have more and more options, the optimal mode defining the level of abstraction we can handle under ideal conditions. Thus learning can be intermodal. We can learn a topic in several modes, either using higher level modes to facilitate learning a lower level (top-down), as in learning motor skills with the help of declarative knowledge or ikonic procedural knowledge (if you can't do it, imagine doing it); or using lower level representations as a ladder to climb up to abstract targets, as in learning maths with concrete aids.

The processes of developmental growth

Why do people shift from one mode to the next? Physiology no doubt makes a shift possible, but doesn't cause it. Other factors help. We need to know a lot about the topic that is subject to the more abstract treatment; we don't shift upwards across the board irrespective of topic, contrary to what Piaget might have implied. Being made to look a fool by being confronted with our submodal bloopers motivates a change. Interacting with other people—peers, parents and teachers—tells us which way to go. School can help with all but the physiology.

The course of cognitive growth in adulthood

Adults do differ from adolescents in the way they learn, but are they a different species? The bad news is that brain cells die off progressively faster with age; the good news is that adults develop world knowledge and strategies of self-management that more than offset the losses. Adult cognition is directed towards handling the choices and decisions that society presents them with. But should we create learning institutions that cater for adult–child differences in learning? No! The aim of child learning institutions is to make children behave ultimately like adults, so why not make the institutions adult-mode but child-friendly in the first place? That theme is addressed throughout this book and particularly in Chapters 12, 16 and 17.

Learning activities

1. Modes and thought

Central to this chapter has been the notion of levels of abstraction, or mode in which thought is represented. We make the point that modes are the stuff of which learning is made. The purpose of this particular learning activity is to get you to understand the concept and more specifically, to understand the five basic modes: sensori-motor, ikonic, concrete-symbolic, formal and post-formal. If done as a class activity, five groups could be formed with a group assigned to a mode. Each group could then prepare say an overhead transparency or a 'butchers' paper presentation for the whole class, describing their assigned mode.

An extension of this could be to have a fifth group providing input on how the modes work together, what we have called the 'accumulation of modes'.

2. Schooling and abstract thinking

When we looked at the role of the school in this chapter we noted that extended abstract thinking could be promoted in the following ways (assuming the biological hardware is in place): establishing well-structured prior knowledge; providing challenging problems; and providing social support.

As a group or class activity, give examples of each of the above three ways of extending thinking. An extension of this activity could be dramatisation of the examples (e.g., How would well-structured prior knowledge be developed? How could motivating problems be presented? How could social support from peers be incorporated into teaching?)

3. 'Top-down' and 'bottom-up' processing

In intermodal learning we examined the notions of top-down and bottom-up. Earlier in the chapter we gave some examples of top-down processing (skill learning) and bottom-up processing (the work of Resnik et al. 1992). Generate a number (say five) other examples that are top-down or botttom-up in orientation. What characterises top-down and bottom-up?

4. Egocentricity

As we saw earlier in this chapter, ikonic thought has been described as egocentric (Piaget 1926) in that small children see things very unidimensionally. We used the mountain experiment to demonstrate how children under 7 draw the same picture, irrespective of the perspective they have been asked to take (from their side or from the opposite side).

In this task we challenge you to gather some drawings from young children (say, 5, 7, 9 year olds) to see if they perform the way Piaget's children did. You will need to make some form of model (a mountain and a tree near it, for instance) and sit it in the middle of a table. Ask the child to draw the scene as they see it, then ask them to draw it as if they were on the other side of the table. Can the older child draw both perspectives? Good luck.

5. Social support

Writers such as Vygotsky (1978) see social support as being important for spurring development. In this activity we urge you to observe 'snippets' of language exchanges between adults and children to see how much scaffolding (the provision of supportive structures) occurs. We used the macaroni example to show support and non-support.

You could do the observations during practice teaching and, say, pick a couple of minutes of teacher/student exchange to see how much the teacher supports the student. We would think that news telling time in infants' classes would provide an excellent opportunity to examine such interactions. Share your findings with your colleagues.

Alternatively, you could observe adults talking to young children. One of us is reminded of such an interaction that we experienced. A small boy was sitting in the gutter complaining bitterly (among sobs) to a parent about all the walking he had to do while they were out shopping. The parent responded by saying, 'If you don't get up, I'll knock you down'!!!

6. Formal modes of thought

The purpose of this activity is to examine the relationship of levels of thought, particularly abstract thought, to political cartoons. Clearly some cartoons require greater levels of abstraction than others, you have to work harder to abstract the implied principle. For this activity collect a range of political cartoons and either at a group or class level, rank them from the most abstract to the least abstract. You will need to determine what is meant by abstraction and you will need to defend your rankings.

If done as group activity, each group could be given the same cartoons and the rankings for each cartoon compared across groups. If there are differences, why might these have occurred? Would the level of 'political' knowledge you have make any difference to the rankings?

Further reading

On cognitive development
Evans, G. T. (ed.) (1991). *Learning and Teaching Cognitive Skills.* Hawthorn, Vic: Australian Council for Educational Research.
Demetriou, A., Shayer, M. & Efklides, A. (eds) (1992). *The Neo-Piagetian Theories go to School.* London: Routledge & Kegan Paul.
Ginsburg, H. & Opper, S. (1987) *Piaget's Theory of Cognitive Development.* Englewood Cliffs: Prentice Hall

Piaget was the father of modern theories of cognitive development. Some even say that he had no legitimate 'offspring'; that he said all there was to say. If so, no one could say it as well as Ginsburg and Opper in as short a space. But even if you do think there is life after Piaget, you should know how it evolved.

Demetriou et al. provide the most recent collection of neo-Piagetian theories presented with particular reference to their applicability to school. Some chapters speak generally of ways in which Piagetian theory has become modified. Bidell and Fischer emphasise how learning and development are specific to context and to task; Biggs argues that the Piagetian 'stages' are modes of thinking leading to different kinds of knowledge; Demetriou, Gustaffson, Efklides and Platsidou present an elaborate model of domain specific areas of development. Science and mathematics learning is a common concern. Case emphasises the role of 'central conceptual structures' in science and mathematics, which contrasts with Bidell and Fischer's context specific position. Halford and Boulton-Lewis analyse why 'analogs', such as the Dienes and Cuisenaire blocks, may and may not be helpful in teaching early number. Resnick, Bill and Lesgold describe the study referred to above, whereby using the 'protoquantitative' (ikonic) understandings inner-city kids have of maths brings about amazing gains in achievement (but you'll only be amazed if you haven't read this chapter).

Evans' fine collection ranges over topics relevant to several chapters in the present book. For this chapter, Boulton-Lewis and Halford outline the theory that what develops are 'structure mappings', the basis of at least mathematically oriented thinking; their conclusion that concrete aids in teaching, used unthinkingly, may occupy more mind-space than the mappings they are supposed to teach and confuse rather than illuminate. Too much bottom and not enough up top. Collis and Biggs review development through the various modes, but we'll save that one for the next chapter.

On adult learning
Candy, P. C. (1991). *Self-direction for Lifelong Learning*. San Francisco: Jossey-Bass.
Knowles, M. (1978). *The Adult Learner: A Neglected Species*. Houston: Gulf Press.
Levinson, D. et al. (1978). *The Seasons of a Man's Life*. New York: Knopf.

Candy's is undoubtedly the definitive book on adult learning, whereas Knowles was once the ground-breaker, linking adult learning to broader psychological theory. Candy's book is highly relevant to various other chapters, especially Chapter 12. Levinson is in a different stream; if you want to pick up the thread of adult development, this book, despite its age and gender-bias (a function of circumstance not ideology), is the place to start.

THE DEVELOPMENT OF UNDERSTANDING

The development of understanding

Cleverness is doing things
better and better

But

How can we understand the
development of cleverness?

What is the
structure of
clever responses?

Novices and experts.
Can we learn
from experts?

Children's
views on science.
Are they naive?

THE DEVELOPMENT OF UNDERSTANDING

In this chapter you will find out:

- that the structure of what is learned changes characteristically during learning;
- what experts do that novices don't do;
- how what children think about natural phenomena differs from what they are taught;
- why science is peculiarly difficult to teach;
- how to describe different curriculum objectives in terms of learning and developmental level.

What goes on within modes?

In Chapter 2 we looked at the big picture: what goes on across modes during cognitive development. We now zoom onto what happens within a mode, during learning itself. This involves what is known as 'becoming cleverer'. Vosniadou and Brewer (1987) have already given us the broad picture with their steps of *accretion*, where new factual information is acquired; *weak restructuring,* where cognitive structures accommodate (to use Piaget's term) to better interpret the information; and *radical restructuring,* where different cognitive structures that are structured within a higher mode are used to reorganise the problem or topic.

These three steps form a hierarchy, accretion being prerequisite to weak restructuring, which is in turn prerequisite to radical restructuring. At the end of accretion, students are competent. After weak restructuring they are clever. But after radical restructuring they are very clever indeed. This chapter explains what is involved in this evolution of cleverness.

There are several theories that are relevant in understanding these matters, which must be admitted as central to any concept of schooling; what is going to school if it is not being made clever? First, we look at the SOLO Taxonomy, which is a way of categorising levels of learning in terms of increasing cleverness. Then we look at a specific issue in becoming cleverer, which children do on their own, outside the framework of what is taught in school. This is the evolution of children's thinking about the natural world, which children do think about from a very early age, thus serving the immediate purpose of helping them come to understand their own environment. However, it helps defeat a longer term purpose of educators, which is to get them to accept the science that we would like them to learn.

So teachers have to be clever too, because the understandings children construct out of school are so plausible that the onus of proof is on us to convince them otherwise. What a job! How do you tell an intelligent child who is sitting on a solid, wooden chair that he is not; that he is sitting mostly on empty space, except for a whirling field of electrons and atoms? One false move and he'll fall into the abyss.

One way of helping you do this is to be clear about what level of cleverness you are trying to teach and to structure your curriculum goals accordingly. Finally, we look at novices (who are unclever at the task in question) and experts (who have radically restructured and are awfully clever). In this chapter, then, we look at cognitive development in a much more task-specific sense than we did in the last chapter, which simply set the backdrop for the general way in which children's thinking develops. Here, we see how learning becomes more structured with the growth of competence and how knowledge of the ways in which this happens can be used to structure our thinking about student progress. The complement of this, how this knowledge can be used for assessing learning, is directly addressed in Chapters 14 and 15, in Part 5.

The structure of the observed learning outcome: The SOLO taxonomy

When people learn, they display a *consistent sequence,* or learning cycle, in the way they go about learning; this sequence applies over a large variety of tasks and particularly school-based tasks (Biggs & Collis 1982a). This sequence, which is not unlike Vosniadou and Brewer's sequence of accretion and weak and radical restructuring, can be seen in infants learning to handle a toy, in school-age children mastering content taught to them in school, and in undergraduates coming to grips with understanding a new theory.

- First, there is preliminary preparation, but the task itself is not attacked in an appropriate way. This is called *prestructural.*
- Next, one *(unistructural)* and then several *(multistructural)* aspects of the task are picked up (but in a serial or unrelated manner). This is equivalent to accretion.
- Then these several aspects are integrated into a coherent and interdependent whole *(relational),* as in weak restructuring.
- Finally, that coherent and interdependent whole may be generalised to a higher level of abstraction *(extended abstract),* as in radical restructuring.

Let us take some examples: the first two, discussed in Chapter 2, are based on Piaget's observations of babies seeking hidden objects and of the concept of reversibility; the other example is taken from a school subject.

The development of object permanence

You will remember Piaget's preoccupation with snatching toys from little children (pp. 37–8). Let us look at the five levels in the ways the children handled that ripple in the even tenor of their lives.

1. The toy is removed while the baby is playing with it and it is not missed. What SOLO level is this? Right, *prestructural:* the child's actions are related to the object only in an immediate and transitory sense. Take the object away and the child seems not even to notice.
2. The toy is removed and the baby does notice, because if placed under a cushion (the toy, that is), the baby crawls over to retrieve it. Next the toy is visibly transferred to another hiding place, but the baby goes to find the toy under the *first* cushion.

This is *unistructural* because once the first action, based on the first perception of where the toy is hidden has been run off, that's all there is. End of object search. But at least it's something.

3. The toy is missed, whether or not it is being played with and transferred as above. The child first looks at the initial hiding place but persists until it is found. This is *multistructural*. The child has first to act on the first information about the hiding place, but can then put the perceptions of object removal into sequence and act upon that sequence.

4. The toddler seeks to find the toy where it was *seen* to be last hidden. This is *relational*. As long as the transfers are physically visible there is no necessity to run through the previous sequence; the information is integrated and action based on where the object was *last* hidden follows directly.

5. The toy is hidden while the toddler is *not* watching. The first search is where it might be thought to be, but if it isn't there, other likely hiding places are investigated. This is *extended abstract*, because to find the object when its transfer has *not* been physically witnessed is to internalise and hypothesise, by imagining where it *might* be. That requires thinking in the ikonic mode, not the sensori-motor mode.

Reversibility: Tube turning

Now take the tube-turning experiment (pp. 42–3). The corresponding levels of cleverness require increasingly complex use of two abstractions: (a) to consider only whether the colours are reverse order and same order (as opposed to coding the particular colours in an image) and (b) to relate the number of turns to the outcome (reverse or same).

1. *Prestructural.* Abstractions (a) and (b) are not used. The child tries to imagine turning the ikonic representation of the marbles in the tube. It works only for one or two turns.

2. *Unistructural.* Simply take these two abstractions and coordinate them mentally, trying to match each turn with whether it makes it reverse or same.

3. *Multistructural.* Count the turns and match with reverse/same. Thus, one gives reverse, two gives same, three gives reverse, four gives same. This is only a marginal improvement on (2).

4. *Relational.* Code the number of turns as an *odd* or an *even* number. All you then have to do is to count the number of turns and note if that is odd or even.

5. *Extended abstract.* Do something fantastically clever with the set-up, like show that it's a special case of a Fourier series, or write a Tom Lehrer type song about it.

These examples are used to show how SOLO can apply to the sensori-motor and to the concrete-symbolic modes respectively, in tasks that have been used in studies of cognitive development. Now an example from the classroom.

Year 9 geography

A lesson to a Year 9 class has been given on the formation of rain and the question is asked: 'Why is the side of a mountain that faces the coast usually wetter than the inland side?' The following responses are given by students:

1. Because it rains more on the side facing the sea.
2. The sea breeze hits the coastal side first.

3. Well, the sea breezes pick up moisture from the sea and as they hit the coastal side first, they drop their moisture so that when they cross to the other side there's no rain left for the inland side.

4. Because the prevailing winds are from the sea and when they blow across they pick up water vapour and, continuing, hit the coastal ranges. They are then forced upwards and in so doing get colder so that the moisture condenses forming rain. By the time they cross the mountains the winds are dry.

5. Only if the prevailing winds are from the sea, which is likely to be the case. When this is so, the winds pick up water vapour evaporated from the sea, where it is carried to the coastal slopes, rises and is deposited in the form of rain. Not only is the wind now drier, but as it is carried up the mountain further it is compressed, which has a warming effect so it is relatively much less saturated than before. The effect is similar to the 'Chinooks' or warm spells experienced on the eastern slopes of the Canadian Rockies in winter. However, all these effects assume certain wind and temperature conditions. If these changed, then so would the energy exchanges and the effects would then be different.

Let us consider each response as before. The same structural principles emerge.

1. *Prestructural*. It misses the point, simply restating the question. No new knowledge is given ('It's wet because it rains more ...'), which is a tautology. Other responses at this level may be based upon personal anecdote (e.g., 'Well, we have a week-ender on the coast side and it always rains more there ...') or denial ('Dunno'). All three illustrate an inadequate link between response and original context. Prestructural responses are always unsatisfactory.

2. *Unistructural*. It extracts one relevant fact ('the sea breeze hits the coastal side first'), equivalent to the baby coping with one perception linking the object with its hiding place. The student here has linked wind and deposition, but that is all.

3. *Multistructural*. It contains several relevant facts, but considers them in isolation from each other, again just as the toddler tried first one then another hiding place. In the present example, the structure is the same; there is little explanation, just a description of a string of events whose interrelations are not made clear.

4. *Relational*. It relates temperature change to the picking up and deposition of moisture, just as the coordination of previous perceptions led straight to the correct hiding place. Here, most or all of the various aspects of the situation are tied together with a relating concept. The explanation, however, is valid only for the given context.

5. *Extended abstract*. It goes to the next mode, a shift from concrete-symbolic to formal, where a higher-order principle involving temperature and pressure is used. This principle is applied not only to the given problem of coastal rain, but also to such phenomena such as the Chinooks in Canada. No doubt this student could have generalised further to include coastal fog and various other natural and scientific phenomena. This response generalises across contexts and typically admits the possibility that things could be otherwise (e.g., 'However, all these effects assume ... If these changed ... the effects would then be different.'). Very clever, but some teachers might be irritated by extended abstract responses and may even mark them down: the students weren't *asked* about Chinooks in Canada.

To summarise, then, five levels in the cycle of learning any particular task can be distinguished: prestructural, unistructural, multistructural, relational and extended abstract. Prestructural responses indicate that learning is at too low a level of abstraction; it is in a mode that is too concrete for the given task. The middle three fall within one mode (called the 'target mode') and contain Vosniadou and Brewer's first two levels. Accretion, or the acquisition of new factual information, is a 'horizontal' process of broadening and corresponds to the shift from uni- to multistructural; and weak restructuring, in which cognitive structures evolve to interpret the information better, is a 'vertical' process corresponding to the shift to relational. The essence of the relating concept is that it incorporates what is common to the multistructural aspects so that they are no longer disconnected. Radical restructuring involves new higher order or extended abstract structures.

The target mode

Let us look at the matter of the 'target' mode. This is the mode at which teaching is aimed, and in which unistructural, multistructural and relational responses occur. In the first example the target mode was sensori-motor, with the extended abstract response therefore being ikonic; and in the last two examples the target mode was concrete-symbolic, with the extended abstract response being in the formal mode. Instruction usually aims at accretion (acquiring information) and weak restructuring (organising it), so that instructional goals can mostly be construed as multistructural or relational: this is an important point and will be developed later in this chapter. Extended abstract responses overshoot the target mode, usually being more abstract than instructional purposes currently require.

Table 3.1 describes these levels in relation to the target mode. Note that the levels are *task specific*; they do not describe an individual's characteristic way of operating.

Table 3.1   *Modes and levels in the SOLO taxonomy*

Mode	Structural level (SOLO)
Previous	1. *Prestructural*. The task is engaged, but the learner is distracted or misled by an irrelevant aspect belonging to a previous stage or mode.
	2. *Unistructural*. The learner focuses on the relevant domain and picks up one aspect to work with.
Target	3. *Multistructural*. The learner picks up more and more correct or relevant features, but does not integrate them together.
	4. *Relational*. The learner now integrates the parts with each other, so that the whole has a coherent structure and meaning.
Next	5. *Extended abstract*. The learner now generalises the structure to take in new and more abstract features, representing a higher mode of operation.

In learning contexts, whether everyday or institutional, the focus of learning is the target mode, in which levels 2, 3 and 4 describe various points in the course of learning a task. It is therefore important to distinguish between mode and learning cycle quite unequivocally, and to be quite sure about what mode we are referring to as target.

Take, for example, two interpretations of the meaning of a poem, *The Man in the Ocelot Suit,* by Christopher Brookhouse, that were given by a 14 year old Year 9 student and a 35 year old student (Biggs & Collis 1982a: 97). When asked what the poem 'means to you', the Year 9 student replied:

(a) 'Nothing very much I'm afraid but it does seem like a new style of writing.'

And the mature age student:

(b) 'Life must contain some eccentricities.'

What is the SOLO level of each response? (a) is clearly unistructural, but is (b) unistructural or extended abstract? In (a), the student doesn't understand the content, but recalls something from poetry lessons about style and suggests that that is what the poem is about: not very much, but it derives from the target mode. In (b), the student has reinterpreted the story as a comment on life itself, but only a single and rather simple comment. Yes, both are unistructural, (a) unistructural within the target mode of the lesson, (b) within the target mode imposed by an adult reader (formal), but, in terms of the concrete-symbolic mode, (b) is extended abstract. What defines whether a response is unistructural or extended abstract, then, is the mode which is the target.

Target modes thus vary considerably from primary, through secondary, to tertiary levels of education, but the unistructural–multistructural–relational learning cycle repeats itself within all modes. The prestructural and extended abstract levels indicate that the target mode has been missed in the former case and surpassed in the latter. As discussed below, it is possible to specify curriculum objectives according to the desired SOLO level within the appropriate mode.

Structuring curriculum objectives

Once we have decided the target mode, SOLO provides a way of structuring curriculum objectives. In most academic subjects, the target mode will be concrete-symbolic, but note that this does not rule out using the 'lower order' modes of sensori-motor and ikonic in the teaching *method*, as discussed in Chapter 2.

Much of the secondary school curriculum is expressed and tested as declarative knowledge, and SOLO provides a means by which curriculum objectives can be stated in which qualitative levels of performance may be stipulated. This is an important step as it enables one to state in qualitative terms what the level of performance might be at a given year level on a topic by topic basis. Defining the criterion performance in terms of a SOLO level indexes performance at a specified grade level to a point in the learning cycle of that topic. Some implications of the model have been spelled out elsewhere: for setting curriculum objectives at a systemic level and with reference to school-based curriculum development in Biggs and Collis (1989), and for science education in Collis and Biggs (1989). Let us briefly look at how SOLO can be used in this way.

After determining the mode—in secondary school, this will be concrete-symbolic in academic subjects—the next thing to decide is whether the aim is to *increase knowledge* (a unistructural, then a multistructural, outcome) or to *deepen understanding* (a relational, possibly an extended abstract, outcome). In teaching a particular topic, the issue is to decide what SOLO level the students might reasonably be expected to attain for that topic in the year level in question.

The 'natural' end-point of the learning cycle is relational, which is when the aspects of the task in question have been functionally integrated. The curriculum objectives at that level might contain the verbs: 'understand,' 'apply', 'integrate', 'compare and contrast',

In teaching, the issue is to decide what level the student might reasonably be expected to attain.

'explain the causes of ...' and so on, all of which imply *doing something meaningful* with the given aspects of the task. The material has been internalised and can be used effectively.

A multistructural objective would relate to the accumulation of knowledge—'knowing something about' rather than 'understanding'—and might stress the following kinds of verbs: 'enumerate', 'list the principal features of ...', 'what are the ...'.

A unistructural objective would relate to the first steps towards acquiring knowledge or a skill: 'identify', 'what is the correct term for ...', 'what prominent feature ...', 'calculate ...'(when given the data and the formula).

In deciding what are appropriate objectives, then, it is necessary to be clear about the level of understanding that is reasonable for the topic in question. As an example, Table 3.2 shows some topics from the science curriculum (adapted from Shayer & Adey 1981).

To get an idea of what proportions of students might respond at these levels, Collis and Davey (1986) surveyed Year 7 and Year 9 students in five Tasmanian high schools using 19 concepts from biology, chemistry, physics and geology, taken from the State Education Department Science Guidelines. Table 3.3 shows their findings.

Table 3.2 *Learning cycles and modes for some science curriculum topics*

Column groupings — Concrete-symbolic mode: Unistructural, Multistructural, Relational. First order formal mode: Prestructural, Relational, Unistructural, Extended abstract. (The Relational/Prestructural and Extended abstract/Unistructural levels share a column where the cycles overlap.)

Topic	Unistructural	Multistructural	Relational / Prestructural	Extended abstract / Unistructural
Kinetic theory	Discrete items of information: for example 'solid turns to water'; 'liquid turns to gas'.	Change of state reversible: ice-to-water; water-to-steam by *heating*; steam-to-water, water-to-ice by cooling.	Energy speeds particles. All matter might exist as solid, liquid or gas depending on particle state.	Melting and vaporisation, equilibrium processes. Latent heat the energy required to change state.
Experimental design	To see if something produces an effect, try it. No attempt to compare across situations, only before-after.	Sees need for a comparison but satisfied with 'one with and one without' design. Ignores other variables when testing for one.	Controls obvious variables, but not for possible ones that are not present.	Sees system as a whole and controls for all possible combinations. Sees variables may interact: need for sampling to control natural variation.
Velocity and acceleration	Speed and relative position undifferentiated: faster object is the one ahead. Acceleration not differentiated.	Speed relation between distance and time (kph). Intuitive notion of acceleration (push in back).	Acceleration is rate of change of velocity. Can equations involving acceleration as algorithm $(S = ut + \frac{1}{2}at^2)$.	Acceleration is the Limiting value of: $\dfrac{\Delta v}{\Delta t}$
Acids and alkalis	'Acids' are substances with properties (turn litmus paper red, sour taste, attack metals) that work one at a time.	Acids and bases are opposites: neutralise each other in same quantities if teacher makes equivalent solutions. Metal oxides are alkaline, non-metal oxides are acidic.	Base + acid = salt + water because H^+ in acid + $OH^- = H_2O$. Nothing is lost during neutralisation.	Acid-base reactions due to disturbance of equilibrium between H^+ and OH^- ions in water Use of quantities for finding equation of reaction.

Source: Adapted from Shayer and Adey, 1981

Table 3.3 *Percentage of students successfully completing science items at various levels*

Mode	Ikonic		Concrete-symbolic		Formal
Level	Pre-	Uni-	Multi-	Relational	Extended abstract
Year 7	24	34	22	16	4
Year 9	15	23	32	23	7

Source: Collis & Davey, 1984

Overall, the most common level of responding in Year 7 is unistructural and in Year 9 is multistructural. Nevertheless, 38% of the Year 9s are still finding multistructural too difficult. Pallett (1985: 3) thought that for the topics in question:

> The object should be to raise the level of all children at Grade 10 to the relational level. There should also be provision for a small percentage to attain the extended abstract level.

Collis and Davey, however, saw the prospects of most students responding at the relational level by Year 10 as 'remote'. So either Pallett's goal is too high, for all but the academically inclined students, or something is seriously wrong with the standard of learning in schools. If, on the other hand, the goal for a general education may be taken as multistructural then the Collis and Davey figures are more acceptable. That would then mean that students will know some important things about most topics, but mastery in the relational sense would be expected only on particularly important ones. Clearly, then, we need to decide what topics should be mastered (at relational level) and what should be knowledgeable background (multistructural). Perhaps most school-leavers would need only to 'know something about' acids and alkalis, but to understand and apply some topics in nutrition and ecology (the phenomenon of acid rain might then click into place with the background of knowledge of acidity). Table 3.2 however will add a dash of realism: the relational level in all topics listed there represents a very large investment in time and effort.

Given all this, then, what might be reasonable levels to aim at in the various school years?

Primary school

The primary years operate horizontally. Students acquire skills and knowledge that broaden throughout the primary years. The basic rules of tools for working in the concrete-symbolic mode—reading, writing and the four rules of number—are acquired and applied to more and more topics and subjects. The parallel between tool-using and experience is the essence of the concrete-symbolic mode, but the relational level is typically reached well after primary school. Year 6 would not be expected for the most part to go beyond multistructural responses, although some students might do so, especially in mathematics.

Secondary school

By the time students are ready to leave school and enter the workforce, they should know about much of their world and understand some of the more important aspects of it. They should have mastered the basic mathematical techniques and operations, and have the procedural knowledge to use them in solving the kinds of problems they are likely to meet: fencing a block of land, painting a house, calculating tax, estimating the cost of extensions to the house. This is not a matter of knowing how to do lots of different sums (multistructural) but getting mathematics to work for you (relating the procedures to particular problems). History is likewise taught not to have a fund of entertaining stories about weirdos like Sturt trailing a boat through the desert, or Buckley giving the lie to Buckley's chance, or Eliza Fraser's tongue striking terror into all her associates, whether sailors or Aborigines, but to help students form a view about themselves and their country. Certainly some multistructural story-telling will help provide the background, but it will take more than that to make Kevin Smith from 4C form a sense of non-chauvinistic identity (actually, history is a hard one for adolescents; it becomes more relational as one becomes part of it oneself).

The goals for students going on to Year 12 are different. They used to be exclusively aimed at meeting tertiary requirements, in which case students should show evidence of formal thinking in their specialist subjects (Collis & Biggs 1983). There are now, however, increasing numbers of students in Year 12 who do not need to think formally; for these, the goal might be to consolidate relational thinking in those topics which were only multistructural at Year 10.

Children's science: Alternative frameworks for understanding

While it is certainly the case that most curriculum objectives are structured in the concrete-symbolic mode, the SOLO learning cycle, unistructural–multistructural–relational, works through all modes, independently of formal instruction. Further, as may be seen from Figure 2.1 in the last chapter, the concrete-symbolic mode evolves from sensori-motor and ikonic foundations, so that any topic raised at the concrete-symbolic stage has an ancestry in the earlier modes.

'Bottom-up' instruction uses this pre-concrete-symbolic ancestry, but in secondary schools especially this is too frequently neglected and direct instruction in declarative knowledge—sentences and propositions saying that such-and-such is the case—is very common. Such direct instruction inevitably short-circuits the experiential knowledge the child already has, substituting a network of concepts and propositions that are self-referential and that co-exist within the concrete-symbolic mode itself. In other words, children learn a bunch of sentences that link up with a bunch of other sentences, that seem to have little to do with experience. Ultimately they do link to experienced knowledge, but until they do, children explain the world with two kinds of theories, depending on who is asking them:

1. those taught in school, which until integrated with experience will remain as verbal explanations, cued by other verbalisations. These verbal explanations are given to teachers and such.
2. those that their peers and 'common sense' know to be the real reasons for things.

A story of the American educator John Dewey captures the difference. Visiting a class being taught science, with the teacher's permission, he asked the question: 'What would you find if you tried to dig for oil in your backyard, and kept digging and digging until you reached the centre of the earth?'

Silence. The teacher was annoyed and said: 'Come on class, what is the state of the earth's core?'

'Igneous fusion!' was the immediate chorus.

Marton and Ramsden (1988) give a similar example; high school students could describe with great accuracy and with diagrams what photosynthesis is and how it works, but they could not explain the difference between the way in which animals and plants obtain food.

This 'schizophrenic' nature of learning, comprising on the one hand propositions that may link (more or less richly) to each other, and everyday learning based on personal experience on the other, creates problems in teaching, in science in particular, which we look at in this section.

What it is to explain something

An explanation for a young child is not what scientists mean by an explanation. The first 'why' questions are to seek reassurance:

'Why have all the lights gone out?'
'Because we are having a blackout.' (Solomon 1985).

Another form of explanation is 'reaffirmation' (a form of tautology) which persists until high school:

'Gold can be found as the pure metal in the earth's crust. Iron cannot be found as a pure metal. Why is this?'
'Because iron is not found in the earth's crust.' (op. cit.)

Referring back to the example of coastal rain the Year 9 student reaffirmed the question when she replied, 'Because it rains more on the coastal side'. Better explanations come when children explain by substituting one word for another. 'Vinegar protects food from going bad because it pickles them' may be suggesting that vinegar is one example of a superordinate class of pickling fluids: or it may cleverly be concealing ignorance (Solomon 1985). Children accept loose 'explanations' and are satisfied with them; the educational task is to make them dissatisfied.

The first explanations are couched in narrative in the ikonic mode, which results in animism (Piaget 1926). Children use the ikonic mode to explain things, as do preliterate societies, by projecting human characteristics onto animals, plants and inanimate objects and weaving stories around them. Then, particularly if assisted by interaction with adults, it is seen that these animistic explanations do not make sense; they lead to too many contradictions. For example, an early explanation for wind imputes intentionality to trees, and is constructed by putting together quite correct observations: that when there is a wind, the trees wave around, and when I wave my hand there is a wind. Therefore, the trees wave when they want to make a wind.

In between the use of animism and myth to explain the world and the models taught in high school, children create their own science as best they can (Gilbert, Osborne & Fensham 1982), forming what are now referred to as 'children's science', or more usually, *alternative frameworks* (Driver & Easley 1978; Driver 1981). Rather like the wind explanation, which is based on valid observation, children focus on aspects of a phenomenon that are close to their own experience. These explanations are remarkably:

- similar to each other;
- similar to explanations used in the history of science, from Aristotelian, through Newtonian, to currently accepted frameworks (Clement 1983; Strauss 1988);
- resistant to change.

In forming these explanations, students seize on aspects that are striking and what strikes one student is likely to strike another. One major reason for their similarity is that they are socially constructed.

When children discuss shared experiences such as a TV program, they don't argue so much as reconstruct the event (Solomon 1984). They share their views and when they agree, that is what goes down as what the program was about; its meaning is validated by consensus. Children—in story, discussion, play and finally consensus—construct accounts of what the world is about. Consensus can however work for the accepted frameworks as well as for the alternative frameworks:

> A Second Year (Year 8/9) group was discussing the nature of energy. Asked if a piece of bread lying on the bench had energy, Mark volunteered the opinion that it could not because 'it couldn't jump about'. This meaning of energy was familiar to most of the others who leapt eagerly into the fray using the same argument against petrol having energy. Errol [is] trying to disagree but his view is ignored...
>
> Two years later, when these pupils were about to start their first course on energy, the same question was put to them. At once Mark staked out his previous claim that food could not have energy but this time his was the view that was to be ignored. Errol offered the idea that the energy was contained in the food but that it was stored and the others agreed with him. One week later, in the next discussion on energy, Mark changed his mind and came into line with the rest of the class (Solomon 1984: 8).

However, by the time Errol's view has become the consensus, we are into Year 9 or Year 10. Meantime—throughout primary and secondary schooling to Year 9—mistaken conceptions of the world have dominated the children's thinking.

Another perspective on the social construction of knowledge is given in Box 3.1:

Box 3.1 *Student is to child as teacher is to adult*

The kids do not treat the teachers as normal adults. Arlette herself spells out a striking example of the consequences ... The school set up special classes about sex and contraception. They don't work. Arlette heard one girl tell her girlfriends that her older sister had told her, 'Don't go on the pill, it screws up your insides and later on you can't have any babies.' The girls, Arlette says, will believe a mother, or a virgin aunt, or a sister. They will not believe the scientific information they are given in the special classes, as she pointed out to the teacher in charge, 'because you are a teacher'. The curriculum breaks down because there is no trust.

Source: Connell 1985, p. 105.

It is not surprising, then, that teaching science can be peculiarly difficult.

Some common alternative frameworks

Clough and Driver (1984) set out to determine what frameworks adolescents used to explain the same situation; and the extent to which the same framework was used across different situations. They gave a series of tasks to groups of students aged 12, 14 and

16, who were to explain what was happening. The tasks illustrated movement of fluids from regions of higher to lower pressure and included:

- drinking from a straw;
- placing a syringe under water and withdrawing the plunger;
- placing hot glasses upside down on a soapy sink.

In the straw task, the way the question was put suggested that the students use the idea of atmospheric pressure; at all three ages, the majority response was based on pressure ('the air pressure forces it up'). With the other two tasks, however, with no leading questions, about half the respondents used the idea, or framework, that the vacuum actively sucks, rather than that the atmospheric pressure stabilises the difference. While more 16 year olds used the atmospheric difference framework, the 'sucking vacuum' was the most popular response at all ages.

Another situation involved the conduction of heat energy through solids. These three tasks were:

- plastic, wooden and metal spoons standing in a cup of hot water: explain why the metal spoon felt hotter than the other spoons;
- explain why a metal plate felt colder than a plastic plate;
- explain why, on a cold day, the handlebars of a bicycle felt colder than the plastic grips.

The spoons question attracted the accepted framework (heat energy travels through different materials at different rates) much more readily than did the plates and handlebars questions. The latter task especially was put in the framework that metal attracts coldness, that is, that cold is a property just like heat. Again, older students increasingly used the accepted framework (heat energy travels through different materials at different rates).

Tasks with which the students were familiar (like the bicycle handlebars) were explained with incorrect but stable frameworks (metal conducts or attracts coldness), which were hard to change: 'Many incorrect scientific conceptualisations are resistant to instruction, even when the teaching has been deliberately structured to incorporate or confront children's ideas' (op. cit.: 21).

Some frameworks become folklore, particularly those to do with health:

'Sugar gives you energy.'
'If milk is good for babies it's good for everyone.'
'You can't work well on an empty stomach.'

These are even more difficult to counter. What frequently happens is that we *talk* the accepted framework and *act on* the alternative framework. We 'sort of know about' electrons, but actually operate on the world using a hydraulic framework, according to which electricity flows through the wires. Remember James Thurber's story of his aunt? She left dead light bulbs in their sockets so that electricity didn't leak into the room.

Gunstone and White (1981) found that physics students entering Monash University— the 'successful fraction from 13 years of schooling'—had quite serious misunderstandings about gravity.

Students know a lot about physics but do not relate it to the everyday world … much more attention may have to be given to integrating the knowledge acquired in school to general knowledge (op. cit.: 298).

These students had passed their HSC in physics, but their knowledge did not permeate their experience. They 'observed' what they expected to happen not what did happen; 'some even managed not to observe at all and gave mathematical equations when asked what they had seen'.

To sum up, then, alternative frameworks are constructions that stand in for scientifically accepted explanations, where the latter involve at least relational thinking in the concrete-symbolic mode. Alternative frameworks are lower order, being constructed around one, few or several aspects relevant to the final concept, or around quite irrelevant ones.

Dealing with alternative frameworks

Establishing a framework for making sense of the world is something that the learner does spontaneously (Driver & Bell 1986). If a teacher insists on a view that does not evidently make sense, the learner will as we have seen, simply learn the symbols of the accepted framework, while interpreting the world through the alternative framework. Driver and Bell insist that students need to *reconstruct* their frameworks, not simply correct them. But first, they need to be convinced of the need to do so. As the following study shows, this is not easy.

Establishing a framework for making sense of the world is something that learners do spontaneously.

Gunstone, Champagne and Klopfer (1981) worked intensively with 12 Year 7 and Year 8 students, who were specially selected for their interest and ability in science, for one day a week for eight weeks. They first found out what the students believed about force and motion and then provided a rich program of activities, including a computer simulation, that challenged those beliefs. They seemed to be successful, for the students appeared to have adopted the accepted frameworks. However, on retesting with a new set of demonstrations, most retained their Aristotelian (incorrect) frameworks—*alongside* the newly acquired Newtonian knowledge. They retained the belief that, for instance, force implies motion; if there is no motion then there is no force. Well, what do you think? Are there any forces acting on a car that is parked on a hill? Aristotle would have said no; Newton would have said yes.

If students can be so rigid under such ideal circumstances, what can science teachers in general do? There are three possible strategies:

1. *Nothing.* If ideas work, why change them? As Driver and Bell (1986) point out, electricians operate effectively in their calculations of conductivity of materials in terms of a flow model. This is a bottom line argument. If teaching is a matter of helping students get by, it may not be a bad idea, but *should* teachers be endorsing known error? You would have to be very selective about that.

2. *Build on what is there.* Remember Bruner's challenging statement that he could teach anything to any child in an 'intellectually honest form'? He meant, as we saw on p.51, that any concept in concrete-symbolic or formal modes has sensori-motor and ikonic prototypes. Driver and Bell (1986) have the same idea when they talk of the 'spiral curriculum' and Carmi (1981) when he talks about the 'onion principle'. Alternative frameworks enable the child to make some sort of sense of things: not *our* sense, to be sure, but sense nonetheless. Their frameworks aren't *wrong* so much as *incomplete*. Carmi suggests that many concepts can be used and built on. Cognitive development involves the *gradual* widening of that range of applicability until it finally results in a context-free handling of the concept:

   > In my Israeli work I teach 'qualitative physics' in kindergarten and grade one, 'gradative physics' in grades two and three, etc. Each such stratum of physics is a self-contained science, with its own experiments, definitions, etc. and is in no sense 'less rigorous' a discipline than fully fledged quantitative physics (Carmi 1981: 48).

   He designed a spiral curriculum developing these views. Resnick, Bill and Lesgold's (1992) primary arithmetic classes using ikonic or 'protoquantitative' understanding are another excellent example (see p. 52).

3. *Confront.* Because students distort their observations to fit their existing frameworks, it seems reasonable to confront them with what really happened. This may be difficult. Driver and Bell (1985) mention a 14 year old boy who was asked to observe Brownian movement through a microscope; he reported 'smooth' particle movement. When asked to have another look, he observed 'smooth' movement once again. He shrugged: 'Oh well, everyone sees different things I guess' and wrote 'jerky' in his lab report, which was what he was supposed to observe. He saw no need to revise his ideas, as long as what he committed to writing was the official version. Confrontation must challenge the student's own construction to such an extent that a *perceived need* for change is created. This boy's perceived need was to put down the correct answer.

D. Tang (1991) modified Driver's CLISP program, which emphasises confronting with examples that counter already held notions, clarification and exchange of ideas by peer interaction, construction of new ideas, and evaluation of the newly constructed ideas. He focused on the framework 'motion implies force' over a series of eight lessons with 32 low ability students in a technical institute in Hong Kong, giving a comparable control class equal time with revision. 73% of the students in the treatment class showed conceptual restructuring while there are none in the control class. So what strategy to use? All three have their place, but the overriding question remains: How do you create the perceived need to give up the incorrect conceptions? The following suggestions are derived from several sources (Driver & Bell 1985; Fensham 1980; Gilbert & Watts 1983; Watts & Bentley 1984):

1. *Find out what common alternative frameworks exist and what your own students think.*

Table 3.4 lists some references that present common frameworks for some basic topics in the science curriculum. Science teachers should be aware of these and then find out what their own students think.

Table 3.4   *Some sources for alternative frameworks on various topics*

Force: Watts (1983), Driver (1985), Watts and Zylbursztajn (1981)
Heat: Clough and Driver (1985a)
Pressure in fluids: Clough and Driver (1985b)
Energy conservation: Driver and Warrington (1985)
Mechanics: Driver (1985), Gilbert, Watts and Osborne (1982)
Evaporation: Beveridge (1985)
Children's learning in Science Project (CLISP), Centre for Studies in Science and Mathematics Education, University of Leeds, LS2 9JT, has collected material for teaching and curriculum development based on alternative frameworks about: particles, heat, plant nutrition, energy and chemistry.

2. *Present them with events that challenge these ideas.*

Now knowing what they think, design a demonstration that does *not* happen according to prediction and ask them to explain that. The explanation then elicits the students' frameworks for interpreting the event. For example, Gunstone and White (1981) for one of their situations slung a rope over a freely running bicycle wheel mounted as a pulley, with a bucket of sand at one end of the rope and a block of wood, the same weight as the sand, at the other. The bucket was then adjusted so that it was higher than the block (Figure 3.1):

> *Question 1:* 'How does the weight of the bucket compare with the weight of the block?'
> *Question 2:* 'Now predict what will happen if this small spoon of sand is added to the bucket.'

Look carefully at Figure 3.1 and think carefully how you would answer the questions. Well, how do you compare with Gunstone and White's students (who were first year physics students who had done well in HSC physics the previous year)? In answer to Q1, 27% said that the block was heavier; and to Q2, 46% did *not* say that the bucket would accelarate smoothly to the floor. After the bucket *had* accelarated smoothly to the floor, the students were asked to explain what had happened; 46% of them had some explaining to do.

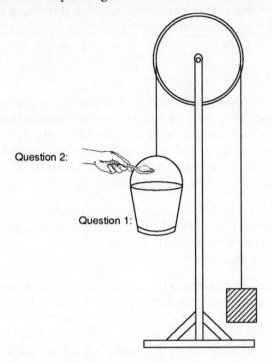

Figure 3.1 *Probing the understanding of gravity*
(from Gunston & White 1981)

3. Encourage hypothesising and the generation of explanations to replace those that have just been demonstrated to be inadequate.

While the discovery that one has predicted incorrectly may be challenging, it is also threatening. Students can easily be made to look foolish by these demonstrations and then either clam up, or do other defensive things, such as the 14 year old boy who simply complied with expectations to write down what he was supposed to have seen. The environment for these explorations of alternatives must therefore be non-threatening. Students have to be able to admit their mistakes without shame and explore alternatives without inhibition.

4. Teach science through the history of science.

It helps to point out where scientific definitions conflict with those in common use; and to point out that the scientific Greats (Parmenides, Aristotle, Dalton, Newton ...) in fact trod the same road they are treading. Alternative frameworks recapitulate with surprising accuracy the history of science (Clement 1983; Strauss 1988).

5. Explain scientific method.

Scientists *oversimplify*: They invent idealised solutions and concepts, such as absolute zero or a perfect vacuum. They use abstract principles that are not observed in the situation to explain why, for instance, pieces of paper are attracted to a plastic comb that has been whisked briskly through a dry head of hair. Children generally use what they see: 'the rubbing makes the paper stick'. Electrons and fields aren't visible. As students realise what scientists actually *do* and that it is not so weird after all, scientific explanations may become more acceptable.

Experts and novices

Another approach to the study of cleverness, and how we might help people become much cleverer than they are currently, is that adopted by Glaser and his team in Pittsburgh (Chi, Glaser & Farr 1988; Chipman, Segal & Glaser 1984) who studied all sorts of problems, including chess, mechanics and radiology. Others have applied the expert–novice model to teaching itself (Borko & Livingston 1989; Leinhardt & Greeno 1986). The approach seems engagingly simple:

1.   Study what experts do when handling the task they are expert at.
2.   Study what novices or beginners do when trying to handle the same task.
3.   Pinpoint the differences between (1) and (2).
4.   Teach novices how to do (3).

The first step anyone takes in solving a problem is to understand it by representing it in some way. Novices use concrete representations, such as aspects of the problem that are explicitly given, whereas experts use extended abstract concepts that are more abstract, radically restructured from their much greater experience. Novices work at a lower level of abstraction and do the wrong things. Typically, they use a 'means-end' analysis, whereby they focus on the desired end state, the solution or a formula for the solution and reason backwards from that to the givens, trying to close the gap (Sweller, Mawer & Howe 1982). Logical, maybe, but inefficient; and it's not what experts do, which is to use forward reasoning from the given particulars, their greater experience enabling them to categorise the problem top-down as belonging to a certain class, the strategies for solving the problem at their fingertips (Perkins & Salomon 1989).

Experts know what is relevant what is not and infer from what is given to principles that can be used to solve the problem. Thus, novice chess players take each move as it is given; an expert might instantly recognise the Slobovsky Gambit and reply with the Borovansky Feint. All might use the general strategy, 'control the centre', but to the novice this involves only weak restructuring, while to the expert it is the source of radically restructured and paralysing surprises.

Expertise built through radical restructuring is built up cumulatively through personal experience, often from lower level modes and then involves a shift to a qualitatively different, more powerful, way of operating. Such knowledge is often tacit; it cannot be described or treated as declarative knowledge. The expert teacher 'knows' when to switch to a different example: 'I could just tell. They weren't with me.' That sort of expertise needs first-hand experience.

Teaching novices how to be experts may be a little like the story of the Australian tourist visiting King's College in Cambridge. The tourist was mightily impressed by the College lawns and asked a gardener weeding the border how he got the lawns looking so magnificent.

'Oh, we just water them, mow them, and roll them, sir.'
'But that's exactly what I do to my front lawn back in Templestowe. True. Looks nothing like this. I mow it, water it and roll it, just as you said.'
'For four hundred years, sir?'

But if there's no substitute for hands-on experience, it may be possible to alert the novice to the things the expert has acquired more slowly. The task is making the novice sensitive to crucial aspects of the task rather than creating an instant expert.

There is, then, much that the experts do that can be taught. Taylor (1991), for example, used the novice–expert paradigm to teach 37 industrial sales representatives sufficient metallurgy to enable them to talk knowledgeably to their clients, in an average of three-and-a-half hours' study time. He analysed the frameworks and cues that experts used when classifying metals and put this material into tapes and diagrams that could be used in a distance-learning mode. The technique was most successful and far superior to the traditional methods of training the salespeople.

Amazingly, there have been relatively few comparable analyses. This sort of detailed task analysis could probably be applied to many topics in the curriculum, to become part of the procedural knowledge of the subject and to be used in helping students on the road towards expertise.

The novice–expert studies, then, show that expertise is not simply a matter of knowing more. It does involve knowing more, but it leads to a qualitative shift in the way the problem is handled. This explains why students do not move wholesale into a new mode: they only do, if they do at all, in those areas in which they have experience and expertise.

Summary

What goes on within modes?

Learning, is what. We become cleverer by doing particular things better and better, not in developing new modes as such. What we need is a framework for helping us to see what is involved in getting cleverer at doing things. Children become cleverer both within school, by learning what we want them to learn, and out of school, when what we teach them doesn't answer the questions that burn within them and so they seek out their own answers.

The structure of the observed learning outcome: The SOLO taxonomy

The SOLO taxonomy provides a general framework for showing how learning outcomes grow progressively more complex at all age levels as learning proceeds. A consistent cycle occurs from prestructural (out to lunch), through unistructural (a one-eyed view of things), multistructural (all bricks, no house), relational (home and hosed), to extended abstract (pastures new). This cycle can be used to describe sensori-motor learning in infancy or progress in many school subjects, by defining curriculum objectives and performance outcomes. Much schooling is concerned with reaching objectives in the concrete-symbolic, and in later high school years, the formal mode, as declarative knowledge. Saying what unistructural, multistructural and relational objectives would mean on a topic-by-topic basis effectively defines for the teacher the quality of performance outcome that might be expected: simply knowledge acquisition, weak restructuring, or radical restructuring of knowledge. The assessment of outcomes is left for Chapter 15.

Children's science: Alternative frameworks for understanding

Scientific explanation requires students to understand the world in a way that is beyond them, so they create their own explanations that are located in less demanding structures. They use the ikonic mode, animism and narrative, or selected aspects of the phenomenon cemented by consensus, to satisfy 'why?' In this, they recreate the history of science, if only they knew it. All this makes the teaching of science difficult. Teaching is derived from two complementary strategies: to build on what the students already know at a sub-optimal level; and to motivate the need to change by confronting them with the inconsistencies their present position propels them towards.

Experts and novices

Experts are people who are extremely clever at handling particular tasks; novices are fumbling beginners. Although expertise is very task-specific, the differences between the way experts and novices handle tasks are strikingly similar. The first prerequisite for expertise, but not its guarantee, is a vast amount of hands-on experience. Experts radically restructure that experience so that they can recognise immediately the way the parts of the problem interrelate; they work top-down. Novices get stuck with the givens. It seems, however, that some of the knowledge gained by experts *is* transferable: and lucky the novice to whom it is transferred, because it will save lots of time in reaching expertise. This is what teaching should be about: getting students there faster than they would otherwise. The unfortunate thing, however, is that all this is very task-specific and so we need procedural knowledge for each topic and we don't yet have it on file. Hopefully somebody is working on it.

Learning activities

1. Alternative frameworks I

The purpose of this activity is to introduce you to the nature of alternative frameworks. The starting point is the work of Clough and Driver (1984) referred to in this chapter. We drew upon two of their tasks for 12 to 16 year olds: fluid movements due to changes in pressure and conduction of heat through solids. You could replicate this research by asking a couple of 12, 14 and 16 year olds to explain each phenomenon. The individual responses could be brought back to a class session where the alternative frameworks could be discussed. In that discussion you would obviously want to focus on what teachers can do about students' alternative frameworks.

2. Alternative frameworks II

In this activity you are to seek infant and primary aged children's explanations for natural phenomena. If you can question pre-schoolers, all the better. Here you could gather explanations for phenomenon such as the wind, the sun, the tides, the moon, etc.

You could use question such as: 'Where does the moon go in the day?', 'Where does the sun go at night?', 'What makes the wind?', 'Where does the rain come from?', 'Why does it get cold in winter?' to get you started.

You will be surprised at the range of explanations. What are the implications for teaching young children?

3. The Structure of the Observed Learning Outcome (SOLO)

While we do deal with SOLO in later chapters, it is appropriate to have a learning activity here to help your understanding. In this chapter we used two examples (object permanence, school subject—geography) to show how responses can vary from pre-structural to extended abstract and more can be found in Biggs and Collis (1982a). In this activity you are to gather some data from students (practice teaching might be an appropriate time) and analyse the responses using the SOLO taxonomy. If possible, use SOLO to analyse levels of learning after you have given a lesson.

This activity could be done as a class assignment for presentation and discussion.

It might be useful to consider, in more detail, the Biggs and Collis' work before you go about this task. You will find a range of examples across school topics (e.g., history, mathematics, English, geography, modern languages) and good examples at each of the levels of SOLO. Might we suggest you start with the history example (pp. 36–7) where student responses to a lesson on the role of the squatters are presented.

4. Post-compulsory schooling

More and more students are continuing into Years 11 and 12, the post-compulsory years of schooling. We made the point (p.76) that in the past, Year 12 was aimed exclusively at tertiary education requirements, a demonstration of formal thinking in specialist subjects but now many students continue for reasons unrelated to tertiary aspirations. The question for discussion here is: 'should Years 11 and 12 aim to develop formal thinking in all students? If not, what might be a reasonable level (relational, multi-structural) to try and achieve? In addressing this question, consider ways in which you could write curriculum objectives to achieve such levels. You could write objectives reflecting multi-structural, relational, and extended abstract levels.

5. Novices and experts I

Are there differences in the ways that expert and novice teachers think about solving classroom discipline problems? You'd be surprised if there were not, given our discussion and your own experiences (as a student and during the practicum). This activity uses a recent research paper by H. L. Swanson, J. E. O'Connor and J. B. Cooney (1990), 'An information processing analysis of expert and novice teachers' problem solving', *American Educational Research Journal,* 27, 533–66. This paper shows that experts place a priority on defining the problem and then representing it, whereas novices tend to focus on possible solutions. The results are discussed in terms of declarative and procedural knowledge.

You could summarise the paper individually but we think that group work might be a better way to handle the 'complexity' of the paper. Groups could be assigned to present parts of the paper (e.g., Introduction, Method, Results, Discussion) to the class.

An extension of this could be to take the scenarios presented on page 537 of the paper and discuss in class how the problems could be solved. You could then compare your own problem solving strategies with those presented by Swanson et al.

6. Novices and experts II

This activity also is based upon the paper by Swanson et al. but here the focus is on making up your own scenarios and finding how expert and novice teachers say they would solve the problem. You could develop infants, primary or secondary level cases, dependent upon your interests. We provide an infant grade scenario to help get you started.

'During morning story time, when you read stories to the whole class, you notice that one youngster is consistently poking, pushing and hugging other children around her. This happens frequently.' What are the things you think about in solving this problem and how would you solve it?

Further reading

On the SOLO Taxonomy

Biggs, J.B. & Collis, K.F. (1982). *Evaluating the Quality of Learning.* New York: Academic Press.

Biggs, J.B. & Collis, K.F. (1989). Towards a model of school-based curriculum development and assessment: using the SOLO Taxonomy. *Australian Journal of Education*, **33**, 149–61.

Collis, K. F., & Biggs, J. B. (1989). A school-based approach to setting and evaluating science curriculum objectives: SOLO and school science. *Australian Journal of Science Teachers*, **35** (4), 15–25.

The 1982 reference is the first and major publication on SOLO, outlining the theory with reference to the subjects of history, mathematics, English, reading, geography and economics. Biggs and Collis (1989) expands on the general application for defining curriculum objectives described in this chapter, and Collis and Biggs (1989) on the specific application to science.

On alternative frameworks

Driver, R. (1983). *The Pupil as Scientist.* Milton Keynes: Open University Press.

Pozo, J. & Carretero, M. (1992). Causal theories, reasoning strategies and conflict resolution by experts and novices in Newtonian mechanics. In A. Demetriou, M. Shayer & A. Efklides, (eds.) (in press), *The Neo-Piagetian Theories go to School.* London: Routledge & Kegan Paul.

White, R. (1988). *Learning science.* Oxford: Basil Blackwell.

Alternative frameworks are not the preserve of the physical sciences (there are plenty in the biological sciences, economics and mathematics), but they are much better researched and documented in physics and mechanics. Driver's book represents the classical study of the area; White relates his own research and the implications it has for science teachers, with style and panache. Pozo and Carretero describe a series of studies comparing misconceptions held by scientists of varying ages and by undergraduate non-scientists (historians); no, misconceptions are not more common in the young, but in the ignorant. But the young are usually more ignorant.

Experts and novices

Chi, M., Glaser, R. & Farr, M. (1988). *The Nature of Expertise.* Hillsdale NJ: Lawrence Erlbaum.

Taylor, J.C. (1991). Designing instruction to generate expert cognitive skill performance. In G. T. Evans (ed.), *Learning and Teaching Cognitive Skills* (pp. 164–184). Hawthorn, Vic: Australian Council for Educational Research.

The expert–novice literature is scattered throughout the journals; the Chi et al. book is one of the more comprehensive and most recent. It deals with the general question of expertise and contains chapters dealing with several specific subjects. The Taylor article describes the experiment in teaching expert knowledge to novices in a metallurgy context.

CHAPTER 4

MORAL AND SOCIAL DEVELOPMENT

Moral and social development

The development of our relationships with others.

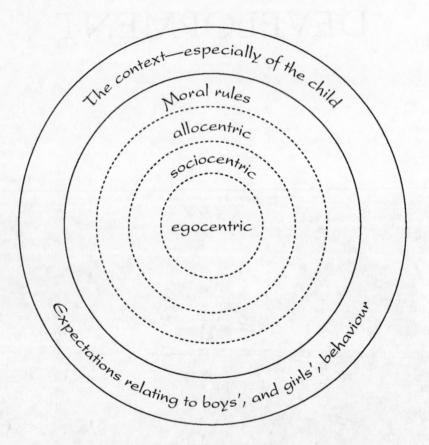

How can teachers cope with:
- what they think is fair?
- what you think is fair?
- teaching students to do the right thing?
- knowing what is the right thing?

MORAL AND SOCIAL DEVELOPMENT

In this chapter, you will find out:

- how moral reasoning develops;
- if you'd be likely to electrocute a stranger if you were told to;
- the nature of children's culture;
- if girls are genetically less able to do science and maths;
- if girls are advantaged or disadvantaged in coeducational schools.

Social development in general and in particular

In this and the next chapter, we look at development from the social point of view: how we develop in our relations with others. Our thinking on this parallels the way our thinking has developed in the area of cognitive development. First, and mainly through the influence of Piaget, psychologists looked at more general processes of social and moral development, where the question was: Are there general stages of development, through which all students will pass on their road to becoming socialised individuals? Several psychologists think that these stages exist and can be discerned in the study of the development of moral reasoning: how individuals come to think the way they do about what is right and what is wrong.

Then thinking began to become more contextualised and problem oriented. As when psychologists began to study children's learning in the context of school, the general structures that appeared so powerful in the 'pure' or decontextualised tasks that Piaget used began to seem less important. When children's social thinking was looked at in context, that too began to seem less dominated by general stages, but more determined by context.

A very important and topical aspect of children's social thinking concerns gender: how children acquire expectations about how boys should behave and how girls should behave. Such expectations have an obvious effect on school performance, particularly in how students perform in 'male' and 'female' subjects. Teachers should know about many implications arising from the research done so far and relate them to their own teaching.

In this chapter, then, we deal with general issues of social and moral development first, and subsequently with the more contextualised aspects of social and moral development, with particular reference to gender. In Chapter 5, we focus on the question of culture itself and what research says about multicultural and bicultural education, concluding with an examination of the school's role in socialising and acculturating.

The development of moral reasoning

One of the pioneers of the study of moral reasoning was Piaget (1932); this was before he attempted to describe thinking in terms of logical systems. His methodology then was more observational and naturalistic, asking children what they thought about various aspects of their daily life: such as playing games, natural and social phenomena, very much as do contemporary ethnographers and qualitative researchers.

In the case of moral reasoning, he argued that 'morality' was simply the tendency to accept and follow a system of rules governing interpersonal behaviour. How then do children come to accept and understand those rules? Let us start with a simple prototype of interaction requiring that those involved stick by the rules: the game of marbles. He asked children of various ages where the rules came from, why they had to obey them, and so on. He also asked more obviously 'moral' questions, such as: Why is telling lies wrong? Who of two children in the following story was the naughtiest?

> Mary did the washing-up for her mother to give her a nice surprise, but broke 16 cups in the process. Jane was forced to do the washing-up, so she showed her resentment by deliberately breaking one cup. But she did the rest very well.

Who was naughtiest, Mary or Jane? (Wait for it: we'll let you know).

Piaget believed that the *intention* behind the action determined if it was moral or not. The *fact* of lying is not as important as the intentions leading to the lie. To lie in order to gain ('I lost that wallet you found') is morally different from lying in order to protect someone else ('Sorry she was late, it was my fault for forgetting the time'). This places the focus on what people *think* about behaviour rather than on what they *do*. Piaget found that moral thinking fell into stages of development that not surprisingly correspond in general outline to the four modes of development: *amoral* (based on the sensori-motor mode), *egocentric* (ikonic), *sociocentric* (concrete-symbolic) and *allocentric* (formal).

The sensori-motor mode: Amorality

Behaviour in the sensori-motor mode can only be *amoral*. As it is concerned only with doing, intentions are excluded. Control over behaviour is thus quite external. Hot things burn, so the infant very quickly acquires a 'Don't touch hot things' rule. Simple conditioning, through the use of arbitrarily assigned rewards and punishments (see Chapter 10), is used to establish a general class of 'no-nos'; thus, some things, like hitting baby brother, become no-nos. Morality is not involved. Dogs can be trained to avoid no-nos.

The ikonic mode: Egocentric morality

The main characteristics of ikonic thinking you will remember from Chapter 2: rigid unidimensional thinking based on a strong percept, emotion, or both, with strong self-reference or *egocentrism*. Piaget observed that two little boys playing marbles did not understand the rules; each played by his own set of rules which was different from the other. They were mimicking what they thought older children were doing. Yet each set of rules was absolute, laid down by unimpeachable authorities: 'Where did the rules come from?' 'God' said one. 'The Mayor of Geneva' said another. 'Daddy' said one loving son.

Morality at this stage is rule-bound, the strict letter of the law: what Piaget calls the morality of *unilateral respect*. Ikonic laws demand instant obedience; they are sacred, infallible, and unchangeable. What is written is written. As in egocentric thinking, the point of view of another is not taken into account, their intentions unkown and irrelevant. In these circumstance, naughtiness can only be judged on external criteria. Who broke the rules? Who did most damage? In the washing-up story, Mary broke 16 cups and Jane only broke one. Naughty Mary.

Lies are wrong, because they do not correspond to objective fact. Adolescents see that a lie is wrong because it is intended to mislead. In one of Piaget's stories, a little boy came racing home to say that he had received good marks in school when in fact he had done badly; another to say that he had seen a dog as big as a cow. Children aged around 8 years regarded the second boy as telling the worse lie: dogs as big as cows just do not exist, so that was very naughty. The first child, on the other hand, *might* have got good grades, so his was not so bad a lie.

How do children view punishment? Piaget distinguished two kinds of punishment: *expiatory* and *reciprocal*. According to the first, wrongdoing demands a natural price, the currency of which is pain. Up to about 10 years of age, children tend to regard the fairest punishment as the most severe, which is consistent with their morality-by-consequences. They accept punishment for lying long before they understand that they are lying. After 10 or so, however, children acquire the reciprocal view: the punishment should involve the wrongdoer in making good any damage caused. Some adults retain the expiatory view of punishment: prisons should be as unpleasant as possible, to 'teach a lesson'.

An authoritarian parent who lays down the law and regularly responds to 'why?' questions with 'Because I say so, that's why!' is encouraging a morality of unilateral respect. If the parent also punishes according to the extent of material damage, the child is being encouraged to remain at the egocentric stage: evaluate right and wrong in terms of results not intentions and to regard the law as arbitrary, immutable, imposed from outside. Personal responsibility is pre-empted.

The concrete-symbolic mode: Sociocentric morality

In the socialisation process, rules and codes are assembled to cover particular contexts and situations; eventually they cover society itself, with the relational system of law-and-order. On the way, sets of rules govern particular contexts—family, peer group, school, neighbourhood—each sitting multistructurally alongside the other. There are different codes for playground, home, school, the beach, the footie, church. Love your neighbour when in church and kick his head in on the playground.

Sociocentric morality differs from egocentric morality in the generality of the rules, not in their felt power to command obedience. The rules apply equally to all members of the peer or reference group. Whereas earlier the adult was the authority who commanded obedience, now it is the peer group. Children must live with adult authority in most homes and schools, but this is just an inconvenient fact of life: their major loyalty is to their group and the rules apply to all within it (Davies 1981). The rules include the immediate group, without exception and with rigid uniformity. Even rules to cope with biscuit-eating: if one gets a biscuit, then all get a biscuit. This can lead to such democratic lengths that a biscuit is refused because then *'she'd* get an extra one'. One in, all in.

While there are social-class differences in the *rate* of moral development, possibly because of the more frequent use of external control techniques in lower-class homes, these differences tend to disappear when children join clubs and organisations (Hess 1970). Such memberships tend to encourage a new perspective whereby behaviour is considered from different points of view and thus egocentric orientation begins to be broken down. Similarly, children's experiences in the school community teach them that what applies at home does not apply to everyone. Other children, other parents, have different rules. They believe different things; do not go to church; go to bed at different times; are not forced to do their homework. In the face of that, by the age of 12 some allocentrism should begin to soften the democratic, neo-fascism of earlier years.

The formal mode: Allocentric morality

What makes a rule a rule? We can question the question here as we did in Chapter 2. Justice is not the letter of the law—if you get a biscuit then I get a biscuit—but the *spirit*; for each to be served equally in principle, justice might better be served by apparent inequality in practice, as is recognised in the notion of diminished responsibility. You don't apply the same penalties to those who aren't responsible for their actions. The citizens of Erwin, Tennessee, however, did not recognise this principle, generously including elephants within the range of their sociocentric rules (see Box 4.1).

Box 4.1   *The cruel death of 'Five-ton Mary'*

There are ancient records of the hangings of bulls and oxen, but there is only one known case of the hanging of an elephant—it happened in Erwin, Tennessee, on 13 September 1916. The Sparks Circus was stationed in Kingsport, Tennessee, when Mary, a veteran circus elephant, was being ridden to water by an inexperienced trainer, Walter Eldridge. On the way, Mary spotted a watermelon rind and headed for this snack. When Eldridge jerked hard on her head with a spear-tipped stick, Mary let out a loud trumpet, reached behind her with her trunk and yanked the trainer off her back. Mary dashed Eldridge against a soft-drink stand and then walked over and stepped on his head. A Kingsport resident came running and fired five pistol shots into the huge animal. Mary groaned and shook but didn't die—in fact, she performed in that night's show. The next day the circus moved to Erwin, where 'authorities' (no one is sure who) decreed that Mary should die on the gallows, to the great sorrow of her friends in the circus. She was taken to the Clinchfield railroad yards, where a large crowd was gathered. A $7/8$-inch chain was slung around her neck, and a 100-ton derrick hoisted her 5 feet in the air. The chain broke. The next chain held and Mary died quickly. Her five-ton corpse was buried with a steam shovel.

Source: Wallace, Wallechinsky & Wallace 1984, pp. 67–9

The application of principle requires *allocentric* thought: the ability to place oneself in the position of another, a notion already introduced in Chapter 2, and to observe oneself from the position of another. Formal thought also permits people to think in terms of the possible: what might be, rather than what is. Thinking adolescents and adults can see that society can be different and maybe should be different. Sociocentric thinkers, on the other hand, are conformists on social issues. If an elected government has decided to allow foreign companies to clearfell a section of a national park for woodchipping, so be it: it is a government's job to make those decisions, even if you personally disagree. Allocentrics and egocentrics would challenge that decision if they disagreed: allocentrics because of a stand on principle, egocentrics on whether they personally stood to gain or lose. Sociocentrics can't see the allocentric point of view, but they can see the egocentric point of view; they've been there, done that. Hence, they interpret the actions of allocentrics as egocentric; they simply cannot conceive that the Bob Browns and the Peter Garretts can be doing more than stirring and grandstanding to feed their own egos. Allocentrics may see times when it is right to challenge law and order and to disobey the law of the land. This makes sociocentrics absolutely furious.

Kohlberg's stages of moral development

Kohlberg (1969) built his system around Piaget's ego-, socio- and allocentric levels, sub-dividing each so he arrived at six levels (see Table 4.1).

Table 4.1 *Comparison of Piaget's and Kohlberg's stages of moral development*

Judgment		
Piaget's stages	Kohlberg's stages	
Egocentric	Pre-conventional	1. Punishment
		2. Reward
Sociocentric	conventional	3. Conformity
		4. Law and order
Allocentric	post-conventional	5. Contract
		6. Autonomy

He used moral dilemmas to assess level of moral judgment. In one example, Hans has a very sick wife who can be cured only by a certain drug which has been developed and patented by the local pharmacist, who requires an enormous sum of money for the drug, although it is cheap to produce. Hans does not have this amount available. What should he do?

In assessing the responses, the decision itself, to steal or not to steal, is not the point but how the subject justifies whatever decision is made. Kohlberg classified the replies he obtained (mainly from a sample of 78 boys studied over a period of 12 years) in terms of his six stages. He judged the individual's stage of moral development as that level in which 50% of a person's replies could be classified.

Pre-conventional morality

This general level is said to characterise children's thinking up to 10 years of age. Good and bad are defined on the basis of *actual consequences,* whether they are rewarding or punishing, rather than in terms of standards of right and wrong.

Stage 1: Punishment. The likelihood of punishment determines whether an act is wrong or not. The stage 1 delinquent believes that the crime is being caught. In terms of the Hans story, a typical stage 1 reply would be that 'Hans should steal the drug because his father-in-law might punish him if he let her die'; or he should not, because he'll be punished by the law if he does. People act in this way when they walk across an empty street against a red light. They would be stage 1 in their moral development if they behaved in this way in all situations: if you can get away with it, do it.

Stage 2: Reward. Enter an element of reciprocity. Stage 2 acts out of self-interest, but often modified in the light of mutual advantage: 'I'll scratch your back if you'll scratch mine'. Hans would steal the drug and save his wife because she'd then be a very grateful little wife to have around and he'd look great. On the other hand, he might not steal it because that would render him *persona non grata* with the pharmacist, whose services he might well need in the future.

Conventional morality

Conventional morality is sociocentric. There is some reciprocity and the recognition that objective standards apply both to oneself and to others, but other people dictate what is right and what is wrong; one's own views are unimportant.

Stage 3: Conformity. Stage 3 is the quintessential Good Boy. Hans would do what any 'decent husband' would do: protect his wife even if that meant breaking the law. His not to reason why, his but to do and die. This kind of reasoning is typical of the bureaucrat whose job is zealously to carry out orders; an Adolf Eichmann (whose orders included genocide). The morality of the orders is the responsibility of those who issue them. As Lieutenant William Calley said on reporting back to base after the infamous My Lai massacre during the Vietnam War: 'I did my duty. *Sir!*'

Stage 4: Law and order. Stage 4 is also other-directed, but is more sophisticated than stage 3. Stage 4 would demand to know what is the lawful authority, wherever a conflict exists between two lines of apparent duty. In the Hans story, stage 4 might reply that he should steal the drug in light of his marriage vows; or that he should *not* steal the drug in light of the laws of the land that allow the pharmacist to charge what the market will take.

Post-conventional morality

Stages 3 and 4 do not question the law: post-conventionals do. Using the formal mode, they see that there are higher principles applying.

Stage 5: Contract. Stage 5 recognises that the rules of any particular society are arbitrary; behind each rule system are general principles of justice, love and humanity that transcend the particular. Stage 5s see society in terms of a legal contract between various factions, the particular clauses of which are open to change by virtue of the arbitrary nature of particular rules, just as adolescents invent new rules for a game and modify them as experience suggests. In the Hans story, the stage 5 person would argue that Hans and his wife committed themselves to each other for better or for worse and this contract overrides the social–legal contract of payment. The pharmacist is being unreasonable in terms of natural law and thus the existing law is wrong and Hans must stand by his greater obligations. Or stage 5 could uphold the existing law and justify that.

A judge trying a case ideally operates at stage 5; the particular case may well have extenuating circumstances that make the literal application of the law as it stands unfair.

The judge, mindful that the ruling will create a precedent for future cases, has to make a judgment acceptable to society and in keeping with abstract principles of justice.

Stage 6: Autonomy. Stage 6 represents the highest level of morality, which few reach: it may be regarded as a post-formal mode, in which the individual recognises that there may be principles higher than those that underlie society itself. Thus, stage 6 might recommend that Hans steal the drug, but publicly. In that way he would be saving his wife and also making the point that the free enterprise system may be destructive of human relations (if that's the point driving stage 6) and therefore should be changed. Or possibly that Hans should not steal the drug because, er ... well, actually this is one case where the alternative response is hard to reconcile with a stage level. Could a stage 6 *not* steal? (see Box 4.2)

Box 4.2 *Roll up, roll up, all you stage sixes!*

The first lucky reader to write in convincing us of such a case—that is, of a stage 6 who would NOT steal the drug—will get a FREE mention in the next (fourth) edition of *Process of Learning*!

But just a minute. Wouldn't that stage 6 be then driven by stage 2 egocentrism? Very well, that first lucky reader will get an ANONYMOUS FREE MENTION in our next edition.

What could be fairer than that, folks?

The difference between stages 5 and 6 is nicely illustrated in the famous exchange (quoted in Feigelson 1970: 146) between two friends, Thoreau and Emerson. Thoreau (6) was a radical and idealist; Emerson (5) a famous jurist and poet. On this occasion, Emerson was being conducted through a new prison and saw his old friend locked up. Shocked, he asked the jailed Thoreau: 'Why David, what are you doing in there?' To which Thoreau replied: 'Why Ralph, what are you doing out there?' A modern example is provided in Box 4.3

Box 4.3 *Do individuals have the right to place their own principles above the law? Stage 6s think that they have.*

The peaceful arrests climaxed a week of tension at Farmhouse Creek where a timber company plans to build an access road past the creek that Dr Brown calls a wilderness gateway.

During the week, more than 60 forest workers dragged conservationists away from the paths of earthmovers and two shots were fired toward Dr Brown.

These two incidents contributed to heated responses from members of a lunchtime crowd that spilled over the lawn in front of State Parliament in Hobart yesterday.

The crowd was estimated by police at 2000 and by the Wilderness Society at 5000.

It cheered Dr Brown as he said: 'When the law is wrong, the only place for a true citizen to be is in jail.'

Source: The Newcastle Herald, 14 March 1986

Evaluating the cognitivist position

In considering the Piaget/Kohlberg position on moral development, some questions emerge:

- Do people go through the stages as outlined and make judgments over a variety of situations according to their current stage?
- Does egocentrism in young children pre-empt altruism?
- Are there gender differences in these stages, given that Kohlberg's data at any rate were based on males only?
- Do people *actually behave* in the way they say others should?

The question of stage

We saw in Chapters 2 and 3 that, when handling cognitive tasks in school, students tend to operate unevenly, at different levels according to their interest in the task, their previous experience and so forth. Moral judgment varies even more across situations. The stage of moral reasoning based on an individual's responses to one story may have little or no correlation with the stage of the same individual based on another story, contrary to Kohlberg's claim that 50% of a person's responses will fall at the one stage (Kurtines & Greif 1974). By scoring responses in an open-ended way, it is frequently possible to find evidence of *all six* stages in a person's responses (Phillips & Nicolayev 1978).

Thus, the way a person thinks about a moral situation is like any other aspect of thinking; it depends on the *situation,* as much as on the person's stage of cognitive or moral development. As we see below, a number of contextual factors influence both what people say and what they actually do, especially the perceived *costs* for acting or not acting in a certain way.

Can young children be altruistic?

Altruism refers to helping or giving pleasure to others when there is nothing in it materially for oneself, and seems to result from sophisticated moral judgments: sociocentric thought allows us to be altruistic to our group, and only when allocentric thought develops can we be altruistic to people in general. It would seem to be impossible when thinking is mainly egocentric. Yet young children do seem to feel for the pain of others:

> One woman who accidentally bit her cheek and winced reported that her daughter's face was 'an exact mirror of the pain' ... When one woman bumped her elbow and said 'Ouch', her 20-month-old son at once screwed up his face, rubbed his own elbow and said 'Ow'. Only then did he begin to rub *her* elbow. (Pines 1979:74)

These children's altruism was inspired by feelings, not judgment or reasoning. They felt sympathy and behaved in a way that is in anyone's definition morally or socially appropriate. Thus, too, the more children are exposed to incidents where models are altruistic, for example offering sweets to others, the more likely the children exposed will be more altruistic with their sweet supply (Rushton & Littlefield 1979).

Nevertheless, there are striking individual differences in the readiness of young children to display altruism. Some do so from a very early age, even before social learning and imitation might play a part, while others show little altruism or even concern for the distress of others. Although such differences might in part, even a large part, be explained by childrearing and social learning, Pines suggests that genetic factors may also contribute.

Can young children be altruistic?

Gender issues

Kohlberg's data were obtained from an all-male sample and the post-conventional levels for female moral development were simply not examined (Gilligan 1982). Gilligan postulates a 'network of caring' which operates at the higher moral levels and through which girls and women make sense of their lives. This network is not a stage 3 conformity to avoid disapproval and the dislike of others. The frameworks girls use to construe their relationships with other children, teachers, parents and adults in general are *different* from those used by boys. How's this for a 'sociocentric' comment from Suzie (age 10):

> Some people tease Aborigines, well for instance, a long time ago Sherryl Grimes was at school and there was a lot of people teasing her and this Aborigine Susy she used to go around with … and that's what happened to a lot of Aborigines at D school, and that's why I feel sorry for them and I let them play with us, cos they were always being teased. (Davies 1984a: 290).

Egocentrism, or sociocentric peer pressure, evidently is not the only spring to action. *Feelings* matter, and guide children's and female morality in general, in ways that are different from the way male morality is guided. Gilligan, Ward, Taylor and Bardige (1988) summarise by postulating two perspectives on moral development:

- a *justice* perspective, which is chiefly male and is based on moral reasoning à la Piaget and Kohlberg; and
- a *care* perspective, which is exclusively *(sic)* female and is based on feelings of concern.

Maybe there's an egocentric streak in stage 6 male moralising: '*I* believe in *my* conscience … *I* rely on *my* moral judgment. Out of my way, lesser mortals, while *I* straighten you out!' Gilligan at any rate believes that the justice perspective of the crusader omits a crucial aspect of morality: how others might be affected by this highly principled, relentless, moralising. But maybe, too, caring isn't *exclusive* to females.

From judgment to action

Do people act in the way they say others should in these moral dilemmas? Sometimes and more particularly at the top end. Students who successfully resisted conforming to peer group pressure in judging the length of lines (see below the Asch experiments on conformity), or to authority pressure to inflict punishment on someone else (the Milgram experiments on electric shocks) were at higher Kohlberg levels than those who did conform. On the other hand, in other situations—such as cheating in examinations and in helping others—little or no relationship exists between moral judgment and moral behaviour.

In the case of helping others, there are striking differences between the actual behaviour of kindergarten children and senior high-school students. 100% of (egocentric?) kindergarten children helped a student carry a large pile of books across a crowded classroom, whereas only 5% of (sociocentric? allocentric?) high-school students did so; yet most kindergarten children said they would not help and most of the high-school students said that they would (Blasi 1980)!

Kohlberg and Piaget are simply incorrect in asserting that people behave consistently across a variety of situations according to the stage they are currently occupying. First, people do *not* make consistently similar judgments across a variety of situations; circumstances can make an enormous difference to what people judge as right or wrong. Second, judgment is only one of several determinants of behaviour. Hartshorne and May (1928) found that student cheating was unrelated to students' expressed values or honesty, but rather related to whether or not they thought they were under surveillance.

The cognitive position is however useful in categorising the different *kinds* of moral judgment that people may make. A person may decide in a particular situation to act out of self-interest; in another out of a sense of either loyalty or conformity to the group; in yet another out of conscience, in defiance of group or self-interests. But those decisions are not so much a function of moral developmental levels as of situational factors in particular. Conformity, the key process in sociocentric morality, is an excellent example.

Conformity: The importance of context

Conformity

Conformity is:

a change in a person's behaviour or opinions as a result of real or imagined pressure from a person or a group of people (Aronson 1984: 17).

The classic study of conformity was by Asch (1956); the task involved judging which one of three presented lines was closest in length to a standard. The task seems extremely simple, with the correct answer being quite clear. The subject who is to make the judgment is required to speak last, after four others (stooges) have confidently announced the 'correct' answer to be an *incorrect* line and to announce their choice publicly. Over one-third of Asch's undergraduate subjects conformed to the group judgment. Note that they were not *persuaded* that they were incorrect because, when asked to make their judgments privately, they said what they really saw.

Much research has been done to see what factors influence conformity in this situation (summarised in Blasi 1980; Aronson 1984):

- If the subject is required to give a public commitment first, before the group give theirs and again afterwards, the last judgment conforms less. People figure that they would make even bigger fools of themselves if they changed.
- If people are trained to believe that they are good at the task, by prior runs, they are less likely to change to the group norm opinion: their self-esteem is sufficiently strong to withstand the tendency to follow the mob.
- Subjects at post-conventional levels on the Kohlberg scale conform less.
- Whereas in earlier (pre-women's lib) experiments, women were found to be more conformist, more recent experiments show this to occur only when either the experimenter is male, or the task male-oriented (as in the Milgram task below).
- Conformity increases where the group is of higher perceived status than the subject.

Conformity to authority: Obedience

Perhaps the most stunning experiments on obedience were those initiated by Milgram (1964), repeated with variations many times since. Let us return to the stage 3 reasoning that the 'right thing' is following orders. In the trials of Eichmann (a Nazi officer who directly ordered the execution of thousands of Jews) and Calley (an American non-commissioned officer who directly supervised the rape and massacre of a Vietnamese village), what shocked many people, possibly as much as the acts they committed, was the evidence given by psychiatrists that neither Eichmann nor Calley was sadistic or even unbalanced. They were normal to the point of banality. They saw themselves as *agents*: super stage 3s. Most individuals would imagine that they themselves would refuse to carry out orders that were clearly morally obnoxious. Milgram actually set out to demonstrate that there must be some basic flaw in German society that allowed 'normal' men like Eichmann to operate in the way he did, but his pilot studies in America told him not to bother going to Germany.

Milgram (1964) advertised for subjects for a 'learning experiment', at $4.50 per session (that was when $4.50 was considered good payment). The respondents were told they were to take part in an experiment on the effects of punishment on learning. Each subject, tested individually, was to act as 'teacher' by reading out a list of words and when the 'subject' (who was in fact a stooge of Milgram's) made an incorrect response, the 'teacher' was to throw a switch that would administer a shock. After each mistake the shock was to be increased: the 'teacher' used a switchboard that ran from a harmless 15 volts to 450 volts, with warning signs (DANGER: SEVERE SHOCK) written at the high-voltage end. The 'subject' initially informed the 'teacher' that he had a weak heart.

The 'teacher' was requested as part of the procedure to increase the shock after each error and to continue the experiment until either the 'subject' learned the word list or the extreme 450-volt position had been reached. After each shock, the 'subject' registered pain. At medium shock levels, the 'subject' was already screaming, groaning and begging for the experiment to terminate; at the extreme end, he lay slumped in his chair, apparently either unconscious or dead. (There were no shocks received, in actual fact.)

Milgram initially estimated that about 5% of people might continue to the 450-volt mark. In one study he found that 65% did so: in another, 48%. He thought sadism could not be the reason for these astonishing figures, as his 'teachers' were clearly distressed about what they were doing.

> If, in this study, an anonymous experimenter can successfully command adults to subdue a 50 year old man and force on him painful electric shocks against his protest, one can only wonder what government, with its vastly greater authority and prestige, can command of its subjects (Milgram quoted in Meyer, 1970:132)

Might it not be even more alarming if people did *not* obey? Meyer (1970) thought that without this strong tendency in people, everyone would be a law unto themselves and total anarchy would result. But this is to assume that the alternatives are: (a) pre-conventional behaviour, or (b) conventional behaviour based on obedience and duty. But you will remember the post-conventional stage, which may make disobedience the more moral alternative, even if Meyer didn't.

It is thus not a question of being an agent or not being an agent; it is *when* to be an agent. Is it right for us to carry out orders unquestioningly in *this* situation? That is the question and the stage 3 answer is an unequivocal 'Yes. There are *no* situations in which it is right to disobey orders from a higher authority.' This answer was endorsed by 65% of the people involved in Milgram's research.

Yet there are aspects about the situation that allow us to maintain some faith in humankind. Here, the victim had given prior assent and we may assume that few of the Jews or Vietnamese villagers did so. Further, the experiment was conducted by a scientist affiliated to the highly prestigious Yale University (Aronson 1984). When the experiment was repeated in a rundown commercial building in an industrial city, the figure of obedience dropped from 65% to 48% (still disturbingly high, you might think). When subjects witnessed other subjects (stooges of course) refusing to comply, conformity appeared on the side of the angels: those who went along with the experimenter dropped to 10%. And when the experimenter was out of the room, his orders delivered by telephone, only 25% actually complied, a substantial number delivering lower-level shocks than instructed. If they can disobey with honour, many people will.

Conclusions

We have been looking at general factors in social and moral development independently of specific cultural factors. We have seen that:

- There is a progression in developmental level of moral reasoning that roughly follows characteristics of the modes considered in general cognitive development, but it is rather more difficult to tie to ages. The levels of moral reasoning are more useful as a typology of moral decision-making than as a guide to development.
- Interpersonal feelings play a large part in moral development, possibly playing a larger part in female than in male decision-making
- The immediate context also significantly affects how a person will behave, particularly in relation to conformity and obedience to rules.

Social development in the child's context

Now let us look at social and moral behaviour within the natural context in which children work: their own culture. Davies (1982, 1983, 1984b), after observing and talking with children in a country primary school for a whole year, concluded that children have their own valid culture, with its own values and which they bring into the class-room. What values does the typical playground peer group impart? Do peer groups impede or facilitate classroom interaction? What use can teachers make of this? We start with the sociocentric nature of children's socialising.

The development and nature of children's friendships

Schofield and Kafer (1985) interviewed 166 primary students (Years 4 to 6) about their friendships, using the SOLO taxonomy to analyse their responses. Their results showed that:

- children were situation-specific about their understanding of friendship;
- popular children were more advanced socially than unpopular children;
- girls were more advanced socially than boys (at this age);
- 74% of all responses were at the multistructural level;
- a multistructural 'fair weather cooperation' seems to be the cement binding peer groups together in the upper primary groups of middle childhood.

Children recognise a wide range of appropriate and inappropriate behaviours but, truly multistructural, they are less concerned with consistency from individuals than with consistency within *situations*. They are not bothered if a friend's home behaviour is different from the same friend's behaviour in school, or if 'friends' are unfriendly if the situation demands it.

The following interchange focused on the question: How can the same individual behave so differently between school and home?

Linda:	At home I sort of do everything, I sorta show off a bit at home ... I don't show off at school 'cos you get called ...
Terry:	Poser! Poser! (said sing-song)
Linda:	Yeah 'Poser! Poser!'
Davies:	So what the other kids say about you at school has a big effect on what you are at school?
Suzie:	Yes, see, whenever I'm being called a name or somethin' like that, I dunno what happens, but it feels horrible.
Linda:	I sorta really go. I really get the snobs.
Terry:	Yeah, me too. (Davies, 1984b: 256).

The pressure is powerful not to pose: doubly powerful, because if you are teased and withdraw, that brings on more teasing. But when is posing posing? There are subtleties. 'Bashing up' can be seen either as posing (by the victim) or as being tough (by friends): being tough is good, posing is bad. *Circumstances* determine whether bashing up is good or bad: not the person or the act itself.

These are some of the characteristics of the culture of childhood:

- Reciprocity: 'I should behave to you as you behave to me', as in the old law of talion ('an eye for an eye, a tooth for a tooth'). Repayments are instant, so that who started it rapidly becomes unanswerable. Fights are self-maintaining.
- There is only one account of what 'really' happened. Children's talk is often negotiating a consensus view of what happened; that is then the official record (see also Solomon 1984). The allocentric view of participants having valid but different perspectives is beyond them.

- People are what they are because of the situation. What is true of someone today may be untrue tomorrow. You behave to people as they are now, not what they might be tomorrow.
- Children inhabit at least two cultures: their own and, when they have to, adult culture.

Davies sees children's culture as valid in its own right, not an immature version of adult culture. She thinks that in a similar here-and-now culture, adults would behave identically. There is evidence that this is so, for example, the treatment and behaviour of inmates in old people's homes (see Peterson 1984), or as vividly brought to life by Ken Kesey in the behaviour of the asylum inmates in *One Flew Over the Cuckoo's Nest*.

We now need to look more closely at the interface between child and adult cultures: that is where teachers have to work.

The rules of teacher–child interaction

Children participate in two agendas: their own and the teacher's. The framework which they see as the most important and relevant is their own. Carrying out the teacher's agenda, involving the teacher's rules, has to fit in with their own and more important set of rules. At the same time, children acknowledge the importance of learning about the adult world (Davies 1981). At best the two agendas run alongside each other. How that may affect student teachers may be seen in Box 4.4.

Box 4.4   *From the horse's mouth*

Question: What's the most important advice you'd give a student teacher?
Paul: Don't treat kids badly, or else they'll treat you worse than you treat them. If you treat them badly on the first day, they'll absolutely murder you.
Friend: Oh well, if they be nice to us, we'll probably be nice to them, you know, we wouldn't be naughty or anything. Any teachers that can take a joke we really like and we treat them really well.

Source: Davies 1982, p. 172.

Another complication is that *two* layers of adult rules exist: the explicit stateable rules, such as those of classroom interaction; and the tacit rules that are not clearly stated, which form the way adults behave and are learned only after long exposure to the culture. The school Davies visited was an experimental school; the principal (Mr Bell) encouraged reciprocity in interaction between children and teachers, treating each with 'respect', explaining why something needed doing rather than issuing unilateral orders. Mr Bell was well-liked: until the day when in the music room he found some boys and girls listening to music under a blanket. Mr Bell misunderstood. His misunderstanding was based on what adults of opposite sex are likely to do under blankets. He flipped; and punished harshly. The children were mortified, not because their teacher had punished them, but because he had become 'unpredictable' (1982: 121). They did not understand the tacit set of rules that made Mr Bell act out of character. They did not ask the allocentric question: 'That's not like him… How could he have seen fit to act like that?'

In school, then, there are many interfaces between the stable and known childhood rules and the adult rules, which either keep changing from adult to adult or, as in the case of the blanket incident, the tacit rules suddenly and unpredictably surge up to make adults act out of situation: unpredictably and capriciously.

Implications for the teacher

The most important implications revolve around reciprocity. Children are naturally willing to learn an adult's particular rules and about the adult world in general; at the same time, their own rules are most salient to them. Adults must therefore show sensitivity and respect for children's rules (Davies 1981). Teachers should therefore find out what they can about their students' rules, show that they know and respect them, make their own rules absolutely clear and explicit and be ready to negotiate the obvious mismatches (see Box 4.5).

Box 4.5 *How one teacher entered Jacob's framework, chopped him up—and was greatly admired*

Jacob had been asked by this teacher to write out 10 times that he must not talk. Jacob wrote his lines hurriedly and in his worst possible writing. The teacher wrote across the page in perfect handwriting, 'Jacob your writing is 'orrible (just like your face, yuk, yuk)' and signed his name with a beautiful flourish. Jacob's comment was, 'He's great. He really knows how to chop people'. The teacher had corrected Jacob, shown himself very correct on the point at issue, made a joking insult (using the 'yuk yuk' to ensure it was recognised as a joke) and displayed at the same time a capacity to play the pupils' game of chopping each other up. In other words he had pursued his central purpose of teaching (in this case, how to write properly) and had at the same time revealed a knowledge about and acceptance of the pupil's perspective in which neat writing, especially the writing of lines, is an awful bore and where being artfully chopped up is infinitely preferable to being punished ...

Source: Davies, 1982, p. 172.

There are basic ground rules for negotiating between any two responsible parties. If schools are to induct young people into the world of adulthood it seems appropriate to use the management metaphor from the world of business: teachers are managers of learning and classroom management is their profession. We explore the full implications of this in Chapter 17.

The perception of gender differences

The largest subcultural difference between people, determining so many expectations as to how others should behave, what they hold to be important, what they believe in and how they should dress and talk, is gender. Just how powerful these expectations are and how early in life they exert an effect can be gauged by Box 4.6.

> ### Box 4.6   *Getting gender right*
>
> Spread out on the grass under the trees was a picnic with convivial adults sipping wine and children playing around in the forest. I … joined the picnic, since these were friends I rarely had a chance to see. There was a child there whom I had not met before. The strawlike unkempt hair, old jeans and checked shirt, the rough way of talking and eating, left me in no doubt that this was a boy. When someone who knew her called her Penny I was startled, but one of the 5 year old children, who had not met Penny before either, was shocked and outraged. She asked her mother to take her to the toilet and when they were out of earshot asked her, with tears in her eyes: 'Mummy, why are they calling that boy Penny?' …
>
> What is so important, I wondered, about getting one's own and other people's gender right?
>
> (Davies 1990: 318–19)

The easiest and most long-standing explanations for gender differences have been biological, but it is also very clear, given gender role differences that exist across societies, that the precise characteristics of what it is to be 'typically masculine' or 'typically feminine' are learned from a very early age, through modelling and other forms of social learning.

One of the most comprehensive studies of gender differences was that by Maccoby and Jacklin (1974), who concluded that there were only four areas where culture and social learning could not be invoked to explain observed (non-physical) male–female differences:

- *verbal aptitude:* females superior;
- *visual–spatial aptitude:* males superior;
- *mathematical aptitude:* males superior;
- *aggression:* males more aggressive.

That was nearly twenty years ago; the critics and researchers moved swiftly. Today, all four areas are questioned, the last least convincingly as there is considerable biological evidence that aggression is related to levels of sex hormones. The previous three, however, are of considerable educational significance and we should examine them in more detail.

Whether she is better than he at English, or he than she at maths, is not the really important issue. Mean or average differences obtained when testing large populations may well be statistically significant (that is, such differences exist in that they cannot be attributed to chance), but in actual fact involve a matter of only a few standardised test scores. While an average (hypothetical) boy may score 102.3 on spatial ability and a hypothetical girl 99.8, the *fact* would be that considerable numbers of girls would be obtaining scores higher than considerable numbers of boys: and of course, *vice versa*. Translate that into a classroom of 20 and it *should* not affect how you would deal with any single individual, or group of girls or boys, in any way at all.

So does that make the whole question of gender differences a massive non-issue? Not at all:

- First, there is the task of *demythologising*, that is getting straight what is myth and what is true, as far as we can tell by current research.
- Second, there is the question of the *mechanisms* that might account for apparent gender differences.

- Third, there are the *implications* they hold for the organisation of teaching. One major issue here is to do with mixed or single sex groupings for teaching purposes, and there is accumulating evidence that these do have an impact, not only on students' performance but on their attitudes and self-concept (e.g., Jones 1990).

Gender differences in mathematics–related areas

First, we deal with the complex of issues dealing with the related spatial, mathematical and technological areas. We have seen that although there is undoubted evidence for social learning effects that account for lower expectations from females, in both their performance and in their attitudes (Fennema 1983), the state of the art in 1974 suggested a biological bottom line:

> The one mental difference between men and women that experts can agree upon is that women are generally superior at verbal tasks and men are superior at spatial ability. Blakeslee (1980: 103)

Do the experts still agree?

Many subsequent studies have compared males and females on their performance in standardised tests of mathematics, science and spatial abilty (which is closely related to mathematical performance). Friedman (1989), and Linn and Hyde (1989), summarised the results of a number of studies. Other writers have focused on studies of possible causal factors: different curricula typically pursued by girls and boys (Pallas & Alexander 1983); classroom interaction and teacher-time (Leder 1987; Nix 1986); motivation (Steinkamp & Maehr 1984); general and specific self-concepts of males and females (Marsh 1989a); and growth in different mathematical skills (Willms & Jacobsen 1990); and all of the above (Oakes 1990). The question of coeducational versus single-sex schools or classes in accounting for differences is particularly pertinent and is dealt with separately. What emerges is the following:

- The overall sex differences observed in the 1970s in *both* verbal (once favouring girls) and mathematical ability (once favouring boys) have in the last twenty years declined dramatically, now approaching zero.
- Some differences in spatial ability still seem to remain, favouring males; and in particular subjects: computational skills increasingly favour females, and maths concepts, males.
- The recent narrowing of differences is linked at least partly to less gender-typed curricula, in which boys were steered into technical/scientific, girls into home economics and 'life force' sciences (biology, botany). Test items in mathematics and science now much less reflect male-biased content (e.g., sport).
- From primary to early secondary school, mean scores in mathematical ability increase fairly evenly in both sexes; what differs is the *spread* of scores, boys fanning out more than girls, particularly in concept performance. The resulting sex difference is that more boys occupy the high *and* low scoring ends. The nursery rhyme is wrong: when talking about mathematical ability, at any rate, boys are more likely both to be very, very good and to be horrid.
- But if mean or average gender differences in verbal and mathematical ability have in general declined in the last twenty years, self-concept and motivational differences have not. Despite what their test performances say, girls *believe* they are less competent than boys in maths/science areas and more competent in languages/humanities. Girls express more positive motivation towards biology, botany and (surprisingly?)

chemistry; boys towards physics and general science. That was in the United States. In Israel, girls were found to be more positively motivated than boys in *all* science subjects. Clearly, cultural factors operate.

- Microcultural factors also operate in the classroom. Teachers spend more time interacting with boys than they do with girls; boys demand more time, both positively and negatively.

Just to spice up the picture, Linn and Hyde (1989) point out that gender differences favouring males in height and strength are 400% of those favouring males in any cognitive area. The earning capacity of females is however 59% that of males. But that differential is not limited to jobs requiring height or strength.

The above findings were concerned with mathematical and scientific performance as measured by norm-referenced *ability* tests, which tend to measure what students bring into a course, not what they take from it. What is the picture when we look at classroom-based criterion-referenced tests? (See Chapter 14 for an elaboration of different kinds of test: essentially, one is concerned with a general ability for mathematics, the other with the specific content that has been learned.) Farkas, Sheehan and Grobe (1990), in a comprehensive study of a whole school district over several years, found that girls in Years 7 and 8 were significantly better than boys in *all* subjects, maths and non-maths. They also found that Asian students (both boys and girls equally) were very much better than Anglos, and Anglos usually better than Blacks and Hispanics. They suggest that 'teacher pleasing' behaviours, such as willingness to expend effort and manageability, explain their findings much more adequately than explanations in terms of ability.

Similar explanations apply in a closely related area: computer participation. Girls are much less likely than boys to use computers in home or school, for educational and recreational purposes, although they will use them in offices (Clarke 1990). Remember: ability differences are minimal, but subjective beliefs about differential abilities and resulting motivation are powerful. Whereas many girls are disproportionately scared of computers, boys associate computers with being clever; especially is this true in coeducational schools (Hattie & Fitzgerald 1987). A completely false belief exists that boys are more likely to have 'some innate capacity for working with computers' (Clarke 1990: 56).

In the case of computer participation, the remedy is clear. Computers should not be associated so easily (in many schools exclusively) with mathematical and technical studies or (at all?) with male-type, aggressive, war games (Clarke 1990:56). Word-processing in connection with essay and creative writing is an obvious area where languages and computing can be brought together in a frontal assault on gender/subject stereotyping.

Where do we stand, then? There may be a biological bottom line. Blakeslee (1980) claims that the female brain and nervous system matures faster than the male, with reduced lateralisation between the hemispheres. Thus, the average levels remain the same, but there are more males at the extremes, both at the genius and at the learning-disabled end. Certainly, there is evidence for male predominance among both the highly gifted (Benbow & Stanley 1982) and the retarded (MacMillan 1982).

As to the verbal/spatial difference it may exist physiologically (op. cit.), but within the 'middle' 95% of the population, with which we are overwhelmingly concerned, it is not a major or even a minor issue. What is clearly an issue is the *context*. The presence of motivational and self-concept differences (Marsh 1989; Steinkamp & Maehr 1984), which are sharply focused in the computer participation issue (Clarke 1990), tells us that we still have a long way to go in providing perceived equal access to the full range of school subjects. Equal opportunity campaigns can even be counter-productive, reinforcing the very thing they are attempting to overcome (see Box 4.7).

Box 4.7   *Equal opportunities for boys too*

... it is the underlying assumption in much current educational rhetoric that concerns me—that is, that the path to educational and employment success is through
the maths and sciences ... This ideology seems to have permeated most equal opportunity programs and to be the major impetus behind the 'Girls into science and
technology' campaign ...

Why don't we see headlines proclaiming the alarming fact that male enrolments
in Arts have fallen to 27%? Why is there no awareness of the fact that boys, too,
need to 'multiply their choices'? ... little attention is being given to the need to
open up different sorts of opportunities for boys ... The effect is to 'privilege' traditional male areas, to reinforce the assumption that they are indeed *better*.

(Baldwin 1990b: 11)

The way the whole question of girls and maths has changed over the year is summed up
pithily by Horin (1989: 12). Twenty years ago the question assumed genetic inferiority:

- Why *can't* girls do maths?

Now the emphasis is on social factors discouraging girls even when they do well up to
early secondary:

- Why *won't* girls do maths?

The computing example seems to highlight the importance of context and in particular social attitudes, both inside and outside the classroom, which change a don't-do
from a can-but-won't-do.

A particularly significant part of that context is the kind of schooling provided: coeducational or single sex?

Are gender differences minimised in coeducational schools?

You would think that teaching boys and girls together, in the same class, would help minimise attitudinal and curricular differences to specific subjects and lead to better social
development in general. You would, now, wouldn't you?

A study of Sydney adolescents by Phillips (1979), however, indicates otherwise.
According to her girls were better off in single-sex schools. In co-ed schools, boys usually won the leadership battles and imposed their rotten little chauvinistic rules, leaving
girls with the self-concepts of losers. Maths/science subjects were (and still are) most frequently taught in co-ed schools by males, who were all too happy to communicate their
views on female suitability for these esoteric realms of academe, while in single-sex
girls' schools, subject mistresses were often female, communicating a very different message. More simply, in single-sex schools girls interested in maths are more likely to have
a positive role model; in co-ed schools they are distinctly likely not to have one. Boys
have a positive like-sex role model whatever school they attend.

But that was in the 1970s. The sensitivities of teachers may have changed since then,
with sharp increases in public awareness of anti-discrimination. Also, socioeconomic
status (SES) and type of school are confused; single-sex schools tend to be exclusive

independent schools and co-ed schools to be government. In fact Jones (1990) confirmed that girls do better in independent, single-sex schools; it is at low SES levels that girls are disadvantaged. In another study of 16 independent Melbourne schools, Foon (1988) showed that in the single-sex schools girls preferred science to English and rated their own science performance highly, but in the co-ed schools girls preferred English. Boys in single-sex schools preferred English to science. In co-ed schools, girls were lower in self-esteem than boys; in single-sex schools, girls had higher self-esteem than boys. Yes, it looks like single-sex schools beat the gender stereotyping and co-ed schools enhance it, as Phillips suggested in the first place.

Are gender differences minimized in co-educational schools?

So would you expect girls from single-sex schools to opt for maths/science/engineering at tertiary level; girls from co-ed to opt for arts/law/humanities? Wrong; Baldwin (1990a) studied over 20 years of enrolment patterns at Monash University and found precisely the opposite. There were proportionately more females in science/engineering than in arts/law. But as these figures exactly reflected the proportions from independent (mostly single-sex) and government (mostly co-ed) sectors, Baldwin reanalysed within sectors and found no difference between faculty enrolments and type of school.

Some studies have looked at schools who have shifted from single-sex to co-ed, or vice versa, which simplifies the social class issue. Marsh, Owens, Myers and Smith (1989) looked at several schools that shifted from single-sex to co-ed and found that achievement, self-concept and teachers' perceptions were all favourable to the change. Girls did not appear to be disadvantaged. In a shift from co-ed to single-sex classes, however, Rowe (1988) found that both boys and girls did better in single-sex classes. Rowe and his team changed 12 Year 7 and 8 mathematics classes from co-ed to single-sex, with 4 classes remaining co-ed; teachers and students were randomly allocated to all 16 classes. Both boys and girls in the single-sex classes gained in confidence and performance in maths, were much more likely to choose Mathematics A rather than General Maths later on, and management problems were sharply reduced. It wasn't quite so much the case that girls did better in single-sex classes; they did, but so too did boys. In interpreting these results, it must be remembered that coeducation in general was not abandoned: only maths classes were scheduled as single-sex. This could possibly have led to a 'Hawthorne Effect': maths is special, the treatment is special, and we are special to have been given this treatment, so we'll put more into it.

In a commissioned study to review the evidence on single-sex versus co-ed type of school, Gill concluded:

> At this stage, it is not possible to give a clear-cut answer to the question of the relative merits of single-sex schools and coeducation from the perspective of optimal education for girls. (Gill 1988: 15)

The studies produced since then take us little further, except to show that teachers should be aware of the issues and be prepared to experiment. The Rowe study at school level suggests (Hawthorne Effect or not) that the results might be gratifying.

Conclusions

The issue of gender differences involves three tasks: demythologising and identifying, then using, the mechanisms. As to the first, we have made progress. As far as cognitive differences are concerned, possibly verbal (favouring female) and spatial (favouring male) differences exist, but their effect is residual. It's not a matter of can't-do-maths but of won't-do-maths. Why not? This brings us to mechanisms. Social attitudes and stereotyping are the culprits and they work with differing efficacy according to their context. They do seem to be more powerful in coeducational rather than in single-sex learning situations; which implicates teachers, particularly male teachers.

So let us look at teacher education students. We find that indeed males hold much stronger stereotypical attitudes than do females (Christensen & Massey 1989). We also find that students in the final year of their course are no less stereotypical, either males or females, than first year students (op. cit.). So maybe we should start with teacher education programs.

Summary

The development of moral reasoning

An essential part of transmitting social values is achieved through moral development: the assimilation of those rules that govern interpersonal behaviour. These rules form unstable systems, which can be overridden by situational cost-benefits with more or less ease, but they can be seen to develop in three broad stages that are partly age-related and that parallel the major modes of development: *egocentric,* where the system is ikonically based, and moral judgment is in terms of literal adherence to external laws but moral behaviour is governed by self-interest; *sociocentric,* where the system is governed by conformity to peer or other reference group definitions of right and wrong; *allocentric,* where the system is governed by formal principles designed for the general good. Behaviour in particular situations, however, depends on other factors, particularly on immediate pressures and on a person's feelings, so that these categories and the more finegrained elaboration developed by Kohlberg, are best seen as descriptions of types of moral judgment than as ways of predicting how people will behave.

Conformity: The importance of context

Conformity is the mechanism of sociocentrism; situations commonly occur that exact conformity and its vertical derivative, obedience. It is not very hard to devise a situation in which about half the population would obey orders to kill the other half. They would hate doing it, but they would do it. Exceptions to that horrible generalisation include those who tend to give principled, allocentric, interpretations to moral dilemmas.

Social development in the child's context

Children form their own sociocentric culture, which adults can either ignore or work with. Children's expectations of each other and of adults derive from their own culture, not from their understanding of adult culture, with which they will interact only if they have to. The implications of this for the running of schools could be radical, but even within normal student–adult interaction there are important implications about how best one should interact. Children value reciprocity. Thus, once a teacher recognises that the student culture exists, negotiation becomes the means of bridging the two; here is a key to managing classrooms, as we see later.

The perception of gender differences

Girls are both not choosing and doing as well proportionately as boys, in subjects like maths, science and computing studies. Twenty years ago the general belief was that this was because girls tend to lack, for genetic reasons, the appropriate abilities underlying successful performance in these areas. That theory has now very little support. Biological factors may operate at the extremes of ability, but for the great majority of the population social attitudes and resulting motivational difficulties are overwhelmingly important. Do these unfavourable attitudes have a stronger effect in a coeducational environment? In the past, this seems to have been so; it is not a necessary consequence of coeducation, however, but of the attitudes of teachers and students within it.

Learning activities

1. Piaget and Kohlberg on moral development

Table 4.1 compares Piaget's and Kohlberg's stages of moral development. The purpose of this activity is to take that table and use it to summarise both the Piagetian and Kohlbergian perspectives. Perhaps a large piece of butchers' paper could be used if done as a class activity, or alternatively the table could be copied onto an overhead transparency.

In summarising the theories it will be useful to provide examples of each of the stages. Gather examples from the classroom or from home. For example, under Piaget's stage of allocentric thought, you could include something like 'the application of principle… tensions between individual and society'. The construction of such an elaborated table should give you a better understanding of the theories and the relationships between them.

2. Conformity–obedience

Milgram's (1964) study, discussed earlier in this chapter, clearly illustrates that many people believe there are no situations in which it is right to disobey orders from a higher authority. (Remember, they continued to administer 'shocks' to others who made mistakes while learning—up to '450 volts'.) In this task you could prepare a poster, perhaps in a cartoon format, that shows what the Milgram study was about and how we see it fitting in with the stages of moral development (say of Kohlberg). Are there implications for what happens in schools, in terms of conformity to authority? Should teachers discuss non-conformity with their students??

3. Children's friendships

This activity emerges from the Schofield and Kafer (1985) research on children's friendships. See if you can 'interview' students at different levels of schooling, say at preschool, infants, primary, early secondary and late secondary. Many questions could be asked about friendships but you can probably get started with two: 'Who is your best friend?' and 'Why is he/she your best friend?' Relate your responses to stages of moral development.

An extension of or alternative to this activity could be to observe young children's play to see how friendships develop. You will notice the somewhat transient nature of friendships ('You're not my friend any more!').

4. Gender differences in mathematics-related areas

We have presented a fair amount of literature addressing the issue of whether or not males differ from females in their performance and abilities related to maths, science, etc. In this task you are to summarise that information and present it in the most novel fashion possible. The challenge here is to be as creative as possible in teaching your peers. If done as a group activity, each group could present its results and the presentation could be rated (say on a 5 point scale) for originality, content, presentation, audience involvement, etc.

5. Equal opportunity

Box 4.7 presented Baldwin's (1990b) concerns about gender equality. Do you agree with the comment that 'little attention is being given to the need to open up different sorts of opportunities for boys'? We see this activity as being discussion oriented and leave it at that.

6. Coeducational or single-sex schools

The purpose of this activity is to gather and interpret data from interviews with students concerning their feelings about coeducational and single-sex schools. This could be done as a class project, for example, with the class discussing which questions would be asked (based upon the types of studies we have presented in the chapter) and then selected members interview say 10 male and 10 female students. The results could then be presented back to the class.

An interesting extension would be to compare responses from students at primary, early secondary and late secondary levels. Would you predict differences? If so, what might they be?

Further reading

On the development of moral reasoning
Aronson, E. (1980). *The Social Animal.* San Francisco: Freeman.
Gilligan, C. (1982). *In a Different Voice: Psychological Theory and Woman's Development.* Cambridge, Mass.: Harvard University Press.
Gilligan, C., Ward, J., Taylor, J. & Bardige, B. (1988). *Mapping the Moral Domain.* Cambridge, Mass: Harvard University Press.
Ginsburg, H. & Opper, S. (1987). *Piaget's Theory of Intellectual Development.* Englewood Cliffs: Prentice Hall.
Graham, D. (1972). *Moral Learning and Development.* Sydney: Angus & Robertson.

Ginsburg and Opper have an excellent chapter on Piaget's theory. Graham covers Piaget, Kohlberg and social learning theory. Gilligan's critique of the Kohlberg position is outlined in her book, a landmark in gender issues and moral development. The amount of readable recent material on moral reasoning is however disappointing. The Asch and Milgram studies on conformity are put into excellent perspective by Aronson, whose approach is strictly social learning theory.

On children's culture
Davies, B. (1982). *Life in the Classroom and Playground: The Accounts of Primary School Children.* Henley: Routledge & Kegan Paul.

This book describes Davies' first ethnographic studies of children's perceptions of their social environment in the New England plateau. A view of what children think of teachers that is not only usefully direct, but directly useful (see Chapter 17 for confirmation).

On gender issues
Curriculum Development Centre (1988). *Gender Equity in Mathematics and Science.* Woden: Commonwealth of Australia.
Gilbert, P. (1989). *Gender, Literacy and the Classroom.* Carlton South: Australian Reading Association.

The Curriculum Development Centre's publication is the culmination of work carried out in Victoria by the Girls and Maths and Science Teaching Project (GAMAST). The project materials are designed to raise teacher awareness of issues in the participation and achievement of girls in these disciplines. Gilbert's book also offers suggestions for teachers in the literacy domain. Gender bias in textbooks is examined in some depth.

CHAPTER 5

CULTURE, LANGUAGE AND MULTICULTURALISM

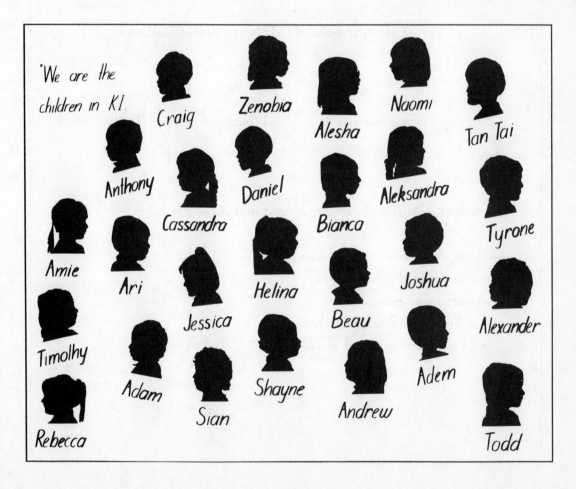

'We are the children in K1.

Craig
Zenobia
Alesha
Naomi
Tan Tai
Anthony
Daniel
Aleksandra
Cassandra
Bianca
Tyrone
Amie
Ari
Helina
Joshua
Jessica
Beau
Alexander
Timothy
Shayne
Adem
Adam
Andrew
Sian
Rebecca
Todd

Culture, language and multiculturalism

What is Oz?   What is definitely not Oz?

What should schools do with Ozness?

|

What should schools do with non-Ozness?

/   \

Encourage?   Discourage?   (both?)

So, what can teachers do about issues such as:

—class differences and language?
—multicultural education?
—Aboriginal education?
—dealing with race related
   and gender related biases?

CULTURE, LANGUAGE AND MULTICULTURALISM

In this chapter you will find out:

- what is meant by 'culture';
- and what is meant by 'acculturation';
- and what schools are meant to do about each;
- why working-class children are more likely to do poorly in school;
- how immigrants perform academically;
- what multiculturalism is;
- what particular difficulties Aboriginal children face in school;
- what schools can do about educating in moral values.

What is culture?

A Melbourne tram; the Opera House hunched under the Sydney Harbour Bridge; sunset on Ayers Rock; the scent of eucalyptus; sizzling brown bodies on a dead white beach; another shrimp on the barbie. These are some ikons of Australian culture. Visit another country and you will collect another set of ikons, that collectively create a quite different and equally distinctive feeling for that culture.

What do we mean by a culture? Culture is:

> … the sum total of ways of living built up by a group of human beings, which is transmitted from one generation to another. *(Macquarie Dictionary* 1982: 163)

This network of attitudes, symbols and ways of behaving is treasured by most inhabitants of a particular culture, and its institutions of learning are geared deliberately to play an important role both in valuing its ikons and in transmitting its contents. That process of transmission is at the heart of social development, but it is not the whole story.

The term 'acculturation' refers to a rather different, almost opposed, process:

> … the process of borrowing between cultures, marked by the continuous transmission of elements and traits between different peoples and resulting in new and blended patterns. *(Macquarie Dictionary* 1982: 14)

That process has been carrying on furiously in Australia. The ikons of the 1940s and 1950s—Great Britain as the 'Home Country', aggressive monolingualism in 'the King's English', and overcooked, stodgy food—have been replaced by those deriving from an extraordinarily diverse population, comprising 140 ethnic backgrounds speaking over 80 languages (Callan 1986), which has provided us (for one thing) with the greatest variety of international restaurants outside Hong Kong.

The school has now two very different roles to play in the social development of students:

- to transmit existing culture in order to socialise or 'tame' individuals so that they conform to what is socially acceptable;
- to acculturate, by facilitating the process of blending minority and majority cultures within society.

We are interested here in both the socialising of individuals, in the sense of assimilation to existing cultural norms, and in the valuing of diversity, as in the process of acculturation. In fact, that last process has become the official policy of *multiculturalism,* which holds that it is beneficial to the majority culture to value and foster minority cultures within it.

In this chapter we look at social development in the macro context of culture itself, focusing on the inevitable tension between subgroups, with their various values and centres of gravity and the mainstream culture of modern Australia. Finally, turning to the 'public' side of moral development, we look at the school's official and unoffical roles in transmitting culture.

Class differences in society

The first tension between subgroups in mainstream Australian culture involves social class. Contrary to another old ikon, Australia is not a classless society. Social class, or socioeconomic status (SES), is defined by several indices: income, occupation, education and general prestige in the community, which in turn might include things like family background (e.g., being born into 'the squattocracy'), accent and many lifestyle attitudes and preferences. The Broom-Jones scale assesses SES by occupation, forming 16 ordinal categories (Broom, Duncan-Jones, Lancaster-Jones & McDonnell 1977). More usually, SES is ordered along fewer categories: such as upper middle class, middle class, lower middle class, upper working class and working class. In common speech, two categories: working class and middle class, workers and bosses.

Whatever the categories, such rank orders are closely related to educational attainment (Connell, Ashenden, Kessler & Dowsett 1982; Graetz 1990; Williams & Carpenter 1990). The sectors of schooling themselves are class-related: independent, which charge high fees although there are direct and indirect charges on the public purse; Roman Catholic, access to which is usually on religious grounds and which receives some considerable public funding, and state, which is provided for everyone else out of the public purse.

Private and public sectors and educational attainment

It is common to find that students from independent schools outperform those from Catholic schools and both greatly outperform state school students (Graetz 1990; Williams & Carpenter 1990). Does the private sector provide a better education? Or are private sector students more highly selected in factors relating to educational achievement (are more able, better motivated and come from middle-class homes that value and strongly encourage educational achievement)?

Certainly students at independent schools are more favoured than those at government schools and, after allowing for these factors, Williams and Carpenter found that some schooling quality differences did exist, but probably not to the extent that parents believe when purchasing private education. Nevertheless, an 'old school tie' factor seems to operate: children attending the Catholic or independent sectors in their parents' foot-steps did relatively better than first generation attenders (Graetz 1990). Contrary to what you might think, differences between state and private sectors have actually increased from prewar days to the present, but have decreased between Catholic and independent sectors (op. cit.). Sectoral differences are greatest when looking at retention rates and performance up to Year 12; that is, proportionately less students from state schools make it to Year 12. Sectoral differences are much less apparent when looking at tertiary performance. At all levels, type of school is not as important as *social background,* measured by parental education, parental occupation, wealth, family size and number of books in the home, and *ability* (Graetz 1990).

How does a factor like social background work to bring about such powerful effects on student attainment? The factors looked at by Graetz provide a clue: middle-class parents, themselves well educated, are likely to be very conscious of the economic and other advantages of good educational qualifications. They themselves enjoy using the tools of literacy and can afford to stock the home with books and now, with computer software. They provide a strong motivational context, which encourages high achievement; they push their kids (McClelland, Atkinson, Clark & Lowell 1953; see also Chapter 10).

Another important dynamic that underlies class differences and educational processes is language use.

Language use in schools

Standard and non-standard English

Within any given language, such as English or French, there are different *kinds* of language: the variations of language found between social classes, formalised as *standard* and *non-standard* English (Bernard & Delbridge 1980). Standard English is that used by the 'establishment'; non-standard English is some dialectical variant, such as Cockney, Southern American, or 'Strine'. While standard Australian English is now recognised as different from standard British English, this was not the case as little as 40 years ago, as recordings of news readers will confirm.

Elaborated and restricted codes

Schatzman and Strauss (1955) studied interviews with 10 working-class and 10 middle-class people whose town had been devastated by a tornado. The two sets of accounts were strikingly different. The working-class reports tended to be unorganised, describing events as they happened to the interviewee: they did not take into account the fact that the listener had not shared those experiences. There was a great deal of exophoric reference: that is, applying words like 'it' and 'he' to events and people out of the immediate context and baffling to a listener.

Bernstein (1961, 1965) formalised these and his own observations in the UK into a theory of *elaborated* and *restricted* codes, which were used by the middle and working classes, respectively. Essentially, an elaborated code bridges the gap between speaker and listener by explicit speech, governed by public rules and referents; a restricted code presupposes a common context or background of shared experiences and is, consquently, less subject to the rules of formal grammar, less abstract, and dependent on the context.

It appears also to apply to Australia, even in such a selected group as university students. Poole (1971) categorised students into middle and working classes (on the basis of father's occupation), interviewed 40 of each and analysed their speech. The middle-class students used more complex syntax, more uncommon adjectives and adverbs, more first-person references, and fewer fragmented or repetitious sequences.

To illustrate how these codes may have developed, let us eavesdrop. The scene is a bus.

Mother 1:   Now sit down darling, the bus will start in a moment.
Child 1:   Why?
Mother 1:   Because the bus will start in a moment and you might fall over and hurt yourself.
Child 1:   Why?
Mother 1:   Do as I say and don't worry Mummy any more.

Now take another pair:

Mother 2:   Siddown.
Child 2:   Why?
Mother 2:   Because I say so. Now siddown.
Child 2:   Why?
Mother 2:   Siddown or you'll get what-for.

The example (fictitious but verismo) illustrates two techniques of child control, in which language is used in quite different ways. Mother 1 controls her child's behaviour by appealing to reasons the child will hopefully understand, implying consideration for others (that is, Mother), and self-control as an ultimate end ('My actions may result in quite awful consequences, so I'd better be careful'). Mother 2 uses external methods of control, in particular conformity to rules imposed by authority (that is, Mother) and keeping out of trouble as an ultimate end ('Is she watching?').

It is possible that different sections of society see themselves and their children occupying differing roles (Edwards 1976). Working-class parents tend to perceive their role as subservient and train their children to follow instructions, not to question matters they scarcely understand. Middle-class parents, on the other hand, see themselves (and, in time, their children) as the givers of instructions and as the providers of reasons for those instructions. Working-class children are not used to having their motives probed, to responding to indirect commands, to exploring alternatives to those given, or to solving problems where the solutions are diverse or uncertain; teachers are seen to be there to instruct, from a position of authority, not to explore alternatives provided by the child.

Deficit or difference?

The names, restricted and elaborated, imply that restricted codes address lower cognitive levels, elaborated codes higher levels. It is a short step from there to say that restricted codes, in non-standard English, are substandard or deficient versions of the language, such that non-standard speakers are less able to solve complex problems which require a fine language structure. Bernstein (1970) regretted that this implication was drawn from his earlier work, but many educators have adopted the deficit model, seeing it as one of their roles to get their charges to 'talk proper' in the language of schooling, that being the elaborated code of standard English. If one of the major functions of school is to pass on the cultural traditions and accumulated knowledge of society, it must use a disembedded language that assumes a lack of both shared personal experience and non-verbal supports between communicator and learner. This presents the educator with two related and complex decisions to make:

1. Is the difference between non-standard and standard English one of deficit or difference? Have speakers of non-standard English failed to acquire abilities needed to cope with society? Or have they simply learned a different grammar and vocabulary that serve their functions just as well as the elaborated code serves its own?
2. Whether deficit or difference, what should the school do about it? Teach in a context with which the child can relate most meaningfully (which will often mean for working-class or immigrant minorities using a restricted code); or use the elaborated code from the outset?

Linguists object strongly to the notion that any language, standard or not, is 'inferior' to any other (Labov 1970; Shuy 1973). A language within a cultural or subcultural group develops to allow communication within that group. One cannot apply the rules of one group to claim that usage in another group is 'wrong':

> Children who speak the regional and social dialects of their home communities cannot be considered pathological ... A child speaks the language that he hears and reveres. (Shuy 1973: 25)

To tell people that they will have to change their manner of speaking if they want to get on in the world is to criticise them for what they are now. Many working-class children do possess strong ambitions to 'get on' but, as the English writer Hoggart (1959) pointed out, the cost was high in personal terms. Grammar (selective) school children in Britain acquired two dialects, standard English for school and outside and non-standard for home. The net result was commonly for children to grow away from their cultural and familial roots. Yet:

> It is just not possible to see non-standard English as the language of literature or scholarship ... Accordingly, the school should do as it has always done and try to give its pupils command of the standard form as the tool to their own advancement. If it has not been as successful with some groups in the past as it would like, the reason may lie less with matters of technique than of attitude and in particular with a complete refusal to give any honour at all to non-standard forms. (Bernard & Delbridge 1980: 269)

So what should the school do about non-standard English?

The dilemma is revealed when Chris is asked to read aloud the words: 'And then he came home'. He reads: ' 'n then 'e come 'ome'.

Chris has achieved two tasks perfectly. He has correctly decoded the script; and he has translated equally correctly into the dialect of his community. Many teachers, however, would consider his reading wrong on two grounds: lexical (reading *a* for *o*) and phonetic (/e/ for /he/). Chris is now both bewildered (*'Wrong!* But I thought I understood!') and insulted. He learns very quickly that school is not his thing.

Di Vesta and Palermo (1974) recommended concentrating initially on learning through the student's non-standard language. Standard English would then be introduced later. This approach, which presupposes a large qualitative difference between non-standard and standard English, does not appear to have been used in Australia. Possibly standard English is sufficiently familiar here to (native speaking) non-standard speakers for it to be focused on directly. This is not the case for students whose first language is not English, as we see below.

Alternatively, then, one teaches solidly for standard usage from the outset, but avoiding denigration or sarcasm. Regular correction of the non-standard form should be avoided; the regularity implies criticism rather than correction. Bereiter and Engelmann (1966) emphasised the need to lift language development by changing pupils' attitudes, values and behaviours to those of middle-class children. In an outback pre-school project at Bourke, New South Wales, called 'Enrichment of Childhood', two concurrent programs were run with matched groups of children: one typical of those offered in New South Wales kindergartens, the other based on the Bereiter drill techniques (de Lacey 1974). A teacher was appointed to communicate directly with parents in their homes and to explain homework tasks. Sessions of 20 minutes, in which the students provided chorus answers when asked to identify objects and sentence responses, were varied by free play or songs which reinforced the language skills. Aboriginal people constituted 25% of the population and spoke what de Lacey termed 'a variation of low-income rural English'. The Bereiter–Engelmann group showed 'spectacular' gains, which were still in evidence two years later.

The Bourke approach exemplifies 'closed' instruction based on the *deficit* model of non-standard English. The problem is seen as a lack of skill in standard English, and direct instructions and drills are thus used to build up competence in standard English as quickly as possible.

An 'open' alternative has been suggested by Evans, Georgeff and Poole (1980). These writers argued that working-class (particularly immigrant) children do not use standard (or elaborated-code) English because their environment is full of non-verbal clues and so they do not have to. They placed children in a discovery-learning situation which offered no facial or bodily clues. To communicate at all, they had to use the public, elaborated code. Pupils were grouped into four or six and then subgrouped by means of a physical partition; all non-verbal communication was prevented. Four tasks were set:

1. Speakers and listeners were given identical sets of six to eight items such as plastic shapes or pictures. Speakers were then asked to describe specified objects so that listeners could correctly identify them.
2. Listeners had the task of building a pattern of shapes identical to that of the speaker.
3. Listeners were required to carry out an everyday task (such as fitting a baby's nappy) on the instructions of the speaker.
4. More general activities included a game in which a blindfolded child had to be verbally directed past obstacles, or drawings were reproduced.

The results strongly favoured the experimental discovery learning approach, with children significantly improving their language skills and ability to communicate.

The Australian research, then, has worked on building up standard English from the outset. The success of this strategy depends on the degree to which one's students can cope with standard English. For those whose mother tongue is not English, the gap between their first language (L1) and standard English (L2) is profound and some bridging is certainly necessary. This is, however, a different order of problem from that of non-standard L1 speakers and is dealt with under ethnicity and multiculturalism and, in the case of Aborigines, biculturalism.

Teaching in disadvantaged schools

Since the mid-1970s Education Departments have allocated funds for special programs at selected disadvantaged schools in an attempt to promote more effective learning, more enjoyable and relevant schooling, and closer liaison between school and community. Such schools are selected on the basis of socioeconomic factors operating in the communities they serve and the funds are provided in response to school/community initiatives. Funded programs cover a vast range of actitivites, including staff development, special curriculum packages, new teaching materials and equipment.

Teaching in disadvantaged schools has its own challenges, as does all teaching, but there are indications that teacher stress is quite high in such schools. Further, the greatest sources of stress for teachers in disadvantaged schools are student problems, demands and behaviour. In contrast, the main causes of stress for teachers in non-disadvantaged schools are teaching loads and time pressures. (Pierce & Molloy 1990a)

Multicultural education

In the early days of postwar immigration, the community firmly believed in the transmission model, applied to both language and culture. New migrants were strongly encouraged to *assimilate* into the Australian Anglo-Celt community, 'on the myth of the homogeneous Australian' (Grassby 1978). The assimilation model reckons on the virtual annihilation of the minority culture, as its members take on the values, modes and attitudes of the majority: no acculturation. A multistructural flirtation with acculturation is the 'mosaic', where each group retains its beliefs and ways within the majority culture, with little modification of values (de Lacey & Poole 1979). The mosaic is however unrealistic. Multiculturalism leads almost inevitably to the 'melting pot' view of acculturation, where both minority and majority cultures are mutually permeated and changed, with each retaining a core of self-identity.

Multiculturalism is currently official policy, which encourages immigrant groups to retain their cultural identity; it is endorsed by a majority of Australians, but with rather mixed feelings (Callan 1986). Some ambivalence still exists among teachers: while 84% feel that migrant children should be given opportunities to learn their community language, 44% felt these opportunities should be given *outside* school hours (Callan 1986), as happens in the government supported 'Saturday school'. Less ambivalence appears to exist in the teachers' attitudes towards assimilation. Teachers in the western suburbs of Sydney showed strong support for interaction between minority and mainstream groups rather than that the minorities conform, giving up their own culture, or that they keep to their own culture (McInerney 1987).

Multiculturalism represents an enormous challenge to educators, in terms of provision of services, which includes teachers familiar not only with the mother languages (L1s) but with the values, customs, folkways and mores that make multicultural education possible. Teachers intending to serve in multicultural and Aboriginal education obviously need specialised training.

The problem facing teachers in multicultural education is essentially one of attaining the basic goal of schooling: both to perpetuate Australian culture and to retain the cultural identity of ethnic minority groups. As Australia has the most diverse workforce in the industrial West, excluding Israel and the OPEC Arab regions, this dual goal is difficult to attain.

The policy of the Commonwealth Schools Commission has two aspects:

1. That schools will attempt to reflect within their curriculum the realities of the differing lives of their students and within their organisation provide ways to support student self-esteem and confidence.

2. That schools will attempt to provide opportunities for students to broaden and
    enrich their lives through acquisition of at least some aspects of another culture
    (Education Commission of NSW 1986)

Multiculturalism represents an enormous challenge to educators.

These points have been reaffirmed by state and territory education authorities through
policy statements which incorporate aims to develop in students understandings such as:
Australia's multiculturalism has been part of its history, both before and after European
settlement; people from different cultures have made and are making contributions to
the nation; and different cultures have different beliefs, values and attitudes (NSW
Department of Education, 1983). Recent authors, however, have criticised the rather narrow way in which policies have been implemented in some areas with their focus on ESL
and economic/community languages (Khoo 1990).

Cazden (1989) provides a case study of one inner-city New Zealand multicultural
school, Richmond Road: the vision of its recently deceased Maori principal. The
school contained 269 primary students: one-third Maori, the rest split between Anglo,
Samoan, Indian and other Polynesian. The extended family was the model, the structuring vertical. Four large groups speaking the same language were formed, each covering the full age range and each split into smaller home groups, with its own teacher.

The curriculum was school-based, the dynamics cooperative and non-authoritarian, the outcomes inspirational. The subheads of her article give a taste of Richmond Road:

- The kids always come first.
- But it's actually an agenda for everyone.
- Learning about teaching.
- Learning about other people in other cultures.
- Learning about oneself.
- 'This is the way we learnt at home': vertical groupings of children.
- Whoever has knowledge teaches.
- 'The teachers, they all work together'.
- 'I can't tell you how old that child is; but I can tell you exactly where he is working in maths and in reading': monitoring progress.
- 'The point of dual immersion is to offer that variety';-.
- 'The parents have a place here too. The door's always open.'
- 'The people who want to learn offer you heaps.' …
- A final image: Jim's tree.

Richmond Road is such an exemplary school that Cazden, a distinguished Harvard academic, went to Auckland to study the school.

Immigrants in the classroom

Australia, contrary to its older ikons, is one of the most cosmopolitan societies in the world. Earlier migrant groups were mainly British, Italian, Greek and Yugoslav, but today the Southern European immigration has slowed and that from South East Asia has increased markedly. Of the 750 000 students in NSW government schools, 130 000 or 17% have a non-English speaking (NES) background; 89% attend schools in metropolitan Sydney. In the average Australian classroom, 5 or 6 students would come from NES homes; in some areas, the figure would be as high as 90%. How do they get on: with their studies, with their teachers, with their classmates?

A number of surveys in the 1970s provided evidence of the academic achievements of migrant children in Australian schools (Bourke & Keeves 1977; de Lemos 1975). About one-third of the school migrant population in New South Wales was being impeded because of language difficulties, primary pupils more than secondary students, but not surprisingly NES students did better in non-verbal and arithmetic tests than in literacy tests, and on one ACER numeracy test there was no significant difference for 10-year-old NES and Anglo-Australians.

Basically, however, that is not an encouraging picture. More recent work gives a different but conflicting perspective. Probably the most important change in the multicultural classroom today is that the pattern of ethnicity has changed. The Southern and Middle European NES groups are more likely to be well established, the newer arrivals are chiefly Asian. Each NES group—the older European or the newer Asian—has quite different characteristics and problems. If we only consider classroom performance, the older European groups appear to have fewer problems than they once did, but the Asians are scooping the pool: of 240 Chinese Year 12 students in Melbourne, over half were in the top 20% of HSC performers, girls doing as well as boys (Jopson 1990). Anglo-Australian students resent this, referring to Asians disparagingly as 'brainy' (Bullivant 1988).

Asian students, especially at tertiary level, have a mixed press. Some tertiary teachers seem very willing to stereotype, others to reward (see Box 5.1).

> **Box 5.1** *Tertiary teachers' views on overseas Asian students*
>
> In my discipline they all want to rote learn material rather than think. (Animal Science and Production)
>
> Students from Malaysia, Singapore, Hong Kong appear to be much more inclined to rote learning. Such an approach does not help problem solving. (Dentistry)
>
> (Asian students) tend to look on lecturers as close to gods. Often they are very reluctant to question statements or textbooks. (Parasitology)
>
> (Samuelowicz 1987: 123–5)
>
> On the other hand, other teachers seem very willing to give the First Class Honours and the Gold Medals to Asians. Not a likely reward for relentless rote learning. At my last graduation ceremony ... I took particular notice of the quite disproportionate number of Asian names in the First Class Honours and University Medal lists, in Science, Mathematics, Engineering and Architecture.
>
> (Biggs 1990: 4)

Accumulating evidence suggests that Asian students have an approach to learning that derives from beliefs in the importance of effort rather than ability in achieving success (Hau & Salili 1990; Holloway 1988), and that this predisposes them to a 'deep' (or meaning-oriented) rather than a 'surface' (or rote-oriented) approach to academic learning (Biggs 1990). Approaches to learning are explored in more detail in Chapter 12.

In the inner-city suburban schools that Bullivant (1988) studied, Asian students were in fact perceived as exemplary by their teachers: quiet, diligent, highly motivated, and valued as members of the classroom. Other NES students, mainly from Southern and Middle Europe, were likewise valued, particularly for their high motivation, but they were criticised for their macho and sexist behaviour, particularly as directed towards girls from their own culture. The major source of negative prejudice came from Anglo-Australian and British students, who seemed to resent most the diligence and high performance of the NES students. Anglos, for their part, were criticised by NES students for being lazy and disruptive and for lacking parental support and ambition. The major source of peer prejudice, however, came from within subgroups of NES students.

The picture of migrant education has thus changed, from being a matter of providing linguistic support, although that is of course still important as we explore further below, to a complex interplay between cultural and motivational factors. It is these that in fact provide the teacher with the greatest challenge: to avoid stereotyping and to understand the values and role perceptions that migrant children bring into the classroom.

Learning a second language

Second language learning, and particularly English as a second language (ESL) is central in multicultural education.

Do children learn a second language more easily than adults? Di Vesta and Palermo (1974) reviewed the evidence then available:

- Pronunciation is learned more easily by children.
- Vocabulary is learned more easily by adults.
- Grammar is learned equally by both children and adults.
- There are marked differences between children in the ease with which they acquire a second language, even when they are equally bright in other ways.

Learning a second language (symbolised as L2), after the individuals have gained some sort of fluency with their first, or mother-tongue, language (L1), has two different aspects. The first is where (in an English-speaking culture) a native English speaker learns a foreign language at school. The second, and much more complex, case is where a non-English speaker migrates to an English-speaking country and has to acquire English as a second language. While there are certain factors common to both cases, the second involves many additional problems, some of which are common to those already mentioned in connection with non-standard and standard English. It is the second case that concerns us here.

Immersion or submersion?

Much L2 learning is carried out in *immersion* programs, where L2 is the only language used for all communications. In reviewing their effectiveness, Cummins (1979) attempted to account for the common finding that learning L2 by immersion usually results in *better* language competence and academic achievement generally in the case of middle-class majority-language children, but *worse* learning by minority-language children. Worst of all, minority-language children may deteriorate in their mother tongue (L1) competence as well.

Thus, while a bright native-English speaker in an English-speaking country *benefits* on all fronts from learning French, German or any other language by immersion, a Greek speaker in an English-speaking country is often *dis*advantaged by attempts to teach English as a second language. Why the difference?

In the case of the bright English-speaking child learning French by immersion, L1 (English) is not denigrated by the teacher. In fact, its importance is recognised by the fact that it becomes a school subject in its own right, whereas the migrant child's L1 becomes so only rarely. For example, Australia has many migrants from Greece, Italy, Yugoslavia, Lebanon and non-German-speaking Europe, but very few from France or Germany. Yet the high school language subjects (after English) are: French, German, Indonesian and Japanese. Migrant students might see a hidden curriculum in that (see below; also Box 5.2).

In short, a complex of attitudes and value judgments favour the English-speaker learning French by immersion, but inhibit the Greek-speaker learning English. The latter learns by submersion rather than by immersion.

But this is not the full explanation. The effectiveness of L2 learning also depends on *competence in L1*, on the stage of development in L1 before exposure to L2. There is a threshold effect (Cummins 1979):

1. If a person is *already competent* in two languages, further learning in any one language will enhance that person's general competence even further.

Box 5.2 *Wog Boy*

An autobiography

Wog Boy
sits in a crowded bus
close to his old mother
clad all in black.
His face is one of embarrassment,
why he knows not.
But he can feel
them all,
watching him,
fifty pairs of eyes
eagerly plotting
his mental destruction.
And their laughter
is like a hot knife;
and his feelings are but butter;
and they are cutting
those feelings to nothing.
Sounds,
are all magnified
one hundred times over
and the walls

of that old bus
are starting to move,
intent on crushing
him to death.
He feels terribly confined;
no room
in which to cry out,
to cry out for mercy
from some two-bob god
who has pre-plotted his destiny.
And he looks for some way out.
There's no one to turn to
but his old mother
clad all in black.

Ali Eyian,
Form 6
University High School, Melbourne

By permission of the author.

2. If a person is competent in only one language, second-language learning will have no marked effect on either, until the point when bilingualism is reached in the second language (as in point 1.).
3. If a person is minimally competent in L1, further learning in L2 will have *negative* effects on L1, on L2 *and* on competence in general cognitive tasks.

In case 3, the negative effects become general because L2 is usually the language of instruction. This is the unfortunate situation in which many migrant children find themselves.

Skutnabb-Kangas and Toukomaa, in a series of studies conducted in Scandinavia (reported in Cummins 1979), found that Finnish children of average (non-verbal) ability who migrated to Sweden at the age of 10 maintained a level of Finnish (L1) comparable to that of Finnish students who remained at home. They *also* achieved a level of competence in Swedish (L2) comparable to that of native-born Swedes and surpassed the competence in Swedish of *Swedish-born* children of Finnish migrant families. In fact, the ability of these students in Finnish (which they maintained) was a better predictor of mathematics achievement than Swedish; although the mathematics exam was in Swedish! Children whose families migrated to Sweden when they were younger not only learned to speak Swedish poorly but also lost competence in Finnish. Similar results have been found in the case of Spanish-speaking immigrants to the United States and Canadian Indians (whose L1 was Cree) and French Canadians learning English (op. cit.;).

There appear to be *common processes* in learning L1 and L2, so that as children spontaneously improve their competence in L1, they will also develop their L2 competence if allowed to do so by immersion (Cummins 1979; Dulay & Burt 1974). Acquiring L2, L3 and L4 on top of L1 results in mutual interference only at low levels of competence; otherwise, each reinforces a general language handling ability.

Collectively, this research strongly suggests that the child's mother tongue (L1) is the basic tool for developing strategies for scholastic and general intellectual achievement. Thus, basic instruction should continue in L1 (the native tongue) until sufficient competence is reached that it will not suffer when L2 learning begins.

Take reading skill; if gained sufficiently well in L1, it is transferred readily to L2. If, however, reading skill is not developed to the point where the child can read fluently in the mother tongue, total immersion in L2 will be likely to damage what reading skill already exists and make it extremely difficult to learn reading in L2. The child loses on all fronts. Existing skill in the mother tongue is lost and progress in the adoptive tongue severely hampered.

Thus, migrant children should continue to be taught in their mother tongue to a high level of competence before immersion in L2. But it is unwise to ignore L2; it needs to be taught alongside L1 but not replace it. There is a threshold of competence in L1 which is *necessary* for cognitive survival if immigrant children are immersed in L2: otherwise, immersion becomes submersion and both L1 and L2 are drowned.

Educationally speaking, then, the most important factors that emerge in learning L2 by immersion, as do all ESL migrant children, are:

• positive motivational attitudes to the L2 language and culture;
• developed competence in their own language.

These are the functional goals of multicultural education.

Bicultural education: Aboriginal education

Bicultural education seems at first a simpler variant of multicultural education, but it is in fact more complex and more difficult. In both Australia and New Zealand, bicultural issues arise out of colonisation and are imposed on an indigenous people, whereas multicultural issues arise from (more or less) voluntary migration post-colonisation (Rikys 1990). In New Zealand, bicultural problems arise from treaties drawn up last century, and from the facts that the Maori language has now some official recognition, is the medium of instruction in some schools and the Maori population is 14% and growing (op. cit.).

In Australia, the problems of bicultural education are not so clearly focused. Lacking official clout deriving from legal treaties, a single official language, or population size, Aboriginal education has remained relatively undeveloped, with two very broad aims:

1. to enhance the learning and development of Aboriginal students;
2. to enable all students to have some knowledge, understanding and appreciation of the Aboriginal culture (Directorate of Special Programs, 1985).

Realising the first of these aims is difficult. Three Aboriginal communities, Dandenong and Shepparton in Victoria and Bourke in New South Wales, pointed to differences between so-called Anglo education for Aborigines and Aboriginal education for Aborigines (Fesl 1983): the term 'Aboriginal education' needs to be used with discretion (see Box 5.3).

Box 5.3 *Involvement of the Aboriginal community in education*

Like faded dots of confetti strewn along a path from the altar to the car, lie the skeletal remains of a cession of Australian education programs.

The High Priest of Knowledge has watched the marriages and divorces between 'Perceived Educational Needs' and 'Social Realities' since the arrival of the First Fleet—through the early days of 'moral' education for the convicts; through the battle of the churches for control of the education system, the temporary Anglican victory (whose monuments—Geelong, Melbourne and other grammar schools—still stand); tugs-of-war between the free, compulsory and secular systems of the latter part of the Nineteenth Century; the Twentieth Century's reforms in teaching methods, curricula and schools; and now he anxiously presides as the bride approaches her latest marriage with—Multicultural Education.

Suffering far more than their white counterparts, whose own systems are still unsettled, are the Aboriginal people of Australia upon whose lifestyles and own education system have been imposed the assumed needs and experiments of the ruling classes of the white society.

The attempts at imposed Aboriginal 'Education' can be roughly summarised as follows:

- Elimination—of language and culture
- Assimilation—into Christian ideology and the white man's way of life
- Integration and acquisition—of enough literacy skills to make Aborigines useful tools of the white economy.

Successive attempts over nearly two centuries to interest Aborigines in the white education systems have failed—failed because Aborigines' interests and goals were neither sought nor contemplated.

It is hoped that the present project will contribute usefully to change long overdue; a closer involvement of Aborigines in the shaping of their own education.

Source: Introduction to Bala Bala: Some Literacy and Educational Perceptions of Three Aboriginal Communities (Australian Government Publishing Service), quoted by Fesl 1983, p. 15.

Aboriginal studies focus on the history, cultures, languages and lifestyles of Aboriginal and Torres Strait Islanders, but a survey of over 1200 schools (with 72 known to have programs in Aboriginal Studies) showed uncertainty about how increased emphasis should be given to Aboriginal Studies in schools (Budby 1982). The survey showed that most of the schools emphasised social and cultural aspects of the traditional culture and involved Aboriginal people, but that teaching is mainly undertaken on an ad hoc basis according to teacher interest.

One point is worth establishing from the start, in view of evidence that Aboriginal students are disadvantaged when handling school subjects (Bourke & Parkin 1977) and existing beliefs that this is due to inferior intellectual capacity (see Chapter 6). Boulton-Lewis and Halford (1991) showed that measures of structure-mappings, which underlie and correlate strongly with mathematical performance, are not only not deficient in Aboriginal children, but when the structure-mappings are exemplified, using situations that are culturally familiar to the Aborigines, the latter are greatly superior to non-Aborigines. They had the wherewithal to do mathematics, no mistake. Boulton-Lewis and Halford conclude:

> ... the lower school achievement of Aboriginal children cannot be attributed to lack of capacity or inability to cognise mathematical concepts. The most compelling reasons for lower school achievement therefore appear to be educational and social. (Boulton-Lewis & Halford 1991: 36)

Just how these educational and social factors operate is seen in the following study.

Probably the majority of Aborigines live in urban areas and they will attend mixed schools. Malin (1990) conducted a sensitive ethnographic study in an Adelaide school over several years showing how children from 'pure' Aboriginal homes brought with them attitudes and learned roles that transformed them from 'three physically attractive, bright, energetic, curious 5 year olds ... confident, assertive and socially competent' to 'below average achievers, considered troublesome by their teacher and were largely ostracised by their peers' (Malin 1990: 312). This happened all in the space of one year. This did not happen to children even from 'bicultural' (mixed Aboriginal/Anglo) homes. The major reason for this disaster was that the traditional beliefs about autonomy between adult and child they had learned in their homes were read as disrespectful by their teacher. For example, an Aboriginal child does not have to make eye contact with an adult who is talking to her; she may walk away if she wishes. That infuriated one naive Anglo teacher beyond endurance. The wiser Ms Barker:

> ...would grab the departing student with a bear hug and hold them close to her and finish off what she was saying without letting them go ... She thus accomplished her communication with them without making an issue of what many teachers would misrepresent as an act of disrespect. (Malin 1990: 326)

And another teacher:

> Michelle (Aboriginal) won't answer a question when asked if she doesn't know the answer or doesn't feel like it ... I feel if I pushed her into a corner she'd likely blow up so I don't do that. I treat Aboriginal kids differently, for better or worse, than the other kids. I don't ride them as you can other kids ... (op. cit.: 327)

As a result of such clashes with teachers who are less wise than the above two, what usually happens is that the classroom 'resources'—time, affection, responsibility and positive expectations—are dealt out disproportionately; the most culturally different Aborigines receive less and are perceived as receiving less by the other children and are hence accorded lower status. And all by 5 years of age.

Malin's work highlights clearly the desperate need for teachers to receive culturally relevant training. It also supports those who, at the other end of the educational ladder, perceive a need for bridging programs specifically designed for Aborigines entering higher education (Munn & Stephenson 1990). Support structures would include:

* academic, involving discussion of course content, different teaching methods, study skills;
* personal, help in maintaining identity;
* space, or an enclave, allowing students to work at their own rate and to provide social relaxation;
* institutional support for these in the form of funds, staff.

As with multicultural education, bicultural education is concerned with a specific context and set of values, the successful management of which requires not only the declarative knowledge but sensitive procedural skills.

The role of the school in transmitting and acculturating

Class, ethnicity and (as we saw in the last chapter) gender have their effects on student attitudes, performance, and career options. That is one problem. Another is to return to where we came in: to transmit those aspects of our culture we wish to preserve and to incorporate and value aspects of subcultures who live within the main culture. The school has a key role in these functions.

The socialising role of the school has changed considerably over the years:

- **from** deliberately teaching 'the principles of morality ... to avoid idleness, profanity and falsehood' (1886 *Public Instruction Act*, see Box 5.4);
- **through** the 'neutral grounds for rational discourse' position, provided the rational discourse excludes 'any issue on which the community is divided' (the 1975 Buggie directive, see Box 5.5);
- **to** encouraging minority students to maintain their cultural diversity and majority students to *value* that diversity (the present multicultural position).

Box 5.4   *Nineteenth century views of the involvement of schools in moral education—and why*

... to impress upon the minds of their pupils the principles of morality, truth, justice and patriotism; to teach them to avoid idleness, profanity and falsehood; to instruct them in the principles of free Government; and to train them up to a true comprehension of the rights, duties and dignity of citizenship.

Source: New South Wales Public Instruction Act 1886, quoted in Bessant & Spaull 1976, pp. 1–2

I have never considered mere knowledge ... as the only advantage derived from a good Common School education ... [Workers with more education possess] a higher and better stage of morals, are more orderly and respectful in their deportment, and more ready to comply with the wholesome and necessary regulations of an establishment ... In times of agitation, on account of some change in regulations or wages, I have always looked to the most intelligent, best educated and the most moral for support. The ignorant and uneducated I have generally found the most turbulent and troublesome, acting under the impulse of excited passion and jealousy.

Source: A manufacturer writing to the Massachusetts State Board of Education in 1841, quoted in Katz 1968, p. 83.

Box 5.5 *What one Australian Director-General thought about the neutrality of schools and the autonomy of teachers*

Schools are neutral grounds for rational discourse and objective study and should not become arenas for opposing politics or other ideologies ... The teacher's personal view should not intrude into discussions of controversial subjects ... [These controversies] would include politics, sex education, high rise development, open spaces, media bias or any other issue on which the community is divided ... We're saying implicitly that the teacher is not an autonomous person.

Source: J. Buggie, reported in The Australian, 18 November 1975; from a letter addressed to all schools in New South Wales. (Note the date: There was an interesting election campaign in full swing!)

Discussion point
• Has the role of schools and teachers changed significantly since 1975?

The inherent conflict between these positions of conformity to the majority culture vs. the tolerance of diversity within it has always been present. The 1973 New South Wales statement of aims of schooling, promoting 'individual development in the context of society ... towards responsible self-direction and moral autonomy' (published exactly two years *before* the quite incompatible statement appearing in Box 5.5) raises problems for stage 3s. To them, moral autonomy *isn't* what schools should foster. Thus a tension between individual (post-conventional) and societal (conventional) goals, between self-fulfilment and social conformity, arises and is difficult to resolve.

Let us look first at unofficial and implicit means of teaching values, then at explicit means.

The implicit curriculum

Teaching 'the principles of morality' (Box 5.4) is, in government schools at any rate, not on. Neither now is neutrality (Box 5.5). However, there are the tacit or unspoken rules that need to be learned; the sort of rules that proscribe the use of blankets under certain circumstances because of the values implied. Such rules are not usually taught explicitly, but by the implicit or hidden curriculum:

> ... every classroom really has two curriculums that the students are expected to master. The one that educators traditionally have paid most attention to might be called the official curriculum. Its core is the three Rs and it contains all of the school subjects ...
>
> The other curriculum might be described as unofficial, or perhaps even hidden ... This hidden curriculum can also be represented by three Rs, but not the familiar ones of reading, 'riting and 'rithmetic. It is instead the curriculum of rules, regulations and routines, of things teachers and students must learn if they are to make their way with minimum pain in the institution called the *school*. (P. Jackson, in Silberman 1971: 19–20).

Learning the rules, routines and regulations that mould individual behaviour to the requirements of institutional living has a dual purpose. The first is functional; they make the school run more efficiently. Students are required to raise their hand in class because things would become chaotic otherwise. Second and more subtly, they convey values. Many school rules (e.g., as to dress, conventions of approaching an authority figure, meeting deadlines, etc.) are arbitrary for a reason:

> The very point about such rules is their pointlessness. It's not *what* you're taught that does the harm, it's *how* you're taught ... the real lesson is the method ... the method that currently prevails in schools is standardised, impersonal and coercive. What it teaches best is ... itself. (Farber 1970: 19–20)

It teaches the child to obey and obedience is desired by those, perhaps a majority of the population, who think that obedience, in and of itself, is *morally right*. A school that enforces many rules gives important lessons in morality. Perhaps, too, a majority of leaders desire automatic obedience; their power derives from their ability to exact obedience.

Just how desirable or undesirable you think this is depends on whether you take a conventional or post-conventional view of schooling. Should the focus in education be upon the maintenance of society as it is, or upon the growth and sophistication of the learner? If the latter, you might conclude that growth is likely to be hampered by an emphasis on obedience to given values regardless of situation, and thus conclude that the influence of the typical hidden curriculum cannot be beneficial.

Biased textbooks

Racism

Another way of transmitting a value system is through biased textbooks. McDiarmid and Pratt (1971), in a book appropriately entitled *Teaching Prejudice,* analysed pictorial and prose treatments in 143 social studies texts, in use in Canada from Grades 2 to 13. They focused attention on six 'target' groups—Christians, Jews, immigrants, Moslems, Blacks, and Indians—and found striking differences. Christians and Jews were dealt with favourably, in terms of number of evaluative comments, and were not different from each other. Blacks and Indians, however, were dealt with unfavourably and indistinguishably from each other. The other groups fell in between.

Closer to home, Spalding (1974: 26–9) found some interesting examples of race bias in social studies textbooks then used in Australia. These are two examples:

> *For secondary students:*

> Over the 25 000 years during which the Australian natives occupied our land before the coming of the white man, they never advanced beyond the stone age or hunting stage of development. (Sparkes et al. 1970: 52)

> *And for junior primaries:*

> People who live together in tribes like the early Aborigines are called PRIMITIVE people. (Lloyd, 1970: 49)

For the teacher the choice of texts should be dictated by race relation considerations with the fundamental question being: 'Does the material reflect the universality of human experience, transcending colour, class and caste?' (Office of the Commissioner for Community Relations 1979)

Sexism

Much children's reading material is biased because of discrimination based on gender. For example, Tibbetts (1978) found five sexist devices:

- presenting more male than female characters;
- portraying males in a greater number and variety of occupations;
- depicting most female characters in passive, subordinate, incompetent roles in contrast to most male characters being active, dominant and capable;
- attributing desirable traits to males and undesirable traits to females;
- presenting females as people to be denigrated.

How do the reading materials commonly used in infants schools in Australia rate on gender bias? Have things changed in the last ten to fifteen years? An answer to the first question can be found in Baker and Freebody's (1989) examination of 163 basal and supplementary beginning readers used in New South Wales schools; they analysed nearly 84 000 words. 'Boy/s' appeared more frequently than 'girl/s' by a ratio of about three to two and verbs related to males exclusively included 'hurt', 'shout', 'think', 'work', 'jump', 'play' and 'talk', while only 'hold on to' and 'kiss' were exclusive to females. Also males were more likely to be 'brave' and 'naughty' whereas females were associated exclusively with 'young', 'dancing' and 'pretty' (full details on p. 55). Conversations in these stories demonstrate a similar bias with males being dominant. The point to be made is that the material analysed broadly represents the reading matter experienced by young children in Australian schools.

Have things changed much with respect to biases such as those presented above? No and Yes. A comparison of a mid-1960s Australian edition of a widely used reading series with its 1980 'update' showed less emphasis on female characters with occupational roles for women only increasing from two to three. At the same time the increase for males was from eight to nineteen (Anderson & Yip 1987). On the other hand a look at award winning novels for children in the United States from 1971 to 1984 shows that the portrayal of girls and women are less stereotypic and roles are less biased (Kinman & Henderson 1985).

How can sexist bias in textbooks be overcome? When selecting texts for use in your classes ask questions such as: Are men and women portrayed in roles other than traditional ones? Is there a variety of people and lifestyles (e.g., single-parent families, nuclear families)? Do men and women share in activities? Are females independently insignificant? What emphasis is given to traditional female values such as compassion compared to male 'toughness' and domination? Are decision-making and problem solving distributed across the sexes? (NSW Department of Education 1985) The list in Box 5.6 provides a means of checking the extent to which sexist bias could be part of the hidden curriculum in your school.

The report of the committee investigating sexism in education in New South Wales (Guthrie 1977) saw a need for revision of the materials used in schools if 'young people are to gain a balanced view of their past and present' (p.30). This committee found that male and female stereotypes are shown in most published school materials, especially those used in reading, mathematics and social studies. The committee drew attention to such examples as the following:

- girls cook, sew and look on while boys climb, race and are generally adventurous;
- women cope with washing powder, eggs and unpleasant minor disciplinary actions while men are astronauts, scientists and policemen;

Box 5.6   *Towards non-sexist education in schools*

School organisation

- School uniforms need not be the same, but should enable students to comfortably participate in a variety of activities.
- Assemblies should consist of mixed groupings with female as well as male staff leading.
- School awards should be made on the basis of merit irrespective of sex.
- Sports and physical education should be equally available to all students—but contact sports (such as rugby) are not considered suitable for co-educational sports.
- Curriculum and timetable should not restrict the choices of boys or girls.
- Discipline should be similar for boys and girls.
- Careers advice/counselling should be on the basis of ability, interest and personality regardless of sex.
- School displays should maintain a reasonable balance in relation to the sexes.
- Playgrounds should be open in all areas to both boys and girls.
- Staff duties should be distributed so that both women and men are equally encouraged to undertake duties and responsibilities.
- Visiting resource people should exemplify appropriate attitudes, language and methods.

Classrooms

- Teachers should examine their own assumptions about the academic achievement, future employment and general behaviour of boys and girls.
- Teachers should be sensitive to the language and tone of voice they use with girls and boys, and their differential use of praise and criticism.
- Pupils should be encouraged to be considerate of each other as people.
- Assertiveness and independence in girls, and gentleness or caring in boys, should not be discouraged.
- Sexist comments should be checked.
- Class programs should reflect a balance of interests and both sexes in language.
- Non-sexist resources should be used when possible: with attention being drawn to sexism if it exists. For example, a picture of a male airline pilot could prompt discussion of whether there are women airline pilots.
- Examples, exercises and test questions should make balanced reference to both sexes.
- Assignments should raise questions about sex-roles and sex-stereotypes in life, literature and media.
- Historical contributions of women should not be overlooked.
- Real-life situations (such as males portraying a doctor and females portraying a nurse) should be used to investigate student attitudes and concepts.
- Visual materials should depict people in non-traditional roles
- Boys and girls should be given opportunities to carry out similar tasks (such as decorating a room or arranging furniture).
- Sex should not be the criterion for line formations or seating plans.

Source: Adapted from NSW Department of Education, 1980.

- girls jump skipping ropes, weigh flour or buy fabric while boys show girls how to solve their technical, mathematical and mechanical difficulties.

The argument works both ways. Thus Conway (1975) saw a need for boys to have more exposure to a curriculum which emphasises sensitivity towards others and a responsiveness to cultural subjects such as art, music, history, drama and social problems. The 'biology for girls' and 'physics, chemistry and maths for boys' stereotypes need to be challenged. Conway reserved the most vigorous challenge of all for the 'iron jock-strap' syndrome of sport-obsessed boys' schools.

Teacher expectations

Teachers teach values about what, and who is right or wrong by setting up self-validating expectations. *Expecting* a certain outcome can make it more likely to become a fact: if a child is expected to under-achieve, then it is more likely that failure will be the outcome (Good & Brophy 1987; Finn 1972; Rosenthal 1971; Rosenthal & Jacobson 1968). Guess who'll fail at working out a sum on the blackboard before the whole class, when the teacher first announces: 'I bet I can pick those who can't do it!' (Silberman 1970).

How do self-fulfilling prophecies work? Teachers might spend more time with pupils they expect will do well; we have seen that this is one of the mechanisms whereby girls tend to be disadvantaged. They might be more inclined to give particular pupils the benefit of the doubt, which is the kind of reinforcement that will help them try harder, but set more trivial goals for other students, thus never giving them the opportunity to show how good they are. Judgments relating to pupils' self-worth may be communicated non-verbally: by *not* calling on a student ever to make a contribution in class, by ignoring questions asked by a student. Where the student may easily be 'typed' (e.g., comes from a Commission area, is black, parents are divorced or divorcing, has a foreign accent, etc.), the teacher may unintentionally signal what may be interpreted by the student as negative evaluations.

Unfortunately discriminatory messages are often not as subtle:

Angela, Maria's sister, repeating Form 6, adds, 'In the lower forms teachers are forever telling the Australian girls how well they are doing and denigrate the Greek girls: they refer at times to wogs and then say 'I'm sorry', to the Greeks in the class. (Isaacs 1979: 219)

The communication of teachers' expectations of failure may sometimes only have the effect of postponing the students' achievement until they are clear of the school and can handle their education in their own time:

Steven says, 'I wanted to do medicine and I was doing well at school ... I remember one day getting 16/20 for my English essay, but because of flu I handed my work in a few days late, the teacher took off fourteen marks and this pulled me down to a failure and when I said to the teacher she shouldn't do this, I got six cuts. This happened often. I lost marks for silly things; I had to leave school, because I was frightened that, if they provoked me enough, I'd do something stupid and I would regret it. I am working and attending evening school and I have a good chance of passing the School Certificate and I might get to medicine yet.' (ibid: 218)

Steven's account poignantly demonstrates the two curricula. He was doing well in the explicit (official) curriculum, but at least two teachers thought there were more important things to schooling than doing well academically, such as not handing in assignments late and not querying the decisions of a teacher.

Evaluation

Evaluation methods convey strong messages:

- It is better to beat others in competition than to write essays for the sake of their quality and interest.
- It is not important how you do it, as long as you get an acceptable result.
- It is not what you do, but whether you beat the opposition.
- Nothing is worth learning unless it is tested.

While these are oversimplifications logically speaking, the implicit curriculum is a matter of feeling and psychology rather than of logic. Routines of testing usually have strong negative effects on academic motivation. Further effects of evaluation on students are dealt with in Chapters 14 and 15.

Values education

The implicit curriculum, text bias, expectation and evaluation methods, teach sociocentric values. Official policy in most states, on the other hand, is that allocentric or post-conventional moral reasoning is the desired goal, not conventional or sociocentric reasoning. There is thus a conflict between means and ends. While some specific programs on moral education in religious schools also stress conventional values, moral education programs in the public sector are mostly aimed at raising the level of moral judgment from egocentric to allocentric.

Kohlberg programs

Several researchers have directly adapted programs from Kohlberg's theory. Essentially, the technique is to present a moral dilemma in group discussion: if change is to take place, there must be an element of conflict (or mismatch) that forces participants to confront their own beliefs and values. However, the timing and extent of the conflict are said to be crucial, for people will simply reject an argument if it is *too* far above their present level. Kohlberg and his colleagues (Rest, Turiel and Kohlberg 1969; Turiel 1966) proposed the 'Plus One' hypothesis: people are most likely to change when an argument is presented at one stage above that at which they are currently operating. Preaching law and order (stage 3 or 4) to a punishment-oriented stage 1 is likely to be ineffective; instead, one would show that it is worthwhile (stage 2) to cooperate. Then, when they are at Stage 2, they should be presented with a 'being good' argument, not one based on abstract principles. While this seems to make good sense, there is little experimental support for Plus One (Kurtines and Greif 1974), and further, it is impractical to monitor several individuals simultaneously and present Plus One arguments to suit each (Rest 1974).

Schlaefli, Rest and Thoma (1985) reviewed 55 studies in which the experimenters discussed moral dilemmas with the students:

- the intervention was successful with all subjects, but especially with subjects aged 24 years and older;
- interventions worked when they lasted 3–12 weeks, but had no effect if they were under 3 weeks long.

There probably are benefits in discussing moral dilemmas. Effects will be longer and more marked with older students; more research is needed to clarify the situation in secondary schools.

Values clarification

Other programs have been advocated that are more flexible than the Kohlberg programs themselves. In New South Wales, moral education is not addressed as such, but role-playing and the clarification of values are taught in social studies (Hepworth 1979) and Bruner's *Man: a Course of Study* (MACOS), which was adapted by including Aboriginal content. A similar course is SEMP, which involves role-playing by students in situations involving moral dilemmas or the kinds of cultural conflicts faced by some minority ethnic groups in our culture.

Such programs help students become aware of the values they espouse. They are led to recognise what they prize, to be able to defend that choice and be prepared to act upon it. Brady (1979) presented a comprehensive program that incorporated values clarification. He included a variety of approaches, including role-playing and moral dilemmas covering most aspects of modern urban life in Australia (see Box 5.7).

Box 5.7 *Values education: Getting along with people*

'We shouldn't really be doing this.' Scott looked at the other five boys who were already busy tying a rope to the tree trunk.

'But it'll help our fathers', said John. 'They've been mighty good about building this tree house for us! The least we can do is help them by moving this big tree trunk out of the way!'

The boys went on working. That is all except Scott. Help or not, he thought, they were being disobedient.

'John, your father said to keep away … and Brett, your dad said that we should not try to do anything by ourselves.'

'We're here now!' one of the other boys said. 'Are you going to help us or not?' Some of the boys were getting cross with Scott.

So when the rope had been tied to the tree trunk, Scott helped the others pull.

'We're not moving it at all,' John said, grunting as he pulled. 'One more time,' said Brett. 'After three … one, two, three.'

The boys pulled as hard as they could and the tree began to move. 'Keep pulling,' John shouted. But the tree slid sideways and began to roll down the hill. The rope was ripped from the boys' hands.

Scott didn't have time to curse the rope burn on his hands. There was a loud crash, like a cannon firing, and the tree crashed through Mrs Kelly's front fence and came to rest against the front of the house.

For a second the boys were frozen with shock. They looked down at the mess they'd caused. Then they started, some more slowly than others, to run over the hill and out of sight.

But Scott was the last to move and, as he disappeared over the hill, he could see Mrs Kelly standing in her front doorway. She held her hands to her head and was looking towards him.

When the boys were safely away, they met again, panting and white with shock.

'We mustn't say a thing,' said Brett. 'We mustn't own up.'

'If our fathers find out,' said another boy, 'We'll be in terrible trouble.'

'And that will be the end of the tree house,' said John.

'But I think Mrs Kelly saw me,' moaned Scott, rubbing his hands.

The boys were quiet for a while and then Brett spoke. 'We've got to take a chance,' he said. 'We've just got to hope that Mrs Kelly didn't see anyone.' The boys all nodded.

'But what about Mrs Kelly's front fence?' Scott asked.

'We've all agreed to say nothing, Scott,' Brett said sternly. Again the boys nodded.

Scott wasn't sure what to do. He was the one who might have been seen! He felt sorry for Mrs Kelly, but the boys had said to say nothing. They'd all been disobedient and now someone else was paying for it. People might believe that the tree had blown down in the wind ... as long as Mrs Kelly had not seen him!

What should Scott do?

Now talk about

A If the boys owned up to their fathers, what should their fathers do?

B The boys were disobedient, but their reason was a 'good' one, that is, they wanted to help their fathers. Should this make a difference to how they are treated?

C If Scott knew he had been seen and recognised, should this make a difference to what he does?

In the story about the boys and the tree house, role-play a talk between Scott and Mrs Kelly. Pretend that Scott has decided to own up. In one role-play, make Mrs Kelly kind. In another, make her very angry.

Put a tick in the column which is closest to the way you feel about each of these. You may answer: Strongly Agree (SA), Agree (A), Disagree (D), Strongly Disagree (SD).

	SA	A	D	SD
A People shouldn't ask you personal questions.				
B People shouldn't be completely honest all the time.				
C People should share everything.				
D People should be able to laugh at their own silly ways.				
E People shouldn't have to give others a turn before they have their own.				
F I want my own way most of the time.				
G I'm not shy with big groups of people.				

Discuss your answers with others.

Source: Brady, 1979.

Group interaction

A number of small group methods are designed to promote the social development of students. In small groups, students can be given a structured experience, 'an organised game-like activity designed to produce group processes that can easily be understood by participants and which can greatly assist in the development of effective group interaction' (Watson, Vallee & Mulford 1981). An effective group has to attain its goals by completing set tasks and at the same time it has to maintain itself internally (through human relationships) to enable it to remain effective.

Students learn distinctive social skills in group situations when they have the opportunity to practise them and gain feedback. This learning follows a cycle in which concrete personal experiences lead to observation, reflection and examination; then comes a formulation of abstract concepts, rules or principles and, finally, a personal theory to be tested in new situations (Johnson & Johnson 1990).

Structured experiences are not only used in schools, but in a number of business and service organisations to develop skills in communication, decision-making, problem solving, leadership, and team-building. A typical structured experience on communication would enable students to test both sending and receiving skills, verbal and non-verbal messages, seeking and gaining feedback, and non-evaluative paraphrasing of the content of a message and the feelings of the sender (ibid.).

An example of a group interaction using social processes is 'The Prisoner's Dilemma', designed to explore trust between group members and the effects of betrayal of trust. The game shows the effects of interpersonal competition and the benefits of collaboration (Watson, Vallee & Mulford 1981). Groups are told that they are going to experience the risk-taking faced by guilty prisoners being interrogated by police. Questioned separately, the prisoners are each told that the other has confessed and that if they collaborate, they will be treated more leniently. The dilemma is whether to confess when they should not, or fail to confess when they should. Teams are given time to make decisions and coloured cards by means of which members indicate their preference in a series of rounds, during which representatives of each team act as negotiators. After the final round and the totalling of points, the teams combine for the first time to discuss as a group who the winners were in the win/lose situation, what were the benefits of collaboration versus competition, and the effect of high or low trust on interpersonal relationships.

In group interactions the role of the teacher switches: teacher–student interaction, decisions on curriculum content and procedures are not relevant. The interaction between students is all important. The teacher may establish objectives, provide materials and facilities and explain the cooperative goal structure, but during the group interaction itself, the teacher's role is that of observer, only intervening as a consultant to help a group solve problems of working together and, finally, helping the group to evaluate the products.

Role-playing in groups integrates judgment and feeling, cognitive and affective. For example, it is one thing to discuss racial *prejudice* rationally: it is another to dress up as a black and feel prejudice (Raucher 1970). In one enterprising experiment (Peters 1971), the teacher designated 'niggers for the day' (on Monday, say, all blond children were to be discriminated against and called names; the next day, it was the turn of children who had brown eyes; then those who had freckles ...). The children learned just what it felt like to be discriminated against. Racial prejudice and, even more important, prejudiced *behaviour*, decreased markedly, but the experiment was called off because of parental prejudice.

Encounter groups use a similar process. Here, the group members are instructed to provide valid feedback to each other about how each person comes across to the others. Our normal roles in society prevent us from getting information about our interpersonal effectiveness, which sometimes makes it difficult for one's self-concept to be firmly based in reality. However, participants need to possess a robust self-concept already if they are to handle information that challenges what they would *like* to think about themselves.

Grainger (1970) describes a loosely structured group encounter for the whole class called 'The Bullring', so-called because, as one student wrote: The speaker and person being spoken to are all alone, like the bull and the matador in a bullring (op.cit.: 29). In this situation, 'bull' and 'matador' keep changing roles: the idea is that students will come to recognise their own (and others') motives and failings. As one Year 9 boy expressed it:

> Because some people dislike others they oppose them in the Bullring ... I believe that the only thing we can do is to speak to anyone we dislike and try to understand why we don't like them. Then perhaps we could discuss things without feeling we have to oppose the speaker. (op. cit.: 130)

Grainger found the technique highly successful from Years 7 to 10; and, interestingly, with children of low intelligence as much as with those of high intelligence:

> I have learnt that i am a bit shy to speak to, i join the noisey lot I speak to my next door nabourgh and he speak to me we have confersaisions which I dere not speak out—also I have learnt that also i throw things about and try show of a bit like going up to the teacher and pulling his ear or talking to him in a funny way also when I sujest something the group does not carry on with the confersation and that's why I dear not speak up ... (op.cit.: 140)

Evidence for the success of such encounter group programs is largely impressionistic: that is, the participants enjoy them (even when they are painful) and seem to believe in their value. But 'hard data' are difficult to obtain and are often regarded by the participants as irrelevant or inappropriate. Such experiences clearly should be handled by teachers who are skilled in group dynamics and who have pretty robust self-concepts themselves.

Moral education across the curriculum

More important than special programs, however, is providing a school climate, or as Kohlberg put it 'the moral atmosphere of the school', that encourages moral autonomy. Moral education is achieved by immersing young people in open social situations where their validity can be discovered in action: across the curriculum, not in special 'values classes':

> ... moral education calls for much more than competent teachers with a battery of items to dispense; it needs a civilised school community and teachers whose quality of life are models of moral feeling and intelligence. (Hemming 1980:75)

In order to run a complex institution such as a school, it is necessary as we have noted to set up rules, routines and regulations that make smooth running of that institution possible. That task is made very much easier by the structuring of sociocentric norms that exact their own obedience, by discouraging the questioning of rules and the reasons for them. Thus, the rules become autonomous, rather than students' morality, and their reasons forgotten; righteousness becomes identified with a purposeless conformity. The difficulty is that while official aims dictate moral autonomy or post-conventional judgment, everyday interaction requires conventional behaviour and, if that is not forthcoming, the resulting sanctions call out pre-conventional morality.

Fully to explore the moral atmosphere of the school in all its realisations would require quite a different book. Our present purpose is sufficiently met if the means by which values may be transmitted are identified and, perhaps more importantly, the means by which they can be expanded and enriched. While the Kohlberg theory as a model of stages of moral development leaves much to be desired, it is very useful in helping us decide what the NSW Education Department (for example) might have been on about when making 'moral autonomy' a major educational aim, in providing us with a means of describing different kinds of moral decision-making, and therefore in helping us realise the kind of moral atmosphere we might wish to foster in our own classrooms.

Summary

What is culture?

We are all born into a culture: a network of attitudes, symbols and ways of behaving that we treasure and try to preserve. The school is a major instrument in preserving culture and is therefore an instrument of *socialisation*, taming the young into ways of being that society will endorse. But society now comprises those from many cultures; they bring their ways of being with them and, through the process of *acculturation*, enrich the dominant culture. So culture is preserved as it changes and the school plays its part in both processes: of transmitting what is and of transforming what is to be.

Class differences and language use

Schools tend to favour middle-class learners. There are several reasons for this, including the obvious one that the motivations of middle-class families, and the tools they use to pursue their goals, are those also favoured in the classroom. Working-class students more frequently lack a support structure at home that provides motivation, books, computers—or an inherited school tie. Another reason is that schools use standard English, the language of the middle classes, as the medium of instructing. Users of non-standard English have to learn both the medium itself and the content the medium is addressing, which makes their task all the harder.

Multicultural education

Multicultural education picks up the acculturating role. It aims to encourage immigrant groups to retain their cultural identity and especially their language and to sensitise the majority culture to the minority groups, thereby encouraging acculturation on all sides. There is evidence of much success in this, 'older' (European) immigrants now having established roots and 'newer' (mainly Asian) immigrants doing well academically. And our restaurants are as varied and as good as those anywhere.

Learning a second language

A central aspect of multicultural education revolves around language and particularly when NES children are required to speak English. Conventional wisdom holds that the less L1 you know, the more room for L2; certainly the assimilation model of coping with migrants worked on that principle. It couldn't be more wrong. A general language-handling ability seems to be developed on the basis of a good command of L1. Thus, multicultural education should keep children speaking and indeed reinforcing their mother tongues, while at the same time developing skill in English.

Bicultural education: Aboriginal education

The aims of bicultural education are similar to those of multicultural: to preserve existing Aboriginal culture and to have that culture valued by the majority culture. There are however particular problems, partly deriving from history and its residual emotional fallout and partly because the role structures involving child–adult interaction in traditional Aboriginal culture cut right across those assumed in school. Special training in handling cultural differences is important in any multicultural enterprise, but is particularly so in Aboriginal education.

The role of the school in transmitting and acculturating

Values are transmitted these days less by direct instruction than by the hidden curriculum, which permeates the whole school: teaching and assessment methods, the rules of student–teacher interaction, the routines of school life, biased textbooks, teacher expectations and so on. Such factors are inevitable, as they have a function in making the school workable, but their over-zealous definition and application teaches a sociocentric morality.

Acculturation, the clarification of existing values, and the forming of new ones, are usually handled in school by special programs, such as values clarification, Kohlberg programs and many different kinds of group experience. Basically, though, allocentric morality (espoused by many systems as an educational goal) is best developed in the same way as sociocentric morality: through the structures and atmosphere that permeate school life.

Learning activities

1. Learning a second language

We have made the point in this chapter that if an individual is minimally competent in L1, the introduction of learning in another language will have adverse effects upon both L1 and L2 and on competence in general cognitive tasks. Why is this? What does the research have to say about the problem? From a teaching perspective, how should learning in L2 be approached? In this activity generate a set of questions that teachers should know the answers to before they embark upon any L2 teaching(e.g., What is the child's competence in L1? Can you get ten questions (and answers) ?

2. Multiculturalism

As we noted earlier, most state and territory educational authorities have multicultural policies. In this activity you are to analyse that policy in the light of our discussions. Is the policy, for example, essentially aimed at ESL issues or is it broader in perspective? What are the aims of the policy? Is there any indication of how the policy is to be implemented or monitored, etc.? If there were access to teachers, a survey could be conducted on their views of the policy and its implementation in schools. An additional activity would be to organise to video-tape multicultural activities in a local school for presentation to the class.

3. The implicit curriculum: Part 1

Now is the time to reconsider your own primary and secondary schooling. In particular pay attention to the implicit curriculum, the curriculum of rules, regulations and routines as Jackson called it. What things happened to you that were not included in the official curriculum? Lining up for assemblies, males in one line, females in another? Wearing school uniform? Standing when another teacher came into the room? Writing out lines for disobedience, etc.? This activity could be done as a group project with groups listing implicit curriculum activities, then categorising them. In addition, the *intent* of the activity should be identified. For example, standing when a teacher came into the room could be interpreted as respect for authority. An extension activity could focus on the Piagetian or Kohlbergian stages related to the '3R's' identified by the group.

4. The implicit curriculum: Part 2

This activity takes you from the past to the present in your consideration of the implicit curriculum of rules, routines and regulations. During the practicum, or in your own school, gather information on the types of implicit curriculum activities carried out and compare them with the results of Part 1 above. Have things changed much? If so, in what areas have there been changes? Can you identify the factors that may have produced any changes? A comparative chart could be produced to show 'Past' and 'Present'.

5. Biased textbooks

We looked at both racism and sexism in the section on biased textbooks. The purpose of this activity is twofold: to examine some of the commonly used textbooks, or early readers, for both racist and sexist biases; and to produce a checklist that teachers could use to help them select non-biased books for use in their classes. Again the activity could be done individually or in groups by selecting 5 commonly used infant school readers and then examining them, say, for the roles that males and females play. (You would need to examine both the words and the illustrations.) If you can get access to Baker and Freebody's (1989) book, *Children's First School Books,* it might prove helpful as you could link your findings with those reported by them. (Also their work will give you ideas on what aspects, at least of sexism, you can look for in your texts.)

6. Aboriginal education

Earlier in this chapter we introduced a study by Merridy Malin (1990) in which she investigated the first year of school in two urban classrooms for several Aboriginal students. As we noted then, the research is a sensitive ethnographic study that highlights the culturally based skills, values and assumptions that the students brought to the classroom and the ways in which the teacher and peers interacted with these Aboriginal children. In this activity you are to summarise that report and draw out the implications for teaching in a bicultural context. You will note that Malin has organised her paper into six major sections: Introduction; Home Socialisation; Culturally Based Responses to Classroom

Life; Micro-political Processes in the Classroom; Repercussions for those who do not Share Co-membership; and Conclusion. If done as class activity, groups could be responsible for reporting on sections of the paper.

Further reading

On social disadvantage
Bernard, J. & Delbridge, A. (1980). *Introduction to Linguistics: An Australian Perspective*. Sydney: Prentice Hall.

Does Bernstein fit the Australian context? What do you do about non-standard Australian English? Two sociolinguists provide food for thought.

On multicultural education
Department of Employment, Education and Training (1987). *Ethnicity, Education and Equity*. Canberra: Commonwealth of Australia.
Lynch, J. (1986). *Multicultural Education*. London: Routledge & Kegan Paul.
Sherwood, J. (1981). *Multicultural Education*. Perth: Creative Research.

The Commonwealth publication provides data on the situation of members of ethnic groups in relation to education. It examines the implications of the findings for multicultural education and multiculturalism generally. Both Lynch's and Sherwood's books examine the multicultural concept and highlight educational implications and strategies: Lynch in the United Kingdom; Sherwood in Australia.

On Aboriginal education
Hart, M. (1974). *Kulila on Aboriginal Education*. Sydney: Australia and New Zealand Book Company.
Malin, M. (1990). The visibility and invisibility of Aboriginal students in an urban classroom. *Australian Journal of Education*, **34**, 313–29.
New South Wales Department of School Education (1990). *Aboriginal Reflections from ELIC*. Sydney: (Series of seven pamphlets).

Hart's book is important from an historical perspective examining a range of issues in education for Aboriginal people. Malin's work we have already referred to but we consider it worthy of repeating here: its messages are strong. The ELIC (Early Literacy Inservice Course) documents challenge deficit assumptions and propose what they call 'risk-taking, risk-breaking' approaches to literacy in Aboriginal education. Pamphlet 6 may be particularly useful as it provides information on ways in which teachers can organise literacy learning environments for Aboriginal learners.

On teaching values
Goodnow, J.J. (1991). Cognitive values and educational practice. In J. B. Biggs (ed.), *Teaching for Better Learning: The View from Cognitive Psychology*. Hawthorn, Vic: Australian Council for Educational Research.
Brady, L. (1979). *Feel–Value–Act: Learning About Values, Theory and Practice*. Sydney: Prentice Hall Australia.

Goodnow deals with how many sorts of values about gender, working alone, finding out what is valued by teachers and what is the 'proper' way to learn, are conveyed through practices in school. Brady tries to make all these things explicit, so children know and can hopefully deal with what they come to believe.

CHAPTER 6

INTELLIGENCE
AND THE IQ

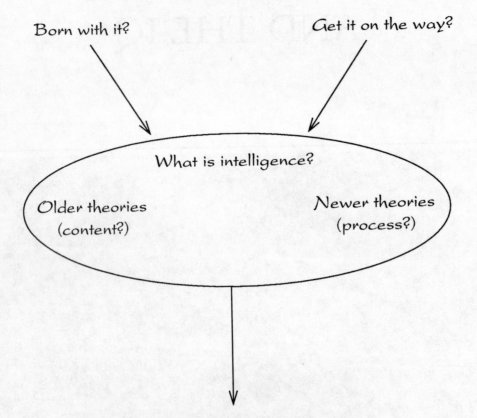

Intelligence and the IQ

Born with it?

Get it on the way?

What is intelligence?

Older theories
(content?)

Newer theories
(process?)

What do teachers need to know about:

— IQ testing?
— grouping kids in class/school?
— effects of teachers' expectations on kids?

CHAPTER 6

INTELLIGENCE AND THE IQ

In this chapter, you will find out:

- that psychologists disagree about whether intelligence is general or specific to particular areas;
- what the IQ is and if it is useful;
- what is meant when intelligence is said to be determined by heredity or by environment, and why that question is not very important for teachers;
- some theories of what is involved in being intelligent;
- what the effects of grouping students by ability (streaming) are, compared to mixed ability classes.

Abilities and intelligence

Every teacher's theory-in-use assumes something about students' differing abilities:

- 'He's an academic type, should be in the A stream.'
- 'Of course girls are no good at real maths—you've only got to look at the drop-outs after Year 10 to see that.'
- 'I like teaching the slow learners; it's a real challenge.'
- 'Fred's the class clown; too smart for his own good.'

Such statements rely on theories-in-use, the commonsense of experience. Only sometimes are they congruent with espoused theory, based on the findings of psychology.

Most teachers categorise their students along two dimensions: bright–dull and cooperative–nuisance (Holland, 1959). The ideal student is bright–cooperative; the class clown, bright–nuisance. The bright–dull dimension presumes that something called 'ability', or 'intelligence', is present in individuals in different quantities and that its presence crucially affects the efficiency and the quality of different students' learning. We look here at the question of abilities and intelligence, and at how teaching decisions may be affected by our theory of students' abilities.

The terms 'ability' and 'intelligence' refer to a tendency to perform well across the board. But to what extent do people perform well over different tasks?

- Jill is good at maths but hopeless at English; is she 'intelligent'?
- John was a poor student, but is now one of the most sucessful real estate agents in town; is he 'intelligent'?

In trying to resolve such questions, psychologists have come up with several different models of intelligence. Some theories postulate several autonomous intelligences, others one or few components of intelligence.

149

Different kinds of intelligence

Gardner (1985) identified seven autonomous intelligences, or 'frames of mind', within which some people manifest prodigious performance, often from an early age. These frames are content based:

- bodily-kinaesthetic (gymnasts and dancers)
- musical (composers, performers)
- linguistic (poets, writers)
- logico-mathematical (scientists, mathematicians)
- spatial (architects, artists)
- interpersonal (skilled negotiators)
- intrapersonal (mystics).

Gardner identified these areas on the basis of studies of brain localisation (e.g., particular lesions resulting in specific behavioural impairments) and of exceptional attainment in specific areas (e.g., child prodigies in music, mathematics and language). These frames are autonomous, or in other words, prodigies within one frame perform little different from anybody else in other frames. Mozart was not a particularly good mathematician. Such specialised talent suggested to Gardner that prodigies 'had' something, genetically based but also requiring strong environmental support from a very early age, that other people did not have.

Gardner's work is interesting, but as far as teaching is concerned it is limited, because as you might have observed, school focuses significantly on but two frames: logico-mathematical and linguistic. That suggests to Gardner that schools *should* address the other five, otherwise we develop in a lopsided way, ignoring the potential that we might have in the other five frames (Gardner & Hatch 1989). He's probably right, but that's no help to us right now.

Academic and everyday intelligence

Like Gardner, Sternberg and Wagner (1986) were disturbed at the fact that although many examples of prodigious performance in everyday life show a very high degree of skill and complexity, almost all traditional theories of intelligence were developed in the academic context. As we shall soon see, 'intelligence' or IQ tests were deliberately developed to predict performance in school, where the focus is upon tasks that relate to the more abstract modes dealt with in Chapter 2: concrete-symbolic and formal. High quality performances in sensori-motor and ikonic tasks are accorded lower status in school; their cultivation is not a priority in the curriculum of the public school system.

High level performance outside the academic context often uses the 'lower' modes, ikonic and sensori-motor. Scribner (1986), for example, found that the warehousemen most skilled in estimating the number of crates that can be stored in a given space didn't use the school-taught algorithms to calculate area. They looked at the spot and 'saw' how many crates would fit: 'When a large array was not a solid rectangle, but had gaps, the men mentally squared off the array by visualising phantom stacks and counting them' (op. cit.: 20). Such performance was very fast and accurate, but it took years of experience to perfect.

Ceci and Liker (1986) describe how professional gamblers estimate the odds on horses' performance given their form over the past few years, their handicaps on the present and past races, the weather and state of the tracks in previous races—up to 16 variables were included in their 'calculations'. A single calculation could take days of hard mental effort, with the aids only of racing guides, pencil and paper. A statistician could also do it, with the aid of a computer, but almost certainly not as accurately; Ceci and Liker's experts were able to predict the winning horse in 93% of races. If statisticians with their little IBMs could do that they undoubtedly would, using routine regression equations. But to say that is to assume that gamblers were handling the problem in the same way that a statistican would. Clearly the modes of operating are entirely different, the gamblers tapping an ikonic mode of handling the problem, that was independent of concrete-symbolic and formal algorithms, and indeed of schooling. Those who were good at this were not better educated, and did not have higher IQs, than those who were not. What characterised them was motivation and a huge amount of experience, much of it non-teachable.

Such examples of prodigious everyday intelligence are *highly specific* to the content area and the context in question. This is opposite to what schools are about, as we saw in Chapter 1. Schools are charged with teaching content and operations that transfer across contexts; hence their focus on the concrete-symbolic and formal modes, and on the two 'frames' that are expressed in those modes, linguistic and logico-mathematical.

From general abilities to particular competencies

Let us then look at different levels of ability within the concrete-symbolic and formal modes. Levels in descending order of generality are usually referred to as: intelligence, ability, attainment and competency.

Intelligence is the most general; it is defined as a tendency to do well over a wide range of performance tasks.

Ability refers to a characteristic derived from a narrower range of tests, such as verbal, spatial, or musical tests. Abilities are hypothetical characteristics that are invoked to explain why some individuals do better on specified kinds of performance. The relationship between ability and intelligence has been one of the most enduring issues in educational psychology this century.

Abilities have traditionally been distinguished from each other on the basis of the *content* addressed: those doing well on musical tests seen as being high on musical ability, on arithmetic tests, as high on number ability, on verbal tests as high on verbal ability and so on. The justification for this was that one could predict performance on a test requiring that ability by using scores from another, 'marker', test of that ability. Such an approach is almost entirely non-theoretical; it predicts actuarially, strictly on the basis of recorded fact, in the same way as an insurance company calculates premium against risk. Thus, what nominates an ability is the content area tested.

Abilities may also be conceived in terms of the *processes* involved. Process theories, such as the information integration theory of Das, Kirby and Jarman (1979) and Sternberg's (1985) componential theory of intelligence, have much more promise for guiding classroom intervention, because they engage the question of *how* students learn.

Attainment refers to a very particular kind of performance that has been the subject of specific instruction. An ability test is meant to indicate a person's potential for a particular range of performances, independently of any instruction. Ability tests are thus meant to be instruction-free; attainment tests are instruction-dependent.

Competency refers to 'a particular skill, something an individual knows how to do' (Tyler 1978: 99). Tyler, like many educators, was unhappy about the reliance educators placed on ability testing and thought that individuals could be more helpfully understood in terms of their repertoire of competencies.

Core competencies are those that should be mastered by all school leavers; *individual* competencies reflect a person's interests, abilities and lifestyle, and may be acquired with the help of schooling. Abilities would then only set broad limits, beyond which certain competencies may not be easily learned by a particular individual.

Many school systems in the United States specify core competencies: 'Read well enough to follow an instruction manual', 'Write a job application using correct grammar and spelling', 'Calculate the total square footage of a room' (Tyler 1978). The ACER literacy and numeracy studies used competencies of this kind (Keeves & Bourke 1976).

Competency-based education has a logical appeal. The particular competency has to be specified, its components analysed and taught to mastery. However, there are hidden problems. In an abilities-based model of education, student performance is held to be due to the student's ability (or lack of it), in which case teachers cannot reasonably be held accountable for their student's learning (or lack of it). In a competency-based model, on the other hand, student performance is held to be due to the teaching received, and in that case teachers can be held accountable. As we shall see in this chapter, there is evidence to allow for both positions. A student's ability in a subject does set limits to what may profitably be taught, but there are core skills that should reasonably be mastered by most students.

Intelligence and the IQ

The concept of a single 'super-ability', or of a few general abilities underlying the successful performance of a wide range of tasks is surprisingly modern. It was the introduction of compulsory schooling at about the turn of the century, and its social consequences, that led people to ask whether finer distinctions might be made about intellectual functioning. Once schooling rather than family connections became the route to high-status occupations, it became important to ask just what it was that the more successful students might have 'had'.

It was precisely this question that the French psychologists, Binet and Simon, were asked in 1904 to investigate. Teachers and administrators were concerned by the fact that some children appeared to be gaining much more from their education than were others. Please, could Binet and Simon suggest any tasks that might sort out those likely to experience difficulties in school from those who were likely to be successful in school? They could and did. Thus, Sternberg and Wagner were quite right in saying that the theory and measurement of 'intelligence' had been restricted to academic contexts. Historically, the first tests were designed and used in the context of predicting school performance. This focus has undoubtedly discouraged us from looking at 'intelligent' behaviour in other contexts.

But back to Binet and Simon (1908), who concluded that the sorts of tasks psychologists then used (such as reaction times and learning nonsense syllables) and the processes they engaged (such as memorisation) did not relate to the kind of thinking required in schools. Instead, Binet and Simon used words and numbers as content, in tasks that required 'commonsense' reasoning, but which were not directly taught in school; the familiar verbal analogy ('X is to Y as A is to ?'), for example. They then selected particular items of these kinds that best predicted school performance and agreed with teachers' ratings of educability or 'intelligence'. Binet's conclusions about the nature of the kind of thinking required in school were remarkably good; so much so that his basic items are still in use today. One of the most widely used tests (the Stanford Binet) is a direct descendant of the original Binet–Simon test.

The Intelligence Quotient (IQ)

Binet and Simon then gave their selected items to large samples of children to find what the average performance was from 4 year olds, 5 year olds, and so on. A child performing at the level of an average 6 year old was said to have a 'mental age' of 6. If, however, the actual chronological age of the child was 8, this child would be *below* average. The *Intelligence Quotient*, or IQ, was found by dividing mental age by chronological age and multiplying by 100 (to get rid of decimals). The 8 year old performing at a 6 year old level would thus have an IQ of 75 (6/8 x 100 = 75). If a 4 year old passed the items expected of a 6 year old, that child's IQ would be 6/4 x 100 = 150.

The concept of IQ was very convenient, but it had one fundamental problem. After the age of 16, performance on these tasks tends to stabilise, so that mental age remains relatively constant: according to this formula, a 'normal' 32 year old would automatically have an IQ of 50. One way out of this is to allocate anyone over the age of 16 a chronological age of 16 regardless of their actual age, but this is rather arbitrary. More common today is using a different means of calculating IQ based on the extent to which an individual's standardised test score deviates from the appropriate peer population mean, rather than on the ratio of mental to chronological age. This latter method is called the *deviation* IQ. The derivation of an IQ score either by deviation or ratio methods does not however affect its functional meaning.

So what does an IQ score functionally mean? According to Wechsler (1949), who devised the widely used Wechsler Adult Intelligence Scale (WAIS) and the Wechsler Intelligence Scale for Children (WISC), intelligence is an aggregate or global estimate of an individual's capacity for schooling, relative to age peers in the normal population. The items used in the tests were selected because they predicted school performance; they were not based so much on a theory about how intelligence 'works'.

We are now much more interested in this last question, because it has more to do with how we might adapt teaching, whereas the predictive or actuarial approach to the measurement of intelligence actually distracts us from the question of the quality of teaching. For example, if a low IQ student were helped to perform well by excellent teaching, the IQ test would in this case be a *poor* predictor of academic success. Indeed, in the old days such a student would be called an 'over-achiever' and would be *dis*couraged from doing so well. This was argued on the crude 'pint-pot' metaphor; the IQ measured the individual's 'capacity' for learning. It was easily understandable if a person was not 'working up to capacity'; such people were called 'under-achievers' and clearly needed further pushing. But to work *over* capacity suggested that something quite weird was happening; certainly over-achievers (i.e., those performing at a higher level than predicted by their IQ) should not be pushed. They might blow up or something.

Over the years, indeed very rapidly after Binet's work and perhaps particularly as a result of massive testing of American army draftees in the First World War, it was found that racial and cultural groups differed widely in performance on IQ tests (e.g., Kamin 1974). As a result, IQ scores came to be seen as a measure of an individual's *innate capacity* for intellectual functioning (i.e., one which had a biological foundation and was largely determined by heredity). When it was found that the IQs of northern European immigrants to the United States were superior to those of southern European immigrants to the United States, it was taken as evidence that the Nordic races were genetically superior to southern Europeans. Further analysis showed, however, that the difference between northern and southern Europeans was entirely accountable for in terms of the number of years of residence in the United States (Kamin 1974). Northerners had migrated earlier than southerners and had better English—and the tests were in English!

Such crass over-generalisations made their mark. A test score shifted in meaning, from an empirically derived index that predicted educability to a biological entity. The resulting misunderstandings are still common, the over-/under-achiever misconception being one. Hebb (1949) brought some conceptual clarity into things when he distinguished:

- *Intelligence A:* a biological capacity that is never measured directly.
- *Intelligence B:* the capacity for acting intelligently, which is a function of A (innate capacity) and learning.

To which Vernon (1969) added:

- *Intelligence C:* what intelligence tests measure.

Intelligence C is derived from a highly specific subsample of Intelligence B behaviours and is two steps removed from innate capacity. Yet for years many people believed IQ measured innate capacity. Some still do today, but they wouldn't after reading the rest of this chapter.

The structure of intellectual abilities

Terman (1954), a psychologist at Stanford University, in 1922 selected 1400 Californian children with IQs of 130+ and followed them through their school years to adulthood. Those children have now retired and although Terman himself is dead, Robert and Pauline Sears took up the study, and subsequent findings were reviewed by Goleman (1980). These highly intelligent people were not only superior in school, but in a variety of ways throughout their life span: longevity, low rate of physical and mental illness, sporting ability, even happiness and marital harmony. How unfair!

Terman was dealing with a highly selected group of people in selecting those with an IQ of 130+. What happens within more normal ranges? Are people who are good at mathematics also good at languages? Or are these different and unrelated frames as Gardner suggested?

A common approach to researching such questions is to give a randomly selected group of students a battery of tests on such activities as memorising, reasoning, following instructions to make patterns, —all factors which relate to 'educability'—and then analysing the results (usually by a technique called 'factor analysis') to find the most economical way of weighting and grouping test scores. The aim is to find the smallest group of factors that gives essentially the same information as do the original item results. Each such weighted group is identified as a particular factor or 'ability' that explains the results, for example a factor called 'number ability' might well give the same rank ordering of people as if we ordered them by their performance on an addition test ('adding ability'), a subtraction test ('subtracting ability'), a multiplication test—and so on. 'Number ability' is so much easier to conceptualise and to use.

No single factor (or ability) can be discovered to account equally for all tests of the kind relevant to schooling, but one factor can usually be found that accounts for some variability in many tests. This factor was called 'general intelligence', or *g*, by Spearman

(1927). The extent to which any particular test 'loads on' or correlates with *g* is not a simple matter to determine, as it depends on other tests in the battery and the method of factor analysis used, which is itself 'a matter of taste' (McKenzie 1980). Basically, there are two positions: the *hierarchical* and the *independence* models.

A very influential hierarchical model was Vernon's (1950), which distinguished *g* and then layers of increasingly specific factors. In his view, performing a particular task required:

1. some underlying *g*
2. some verbal or practical ability *(v:ed* or *k:ṁ)*
3. a particular subgroup of verbal or practical ability, and
4. less importantly, any task specific components.

Thurstone's (1938) theory of *primary mental abilities* was historically the most important version of the independence model, and in content, but not in structure, came up with a somewhat similar list to Vernon:

- *N*, the ability to use numbers with speed and accuracy
- *V*, verbal understanding
- *S*, spatial ability
- *W*, the ability to use unrelated words rapidly
- *R*, inductive and deductive reasoning ability
- *M*, ability to memorise rapidly and accurately.

Unlike Vernon, however, and rather like Gardner, he saw these abilities as unrelated to each other.

The difference between the two views has obvious implications for how we teach; for example, do we group students by specific (Thurstone-type) abilities, thus forming different groups or sets for different subjects? Or do we group by general intelligence of *g*, *à la* Vernon, forming streams for all subjects? Most Australian schools seem to be Vernonites, rather than Thurstonians. We examine this very question later, but just to anticipate our little secret, note that the practical evidence from classrooms suggests *neither* form of grouping; but if you must, do it *à la* Thurstone (see p. 155).

Fluid and crystallised intelligence

Cattell (1971) and Horn (1968) distinguish between fluid and crystallised intelligence. Fluid intelligence is rather like Hebb's Intelligence A; it is highest at birth, when the brain is in its most pristine state and declines as the brain suffers trauma, due to whatever causes, but most predictably with ageing and with lifestyle factors such as drug and alcohol abuse. That is the bad news.

The good news comes twofold. First, fluid intelligence 'crystallises' with acculturation, experience and especially schooling; it is the form of intelligence involved in everyday decision-making. Crystallised intelligence increases with age and continues to develop well into old age. Second, fluid intelligence is trainable, even in old age. Training studies with the elderly, incorporating both explicit instruction and self instruction, suggest that they have a repertoire of fluid intelligence strategies that need 'reactivation' (Baltes, Kliegl & Dittman-Kohli 1988).

Any performance in a task is thus a function of two factors: the basic 'smarts' (fluid) and the particular knowledge and acquired skills that are necessary for the task in question (crystallised).

Different tests tap the two types of intelligence in varying proportions. Tests of reasoning in a spatial mode, which do not rely on vocabulary, such as Raven's Progressive Matrices test, are good tests of fluid intelligence. In this test, a series of diagrams is presented that change according to a rule; the testee has to abstract the rule and apply it to a new diagram. Sometimes two or three rules are embedded simultaneously, so that correct performance can become very complex. Essentially, what is involved is nonverbal reasoning in a task unlikely to be presented in school (see Box 6.1):

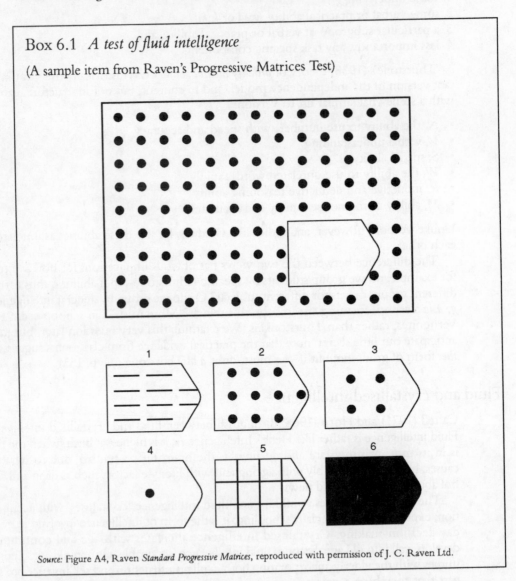

Box 6.1 *A test of fluid intelligence*

(A sample item from Raven's Progressive Matrices Test)

Source: Figure A4, Raven *Standard Progressive Matrices*, reproduced with permission of J. C. Raven Ltd.

Tests of verbal ability, on the other hand, are held to be good indicators of crystallised intelligence (Snow, 1976); performance in such tests is strongly affected by amount of schooling. This distinction is therefore closely related to Vernon's *v:ed/k:m* distinction.

Level 1 and Level 2 abilities

As noted earlier, abilities can be categorised according to the processes involved. Jensen's (1969, 1970) theory of Level 1 and Level 2 abilities is a process theory. Level 1 is the ability to read in input and reproduce it exactly, as in memorising by rote. Level 2 is the ability to transform input so that the output is different and reasoning is the main process involved. Jensen regards Raven's Progressive Matrices (which Cattell regards as a measure of fluid intelligence) as a good measure of Level 2. Unlike Cattell, however, Jensen regards Level 2 as the ability, reasoning, most required in school tasks. What do you think? Do schools mostly require reasoning, or rote-memorising?

Jensen saw the two abilities as hierarchical, with Level 1 as a prerequisite for Level 2. Somebody who is good at memorising may or may not be good at reasoning, but someone who is good at reasoning must be good at memorising as well. You need to retain in memory the contents of thought in order to reason about them, but simply retaining items in memory does not necessarily mean that they will be subject to higher order processes.

Jensen (1969) created considerable controversy when he claimed (a) that both abilities were primarily inherited, with 80% being the figure placed on the amount that can be attributed to genetic inheritance; and (b) that there were racial and social class differences in Level 2 ability (reasoning) but not in Level 1 (memory). Both claims have been disputed in the literature, the racial reference especially hotting up the debate (e.g., Eysenck, 1971 [for]; Kamin, 1974 [against]; refer to the readings at the end of this chapter if you want to follow this further). In 1976, when Jensen and a like-minded psychologist, Hans Eysenck, came to Australia, there were huge demonstrations against them and the police were called to the University of Melbourne where Eysenck tried (unsuccessfully) to give a lecture. Today the racial issue is regarded as raising the kind of questions that do not permit confident answers.

What that might mean becomes clearer when we look at the heritability of different abilities and of IQ in particular.

The nature–nurture controversy

What are the relative effects of heredity and environment upon intelligence? This is a very difficult issue to review dispassionately, because, more than any other in psychology, it plugs into political and philosophical theories about equality, the racial issue being one example. Take the hereditarian view and you are committed to a certain view of society and school's place in it; take the enviromental view and you have an opposite opinion about the consequences for schooling and society.

Jensen and Eysenck are perhaps the best known proponents of the hereditarian view, which is simply that IQ scores are determined more by the biological basis of intelligence than by any environmental influences. Supporting evidence is obtained from data which express the relationship between the IQ scores of individuals who are related by blood. It is also possible to estimate what this relationship would be if genetic factors alone were operating. Jensen (1969) collected the median value for these correlations, obtained over a number of studies, some examples of which are given in Table 6.1.

The theoretical value, as determined on the assumption that *only* genetic factors operate, for unrelated individuals is 0.00, whether or not they live together. Thus, the fact that the correlations between individuals who live together are higher than zero shows that environment exerts some effect on IQ scores. On the other hand, as the

Table 6.1   *Obtained and theoretical correlations for IQs of people of varying kinship*

Correlations between	1 Obtained median relationship	2 Theoretical value of relationship
Unrelated people		
Children reared apart	− .01	0.00
Foster parent and child	+.20	0.00
Children reared together	+.24	0.00
Related people		
Second cousins	+.16	+.14
First cousins	+.26	+.18
Uncle/aunt and nephew/niece	+.34	+.31
Siblings reared apart	+.47	+.52
Siblings reared together	+.55	+.52
Fraternal twins (different sex)	+.49	+.50
Fraternal twins (same sex)	+.56	+.54
Identical twins reared apart	+.75	+1.00
Identical twins reared together	+.87	+1.00

Source: Jensen (1969)
Note: Column 1 refers to the **obtained** median of all observed correlations. Column 2 refers to the **theoretical** value of the correlation on a genetic theory (i.e., if genetics explained the relationship totally, this is what the correlation should be).

degree of kinship increases from, for example, cousins (who are partially related) to identical twins (whose genetic make-up is the same), one can see the correlations rise, from .16 for second cousins to .75 for identical twins reared apart and .87 for identical twins reared together. These last figures are, however, mainly derived from studies carried out by Sir Cyril Burt (the latest being in 1966) and there is considerable controversy about the genuineness of Burt's data (anti-Burt: Hearnshaw 1979, Kamin 1974; and pro-Burt: Joynson 1989).

The *heritability* of intelligence, which when multiplied by 100 gives the percentage of variance in IQ scores that can be attributed *directly* to genetic factors, may be calculated from these correlations. Jensen arrives at the figure .82, so that in this case 82% of IQ score variability is genetically determined. Vernon (1979) puts the figure at .6, but warned that such a figure must be tentative because estimates of environmental effects assume that they are constant.

But more important than batting figures around is the recognition that a heritability estimate, whether for achievement or for IQ, is *relative* to the environmental conditions prevailing in the sample tested. In most developed countries, environment is relatively constant; few children experience drastically impoverished environments and virtually all attend school for a minimum of nine to ten years. Thus the effect of environment is underestimated because it is moderately constant. Yet individuals may still experience radically different environments and IQ can change accordingly. Newman, Freeman and Holzinger (1937), in following identical twins separated at birth, found one pair where one twin had been reared by a relative in the country, the other in the city. The country girl left school early and settled down quietly to life on the farm. Her twin sister in the city had a busy life and went to teachers' college, and her tested IQ was over 20 points higher than her sister's.

So what does all this mean? Let's look at some data on the heritability of *achievement*, instead of IQ. Estimates of heritability range from .15 to .41 for general achievement; and in particular subjects, from .04 to .57 (reading) and from .23 to .74 (arithmetic). Such ranges are enormous and probably reflect (apart from the unreliability of the data) genuine variation in environmental effects. If teaching were totally ineffective, arithmetic or reading would only be acquired to the extent that students taught themselves (i.e., the smart ones would end up knowing these subjects well and the not-so-smart would not). If, on the other hand, teaching were totally effective, then heritability would drop to zero; no matter how dull the student, good teaching would result in good attainment. These different estimates tell us, then, not so much about genetics as about the effectiveness of teaching. If .3 is accepted as a general estimate, then schooling may have over *twice* the effect of heredity on determining a reading or arithmetic score.

However you look at it, then, heritability arguments are not an issue when it comes to pragmatics in the classroom. They do not let educators off the hook (Kamin 1974). There's plenty of room for you to pitch in there.

IQ and education

How come, then, that the single most effective predictor of academic achievement is indeed the IQ? This is not because the IQ in some mysterious way measures an individual's innate potential. IQ tests predict school performance because they are designed to do so, independently of qualitative differences in students' approaches to learning, of different methods of teaching, or of task structure.

However, as we have seen in the matter of over-/under-achievement, the cart eventually preceded the horse. Only under-achievers were given remedial work, as the over-achievers were already working beyond their presumed capacity. The IQ test, developed to predict school performance, somehow became the criterion for *setting* school performance.

The actuarial approach to intelligence and abilities dominated psychology's contribution to education for the greater part of this century. Jensen (1974) even saw intelligence tests as 'the most important single contribution psychology had to make to educational practice'. Today, most educators are rather more sceptical about the value of intelligence tests and about the assumption that the outcome of schooling is mostly dependent on a stable factor that is inherent in the students. As we see in Chapter 11, attributions of success and failure are more helpfully made to factors such as effort, strategy and to teaching itself. If the outcome of teaching is crucially dependent on something quite beyond the control of the teacher, what is there to being a teacher? The demythologising of this notion is therefore central to developing a professional conception of the role of teacher.

Just how important this is can be seen in the study by Beez (1970), reported in Box 6.2.

More recent theories of intelligence

More recent theories of intelligence take a more process-oriented view of intellectual functioning by nominating the *processes* involved, rather than the content of the items used (spatial, verbal, number, etc.). This has the enormous advantage of telling teachers how intelligent behaviour 'works' and therefore gives some insight into sensible ways of intervention: of beating the predictions, rather than confirming them.

Box 6.2 *Should teachers have access to students' IQ scores?*

Beez (1970) randomly selected high school students for individual tutoring by teachers on a simple symbol learning task. The only information about the students the teachers were given were false IQ scores, which ranged only from 90 to 110, and a misleading interpretation of each score: 'Sue, IQ 94, a dull, slow child', 'Bill, IQ 107, verbally quick, promising academically'.

The teachers produced results that matched their expectations. The Sues learned much less than the Bills. One student with a real IQ of 74, but labelled 'bright', was given 14 symbols to learn and learned 7; another student with a real IQ of 127 but labelled 'dull' was given only 5 symbols and learned 3. The teachers' preconceptions were confirmed: the 'bright' student learned 7, the 'dull' one 3. The teachers did not realise that a variation in IQ from 90 to 110 is entirely within the 'normal' range—such deviations can be expected from a mean of 100—so that the comments were quite inappropriate. The comments and their match with a misinterpreted IQ took over reality; their effect on the teachers was to make them come true.

Intelligence-in-context

One such approach is to take the expert–novice work (pp. 84–5) to its logical conclusion (Glaser 1991). Experts are clearly working intelligently within their domain, so what then becomes the issue is how they perform in *unfamiliar* domains. 'Intelligent' experts do two main things: they represent the new domain using analogies with systems they understand well and they use general problem solving strategies with a high degree of metacognitive processing (see Chapter 12).

This approach thus sees intelligence as a way of behaving towards particular tasks, rather than as a 'something' residing in individuals. Thus, Jethro is not a stupid boy; he simply behaves stupidly in many of the tasks we have seen him undertake so far. Give him plenty of experience, a knowledge base, structured teaching and the chance to interact differently, and he'll behave intelligently. Practically speaking this approach has much to be said for it. It throws the focus on the learner-in-context and on such factors as motivation, task difficulty and other contextual factors that can be controlled, rather than on internal factors that cannot. After all, that's what teaching is all about, isn't it?

Information integration theory

Information integration theory does refer to internal factors, but to processes, not content factors. Das, Kirby and Jarman (1979), following Luria's (1966) model, proposed two modes of information-processing:

1. *Successive synthesis*, where information is held in working memory (see Chapter 8) for processing when there is no interrelationship between the data other than their sequence. This is very close to what happens during rote memorising and acquiring skills; we rote-learn on the basis of which item follows what. Successive synthesis is involved in understanding spoken or written sentences, or whenever we transform several word units into a single meaning unit; the words have to be placed in order.
2. *Simultaneous synthesis*, which is an ability to hold two or more items in mind at once, while attempting to find a relationship between them. Thus, the meanings of

many words have to be changed into a single meaning to get the meaning of a sentence. Reasoning, such as the verbal item 'Cat is to kitten as dog is to ...', is another example of this process. You have simultaneously to abstract what relates cat to kitten and match that with what might relate dog to ...

Luria located these two processes in different parts of the brain and has shown how inadequate successive or simultaneous functioning in patients may be related to injury in the appropriate brain areas.

Simultaneous and successive synthesis are processes that are involved—either one or both—in virtually every cognitive task. In doing anything, we have either to follow through one step after the other, or to react simultaneously to the aspects that are presented; sometimes each process is involved at different stages of the same task.

We can talk about these processes as 'abilities' when we measure them and see *how well* people perform in simultaneous or successive tasks with respect to a particular content domain. Thus, an individual may be measured on performance in verbal tests and it is usually found (as we saw above) that good performance at one or other process generalises across several verbal tests. It may seem that we are back into dealing with fixed abilities again, but there is a difference. Now we are looking at how well people go about a group of tasks in a *particular way*. Are they good at handling the simultaneous aspects, the successive aspects, or equally good at both? As many tasks may be approached with either a simultaneous bias or a successive bias, this model provides a way of generating alternative approaches to a particular task.

The key to the use of either, and when the right mix of process is best for the task in question, is *planning*. Plans are analogous to computer programs (Kirby 1984b); they mastermind the use of particular simultaneous or successive strategies which are appropriate for the task in question. The word 'mastermind' is used advisedly: one of the tests of planning ability is in fact the game 'Master Mind', in which one has to match a hidden array of coloured pegs in as few moves as possible on the basis of feedback provided on the correctness of the guesses so far. Poor planners use superstition ('Red seems to be working for me today so I'll use that') and they tend to ignore feedback, replaying a colour they should know to be wrong. Good planners use their prior knowledge to work out their strategy (for instance, do they change their strategy if they know the opponent consistently selects colours systematically or randomly?); they vary few variables at a time; they take a logical set of alternatives and exhaust that before trying a different set.

Other planning tasks include searching for targets in a large visual array, planning composition and connecting up letters and figures systematically. A variety of possible tasks can be used, but they have in common: systematic and reasoned forethought before making a move; making use of feedback as one progresses and use of other relevant prior knowledge; a concern to be economical or 'elegant' in solution and so on. Planning invokes that often mentioned process *metacognition* (Chapter 12).

Planning may operate at different levels of generality. As we shall see when we look at planning an essay (see Chapter 13), the writer may plan at the level of the main ideas or theme of an essay and/or at the level of detail (e.g., sentence construction). Strategies may be regarded as components of a plan, or subplans, that are set up to handle a particular kind of task (Kirby 1984c).

What is the relationship between planning and intelligence? High level, abstract planning seems clearly to be closely related to what we mean by 'intelligent' behaviour, yet:

traditional tests of intelligence appear to minimise the input of planning, in that they do not assess how the subject solves the task, only how well. (Kirby 1984c :85)

The information integration model, then, adds an important dimension to the concept of intelligence: planning and coordinating behaviour. This can be used to help design instruction.

For example, let us look at the case of reading. The early stages of decoding involve letter–sound blending, which is an essentially successive task: letters are taken in one after the other and run together to make a sound. Then, with practice, word identification becomes more a matter of recognising the whole word: the letters are taken as a simultaneous whole that is instantly identifiable as a known word.

Comprehension involves both simultaneous and successive processes, and these operate differently at different stages of reading skill development. A young child comprehending a sentence relies heavily on tracing word by word and then holding the gists of individual words and phrases in mind at once to see what their collective meaning is. A practised reader who is focusing on a main idea, on the other hand, holds that idea in mind simultaneously with the sentence meanings as they are rapidly processed. Meaning is thus added to or clarified simultaneously.

Successive processes thus tend to precede simultaneous, in both word identification and in comprehension, and this is important information for teachers of reading: clearly strategies of approach should reflect the balance of simultaneous and successive processes required currently. For example, Krywaniuk (1974) found that Canadian Cree Indian children were higher on simultaneous processing and lower on successive than Caucasians, a difference reflecting the way they were brought up to respond to their environment. A similar imbalance exists with Australian Aboriginal children, undoubtedly for the same reasons (Klich & Davidson 1984). The Cree children (again like Aboriginals) tended to score very poorly on early reading tests. Could it be that the failure to learn to read was due to a simultaneous-based attack on a task that at this stage required a successive approach? Krywaniuk thought so: and in that event, the appropriate strategy was to build up successive processing by providing practice on a variety of successive tasks, which Cree children in their normal habitat do not experience but European children do. The tasks and activities were built into games, such as laying out toys in series. It was found that after such practice, the children began to adopt more appropriate successive-based approaches to word identification and their reading skills improved accordingly.

A parallel study does not yet appear to have been attempted in this country, but the potential is clearly there. The general paradigm for the design of instruction, then, is to match the approach to the appropriate balance of simultaneous and successive processing that is required for the level of skill demanded at that point.

Sternberg's triarchic theory of intelligence

In his 'triarchic' theory, Sternberg (1985; 1991) takes into account both the cultural side of intelligence as well as the mechanisms that underly intelligent behaviour. He postulates three 'sub-theories':

- a contextual sub-theory
- an experiential sub-theory
- a componential sub-theory.

The contextual sub-theory attempts to specify how intelligent behaviour reflects a process of purposeful adaptation to the environment and the shaping of the environment in an attempt to make it best fit one's skills, interests and values. In modern Western society the contextual theory of intelligence would focus on problem solving and academic skills, whereas in other cultures, hunting skills or navigational skills may be more valued. The point is that different socio-cultural contexts value different adaptive, intelligent behaviours. Krywaniuk's study of Cree children is exactly a case in point; they had developed simultaneous but not successive skills.

The experiential sub-theory states that intelligence is seen at its best when the task being attempted is relatively novel. This is a different emphasis from Glaser's work on experts, which concentrates on competent performance in the familiar domain.

The third is the componential sub-theory, which refers to the cognitive structures and processes that underlie intelligent behaviour. A component is 'an elementary information process that operates upon internal representations of objects or symbols' (Sternberg 1985: 97) that allows the specification of the mental mechanisms that underlie intelligent performance. There are three types of components:

- *metacomponents*, which are at the highest level and involve the metacognitive skills of identifying the problem, planning, working out a strategy and monitoring: rather like planning in information integration theory.
- *performance* components, which comprise the procedural knowledge needed to solve a particular task.
- *knowledge acquisition components*, which are used for acquiring new information.

First, the metacomponent of identifying the nature of the problem is involved; a negative example occurs when students do not identify what is required of the task. A study by Sternberg and Rifkin (1979) nicely illustrates the outcomes of not knowing the nature of the task; a group of second-grade children were asked to solve a pictorial analogies task requiring them to circle one side of an analogies problem. Some children consistently circled the wrong set of terms. It turned out this group attended a Jewish school, having their lessons in English in the morning and Hebrew (which is read from right-to-left) in the afternoon. The children had been tested in the afternoon!

Monitoring the solution, as another metacomponent, is also important for successful performance. As students progress through the problem they have to be conscious of what they have done up to date, how well that has been going and what they are to do next to produce a successful outcome. Take solving an analogy problem of the type lawyer: client: doctor: ... (medicine, patient). The performance components involve encoding the terms (lawyer, etc.) and forming them into internal representations that can then be operated upon. Next, the student infers the relationship between lawyer and client (a professional relationship) and then maps the higher order relation between the first section of the analogy and the second (lawyers and doctors deal professionally with people). This is then followed by the application of this relationship (i.e., professional) to the doctor and the two alternatives (medicine, patient) with the choice of patient (as doctor and patient are related professionally to each other). More generally, performance components tend to organise themselves around stages of task solution: encoding, combination and comparison, and response. Encoding is concerned with the initial storage of information. Combination and comparison occur next in the sequence of operations (such as lawyer: doctor relationship) and finally the individual responds. Each of these components is a source of individual differences in cognitive operations.

Summary

This brief overview of recent theories makes several important advances over the traditional ones:

- Intelligent behaviour involves questions of value: what is or is not considered intelligent is cultural and contextual.
- 'Being intelligent' involves going about problems in a particular kind of way, rather than 'having' more or less of this or that kind of ability.
- The relative importance of each kind of component in behaving intelligently depends upon the nature of the task, the nature of the individual and the expected outcome. Effective use of components is measurable and is a major source of individual differences, but there is plenty of scope for alternative solutions and for individual creativity in devising solutions.
- Theories of intelligence therefore do not pre-empt teaching by predicting the outcomes of teaching, but should actually help educators design the context for better learning.

Unfortunately, educational practice hasn't yet caught up with this contextual view of behaving intelligently. Ability is still commonly seen as a static quantity residing in little heads. Grouping children in terms of ability is based on exactly that assumption and the practice is widespread.

Catering for individual differences in the normal classroom

Once we assume that children differ according to general or specific abilities, we can allow for differences in these abilities in two ways: in the formal structuring of classes (ability grouping) and in informal student–teacher interaction.

Ability grouping

Grouping students by ability or achievement can take several forms:

1. *Between-class grouping*, which may be of two kinds: *streaming*, where a general ability measure is used to group students over most or all other classes; and *setting*, where students are grouped by performance in particular subjects (e.g., Cathie may be in the top maths class, but in the middle ability class for history).
2. *Within-class grouping*, where students are formed into small groups within a class for particular purposes, such as reading or mathematics.
3. *Mixed ability classes*, where no attempt is made to group students according to ability.

The aim of any form of ability grouping is to tune the pace and level of teaching to the ability of the students, which sounds fine in theory. Let us take between-class grouping first.

Between-class grouping

Two arguments are used for both streaming and setting:

1. *Classes of homogeneous ability are easier to teach.* Students are more likely to be working at the same pace and so the teacher can adjust the pace and level of instruction to suit the maximum number of students.

How can teachers cater for individual differences in the classroom?

2. *The students are more comfortable;* the bright are less likely to be bored, the dull to feel lost. In particular, the less bright student is protected from the humiliating knowledge of how far ahead the brighter students really are.

The evidence contradicts both arguments. (1) is plausible on the assumption that only expository whole class methods are used. If the teacher mostly focuses on small group work then this point becomes irrelevant. More compelling, streaming by a general ability measure such as IQ does not in fact reduce the variability of *particular* classes, so that in practice there is considerable overlap in performance levels between classes (Rosenbaum 1976). This argument applies less readily to setting, where the grouping is on the basis of performance in particular subjects. The matter clearly depends on the nature of the content being taught and how it is taught.

(2) is true only of the students in the top streams (Corno & Snow 1986). The evidence otherwise is not only that students feel less comfortable when streamed, but perform worse (Biggs 1966; Good & Marshall 1984; Rosenbaum 1980). The reasons for this are not hard to find. The quality of teaching in lower streams is usually worse; frequently the 'Ds' and 'Es' are assigned to newer, inexperienced teachers because these classes are less popular, while good teachers are rewarded by being assigned the 'better', more manageable, classes (Good & Marshall 1984). But not only are they likely to be taught less well, the low stream classes are taught lower level content; for their ability, then, they achieve at a lower level than they would if placed higher in streams, or even in unstreamed classes, because the quality of instruction in mixed ability, unstreamed, classes more closely resembles that of high stream than low stream

teaching (op. cit.). Teachers adjust *upwards* to cope with mixed ability classes, *downwards* to cope with low ability classes, so that low ability students are exposed to better teaching and better role models when in mixed ability classes, while the good students are better taught and achieve well, anyway.

Possibly even more influential than these teaching factors is how the students *feel* about being assigned to lower streams. As we shall see in Chapter 11, when discussing motivation and self-concept, these feelings can have very damaging effects on student motivation (see also Weiner 1967). These effects are largely due to the fact that the students too readily believe the 'E' label, which says 'I am no good at academic work', a tendency frequently reinforced by the teachers who take these classes and who deliberately or unintentionally communicate to students their low expectations of them (Good & Marshall 1984).

These problems are exacerbated because once a student is assigned to an 'A' or a 'C' stream it is usually very difficult to be re-assigned, as the curriculum and pace of differently streamed classes rapidly diverge. The students become locked into a grouping that, for the less than very bright, attracts a pejorative label. Calling the classes 'Possums', 'Wallabies', 'Emus' or 'Galahs' (whoops, change that to 'Wombats'), instead of 'Cs', 'Ds', 'Es' and 'Fs', fools nobody for very long. As we shall see below, the self-fulfilling prophecy tends to make its own expectations come true.

Within-class grouping

Within-class grouping is more common in primary than in secondary schools. It is used when it is particularly important that students focus on a structured task that requires detailed step-by-step mastery, as is frequently the case in reading and mathematics. Such groupings are usually temporary, and for quite a specific purpose, so that the problem of labelling does not seem to arise. Research shows that it is highly effective, provided certain conditions are met (Slavin 1987a):

1. Students should remain in mixed ability classes for most of the time and be regrouped within the class only for particular purposes when homogeneity of achievement is important.
2. Assignment to groups should be on the basis of a *specific skill*, not a general measure such as IQ.
3. Assignments should be flexible, so that re-assignment of individuals is easy if their performance warrants it.
4. The number of sub-groups within a class should be small, say two or three groups. If there are larger groups, then more groups of children are left unsupervised at any given time.
5. Clearly, the teacher needs to be flexible enough to adjust to the pace of the particular group.

The important thing is that within-class grouping does not encourage students, or teachers, to build up long-term expectations or messages that create damage.

Self-fulfilling prophecy

So far, we have been talking about using data on abilities to make formal decisions about teaching. How does such information affect informal student–teacher interaction? The Beez study (see Box 6.2) shows very clearly how information from IQ cards—whether false or correct—can affect the way teachers react to students on the basis of what is called the *self-fulfilling prophecy*, or the Pygmalion Effect (Rosenthal & Jacobson 1968), in which the fact of labelling students makes them behave in ways appropriate to the label given.

In their original study, Rosenthal and Jacobson supplied teachers with false information about which students in their classes were 'spurters' (i.e., likely to make a spurt in academic progress). By the end of the year, those designated as spurters made slight but significant progress ahead of the non-spurters. In fact spurters and non-spurters were selected at random; there was no intrinsic reason at all why those so designated should make more rapid progress.

While the Rosenthal and Jacobson study has been severely criticised on methodological grounds (Elashoff & Snow 1971; Thorndike 1968), the concept of the self-fulfilling prophecy is an important one and better work has established its validity (Beez 1970; Finn 1972; Meichenbaum, Bowers & Ross 1969). Simply, the expectations we have affect the way we behave and the way we behave affects the way other people respond. Good and Brophy (1987) suggest that:

- teachers acquire different expectations about students in their classes;
- teachers therefore behave towards different students in different ways, which tell students how they are expected to perform. Smiling encouragingly to a student expected to give a good answer to a question is likely to elicit one; quickly turning to another student with 'You tell him …' before a presumed dullard has a chance to respond is guaranteeing the latter's future silence;
- unless the student actively resists, or is determined to prove the teacher wrong, such interactions over time will convince the student to behave in keeping with the communicated expectation: as a non-answerer of questions, as a clown, or whatever has been consistently communicated;
- the teacher's expectations are consequently confirmed and reinforced; students have more often conformed to them than not.

Girls' lower performance in mathematical and scientific tasks is almost certainly maintained by these mechanisms (see pp. 107–9). The self-fulfilling prophecy does not of course only work with academic behaviour based on assumptions about ability. Giving dogs a bad name will keep you well supplied with misbehaving dogs.

Some of the mechanisms that convert expectations into changed behaviour are:

1. *Goal-setting.* As Beez's study shows clearly, the 'bright' students were given more problems to solve, so they obtained higher scores than those were who given fewer problems.
2. *Reinforcement.* Students of whom much is expected receive more praise, while those of whom little is expected receive more criticism for incorrect responses (Good & Brophy 1987).
3. *Quality of input and of task set.* Teachers of low stream classes teach more facts and provide less higher level conceptual input, and set less demanding tasks (Good & Marshall 1984).

There are several ways in which the self-fulfilling prophecy can be turned to good effect and the bad effects avoided. Simply having high goals for all students is positive, although one cannot be a Pollyanna, blind to all negative information about students. Where one does receive negative information, however, it is important to know: (a) if it is valid and (b) how to minimise conveying negative expectations. Knowledge of the ways in which expectations are conveyed is a first step.

Summary

Abilities and intelligence

Theories of intelligence tend to emphasise either the specificity of several different intelligences, or the general nature of intelligence. It is generally agreed that competencies occupy the most specific end, with abilities such as mathematics or music midway, and intelligence the most general end. Several writers today speak of 'academic' and 'everyday' intelligence as two unrelated forms of intelligence.

Intelligence and the IQ

The first intelligence test by Binet and Simon was specifically tied to predicting school performance; that set the pattern for subsequent work on the IQ until very recently. IQ tests thus reflect performance on particular sorts of items (Intelligence C), not how intelligently we behave in real situations (Intelligence B), or how good our brains are (Intelligence A).

The structure of intellectual abilities

Even within the rather scholastic interpretation of IQ, there are two models: several relatively independent factors based largely on item content (number, spatial, verbal, memory, etc.), or one major factor of general intelligence (*g*), with various subfactors coming in depending on the nature of the task. Other theories compare fluid (basic) and crystallised (schooled) intelligence, the former declining and the latter increasing with age; and Level 1 (memory) and Level 2 (reasoning), with different races said to inherit different levels of reasoning, but not memory.

Such salty speculations lead to the age-old 'nature–nurture' controversy: is intelligence mainly inherited, or mainly shaped by the environment? Mindblowing implications for education lurk in the answer; or so it was once thought. We tend not to think so today, because wherever the real answer lies precisely, there's always enough room for intervention to have an effect.

More recent theories of intelligence

Modern approaches to intelligence ask a different question: What is involved in being clever? Such a question implies process and its answer is clearer about the nature of educational intervention. Information integration theory refers to planning and the use of two ways of processing, simultaneous and successive. These ways of processing are drawn upon differently in various stages of learning, which is helpful when designing instruction.

Componential theory suggests that being clever involves several components: knowing what to do, how to do it, and masterminding the whole process. It also suggests that contexts are very important: being clever in school, at a party, and at the racetrack are all very different things.

Catering for individual differences in the classroom

Not to stream; that's what the research evidence says loud and clear. Some form of ability grouping is consistently advocated by administrators and by teachers themselves, but the evidence is that low ability students do worse with ability grouping, while high ability students perform the same. The reasons are clear; low ability groups frequently suffer from poorer teaching, a lower level curriculum, and a self-fulfilling prophecy. It is better for teachers to understand different ability patterns and react to student differences informally, one to one, than to homogenise classes, because that usually means homogenising teaching methods. And that usually means poor teaching.

LEARNING ACTIVITIES

1. Abilities and intelligence

Earlier in this chapter we looked at the distinction between *academic* and *everyday* intelligence (pp. 150–1). Can you draw out the major differences between these two 'intelligences'? Sternberg and Wagner's (1986) *Practical Intelligence* looks at intelligence in the workplace, in other everyday settings, across the lifespan, and also the relationship of practical intelligence to culture and society.

A list of occupations and everyday activities follows. Next to each indicate at least two 'practical intelligence' behaviours. The first has been done for you.

Occupation/Activity	Practical intelligence
Waiter/Waitress	Use of external memory by writing orders in seating sequence around table.
	Remembering distinctive features (e.g., clothes) of person from whom the first order is taken.
School principal	
School teacher	
School secretary	
Punter	

You probably realised when you were doing this task that you needed to think of a situation for each. This raises the important issues of the context of practical intelligence and the use of setting-specific knowledge. Scribner's chapter in Sternberg and Wagner (1986) discusses these aspects.

A final question. Can practical intelligence be taught and, if so, should schools explicitly teach to increase practical intelligence?

2. Tests of intelligence

The aim of this activity is to acquaint yourself with tests of intelligence and more particularly the types of items that are used in such tests. We presented an item from Raven's Progressive Matrices Test (p. 156). What types of items are used in other tests? If you can get access to the Binet and the Wechsler tests you will see that they have many different types of items. Other tests, such as the Australian Council for Educational Research's TOLA (Test of Learning Ability, 1976) give a different slant on intelligence. How do the tests fit with the 'models' of intelligence we presented?

3. The structure of intellectual abilities

Intelligence has been described as a group of abilities that underlie successful performance in school. Below each of the following theorists, list their 'structures' of intellectual abilities. Compare them with the newer theories of Das, Kirby and Jarman (Information Integration theory) and Sternberg (Componential theory).

Vernon   *Thurstone*   *Cattell/Horn*

4. More recent theories of intelligence: Information–integration theory

The work of Das and his colleagues (Kirby, Jarman) has provided an alternative way of thinking about mental processes. As noted in this chapter, simultaneous processing is the synthesis of separate parts or elements of information into wholistic representations that can be mentally surveyed while successive processing is concerned with sequential ordering and the individual component parts.

There is an excellent article by Robinson and Kirby in the *Australian Journal of Reading* (1987, **10**, 32-44) which shows how simultaneous and successive processing are involved in reading. The section on remediation is interesting and we have adapted the important elements below.

Successive processing:

- picture and object sequencing—ordering ever increasing or decreasing numbers of pictures or objects.
- letter sequencing—analysing compound words into component parts.
- word sequencing—identifying incorrect syntax in word sequences. Use of close procedure.
- Story sequencing—retelling story in sequence. Identifying story components out of sequence. Ordering of story components.

Simultaneous processing:

- pattern synthesis—reproducing patterns with blocks or drawing. Draw or reconstruct after object has been removed.
- picture and object synthesis—explanations of differences between objects. Identification of objects partly exposed.
- letter and word synthesis—identifying differences between various letters and common sight words.
- sentence or plot synthesis—identifying word meanings, close choice procedure. Making mental images of phrases, sentences, paragraphs. Identifying the main ideas, summarising.

For each of the 'levels' within the simultaneous and successive areas, generate some teaching tasks. The levels, you will note from the above, are from lower levels (e.g., letters, words) to sentence and whole text levels. Show how the task relates to either simultaneous or successive processing. Share your work with your colleagues.

5. Catering for individual differences

Grouping students by ability or achievement are ways in which we can move to accommodate individual differences. We discussed streaming, setting, within-class and mixed ability classes in this context. This activity is aimed at drawing out the advantages and disadvantages of each, using the research we have cited as well as your own experiences as a student and as a teacher. Of course, the advantages and disadvantages relate to the student, the teachers, the school organisation, etc., and more than academic performance would need to be commented upon (e.g., self-concept). If done as a class activity, groups could be assigned specific grouping types. The results of the discussions could then be brought back to the whole class.

6. Expectations into behaviour

We spent some time in this chapter discussing self-fulfilling prophecies, that expectations affect the ways in which we behave. This activity encourages you to examine classroom activities to see if you can identify some of the mechanisms that convert expectations into changed behaviour (see pp. 166–7): goal-setting, reinforcement, and quality of input and of task set. Perhaps this could be done in an informal manner, observing classrooms during practicum or by reflection on your own schooling. Questions to be addressed include: Do the 'brighter' students have more work to complete? When the faster students are finished are they given more of the same type of work to complete? Is more praise given to the 'better' students in the class? Does the teacher give different types of responses to those of lesser ability? Class discussion could develop a set of questions to guide the investigation.

Further reading

On abilities and intelligence

(a) *Traditional*

Eysenck, H.J. (1971). *Race, Intelligence and Education*. Melbourne: Sun Books.
Hearnshaw, L. S. (1979). *Cyril Burt, Psychologist*. London: Hodder & Stoughton.
Joynson, R.B. (1989). *The Burt Affair*. London: Routledge & Kegan Paul.
Vernon, P. E. (1979). *Intelligence: Heredity and Environment*. San Francisco: W. H. Freeman.

For a thoroughly straightforward account of traditional intelligence test theory and a balanced discussion of nature–nurture, Vernon's book is still unbeatable. Where traditional theory went off the rails—maybe—is juicily described in Hearnshaw's attack on and Joynson's defence of the hapless Sir Cyril Burt: Did he, or did he not, fake the data that most strongly supported the hypothesis that intelligence is inherited? Eysenck's book is, as is annoyingly usual for him, a very clearly written account of the hereditarian point of view: truly, he is the psychologist you love to hate.

(b) *New wave*

Gardner, H. (1985). *Frames of Mind*. London: Paladin.
Kirby, J. (ed.) (1984). *Cognitive Strategies and Educational Performance*. New York: Academic Press.

Rowe, H. (ed.) (1991). *Intelligence: Reconceptualisation and measurement*. Hawthorn: ACER/Hillsdale: Lawrence Erlbaum.

Sternberg, R. (1985). *Beyond IQ*. Cambridge: Cambridge University Press.

Gardner's book contains his interesting but quirky theories of 'frames'. Kirby's contains several papers focusing on the Das-Kirby information–integration model, with a recent restatement by Das and Jarman in Rowe. Sternberg as always, brilliantly describes his own theory at length in the book, and an overview is also included in Rowe. Rowe's book contains papers given at a seminar on intelligence held as part of the Bicentennial celebrations in 1988 and provides an update on aspects of theory and measurement both from within Australia and prominent overseas contributors.

EXCEPTIONAL CHILDREN AND THEIR NEEDS

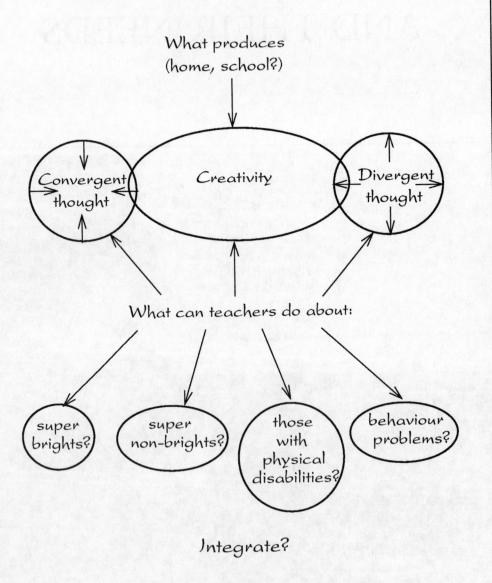

Exceptional children and their needs

What produces
(home, school?)

Convergent
thought

Creativity

Divergent
thought

What can teachers do about:

super
brights?

super
non-brights?

those
with
physical
disabilities?

behaviour
problems?

Integrate?

EXCEPTIONAL CHILDREN AND THEIR NEEDS

In this chapter you will find out:

- who 'exceptional' children are;
- what processes are involved in 'being intelligent' and in 'being creative';
- how convergent and divergent ability differ;
- why teachers can ignore cognitive styles;
- what regular teachers should know about learning disabilities and emotional and behavioural disorders.

Who are exceptional children?

In the last chapter, we dealt with various conceptions of ability and intelligence and what research suggests might be useful strategies for teachers in handling children within 'normal' ability ranges. But what about those who lie outside those ability ranges: the top 1% (the really high fliers), or the bottom 5% (the learning disabled)?

Clearly, we have by no means explored the whole field of individual differences. Individuals differ in more than just academic ability, in more even than the seven frames of intelligence that Gardner described. Let us look at two examples of student performance, both of which would be regarded as 'good', if not actually exceptional.

The following essays, obtained from a Year 8 history class, were written after a series of lessons on Columbus's discovery of America. The teacher set the topic, with detailed guidelines to help the students. He then marked the essays on the basis of adherence to the guidelines. The students' names are fictitious, but not their essays.

The topic and guidelines
As Christopher Columbus, write an account of your voyage.
State: The reasons for the voyage (2 marks)
            The name of your second in command (1 mark)
            A mistake you made with the rations (1 mark)
            The crew's attitude to the voyage and how you tried to fool them (2 marks)
            The first signs that land was near (1 mark)
            Describe the sighting of land (time of day, who sighted it, the reward) (3 marks)
            What you called the land and its inhabitants and the reasons behind the names you chose (3 marks)
            What you brought the natives (1 mark)
            Who you claimed the land for (1 mark)

Total = 15 marks

Let us take two of those essays: first Merelyn's, then Steve's.

Merelyn's essay

I went on this voyage because when the Turks invaded us they blocked off the traditional route to the East Indies. Perizon was my second in command. I left out Vitamin C in my rations so my sailors got scurvy. My crew didn't want to go on the voyage and wanted to turn back. I tried to fool them by saying we were closer to home and that anything and everything was a sign of land. They mutinied but we made a proposition to stop them. We saw a branch bearing leaves and berries, a plank and a piece of carved wood. Later we saw landbirds. Rodrigo de Triano sighted land at 2.00 a.m. The first person to see land was to get 200 pounds a year from the slaughter houses of Cordova which is why I said I saw lights first. I called the islands the Indies and the natives Indians because they lived here. I brought the natives crosses and other religious things. I claimed the land for Isabella of Spain.

Steve's essay

As you kn-kn-know, my n-n-name is Christ-topher Seymour Herman Louis Gilbert Bono Edge Cl-Cl-Clo-Columbus. I also st-st-stutter & I can't spell neethur.

I went sai-sai-sailing one d-day in the 1400s and g-got lost. No, just jo-jo-jok-ing—I rea-rea-really went explor-splor-sploring for Quee-Queen (cool band) Isabella. My se-second in command was Fredrico Edebella Lasagna.

I left out vit-vit-vitamin C from my cre-crew's rations and half of them die-die-die-d-die-croaked-it because of this stu-stu-dumb mistake. My crew were so easily foole- easily foo-gullible that I told them we were'nt going very fa-far and they belie-belie-be-believed me.

One day, we fou-found some branch-bra-branch-twigs floating around in the wat-wa-wat-ocean so we knew that land was ne-near-ne-not far away. Yes folk-fol-folk-people we found America. I called the place the Indies and I called the natives indi-in-ind-Indi-india-niggers because they were black.

I brought the na-nat-nativ-niggers gifts of gold, f-franken cents and m-mur ... OOPS-SORRY WRO-WRO-WR-WRO-DIFFERENT P-PERSON. No, really. I ga-gav-go-g-brought them beads and mirrors. In retur-retur-ret-exchange, the retards g-gave me gold. Unfortunately, It turned out to be fools gol-f-foo-fools go-Iron Pyrites, So I k-kill-k-kill-murdered them all.

Let us now look at the teacher's response:

Merelyn: 13/15. 'Great work, Merelyn! Clearly written, displaying a sound knowl-edge of the voyage. Perhaps *you* were Christopher Columbus in a past life?'
Steve: 7/15. 'Very amusing, especially the Iron Pyrites line. Do you know, humour doesn't count for a lot of marks in history (you needed more facts). But it was fun to read!' (He also ringed the work 'niggers' and wrote 'RACIST' in capitals.)

The marks and comments duly reflect the clear guidelines set up by the teacher. We hesitate to take this further, but here goes.

Who has answered the question in terms of the given criteria more effectively? Merelyn, we think you will agree. Who has assimilated the lesson more effectively? Probably Merelyn; there is perhaps more doubt here because the guidelines are so tightly structured. Which student shows the greatest—what can we say—talent? Steve, we think you will agree. In fact, he became deeply involved in student drama when at University a few years later and became well known locally.

Who best understands the implications of Columbus's voyage for the people involved? The essays were written in 1985; this year (1992) it is now emerging that Steve's quick brushstrokes appear to have captured the incompetence, ruthlessness and racism that Columbus is now thought to have displayed more effectively than Merelyn's straight replay. Yet Merelyn has played the game required of students much better than has Steve, as her marks show. Steve's essay showed clear evidence of an exceptional talent; Merelyn's of a quite ordinary but institutionally rewarded talent.

The point about all this is that exceptionality shows varying forms. Exceptionality is not a matter of being exceptionally bright or exceptionally slow. There are qualitative aspects to being exceptional. Let us first take the kind of exceptionality manifested by Steve. Later we deal with quite different forms of exceptionality, in children with special educational needs brought about by disabilities. This last area is however one that requires specially trained teachers and so the main concentration in this chapter is on the kind of exceptionality that most classroom teachers are likely to meet.

Convergent and divergent abilities

Research into the psychology of giftedness and creativity used to be very popular; much of the underlying research was conducted twenty or so years ago and now seems a little old-fashioned, which is a pity, because the provision of programs for the gifted is certainly of current concern. In order to understand this area, it is still important to consider this earlier work. The point of departure is Guilford's (1967) distinction between convergent and divergent ability, high levels of each being manifested in Merelyn and Steve, respectively.

Convergent and divergent productions are terms used by Guilford to distinguish the processes used to produce two different kinds of performance. Convergent ability is required to solve problems that have a particular, unique, answer; most items in intelligence or attainment tests are of this kind. Many tasks in school require the application of specific rules to produce a single correct answer, such as working out a sum, spelling a word correctly, or inducing a rule to obtain the correct answer ('Kitten is to cat as ... is to goose') and therefore address convergent ability. However, the fact that there is only one correct answer does not mean that only low level processes are involved. Tests requiring rote memorising are examples of low level convergent processes, but some tasks require quite complex and abstract levels of convergence (see Box 7.1).

Merelyn shows convergent ability in the way she took each particular mark-bearing cue provided by the teacher and dealt with them in order, correctly but unimaginatively.

Divergence involves quite a different process. The person who is good at this kind of thinking generates alternatives and suggests different answers from those given; this ability has a lot to do with creativity. Such people would be good at problems of the kind: 'How else could this story have ended?', 'What explanations can you think of that might account for the failure of that experiment?' Certainly some alternatives would be preferable to others, but the point here is to entertain alternatives, not to say that one is correct and all the others wrong. Steve simply reinterpreted the task as something to enjoy, using his topic knowledge as his material; being 'correct' was not his foremost concern.

> Box 7.1   *An example of high-level convergence*
>
> Two brothers lived in a cottage situated at the fork in a road, one branch leading to Conville, the other to Diville. One brother always spoke the truth, the other brother always told lies. A traveller arrived at the fork, wanting to get to Conville but did not know which brother was the liar and which one spoke the truth. He was only allowed one question: what question could he ask *either* brother and be sure of taking the right track to Conville?
>
> *(The answer is given below—upside down.)*
>
> 'If I want to go to Conville and I asked your brother, what would he say?' When you hear the answer, take the opposite fork.
>
> *Answer*

Measurement of divergent ability

When, as in convergent thought, there is one correct answer, measurement is in principle straightforward. But when the product of thought is novel, we need to assess the process itself. Divergent thinking is thus more difficult to measure. In Guilford's Uses of Objects Test, common objects are mentioned one at a time and subjects have to think up as many different uses for it as they can. For example, given *brick*, one person might list: to build a factory, to build a house, to build a garage, to build a wall, to throw at people, to throw at stray cats, to drop on spiders. Another person may list: to build houses, to use as a weapon, to grind into powder to make paint, to make a tombstone for a mouse, to put into cisterns to save water, to use as a paperweight, to stand on to gain extra height. The total number of *responses* (the fluency score) is the same in both cases, but the total number of *categories* is clearly different. The first person has listed only two categories (building and missile), whereas the second person has produced seven different categories (building, missile, paint, tombstone, displacement, weight, height). Accordingly, the latter is considered to be more divergent, having given an example of each of many different properties, while the former provided only two properties. Although these differences between fluency and category scoring are important theoretically, the two scores correlate highly in practice (Biggs 1970). Box 7.2 lists some examples of responses to a typical item.

Another method of scoring the Uses Test is to calculate the *originality* of the responses. This involves finding out the frequency of each response in the sample tested and then weighting each individual response according to its rarity. This is, unfortunately, quite a tedious procedure. Many people, for instance, do not readily think of the 'tombstone' response, so that would be given a higher originality score than 'build a house' (which is mentioned by almost everyone). Originality scores correlate with fluency and flexibility, but they appear to relate to a different aspect of divergence: all aspects are related to *creativity*.

Another technique requires subjects to complete a half-finished story, or to invent titles for given stories. Read this short story mentioned by Guilford and then give it a title of your own.

A man had a wife who had been injured and was unable to speak. He found a surgeon who restored her power of speech. Then the man's peace was shattered by his

---

Box 7.2 *Some responses to the uses test*

'Think of as many uses for a paper clip as you can'

High divergent
To hold papers and stuff together
To mend fuses with
To make wire sculpture
To unbend and poke at people you don't like
To pick locks
To join several up and make a necklace
To use as weights on science beam balance
To heat red-hot and drop down lower-class backs
To perform operations with (e.g., cauterising diseased genitals)
A frame for a mouse's sailboat
To hold glued surfaces together to dry
A clothes peg for dwarf's washday
A stick for iced lollies
For clamping the flapmouths of psychologists shut ...
(At this point the subject stopped writing)

Low divergent
To fasten letter and papers with
A bookmark
A missile
To hold photos in an album

---

wife's incessant talking. He solved the problem by having a doctor perform an operation on him so that, although she talked endlessly, he was unable to hear a thing she said. (Guilford 1967: 156)

Non-witty titles, from low divergers, include the likes of 'Medicine triumphs', or 'Never satisfied', while witty titles, indicating high divergence, include 'Anything for a quiet wife' and 'A matter of wife and deaf'. There is some subjectivity involved in deciding whether one title is wittier than another; scorers of the test ought not to be low on divergence themselves.

Humour, cleverness and wit are characteristic of the high diverger, as is high aggressive content (Hudson 1966). The response to uses of a paper clip, 'To heat red-hot and drop down lower-class backs' (see Box 7.2), is typical. Steve's essay of course reveals both the humour and the aggression of the high diverger.

Tests of divergence need not be verbal. Another of Guilford's tests involved presenting an incomplete line drawing reproduced 20 times on a page. The task is to complete as many recognisable but different drawings on each outline as possible. This test, like the Uses Test, requires producing several appropriate responses rather than a single correct one.

In sum, the main features of divergent ability are:

1. *Fluency:* the production of many responses, as opposed to settling on any one.
2. *Flexibility:* the production of many *categories* of response, readiness to change categories, to explore different trains of thought. These categories do, however,

have to be minimally relevant; a random list of uses is evidence more of schizophrenia than of divergence.

3. *Originality*: being different is a further characteristic of divergence. This is often displayed as wit, delighting in the unexpected, creating novel responses rather than settling for existing ones.

Factors producing divergence

As with intelligence, we may ask the nature–nurture question: is divergent ability a matter of genes or of upbringing? What are the heritability estimates with regard to divergence? Pezzullo, Thorsen and Madaus (1972) tend to agree with Jensen about the heritability of Level 1 and Level 2 abilities: .54 and .86 respectively. Their figure of zero for divergent ability probably shows that the ability is not inherited.

What about the evidence for environmental effects? In one of the classic studies of creative children (which in this context means high divergent children), Getzels and Jackson (1962) compared students who scored highly on open-end divergence tests and medium to low on an IQ test ('high creative') with students who scored low on divergence tests but high on IQ ('high intelligent'). The 'high creatives' defined in this way were found to come from 'bohemian' homes, in which the rules were few and the children were encouraged to express themselves freely. The 'high intelligent' students, on the other hand, came from conventional homes and were brought up on the Puritan ethic to work hard and do the right thing.

It is likely that children coming from these quite different home backgrounds internalise quite different ways of coping. Anderson and Cropley (1966) suggested that high divergent children are high risk-takers who like being original and who like to shock; hence their freedom with sexual and aggressive content in their responses to open-end tests. It may be not that low convergers are unable to generate these 'shock' responses, so much as that they feel unable to allow themselves to take the risk of expressing them. In this earlier work on divergence, it was consistently found that boys were more divergent than girls, a difference explained in terms of the sex role stereotyping that prevailed in the 1960s; boys were expected to be higher risk-takers than girls (Anderson & Cropley 1966). It would be interesting to know what researchers would now find, but this aspect of gender research seems to have been neglected.

Finally, divergent and convergent ability aren't the polar opposites that Getzels and Jackson seemed to imply. In fact, all their 'high creatives' had IQs at least one standard deviation above the mean; that is, they were in the top 16% of the population on intelligence anyway. Divergent and convergent ability are positively correlated in general (Biggs, Fitzgerald & Atkinson 1971; Cropley 1966). Divergent ability seems to need a *threshold* of convergent ability for it to operate at all, approximately an IQ in the region of 115, or over one standard deviation above the mean (Yamamoto 1965). This is reasonable; divergent responses have still to be relevant, not bizarre or random.

Divergent ability and creativity

The description of divergence as involving fluency, originality, flexibility, intelligence, wit and humour seems to be describing what many people would refer to as 'creativity' and, in fact, the terms 'divergent' and 'creative' were used interchangeably in earlier studies (e.g., Cropley 1967; Getzels & Jackson 1962; Torrance 1963). The terms should, however, be kept separate.

Divergence is a process which may be developed by all students.

The word 'creative' has strong value overtones, recalling the 'sixties, the heyday of creativity research. To be creative is to be: sensitive, artistic, unconventional, unhung-up, a Beautiful Person. Not to be creative is to be: rigid, hidebound, obsessive about rules, authoritarian, a Fascist Pig. All this and more, from patterns of test results. No, the terms divergent and convergent should not be used to label, but to refer to character-istics of thinking that all people display to some extent, in just the same way as all peo-ple are intelligent to some extent. It is impossible to imagine a person with no intelligence. It is almost impossible to imagine a person with no creativity (but not quite...).

Creativity refers to a particular product within a particular area such as painting, music, or mathematics; divergence is a process that applies across areas and is possessed to some extent by all students. Creativity has the following components:

1. Divergent thought. This may subdivide into at least flexibility, originality and fluency.
2. Convergent thought, to some threshold level. The person must be at least moder-ately bright in the normal (convergent) sense.
3. Total immersion in a particular area. Both 1 and 2 apply to general processes that are content-free. A creative *work*, however, is a particular product in an area in which the individual has considerable prior experience and expertise.

4. As a corollary of 3, the creative person is highly intrinsically motivated. Given expertise (which presupposes convergent ability), motivation, plus the bonus of divergent ability, *then* we might begin to talk about creativity.
5. Finally, the world plays a large part in defining whether or not a work is genuinely creative. Someone who was mad might do well in tests 1–4: unless there is the test of expert opinion, whatever that might be, we should still not label the work 'creative'. That test, however, is aesthetic, not psychological.

We must be careful not to confuse the process and the product. For example, training children in divergent thinking (process) *might* make it more likely that they will be creative (product) later on, but not necessarily. Thus, discovery methods are not useful because students are likely to make substantive discoveries. They are useful because the means used and the processes employed may be of value in developing the cognitive processes of the learner.

Cropley suggests that creativity and intelligence are not separate dimensions at all. Creativity he sees as 'a style of applying intelligence rather than as a separate entity' (1991: 269), which arrives at a solution to a problem divergently, by using intuition and by taking chances, rather than convergently, by reapplying the already learned. He thus proposes that intelligence itself can be enhanced by requiring people to exercise their divergent cognitive processes.

Divergent abilities in the classroom

Most subjects at school are taught and evaluated in a convergent manner, with emphasis on mastery of existing skills and knowledge, with correct application of known rules and with evaluation emphasising the one–correct–answer principle. Yet divergent ability contributes to achievement in school, on top of the contribution from convergent ability or IQ, which is quite in keeping with Cropley's view of divergence as one way of being intelligent.

Getzels and Jackson's 'high intelligent' children were over 20 IQ points higher than the 'high creatives', yet the overall performance in school of these groups was the same; and remember, the IQ test was deliberately designed to predict performance in school. Divergers appear to be 'over-achievers', doing better academically than their IQ would lead one to expect. Rather than being freaks filled beyond their capacity, they 'over-perform' with wondrous ease. The contribution of divergent ability to school achievement is higher in verbal than in mathematical subjects (Torrance 1960), and greater in more permissive schools (Haddon & Lytton 1968, 1971; Hasan & Butcher 1966).

The higher the academic ladder, the more important divergent abilities seem to become (Wallach & Wing 1969). University students specialising in arts score relatively higher on divergent than on convergent tests; those specialising in science are more convergently biased, with subjects such as languages falling somewhere in between (Cropley & Field 1968; Field & Poole 1970; Hudson 1966; Mackay & Cameron 1968). Divergence, but not convergence, relates to the following extracurricular activities: leadership of student societies, art interests, social service, writing and science (Wallach & Wing 1969). Convergent test results relate only to formal grades, while divergence relates both to formal grades *and* to activities pursued out of interest—even in science, where the activity itself may require convergent thought.

The full power of divergent thinking is more likely to emerge at the end of undergraduate, and during graduate, days. Many high divergers who were so-so in their first year at university, emerged finally as significantly ahead of very able convergers who had actually outperformed them early in first year (Hudson 1966). This is easy to understand. The undergraduate years in many science subjects tend to be a matter of mastering existing content, of getting it right. In higher and postgraduate years, one is required to query experiments and ask open-ended questions such as 'How can I design an experiment that will control these factors?' In the case of genuine research these are divergent questions. Nobody has done it before; there are no single right answers.

Divergent methods of evaluation

Measures that emphasise divergent ability have an open-ended format: for example, 'Think of as many —— as you can', the blank being filled as appropriate to the subject. The blank might refer to maths (ways of building a garage for $5000 given a materials price list), English (synonyms or antonyms for supplied words), or science (factors to control in a given experiment; things that might happen if water froze at -5°) and so on. The responses can be scored according to fluency, flexibility or originality, although busy classroom teachers might find it convenient to score only according to the total number of responses (fluency). The general strategy is that the one-correct-answer restriction be removed so that students are free to structure their responses.

Very little work has been done on the reliability and validity of these techniques. Usually they have been used for the purpose of assessing divergence in general, not for allowing divergers to express themselves comfortably in given content areas, which is what educational evaluation is concerned with. There is much potential for divergently oriented assessment in the classroom. The positive backwash effects on teaching technique and student contact could be considerable (see Chapter 14).

It should not be assumed, however, that essay methods of assessment, being open-end (at least in theory), necessarily favour divergers. Biggs (1973b) found that while students who did relatively well on objective tests had convergent characteristics, those who did relatively well on essays were not all happy little divergers. It depended on the kind of question asked and on what the marker of the essay valued. Too frequently, essay marks are awarded according to the fit of the essay to a model answer in the marker's head, marks being awarded for each fit correctly listed: witness Merelyn.

Student–teacher interaction

Given the humour and playfulness, yet good attainment, of the high diverger, one might think that divergers would in general be popular with teachers. But consider the following exchange:

> *Teacher:* And now can anyone tell me what infinity means? *(Silence)* What is infinity?
> *Billy:* Uh. I think it's like a box of Creamed Wheat.
> *Teacher:* Billy, don't be silly. (Jones 1968: 72)

Many studies have found that high divergers tend *not* to be liked by their teachers. Teachers tend to rate achievement, persistence and leadership as the most valued qualities in students, a picture not of the creative person but of the conventional conformist (Holland 1959). High divergers tend to be rated as 'undesirable' students to have in class, despite the fact that their actual attainment is as good as and often better than that of high IQ students, yet only the latter are regarded as 'highly desirable' (Getzels & Jackson 1962; Hasan & Butcher 1966; Torrance 1963). In fact, the

Box 7.3 *What creative students see as desirable qualities in teachers*

'They need patience, that's for sure. I guess they would have to have a very creative mind and an ability to judge because for a teacher to go home and mark 32 pieces of writing is not the thing that most people would want to do. So they've got to be able to judge whether it's good, but they've got to keep an open mind about it because they can't just say—well that piece of writing it's no good because ... it's written in some other form than everybody else's.' (Student 8, M, Yr 9)

'... my teacher last year used to always read out my writing because he thought it was good, and that really made me mad ... I didn't mind it when it was fiction but when it was something that said my feelings about something I didn't like that ... He didn't have any right to tell everyone in the world how I felt ...' (Student 12, F, Yr 8)

'Someone who can persuade other people to express themselves, someone who can, yes, bring out the creativity in the kids. Because I think probably everyone's got creativity they don't use, and I think it's how good the teacher is that they can show that creativity to the person and persuade them to use it.' (Student 34, F, Yr 11)

'... The ultimate thing ... is the ability and the willingness to sit down and talk to students, because you find some English teachers (they're in a minority, thank God) aren't willing to talk to their students on a level ... you get people who talk down ... which is the worst thing possible for the writing of English because you need to be able to discuss things absolutely straight.' (Student 35, F, Yr 11)

The quality most mentioned by students (15 responses; 43%) was that English teachers more than anything else should be 'tolerant', 'fair' or accepting of individual points of view, styles and opinions.

'It's so important to know that whatever you say will be listened to and considered. I think an English teacher should be willing to put aside their own point of view and consider somebody else's point of view solely on its own merits.' (Student 35, F, Yr 11)

'Just being cheerful and fairly funny, or doing little things that probably other teachers wouldn't do ...' (Student 5, F, Yr 8)

'Being able to be different—all maths teachers are the same and all science teachers are the same—but all English teachers are different—they've got their own character and personality ...' (Student 28, M, Yr 11)

Source: O'Neill & Reid 1985, pp. 131–3.

non-conforming, divergent student is regarded as a threat to the established order, rather than as clever and amusing and good to have around.

It is understandable that teachers should react in this way. Divergers are likely to raise issues and possibilities that may not occur to anyone else in the class (including the teacher) and thus to upset the lesson if their comments and suggestions are taken seriously. They will lead the train of thought into directions that the teacher may not have anticipated. The teacher who is anxious to cover a set number of topics in a given time and in a given order is bound to be irritated by someone who would, if permitted, make this reasonable goal impossible.

Such a situation may be threatening to an insecure teacher. If apparently whacky comments are actually sound, the teacher has to be constantly on guard. Billy's Creamed Wheat answer is an excellent one; the packaging has a picture of a man holding a Creamed Wheat box, on which there is depicted a man holding a Creamed Wheat box ... The point of many such remarks may not be seen immediately. While they *might* happen to be good ones on reflection (or might not), a time-effective (and face-effective) strategy for the teacher is to dismiss them as insolent or foolish. The high diverger may thus become typecast as the class nuisance, the class clown, or both. Torrance (1965) describes a case of a boy who was regarded by his parents and pediatrician as gifted, but whose teacher classified as retarded; he did not accept the tasks he was assigned and was continually awarded failing grades. As for what creative students think of teachers, see Box 7.3.

Divergence, then, leads to behaviours that may be seen as undesirable: even, as Torrance pointed out, to confusion with mental retardation Such labelling can easily become a self-fulfilling prophecy. If a teacher does decide that highly divergent Liza is a rebellious and evil-minded little girl, Liza may behave in keeping with those expectations. So next time the teacher tells the class to draw a human head and Bart inquires: 'From the inside or the outside, Miss?' (Cropley 1967), consider the possibility that he is asking a genuine question. Then kill him.

In a large-scale survey of British teachers, those who are themselves oriented to creativity in their teaching see 'deepening pupils' understanding of their world' as highly important and, not surprisingly, prefer student-oriented teaching methods; creative teaching was seen mainly to be important in the creative arts, rarely in science amd mathematics teaching (unlike in the USA) (Fryer & Collings 1991). Fryer and Collings see the connection between creativity orientation and teaching preference through the teachers' value systems; you have to be a certain sort of person to want to teach for creativity.

Do convergent children work better with a convergent teacher and divergent children with a divergent teacher? Yamamoto (1963) showed that they did. He matched low divergent children with low divergent teachers and high divergent children with high divergent teachers, and deliberately mismatched low divergent with high divergent, finding that (with IQ held constant) matched students and teachers did better than mismatched on Grade 5 arithmetic. It seems that the divergent-teacher/ divergent-student match meant that the teachers and students were all on the same wavelength, which facilitated the educational process.

However, this raises the important question as to whether this kind of match is in the long term the most *desirable* one. Perhaps divergent children should be exposed to other people who are convergent; they certainly will be when they leave school. And similarly, should not convergent children acquire tolerance for divergent behaviours and perhaps even become more flexible and spontaneous themselves? There is little research reported that speaks directly to this question, so the issue of who to match with whom remains at this stage rather a matter of opinion and one's views on the function of schooling: to maximise achievement, or to experience and be modified by diversity.

Training in divergent and convergent abilities

We have seen that home background has a major effect on divergence in children. What evidence is there that school has any such effect?

First, one needs to be careful about measuring the effects of change. Hudson (1968), for example, showed that scores on the Uses Test could be boosted simply by telling students to be as 'original' as possible. He also achieved the same effect by pretending to throw a tantrum while administering the test. It is easy to train students to be more divergent on one kind of test, to find that there is no transfer to other kinds of divergence test (Anderson & Anderson 1963). Effects need therefore to be shown across a variety of tests and conditions.

Divergent thinking seems to be affected by the nature of the school environment. Torrance (1961) classified the teachers in a primary school as being basically 'creativity-motivated' or 'power-motivated' in their teaching. The first group emphasised flexibility in problem solving, were keen to have children produce their own solutions and so on; the second emphasised adherence to rules, firm discipline and had no tolerance for distracting or time-wasting questions. He found that at kindergarten and Grades 1–3 divergence increased in the children taught by the 'creativity-motivated' teachers, but decreased in the 'power-taught' children.

Does a highly formal, authoritarian classroom inhibit divergent productions, an informal, warm, classroom climate permitting children to express divergence? Haddon and Lytton (1968, 1971) set out to find out in several formal and informal primary schools; and four years later, followed up 200 students from their original sample now in secondary school. They found:

- strong evidence for the threshold effect; divergence was most evident in those students who scored high on a convergent test of verbal ability.
- after allowing for verbal ability, the most important factor accounting for current divergent thinking was whether the *primary* school attended was formal or informal; the effect of the current secondary school was negligible.

Haddon and Lytton concluded that schools fail to develop divergent thinking abilities in the most able and promising students, and that primary school has a much more important role in this than secondary. School does not appear to *make* children divergent so much as allow them either to manifest their existing divergence, or to suppress it.

Several teaching practices appear to inhibit divergent abilities (Cropley 1967):

1. *Emphasis upon being right*. Naturally enough, where insistence is upon one correct answer, divergent children are not capitalising on their abilities.

2. *External evaluation*. 'Being right' implies an external criterion of truth (i.e., what the teacher or the textbook lays down as truth). Such an approach encourages the learner to adopt a pawn-like stance which is inimical to personal involvement and the development of intrinsic motivation (see pp. 270–1). It is likely that excessive reliance on external sources of truth will make it more difficult to cope later when such sources do not exist.

3. *Impatience with wasting time*. When teachers are anxious to get on with the lesson and to cover the set curriculum, they will be disinclined to allow time to follow up novel suggestions or interpretations by the high divergers. Some of these may be worth fol-

lowing up, others may not; but if they are not pursued the diverger will increasingly be discouraged. It is a short step from there to sabotage, or to the role of class clown.

4. *Conformity pressures.* One major attribute of divergent thought is originality, a tendency which is obviously discouraged where there are strong pressures to conform to the established standards.

5. *Distinction between work and play.* Another notable characteristic of divergent thought is humour, wit and playfulness. If work is maintained as solid and serious, with play treated as a separate area where frivolity is permitted ('All right Class, settle down. Joke over'), the play–work mix so characteristic of divergent thinking will not happen.

Every teacher can reflect on that list and decide what to do about it. More positively, Torrance (1965) believed that the teacher can do more than simply avoid inhibiting divergence. 'Guided self-evaluation' embodies a cognitive *acceptance* of the child's efforts and an affective *approval* of them. When children offer solutions to problems or write stories, teachers would not dismiss them out of hand or vigorously correct them, even if they can see glaring faults. Rather, they welcome the fact that the child has tried, praise the effort and then turn the evaluation itself back onto the child (hence the term guided self-evaluation): 'Do *you* think this would work? ... Are there other ways you can think of that might improve your idea? ... Try it out and see what happens ...' Torrance and Myers (1970) list several practices that help produce divergent responses (see Learning Activity No. 4 at end of this chapter).

There is, then, clear evidence that schools affect the expression of divergence and that the major effect is in the primary grades rather than in high school (which is not to say that high school teachers need not worry about de-inhibiting divergence). A student brought up to believe that every question has a correct answer—whether about maths, the nature of the universe, or the choice of a spouse—may find it unsettling to land in a class where these ideas and the values behind them are open to question.

Brainstorming is one way of bringing home the message that ideas are free and that their 'correctness' is relative. Divergent teachers would no doubt find it easy to think up their own flexibility exercises. Cropley (1991) lists several studies where creativity in everyday settings has rubbed off in some measurable way. These settings include: cognitive games, craft projects, sports coaching and playing jazz. One famous physicist developed a technique for improving his tolerance for novel ideas, by writing on cards as many physical principles as he could think of—one per card—and placing the cards in a goldfish bowl by his front door. When he left for work each morning, he would shake the bowl, extract three cards at random and spend the first hour of the morning thinking up ways in which the three principles could be interrelated. What could you do to improve your creative potential?

Cognitive styles

We have seen that Cropley (1991) referred to creativity as a 'style': a consistent way of handling problems. Creativity isn't the only such style: there are probably several dozen reported in the literature somewhere. Cognitive style research again is one of those areas that was once thought to have great potential for education.

Cognitive styles reflect consistent individual differences in the way people perceive the world, conceptualise meanings, learn a range of tasks or solve problems (Gardner, Holzman, Klein, Linton & Spence 1959). People are classified as 'high' or 'low' on the style according to their performance in a given task or test; highs and lows are then compared on how they handle other situations, especially educational ones. Although much of the work on divergence was of this pattern, divergence is regarded as a process *ability*, and cognitive style research attempted to use tasks and tests that tended not to correlate with ability (Kogan 1971).

Many studies have been conducted along these lines. The following is a brief overview of some of the more common findings.

Field dependence–independence

Field-dependent individuals are unable to separate relevant from compellingly irrelevant cues in perceptual tasks, such as perceiving a geometrical figure embedded in a complex background (the Embedded Figures Test, familiar in various versions in Sunday papers), or judging verticality when seated in a tilted chair (Witkin, Moore, Goodenough & Cox 1977). Field-dependent people perform poorly in low structured or informal classrooms compared to field-independent, but are more socially competent.

Reflection–impulsivity

This style contrasts slow and accurate scanning of information (reflection) with rapid and inaccurate scanning (impulsivity) (Kagan 1966). This diagnosis is made on the basis of the Matching Familiar Figures test, versions of which are likewise familiar in the Sunday papers, where the game is to spot the one figure in an array of several very similar ones that matches a criterion figure. Children who are good at this test (reflective) tend to be better readers than impulsive children of the same IQ (Kagan 1965).

Cognitive complexity

Cognitive complexity (Harvey, Hunt and Schroder 1961) is based on Kelly's (1955) theory of personal constructs, which refers to the number of dimensions people use to make judgments. People who are cognitively simple use one or few dimensions to make a decision; the cognitively complex use several. Unfortunately, the decisions of the cognitively simple are made rapidly, with little reflection and with huge authority; those of the cognitively complex are made slowly, analysing the issue from many angles and with a willingness to re-examine. The former therefore beat the latter hands down when it comes to practical politics; they tend therefore to become leaders of political parties and, in academe, senior administrators. The leaders tend therefore to be cognitively simpler than the led (see Box 11.1).

Hunt (1971) later produced a variation he called 'conceptual level', which he used to match students with classroom environments; high complexity students doing better in low structure classrooms and low complexity in formal, authoritarian classrooms (again see Box 11.1).

There has been much work on these and many other styles, and all can be shown to have some relevance to education, some more so than others. However, cognitive styles proliferated to such an extent that anyone who wished to 'discover' a new cognitive style devised an interestingly different test situation to operationally define the style. They then compared high and low scorers on the test on whatever they could think of to find in what other ways they might happen to differ from each other. In 1971, one of the authors attempted to review the cognitive style literature, thence to draw educational implications. He reached 18 different styles and added another 8 or so when Kogan's (1971) review appeared. After this, the reviewing ended; there had to be a better way of looking at individual differences.

Learning style is another, closely related concept described by Kolb (1976) as a permanent personality characteristic or trait that is displayed over a range of tasks and situations; its origins lie in an individual's psychodynamic history rather than in academic contexts. A different meaning of style is that of a *preference* for verbal or visual data, which correlates differentially with verbal and spatial abilities (Kirby, Moore & Schofield 1988).

One helpful conclusion comes from the otherwise confusing style literature; learning outcomes are determined by more than general intelligence or even specific abilities. In other words, the *way* one goes about a task is an important consideration, on top of the sheer power or speed with which one tackles the task. Indeed, this notion is at the centre of much recent research into student learning and we examine it in detail in Chapter 12. There we see that a student's *approach* to learning, as it is called, is a resolution of several factors, both personal to the student and built in both to the teaching context and to the task in question. An approach is not so much an individual difference variable, then, as a resolution between individual differences, goals, task knowledge and the teaching/learning context itself. Styles oversimplify what is going on and, because there are so many of them, they simultaneously complicate things.

Special educational needs

We have dwelt so far in this chapter on the nature of abilities and processes that might be used to define exceptionality, in either direction. We now turn to the question of providing for those whose educational needs are 'special', either because they are supremely gifted or, more commonly, because their exceptionality is in some sense handicapping. Why do teachers need to be aware of the range of 'exceptionalities'? What can teachers do to develop the full potential of students who are exceptional?

Our intention here can only be to raise your level of awareness of these issues, not to provide in-depth analyses of children with special needs, the exceptional students. Recent works by Butler (1990), Ashman and Elkins (1990), and particularly Cole and Chan (1990) deal with these issues more comprehensively. In translating theory to practice and providing teaching methods and strategies, again we draw attention to Cole and Chan (1990). They discuss a wide variety of teaching methods and strategies from behavioural, mastery, process, cognitive and metacognitive approaches to peer tutoring, cooperative learning and applications of computers to special education.

First, let us deal with giftedness.

Giftedness

The clear definition of giftedness has proven to be an elusive and challenging task. While the layperson's view of gifted individuals might be reflected in terms such as 'more intelligent', 'brighter', 'smarter' or 'sharper', theorists continue to debate the nature of giftedness.

The earlier pioneering studies of intellectual giftedness (e.g., Terman 1925) used Stanford-Binet Intelligence test scores, whereas more recently we find giftedness defined as multi-dimensional incorporating above average general intelligence, extremely high degrees of task commitment, and creativity (Renzulli 1986). Sternberg's (1985) triarchic theory also offers insight into the nature of giftedness. According to Sternberg there

What can teachers do for the gifted student?

are three main foci of intellectual giftedness: in analytical abilities, in synthetic abilities, and the ability to apply analytical and synthetic abilities to practical problems. In these terms giftedness is typified by more of the lower level processes running 'automatically', the effective operation of superior metacomponential skills (such as indentifying the problem, planning how to attack the problem, monitoring the success of the strategy) and superior ability to use the knowledge one has about a topic (Shaughnessy 1990).

Is giftedness an all-pervasive phenomenon? If students are gifted in one intellectual domain are they gifted in others? Not according to Gardner with his seven frames of mind, but it partly depends how you define giftedness. If a measure of general intelligence is used (say an IQ over 130), they would tend to be gifted in several areas, as Terman found. However, if we look at Gardner's autonomous intelligences, students gifted in one domain (e.g., logico-mathematical) are not particularly gifted in others (Colangelo & Kerr 1990).

While the problem of defining giftedness will probably be with us for some time, the more pressing problem for teachers is how best to develop the potential of such students in our schools. In Australia, state Education Departments have recognised this challenge and produced policy statements in support of gifted and talented students. For instance, in New South Wales the *General Policy Statement for Students with Special Talents* (School Manual on Educational Management 1988) emphasises the role of individual school policies with respect to the curriculum, the teacher, parents, and the community. Such policy statements stress that giftedness and talents be identified as early as possible and special provision be made, within the constraints of resources available to the school, so that special talents can be fully developed.

For the gifted in Australia there are a variety of forms of curriculum provision: enrichment, cluster groups (a number of schools combine to offer a special program at a centre), special classes/groups, special interest secondary centres, acceleration, and mentor programs (Braggett 1985). Acceleration is an option that seems to be gaining attention from educational authorities. In some Australian states there are moves to encourage individual progression and the completion of the set syllabus in a shorter period of time for those who are gifted.

The teaching of the gifted is more fully developed in Davis and Rimm (1985) and Gallagher (1985).

Impairment, disability and handicap

We now need to clarify the other end of the scale. Impairment, disability, and handicap are key words in this context. The World Health Organisation's (1980) classification is helpful:

• *Impairment* is a loss or abnormality of psychological or physiological structure or system function which represents disturbances at the organ level.
• *Disability* is a lack of ability (resulting from an impairment) to perform within the range considered normal for humans.
• *Handicap* is a disadvantage experienced by the individual resulting from an impairment and/or disability that restricts the fulfilment of a role.

Whether or not a disability becomes a handicap depends upon many things including the nature of the disability, the nature or demands of the environment in which the individual is placed, the confidence of the individual and societal attitudes (Hickson 1990). An individual may have an impairment but whether it constitutes a disability, which in turn may lead to a handicap, depends upon the particular environment.

Exceptionality thus encompasses a wide range of abilities and disabilities associated with giftedness, mild, moderate, severe or profound intellectual disabilities, specific learning disabilities (e.g., in mathematics or reading), and emotional and behavioural disorders that impact upon abilities being fully realised. Consideration also needs to be given to the effects on cognitive development of physical disabilities and visual, hearing, and speech impairments.

Intellectual disabilities

Intellectual disabilities, specific learning disabilities, physical disabilities, and behaviour disorders are not necessarily mutually exclusive categories. The term *intellectual disability* describes individuals who do not have the complete range of abilities seen as necessary for functioning in society. Earlier definitions of intellectual disability focused solely upon the IQ. Individuals with mild-to-moderate intellectual disabilities typically scored more than two standard deviations below the mean on a IQ test (a score of 69 on the Stanford–Binet Test). In a similar way individuals with severe-and-profound intellectual disabilities scored less than 30. However, over the last twenty years, two criteria have become important in defining intellectual disabilities: intelligence (as discussed above) and adaptive behaviour (Kramer, Piersel & Glover 1988). Individuals may score low on an intelligence test but be able to adapt adequately to their environment in terms of their ability, for example, to help themselves, to effectively communicate, and to socialise with others.

As it is likely that students with such severe disabilities would be in special classes within regular schools, we will leave discussion of such students to more specialised texts (e.g., Butler 1990) and focus on mild-to-moderate disabilities.

The student with mild-to-moderate intellectual disabilities is likely to exhibit lower levels of intellectual functioning and adaptive behaviour, a general lack of learning strategies, generally lower rates of skill acquisition, and also a lack of ability to transfer or generalise what has been learned in one context to another. We can turn to several traditions of research to explain the disabilities.

Information processing perspectives (e.g., Hunt 1978; the terms referred to below are elaborated in Chapter 8) suggest that sensory register size is typically smaller and duration may be shorter in those with intellectual disabilities. Further, the capacity of working memory, speed of information manipulation, access to long-term memory and executive control operations (metacognition) are inferior in students with mild/moderate intellectual disabilities when compared to their non-disabled peers (Kramer, Piersel & Glover 1988).

Information Integration theory, described in Chapter 6, helps us understand the nature of intellectual disabilities. Low levels of simultaneous and successive processing abilities have been reported in those with mild intellectual disabilities (Kaufman & Kaufman 1983) and such children may spontaneously select modes of processsing (simultaneous, successive) not appropriate to the particular task being undertaken (Kirby & Williams 1991; Robinson & Kirby 1987).

Specific learning disabilities

Specific learning disabilities, or 'learning problems' as Kirby and Williams (1991) call them, include a range of disorders related to failures in school which cannot be attributed to general low levels of ability. While the distinguishing characteristic of students with mild intellectual disabilities is this low level of ability across many measures of intellectual functioning, the student with specific learning disabilities is sometimes characterised by an uneven pattern of abilities as well as discrepancies between their expected potential and actual school achievement. What is clear, though, from the literature on specific learning disabilities is that there are problems in 'bolting down' the concept. Indeed, there has been a proliferation of conceptualisations and definitions of the phenomenon leading to a current focus on three process-oriented deficits: visual perceptual/perceptual motor, linguistic and auditory, and mixed perceptual/linguistic deficits (McKinney 1988).

For teachers, an understanding of the effects of specific learning disabilities on reading and mathematics achievement is important. To gain some flavour of the problems in reading, 'retarded' readers seem to rely too much on simultaneous processing in the early stages of reading whereas 'normal' readers employ sequential or successive processing to greater benefit (Robinson & Kirby 1987). This inappropriate processing may be due to deficits in the skills of successive processing, the lack of successive strategies or a combination of both. (One of the learning activities for chapter 6 is based on Robinson and Kirby's research.)

Teaching methods and strategies for those with specific learning disabilities are discussed at length in Cole and Chan (1990), Chan (1991) and van Kraayenoord and Elkins (1990), while Kirby and Williams (1991) provide an excellent conceptual framework for understanding the problems some children have with learning, which adds considerably to the teacher's power in diagnosing and handling such problems.

Physical disabilities, visual and hearing impairments

In the context of abilities and disabilities teachers also need to be aware of the effects of physical disabilities (e.g., cerebral palsy) and visual and hearing impairments on abilities and school performance.

The term *physical disabilities* encompasses a wide range of disorders that may or may not influence cognitive abilities and subsequent performance. Conditions such as cerebral palsy, muscular dystrophy, spina bifida, epilepsy and injuries to the head or spine through accidents are recognised for their likely effects upon development. For instance, cerebral palsy is often associated with mild intellectual disability and it may be associated with speech impairments and other disorders (e.g., visual and hearing). Other conditions such as bowel disorders due to malfunctioning of the large intestine are not likely to directly influence abilities, although they may influence affective personal variables such as self-confidence. For further information on physical disabilities we suggest you refer to Butler (1990).

Impairments in vision and hearing also vary in their degree and age of onset, and these two factors play a large part in determining the magnitude of the effects on abilities. In vision the range is from total blindness to presbyopia (the need in middle age for reading glasses). For the totally blind, the lack of visual representations of the world seems to delay the development of concepts and cognitive operations such as conservation and classification (Warren 1989).

Let us now turn to hearing. If impairment is extreme to profound and the onset of the problem was before the child was 2 to 3 years old, language acquisition is significantly delayed. It is not surprising that such delays influence performance in literacy tasks where linguistic abilities are required. An 18 year old who became profoundly deaf before the age of 2 or 3 tends to read and write at a Grade 3 or 4 level (Quigley & Paul 1989). A range of teaching approaches have been adapted for those with hearing impairments and these include total communication, which combines oral, aural and manual modes of learning and instruction (Lowenbraun & Thompson 1989). Linguistic abilities may also be enhanced by the use of various hearing aids and cochlear implants.

Behaviour disorders

Behaviour disorders are major concerns for the typical teacher. If you think back on your own school career you can probably remember the persistent attention seeker, the hyperactive, impulsive student who just would not sit down, and the aggressive, bullying student. Equally, you can probably remember the frustration of the teachers as they attempted to manage these students. There is a wide diversity of behaviour disorders from the mild to the severe, the latter often associated with emotional disturbances and requiring placement in special educational settings where both health and educational professionals work hand-in-hand (Conway 1990).

Four major clusters of traits are related to behaviour disorders: conduct, anxiety–withdrawal, socialised aggression, and maturity traits (Quay 1979). Students with conduct disorders are likely to show restlessness, irritability, selfishness and destructiveness of their own as well as others' property. On the other hand, feelings of inferiority, anxiety, depression and general unhappiness seem to characterise those students in the anxiety–withdrawal cluster. Such students tend to be hypersensitive and shy. Socialised aggression may be characterised by stealing, especially in the company of others (perhaps gang members) and persistent truanting from home and school. The fourth behavioural dimension, immaturity, is characterised by problems with attention span and concentration, daydreaming, and clumsiness which may in turn lead to very untidy school work (Quay 1979).

Mainstreaming and integration

Mainstreaming and *integration* refer to policies of educating students with disabilities and their regular school peers together rather than having those with disabilities being segregated in separate institutions or sections of institutions. The term 'mainstreaming' has its origins in North America while 'integration' emerged from the United Kingdom. Both concepts imply more than mere physical presence of students with disabilities in regular classes. As Cole and Chan (1990) note, integration aims to develop positive social relationships among all students and it also aims to provide each individual, irrespective of disabilities, access to a common instructional program.

Integration does not mean, however, that all students with disabilities will be in regular classrooms for the full duration of their schooling. According to the concept of the 'least restrictive environment', best understood by reference to the 'cascade' model of

---

Box 7.4 *Extract from New South Wales Department of Education's integration statement*

Policy
It is the policy of the Government of New South Wales that people with disabilities should be able to live and be educated within their own communities. This policy is based on the principle of 'normalisation', that is the creation of a lifestyle and set of living conditions for people with disabilities which are as close as possible to those enjoyed by the rest of the population.

The regular school environment has been found to be advantageous for many students who are disabled. A secondary benefit will be that the school community will learn about disabilities and develop a greater acceptance of diversity and, in particular, a greater acceptance of people who are disabled.

Implementation

The Department of Education will promote this policy by making educational placements for students with disabilities in the regular neighbourhood school when this is possible and practicable and in the best interests of the student.

The Department has been moving and will continue to move from the provision of predominantly segregated educational settings to the provision of services in the regular neighbourhood school for students with disabilities. This is being achieved by:

1. the provision of services to support students with disabilities in the regular classroom; and
2. the provision of support classes in regular schools where students with disabilities can receive appropriate educational support while experiencing the daily activities of their local community peer group.

Parents are encouraged to consider the neighbourhood school as an enrolment option for their child. The needs of the child will be assessed by Departmental and school personnel in consultation with the parents to ascertain the appropriateness of enrolment in a regular class. These principles are embodied in the policy on Enrolment of Children with Disabilities.

Parents have the right of appeal to the Regional Director regarding any placement decision and ultimately to the Director-General of Education.

Where an optimal educational environment cannot be provided for the student in a mainstream class, the parents will be offered an alternative placement in a support class in a regular school or a school for specific purposes.

When students with disabilities are placed in regular schools with support classes or in schools for specific purposes, the principal will ensure that the curriculum is organised to develop in each student as much independence and integration into the community as is possible.

The principal of a regular school with a support class will involve the students, their teachers and their parents as members of the total school community to the maximum extent possible. Regular school programs will reflect this commitment to integration.

The principal of a school for specific purposes will design activities to promote interaction with non-disabled students, especially similar age peers. Such activities will need to be developed in cooperation with neighbouring regular schools and community groups.

Source: New South Wales Department of Education (1988). School Manual on Educational Management.

service delivery (Reynolds 1976), there are six levels of management: in the regular classroom; in the regular classroom with counselling advice; in the regular classroom with specialist advice; in the regular classroom with withdrawal; in full-time or part-time specialist classes; in residential schools with health and community services involved as well. The least restrictive environment would be the level at which the student, would receive a program commensurate with and challenging to, their abilities and skills in a context where positive associations with regular class students could be developed.

Integration then can be full or partial dependent upon individual needs and of course at the practical level, the availability of appropriate support services. Departments of Education in Australia and New Zealand have developed integration policies that reflect various philosophical and educational perspectives and, while there is diversity, there are many common features. Cole and Chan (1990) identify five common threads: assessment of personal and academic needs, access to regular class programs, provision of a range of educational services and programs, provision of appropriate quality educational services, and personal and professional advocacy of the rights of special needs students and their parents. (Box 7.4 shows extracts from the New South Wales Department of Education's Integration Statement.)

Summary

Who are exceptional children?

Exceptional children are defined as those at either end of intellectual abilities or other dimension (such as physical disability) who need special education. We concentrate in this chapter on clarifying two main kinds of ability, convergent and divergent. We then look at provision for those with special needs.

Convergent and divergent abilities

The ability to get it right, convergent ability, which underlies most IQ-type items, is not the only one that teachers should understand. Divergent thinking generates rather than eliminates alternatives; it comprises fluency, flexibility and originality, processes underlying what we mean by creativity. Divergence seems to have little to do with inheritance, except that high divergers do have to be clever at convergent thinking as well as have a risk-taking personality and background.

Divergent abilities in the classroom

Teachers tend to loathe high divergers. Although they do better in school than their IQ would lead you to expect, divergers like to be funny, to ask what seem to be irrelevant questions, and to do their own thing: all of which is tough on carefully prepared lesson plans. Yet the official aims of education often emphasise the sorts of bright, creative, autonomous things that divergers do. No wonder teachers loathe them.

Cognitive styles

Cognitive styles are consistent ways of handling information that would seem to have important educational implications. Actually, so many different ones have been reported that they are a pest; the teacher is simply overwhelmed with information, unlike in ability itself, which suggests quite clear cut things to do, such as to stream or not to stream.

Special educational needs

It is also important for teachers to be aware of and understand exceptionality in abilities and disabilities. In a period where mainstreaming, integration and least restrictive environments are government policy, more teachers will be working with children with some form of disability. Exceptionality is diverse, as we have seen, covering giftedness, mild, moderate, severe or profound intellectual disabilities, specific learning disabilities, and emotional and behavioural disorders. The challenge for the teacher is to accommodate such diversity by using a range of approaches to teaching. The challenge for the system is to provide sufficient support services.

Learning activities

1. Giftedness

The aim of this activity is to examine the policy documents in your state regarding gifted children. Do such documents exist? Is the focus on schools developing special provision? Are there special classes, schools for the gifted? How are the gifted identified? If it were possible to gather information from different states, comparisons could be made.

2. Mainstreaming and integration

This activity is very similar to the preceding one but the focus is on policy documents related to integration and mainstreaming. Similar questions to those asked of giftedness policy statements could be pursued. Indeed, it might prove fruitful to combine Activity 1 and 2 to get a general feel for policies regarding exceptionality.

3. Creative teaching

The work of Torrance and Myers (1970) was discussed in an earlier part of this chapter (p. 187). In their studies of teaching contexts that encouraged divergent or 'creative' responses from the students, they identified a number of factors. The major factors are shown below (from Torrance & Myers, 1970: 35).

Item	You	Teacher
• Recognising some heretofore unrecognised potential		
• Respecting a child's need to work alone		
• Inhibiting the teacher's censorship role long enough to permit a creative response		
• Allowing or encouraging a child to go ahead and achieve success in an area of interest		
• Permitting the curriculum to be different for different children		
• Giving concrete embodiment to the creative ideas of children		
• Giving a chance to develop responsibility		
• Encouraging deep involvement and permitting self-initiated projects		
• Reducing pressure, providing a relatively non-punitive environment		
• Approving the pupil's work in one area to provide courage to try the others		
• Voicing the beauty of individual differences		
• Respecting the potential of low achievers		
• Showing enthusiasm for pupil ideas		
• Supporting the pupil against peer pressure to conform		
• Placing an unproductive child in contact with a productive, creative child		
• Using fantasy ability to establish contacts with reality		
• Capitalising on hobbies, special interests and enthusiasms		
• Tolerating complexity and disorder, at least for a period		
• Permitting oneself to become involved with pupils		
• Communicating that the teacher is 'for' rather than 'against' the child		
• Giving stimulating or provocative examinations		

Consider the list from Torrance and Myers and select the *five* factors that YOU think are the most important for 'creative' teaching. Mark these in the YOU column with a 1 for the one you think most important, a 2 for the next most important, etc. Why do you see these as more important than the others?

The next activity is to select *five* factors you would have most liked to see in your own teachers at high school or primary school. Use 1 for most like to see, etc. What difference do you think it would have made to your schooling if the teachers had adopted some of the factors you have identified?

If you do this with a small group of your colleagues or friends, see how much agreement there is in the group for the 'most' important ones. (You can do this by getting a tally for each factor across the group.) If this is done in class, each group might want to present its findings on a chart or overhead transparency.

In the above activity you will probably find little agreement. If this is the case, why? Is it all to do with individual differences?

4. Inhibiting divergent abilities

This task should pose a real challenge. You will need access to a video camera/recorder and a small group of your colleagues to teach in a five or six minute lesson. The topic can be of your own choosing.

The task is to teach the lesson in a manner that *inhibits* divergent abilities. Cropley (1966, see p. 186 in this chapter) suggests that there are five major practices that relate to divergence in the classroom: emphasis on being right, external evaluation, impatience with wasting time, conformity pressures, and distinction between work and play. Plan the lesson deliberately to demonstrate these practices and then have your presentation video-taped for presentation to the class. You could lead the class discussion on the negative effects of such practices.

Another possibility is to re-teach (and video) the lesson but this time focus on factors that do not inhibit divergent abilities. It could be interesting to compare the two presentations.

5. Mainstreaming and integration

In this activity we use Cole and Chan's (1990) *Methods and strategies for special education.* Their chapter on integration highlights six studies that we feel are worthy of closer examination. You will see from their book that these studies are concerned with:

- Integrating pre-school children with disabilities
  (Research Study 2.1)
- The integration of children with physical disabilities
  (Research Study 2.2)
- Teachers' attitudes toward the integration of students with disabilities into regular schools
  (Research Study 2.3)
- Parents' thoughts about integration
  (Research Study 2.4)
- Regular students' skills in dealing with severe disabilities
  (Research Study 2.5)
- What determines the success of integration
  (Research Study 2.6)

You could summarise the studies, or if done as class activity, individuals or groups could report the studies to the class. We suggest you go back to the original research after having read the synopses by Cole and Chan. Your opinions then will be informed by fact!

6. How much have you learned from this chapter?

Recent work by Fantuzzo, Riggio, Connelly and Dimeff (1989) shows that learning can be increased through a teaching–learning activity in which two students ask each other questions about the text they have been reading. You can take a section of the chapter or all of it and generate a set of main-idea type questions (say 10) that you then ask of a colleague. In turn, your colleague would also have generated a set of questions that you will be asked. Being able to generate a question, explain the answer to a question, and knowing whether your answer is appropriate or correct gives you an indication of how much you have learned.

Further reading

On creativity and giftedness
Cropley, A. J. (1967). *Creativity*. London: Longmans Green.
Cropley, A.J. (1991). Improving intelligence by fostering creativity. In H. A. H.Rowe (ed.), *Intelligence: Reconceptualization and Measurement* (pp. 267–80). Hillsdale, NJ: Lawrence Erlbaum.
Torrance, E. P. (1965). *Gifted Children in the Classroom*. New York: Macmillan.
Butler, S. (1990). *The Exceptional Child*. Sydney: Harcourt Brace Jovanovich.
Journal of Educational Psychology, 1990, **82**.

Research on creativity and divergence now seems outdated, which is a pity because it has a lot to offer educators: in educational aims, methods and assessment. Cropley's book represents the best of that tradition in a highly readable way; his chapter in Rowe's book deals with how that lack of imagination 'blocks' people's thinking power and what teachers might do about it. Torrance addresses teachers directly in a highly practical way. Butler's book has a chapter dealing with giftedness and two case studies show the issues in supporting and identifying the gifted. Eight research articles covering a range of topics on giftedness are waiting for you in the September 1990 edition of the *Journal of Educational Psychology*.

On special education
Cole, P. & Chan, L. K. S. (1990). *Methods and Strategies for Special Education*. Sydney: Prentice Hall.
Kirby, J. & Williams, N. (1991). *Learning Problems: A Cognitive Approach*. Toronto: Kagan & Woo.
Wang, M. C., Reynolds, M. C. & Walberg, H.J. (1987). *Handbook of Special Education: Research and Practice*. New York: Pergamon Press (3 volumes).
Williams, P. (1991). *The Special Education Handbook*. Milton Keynes: The Open University Press.
Cole and Chan's book, to which we have referred several times in Chapter 7, provides a comprehensive overview of much that a teacher would need to know about special education teaching. The chapter on integration is very useful. Kirby and Williams

is more restricted in that it deals only with specific learning disabilities, which they call 'learning problems'; the book is very clearly written, with a sound theory leading to clear action by teachers. Wang et al.'s three volumes contain the most comprehensive collection of recent research findings in special education. Williams' book is a basic reference for those with professional responsibilities in special education in A–Z form; perhaps too specialised for ordinary mainstream teachers, it is nevertheless very clearly written and should be accessible to all teachers, as some of the problems and issues listed will surely concern them at some stage.

COGNITIVE AND MOTIVATIONAL PROCESSES

CHAPTER 8

LEARNING
AND MEMORY

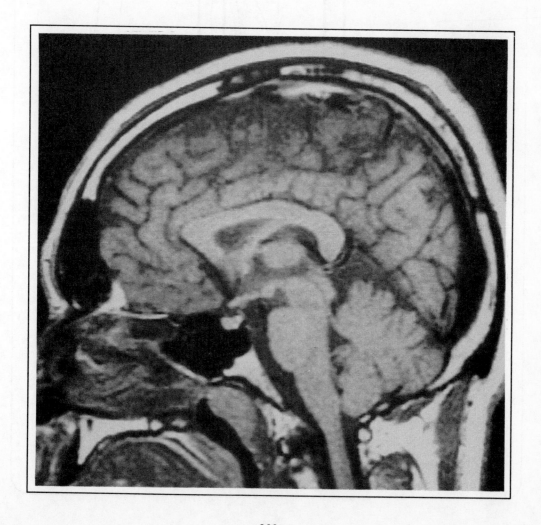

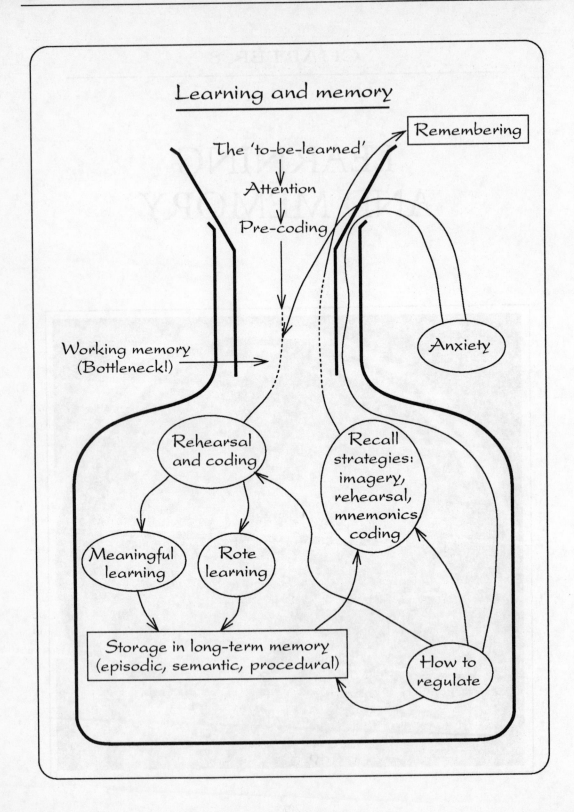

Learning and memory

Remembering

The 'to-be-learned'
↓
Attention
↓
Pre-coding

Working memory
(Bottleneck!)

Anxiety

Rehearsal
and coding

Recall
strategies:
imagery,
rehearsal,
mnemonics
coding

Meaningful
learning

Rote
learning

Storage in long-term memory
(episodic, semantic, procedural)

How to
regulate

LEARNING AND MEMORY

In this chapter, you will find out:

- how many things you can think about at a time;
- why we have to pay attention to selected aspects of our environment;
- how teachers can hold their students' attention;
- how working memory differs from long-term memory;
- how to beat the limits of working memory;
- what makes rote learning different from meaningful learning;
- some useful strategies for remembering meaningful material;
- how teachers may emphasise meaning in their teaching;
- some important factors in forgetting;
- how to use different modalities in teaching and learning.

What is learning?

What is learning? Learning is doing something differently as a result of experience and not because of physical growth, or of other changes in the 'hard wiring'. Putting your hand on a hot stove plate and withdrawing it rapidly is not learning. Not putting your on a hot stove plate ever again is. It may be very difficult to pinpoint any particular experience as crucial, unlike the hot plate example. What particular experiences led to the throat-tightening response to a particular piece of beautiful music?

How does learning differ from development? In Chapter 2 we referred to 'skill acquisition', what goes on within modes, as learning; 'optimal level', what goes on across modes, as development. But of course learning is involved in development; we don't cross modes unless some very important learning has taken place. And in turn development opens up our learning options.

What can we learn? We learn knowledge: *tacit,* which we can do but not verbalise; *intuitive,* which we can use to guide our mental processes but not justify; *declarative,* which we can tell others about, but not necessarily be able to use; *procedural,* which we can use to handle the world; *conditional,* which we can use to handle the world and ourselves. Our knowledge comes variously dressed up in sensori-motor skills, ikonic images, concrete-symbolic systems, or theories. Through learning we construct our experienced world.

How do we learn? We learn things sequentially, as if through a pipeline; we learn things simultaneously, as if through our skin. The first, pipeline or 'conduit', metaphor has been widely used in psychology: the commonly used terms, like 'storage' of learned data and their 'retrieval', suggest a pipeline access to the contents of learning. This metaphor is much used in everyday language: 'you got that idea from me', 'spoon-feeding', 'you must get your thoughts across better' (Iran-Nejad 1990). This metaphor for learning has a 'cold', logical, and sequential connotation, in which the contents of learning are treated as independent entities, packages in transit. It is only half the story; that half is dealt with in this chapter.

The other half refers to learning as 'constructive', 'simultaneous' and 'spontaneous': the simultaneous processing from all the modalities—sight, sound, touch, smell—into a coherent whole, combining context and affect. Learning to love music, learning about how we react to things, and how to control our learning are examples. Pipelines don't explain why we can learn the same thing easily in one context and with much more difficulty in another (Bereiter 1990; Brown, Collins & Duguid 1989), or why learners process information quite differently according to their interest in a task (Hidi 1990). That half of the story of learning is dealt with in Chapter 12.

Information-processing models of learning

Linear metaphors for learning, based on the one-way sequence if-this/then-that, have been around since psychology began. For many years, psychologists based their theories on studies with animals. Not surprisingly, learning seemed to be sensorimotor in nature: learning which stimuli went with what other stimuli, or learning which responses led to reward or not, which is not a bad way of describing what animals learn (but even so there are better ways). But restricting study to animals made it inevitable that psychologists concentrated on behaviour, not on thoughts or feelings. What they chose to see was what they got; their kind of psychology was called *behaviourism*. The environment was seen as sets of stimuli, behaviour as responses to those stimuli. Learning took place when new stimulus-response connections were set up, through a process called conditioning. Hill (1985) reviews different behavioural theories of learning, if you happen to be interested.

Behavioural models are too simple to explain the complexity of human behaviour; they could explain some things, which are actually useful in deriving a technique for getting kids to behave in class (see Chapter 17), but not how people think. Cognitive behaviour, such as problem solving, seemed to Miller, Galanter and Pribram (1960) more like the sorts of things that computers did. The environment provides *information*, which humans attend to selectively, they then process and store it, to access it later. The human mind in this view is rather like a black box. You can see the input and the output, but you can't see how the input is dealt with; it seems to be 'processed' by program-like operations, which change in complexity with the accumulation of similar experiences. Humans seem to operate very like self-programming computers (Biggs 1968); or it seemed so then.

The information-processing model is nevertheless useful for construing some important aspects of cognitive functioning. It even helps us to understand the effects of stress and emotion on our thinking. The one single feature of the model that provides such explanatory power is *channel capacity*, or what we now call 'working memory', which is exactly equivalent to RAM, random access memory on microcomputers. We, like micros, can only handle a fixed amount of information at any one time. From that, all else follows. We cannot attend to this while at the same time we are doing that. We can *recall* a library full of information, if we bother to spend enough time learning it all; but if we overload working memory, we'll momentarily be unable even to recall our own names.

We run with this notion of processing information in the present chapter. It is not the whole story by a long shot, but it helps us understand much about how we learn and remember in school-type situations, where the emphasis is on logical kinds of tasks, dealt with sequentially.

Three stages in learning

The information-processing model gets us to focus on three stages in the learning pipeline, each located in a separate memory system.

1. *The sensory register.* In any situation, we experience a huge variety of sensations; our five senses simultaneously deliver a massive amount of information, much more than we could possibly handle at any one time. We have to be very selective about what we attend to. The sensory register is where we pay attention by selecting information that is important to us. The time scale here is very short, no more than a second.
2. *Working memory* is of limited capacity and is where conscious thinking takes place. It means we can only attend to one major train of thought at a time; we cannot simultaneously hold a conversation and daydream. When we make up our minds to attend to some information we need to *process* it in some way in order to retain it in long-term memory, either by repeating it over and over again (rehearsal), or by linking it to something we already know (coding). Contents may be retained in working memory for up to a minute.
3. *Long-term memory* is where processed information is stored and may be available for recall for periods as long as a lifetime.

These three systems carry out different functions and it is convenient to treat them separately. Nevertheless, they are inextricably linked, in particular by a central *plan*, or executive, which plays a role in governing *what* we attend to (in the sensory register) and *how* we attend to it (in the working memory) by using what we have learned in the past (long-term memory). We might portray the systems and their interconnections as shown in Figure 8.1.

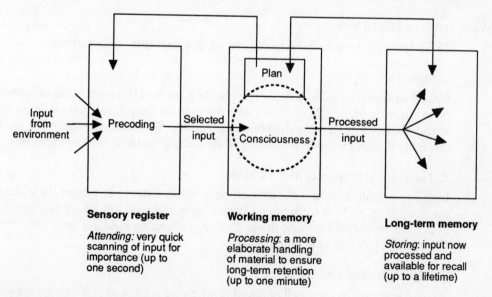

Figure 8.1   *Three memory systems in processing input*

These three systems provide a model for understanding the *cognitive* questions relating to learning and memory: how we select, handle and store information. A fourth system, the *arousal system* described in Chapter 9, helps us to understand how learning and memory can be affected by stress and other emotional factors. Questions relating to self-determination—our planning and awareness and control over these cognitive processes—are *metacognitive* ones (Flavell 1976), dealt with in Chapter 12.

The sensory register

All the information with which our senses continually bombard us has to be screened, as only certain selected features are to be attended to and subsequently consciously processed. Accordingly, all sensory impressions are retained for a period lasting up to one second, pending further processing (Atkinson & Shiffrin 1968). A high degree of selection from within the sensory register is necessary because we can attend to only one train of thought at a time in working memory.

The properties of the sensory register may lead teachers to believe that students are attending when they are not. Johnny is gazing out of the window, apparently miles away; his teacher *knows* that he is not attending.

Teacher: ... and so Captain Cook was killed on the landing at Hawaii ... *Johnny!* What were the last words I said?
Johnny: And-so-Captain-Cook-was-killed-on-the-landing-at-Hawaii.
Teacher: Hmmmm. At least look as if you're paying attention then.

The teacher was sure that Johnny was daydreaming; and she was right. However, she had only probed his sensory register, not his working memory: that is where attention is located. Johnny, on hearing his own name, simply hauled in the jumble of words that was still echoing around in his sensory register and read them off. He could play it back, but that doesn't mean he was paying attention.

Why we pay attention

Three factors determine whether or not we pay attention to something.

1. Mental set

Mental set is established by a deliberate plan (e.g., to read this page, to listen to the radio, or to talk to a friend). It is a conscious decision to attend. It is almost impossible to attend satisfactorily to more than one such activity. With the best will in the world, we can easily slip into a daydream—even while reading material as gripping as this.

2. The physical properties of the stimulus

Low-key stimuli, such as a flat monotonous voice, a dimly lit picture, or a blurred or opaque image, are hard to attend to. Bright lights and loud sounds are easy to attend to. Easier still are varying stimuli; things that keep changing hold our attention very well. We hear the clock ticking when it stops.

3. Physiological or internal states.

We pay attention to the smell of cooking when we are hungry. When we are anxious, we attend both to our feelings of stress and discomfort and to outside stimuli that may conceivably spell threat. Such stimulation is distracting and may make us perform badly. How this happens and how we may take steps to minimise it, are discussed later in this chapter.

What do these three conditions add up to? Each one spells out some way in which external stimuli may be *important* to us; things are important because we decide they are, because they are physically insistent or because they have biological survival value.

This process of sorting out the important from the unimportant stimuli occurs at the gateway of consciousness and is called *precoding*. We allocate priorities to what we are going to attend to by putting stimuli through an 'importance filter' (Deutsch & Deutsch, 1963). Imagine that all inputs to the sensory register are stacked upright; the tallest one at any given moment is the most important and that one is selected for further processing. The rest are dropped through the floor; we don't even know that they were there. To make sure that attention is consistently maintained means that the task-relevant inputs have always to be the tallest.

How does the teacher manage to do that? What you decide is important may easily not be what the students decide is important. For communication between teacher and pupil to take place, each must precode similar information as important. Are they likely to, when to children school means getting the daily tasks done, or at least out of the way, with a minimum of effort and unpleasantness (Holt 1970: 47). Holt thinks not, as he illustrates with the example in Box 8.1 (which took place in the most favourable of circumstances: one-to-one interaction in a progressive school).

Box 8.1 *A problem in communication: Precoding on different wavelengths*

I remember the day not long ago when Ruth opened my eyes. We had been doing math, and I was pleased with myself because, instead of telling her answers and showing her how to do problems, I was 'making her think' by asking her questions. It was slow work. Question after question met only silence. She said nothing, did nothing, just sat and looked at me through those glasses and waited. Each time, I had to think of a question easier and more pointed than the last, until I finally found one so easy that she would feel safe in answering it. So we inched our way along until suddenly, looking at her as I waited for an answer to a question, I saw with a start that she was not even thinking about it. She was coolly appraising me, weighing my patience, waiting for that next, sure-to-be-easier question. I thought, 'I've been had!'.

Holt (1970: 47)

How on earth, then, can teachers get their students to agree with them about which inputs are to be the tallest? How, in other words, do we motivate students? The first step is to grab their initial attention: that is what takes place at precoding. How attention is thereafter maintained is examined in depth in Chapters 10 and 11.

Shock tactics

One of the writers was present at a conference at which a research paper was to be presented. It was after dinner and everyone was tired. The researcher preceded the paper by apparently testing the slides of his results. But they did not present the multifactorial, five-way, stepwise, quasi-orthogonal, discriminant function co-variance matrices. They presented *Playboy* centrefolds. His audience threw off their after-dinner stupor and were attentive that night.

We don't recommend that teachers use erotica on 9C. We do recommend that they tap into the same principle that was used here: *departures from the expected make us pay attention.* Deliberately to incorporate such departures into lessons is to use the principle of *variability*, which can occur in style of teaching, in the media and materials of instruction, and in student–teacher interaction (Turney et al. 1983).

Variability in style of teaching

Variations in a teacher's personal style can be verbal or non-verbal. Effective public speakers constantly change the pitch, volume and pace of their speech. So do effective teachers. To be 'interesting', a speaker should vary speed of delivery, for example by slowing down for emphasis, and vary volume, for example speaking the important bits very loudly, or—double surprise!—speaking the climax very softly so that the audience strains to hear. Tone and pitch provide further contrasts with volume and speed: for example, the teacher's voice can range from sharp emphasis to quiet encouragement. Variation of grammatical style and use of questions at unpredictable moments during the lesson are further examples of ways of creating the unexpected. Of course, variability can be used for other functions as well: unobtrusive shifting from the front of the room when a student is talking, delivering part of the lesson while standing next to an inattentive student. Cathie may be dreaming away in the back row, confident of anonymity, but the brush of eye contact tells her otherwise. Routines are essential in efficient classroom management (see Chapter 17), but don't over-routinise your class or they'll be bored rigid.

Variability in media and materials of instruction

Visual resources include film, actual objects, pictures, maps, charts, videotape, television, overhead projector transparencies and duplicated materials. There is also the school's environment: field trips and excursions take advantage of it to add purpose, variety and interest to lessons—if they are conducted properly (see below). Actual objects are handled as a matter of course in such subjects as science, industrial arts, technical drawing, home science and textiles, but bringing relevant objects to handle in maths, history and English as well adds considerably to pupil interest.

Variability in interaction of pupils and teacher

The final source of variation is the interaction of the teacher and the pupils. This can be considered as a continuum: at one extreme is teacher talk, at the other is independent work by pupils. In between are such variations as group work, pupil presentations to the rest of the class, teacher assistance and so on. Interaction offers the teacher a means of maintaining surprise. The lesson may begin with the teacher introducing the subject, then the groups are formed to discuss it and reach a conclusion which individuals convey to the whole class. Such a lesson has a smooth and purposeful change of interaction every 10 or 15 minutes.

Maintaining attention

Once the students' attention has been gained, it is best maintained by the content itself. That battle is part over if teacher and student agree on what is important. When the *learner* chooses the content there is no problem. When the *teacher* does the choosing, however, the learner may have to be convinced.

The 'centres of interest' approach to the curriculum relies on learner choice. The teacher uses material in which the students are already interested (e.g., playing games, calculating football results, building a play area), when in fact the aim is to increase speed and accuracy in number manipulation. Freire (1970) used such a technique to teach illiterate Brazilian peasants to read. Assembling a group in the village square, he used words of intense common interest, especially those concerned with political disputes involving the local patron. Most of the group became functionally proficient readers after 30 hours of such instruction. Freire's persecution as a subversive was another consequence.

The technique has also been used by Ashton-Warner (1980), the Mt Gravatt Developmental Reading Program (Hart 1976), and the widely used *Breakthrough to Literacy* materials (Mackay 1971). For example, in Ashton-Warner's 'organic reading' program, 5 year old Maori children were asked for their 'own' words (i.e., those which had private importance).

Box 8.2   *Organic reading*

Children have two visions, the inner and the outer. Of the two the inner vision is brighter.

I hear that in other infant rooms widespread illustration is used to introduce the reading vocabulary to a 5 year old, a vocabulary chosen by adult educationists. I use pictures, too, to introduce the reading vocabulary, but they are pictures of the inner vision and the captions are chosen by the children themselves. True, the picture of the outer, adult-chosen visions can be meaningful and delightful to children; but it is the captions of the mind pictures that have the power and the light. For whereas the illustrations perceived by the outer eye cannot be other than interesting, the illustrations seen by the inner eye are organic, and it is the captioning of these that I call the 'Key Vocabulary' ...

Back to these first words. To these first books. They must be made out of the stuff of the child itself. I reach a hand into the mind of the child, bring out a handful of the stuff I find there, and use that as our first working material. Whether it is good or bad stuff, violent or placid stuff, coloured or dun. To effect an unbroken beginning. And in this dynamic material, within the familiarity and security of it, the Maori finds that words have intense meaning to him, from which cannot help but arise a love of reading. For it's here, right in this first word, that the love of reading is born, and the longer his reading is organic the stronger it becomes, until by the time he arrives at the books of the new culture, he receives them as another joy rather than as a labour. I know all this because I've done it.

Source: Sylvia Ashton-Warner, 1980, p. 32–4.

Each child built up a key vocabulary on a set of cards, each word being written on the child's own card. The cards were then rearranged to form stories based on the individual's own chosen words. The child 'owned' that story in a very special way; and as we shall see in the next chapter, that is vital for building intrinsic motivation.

Good teachers, like good conversationalists, recognise the importance of tapping their listener's interests whenever they can.

Adjunct questions and overviews

Another way of highlighting importance is much colder and more cognitive. The teacher can highlight what is likely to be important by asking what are called adjunct questions, which are questions asked before the student commences reading a text, while reading the text, or after it has been read. Such questions can be pitched at a high cognitive level, asking for interpretations or applications, or be quite factual. Overviews are simple statements of the main points to be dealt with, rather like synopses at the beginning of a paper. They put, in abbreviated form, points and issues which will be elaborated in the material to follow. What both adjunct questions and overviews essentially do is channel the learner's attention. Do they work? Reviews of many studies suggest the following conclusions (Faw & Waller 1976; Hamaker 1986; Hartley & Davies 1976):

1. Factual questions asked *before* reading (prequestions) help students focus on content identical with or related to the questions, but inhibit learning of unrelated content. If the material is intended to 'broaden' students' knowledge, then such questions are counter-productive; they only tell the student what is to be tested and hence what to concentrate on.
2. Factual questions asked *after* reading (postquestions) also help learning related content, but have no effect on unrelated content. The student assimilates the content, knowing questions will be asked, but not which ones; the particular ones asked then highlight the related content.
3. The effects of prequestions (1) lessen with longer texts, but effects of postquestions (2) are greater with long texts.
4. Higher order questions have greater positive effects than factual questions especially on higher order outcomes. Asking high-level questions helps learn factual content unrelated to the question, whereas factual questions inhibit learning unrelated content.

So it depends what you want students to learn from the text. If factual detail, ask factual questions first but don't expect anything but better retention of facts. If breadth and depth of meaning, ask higher order questions, either pre- or post.

The overview works like adjunct questions, signalling what particular points are important. *Advance organisers* are a special kind of overview written at a more abstract conceptual level than the text itself, whereas overviews proper are written at the same level. Advance organisers have a different purpose than simply directing attention and are discussed in Chapter 13 in a section on learning from written text (p. 346).

Questions, overviews, or any other kind of device that clarifies to the student what is to be learned, have positive effects on learning (Gagne 1978). Even just telling students what the lesson objectives are is helpful (Faw & Waller 1976; Hartley & Davies 1976).

Working memory

The most important feature of working memory is that it is of limited capacity. Consider the following mental arithmetic problem:

$$333 \text{ multiplied by itself.}$$

Logically, this only involves (1) knowing that $3 \times 3 = 9$ and (2) knowing how to add up. A 9 year old has this knowledge, yet adults find the problem difficult. The difficulty is not because it demands special knowledge, but because we need to hold the various steps in mind simultaneously.

The digit span test, a component in many intelligence tests, gives a good idea of some of the main features of working memory. Glance at the first row of digits below and read from left to right at the rate of about one digit per second, saying the digit to yourself. Then close your eyes and write the series on a scrap of paper.

4 5 7 0 9

Now repeat the performance for the following series, dealing with each series one at a time:

(a)   6 4 0 3 9 5 1
(b   4 2 1 7 3 9 6 0
(c)   5 8 3 0 1 7 9 2 6
(d)   1 3 5 7 2 4 6 8 1 3 5 7 2 4 6 8

Which series was the hardest? Which the easiest? Most people find **c** the hardest and **d** the easier. But **d** needs much more space than **c**: **d** has 16 digits and **c** only nine.

Most people do not of course remember 16 units; they remember *four* (odd numbers, even numbers, 8 the largest number, repeat). The series was coded into a more economical form, using previous knowledge as the basis for the code. These more compact units are technically called 'chunks'.

An individual's digit span (i.e., the number one can hold and repeat back) is remarkably constant. Digit span is typically four digits at age 5, rising to 6 at age 10, settling around 7 in adults. This constancy led to the theory that each chunk took up one 'slot' of working memory, the average person having 'the magical number 7, plus or minus 2' (Miller 1956). We now know that Miller is not strictly correct, as the number of 'slots' seems to vary according to what the items are and how familiar they are to the individual. Adults can typically hold 7 unrelated digits, but only 6 letters and 5 unrelated words (Dempster 1981). Adults taught a new number language have the same span as 6 year olds doing the same task (Case 1985). 10 year old chess experts remember fewer digits than adults but they far surpass adults when the span is for chess positions (Chi 1978).

Thus, while it is true that working memory is limited, the actual *number* of chunks one can retain depends on the material being chunked. In fact, Case (1985) makes this basic to his theory of cognitive development. He maintains that working memory capacity is constant throughout childhood and adolescence: what varies is the informational richness of the unit being handled. In adults, the rough edges are smoothed off with use and so they pack more in a given space. The same is true of experts, whether child or adult. As we have seen, the nature of expertise is to use abstract forms of representation, made smoother by much use.

Optimising the use of working memory

Because working memory is needed for all cognitive activity, more for high level than for low level thinking, and because it is strictly limited, it is vital what you pack into it. Optimising the use of working memory is therefore an important key to successful instruction. If students are to think at a higher level, that is for understanding rather than for memorising, then they will need as much working memory at their disposal as possible.

Working memory should therefore be occupied with the more important rather than the less important aspects of a problem; if your mental purse can hold only seven coins, make sure their denomination is $ and not cents. Students should 'chunk' their material as richly as they can. For this, they need a good knowledge base, and a great deal of experience and familiarity with the lower level contents so that they become automatised, thereby freeing space for higher level activities (Case 1985).

For example, the learner driver has many things to think about at once—remembering the road rules, using signals, pushing the right pedals at the right time—so that it is easy to forget to do something crucial, such as applying the brake in an emergency. Experienced drivers have practised these things for so long that they are automatic; they do not have to consciously decide what to do, so that there is working memory space for other concerns. They can sing with the car radio, or hold a conversation, but they are able to switch into emergency mode if they have to.

When teaching reading, for instance, the lower level process of decoding words by phonics needs to be automated so that the young reader does not have to think about identifying the *word*, but does think about the meaning of the sentence of which it is a part (Kirby 1988; see also Chapter 13 for further elaboration).

Why can an 8 year old typically solve $7 + 9 = ?$ and $16 + 5 = ?$, but not $7 + 9 + 5 = ?$ Because the latter requires more working memory to *hold* the result of the first addition $(7 + 9)$, so that the remaining 5 can be added in. An older child—who has had practice, much practice—chunks the $7 + 9$ into one unit, so that the problem becomes, in effect, $(7 + 9) + 5$; in other words, $16 + 5$. Younger children can, however, be trained to chunk the $7 + 9$ and thus behave like older children (Case 1985).

Students should always be encouraged to use space-saving devices, such as crutches in mechanical arithmetic (which some teachers still frown upon). By writing a tiny 1 in the tens column, the student will remember to include the 10 that is to be carried from the units column. Experienced students are likely to carry the figure without thinking about it, but beginners certainly will not. It is senseless to insist that working memory be cluttered with material that can be 'remembered' more efficiently on a piece of paper.

Working memory is particularly likely to be crowded when the individual is stressed, as in an exam, so a good strategy is to jot down points as soon as they come to mind; they can then be written into the essay at the appropriate time. If one tries to keep them in the head, they are almost certain to be lost. This particular use of space saving to cope with anxiety is dealt with in more detail later in Chapter 9.

In short, one of the most effective ways of improving learning and problem solving is to cut down wherever possible on working memory load. This is not spoon-feeding, but making sure that our limited minds are given the opportunity of handling more complex problems than they otherwise could.

Processes in working memory

Back to our ways of handling the digit span test. Remember, we said that an effective way of remembering the numbers was to code them, for example as odd/even. What other ways are there?

Use imagery. Let the mind go blank and 'hold', without doing anything. This method is suitable if it is only necessary to hold the material for 30 seconds, but if you are distracted, the material will be dislodged from your working memory and it will be impossible to retrieve from long-term memory, for example if you look up a phone number in the directory, and then momentarily think of something else.

Recycle. Repeat the number for as long as necessary to finish dialling it, but not long enough to lodge the number in long-term memory.

Rehearse. Repeat the number until it is fixed in long-term memory.

Code. Link the number to a number we already know: our car registration number, or a telephone number, or the odd–even code. This is usually a much more efficient method, although it too can go wrong by confusing the phone number with someone else's.

Rote and meaningful learning

The last two processes, rehearsal and coding, lead to long-term retention of material; they have the same compressing, or chunking, function, which leads to effective use of working memory.

Rehearsal is used in physical skills, in verbal tasks where there is no intrinsic structure to the material, or where the individual is unable to use what structure there is, in which case it is called *rote* learning (Ausubel, 1968). Rehearsal is also used when the learner wants to make sure that learning is verbatim, or 100% accurate. It is applied to the actual words used, without reference to their meaning. Actors, for instance, rote-learn their lines, not because they do not understand them but simply to ensure accurate performance.

Coding may be used where the material has some kind of structure and when the individual has the relevant background knowledge to make use of that structure, it leads to *meaningful* learning (Ausubel 1968). Obviously, someone who didn't know the difference between odd and even numbers would be unable to make use of that code in remembering the above series. Coding is almost always preferable as a means of chunking if it is available; as we shall see below, arbitrary coding systems such as mnemonics are more efficient for remembering accurately than rote learning based on rehearsal.

Coding and rehearsal aren't necessarily in competition; one can make use of both, as can be seen when we try to remember the following shopping list:

detergent, bacon, scissors, sausages, onions, toothpaste, eggs, garlic, BBQ forks, shampoo, muesli, chops, orange juice, bread, soy sauce, paper napkins, milk ...

This would be difficult if rote learned exclusively. Let us restructure and part rehearse, part code:

food for the BBQ	*food for breakfast*	*non-food things*
sausages	eggs	scissors
garlic	muesli	detergent
onions	bread	toothpaste
chops	orange juice	paper napkins
soy sauce	bacon	BBQ forks
cooking oil	milk	shampoo

The rote learning is focused, first, on the three categories and then within categories. The effort is much less and there is a context to prompt recall, even to generate new items: 'BBQ ... ha! of course. Tomato sauce for the kids'.

Meaningful learning is organised under some form of coding or schematic system such as the above. It is much more economical, more stable, more easily remembered and more enjoyable, than pure rote learning. The focus in meaningful learning is the meaning of the word, passage, or theme (the deep structure), not as in rote learning the word itself (the surface structure). Material learned by coding may be reproduced in a new version: the meaning remains the same, but the words may be different. This, in fact, is a crucial test that distinguishes rote from meaningful learning: rote-learned material cannot be replayed in a greatly changed way, whereas material that has been learned with understanding can be rephrased and transformed.

Meaningful learning is obviously the major goal for school learning; rote learning is a useful tool in achieving that goal, if used appropriately and not as a substitute for meaningful learning. This theme reappears consistently throughout this book; a major section in Chapter 12 concerns students' 'approaches' to learning and these are largely based on whether or not the focus when learning is to seek meaning (deep approach) or to reproduce accurately (surface approach).

Recoding

Coding takes place on the basis of previous knowledge. But how can we code a new experience when nothing quite like it has occurred previously? It all depends on how much the new experience has in common with earlier ones. If there is a very great deal in common, we might code the new experience as 'Uh-huh. Thingamajig again' (William James, 1890, again). Or we might note some differences and in trying to make sense out of them, recombine our past experience in new ways, as when trying to work out the meaning of a new word from its context. That recombination is called *recoding*.

Each new experience, then, is *matched* to what is already known. There are four basic possibilities, each having different and important cognitive and motivational consequences (see also Table 10.2):

- *No mismatch:* the match is exact, or near enough. Recognition occurs, but no rethinking. Coding occurs, but little or no recoding: assimilation but no accommodation, as Piaget (1950) would put it. A boring experience, like hearing an old joke for the hundredth time.
- *Some mismatch:* enough to challenge, not enough to overwhelm. Cognitive reshuffling (recoding) is necessary to cope but not beyond the bounds of capability or willingness to expend effort. An interesting experience, like hearing something new about an old friend. This is the basis for intrinsic motivation.
- *Much more mismatch,* to the point where it cannot be handled. Try communicating with Year 7 French when you are on the platform of a little country station in the heart of the Dordogne and your train to your connecting flight leaves in 5 minutes. Are they telling you the train has '*parti*', or is it '*pas ici*'? *Merde alors!* Desperate recoding; not challenge but flat panic.
- *All mismatch.* You don't understand a word of French, so all this *jabber-jabber* is beside the point. You'll rely on non-verbal ways of reaching your goal, as do many kids in Hong Kong secondary schools where English is officially the medium of instruction. Those who don't understand English when English is spoken, tune out. They sit in the classroom for as long as they have to, then leave and earn money, using Chinese. Much more motivating.

The degree of intrinsic motivation experienced by a student thus depends upon the match between current experience and the knowledge gained from previous ones. The implications for teaching are far-reaching.

Long-term memory

Long-term memory and its opposite, forgetting, have been studied for many years. Most current theories have their roots in the work of Ebbinghaus (1913). There are three main theories: trace decay, associative interference, and structuring.

1. *Trace decay* theory makes intuitive sense; memory traces stored in the brain spontaneously deteriorate over time 'rather like a mark in a pat of butter will gradually disappear in a warm room' (Baddeley 1976: 59). That is not the whole story, as some memories are retained with extraordinary clarity over many decades, while others have gone within days, but it is likely that some kind of fading process does occur.
2. *Associative interference*, and its two forms, retroactive and proactive inhibition, was for years believed to explain all forgetting (McGeoch & Irion 1952). Associative interference occurs when what has already been learned interferes with present learning; the greater the similarity between the two sets of learning, the more likely it is that interference would occur.

For example, if a student learns the French for 'cat' (*chat*) and then the Spanish word (*gato*), the interference (or inhibition) is said to be retroactive if the student recalls the French word: it might appear as *ghat* instead of *chat*, or as *chateau*. In the first case, the Spanish meaning has acted backwards (or retroactively) to change the 'c' and 'g'; and in the second, to create a double confusion between the sound of the word *gato* and a quite different French word, *chateau*. If, on the other hand, the student is required to recall the last (Spanish) word, then proactive interference may occur, for instance, if it is recalled as *cato*.

Associative interference is most likely when the data to be learned are arbitrary—for instance learning new names, symbols or formulae—and is least likely when the data have been carefully learned, understood and related to wider knowledge or structured in a wider context. Associative interference and resulting confusions are most likely to occur in the early stages of learning a topic, before a knowledge network has been built up.

Associative experience can be minimised in the following way:

- Space lessons dealing with similar topics, with dissimilar material interposed; this lessens the chances of confusion.
- When dealing with similar events, highlight the common structure, so that they are coded together, and then highlight the differences, so that they can be distinguished. The structure thus clarified lessens the chance of interference.

3. *Locating events in a structure*. The main determinant of what we remember is what we already know. As we learn, the content actively interacts with related knowledge and becomes coded with it. Chi's (1978) 10 year old chess experts remembered displayed chess positions far more effectively than did adult non-experts.

The difference between associative interference and structuring is given in the following. Say an ancient history exam question asks: 'In what ways were the reigns of Tutankhamun and Akhnaton alike and in what ways were they different?' If the class were taught the reigns of the two consecutive pharoahs in a narrative way, that would be a difficult question to answer. There were a lot of similarities: each overthrew the social and religious structure of his predecessor, each married young, each set himself up as a god. Lots of room for associative interference. However, if the teaching emphasised their differences: one conservative (existing gods), the other radical (Aton, sun-god?); one filthy rich (remember his tomb?), the other only rich rich—then the structure can be used both to remember and to place the reigns of each, while the patterning of the differences makes it clear who was who. Further, any new material, or revised material learned before the structure was in place, can be linked directly to the appropriate place on the overall structure.

Improving semantic memory: The use of mnemonics

When material has no evident or usable structure, such as numbers, dates, formulae, etc., we use rehearsal to remember it in the form of rote learning. But can *coding*, which is more efficient, be used to help memorise such material? It certainly can, in the form of *mnemonics*. A mnemonic system imposes a structure where none exists naturally, thus reaping the benefits of meaningful learning.

A simple example of a mnemonic is an acrostic: a word formed from the first letters of the target words. Thus, the Great Lakes become HOMES (Huron, Ontario, Michigan, Erie, Superior); or the colours of the spectrum become that spunky Minister for Ethnic Affairs, Roy G. Biv (red, orange, yellow, green, blue, indigo, violet). The reverse can also be applied by turning target letters into sentences. The notes in the treble staff are recalled as 'Every Good Boy Deserves Fruit' (the five lines: E G B D F) and 'Dirty Filthy Animals Can't Eat Grass' (the adjacent notes: D F A C E G).

More elaborate mnemonic systems tie visual images of objects with places, letters or numbers. The ancient Greek orators, for example, used the 'method of loci', which involved tying points in their speech with different imagined locations. In this way, they could remember very lengthy speeches by imagining, as they spoke, that they were walking through a temple: the introduction at the temple door, the first point to be argued beside the first pillar on the right, the main argument standing in front of the altar and so on. Their initial memorising was facilitated by associating the strong visual image with the particular content, as was recall: hours of it. Bower's (1970) variant of the method of loci is to remember the day's shopping list, say, by associating each item with a particular location in the kitchen.

Other methods attach visual images to a number or letter, as in the 'pegword' method:

> One is a bun
> Two is a shoe
> Three is a tree
> Four is a door
> Five is a hive
> Six are sticks
> Seven is heaven
> Eight is a gate
> Nine is a line
> Ten is a hen.

The poem is learned to the point where a number immediately recalls its associated object. To remember a number or a date, the objects replace the digits and are assembled in a strong, bizarre—and unforgettable—image. Take the Battle of Waterloo: 1815. Bun, gate, bun, hive. Napoleon lost; he gets a plain bun, which he eats outside a closed gate. On the other side of the gate is Wellington, who scores a bun with honey on it, the hive behind him.

Using techniques such as these, it certainly is possible to 'amaze yourself and your friends' as the advertisements promise; the only (non-financial) catch is that they require a lot of time and trouble to acquire. Such elaborate mnemonics are clearly useful for learning arbitrary formulae or names; beyond that, their usefulness depends on the folklore of a particular teaching subject. One X-rated mnemonic for a trig formula, for instance, begins: 'Sally opens her ...' ... but we forget the rest of it.

Construction and reconstruction

Two processes are postulated in the structural theory of memory, construction and reconstruction (Disibio 1982). The construction process suggests that information is selected and abstracted *before* storing in long-term memory; the reconstruction process that the analysis and synthesis of information occurs at *recall*. It is clear that both processes occur.

Construction is clear from the following experiment. Howe (1970a) read his students an excerpt from a modern novel and they then wrote down what they remembered of it. Immediately after they had done so, the original version was re-read. The following week, the students again wrote their version of the passage and again the original was re-read. This pattern—writing down and re-reading—was repeated for four weeks. You might expect that under such conditions the students would check their errors against each re-reading. In fact, they reproduced a version of their first reproduction each time—yet they had had four opportunities to correct their initial errors. The students were even aware they were doing this but couldn't help it.

The implications of this study are quite important. Teachers need to be very careful about what they say the first time round. If they find they were mistaken and try to correct the mistake, it will be difficult to get the second version across. Have you ever wondered why, when teachers read out the correct answers to a test, the students don't immediately write the corrections in and remember them? Logically they should, but they evidently confuse mistakes with the corrections. One solution is to make sure students do not make mistakes in the first place, which is the teaching strategy recommended by Skinner (1965) in his advocacy of teaching machines and employed in *mastery learning* (see Chapter 14). A 'cognitive' solution is to analyse the *reasons* for those mistakes (Howe 1972): recode the codes that produced the errors, rather than concentrate on the errors.

Reconstruction is illustrated in courtroom practice (Kassin & Wrightsman 1985). 'Leading' questions are disallowed in cross-examination: 'Was the accused still striking the victim when you arrived?' is a leading question, whereas 'What did you see when you arrived?' is not. The first provides a framework telling the witness what to remember. For similar reasons, witnesses are debarred from the courtroom until they give evidence. Expectations guide recall, so a witness could in all honesty assert under oath the existence of a non-event.

Dismembering and remembering

Thus, learning involves 'dismembering' and recall 'remembering'; an event is first taken apart and coded along its constituent dimensions, then reconstructed from those dimensions (Neisser 1967; Pribram 1969). What dimensions might these be? Following are some of the more important, from the most concrete to the most abstract:

1. *Enactive* memory concerns the retention of motor responses, which is remarkably stable. Short of brain damage, is it possible to forget how to ride a bicycle? We often dial a particular number from 'finger memory', but cannot recall the number verbally.

2. *Sensory* memory is of the specific sensations (visual, aural, tactile, etc.) that make up the original experience: the 'bone chips' of experience, which Neisser (1967) compares to the few fossilised bits of bone palaeontologists use to reconstruct the skeleton of a new species, using their knowledge of anatomy and of dinosaurian lifestyles. They might be wrong in detail, but right in general outline. Children are frequently better than adults at storing such detail, using the ikonic mode in the form of eidetic imagery ('photographic memory'). Humans aren't as good as other animals in storing taste or smell sensations. Wine buffs, to counter this unfortunate biological turnaround, prompt their inefficient palates with semantic coding: 'sweaty saddles', 'tropical fruit', 'buttery', 'minty' and the like.

3. *Affective.* We remember feelings and emotions associated with an event as part of episodic memory. These may be powerful; why else do we watch old movies? It is often much easier to recall the 'feel' of an event than its details ('Ah yes. I was happy, that I know. Can't for the life of me remember why …'). Stranger is the nostalgia for desperately unhappy times; the old soldiers, trekking back to Gallipoli and Flanders, where many, many, years ago their mental and physical suffering was intense.

4. *Temporal.* Time sequence helps structure our memory; it is 'natural' to remember things in the order in which they happened. Recall what you did last Friday at 5 p.m.; typically, you would start at some remembered reference point, such as a class or lunch, and then track events thereafter. The strategy works for events that do not even form part of one's own personal experience. It is easier to encode and recall the prime ministers since federation in terms of succession, rather than grouping according to political party or platform.

5. *Spatial.* Spatial encoding is more abstract than visual sensation, relying not on the actual images, but the relationships between objects and events. You can't use visual sensations to guide your way in a place never previously visited, but you can use spatial directions in the form of a map or sketch. Such directions are incidentally much more economically coded than a list of verbal instructions: 'Turn left at the first corner, then straight on for three blocks …' etc.

6. *Semantic.* Semantic encoding, in terms of word meaning, is the most important and most complex aspect of human memory. Semantic memory is organised in quite complex hierarchies from simple, concrete meanings of single words, through meanings of sentences and of paragraphs, to the quite abstract moral of a complex story or the theme of a scientific treatise. One of the most important issues in school learning is targeting the appropriate level of semantic meaning, a point expanded in Chapter 13.

7. *Logical.* The most abstract frameworks are purely logical. Memory is helped considerably if material is encoded in terms of its inherent logical structure. It is much easier to remember logical arguments than illogical ones.

Figure 8.2 represents how a learning episode may be dismembered into these seven dimensions. Not all dimensions will be used at a time. Depending on the nature of the episode and on the capabilities and prior knowledge of the learner, one or more of the dimensions will be used and in varying levels of abstraction. At the most concrete level, the specific sensations, emotions and motor responses will be recorded, giving a fusion of both content, affect and context. Temporal and spatial relations offer the next level of abstraction, whereby the learner begins to separate out contextual from content aspects of the episode; while content becomes more firmly abstracted with focus on meaning and logical structure.

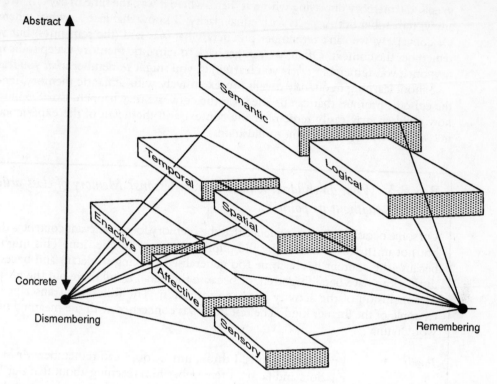

Figure 8.2 *How learning is dismembered and remembered*

Good learning thus implicates (a) a *variety of dimensions* being used for encoding; and (b) the *highest levels of abstraction* that the learner can handle. In turn, good teaching should involve all possible means of encoding: striking images and diagrams to give a spatial encoding; use of mnemonic devices; presenting material in a logical step-by-step structure. Simple repetition should not however be forgotten, especially for those raw picture strips of detail. *Sesame Street* uses visual and auditory surprise, avoiding dullness yet hammering home the message with much repetition. The distinction between procedural, episodic and semantic memory is helpful here.

Procedural, episodic and semantic memory

The above seven dimensions can be simplified into three kinds of memory (Tulving, 1985): procedural, episodic, and semantic.

* *Procedural* memory is of procedural knowledge: remembering how to do things. This usually draws on the enactive dimension in the sensori-motor mode (see Chapter 2).
* *Episodic* memory refers to what happens to us personally, usually recorded in ikonic images.
* *Semantic* memory concerns declarative knowledge, and could include logical and spatial dimensions as well.

The three systems interact. When an event occurs, we seem to record *what* happened (possibly in semantic memory) and the *context* surrounding the event (the images in episodic memory displaying who was there, where it was, the time of day ...). We don't always remember both aspects with equal clarity: 'I know that face ... who? where? ...' Or conversely, we can't remember precisely what was said (the semantics) but we do remember the context. Often, we can get back to semantic memory via episodic memory; once you remember *where* you learned it, you might remember *what* you learned.

School learning frequently dwells too exclusively with semantic memory, ignoring the episodic prompts that can be used. Or the converse may happen. Box 8.3 illustrates how children may easily remember the context and the detail of the experience, but not what the detail was meant to illustrate.

Box 8.3 *What do children remember from lessons? Memory of class activity without its point*

On some occasions there is evidence that the memory for the relevant content is there, but not in the form needed by the pupil to answer the question. This might be because the content has become too generalised (lacking in detail) and necessary distinctions have been forgotten, or because the detail is still there but the purpose or conclusion of the activity has been forgotten. The following transcript is an example of the former kind. The test item was concerned with the meaning of the word 'fauna'.

Pupil:	I put native plants. I think, um ... oh, I can remember Mr H saying flora and fauna. I remember him teaching about that but I still get muddled up which one. And I don't know why I put native plants, but I just did.

An example of the latter kind can be seen in the following exchange. The interviewer uses a prompt to elicit recall of an activity in which the teacher demonstrated the effects of air pollution.

Interviewer:	Do you remember the incense?
Pupil:	Yeah.
Interviewer:	Now, why did he do that? ...
Pupil:	Well, we went into the 'flea-pit' and everyone was all smelling and everyone was going 'Oh God!' and all that, and we were looking on top of the door, and it was all put around the top of the door and everything. It was all up there.
Interviewer:	Why was it there? What did it make you think of?
Pupil:	Um ... Some people thought it didn't smell very nice, some people thought it smelled like flowers and that, and, um, some people just didn't like it and went outside and that sort of thing.
Interviewer:	Did it have anything to do with conservation?
Pupil:	I think it did. I'm not sure and I can't remember

Source: Nuthall & Lee 1982, pp. 11–12

Encouraging meaningful learning

> Teaching is the process of organising and relating new information to the learner's previous experience, stimulating him to construct his own representation for what he is encountering ... (Wittrock 1977: 177).

That is what the coding model means for teaching. The more easily the student can be encouraged to relate new to previous knowledge, in as many modalities as possible, the more easily meaning can be constructed by that student and the more easily and accurately it will be remembered. How well something is remembered depends on the quality of the process used in learning; 'deep' processing (using abstract codes) or 'elaborative' processing (using a variety of codes) produce more effective recall than 'surface' processing (Craik & Lockhart 1972). This notion of deep and surface processes of learning is related to a very important view of learning, which we process deeply and elaboratively in Chapter 12. Here, we look not at processes but at the kinds of codes that are the target of meaningful learning in a subject area: surface and generic codes (Bruner 1957).

Surface and generic codes

Surface codes operate at a low level of abstraction and are not strongly linked to other aspects of the discipline. Material coded in this way is narrow in its range of application or in its transferability to different fields. In order for such material to be remembered, rehearsal will often be required as well: surface coding has few links and requires a proportion of rote learning to 'fix' it.

Generic codes operate at a high level of abstraction, thus allowing the individual to construct connections readily with other parts of the discipline. Let us look at some classroom examples.

Example 1: Year 6 arithmetic

In a Year 6 arithmetic lesson, the teacher says: 'Now take 5 from 3'. Student: 'You can't'. Teacher: 'Oh, yes you can!' Now what?

The problem is that the student has learned a restricted coding of the concept of number based only on cardinal aspects, that is the number of elements referred to. That surface code cannot now handle the new problem. A non-mathematical recoding is that the teacher is lying, which is not helpful: a generic code, please. The teacher might then introduce concrete instances where the student *does* take 5 from 3: as in an overdrawn bank account, or when 2 degrees of frost occur. A crucial piece of recoding is now required, involving the concept of zero. Instead of being the empty set—the absence of something—zero can mean a position on a scale in the directed number system. By stepping up and down that scale, the student learns that all those things that could be done with the old system (of natural numbers) can still be done, plus many new things with directed numbers. The mismatch produced by those experiences has led to recoding under a new generic code.

Example 2: Year 8 science

The formula 'A base plus acid gives a salt plus water' has been taught. The following exam question is set: 'What happens when dilute hydrochloric acid is added to potassium hydroxide?' The example originally given in class involved sulphuric acid and sodium hydroxide, giving sodium sulphate and water.

This time the formula is in itself generic enough, but it has been interpreted in a surface way, where 'acid' means sulphuric acid; 'base' means caustic soda. If taught generically, the formula can be used to access other knowledge: 'A base: ah yes, that's a metallic ion and a hydroxyl ion; an acid, that's a hydrogen ion plus a radical; a salt is a metallic ion plus a radical ... now it doesn't matter what metal is in question, I think, so if we recombine ...' The generic code relates the acid-plus-base-gives-salt-plus-water formula to an abstract structure, from which the solution to many specific problems can be derived.

Such generic codes can be found in every subject and they should become the focus of teaching. In learning generic codes, background knowledge, facts and detail are important, but as a *means* to an end. In learning surface codes, however, the facts are an end in themselves; one is likely to end up being unable to see the wood for the trees. The relationship between factual detail and general principle is well illustrated by Lashley (1960: 497):

> ... every memory becomes part of a more or less extensive organisation. When I read a scientific paper, the new facts presented become associated with the field of knowledge of which it is a part. Later availability of the specific items of the paper depend on a partial activation of the whole body of associations. If one has not thought of a topic for some time, it is difficult to recall details. With a review or discussion of the subject, however, names, dates and references which seemed to have been forgotten rapidly become available to memory.

So it is not facts *versus* structure; it is fitting facts to a structure, thus getting the best of both factual and structural worlds.

Schemata

If generic codes refer to the subject matter, schemata (singular, 'schema') refer to the network of connected ideas or relationships an individual uses (Anderson 1985). Incoming information that fits an existing schema is more easily learned and retained, because it becomes meaningful by virtue of that fit.

Schemata can be formal, referring to structure, or substantive, referring to content. An example of a formal schema is a 'story grammar' (Mandler 1984), which children acquire from a very early age and which makes stories and fairy tales meaningful. The European fairy tale, for instance, has a strict formula for the beginning ('Once upon a time ...') and the ending ('And they lived happily ever after.'). The characters must be Good (with Nordic features) and Evil (with minority or disadvantaged features), and Good must eventually triumph. The fairy tale schema invades adult art on a broad front, from the banalities and fascism of professional wrestling, to the complexity and fascism of Wagner's operas; in both cases, the schema helps our understanding and enjoyment. Story grammars develop beyond the fairy tale schema; they become the *genres* for different forms of literature: the detective story, the thriller, the romance, the saga. All have to follow the schema to be publishable and to make money; truly innovative writing, which challenges the conventional schemata, is publishable but does not make money.

Substantive schemata are important in all meaningful learning. Any concept can be formed into a hierarchical network of higher and lower order substantively related schemata (see Figure 8.3):

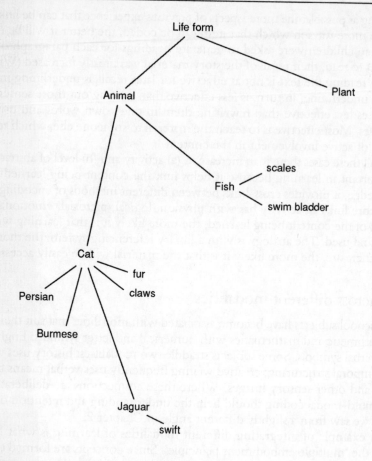

Figure 8.3 *Substantive schematic diagram*

Concept maps

These are similar to schema diagrams. The difference is that a concept map is less formalised; it can be used by teachers for instructional purposes, or may be drawn by students to reveal their understanding of the topic for assessment purposes (Novak & Gowin 1984). In drawing concept maps the learner (or teacher) presents component concepts in the form of nodes which are linked in a variety of ways. For example, a concept map of the food chain would show the major nodes of 'consumers', 'producers' and 'decomposers' with each of these nodes having lower level information linked to it (op. cit). Concept mapping has been used in a variety of teaching settings with some success (e.g., Dupuis & Snyder 1983; Howard, 1987). The chapter overviews in this book are simple concept maps showing the content and organisation of each chapter. The use of concept maps in assessing learning is discussed in Chapter 15.

Generativity in learning and recall

Constructive and reconstructive processes are what Wittrock (1977) calls *generative*. Generativity implies the active construction of meaning using as many dimensions for encoding as possible; the more aspects of previous experience that can be linked to an item and the more ways in which that item can be coded, the better it will be remembered.

When children were asked to generate headings for each paragraph of a story they were set to read, their recall of the story material was greatly increased (Wittrock 1977). Merely reading the text is not as effective for later recall as underlining important sentences; underlining, in turn, is less effective than writing out those sentences; copying sentences less effective than rewriting them in one's own words and using your own examples. Most effective is to teach the material to someone else, which requires a high degree of active involvement in the content.

In all these cases there is an increase in (a) activity and (b) level of abstraction. Activity is important in learning because it helps link the content being learned with existing knowledge; it provides cross-links between different methods of encoding the material. The more links an activity has with physical, logical, pictorial, emotional and sensory aspects of the content being learned, the more likely it is that learning will be remembered and used. The analogy is with a library referencing system; the more cross-references there are, the more likely it is that the material will be easily accessed.

Encoding across different modalities

Most school subjects have become associated with modalities that suit their subject matter: arithmetic and mathematics with numerical and letter symbols; English expression with verbal symbols. Some subjects straddle two modalities: history uses verbal symbols and temporal structuring; creative writing frequently uses verbal means to elicit strong visual and other sensory images. Where these connections are deliberately exploited, such multi-modal coding should help the understanding and retention of subject matter, as we saw from a slightly different angle in Chapter 2.

An example of integrating different modalities of learning is what Dienes (1963) called the 'multiple embodiment principle'. Since concepts are formed through a process of abstraction from concrete experience, he argued that the more varied that experience, the more powerful would be the concept that is formed. Consequently, he illustrated certain basic mathematical concepts with materials and games that had a considerable vogue in parts of the United Kingdom and elsewhere, including several Adelaide primary schools.

The following example is taken from work carried out with Bruner at Harvard University (Bruner 1964; Dienes 1963). The materials were cut out of thick plastic and consisted of small unit squares of constant size; strips of plastic that could be any length, but were unit width; and squares with sides that were as long as the strip (see Figure 8.4). The dimensions of the strip may vary from set to set; the only constraint is that once a particular strip length has been selected, it must also apply to the sides of the square. If we let x be the length of the strip, then, the dimensions of the pieces are: the square is $x \times x$ (or x^2, as it is written); the strip is $x \times 1$, or just plain x; and the unit is 1×1, or 1 (Figure 8.4a).

It is now possible to make a spatial model of quadratic functions by making a rectangle. Let us say we are given the expression $2x^2 + 8x + 6$ (the parts of the expression are shown in Figure 8.4b). They have to be arranged, however, to form a rectangle (Figure 8.4c) and when this is done, it may be seen that such a rectangle has one side of length $2x + 2$ and the other $x + 3$. It can also be seen that such a rectangle is the same as $2x^2 + 8x + 6$ (because it is composed of precisely those parts).

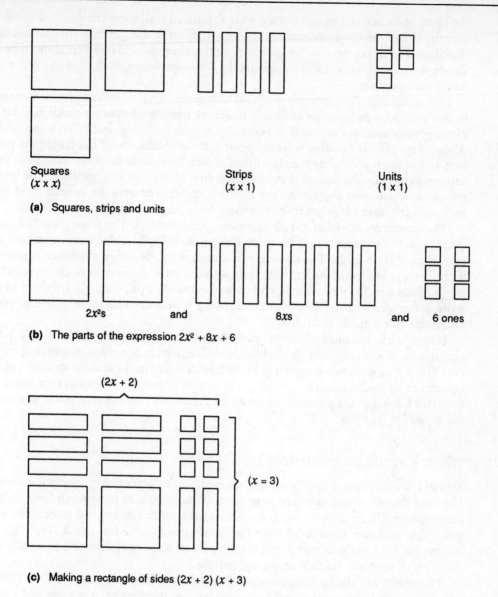

Figure 8.4 *Factorising quadratic functions with concrete materials*

It might be argued that it would be much quicker to do the problem in the old concrete-symbolic way: lay out the brackets, which will have to have $2x$ beginning one and x the other $(2x +)(x +)$. The factors of 6 are 1 and 6, or 2 and 3. We then fiddle around with these combinations, until the addition of xs $[(2x + 2)(x + 3)$ gives $(6x + 2x)]$ makes $8x$. The concrete-symbolic method may be quicker, but it has fewer connections with other items of knowledge. The spatial method, on the other hand, links immediately to several known geometrical concepts. For example, the area or 'size' of a rectangle is the length multiplied by the breadth; when the two sides of a rectangle are the same, the result is a square (hence x^2 is x 'squared'); all these things are true whatever the size of the square or rectangle. Many students find it quite exciting to discover that algebra sums can be done by geometry or by other physical representations. Dienes also explains other ways of solving quadratics, for example, by using cups and beans and hooks on a balance.

How successful is the multiple-embodiment approach? Children taught for two years by this method were superior to closely matched, traditionally taught children in terms of: (a) positive attitudes to maths; (b) conceptual understanding; and (c) computing skill (Biggs 1966). The last finding was unexpected, as the children were not taught the rules, facts and tables, nor did they use algorithms as such for calculation; they worked out the answers to sums on the basis of their understanding of the concepts involved. The longer the children had been exposed to the method, the greater were the benefits; and children with the lowest IQs benefited the most from long exposure to the method.

The generative model of learning explains these findings. The more cross-links into other modes of representation, the more likely students will be able to comprehend and extend their knowledge. The principle of illustrating in as varied a manner as possible is not restricted to mathematics. Any attempt to use activity, illustration, concrete example, the field trip, the experiment, audiovisual aids and so on, simply helps them to use more and wider areas of their brains. Learning is bound to be more efficient, more secure and more usable as a result.

Nevertheless, the method has its limits. As Boulton-Lewis and Halford (1991) point out, the use of concrete aids in teaching itself demands much space in working memory. The correspondence between the structure of the material and the structure of the concept to be taught needs to be made quite explicit, and the procedures for using the materials known to the point of automaticity. Again, it's a question of being able to see the wood for the trees.

Do students learn from excursions?

School learning focuses mostly on declarative knowledge stored in semantic memory. How can the other dimensions of long-term memory be used to help reinforce semantic memory? The field excursion is intended to do just this by helping students to integrate their academic knowledge with their experience of the real world. Typically, the teacher takes the students into the field with a list of demonstrations or features the students are to note, the teacher acting as 'tour guide'.

The results are usually disappointing, according to MacKenzie and White (1982), who argued that observation and demonstration are insufficient. They devised a 'processing' excursion which required the students to be actively involved, including unusual actions such as wading through a mangrove swamp, tasting leaves for salinity, scrambling over cliff platforms. All activities were designed to link with a lesson on coastal geography and were designed to *generate* information to be observed and recorded. Three classes of mixed Year 8 and Year 9 students were given the detailed lesson, addressing 35 objectives. Two classes were then taken on an excursion, one class being given the usual 'guided tour' of demonstration and observations, the other, the processing excursion.

The results, according to the authors, were 'remarkable'. There were no differences between the three classes immediately after the lesson, but three months after, with the excursion intervening, the processing class recalled 90% of the original lesson, the traditional excursion class recalled 58% and the third class who simply had the lesson with

no excursion, 51%. There was also a special test designed to see if students linked experiences or observations with the facts taught in the lesson: the processing excursion
group was far better at this than the other groups.

The passive 'demo' was no better than having no excursion at all; the processing
excursion was very successful in helping students not only to retain previously taught material, but to make the connection between their formal knowledge and their experience
of the world. Students were required to *act,* in as many different modes as possible, to illustrate a set of concepts, operations or principles; without such activity, students learn
formal knowledge insecurely and as alien to the world to which it applies.

Carefully designed excursions require active involvement linked to previously learned material.

Summary

What is learning?

Learning is the process by which we come to interpret the world; development the process that opens out more abstract ways of interpretation. Such a complex process as learning can be understood in many ways. In the school context, a useful way for many purposes is to see learning as a pipeline, where processes follow in sequence.

Information-processing models of learning

A comparison with how computers handle information has given rise to the information-processing family of learning models, which are useful in understanding some aspects of school learning. Three stages of processing, involving memory systems, are postulated: the sensory register, where information is filtered and selected; working memory, which processes information by chunking, using either coding or rehearsal, or both; and long-term memory, where processed information is dismembered, stored and remembered.

The sensory register

The sensory register's function is to sort input information into 'important'/'reject' categories—what to attend to and what to ignore—through a process called precoding. We pay attention because: we decide to, the stimulus is either intense or variable, or the stimulus matches a physiological state. In teaching we focus on encouraging students to consciously desire to attend, by using variability: in teaching mode, in content, in media and in student–teacher interaction. Presentation of content by signalling important features or concepts is facilitated by using overviews and adjunct questions.

Working memory

Working memory, rather than long-term memory, is of limited capacity. Higher order cognitive processes therefore require optimising the use of working memory space, such that information becomes compressed or 'chunked'. One of the important foci of teaching and learning is therefore to derive strategies for making good use of working memory.

Processes in working memory

Two processes for chunking are available: rehearsal and coding. With verbal material, predominance of the first leads to rote learning and of the second to meaningful learning. Recoding is a process whereby existing schemata are changed to accommodate new learning and is related to the degree of intrinsic motivation experienced. Too much mismatch between old and new learning, however, can lead to strong negative feelings.

Long-term memory

Of the three suggested processes of long-term memory—trace decay, interference and structural integration—the latter is the most significant. The most important determinant of what is remembered is what is already known. Information is dismembered and reconstructed along one or more of seven dimensions—enactive, sensory, affective, temporal, spatial, semantic and logical—yielding variously procedural, episodic and semantic memory. Frequently school experiences isolate memory of the context from memory of content.

Encouraging meaningful learning

Meaningful learning is maximised when the content to be learned is of generic rather than surface codes. Meaningful learning should elicit the schemata that structure the content to be learned and utilise as many dimensions for encoding learning as possible. Four generalisations are suggested to maximise meaningful learning:

1. *The task needs to be potentially meaningful.* A poorly structured task, or an ill-chosen task that is out of context or irrelevant, cannot be learned in a meaningful way. Students will not become meaningfully involved in pointless tasks, such as copying notes, practising skills already mastered, looking up definitions of words out of context and learning them, or memorising unnecessarily.
2. *The task needs to be of an optimum level of difficulty.* If the task is too easy it is boring; if too difficult, it is discouraging. Maximum recoding occurs when there is an optimal mismatch between what the task needs for resolution and the existing structures the student can bring to bear.
3. *The task needs to be presented in a way that enables multiple levels of coding.* The more facets and sensory modalities, through which the student can engage the task, the better. However, abstract semantic or logical dimensions should be engaged along with episodic or enactive dimensions so that knowledge is integrated.
4. *The more active the learner the better.* Tasks that require higher levels of learner activity lead to better learning. Passive learning probably means that few dimensions for coding and recoding are being engaged. Good learning requires the output of energy.

So does good teaching.

Learning activities

1. Three memory systems in processing information

Our Figure 8.1 is the focus of this activity. The purpose is to 'decompose' the model, examine its parts and then progressively build up the model. As an individual activity you could check your understanding by redrawing the model, describing each of the major systems as you go. Alternatively, the model could be built up using overhead transparencies in an overlay manner with the sensory register on one, working memory on another and long-term memory on the third. When put together they show the relationships among the parts. A class activity could be to develop a comprehensive model by adding additional information to that we have provided in Figure 8.1 (e.g., long-term memory could include comments about trace decay, interference, structural integration). Are you involved in generative activity here?

2. Memory span

We mentioned digit span earlier in this chapter. Digit span is often seen as a good measure of working memory and indeed forward digit span is used in many tests of intelligence. Backward digit span (repeating the numbers in the reverse of their order of presentation) is also interesting as you can get at the strategies individuals use to solve problems.

The task here is to gather data on digit span across the life span. You will need a child, a teenager, a middle-aged person and a person in their 70s or 80s. For each give them a forward digit span test and a backward digit span test.

You can use the following set for the forward span and make up your own for the backward span. You may want to extend the upper range (say to 9 or 10 digits) for adults. For the test you inform the person that you will be giving them a set of numbers which they have to repeat back to you. If you say '3, 5, 8', then the person should give you back '3, 5, 8' to be correct. You will see that the test has three items at each level of difficulty. You begin at the two digit level and give each of the three items separately, then you move to the three level, then four, etc. You stop testing when all three at any level have been failed. You get a score by adding up the number of correct items.

TEST

(1) 7,5	(2) 2,9	(3) 8,4
(1) 3,7,2	(2) 6,8,3	(3) 5,8,7
(1) 5,2,7,9,	(2) 3,6,2,7	(3) 5,3,1,9
(1) 3,7,5,2,6	(2) 2,4,9,5,1	(3) 3,7,1,9,4
(1) 2,8,1,7,4,9	(2) 4,9,2,5,1,7	(3) 4,8,3,9,5,2
(1) 3,5,9,1,7,4,2	(2) 4,9,1,5,2,6,8	(3) 5,2,7,8,4,1,5

At the end of testing ask the person HOW they were trying to remember the numbers (e.g., rehearsing, imagery, chunking, etc.—all things we have discussed in this chapter).

Give a similar test but the numbers have to be repeated back to you in reverse order. So if you give '5,2,7,9' they should give '9,7,2,5'. Also ask HOW they did the task.

In a whole class activity the results can be plotted on a graph using average correct for child, teenager, middle-aged and older person. What do you notice about the trends? Compare the forward span to the backward for the child, etc. Why is it that backward tends to be done less well? Finally, list the strategies that each group (child, teenager, etc.) tends to use in solving these problems. What do you notice about the range of strategies for each of the groups? What are the implications for school-type learning and teaching?

3. Concept/schematic maps

The challenge in using schematic/concept maps is to develop a comprehensive map for a particular topic or area of study. You could develop one yourself to cover some topic that you are currently studying. At a class level, a schematic map could be used to provide an overview of a seminar presentation, to examine the content of a unit, or to test understanding. If you are involved in teaching in schools you could prepare 'maps' for topics. They are useful in testing knowledge as well. You give a partially completed 'map' to students and they have to fill in the missing parts. Alternatively, students could be asked to generate their own concept maps on a topic.

4. Lesson variability

The purpose of this activity is to take up the section in this chapter on variability, particularly variability in style of teaching, in the media and materials of instruction and in student–teacher interaction (Turney et al. 1983).

The task is to prepare a lesson plan that shows a range of options for variability. This can be done using a set of columns or a set of stems to show different ways in which the lesson could be taught. The beginnings of such a plan are shown below for a lesson on spiders for infant grade children.

Introduction   (1) Show spiders in jars
                    or (2) Read story about spiders
                    or (3) Take class out into grounds to see if spiders can be found
                    or (4) Show stimulus video on spiders
                    or (5) etc.

Lists of activities such as these can be produced and decisions made about which ones to use. This will depend upon resources. In simulated teaching, each of these introductions could be trialled on peers and their reactions sought.

Another way to examine variability is during peer teaching activities. Having presented a short lesson or part of a lesson the 'teacher' descibes what variations were listed before the lesson was presented and which ones were chosen and for what reasons.

5. Excursions

As we noted, field excursions are designed to help students integrate their academic knowledge with real world experiences. We also noted, from the work of MacKenzie and White (1982) that a 'tour' approach to excursions is not beneficial to learning, especially in the longer term. What is required is generative learning. This activity is designed to draw out these issues by getting you to respond to the following scenario:

You have been appointed to a school that has a record of not taking students on excursions because most of the staff believe them to be a waste of time—'Students learn nothing from excursions, nothing …' Some of the more honest teachers admit that their dislike of excursions is due to their not having many ideas about teaching/learning strategies for use outside the classroom.

You have been asked by the principal to lead a 30 minute discussion at the next staff meeting on teaching strategies that could be used on an excursion.

What strategies would you focus on? How would you present the information? (in a short excursion?). Would you talk about the MacKenzie and White study?

As a class activity, the strategies could be listed on the chalkboard. Alternatively, groups could be assigned to respond to the scenario. Indeed, different scenarios could be developed to provide variability, each group responding to a different scenario.

6. Literature review

We referred earlier to Hamaker's review of the literature on adjunct questions, 'The effects of adjunct questions on prose learning' *(Review of Educational Research* 1986, 56, 212–42). This paper is a comprehensive review of the area and is worthy of closer examination. (This is not an easy article to read. Be willing to read it many times before you understand it! Hint: Look at the Discussion after you have read the Abstract.)

Several learning activities suggest themselves. At an individual level you could plot out a schematic representation of the article using Hamaker's major sub-headings (e.g., Major Research Design Features, Method, etc.) then proceeding to put minor sub-headings and details underneath. Alternatively you might move directly to the Discussion section of the paper (pp. 236–8) and summarise the overall findings—there are eight of them. Go back through the paper and find the supporting evidence.

As a class group activity, sections of Hamaker's paper could be assigned to small groups (e.g., one group could consider point 1 in the discussion, another point 2, etc.). Each group would then be responsible for reporting their 'section' back to the whole class. In reporting the sections you should consider the section of this chapter which deals with attention. Make your group's report the 'best' at getting attention at the beginning of the presentation.

Further reading

On attention, working memory and long-term memory
Case, R. (1985). *Cognitive Development*. New York: Academic Press.
Norman, D. A. (1990). *Memory and Attention*. New York: Wiley.

Case, in Chapters 14, 15 and 16, provides a comprehensive review of the nature of working memory and its relation to higher order processes. Norman's book, into its umpteenth edition, is an excellent top-up to the present chapter, giving more detail but in a clearly written way.

On meaningful learning and teaching
Ausubel, D. P. (1967). *Educational Psychology: A Cognitive View*. New York: Holt, Rinehart & Winston.
Boulton-Lewis, G. & Halford, G. (1991). Processing capacity and school learning. In G. T. Evans (ed.), *Learning and Teaching Cognitive Skills* (pp. 27–50). Hawthorn, Vic.: Australian Council for Educational Research.
Wittrock, M. (1977). The generative process of memory. In M. C. Wittrock (ed.), *The Human Brain*. Englewood Cliffs: Prentice Hall.

Ausubel's books was written over 20 years ago, but his account of rote and meaningful learning is classic, particularly on how content can be appraoched in a meaningful way. Boulton-Lewis and Halford approach meaning from the point of view of the structures the learner can impose, which is in part a function of available working memory: keep it uncluttered, they emphasise. Wittrock gives an account of generative learning and how to maximise it.

CHAPTER 9

LEARNING AND PERSONALITY

Learning and personality

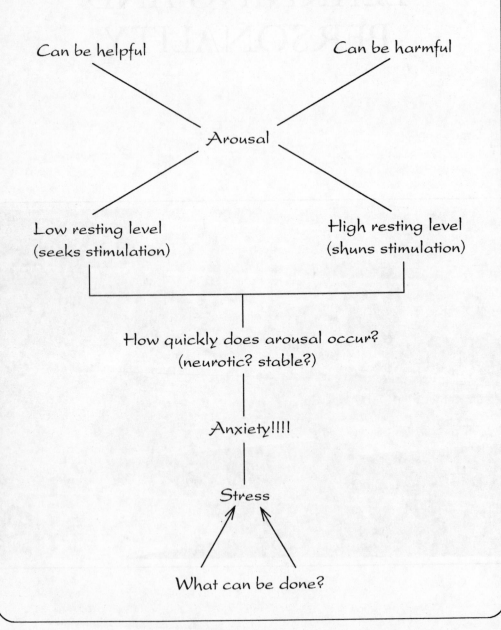

Can be helpful   Can be harmful

Arousal

Low resting level   High resting level
(seeks stimulation)   (shuns stimulation)

How quickly does arousal occur?
(neurotic? stable?)

Anxiety!!!!

Stress

What can be done?

LEARNING AND PERSONALITY

In this chapter, you will find out:

- how arousal both energises and interferes with learning;
- why simple tasks can be done more effectively under stress than complex tasks;
- why some people seem more anxious than others;
- why extroverts tend to socialise a lot;
- how to handle stressful situations;
- whether Australian teachers are more subject to burnout than others;
- when to call in the school counsellor.

Arousal and information processing

So far, we have been looking at 'cold' cognition: selecting, processing, storing and recalling information. We now turn to 'hot' cognition: the energy that drives the system and the effects it has on how we process information. The key is the concept of *arousal*.

So let us now introduce a fourth system into Figure 8.1, the *arousal system* (Figure 9.1), which has links with both sensory register and with working memory. It will be recalled that when something is precoded as 'important' the message goes straight to working memory for further processing. This is marked as pathway 1 in Figure 9.1. In addition, however, another signal goes to the arousal system (pathway 2). It is this boost to arousal that distinguishes important from unimportant messages, in the form of what is called the 'orienting' response, which in effect gives notice that something big is on the way. The arousal system also directly affects working memory (pathway 3), by taking up space in that system. We elaborate on these effects in the present chapter.

The orienting response

As we have seen, some messages are more likely than others to be precoded as important; these are messages that vary from expectations, that signify danger or some biological need, or simply those that we decide are important (pp. 208–9). Such messages are accompanied by what is called the *orienting* response; the individual becomes oriented to pay attention to a new and important event. At the same time, arousal (or cognitive energy) is increased to help handle the new situation.

Input from our sense organs thus takes two routes to the brain:

1. to the cortex, where it is interpreted and stored for decision-making, problem solving or other cognitive processes, as discussed earlier in Chapter 8 and
2. to the reticular arousal system (RAS), which is located in the brain stem (Hebb 1955).

The RAS consists of dense neuronal fibres that operate not in a specific cognitive manner dealing with specific messages, as do the cortical cells, but in a general sense, giving

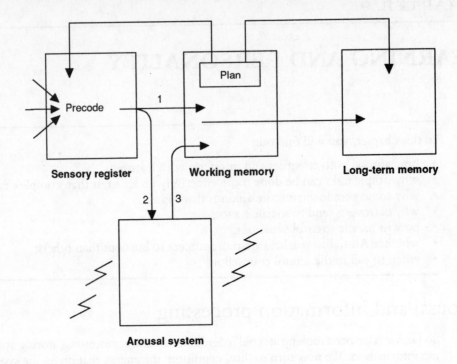

Figure 9.1 *The relation between arousal and information processing systems*

a 'buzz' to the whole system. In particular, the autonomic nervous system is activated, which releases adrenalin to the bloodstream, resulting in increased sweating, heart-rate, rate of breathing and blood flow to the larger muscle systems, eye pupil dilation, and a slowing down of the digestive processes. These changes are useful for emergency action requiring immediate energy, such as fighting or running away. The system returns to normal when the energy has been expended.

However, as most of the stress we endure today is psychological rather than physical, emergency action does not usually demand an immediate, high-energy output. We are forced to deal with emotional or stressful situations with bodily functions that have to be ignored or suppressed in our civilised settings. Instead of lashing out, that energy is dammed up inside, leading to unresolved stress and psychosomatic disorders such as heart attack and stomach ulcers. But well before that breakdown stage, autonomic arousal has immediate effects on cognitive functioning.

Autonomic arousal results in increased heart-rate, sweating, butterflies in the stomach and other strong feelings that signify that something is horribly wrong. We become *aware* of these feelings; that is, they occupy working memory, which you will recall is of strictly limited capacity. Remember, too, that we are also grimly aware of the cause of the autonomic arousal: the threatening event, in other words, that sparked all this off, suddenly remembering that the ghastly staff meeting at which you will have to confront the principal over his new discipline policy is tomorrow. So you can see that under stress working memory easily becomes overloaded with unpleasant and task irrelevant responses. In short, strong arousal is likely to be distracting and to interfere with effective performance.

Arousal, then, has two effects:

- *energising*, which enhances performance;
- *interfering*, which detracts from performance.

These two effects thus work in opposite ways. At low levels of arousal, the interfering effect is least, so energising predominates; we get better and better at the task the more aroused we become. That makes sense. When we are very tired, we can't be bothered to put much energy into it and the more awake we become the better we perform. At higher levels of arousal, however, the interfering effect greatly increases and eventually dominates, so that performance gets worse and worse, as arousal gets higher. That too makes sense. We don't perform well at all when over-excited or jittery. At some mid-way range of arousal, performance is optimal. Precisely where that point is depends on many factors including personality and task complexity. We pick up the point about task complexity in the next section.

Arousal and performance: Simple and complex tasks

The arousal system is comparable to the brightness control of a television set and performance to the picture quality of the tube. If the brightness control is turned down (i.e., arousal is low) there is no clear picture. As brightness is increased the picture becomes clearer up to an optimal midpoint, but then becomes progressively washed out.

The relationship between arousal and performance is therefore an inverted U-curve (Figure 9.2). At low levels of arousal, performance is poor (at extremely low levels we are asleep). As arousal increases, performance improves up to an optimal point after which it deteriorates. On the upward slope, the energising effects of arousal predominate; on the descending slope, the interfering effects take over (Humphreys & Revelle 1984).

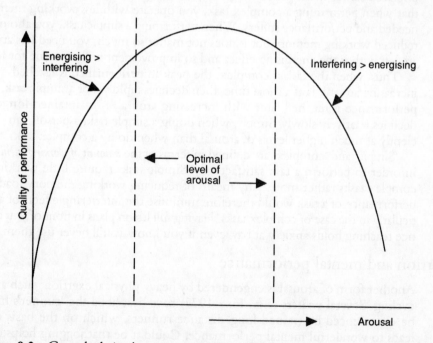

Figure 9.2 *General relation between arousal and quality of performance (the inverted U)*

It is important that teachers strike the best balance, so that students are energised to the highest level possible before interference occurs. In questioning a student in class, gentle probing may well lead to a good response (energising predominates), but heavy or sarcastic questioning is likely to make the student flustered; if answers are forthcoming at all, they will probably be confused or incorrect (interference predominates).

The point at which a student moves from good to flustered responding depends on the nature of the task and the personality of the student. Very simple questions, to which the student knows the answers, are less likely to be affected adversely than complex questions, the answers to which require the integration of a lot of information. Similarly, anxious students are more likely to be adversely affected by heavy public questioning than less anxious students.

Anxiety, as one form of arousal, has an inverted-U relationship to performance. When people couldn't care less, they don't bother to try. Performance is low. When people are 'hyper', they try too hard, become confused and the mind 'goes blank'. Performance is again low. With middling anxiety, performance is best for that person for that task. The Yerkes-Dodson Law states that *simple* tasks are performed better under *high* degrees of motivation; *complex* tasks are performed better under *low* degrees of motivation. In class questioning, a simple question is more likely to be answered satisfactorily under bullying than a complex question.

While arousal is necessary to energise performance, too much invades working memory, thereby impairing performance. Increases in anxiety make us become aware of the physiological and psychological side-effects of arousal; our heart pounds, we have butterflies in the stomach, we feel helpless. These I-feel-awful cues take over working memory to the exclusion of information relevant to the task and, because complex tasks require more relevant cues for adequate processing than do simple tasks, relevant cues are displaced earlier when performing complex than when doing simple tasks. The effect is that when performing a complex task, you operate with less working memory than is needed and performance suffers. When performing a simple task, you also operate with reduced working memory but it does not matter so much; you need less and what you are left with is the energising effect and so improvement will continue for longer.

Thus, when the task is complex, the peak in performance is reached quickly with increasing arousal, lasts a short time, then declines rapidly. For a simple task, the peak in performance is reached later with increasing arousal, is maintained longer and then declines relatively slowly. Simply, when doing a simple task, a person can operate efficiently at much higher levels of arousal than when doing a complex task.

'Simple' and 'complex' are defined in terms of the *amount of working memory* required in order to perform a task satisfactorily. Simple tasks require little working memory, complex tasks rather more. Any means of reducing working memory load during the performance of a task would therefore minimise the interfering effects of anxiety, particularly in the case of complex tasks. Having full lesson plans in front of you during practice teaching holds anxiety at bay, even if you know you'll never use them.

Exertion and mental performance

Another form of arousal is engendered by heavy physical exertion, such as jogging or cycling. Several writers (e.g., Fixx 1977) have described the 'runner's high', said to be experienced by trained long-distance runners, which on the basis of anecdote leads to wonderful mental performance. Could it be that jogging helps one towards the peak in Figure 9.2?

In a series of studies initially carried out on some aspirants to the Australian Olympic Team, Davey (1973) noted that under extreme stress highly experienced athletes sometimes made 'stupid' decisions, such as changing into the wrong lane, sprinting too soon or tackling the wrong player. Davey then set up an experiment using physical education students, giving them two tasks to perform while pedalling an exercise bike. The tasks were:

- spotting odd–even–odd sequences in strings of digits, which demands high concentration;
- a working memory task, requiring the immediate repetition of digits.

He found that performance on the first task increased dramatically for the first 4 minutes of hard pedalling (about equivalent to running a fast 800 metres): working memory was unaffected. After this time, however, most subjects declined rapidly on both tasks.

Tomporowski and Ellis (1986) reviewed many studies, which in general back up Davey's findings, with some qualifications. The facilitating effect of exercise is confirmed, although if the exercise is continued too long, or the subjects are unfit, exercise begins to interfere with performance. Wall (1989) showed that this general pattern generalised to primary school children. She gave memory, spatial, and arithmetic tasks to 60 Year 5 students after various intervals of pedalling on an exercise bike, up to a maximum of 4 minutes. The children were divided, on the basis of a sports day performance, into 'fit', 'medium fit' and 'unfit'. The familiar inverted U began to emerge in the case of the unfit and the medium fit, but even then, after 4 minutes of hard exercise, the children were still *better* at spatial reasoning and arithmetic tasks than when they were at rest. The scores of the fit children were still on the increase.

Are these effects due to arousal in the usual sense? Molloy, Browne, Pierce and King (1990) ingeniously showed that they are. They argued that hyperactive children after exercise should show the same on-task attention that they do after chemical arousal. In the United States, the stimulant methylphenidate (Ritalin) is regularly used to 'sedate' hyperactive children. Molloy and his colleagues showed that 5 minutes on an exercise bike had the same effect, as after that much exercise hyperactive children's attention was 82% on task—near enough to normal—while both they and normal children showed a significant improvement in arithmetic performance (which however washed out after 10 minutes on the bike).

These studies have most interesting implications, both for normal and for hyperactive children. At the least, they question conventional wisdom about the timetabling of PE lessons. Children might concentrate better if the more academic subjects were timetabled *after* PE, not before. A fast jog might be a good idea before an examination. Obviously, there is much room for further research.

Personality differences in arousal

Psychologists distinguish between *trait* anxiety and *state* anxiety. Trait anxiety refers to a *general readiness* to react with anxiety in many situations. State anxiety refers to the anxiety *actually experienced* in a particular situation.

People differ markedly in their tendency to react to stress. Some people overreact and hence tend to seek quietness and solitude in order to work comfortably; others need stimulation in order to work comfortably. Some students are quite distressed by being questioned in public, while others actively seek the limelight. Thus, stress in itself is neither good nor bad. A variety of factors determine whether the stress is *eu-stress* (from the Greek meaning 'good'), in which case the person will be challenged and invigorated by stress, or *di-stress*, which means exactly what it says.

Trait anxiety

Trait anxiety, or neuroticism (see below), is a characteristic predisposition of some people to react with anxiety. It is part of their physiology, particularly of the reticular arousal system and of the autonomic nervous system, and is probably inherited (which is not to say that people cannot develop ways of keeping their general anxiety under reasonable control). People who are high in trait anxiety may or may not actually experience anxiety in a particular situation, but they would tend to react with anxiety more so than people low on trait anxiety.

Eysenck (1957) distinguishes between two arousal-related dimensions:

1. *Introversion–extraversion.* This dimension relates to the *resting* level of arousal. Some people start with a low baseline of arousal; they thus need a great deal of stimulation to bring them up to their working optimal level. Eysenck calls these individuals *extraverts;* they seek excess stimulation (frequently but not necessarily in the form of socialising) because they need extra arousal if they are to function at their best. Other people start with a high baseline or resting level of arousal; these people need to avoid stimulation, otherwise they too easily go over the top and have to operate at supra-optimal levels of arousal. These individuals are called *introverts* (Eysenck 1957).

2. *Neuroticism–stability.* This dimension relates to the *rate of change* of arousal. Whether starting from a low or a high resting level, some people's arousal system reacts rapidly to stimulation; these individuals seem to overreact to stimuli, becoming excited over what to others are trivial issues. Eysenck calls these people *neurotic.* Other people's arousal systems react slowly; such people seem calm, even insensitive; they are referred to as *stable* (op. cit.).

These terms were meant by Eysenck to have a strict, technical meaning and ought not to be confused with the everyday meanings they also have. 'Extraverted' in Eysenck's sense does not mean 'sociable', although sociability is one reliable symptom of extraversion, as other people are a very good source of stimulation. Similarly, 'neurotic' does not mean 'on the verge of nervous breakdown' (whatever that might mean), although excessive worrying is a symptom of high neuroticism. Neuroticism in Eysenck's meaning is in fact very close to trait anxiety; it refers to the readiness some people have of reacting anxiously to a variety of situations.

Introversion and extraversion (note the spelling of the latter: not 'extro-') refer to operating at a steady level under constant conditions; people work out their ways of handling their arousal level, which become characteristic of them and of the ways they come typically to engage the world. (In the following pen-portraits, please note that we are discussing extremes of a continuous distribution, not cut-and-dried categories.) So, in their concern with lifting arousal to an optimal level, extraverts seek stimulation: they tend to be boisterous and noisy, to mix with other people, to study with the radio blaring. They love parties, but in fact have a low tolerance for alcohol (which paradoxically is a depressant: it lowers arousal). Their general orientation is external.

Introverts avoid excessive stimulation and those situations that lead to the discomfort associated with high arousal. Hence they prefer their own company or that of a few friends; they prefer to study in quiet surroundings. They are internally oriented and more perceptive of their own behaviour.

Whereas introversion–extraversion refers to a steady state, neuroticism–stability refers to reactions to changing conditions and especially to temporarily stressed circumstances, like time pressure, interpersonal harrassment, or threat. Thus, we would expect there to be differences in the way introverts and extraverts would react to constant conditions, neurotic and stable personalities to emergencies.

Following on from this, you might think that introverts and extraverts would prefer, and work optimally in, different kinds of educational environment. You would be right. A few years ago, quite a lot of research was done on this question and it was found that whereas extraverts did better in school, introverts did better at university (Naylor 1972). How come? One explanation is that the pressures in schools are more external, coming from teachers and parents rather than from within the student: you do your homework, or else. At university, on the other hand, pressures tend to be rather less external in origin and more internal: it is more up to you to work out your own salvation. Extraverts are more likely to find it on the footy field, introverts in the library. That was the theory then. Whether it would hold today is an open question; schools are much more relaxed than they were twenty and more years ago, and universities possibly more competitive (most definitely, if we are talking about academic staff).

How do neurotics handle pressure?

Wrightsman (1962) divided a group of students into high and low trait-anxious (or neurotic and stable, respectively) and gave them an intelligence test, telling one group (stressed) that the results were so important they could affect their college careers, and the other group (unstressed) that the results were only needed for norming the test and would not be looked at individually. The stable or low-anxious groups performed at the same level under both conditions, but the high-anxious neurotics performed very differently: the stressed group performing at a lower level than the unstressed. In other words, the high trait-anxious did not feel anxious in the unstressed condition, but did when they thought the test results were going to be important to them. Similarly, O'Neill, Spielberger and Hansen (1969) found that high trait-anxious students did better than low-anxious on the easy items in a mathematical concept task, but the low-anxious did better on the difficult items.

Trait anxiety or neuroticism thus affects performance only to the extent to which anxiety is actually experienced. People low on trait anxiety can tolerate more environmental stress before being affected adversely, but those easily aroused to anxiety may only need to be told that the result is important, or to find that the items are difficult, to experience disabling anxiety. It is therefore important that teachers are aware that some students can be subjected to stress without harm, but others need to be handled more carefully. The next point, of course, is to identify which are which.

The task of making personality diagnoses is done on the basis of psychological tests that should only be administered by a qualified psychologist. The role of the school counsellor in this and other functions is discussed later in this shapter. In any case, it is most unlikely that the counsellor would, or should, be involved in screening whole classes for the purpose of identifying which kids can safely and with benefit be monstered and which should be handled with kid gloves. In some cases, the daily round of teacher–student interaction will make the distinction clear; non-anxious kids will perform better under mild stress, such as public questioning, while others will stammer, blush and generally look uncomfortable. You lay off the latter kind.

Other kids will have erected some pretty stable defences that may easily mislead a teacher into thinking they are personally resilient whereas in fact they may be highly vulnerable; introverts, for example, may appear quiet and in control but may very easily be stimulated into over-arousal. One cannot do more in the present context than alert teachers to these kinds of individual difference, and suggest that commonsense and humanity will be adequate for most cases; but that it may be necessary to refer other cases, hopefully few, to the counsellor for special professional treatment.

State anxiety

When anxiety is associated with a particular set of circumstances, we speak of *state* anxiety. Testing is a particularly common example, which strikes some students whenever their competence is laid on the line, by questioning in class or by formal testing; they may not, however, be more anxious than anyone else in other, non-testing, situations. Thus, *test anxiety* is associated with anxiety about doing poorly when being evaluated (Sarason et al. 1960).

Gaudry and Bradshaw (1970) reasoned that students high in test anxiety would do better under progressive assessment (based on class assignments and informal short tests) than under terminal assessment (based on formal examinations). Testing Years 7 and 8 pupils in 14 Melbourne schools bore out these expectations, leading to the conclusion that as terminal examinations are more potentially stressful than progressive assessment, it is unfair on test-anxious children to offer them no choice in the form of examination. Students who are not test-anxious, on the other hand, resent the continual though less severe pressure that progressive assessment brings.

Number anxiety is associated with a fear of arithmetic. One reason why arithmetic, more than other school subjects, can create anxiety is because it is abstract and yet the answers are so definitely right or wrong; one can so easily feel out of control. If a person is prone to anxiety and has little grasp of number concepts, the situation is particularly threatening: one is right, or more usually wrong, for mysterious reasons that one cannot explain (Biggs 1962). When people are test or number anxious they engage in a high degree of 'negative internal dialogue' (Hunsley 1987), convincing themselves they are going to do badly. And of course they do.

Computer anxiety is a state anxiety which shares very similar characteristics to number anxiety, in that one appears to be in the grip of Powerful Other. High tech is a big unknown and software has this terrifying habit of doing things you didn't ask it to do, or so it appears in the early days of getting acquainted with this Other. Thus, many people see computers as threatening, girls rather more than boys (Clarke 1990). Both number and computer anxiety can be prevented if one demystifies from the outset, but once it is there, it is difficult to eradicate. 'Gee whiz' demonstrations, beloved by Ed Tech types, do not help.

Dealing with particular crises is another matter, as we see in the next section.

How to manage anxiety

When a person is faced with stress, particularly in a one-off situation, strategies for handling it can be worked out. It is much easier to learn how to cope with a single stressful event, in which it is important to function well (such as an interview), than it is for a chronic, lifestyle, situation. In the latter case, professional help is certainly advised.

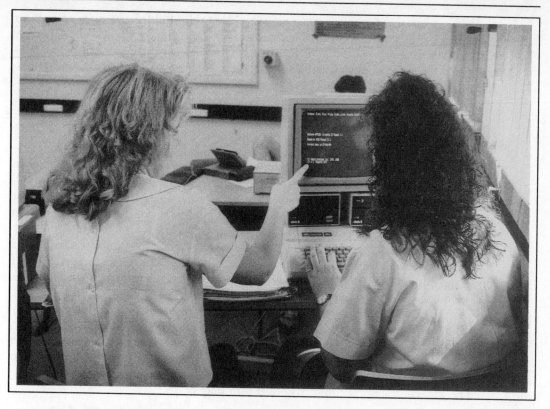

Computer anxiety is a state anxiety in that one appears to be in the grip of a Powerful Other.

The villain in both cases is working memory overload, although in the chronic situation there is much more to it than that. But just to focus on working memory, the poor performance arises because of the felt stress distracting from the important task-relevant cues. Over-learning is one means of reducing the information needing conscious attention.

'Over'-learning means learning way beyond the point necessary for perfect recall. Over-learned cues are much less likely to be displaced when the arousal system is over-activated, as under high stress. In army training, skills such as stripping, cleaning and reassembling a weapon are taught and practised over and over, long after the soldier can perform the task perfectly. The point is that the process will need to be done under battle conditions of extreme stress and therefore the less conscious thought needed to do the task the better. Similarly, rehearsing actors are taken over their lines and perform complicated sequences, many times *after* they have given a 100% performance.

Over-learning thus has two effects: it *reduces the size of the chunk*, thus freeing working memory, and it makes *recall* very much easier. The first function can be achieved in other ways too and that is where the strategies come in. When the unexpected might happen, one must have as much working memory available as possible. The following paradigm emerges:

- *Define the problem clearly.* 'The interview scares me' is too vague. What in particular about the interview is causing the worry—a tricky question? The presence of a particular individual? The unexpected?

- *Devise coping procedures to meet the defined problem*. Use hidden cue cards to prevent 'drying up' or see the individual beforehand on some pretext.
- *Over-learn those coping procedures*. Rehearse under real-life, not artificially restricted, conditions. One cannot anticipate the unexpected (by definition), so the main strategy is to keep as much working memory as free as possible to allow for any such contingencies.

Let us take some examples of stress management.

1. Exam stress

On first reading exam questions, jot down whatever points occur and then make up an outline in logical order and with sub-headings. Once started, relevant information will come rushing back by association, if the material has been learned well. That relevant information will in turn crowd out such negative internal dialogue as: 'Gosh, how am I going to do this? ... I feel quite sick ...'

However, this assumes a solid background of well-learned relevant material. Such a background almost certainly cannot be acquired in the week or two before an exam. If notes and outlines are based on just a week of rote learning, the immediate associations will be quickly exhausted with nothing to replace them.

Generic coding is the answer. A generic code is like a fishing line which has many short lines and hooks attached; and to each hook is attached another line, also with many hooks. By hauling in the main line, a great deal of richly associated material is drawn into working memory and, if it is sufficiently well learned, such material will displace the feeling directly due to anxiety.

The general strategy is cumulative over four stages:

1. *Learning*. This is the initial learning itself (a book chapter, a lecture). The basic material is read and assimilated.
2. *Elaboration*. The learner thinks about what has been learned and relates it to relevant material already known. The old material provides structure for the new; the new helps re-evaluate the old.
3. *Organisation*. Gradually a pattern emerges; the content begins to make sense. This process takes time, but is hastened by much note-taking during elaboration and also during the next stage.
4. *Consolidation*. The learner starts making notes of notes, interrelating all the bits and pieces about working memory, for example, that have been picked up in the references, in discussion and in original classwork. One then makes notes of these notes, uses spatial summaries, or a concept map; an outline of the whole course may, almost literally, be written on a bus ticket. At that point the learner is ready to rote-learn the notes-of-notes-of-notes—not to understand anything better, but simply to make sure those notes can be recalled on cue.

Because of the background of learning, a particular word or pattern in the notes is like one of the hooks on the main line: it is attached by cross-referencing to so much other relevant material.

People who study according to this four-stage process can even afford to be in a state of high anxiety during an exam. Once they get going, and that is the important thing, the relevant information, if sufficiently well coded and established, could rush in and take over. The student would then have it both ways: the advantage of working under the energising condition of high arousal, with a working memory dominated by relevant information.

A four stage process of studying (learn, elaborate, organise, consolidate) can help reduce test anxiety.

2. Stress management during teaching practice

A student, whom we shall call Jim, devised a scheme to cope with his first supervised practice teaching lesson. He was not looking forward to practice teaching; he had always been nervous about speaking in public, but he had also learned that he would get over it in time, as he had with his 'tutorial nerves' by second year. The problem was a matter of getting through the first block practice of four weeks. He followed the above paradigm.

Defining the problem. The problem seemed at first to be: 'It isn't fair that I get nervous and it'll count against me'. Jim could see that to dwell on that just made matters worse. *Why* get nervous? Because of the unknowns: he didn't know quite what to expect. His method lecturer told him he should make early contact with the school: just to find out what he *is* going to be required to do. He met his supervising subject master and class teachers. He was given a list of classes he was to teach and details of the pupils and of the teaching program. He was also told that one of the teachers would be sitting in with him until they were reasonably sure he could handle the pupils. He asked to be shown the classrooms after school. He would need those snapshots for his mental rehearsals. He now knew what the most likely problems were.

- *Content?* No, that had been covered in depth in university; he also knew the class texts and had access to plenty of reference material.
- *Method?* No. He'd done some peer teaching and microteaching and was familiar with a range of skills, how to use the audiovisual aids, etc.
- *Discipline?* Of course, but that was unlikely to be a major problem at this stage with a teacher present.
- *Being centre stage?* Yes, in particular having to cope with the unexpected.

Devising coping procedures. First, he had time on his side, plenty of time to plan.

- *Routinise.* What about all those unexpecteds? Keep everything as *simple as possible*. He decided to follow the same lesson plan and set of routines for every lesson he could get away with: standard set of sub-headings, same number of points, entry into room, diagram with name and pupil seating arrangement for each room propped on his desk in front of him, who was sitting where (check they haven't moved), clean chalkboard ... Too bad if he was marked down for rigidity.
- *Afraid he'll dry up and have nothing to say?* Use materials that would cue him: hand-outs, transparencies, some videos, textbook as a standby.
- *Use dominant body language.* Stand straight, use frequent eye contact (but avoid eye contact with the supervisor: that could really throw you). *Look* dominant, but let the materials do most of the 'talking'.
- *Pupils?* Keep them busy. No gaps. Activities that will make them work, not ask questions ...
- *Over-learn.* There was plenty here to over-learn—all these routines in the context of his mental photographs and the by-now memorised lists of names. So, with his cat and budgie understudying those names, he rehearsed all the routines. He found the odd joke occurring to him—*quick write that down, memorise it* (you never know when that might defuse a tense moment).

Outcome. It worked. There was the odd blip. Announcements over the PA and visitors sometimes disrupted his flow but the routines took over. The supervising teacher withdrew at the beginning of the third week, apparently satisfied now that he could manage. He *did* make a crack about varying the routine: 'Just a little, old son. Keep that up for the next 40 years and you'll die of boredom ...' Which raises the question of teacher stress over the longer term.

3. Teacher stress and burnout

Both beginning and experienced teachers experience state anxiety which has a detrimental effect on both teacher effectiveness and personal happiness (Coates & Thoreson, 1976; Telfer, 1979a, 1981, 1982). Common sources of anxiety among beginning teachers are classroom management and pupil discipline, conflicts with supervisors, popularity with pupils, and their own expertise in terms of content knowledge and teaching skills. Experienced teachers mention discipline as a problem less frequently, being more concerned with their adequacy to handle specific student needs and with industrial issues.

Teacher anxiety adversely affects the quality of the classroom atmosphere (Keavney & Sinclair 1978). Anxious teachers tend to:

- create higher student anxiety;
- teach more dogmatically and rigidly;
- be less friendly to students;

- use negative and critical feedback for poor student performance and behaviour rather than praise for work well done;
- have more rowdy classes;
- award lower grades for the same quality of work than non-anxious teachers.

When such a pattern becomes established, as it may very easily do, we speak of burnout. Burnout describes extreme stress, linked specifically to dealing with other people (Maslach 1976). There are three aspects to teacher burnout:

- increased feelings of emotional exhaustion and fatigue;
- negative, cynical attitudes to students;
- negative self-evaluations, particularly re personal accomplishment (Pierce & Molloy 1990a).

Burnout is an occupational hazard of those whose work is primarily in interaction with other people and is a response to excessive job-related demands. Teachers, like many in the helping professions, are particularly susceptible to burnout (Mandaglio 1984).

Pierce and Molloy (1990b) conducted a comprehensive survey of 1000 Victorian secondary teachers, which confirmed and added to this pattern. Biographical variables, apart from poor physical health, did not distinguish greatly between high and low burnout teachers; sex, marital status, age, teaching subject area, level of secondary teaching, or own educational level, did not relate to burnout. What did were job-related factors such as type of school (much higher in low SES government schools) and perception of the teacher's role. High burnout was associated also with high absenteeism, role conflict, regressive ways of dealing with work problems, low levels of career commitment and of responsibilities beyond the classroom, attribution of the stress in their lives to teaching, and a 'custodial' view of student control.

In another study of Victorian teachers, O'Connor and Clarke (1990) concluded that 'about a third of the sample reported that they experienced a high level of job stress' (p. 49); this they conclude is due to work-load demands, not to personal or demographic factors, with female teachers experiencing more stress in some areas such as work-load and student demands.

Do Australian teachers suffer more from burnout than American and Canadian teachers? On some aspects yes, on other aspects, no, according to Sarros and Sarros (1990). On emotional exhaustion, teachers from 229 Victorian high schools were quite low compared to the other two national groups, but on depersonalisation and personal accomplishment the Australians were significantly higher. Sarros and Sarros attribute these findings to the centralised bureaucracy of Victorian schools, to lack of recognition of merit and to limited career opportunities outside the seniority system.

Burnout is clearly a chronic state, depending on many factors beyond the individual's control. The individual teacher is not however entirely helpless, as there are things that can be done (see Box 9.1): but note the bottom line, the need for professional help.

We should conclude, then, with a discussion of one important resource person for both teacher and student: the school counsellor.

The school counsellor

Many problems and difficulties arising with individual students must be taken up with the school counsellor. Counsellors, guidance officers, or school psychologists as they are called in the United Kingdom, require a great deal more specific training than the

---

Box 9.1 *Countering burnout*

1. Accept the need for taking action about the stressors.
2. Evaluate the dissatisfactions, isolating those that can be remedied.
3. Look for new possibilities to find fresh solutions for problems. Your friends and colleagues may be able to help with such difficulties as finding time for marking and preparation. Other ways of reducing specific teaching anxieties are based on the idea of simulation games. Here, problems are defined and discussed, and solutions tried out in the 'safe' context of a game.
4. Examine your total workload and learn to say 'no' in an assertive but non-aggressive response to suggestions that you take on additional roles without dropping some. Can you delegate some responsibilities?
5. Critically assess your out-of-school lifestyle, hobbies, sport and leisure. Physical work and sport provide a release.
6. Can your workplace be improved? You may be able to effect simple changes which improve lighting, ventilation or lay-out of classroom and staff room. Are you meeting only the same small group of teachers at school? Break the routine. You could also try scheduling yourself some private time.
7. The bottom line calls for professional help and/or strategic withdrawal from the most extreme situations. Teachers with dual qualifications could change teaching subjects from, say, history to English, maths to science, or English to library. A transfer to another school, new staff and new pupils is another alternative.

Adapted from Pines, Aronsen & Kafry 1981

---

classroom teacher normally possesses; their licence to practise normally means registration through the Australian Psychological Society. Most teachers will be at primary or secondary schools where there is a permanent counsellor, either exclusive to that school, or shared with a group of schools (frequently, a high school and its 'feeder' primary schools have the one counsellor).

The traditional or clinical model of counselling is that the teacher is responsible for the general run of students, the counsellor for the problem students who do not get on well in the main system. That model implies a 'production line', with the counsellor straightening out those who fail to conform to the prevailing academic or behavioural or psychological standards; a fairly offensive concept, when you think about it.

Current thinking is more attuned to the 'systems' model: that if the student is having problems then you look at the total system of which the student is but one part (the systems model is discussed with respect to classroom learning as a whole in Chapter 16). Western Australian teachers perceived that psychologists were competent at 'traditional' activities, such as individual assessments and interventions, but not at the systems level, such as 'influencing educational policy, disseminating ideas through the mass media, conducting school-based research and advocating school-wide changes for the benefit of children in general' (Leach 1989: 366). On the other hand, teachers did want 'more system-centred activities, including in-service training and group work with teachers and parents and the dissemination of research findings' (op. cit.: 370). Certainly the shift in counsellor training is recently coming round to the systems viewpoint.

The counsellor may handle several kinds of problem. The initial referral might come about because of one or more of:

- learning difficulties, particularly sudden changes (which might indicate emotional disturbance);
- study difficulties, lack of study skills or facilities;
- behaviour problems, such as delinquency, difficulties in management;
- crisis intervention, where a child gives evidence of emotional upset, or drug usage;
- social problems, such as bullying or being bullied, sexual difficulties;
- home problems, which come to the teacher's attention and seem to require liaison or consultation with the school.

However, the problem and its solution is likely to involve many other people: the teacher, student, administration, and possibly the student's family. Likewise, intervention might therefore involve change in the teacher's classroom behaviour, or in school or departmental policy. Counsellors cannot of course bring about such changes on their own and the structures in the school should allow for the counsellor to act as change agent. The counsellor thus needs to act on a broad front and it is important that teachers understand the counsellor's role and what sort of help might be forthcoming.

Summary

Arousal and information processing

When precoding occurs, the arousal system is stimulated, with two effects: energising the cognitive system and generating its own stimulation. Because of the limitations of working memory, the latter may compete with task-relevant information. These competing tendencies interact to produce the familiar inverted U curve, where performance is enhanced, then diminished, by increasing arousal. The points of inflection will change according to personality and to task complexity.

Personality differences in arousal

It is important to distinguish anxiety actually experienced in a particular situation (state anxiety) and an individual's readiness to react with anxiety to future situations (trait anxiety or neuroticism). Two aspects of arousal have been distinguished that relate to personality differences: a person's typical resting level of arousal (low = extraversion; high = introversion) and a person's rate of change of arousal (rapid = neuroticism; slow = stability). These personality tendencies will determine how a person will react in a given situation and the extent to which anxiety will be experienced under stress.

How to manage anxiety

The main strategy for managing anxiety, so that one benefits from energising but minimises interference, is to protect working memory space. A three-stage paradigm for handling one-off stress situations is:

1. Define the problem clearly.
2. Devise coping strategies appropriate to the problem.
3. Over-learn those coping strategies.

The paradigm was applied to exam stress and to practice teaching. The more intransigent problem of chronic stress, or teacher burnout, was discussed. The bottom line of professional help, for both teacher and student, involves a resource person such as the school counsellor.

Learning activities

1. Terms used in this chapter

While this activity might seem somewhat low level, we think it important for you to understand the more technical definitions of some of the terms we have used in this chapter. We list some of them for you to test yourself. (Yes, you can look back!!)

> arousal (energising and interfering effects),
> trait anxiety and state anxiety,
> introversion and extraversion,
> neuroticism and stability.

2. Arousal and learning

This activity extends Activity 1 from the previous chapter, a model of systems in information processing. Here you need to add the arousal block to the model and then explain the relationships among the component parts of the model.

3. Examination stress

The task here is to prepare a two-page pamphlet for high school students explaining to them how they can reduce examination stress. The idea is to produce a readable, 'friendly' guide for students—make it as informative and interesting as you can. As a base you can use the strategies we developed in this chapter: learning, elaborating, organising and consolidating.

The pamphlet could be developed as part of group work in class or individually. Would you include something on fitness? Are the principles we discussed for management of stress during practice teaching applicable?

Your pamphlet might benefit from a section showing students where else they can get information to help them reduce examination stress.

4. The role of the school counsellor

We think it important for teachers to understand the role that the school counsellor takes within the system. What problems are the province of the teacher and what problems are clearly counsellor problems? How does the teacher make referrals?

To answer these types of questions we suggest that a school counsellor be invited along to class to facilitate your understanding of their role. Such an opportunity would allow you to look back over parts of other chapters as well. For instance, what is the role of the counsellor in mainstreaming/integration? Are IQ tests administered? If so, what purposes do they serve?

5. Stress management and practice teaching

In this chapter we saw how one student, 'Jim', handled the stress of practice teaching. The following activity can be done on an individual, group or whole class basis. The purpose of the activity is to identify the stressors associated with practice teaching and to suggest action that might be taken. (For current purposes we will take a class approach and present it stepwise for ease of understanding. The focus will be on identifying stressors.)

(a) The class is asked individually to identify the factors they think produce stress before practice teaching.

(b) A list of stressors is then compiled on the board from individual responses.

(c) This list is then used to categorise the stressors into those that can be: (i) eliminated; (ii) modified; and (iii) apparently unchanged.

(d) The focus is now on those that can be modified. Either as a class or as individuals, the list of modifiable stressors is ranked (1=highest stressor, etc.). Now you can see which of the stressors should be attended to first—presumably the modifiable one that ranks highest.

(e) Discussions about how these might be modified then follows. It may be that the stressors are specific (e.g., 'What classes am I to teach?') or general ('I feel very tense about the whole thing.') Clearly the former could be addressed by contacting the school whereas the latter might require some relaxation therapy. Books such as Rosemarie Otto's (1986), *Teachers under Stress*, and material produced by the NSW Department of Education (undated) *Managing Stress: A Workshop for School Personnel*, would be helpful in guiding you in stress reduction.

(f) In a similar session the 'apparently unchangeable' category could be ranked and discussions held about how they might be changed.

6. Teacher burnout

In this activity you are to try and identify the factors that teachers feel contribute to their stress and likely 'burnout'. As a mini-research project you will need to interview teachers and/or use a questionnaire which contains items shown to be important in teacher burnout. Your results could be presented individually to the class or they could be part of a class or group project on teacher stress. Pierce and Molloy (1990a; 1990b) could be useful here as could be the information in Box 9.1.

In general, though, sources of stress for teachers can be considered along dimensions such as: classroom management and discipline; career prospects; curriculum demands; lack of rewards and recognition; administration within the school; administration within the system; provision of resources; community concerns; responsibilities beyond normal expectations; interference of school work with leisure activities.

If you wanted to use a questionnaire you might generate a set of items such as:

	Stress level				
	Low				High
Lack of time to adequately prepare lessons	1	2	3	4	5
Insufficient support from community	1	2	3	4	5
etc.					

The preparation of items could be a class activity.

An extension of this activity would be to ascertain how the teachers you have gathered data from 'solve' their stress-related problems.

Further reading

On handling anxiety and stress
Fontana, D. (1989). *Managing Stress*. Leicester/London: British Psychological Society/Routledge.

Identifying and self-managing stress with particular reference to the workplace, with special mention of the classroom. You may think you don't need this ... yet.

Otto, R. (1986). *Teachers Under Stress*. Melbourne: Hill of Content.

Otto's book examines the extent and symptoms of teacher stress in Australia and also aims to help teachers understand that stress is preventable. Worth a read.

WHY STUDENTS ARE MOTIVATED

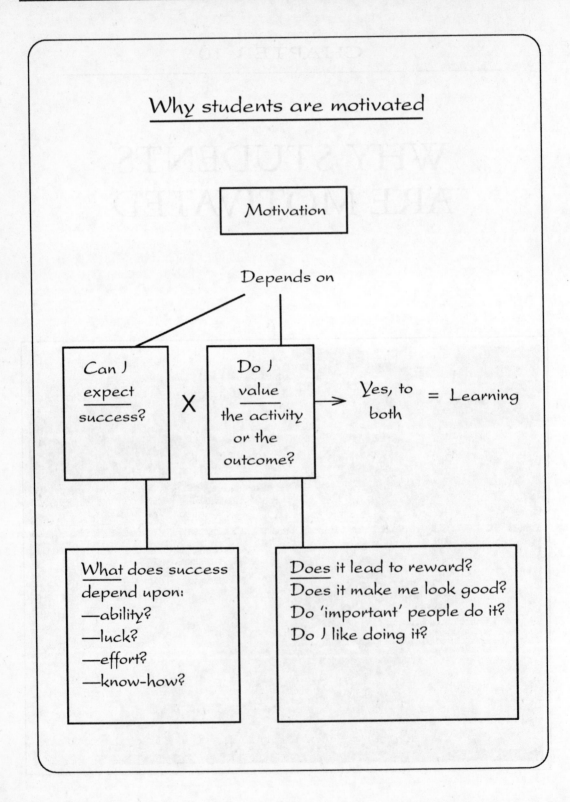

Why students are motivated

Motivation

Depends on

Can I expect success?

X

Do I value the activity or the outcome?

→ Yes, to both = Learning

What does success depend upon:
—ability?
—luck?
—effort?
—know-how?

Does it lead to reward?
Does it make me look good?
Do 'important' people do it?
Do I like doing it?

WHY STUDENTS ARE MOTIVATED

In this chapter, you will find out:

- that motivation involves expecting success in a valued task;
- in what ways students can be brought to value an academic task;
- how other people affect student motivation;
- which students are turned on by competition and which ones are turned off;
- how students' beliefs about their competence affect motivation;
- what students believe about the causes of failure and of success;
- how you can learn to be helpless.

Why do students learn?

A room full of kids can be a black hole of emotional energy, absorbing light years of pleading, cajoling, seduction, encouragement, theatricals, bribery. Teachers are always having to push and push to the end of the lesson, the day, the week, the term.

Teachers crave kids who want to learn. … there is … a deeper human excitement, as deep and as instinctual as watching waves or staring at the fire, the joy of getting a young human being to catch on, to understand, to learn. (Ashenden 1989: 10)

There you have it. First the bad news, then the good news about teaching. The bad news refers to classroom management (what else?), a topic addressed in its own right as our final message in Chapter 17. The good news is the thrill when our students *do* want to learn and when that is so, you need not bother with Chapter 17. Well-motivated children are easy to manage; they just want to get on with their learning. This chapter and the next address the more likely scenario that most students will not be particularly self-motivated and what you might do about helping them become so.

In everyday life, as we have seen in Chapter 1 we do things because of a *felt need*. You don't need a concept 'motivation' to explain why a 17 year old boy wants to learn to drive; you apparently do need that concept to explain why he does—or rather doesn't—want to learn mathematics. The issue is simple; we learn more effectively, and with greater enjoyment, when learning is *functionally important* in our immediate lives. The problem is that to most kids what they learn in school simply isn't seen as important. So we spend a lot of time and trouble trying to make it artificially important; hence the whole structure of exams, penalties, prizes, approval for this, disapproval for that. The problem is that this structure, although necessary, is off-putting to many students. It frequently only elicits a sullen acquiescence.

The problem of low motivation for academic tasks is therefore simple to define. There is no felt need. The students' main aim in tackling an assignment or other activity is to get it finished and out of the way; there is no felt need to try to understand or appreciate what the activity is intended to teach (Brophy 1986). Classroom activities become ends in themselves. For students to be academically motivated, they must find academic activities 'meaningful and worthwhile' (Good & Brophy 1987: 328).

Motivation is thus the starting point for learning. How a student is motivated determines whether or not that student will attempt to learn and how the task is approached. So why do students learn? Because (i) they value either the outcome or the process of learning, and (ii) they expect that they will be successful. Without both elements present—the activity being valued and the outcome being probable—people will not perform. Why should they? That, at any rate, is what the *expectancy–value* theory of motivation suggests.

Expectancy–value theory

Expectancy–value theory states that if anyone is to engage in an activity, they need to expect some valued outcome (Feather 1982). So if students are to be brought to *want* to learn, they will need to develop the expectation that something worthwhile will emerge from their learning.

So the teacher's task becomes twofold:

* to help students see the *value* of what they are doing,
* to give them a reasonable *expectation* of success in achieving it.

Value and expectancy 'multiply' (see Figure 10.1); that is, both factors have to be present. If either one is zero, then no motivated activity occurs. Few are moved by the pot of gold at the end of an impossible rainbow; few, likewise, by the easy capture of the paltry. If students do not value succeeding in the task in question, or do not expect to be successful however much they might want to succeed, then they will not be motivated to handle the task.

In addition and practically speaking, the *context* in which the task is presented needs to be supportive and well-structured. This factor affects value and expectation: a disorganised context implicitly devalues the task, because it conveys the impression that it is not considered worth taking trouble over organising properly and it may also convey an expectation of failure, because if you can't see where you are and how you are going, you are unlikely to arrive.

The general model, then, is presented in Figure 10.1:

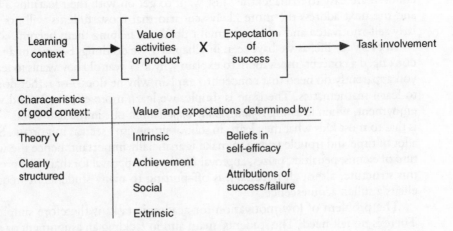

Figure 10.1 *Expectancy–value model of motivation*

In this chapter, we explain the theory and what ways of valuing the task there are and how expectancies of success are conveyed. In the next chapter, we see how strategies for motivating students emerge from this model, and the sorts of things the teacher needs to watch out for in creating a context for learning that maximises both value and expectancy of success. How this relates to students' approaches to learning, their learning strategies and the quality of the learning outcome, is considered in Chapter 12.

Valuing the task

We start with valuing the task. How do we enhance the value of the task to the students? By making their work *important* to them, in the same sense as precoding centres on importance. Importance arises from the value placed on the process, on the product, on what the product brings, or on what other people value. These foci produce four categories of motivation:

1. *Extrinsic motivation.* When students are motivated extrinsically they perform the task because of the value or importance they attach to what the product brings, such as obtaining a material reward, or in avoiding a punishment for not carrying out the task. The focus is not at all on the process, or even on the product itself, but on what is associated with the product. The task itself is incidental.
2. *Social motivation.* Students learn in order to please people whose opinions are important to them. The processes of studying, or the fruits of a good education, can be valued by people important to the student and thereby become important to the student. Motivation here is not focused on material consequences and allows the possibility of closer identification with the task.
3. *Achievement motivation.* Students may learn in order to enhance their egos by competing against other students and beating them: it makes them feel good about themselves and the task. There is more involvement with the task, but the end game is strictly speaking centred on the product, the thrill of victory, not on the task. Like some who mow their lawns meticulously, they may or may not like the process but the product is a source of pride and, incredibly, status.
4. *Intrinsic motivation.* Here there are no outside trappings necessary to make students feel good. They learn because they are interested in the task or activity itself. They do mathematics for the intellectual pleasure of problem solving and exercising their skill, not because the solution is important. The point is travelling rather than arriving.

You will notice an increasing task-centredness from (1) to (4). In (1), an extrinsic reward is something that happens to be at the end of the learning trail (often because the teacher has decided to put it there). In social achievement (2), achievement motivation (3), and especially in intrinsic motivation (4), the student is progressively more able to become personally involved and say 'This is *me!*' People are much more likely to become involved in what they can identify as their very own speciality. Intrinsic motivation and such 'ownership' go hand in hand.

It is important whether we highlight process or product when motivating students because that focus determines the quality of the outcome (see Chapter 12). The more intrinsic or process-centred the motivation, so the student will focus on how to go about the task, the more complex and the more satisfying will be the learning. If the focus is on what the product brings, the important thing becomes gaining the reward or avoiding the punishment, so you do just enough to achieve that end. If the focus is on a highly rated product, then that becomes the goal, to be attained by fair means or foul. Often the best learners are those who are both achievement and intrinsically motivated; they value both the process and the quality of the product.

But we do have to be realistic. Many—probably most—students do not find their school tasks particularly interesting; nor do they feel sufficiently self-confident to compete for the highest grades. Teachers thus usually find that they have to work upon students' more extrinsic motives. But, and this is the thrust of this and the next chapter, they should do so carefully, in ways that do not preclude more intrinsic forms of motivation later on. In fact, students may operate from a continually changing mixture of these motives.

Let us now consider these categories of motivation in more detail.

Extrinsic motivation

Extrinsic motivation is based on instrumental learning (Hull 1943), or what Skinner (1965) called 'operant conditioning' (not to be confused with classical conditioning, see below). Both these psychologists worked mainly with animals; by carefully administering reward and/or punishment, rats learned to run mazes or press levers and pigeons to peck targets. But although the term 'learning' is used, this work can better be seen as manipulating motivation, the rats being motivated to do one thing rather than another: to run along a maze, rather than to run around in circles, or to leap upon Dr Hull and bite him. This is close to what teachers have to do: motivate children to sit still and learn, or solve problems, instead of walking around, kicking the furniture, or biting the teacher. It is a question of motivating them to do this rather than to do that.

The principle of operant conditioning is crudely simple. If you want people to do something, you make it worth their while; a principle well known to parents and teachers. If you want them to stop doing it, you cease to make it worth their while or you make it worth their while to do something else. Not a very noble message, but effective, if followed through consistently. Frequently, however, we are not consistent and we end up rewarding people for doing the very things we don't want them to do (see Box 10.1).

Losing your temper in the face of consistent misbehaviour, for example, might very well be just what is wanted. If you let rip, you are rewarding the student's misbehaviour and it will continue. She is then the one in control and she'll like that a lot. So suppress your rage.

Let us break the situation down into its components. For practical purposes, we may classify behaviour as either desirable or undesirable. Desirable behaviour is that which we wish to encourage: our objective to increase its frequency in a given context. Undesirable behaviour is that which we wish to discourage: our objective to decrease its frequency.

Types of reinforcement

Table 10.1 illustrates the effects of different consequences on behaviour. If we wish to increase their frequency, desirable behaviours should lead to some kind of reward. Rewards may involve gaining something pleasant (*positive* reinforcement), or avoiding something unpleasant (*negative* reinforcement; note that negative reinforcement is not punishment, it is the avoidance of punishment and is thus a form of reward). Both processes strengthen the likelihood that the behaviour will be repeated. For example, one can make children say 'please' whenever they ask for something, *either* by rewarding them

---

Box 10.1   *How to encourage what we like least*

A mother was sorely pressed by her 4 year old's behaviour. He grizzled and whined for biscuits between meals, got them and consequently wasn't hungry at mealtime. The following is a typical scene:

Tony:	(entering kitchen) Mummy, wanna bickie.
Mrs Jones:	Not now, Tony, it's nearly tea-time.
Tony:	But I wanna (sob, sob) bickie *now*.
Mrs Jones:	C'mon, don't be difficult. Run away and play with Cheryl for a while.
Tony:	BUT I'M HUNGRY ...
Mrs Jones:	(harassed and unthinking) OK, OK! Here's a bickie. Now take it and go away until tea-time.

But peace cannot be bought this way. This behaviour was causing endless worry to Mrs Jones and potential malnutrition in Tony. And Tony's whining was being reinforced several times a day, every day. Tony was learning that if he created a fuss, then he got a biscuit—it was as simple as that. The first step, then, is to make sure that Tony *never* gets biscuits by whining.

---

by something positive if they do, *or* by threatening them with punishment if they don't, their reward then being relief that they have avoided punishment.

If we wish to reduce the frequency of an undesired behaviour, we again have two options: ignore the behaviour (no apparent consequences), or make the consequences clearly unpleasant. The first involves the process called *extinction* and the second, *punishment*. Both tend to lead to a weakening of the response, extinction more reliably than punishment.

Table 10.1   *The effects of different consequences on behaviour*

Behaviour	Consequence	Process	Result
Desirable	Gain pleasant	Positive reinforcement	More likely to occur in future (reward)
Desirable	Avoid unpleasant	Negative reinforcement	More likely to occur in future (reward)
Undesirable	None	Extinction	Less likely to occur in future
Undesirable	Unpleasant	Punishment	Unpredictable except in special circumstances

Positive reinforcement

Positive reinforcement involves following desirable behaviour with a reward. Following are some of the things that may be used as rewards:

- *consumables,* such as food, drink, sweets, etc.;
- *money,* but there are obvious limits to which teachers can or will use direct payment;
- *social reinforcers,* which include verbal ones such as 'that's great', 'you're doing really well', or non-verbal, such as admiring glances, eye contact, touching, showing that you are listening closely. Non-verbal reinforcers are often more powerful than verbal ones (Mehrabian 1970);
- *preferred activities,* which are permitted after doing the prescribed activity; for example, no television until the set work has been completed. This is known as 'Grannie's Law' or the Premack Principle: If behaviour A is more probable than behaviour B, the frequency of B can be increased by making A a condition of doing B (Premack 1959);
- *tokens,* which are symbols such as cards or tallies that are given out as the right things things are done and accumulate to be exchanged for a substantive reward, such as a free period. Such tokens are useful reminders that if you continue to do good work, you'll get something you'll really like. Tokens enhance motivation more than giving the one big reward at the end.

The timing of rewards is important. The reinforcement should follow as soon as possible after the behaviour: the longer the delay, the weaker the reinforcing effect. This is one of the reasons why a 'token economy' works well: the tokens can be given out immediately. Teachers should therefore mark assignments as soon as possible. Do not stop a student in the corridor and say: 'Oh, by the way Kathy, that was a good assignment you did last week. Well done!' Tell her last week.

Should every response be rewarded? Oddly enough, no, except in the early stages of learning. Once the behaviour is established it is better to shift to a *partial* schedule of reinforcement, rewarding every so often and on a random basis. The details and technicalities of this are discussed in Chapter 17.

Negative reinforcement

Negative reinforcement is where the consequences of the desired response remove distress and are consequently *rewarding,* not punishing as is so often thought. The reward is relief at *not* being punished. Thus, one of the most widespread negative reinforcers is anxiety, generated by the threat of punishment; it is clearly rewarding to know you are not going to be punished after all. Positive reinforcement is rewarding because the consequence is desirable for its own sake; negative reinforcement because the consequence eliminates something that is undesirable.

Extinction

This involves withholding reward. Whereas reinforcement (positive or negative) increases response strength, no reinforcement extinguishes the response. Extinction, for example ignoring the response, may be extremely difficult to achieve in practice. To ignore a blatant piece of wrongdoing is hard enough for most teachers to do (they may think that ignoring wrongdoing is unprofessional of them); in any case, they often do not have control over all the competing sources of reinforcement. Even if you can be superhuman enough to ignore the 'funny' remarks called out by the class comedian, you cannot easily control the hugely reinforcing guffaws from the rest of the class; so the behaviour, being reinforced, will be maintained.

Punishment

Widely used to stop undesirable behaviour, punishment is in fact a very unreliable weapon. Sometimes it works; other times it actually increases the unwanted behaviour. Punishment is more appropriately discussed in Chapter 17, in the context of classroom management.

A behaviour modification program

Such a program involves systematically arranging the consequences of selected behaviours so that the desired changes are brought about in the behaviour of a student, or of a class. These programs are concerned more with student behaviour than with student learning and again are more appropriately discussed in Chapter 17.

The present concern is how rewards and punishments may affect academic motivation. Clearly, some of the rewards listed above will have quite different effects on valuing the task. A simple monetary reward clearly establishes its price and hence its value: it's only worth doing if you're paid, which is not very compatible with intrinsic motivation's punchline that it's worth doing for its own sake (Deci & Ryan 1985). Negative reinforcement immediately sets up an association with feelings of anxiety, which is worse. Extinction is sometimes quite difficult, but effective when it can be achieved. How the teacher might fine-tune these consequences is developed in this and subsequent chapters.

Social motivation

One of the most powerful influences on the way we value activities or their outcomes are what other people value. We do things because it is important to us that we appear favourably in the eyes of significant others, whether those others be peer group, neighbourhood, boss, spouse, authorities, or whoever. A person who is immune to this kind of influence is called a sociopath. Sociopaths are not at all nice to have around, particularly in your classroom.

Social reinforcement is quite different from material reinforcement. The 'reward' is non-material: its value depends on the relationship between student and teacher (or other reinforcing agent). Praise from someone admired by the student helps the student internalise, to feel a proprietorial ownership about the task in question: 'Gee, I must be good at this if Miss Jones says so!' Material reinforcement, on the other hand, is impersonal and has less effect on the student's feelings of competence.

Modelling

An important mechanism in social motivation is *modelling* (Bandura 1969), which refers to the reliable tendency of people to imitate each other in the absence of direct reinforcement (that is, there is no reward for imitating others). One way of understanding why modelling works is that it makes us feel important to do what other important people do.

Bandura originally used the term 'imitation' to refer to this process, but he decided this was too narrow, implying a direct copy of the model's actions. Modelling occurs throughout life, although the particular model changes. At first, the young baby imitates movements, facial expressions and sounds made by the mother; later both parents are models; later still, other significant people including the peer group, the teacher, the boss and so on, are models. It is a fundamental process for society.

Who are likely to be chosen as models? Models tend to be those most liked or respected; we model on those we like to resemble and can identify with. Typically, different people occupy the role, often in a conflicting way. Thus, adolescents like to resemble their own peers and consequently will model the current fads, fashions and pop heroes. Simultaneously, however, they may want to resemble an admired adult who behaves in quite a different manner. This phenomenon reflects the identity problems of adolescents, and their behaviour swings accordingly, depending, among other things, on who is currently serving as model. They are not yet their own person.

In an academically oriented high school, a minority of children might model some aspects of their behaviour on an admired teacher, but this is unlikely to be true of the majority. Many students stay on until Year 12 not because they are particularly interested in schoolwork, but because there is no real alternative. For these students, teachers playing heavy 'academic' roles will not act as effective models. Also, the power structure in high schools encourages teacher behaviour that is not only unlikely to be modelled by students, but actively resisted. Much teacher behaviour is determined by organisational demands and that is unlikely to be perceived by students to be relevant to themselves.

Certain behaviours are more easily modelled than others. Non-verbal behaviour is more easily modelled than verbal, so teachers have a psychological as well as a moral responsibility to practise what they preach. A colleague once saw a teacher caning a boy for smoking—with a cigarette hanging out of the teacher's mouth.

In fact, aggressive behaviours are more easily modelled than non-aggressive. Liebert and Caron (1972) showed that, after watching television programs with aggressive content, children behaved aggressively towards each other. They did not, however, tend to model loving or cooperative behaviours. Even playground behaviour is different when the preceding lesson is taken by a punitive or non-punitive teacher. Kounin and Gump (1961) found that aggression was markedly higher in the playtime activities of children who had just come from classes taught by teachers who were sarcastic, emphasised negative sanctions and punishment, and who blamed for wrongdoing rather than praised for good behaviour. These aggressive behaviours appeared to have rubbed off on the children and, as most people would agree, this is not desirable; sarcasm and punishment, generally, are therefore not good teaching techniques (see also Chapter 17).

Towards commitment

The effects of social motivation on subsequent intrinsic motivation are probably much greater than was previously thought. The beginnings of our interest in many intrinsically motivated activities—fads, crazes, intensely pursued hobbies, even lifelong obsessions—can be traced to what someone we admired at the time said or did.

Social motivation marks the first move away from what simply happened to be associated with the task, to a more personal kind of commitment to the task. The beginnings of such a commitment are more likely to occur when it is perceived that other people, particularly those who may be admired or seen as role models, are themselves committed to the task. Enthusiasm is infectious; if you like your subject and take care to show it, your students are much more likely to like it.

Achievement motivation

The next step along the road to full personal commitment to a task is to show that one can perform it better than other people. The motivation here is based upon the ego boost that comes about through social competition. Social competition is a motive that is particularly apparent in Western society: it refers to a basic need, greater in some people than in others, to achieve and attain success for its own sake. The rewards are mainly in the struggle to get to the top of the heap, beating others in open competition; it is not so important to gain material rewards as such (although it helps). Neither is it important what the task is; it can be selling cars, winning votes, publishing papers, whatever.

Achievement motivation was first described by McClelland, Atkinson, Clark and Lowell (1953), but Atkinson (1964) later became particularly interested in applying it to the situation in which people:

(a) know that they will be evaluated on their performance;
(b) know that the evaluation will be favourable (success) or unfavourable (failure); and
(c) see themselves as responsible for the outcome.

This is an accurate representation of what goes on in most classrooms. Students are evaluated—by their teachers, their peers and their parents —in terms of success and failure defined by comparison with other students and in tasks that reflect their competence.

To achieve success or to avoid failure?

Two major motives are involved in achieving situations:

• the motive to *achieve success*; in particular, the ego enhancement that success brings;
• the motive to *avoid failure*, which involves the fear of losing face.

In some people, achieving success is a stronger motive than is avoiding failure; such people are called *high need-achievers* (their *actual* ability is a separate question). For them, the greatest glory in winning comes when the chances are about fifty-fifty. If the probability of success is greater than 50% (e.g., 90%), it is like an Olympic athlete competing with the local Under-16s: the ego benefits are slight. If, on the other hand, the probability of success is low (e.g., around 10%), there is not much point in wasting time as you are unlikely to win.

People in whom the motive to avoid failure is stronger than the motive to achieve success are called *low need-achievers*. The relationship between persistence and probability of success is exactly the reverse of that for high need-achievers. Those who fear failure will happily blow their chance of winning, as long as they preserve face: a fifty-fifty chance is thus the most threatening, not the most attractive. When the fear of failure is paramount, it is either better to win cheaply by competing against someone who is certain to be beaten, *or* to fail gloriously by competing when the odds are hopeless. In the first case, success is certain; in the second, failure is blameless ('A real Aussie battler!').

Thus, high need-achievers thrive on competition; low need-achievers adopt any tactic to avoid it. High need-achievers are bored by tasks with high success rates, such as mastery learning or programmed instruction; low need-achievers like them, as a high success program is just what they need to produce better feelings of self-efficacy (see Chapter 11).

Need-achievement in school

Let us see how persistence may change during the performance of an easy task (i.e., when you judge your chances of success to be more than 50%). High need-achievers approach the task, but fail. Now they re-assess their chances of success and judge them nearer 50%; just what they want, a competitive challenge. Thus, high need-achievers tend to be *encouraged* after failure.

Now take low need-achievers; they too fail the apparently easy task. Their chances now become around 50%; just what they don't want, a competitive challenge. Low need-achievers thus tend to be *dis*couraged after failure. Weirdly, they are also discouraged after successfully handling a difficult task. Can you see why? Exactly the same reason; a difficult task successfully accomplished ceases to be perceived as 'difficult' but within the moderate, 50-50, zone—a no-no for low need-achievers.

High need-achievers thus tend to behave 'logically'; the more they succeed, the more they upgrade their aspirations to more difficult and challenging tasks. Low need-achievers behave defensively; under competitive conditions, they give up after success and often persist after failure, to fail and fail again (Moulton 1969). The remedy is obvious; remove the conditions that create competition. These conditions are:

- a goal desired by many,
- which few can attain,
- the attainment of which is defined by public comparison with others.

Schools adopt many practices that nurture competition between students, simply by defining goals ('being top', winning scholarships, prizes and other awards) and limiting access to them (only one person can be top). Such situations positively motivate the high need-achievers, but the low need-achievers do worse than they would otherwise. There are many such situations, the most common and certainly the most enervating being *norm-referenced* testing, where a person's grade is determined by how they relate to others in the class or population. Ranking is the most obvious example (Betty was top, … and Julie was last), but 'grading on the curve' (5% As, 20% Bs…) is equally norm-referenced. In these cases, a person is graded according to public comparisons with peers, which is highly ego-involving. The alternative is *criterion-referenced* testing, where a person's grade is determined by how they match up to an initially determined standard, such as getting so many items correct (for a more complete explanation and relation to other evaluational procedures, see Chapter 14).

Streaming is another case where formal structures in school encourage competition. We have already seen in Chapter 6 that under streaming, the low stream students do worse than they would if unstreamed. Here is one reason why. Placing students of roughly the same ability level into the same class means that the chances of 'coming top' are spread more evenly across the class; competition is maximised. In the case of high need-achievers this simply confirms what they already do; in the case of low need-achievers, again, they are thrown into a competitive situation which is what they try to avoid.

There are also informal ways in which competition can be encouraged and low need-achievers discouraged. The following example of teacher–student interaction comes from the anthropologist Jules Henry's study of American classrooms:

Boris had trouble reducing 12/16 to the lowest terms and could only get as far as 6/8. The teacher asked him quietly if that was as far as he could reduce it. She suggested he 'think'. Much heaving up and down and waving of hands by the other children, all frantic to correct him. Boris pretty unhappy, probably mentally paralysed. The teacher, quiet, patient, ignores the others and concentrates with look and voice on Boris. She says, 'Is there a bigger number than two you can divide into the two parts of the fraction?' After a minute or two she becomes more urgent, but there is no response from Boris. She then turns to the class and says, 'Well, who can tell Boris what the number is?' A forest of hands appears and the teacher calls Peggy. Peggy says that four may be divided into the numerator and denominator.

Only one person can be top. This motivates high need-achievers but not low need-achievers.

Boris's failure has made it possible for Peggy to succeed; his depression is the price of her exhilaration; his misery the cause for her rejoicing. To a Zuni, Hopi or Dakota Indian, Peggy's performance would seem cruel beyond belief, for competition, the wringing of success from somebody's failure, is a form of torture foreign to those non-competitive redskins. (Henry 1963: 243-4)

The real lesson here is how to encourage and cope with competition. If the lesson was in fact to teach fractions, then the teacher was singularly inept: no better way of turning Boris right off the subject could be devised. If it was to teach a lesson in survival values, however, then it was probably quite successful, if not for Boris then certainly for the others.

Family, peer group, mass media and community lay the foundations for competitiveness, which are then built on in the school, so that successful players end with a high need-achievement. Often, this is explicitly stated in political platforms as desirable educational policy; competition in school is necessary in order to prepare people for the 'real' world (that is, the world that is real to the policymakers, the market place). The other side of this is that the unsuccessful ones risk acquiring an incapacitating fear of failure and will avoid situations that are likely to cost them more and more of their self-esteem.

In short, then, constructing academic tasks in an achievement context increases their value to some, but decreases it to others. How one as a teacher (value and political questions aside) can best balance that equation depends on the students one has and the rest of the context in which one is teaching.

Intrinsic motivation

Humans have an intrinsic need to build up competence in dealing with the environment. Biologically, we are built in such a way that behaviours that maximise competence are self-rewarding. Take, for example, the case of a toddler beginning to walk; he stands, totters, falls, stands up again, walks a step or two, falls, back up, same again. Such behaviour cannot be extrinsically motivated; if you practise walking, you fall over and hurt yourself. On an operant conditioning explanation, you would therefore stop trying to walk. Clearly, at that critical stage of development, walking is *self-motivated*; we are programmed that way. Many important developmental tasks are self-motivated in this way; it is adaptive biologically that we should *want* to practise a developing skill (White 1959).

Curiosity is one inbuilt device for helping cognitive development. Curiosity pulls us to experience the new, thereby not only helping us to find out more about our world, but it sets the scene for recoding and further cognitive growth (see Chapter 8; Berlyne 1966).

In such instances, the *process* is what is valued—developing the skill, exploring to see what's there—not the product. The sorts of learnings that occur in school, however, are not biologically crucial: not even socially crucial for some. In the absence of a naturally occurring curiosity, what can the teacher do to help students value the process?

Curiosity is an inbuilt device for helping cognitive development.

Intrinsic motivation, meaningful learning and task difficulty

The first thing is to pick up Good and Brophy's simple statement that academic activities must be seen as 'meaningful and worthwhile' to students. You will of course remember from Chapter 8 some conditions for optimising meaningful learning:

- the task needs to be potentially meaningful;
- the task needs to be of an optimum level of difficulty;
- the task needs to be presented in a way that enables multiple levels of coding; and
- generally, the more active the learner the better.

All apply to the creation of intrinsic motivation. The central issue is optimal difficulty, the mismatch between the task and what is known.

Degree of mismatch and motivation

Self-motivated competencies occur when the conflict or mismatch between environmental demands and developing cognitive structures is just right for recoding to occur (see Chapter 8). When such mismatch is optimal, positive intrinsic motivation occurs. Where mismatch is minimal, so that the environment can be handled without too much internal change, there is no challenge and the task is boring. Where mismatch is too great, the challenge is overwhelming, and negative intrinsic motivation results.

The general cognitive processes presumed to underlie intrinsic motivation are summarised in Table 10.2:

Table 10.2: *Intrinsic motivation and the demands of experience*

Demand	Motivational	Consequence
Too little	Contents of experience all familiar	Boring: been there, done that
Just right	Mixture of familiar and unfamiliar	A challenge; motivating
Too much	Contents all unfamiliar	Overwhelming; can't cope

The degree of intrinsic motivation experienced by a student thus depends upon the match between current experience and the knowledge gained from previous ones.

Positive intrinsic motivation, then, takes place when individuals are placed in a slightly 'difficult' situation involving conflict between what they know already and what they are currently learning. That critical level of mismatch differs enormously between people. A flexible person, for example, can handle a larger mismatch than a rigid person; a person with a rich knowledge base will see more potential connections; low need-achievers find a gap threatening that a high need-achiever would find challenging. The difficulties for the teacher are obvious: the process is internal and different for each student in the class. Yet it is more likely to occur for some students, some of the time, under some classroom conditions than under others. It's worth going for and we explain something about those conditions in this chapter.

Hebb's (1946) experiments illustrate negative intrinsic motivation: he called it 'fear'. He placed a headless chimp torso in a cage containing live chimps, who immediately backed away to the furthest corners of the cage, chattering and squealing with terror. An innate fear of death perhaps? No, because precisely the same result was obtained when two of their well-known and well-liked keepers appeared, dressed in each other's jackets! The mismatch between the expected and the observed was too much for the chimps to handle.

Many school phobias belong in this category. We have noted that children who are motivated by the desire to avoid failure rather than to achieve success will get by using strategies that avoid the task. Such strategies solve the immediate problem of not failing (in the student's eyes), but deprive them of the opportunity of acquiring any task-relevant codes. There comes a time when they realise that they have no idea about what they should be doing; the conflict is too great and they become strongly negatively motivated, to the point perhaps of 'learned helplessness' (see next chapter).

Positive intrinsic motivation has the following properties, which make it educationally so desirable. It:

- signals high-quality involvement,
- involves feelings of pleasure,
- is self-maintaining; external rewards are unnecessary to explain why the behaviour is carried out.

However, intrinsic motivation needs an appropriate affective context in which the right task conditions are placed; students must feel positive about the task, the context and themselves. We discuss self-concept below, and some aspects of classroom and school climate in the next chapter.

Expecting success? Beliefs about the self

The second factor affecting academic motivation relates to students' expectations of success. What they believe about themselves—their competence and the reasons for their previous performances—are particularly vital. Teachers play an important role in forming and maintaining these beliefs. The two major issues are: students' beliefs in their own efficacy and to what they attribute their success and failure.

The self-concept

How students see their chances of success depends to a large extent on how they see themselves. Dale Carnegie emphasised that convincing oneself of one's competence was the first step towards acting competently (and, as he also modelled, much extrinsic reward). This general relationship, between how we feel about ourselves and performance, has clearly been established with respect to schoolwork (Covington & Beery 1976; Purkey 1970). The connection goes like this: If I know I *can't* do it, I won't seriously attempt to; if I know I *can*, I might, depending on other factors. We have already seen what some of those other factors might be: in particular, on how important or valuable the task or the consequences of successful completion might be. Here we look at the question of personal belief in success.

The link between self-concept and intrinsic motivation was clarified by de Charms (1968). He called the intrinsically motivated person an 'origin'. Origins see themselves as the cause of their own behaviour; as self-determining individuals, their locus of control is *internal* (Rotter 1966). Origins see themselves as in charge of their lives; they have ownership over themselves and over what they do. Naturally, they like that. Driven by the belief that an origin's gotta do what an origin's gotta do, they walk tall.

People who see themselves as being directed by other people, more powerful than themselves, or at the mercy of external events, he called 'pawns'. Pawns have an external locus of control, are not self-determining. They do what they believe others have decided for them; they have little sense of ownership and are not easily intrinsically motivated.

De Charms worked with students in a large inner-city high school in the American mid-west and concluded that students saw themselves as Pawns as a result of the demands made upon them from outside. Both their social backgrounds and their school had a cumulative effect such that most saw themselves as very little cogs in a very large machine; their school lives were strongly regimented and they had little or no say in what happened to them at school. De Charms relaxed these conditions and found that, as more and more aspects of their life were decided by the students themselves, the more like origins and the less like pawns they felt—and the more intrinsically motivated they became.

De Charms' view of self-concept depends on how people see themselves being controlled. Other theories refer to the worth or esteem with which we regard ourselves (Covington & Beery 1976). There is, however, a danger of interpreting self-concept theory too simplistically. Consider how these ideas are used by advertisers: *Feel good about yourself! Clean your teeth with Super Brite!* (then you can have your choice of jobs, lovers, bank-loan terms or whatever, the subtext says). Now the 'amateur counsellor' comment: 'No wonder Bill's not doing well at school. He's got such a poor self-concept!' (subtext: if Bill goes jogging, learns macrame, does *something* particularly well, 'He'll get some confidence in himself ...' and up will go his schoolwork, his social relations and wherever else he is performing below par).

But feelings of competence in one area do not necessarily generalise to another. Think for a moment of your perceived self-competence in your best school subject; and then in your worst school subject. What is your academic self-concept? How many shy school teachers are told: 'Oh, you can't be shy. You stand in front of a class and talk to other people all day long!'? Talking to students in a classroom context is quite a different activity from talking to adults in a social context. It depends *what* one feels one is good at that will influence intrinsic motivation.

Self-efficacy

Bandura (1977) proposed a very specific form of self-concept theory: *self-efficacy*. When people approach a task, they form expectations about how well they think they will be able to carry out that particular task. Such expectations derive from a variety of sources, but critical ones are based on:

* how well they have done that task in the past;
* what they *attribute* their past performance to (see below);
* how their teachers and even other students think they will perform;
* how difficult they see this particular task.

Box 10.2 relates how one mature-age student's feelings of self-efficacy were manipulated by teacher communications and relates very powerfully how perceived self-efficacy determines the effort and persistence the student will put into the task.

What this story, a true one, also illustrates is how attributions for success and failure can affect motivation. It's not only *whether or not* they expect themselves to be successful, but the *reasons why* they think they might succeed or fail.

Box 10.2   *Restore a belief in self-efficacy and attribute failure to lack of persistence ...*

'I'd already had several children before coming to uni, and I wasn't sure how I could handle it. I was really interested in psychology, but when we got to the psych. I lectures, the stats lecturer said 'Anyone who can't follow this isn't fit to be at university ...' That was the first message I got. I *was* having difficulty with stats and so I thought maybe he's right, maybe uni isn't for me. I liked the rest of psych. but couldn't handle the stats and had to withdraw.

Next year, funny thing, I did maths I, and we came to probability theory—much the same stuff that I had bombed out in last year. But the lecturer there was a woman and maybe she understood better the difficulties many women have, or anyone come to that, and she said: 'Probability is quite hard really; you'll need to work at it. You're welcome to come to me for help if you really need it ...'

It was like a blinding light. It wasn't *me* after all! This stuff really was *hard,* but if I tried it might just work. That year I got a credit in that part of the subject.'

Bandura's theory differs from simple self-concept theory in its specificity. Thus, a student can hug an area to himself and feel good about that and cheerfully accept that he's 'no good' at maths, cricket and football. Beliefs about self-efficacy are closely tied to particular tasks, which is very fortunate for the self-concepts of many students (Marsh, Cairns, Relich, Barnes & Debus 1984). In the *Self Description Questionnaire* (Marsh 1988), children rate themselves on several areas of self-concept. Verbal, mathematical and academic cover the school-related areas; there are seven others covering social and self-related areas—physical appearance, same sex, opposite sex, parent, honesty and emotional—and overall general self-concept. Norms are provided so that one can see in which particular areas a student has worries about self-efficacy; relationships with performance would depend on how closely the particular self-concept domain is to the task. A student with a poor physical self-concept might perform badly in sports, but very well in other areas.

To what do you attribute success or failure?

A different kind of belief about the self refers to the causes individuals attribute to their previous successes and failures. These attributions relating to previous performance will have a profound effect on encouraging, or discouraging, further involvement. As we saw in Box 10.2, the belief that success in stats was based on ability was crippling; the belief that stats was a difficult task and required effort was challenging. Obviously, we should try to see that students build up sets of attributions that will encourage them in future.

Attribution theory (Bar-Tal 1978; Weiner 1972, 1986) relates future involvement in the task to how one accounts for previous success and failure. Previous successes, or failures, are not so important in themselves so much as why we *think* we succeeded or failed. There are three main dimensions to these attributed reasons:

- *Stability-instability.* If we attribute failure to something that is unstable, such as bad luck, which may not occur in future, expectations about future performance may be unaffected. However, if failure is attributed to a stable factor that will occur in future, such as low ability, then one would expect to continue failing in future.

- *Controllable–uncontrollable.* Some causes are within our control (e.g., the amount of effort we put in), or somebody else's (e.g., the difficulty of the task set).
- *Internal–external.* The cause lies within ourselves (e.g., ability, which in this case is also uncontrollable), or in someone else (e.g., poor quality teaching).

These dimensions of course interact. Let us take the case of a girl in Year 2 who failed in arithmetic. She attributes it to an unstable factor, luck: 'Just my luck to get Miss Smith! It was all her fault; at least I won't get her next year.' Outcome: open and out of her control. Let's now say she attributes her failure to a controllable but unstable factor, insufficient effort: 'My fault: didn't try hard enough. Next year I will though.' Outcome: likely to be more favourable next year.

She could attribute her failure to something stable, such as ability: 'I'm just not good at arithmetic. Never was, never will be.' Outcome: future failure and lack of interest. Or to task difficulty: 'It's not that I'm dumb or anything; the test was just too hard.' Outcome: open, depending on perceptions of the next test.

Similar effects occur for the attribution of success. If success is attributed to luck, the clear implication is that fortune will turn: failure is then the likely prospect. If success is attributed to ability, then intrinsic motivation—ownership—is likely to take over: 'I'm good at this! This is my thing.'

Some common attributions are summarised in Table 10.3:

Table 10.3   *Kinds of attributions, with examples*

	Internal		External	
	Stable	Unstable	Stable	Unstable
Controllable	Typical effort	Immediate effort	Teacher bias	Unusual help from others
Uncontrollable	Ability	Mood	Task difficulty	Luck

It is obviously important that teachers try to influence students' attribution in the most effective direction: failure should be attributed to lack of effort and success probably to ability, but there are problems with both effort and ability attributions. Attributing success to ability could be interpreted as telling students not to put in effort. On the other hand, attributing success to effort could easily mean that you are thick: an attribution students may read into teachers' evaluations that emphasise the effort the student has put in (Meyer, Bachmann, Biermann, Hempelmann, Ploger & Spiller 1979). In Western culture, which puts a high premium on ability, it is therefore more face-saving to put in little effort; if you succeed, then you must be bright, and if you fail, well then, you didn't try, did you? Nevertheless, sensitive effort attribution after failure also seems to work very well with learning disabled children (Dweck 1975).

In more able students, one can avoid these problems by using a *strategy* attribution in the case of failure (Clifford 1986a). In three areas of reported failure—educational, business and sport—students and teachers predicted future success, better feelings about the failure, willingness to try again and restricted generalisability of the failure, when it was attributed to lack of specific skills, such as study skills (Clifford 1986b).

Skill or strategy attributions seem to be particularly important, because then there is always an out, a chance that performance will improve in future, with less of the rationalising that so easily occurs in the case of effort attributions, or the low self-esteem following attributions of failure to low ability. Failing students may be led to believe that they can counter the failure; it is not then a hopeless devastation, or success the glint of fools' gold. The effects of effort, ability and strategy, or any other attributions for good or poor performance, on future motivation and future performance clearly depend on how it is conveyed to and interpreted by the student. This will require much sensitive judgment on the part of the teacher. Teachers should obviously try to structure things so that the most hopeful attribution will be made in the events of success and failure.

Several factors have been shown to relate to different attributions (Bar-Tal 1978). Females tend more than males to attribute their success to luck rather than to ability and to rate their ability lower. Individuals with low self-esteem tend to make internal attributions (low ability) following failure. As might be expected, high need-achievers attribute their success to internal factors—ability and effort, to which greatest pride is attached—and their failures either to external factors, or to lack of effort (but not lack of ability). Low need-achievers, on the other hand, attribute their failure to lack of ability and their success to luck or an easy task.

Many Eastern cultures place a premium on effort rather than on ability, which is the first attribution Westerners make for good or poor performance (Holloway 1988). As one Chinese proverb says: 'If one keeps on grinding one can turn an iron pillar into a needle'; investing huge effort into an impossible task is regarded as admirable (Hau & Salili 1990: 20). In such a context, attributions to effort are more likely to lead directly to improved performance, although exhortations to more and more effort when the student is not very bright could be heart-breaking.

When it comes to academic motivation in the 'normal' range, Asians seem to have a healthier attribution system than Westerners, in the sense that they attribute success to factors which are controllable and modifiable. The top five attributions for success of Hong Kong secondary students were effort, interest in study, study skill, mood and, only fifth, ability (Hau & Salili 1991). The first four are more or less controllable; the fifth, which Western students see as most important for success, is not. In other words, Asian students tend normally to see ways in which they can improve their performance; Western students tend to attribute past performance to things they can't do anything about. It isn't hard to see why Asian students are so disproportionately successful in Australian and American schools (see also Jopson 1990). Less fortunately, this difference in values and motivation gives rise to prejudice on both sides: Anglo-Australians dislike Asians because they work hard and are 'brainy', while Asians are 'contemptuous of Anglo-Australians because they lacked achievement motivation and parental support' (Bullivant 1988: 241). There are lessons here for everyone.

Learned helplessness

A particularly bad form of attribution reduces the student to a state known as 'learned helplessness'. Seligman (1975) observed that when rats are given an electric shock and are trained to turn the shock off (e.g., by pressing a bar), they rarely show signs of distress after they have learned the procedure. However, if the bar is suddenly disconnected and the shocks come at unpredictable times, the rats become very upset, fall comatose and in extreme cases die. When they learn that they have no control over their environment, they become helpless.

Similar states of learned helplessness have been observed in humans when they *believe* they have no control over unpleasant things that happen to them: voodoo deaths seem to be an example. Miller and Norman (1979) distinguish three features of learned helplessness in humans:

- reduced *motivation* to control events;
- impaired *ability to learn* how to control the situation;
- strong fear, which rapidly leads to *deep depression*.

Miller and Norman explained learned helplessness in terms of attribution theory, adding a general–specific dimension to the others. The worst kind of learned helplessness is attributed to internal, stable, uncontrollable and general causes. One is then helpless in all circumstances, an extremely depressing conclusion to have to come to.

Other kinds of learned helplessness are limited to specific contexts, such as school, which is important in the treatment of learning disabilities in school (Thomas 1979). The under-achiever shows all the signs of learned helplessness: persistent failure, lack of motivation to avoid further failure, inability to learn remedial material and apathy bordering on depression. This helplessness being specific to school, however, doesn't prevent students from blossoming once they get into the workforce and fortunately many do.

This pattern of helplessness can be broken by changing the attributions. Dweck (1975) trained the teachers of helpless children to convince them that their failure was due to lack of effort and their success to ability. As a result, the students improved rapidly, making more gains than a group based on a behaviour modification (success only) program. Heckhausen (1975) in a similar program had failing students improve markedly in subsequent performance.

The expectancy–value model can be used to construct classroom strategies for motivating academic learning, as we discover in the next chapter.

Summary

Why do students learn?

In their natural setting, people learn because it comes naturally; they do what they have to do. School learning does not come naturally. Accordingly, we have a problem of 'motivation'. We are not motivated unless we expect to be successful and we value the activity or its outcome. Sensible people pursue neither the impossible nor the unwanted. The teacher has therefore to see that academic activities and tasks are valued in some way and that students can expect a reasonable chance of success if they undertake them.

Valuing the task

We can classify several ways of valuing the task, which refer to different kinds of motivation, according to what is seen as important: the process (intrinsic motivation), the product (achievement motivation), what the product may bring (extrinsic motivation), the importance other people attach to either process or product (social motivation).

Extrinsic motivation

The most direct way of making learning valued is to ensure its consequences eventually lead to something desired. Students (along with rats and pigeons) will learn if you make it worth their while (positively reinforcing), or if they don't learn you will make it horrendously awful for them (negatively reinforcing). The principle here is called operant conditioning and it is the stuff of which behaviour modification programs are made. Motivation is starkly *extrinsic*.

Social motivation

Social motivation is very powerful and depends on imitation and modelling: valuing what important other people value and doing what other people do. Unfortunately, it is easy to model unpleasant behaviours such as aggression; and often adolescents freely model on those whom we would rather they didn't.

Achievement motivation

Those who are achievement motivated value what the product says about them: that they are better than anyone else at whatever it is. The down side is that many of those who are worse than whoever is better are turned off from the entire proceedings. Competition, which is widespread in ways that may surprise, is a selective device. Teachers need to weigh the costs against the benefits.

Intrinsic motivation

In intrinsic motivation, the activity itself is valued. It is bound up with the development of competence; the conditions for meaningful learning simultaneously promote interest. The key is complexity that is optimal for the individual, relating to a task over which the individual has feelings of ownership.

Expecting success? Beliefs about the self

Beliefs about the self may refer in general terms to *self-concept*, or more specifically to *self-efficacy*, which relates more to how good students think they are at specific tasks. Such beliefs, particularly of the latter kind, are very significant in determining future motivation in the task. Self-efficacy is affected by many factors, including past performance (of course) and what their teachers, among others, convey to them.

To what do you attribute success and failure?

Attributions to causes of previous successes and failures naturally enough have a profound influence on future expectations of success and failure and hence on motivation. If students can believe that their successes are due to stable conditions that they can safely assume will operate in future (such as their own ability at the task and their interest in it) then the motivational outlook is good. If they believe that their failures are due to factors which they can control and rectify in future, such as learning appropriate strategies and putting in more effort, failure can be a positive learning experience, rather than a face-losing embarrassment.

Learning activities

1. Expectancy–value theory

For us, expectancy-value theory underlies motivation. What do you understand by the term? Could you explain it to a peer, a parent, a student? We will leave it to you to determine how much you know.

2. Four categories of motivation

In this chapter we have dealt with four major categories of motivation: extrinsic, social, achievement and intrinsic. Prepare an overhead transparency for each category. The transparency should describe the type of motivation, its benefits and disadvantages in the classroom, and it should be presented in an attention-getting manner. (Remember the earlier chapter on information processing?) You could share the overheads with others or use them in class presentations.

3. Attributions

Here we focus on Table 10.3 from this chapter. The table shows internal/external, stable/unstable and controllable/uncontrollable dimensions. The task is threefold: to indicate what a student's comment would be for each of the eight cells in the table; to indicate what the outcomes might be of having made such attributions; and finally to suggest ways in which such attributions (if not appropriate) might be changed. For example, a comment in the internal/stable/uncontrollable cell might be 'I'm not good at reading, never will be'. The outcome might be further failure and lack of motivation to read. Such an attribution might be changed by placing the child in the context where she can realise that effective strategy use facilitates competence in reading (see Chapter 13). The task could be done for both attributions for failure and success. Poster style presentations could be used to 'pull' all the work together, if done in groups or individually.

4. Attributions

This activity is an extension of (3). Gather data on teachers' attributional comments to students during practicum sessions and keep a diary, with the teacher's knowledge of course, of the types of attribution comments teachers make when they teach. You could gather the information over a few days and if possible in a couple of different classrooms. An attributional statement such as 'You're lucky to have worked that out' would represent an external/uncontrollable/variable attribution. 'Yep, you've certainly got the ability' would be what?

You'll probably be surprised at how consistent some teachers are in expressing their own views on attributions. If you provide feedback to the teachers (we'd argue you should), they may also be surprised to find what they say.

5. Pawns and origins

We saw in the work of de Charms (1968) that 'origins' view their learning as being under their own control whereas 'pawns' see that control as being external to themselves. In this activity, identify 'origin' and 'pawn' inducing activities, as they relate to student learning, at three levels: classroom, school and system. Draw up a table with 'Classroom', 'School' and 'System' on the side and 'Origin' and 'Pawn' across the top to make a 3 x 2 table. Within each cell identify, say five activities (e.g., for 'origin/school' cell—range of elective subjects). If conducted as a class activity, groups could be assigned to each cell to then present their findings in peer teaching sessions.

6. Extrinsic motivation

This activity should be a discussion.

In many classrooms, especially those at the infant/primary level, there is widespread use of stickers, stamps, sweets, etc. to reinforce good behaviour and good academic performance. The topic for debate here is: 'There's nothing wrong with extrinsic motivation in the classroom.'

Further reading

On academic motivation
Deci, E. L. & Ryan, R. M. (1985). *Intrinsic Motivation and Self-determination in Human Behaviour.* New York: Plenum Press.
Dibley, J. (1986) *Let's Get Motivated.* Sydney: Corporate Publishing.
Weiner, B. (1986). *An Attributional Theory of Motivation and Emotion.* New York: Springer-Verlag.

Deci and Ryan, and Weiner, expound the declarative knowledge concerning the 'tender' (intrinsic motivation) and the 'tough' (achievement motivation) ways of being academically motivated. Dibley's book on achievement motivation is for the layperson and full of sound procedural advice.

CHAPTER 11

HOW STUDENTS ARE MOTIVATED

How students are motivated

How do we get them motivated??

— Surprise them?

— 'Bribe' them?

— Praise them?

— Get them to compete?

— Get them to cooperate?

— Have 'good' school and
   class climate? (Yes, Theory Y)

But

— Do they expect to succeed?

— If not, why don't they?

HOW STUDENTS ARE MOTIVATED

In this chapter, you will find out:

- how curiosity can be fanned;
- what effects classroom climate can have on student motivation;
- how to praise students effectively;
- if the use of rewards and punishments endangers future interest in the task;
- how students can be led to expect success.

When the task is valued

The most desirable form of academic motivation is intrinsic, but that rare bird is hard to trap. Let us modify our target to motivating the student to engage the task seriously and with more or less enjoyment; that's not a bad compromise and it is easier to attain than intrinsic motivation itself.

First, the student needs to be brought to value the task in some way. The key is that the task meets a *felt need,* which reminds us of the differences between school and everyday learning. Illiteracy to a low need-achiever in school is no big deal; in fact, it's an interesting game laying low in class so that you're not called on to read. Illiteracy to a parent whose primary school child seeks help in homework, or whose promotion depends on some clerical/literary skill, is a mounting, self-annihilating, barrier of shame. Technical and Further Education (TAFE) run literacy clinics throughout Australia with a very simple but effective resource: volunteer tutors with little training and whose only qualification is that they can read themselves. Yet in three months, on a one-to-one basis, they almost always achieve what trained teachers had failed to achieve in nine years of compulsory schooling. The difference is the felt need and a resource meeting that need.

Not all school tasks can be reset in a context of experienced need, but some kind of valuing, if not as high as this, can be achieved. The four major kinds of motivation help define what we might do. It is not a question of what particular kind of motivation we are going to go for — intrinsic, *si!* extrinsic, *non!*—because all interact, sometimes helpfully, sometimes antagonistically. Obviously the kind we call intrinsic is educationally the most desirable, but equally obviously, it is the most difficult for the teacher to instil.

You can lead the horse to water, but can you make her drink? Let us look at some aspects of horse control.

Use intrinsic motivation from the outset

Seeing that she is as thirsty as possible seems a good place to start. In other words, start learning with tasks or content in which the learner is already interested and knowledgable. Allowing students to choose essay topics, or assignments, from a range of offerings is just as possible as saying: '500 words on the settlement at Port Arthur. Don't argue.' If you are teaching in Newcastle, the lesson to be learned, which is the purpose and function of penal colonies in Australia, could equally be learned by studying the Hunter Region. History, or any subject, is much more interesting if you can start from your own back yard. Maths problems, geography, history, writing, economics, virtually any subject, can either start off from where many students already are; current films, pop songs, news items can be used as context rather than the tired textbook context for the problem.

Brophy (1986) refers to 'teachable moments', a nice phrase, which are likely to occur when the lesson is periodically thrown open for comments, suggestions, reminiscences, questions. Nothing may happen on some occasions, but usually something does and in responding you know that at least *someone* is interested, or that point wouldn't have been raised. And if one person is interested, chances are that others may become so. Really superb teachers create their own teachable moments. Mr Keating, in *Dead Poets' Society*, was a master at that, as we saw when he forced the unwilling Anderson to compose his own poetry.

If one word is to sum up intrinsic motivation, it would be 'ownership'. Students become intrinsically motivated about what they can feel is peculiarly 'theirs'—an argument, a position, a responsibility, identification with a career-related step. And remember, public recognition accompanies ownership. Ownership can be encouraged by almost anything that opens out individual choice; for electives, assignment topics, at the obvious level, to class acknowledged expertise in some particular area, arising from some unpredictable interaction, say from a teachable moment. Ownership can be established

Students become intrinsically motivated about what they feel is peculiarly 'theirs'.

and expressed in quite subtle ways in student–teacher interaction, a comment over an essay or in conversation: 'Let's ask Alice to comment on this, as this is her special field.' Alice will glow and even if it wasn't her special field it will be from now on. Such an ambience of ownership obviously brings high personal value to a task.

Creating optimum conflict

Too great a gap between input and code structure leads to avoidance; too narrow a gap, to lack of interest. Berlyne (1966) discussed several teaching techniques that can help create the degree of conceptual conflict that leads to positive intrinsic motivation. One of these is the exploitation of *surprise*.

By surprise we don't mean that the teacher walks in wearing a false nose and a funny hat. We want surprise that is *intrinsic* to the content. Suchman (1961) used intrinsic surprise in science teaching. For a lesson on the expansion of metals the teacher begins by heating a bimetallic strip over a low flame. The strip sags downwards and students are then invited to suggest why this occurs, with the teacher responding with 'Yes' or 'No' to their suggestions. Usually the class agrees that the heat has melted the strip and it sags with gravity. At that point the teacher holds the strip the other way and heats it; it sags upwards! Further question-and-answer produces various hypotheses, until one or two only remain under the evidence. This is the time to bring out the ball-and-ring apparatus and the class then concludes that metals expand when heated, some metals more than others.

Conflict may be particularly appropriate in mathematics teaching. Take, for example, the general rule that any large number, the sum of whose digits is divisible by 3, is itself divisible by 3. It sounds too easy to be true—but after many inductive examples of trying-and-seeing, the students will agree that it does indeed seem to work. Very well, *why* does it work? In this way, the students may be led into a formal proof.

Other techniques involve perplexity ('Which alternative do I choose?'); bafflement ('There are no alternatives to choose—but there must be'); and contradiction ('But this contradicts what we just learned'). Mosston (1972) used questions to create and maintain intrinsic interest; in his view, facts and answers terminate curiosity, so in order to improve teaching he suggested that teachers who supply more than three facts per lesson should be fired. Think about it.

Julius Sumner Miller in his popular TV programs taught by curiosity-through-conflict. Typically, he introduced the unit of instruction by presenting an apparent mismatch between rationality and reality, or by describing a simple but baffling situation. For example, to introduce the issue of heat transfer in liquids he showed two cups: one was three-quarters full of hot coffee, the other a quarter full of cold milk. Which way, he asked, could he obtain the hottest cup of milk coffee: by adding the milk to the coffee, or the coffee to the milk? We teach neither students nor subjects, he said. Our role is to stir interest in the subject and fire the student's imagination. Enthusiasm in a teacher is more important than competence:

> Teachers must, I say, recite less facts, ask more questions, give fewer answers. The drama and beauty and aesthetic of the subject must be pointed up. The intellectual process must be stirred. A feeling for knowledge for its own sake must be engendered. Learning will then be an exciting adventure which few can escape, nor will many wish to. And it will bring the spirit to a great awakening which can likely last for the lifetime. Some of us have seen it. (Miller 1979: 51)

From disinterest to interest

If, as is likely, interest isn't there to start with, students cannot become intrinsically motivated in the task from the outset. They need to be brought or led to the point where they become involved, that is when recoding begins to take place. What does it mean to become involved? Involvement requires:

1. attending to the task in the first instance;
2. having or obtaining the sufficient background knowledge (existing codes) to permit involvement;
3. having the freedom to pursue involvement at the learner's own pace (not that of the teacher);
4. being sufficiently 'motivated' to *want to become* more involved.

The last point focuses on the teacher's main problem: how to obtain a stand-in for interest. This has to be done in such a way that the onset of intrinsic motivation is at least not jeopardised and at best actually facilitated.

This is shown in diagram form in Figure 11.1. The shaded portion of the graph represents intrinsic motivation proper; the unshaded portion all other forms of motivation. Task involvement increases along the bottom line. As task involvement progresses, there are at first fairly slight increases in intrinsic motivation (the shaded area rises). At point 1 there is only a slight degree of intrinsic motivation; the learner is performing the task because of the larger proportion of other forms of motivation. There is then a fairly sudden 'take-off' at point X: 'Hey, this is more interesting than I thought!' After that, intrinsic motivation increases sharply, until towards the end of the task (point 2), the learner is hooked; other forms of motivation aren't necessary.

It may be that point X is never reached. In that case, the student does the task, if at all, entirely because of the non-intrinsic pay-offs. In Figure 11.1 we are looking at the case where the student is not initially interested in the task, but becomes so with increasing involvement in it. The question is: How does the teacher get the student to point X? How, in other words, can the student be seduced into learning?

It helps to seize every opportunity to point out how socially valuable a particular academic task is; a strategy that Brophy (1986) suggests teachers miss so often. This has to go way beyond the fairly futile 'You'll be sorry you can't calculate accurately when you grow up!' In fact, Brophy emphasises that one shouldn't dwell on the negative ('You don't want to look a fool, do you?' 'If you don't learn this, they'll cheat you'). Better to give examples of personally known or famous individuals who got where they are now by dint of success in the task in question.

It is possible to introduce most lessons by showing that the skill in question is important in some way. This obviously requires some homework on the teacher's part. How nice to begin a lesson with an interesting story about the content of the lesson to follow. Often, however, the content or activity is not even presented as meaningful or purposeful; and if teachers themselves do not see the point of an activity then the students assuredly will not. Do not introduce the lesson with: 'You're going to be as bored learning this as I am teaching it. But ... it's in the syllabus and we'll just have to get through as best we can.' That is signalling to the students to tune out. Would you believe that is a direct quote from a teacher educator, no less, who didn't like and didn't see the point of the topic of discourse structure in a course on teaching reading.

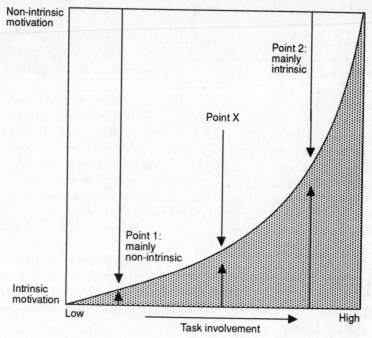

Figure 11.1 *Intrinsic motivation, task involvement and other forms of motivation*

Miraculously, one student didn't agree—she did like and did see the point of discourse structure—and related the incident later in an inservice course.

What about using 'human interest' stories in the text or lesson? Murder, power and sex 'are universally and inherently interesting' (Hidi 1990: 557), but as Hidi points out, the 'seductive details' may in fact take over; they are recalled with relish, the target content with which they have been associated may not be. Anecdote, surprise and human interest may be used, but carefully.

Other ways of getting to point X, where intrinsic motivation may take off, include:

- positive and negative reinforcement (instrumental motivation);
- social motivation;
- achievement motivation.

Not all of these are equally valuable.

We can dismiss negative reinforcement straight away. Threats of punishment if the task is not tackled may result in its being carried out, but the student is unlikely to feel positively towards task or situation (Condry 1977). Positive reinforcement does, however, appear to be a possibility, likewise social motivation, although both have their complications as discussed below. The problem with achievement motivation is that, as we have seen, many students do not see themselves as competitors in the academic stakes, in which case it is likely to be counter-productive.

Perhaps most effective is to combine these in various ways: the clever use of praise, for example, combines elements of reward and social; cooperative games, achievement with social. Some of the possibilities are elaborated below. First, however, we should address an important issue about which there are many divided opinions.

From interest to disinterest?

Does extrinsic reward kill intrinsic motivation? Rewards may get desired behaviour off the ground, but what happens when the reinforcements stop, as they must eventually. Does the behaviour, now hooked to reinforcement, also stop? Does bribery corrupt pure learning?

Many writers are emphatic that it does. According to A.S. Neill, the headmaster of Summerhill Free School, 'to offer a prize for doing a deed is tantamount to declaring that the deed is not worth doing for its own sake' (1960: 162). Festinger (1968) reported an experiment in which some students were given an excessively boring task to do; some were paid quite well, others nothing. Those who were paid said later that they didn't enjoy the task, but those who received nothing at all reported that they found it 'quite interesting'! Festinger suggests that the unpaid students 'over-justified'; they had to explain why they had permitted themselves to be bored to their socks by rationalising and may even have ended up believing they enjoyed it. The paid students could afford to be more honest.

This study may not in fact have to do with intrinsic motivation as much as with how people delude themselves to save face (which is not at all irrelevant to school learning). However, Festinger's study did spark off a long line of research, starting with a classic study by Deci (1971), whose undergraduate subjects did puzzles (Soma cubes) under various conditions:

1. payment for correct solutions;
2. no payment;
3. payment for participating, irrespective of the quality of performance;
4. verbal praise for correct solutions ('That's good—you're doing well') but no payment;
5. verbal praise *and* payment for correct solutions.

He then observed the subjects to see how long they would continue working with the puzzles after the experiment had 'officially' terminated, arguing that the more intrinsically motivated would continue longer. Before reading further, jot down what order you think these groups showed most intrinsic motivation.

Right? Well, what Deci found was that those who were paid for correct solutions only (condition 1) continued the least, but those who received verbal praise continued the longest (4). Those who were unpaid (2) *and* those who were both praised and paid (5), continued for nearly as long as those who just received verbal praise. Those who were paid regardless of their performance (3) came next.

Deci argued that payment for results did dampen interest in the task. It was as if his subjects said to themselves, 'I'll do this for you if you do this for me. That's it, no "overtime" '. Social reinforcement, however, seemed to have quite a different effect: 'If he says I am good at this, I must be. That makes me feel good about these puzzles; I like them.' The other conditions fell in between these two. The conclusion is simple: we like those things that we are led to believe we are good at. Back to ownership again.

It is, however, quite a jump from college students performing Soma puzzles to school students learning maths or reading. What do studies in other contexts and with school students say? Deci's results seem to hold only when the task is interesting already; when dealing with a boring task, like much schoolwork to many students, payment for good results is likely to *increase* subsequent intrinsic motivation (Calder & Staw 1975). It also depends on what the task is. If it is in the nature of the task to receive rewards (e.g., in

Monopoly, or coin-tossing games), then payment greatly increases enjoyment, whereas with tasks that do not naturally lead to payment (such as Deci's) payment decreased subsequent interest (Kruglanski et al. 1975). Lepper and his associates (Lepper, Green and Nisbett 1973; Lepper and Greene 1975) found that motivation in nursery children doing interesting tasks (drawing from numbers) decreased with an expected reward, but was highest when a reward was *unexpected*.

Molloy and Pierce (1980), on the other hand, found intrinsic motivation was unaffected by reward, whether expected or unexpected. They worked with preschool children on a drawing task and had two expected reward conditions and one unexpected. The important difference they found was that children expecting a reward did *better quality* drawings than those who were rewarded unexpectedly. Yet again, Garbarino (1975) studied students tutoring other students. Paid tutors were more critical, impatient, made more demands—and their learners made more errors; unpaid tutors produced a better learning atmosphere and achieved better results. This would seem to agree with one academic's perceptions of his motives (Box 11.1).

Box 11.1   *What motivates academics ...*

Sir: Don Aitkin, chairman of the Australian Research Council, tells us ... that since academics are evidently not in the game for the pursuit of power, sex or cash, it must be the love of symbolic rewards and the esteem of peers.

Since there may be people silly enough to take him seriously, please let me explain what *does* motivate many of us to work an 80-hour week for peanuts.

Some of us like learning and thinking ... the charge that can be got from understanding something, the sudden joy of insight when the little light globe switches on, is one of the greatest pleasures I have found ... ranking about equal with sex (although, regrettably, more strenuous) and well ahead of the transitory satisfaction of impressing the neighbours or pushing someone around ...

... and administrators?
... Who, truly having the choice, would become an administrator rather than a researcher? Only those for whom pushing people around, or contemplating the size of their budgets, gives more pleasure or less pain than does thinking and understanding ...

Dr Michael Alder, Department of Mathematics,
University of Western Australia.
Letter to *The Australian*, 17 May 1990.

Garbarino's study raises real problems; it strongly suggests that people who like their jobs should be paid less than those who don't, because the high pay will cause them to dislike their job, create a tenser atmosphere and work less effectively! Definitely not on. So how can we generalise from these studies to real life? The answer seems to be that it depends entirely on how the individual sees the relationship between reward and performance (Morgan 1984). Reward that is seen as an index of competence in a worthwhile task will encourage motivation; this allows the individual to value the task as his or her personal area of competence. Reward that is seen as an externally controlled 'going rate' on a not otherwise valued activity puts a contract mentality onto the deal; the learner's task is to do so much and no more. In that case, the performance is attributed to factors outside oneself: 'I'm doing this in order to meet the contract'. As we saw in the last hapter, such attributions are alienating from the task.

Finally, an important point to note. Intrinsic motivation is severely depressed when children know they are under *surveillance* (Lepper & Greene 1975). This observation has obvious implications for fostering intrinsic motivation in schools; students are unlikely to feel intrinsically motivated with a baleful eye glaring over their shoulder. That's telling them a truly dreadful message: 'I believe you are incompetent and that if I don't watch over you, you will make a mistake. I know you. But remember this, unwilling and unworthy pupil of mine, you have no choice but to work, because I am here to make damned sure that you do.'

Intrinsic motivation? You have to be joking!

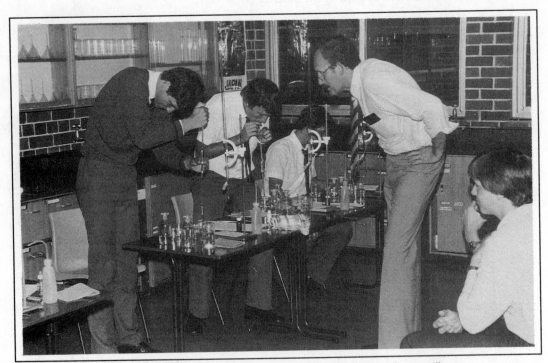

Intrinsic motivation is severely depressed when children know they are under surveillance.

Using social motivation

The effects of praise

Although praise is regarded as an extrinsic reinforcer, it obviously has different effects from material rewards, as the Deci experiments show. Praise is in fact a social not a material reinforcer, and a very powerful one it is too, if it is used carefully. There are two aspects to the delivery of praise:

- *motivational*: it's nice to receive a token of admiration from a valued source;
- *informational*: praise can give important information about ourselves and our performance.

First, then, effective praise must be from a valued source. If a teacher is thoroughly disliked or held in contempt by the student, praise from that source will be seen as irritating, patronising, or just valueless. For a teacher's praise to be effective, the teacher has to be liked or respected, particularly the latter if the informational value of the praise is to be realised. The teacher must be valued if that teacher's praise is to help the student value the teacher's task. Clearly, the classroom climate the teacher has set up is crucial here.

Apart from the general relationship between teacher and student, there is the particular *praising behaviour* of the teacher. Obviously this is partly a matter of the teacher's personality. Some teachers are naturally spontaneous and warm, which is good. Others are reserved, but when they do praise it is like a burst of sun on a cloudy day and that too is good. What is not good is overly frequent praise given without apparent attention to what in particular the student is doing, or how well, and delivered in a monotonous voice. Signals implying that the praise is not sincere will both devalue it motivationally and void it of information.

Second, what makes praise effective and ineffective in giving information? According to Brophy (1981) praise should:

- be given after *selected* performances, not randomly;
- specify what in particular is good, such as effort, or attention to required criteria, not just a global 'Great!';
- give students information about their competence, or about the value of what they are doing;
- relate the outcome to the individual's previous accomplishments;
- imply that similar success will be met in future (attribute success to effort and to ability as appropriate, not to luck or an easy task; see last chapter);
- imply that the students' effort is expended because *they* value the task and are not simply pleasing teacher.

Praise should thus give information about a student's progress, both with respect to the process being used and the quality of the product. This means focusing on specified aspects of the performance. Also, praise can be used to tell the students about themselves, in particular about their sufficiency of effort, competence and future prospects.

Social competition and cooperation

There are three basic kinds of goal structure that can be used to motivate classroom learning (Johnson & Johnson 1990):

- *competitive*, where you believe you can reach the goal only when others can't;
- *cooperative*, where you believe you can reach the goal only if others can too;
- *individualistic*, where you believe your chances of reaching the goal are unrelated to what others do.

The motivational possibilities of all three structures have not been equally explored. Using competition to enhance the value of the product is most commonly used, as in ordinary achieving situations and we have seen that this is effective only for high need-achievers, not for those most in need of motivating. Cooperative structures are used less, despite the evidence that they work very well (Johnson & Johnson 1990; Slavin 1983).

Using *team* instead of individual competition also enhances the value of the final product without putting any single individual's self-esteem on the line. Further, because the team members have to work cooperatively, peer pressure works for rather than against the teacher, and group interaction focuses attention on the process as well as on the product. The challenge for the teacher is to design suitable cooperative learning games in one's teaching subject that are significant academically (see Johnson & Johnson 1990; Slavin 1983).

Apart from the competitive game itself, the interaction induced in small group situations has several features that promote optimal processing:

- a high level of activity; students are less likely to remain passive in well-run groups;
- students provide each other with immediate feedback, at a level they can readily encode;
- students are more likely to be evenly paced in their respective processing capabilities, so that interaction is always engageable;
- students are placed in a context providing a felt need to respond by virtue of group expectations.

Social motivation is not limited to game situations, but can be invoked in many ways, such as peer and reciprocal teaching (see Chapter 16).

Creating appropriate expectancies

So far, we have been dealing with ways of getting students to value the task. We now turn to the second aspect of the expectancy–value model, which is to set appropriate expectancies. This has two major aspects: the task and the student.

Task difficulty and clarity

As we saw right at the beginning, the task set has to be meaningful and set in a meaningful context. After that, the task should be of optimal difficulty: not so easy as to be trivial, not so difficult as to discourage persistence. The key is to get students to make a commitment to reach a goal with that task. Two features greatly enhance goal commitment:

- Goals should be *near,* not far. A task set for tonight is more likely to extract action than one set for the end of next month. More important, a series of subgoals lets students know where they stand and how their performance can be monitored. Bandura and Schunk (1981) produced such a graded program for building the self-efficacy of students lacking confidence.
- Goals should be *clear* and *specific.* 'Write a reasonably long and well-referenced essay on the importance of goldmining to the early settlement of Australia. It should be handed in well before the end of term' is less likely to excite commitment from all but the most internally driven students than 'Write 1000 words on (i) the events leading up to the Eureka Stockade, *or* (ii) the importance of goldmining in the development of Western Australia, *or* (iii) … Refer to at least three different sources from your list and clearly document them. Don't forget to follow the guidelines already handed out. Due: 25th October …'

Of course it is possible to go too far the other way and be overly pedantic and directive, but students cannot be expected to commit themselves to something they perceive only dimly. They should be able to see what the teacher is driving at and also be able to have the criteria spelled out clearly so that they can be continually monitoring their own chances of success. As we shall see in the next chapter, such self-monitoring is a necessary part of serious and committed learning. Driving in a fog is most unpleasant.

Student expectations

The actual clarity and difficulty of the task is one thing. How the student sees it is quite another thing, and that is where the student is operating from. Central here is to build up beliefs in self-efficacy as far as the task is concerned and to attribute the causes of success and failure to factors that are likely to enhance further task engagement. The general lines have been discussed in the previous chapter. If the student has been *successful* in the past, lead the student to believe that future success is likely. It's different strokes, however. If you tell some students that their success is due to their superior ability, then they may cease to put in as much effort in future. But if you tell them it is due to their stupendous and praiseworthy effort, then they may be concluding you are telling them they are not so smart. It's crucial what the *real* factors are, as well as those that are attributed by you and by them.

After *failure*, it is important that the future holds out hope: a new way of handling the task, different teaching, more effort needed, a change of luck (maybe …). If the aim is to improve performance, then performance must be believed to be due to factors that can be changed and strengthed. Ability is a crippling attribution for failure.

De Charms (1976) developed a two-stage program to change pawns into origins:

1. the concepts of pawn and origin, self-worth, achievement motivation and realistic goal-setting, are directly taught (much as in this chapter only in simpler terms); and
2. exercises and assignments illustrating the essential features are given.

Students are asked to set reasonable goals, in the context of a class activity such as a class journal, plan specifically to reach those goals, monitor their effectiveness and to assume personal responsibility for the outcome. They are taught to see themselves as origins, not as pawns; and their enthusiasm for their work increases. In many respects, the program is not unlike other self-management or metacognitive training programs discussed in Chapter 12 in the context of acquiring strategies for learning.

Belief in self-efficacy and attributing success to ability, and failure to lack of strategy or effort, are likely to motivate future achievement. On the other hand, attributions of success to luck or to an easy task, and failure to lack of ability, are likely to kill subsequent interest in the tasks that led to those attributions.

However, as we have discussed above, communicating the appropriate attributions for a successs or failure can be very tricky. Effort attributions can backfire in the sense they could be interpreted as a stupidity attribution. The general rule is to adapt messages—presentation, comments, rewards, evaluations—so that students are given the opportunity to develop a belief in their own efficacy. Even a rat in a Skinner Box may believe it is controlling the controller (see Box 11.2).

> **Box 11.2** *Me origin; you pawn*
>
> Rat, after being trained to press a lever for a pellet of Rat Chow: 'Boy! Have I got this psychologist conditioned … every time I press the lever he slips me some food!'
>
> *Anon*
>
> • Is this rat intrinsically or extrinsically motivated?
> • Is the psychologist intrinsically or extrinsically motivated?
> • Does thinking about either make you intrinsically or extrinsically motivated?

The learning context

School and classroom both must provide an appropriate context if learning is to be motivated positively. Two attributes in particular are important:

• a supportive affective climate,
• a well-managed organisational structure in which the goals are clear.

The school climate

School or classroom climate may be interpreted in terms of McGregor's (1960) Theory X and Theory Y, originally formulated in the context of business management. According to Theory X, people are basically lazy and greedy; they need to be motivated by extrinsic rewards to cater for their greed and to be controlled by threats of punishment and surveillance to counter their laziness. According to Theory Y, on the other hand, people are basically cooperative and trustworthy; they are motivated to develop their intrinsic potentialities and will cooperate with other people to help them develop theirs. The crucial difference between the two theories hinges on the question of trust: Theory X says that you will get best results if you don't trust people; Theory Y says that you will get best results from people if you do.

A state department, principal or teacher operating under Theory X is committed to a system of motivating that relies on extrinsic rewards and punishments. The theory goes: 'Teachers don't teach effectively and students don't learn appropriately, unless they are forced to. The big decisions must be made for them and appropriate incentives, particularly negative incentives, set up to ensure they do what they're supposed to do.' Centralised curricula and external assessments are clearly symptoms of this theory as far as the teacher is concerned and a teacher-dominated classroom as far as the students are concerned; both become pawns in the system (see Box 11.3 for an account of how this may happen).

The University of New South Wales' study of volunteers' reactions to three kinds of prison atmosphere (Box 11.3) shows how the context, and its rules and procedures, can exert a very powerful effect on an individual's sense of identity and motivational disposition.

In the context of school, the 'second set of three Rs'—rules, routines and regulations—likewise affects the student's sense of selfhood. Consider: the school assembly routine, the segregation of boys and girls into single-sex schools, compulsory school uniforms, emphasis on the formal status of staff ('Sir!'), compulsory subjects of study, put-down remarks from staff to student (even if they are facetious, they have their effect), compulsory education for all Australians between the ages of 6 and 15, the interlocking levels of

> ## Box 11.3   *How to produce super-pawns: A simulated prison at UNSW*
>
> Paid volunteers (previously screened for medical and psychological health) were randomly allocated as 'warders' or 'prisoners' for a period of four days, in three different prison conditions: *standard custodial,* which modelled procedures (including warders' uniforms, method of address, food, etc.) in Australian medium-high security prisons; *individual custodial,* similar to standard, except that some respect was accorded prisoners (e.g., recognised by name instead of number); *participatory,* which used joint decision-making by warders and prisoners.
>
> There were, even in the short space of four days, tremendous differences in the 'pawnship' of all participants, both warders and prisoners. Each filled the role the setting created for him. For example, in obtaining action from prisoners the warders could *command, request* or *seek* agreement. In the standard custodial regime, 95% of all attempts to obtain action were by command and 55% by request. In the participatory prison, there were no commands, 52% requests and 48% agreements.
>
> *Source:* Lovibond, Mithiran &Adams (1979).

schooling (infants/primary/secondary/tertiary), the universal progression by grouping in age cohorts called 'Years'. Such decisions are mostly taken for political or managerial rather than for educational reasons and they are not necessarily wrong, but cumulatively they make pawns of us all; they take away self-determination. And the climate they generate tends inevitably towards Theory X.

It's a question of balance. The criteria of a good learning context are positive affective climate and orderliness. You can't be intrinsically motivated in a chaos, because it is simply more difficult to engage the task. Equally, over-emphasis on management can also make us lose sight of the task; task engagement is the important thing either way. So the balance has to be struck somewhere. To simplify: in formal systems one leans more towards a Theory X over-managed system, with the likelihood of producing more pawns than origins, and consequently some motivational but fewer administrative problems. In informal systems one leans more towards Theory Y, with the likelihood of producing more origins but more administrative problems. As we shall see in the next chapter, the quality of learning is likely to differ as well: 'surface' learning under Theory X, 'deep' learning under Theory Y.

So why, if Theory Y is more likely to deliver the educational goods, is there so much of Theory X driven schooling around? The answer to that takes us far beyond the scope of this book and lies in matters of policy, ease of management, and the sociology of institutions. But don't feel a Pawn; the classroom and the school each form mini-systems within the major system itself and there are some degrees of freedom within each mini-system (Biggs 1991a). There is sufficient freedom of movement so that individual teachers *can* make a difference within their own domains (Tobin & Fraser 1988).

It is possible to ease matters at the grassroots, without revolutions within state departments. One example is a commissioned study by a New South Wales mid-coast high school, conducted under the Participation and Equity Program (Telfer 1985). The aim was to look at school organisation and community relations in ways that might encourage retention of potential Year 10 and 11 students. Interviews and questionnaires covered 53 teachers, 207 Years 10 and 11 students and over 350 parents. Emerging recommendations are listed in Box 11.4:

Box 11.4   *Creating a healthier school climate: Recommendations from a pep study of a NSW high school*

Interface with community:

- consultation, interaction, on 'aims of school': conflict on vocationalism;
- reports when problem arises, regular newsletters, use of school facilities (out of hours);
- produce a school service directory giving information to public about facilities, equipment, resources and expertise at the school;
- a map and visitors' guide;
- parental volunteers offering expertise in Year 11 electives;
- work experience outside school, and studies accredited at other institutions such as TAFE;
- parental interviews in a common room—not a formal office, not the long queues and public discussion of parent–teacher nights.

Student facilities:

- a sealed carpark for students;
- shade trees, seats and tables in the playground;
- a sit-down cafeteria, with student notice-board prominent.

Student interaction with staff and decision-making:

- students be involved in choice of library books, texts and equipment such as micros;
- staff accessibility out-of-class at specified times;
- staff–student socials, sporting and hobby clubs, and competitions;
- school counsellor to convene teacher–student discussion groups, to start with the topic 'school discipline';
- student preferences for programs and electives to be canvassed, in relation to each providing a rationale for each subject in 'Why am I teaching this lesson and this subject?';
- provision for free study periods;
- peer support: senior students acting as specific mentors to juniors.

Source: Telfer 1985.

The important thing emerging from this study is not so much the specific points that were changed, but the fact that the school brought in an outside consultant who was open to everyone's views—parents, administration, students, teachers, office staff and canteen staff—and who could orchestrate those views into outcomes in which all concerned could feel some ownership and control.

Classroom climate

As for the school, so for the classroom. Students cannot be expected to find academic activities worthwhile and meaningful if they are alienated, anxious, or cynical about

---

Box 11.5   *Theory X in a Year 11 history classroom*

Teacher: Settle down. Come on, Jonesy, let's get with it. Wakey, wakey, Tony. No sleeping in *my* time! Right—I guess we're as ready as will be—excluding Smith and the other back-row morons.

Today's big question: has 11A done the homework? You recognise the word, I assume. You may remember that yesterday we looked at the achievements of Napoleon and finished up with the section in the textbook which said 'He organised France'. For those of you for whom this is startling information, you might also remember that your job was to investigate the claim and come along this morning ready to justify it. Stand up any who haven't a written summary in front of them. Right, you people see me here at one o'clock and you can do it then. The rest of you make sure I have it before I leave here. Now, who's to be the sacrificial lamb? Yes, you, Thomas—let's see what your summary is like—it wouldn't have to be much good to be better than that last effort you had to rewrite.

Thomas: Well, he ...

Teacher: He? Who?

Thomas: *Napoleon.* He set up a new government and he ...

Teacher: Oh, come on, now. That's just not good enough. Is this Year 11 or Year 7? 'A new government' ... that's so vague it's useless. Facts, specific facts, that's what I'm after. Weak effort, Thomas.

Let's take another ticket in the lottery. What's your story, Julie? You seem to have plenty to say. Try saying something useful for a change.

Julie: Napoleon organised France through, ah, a reform, no, reforms, under a new constitution he ...

Teacher: A bit closer than Thomas, but still a long way from what I need. Where are the *facts? Specific facts?* What reforms? What government? You were asked to read your textbook, underline the key words and phrases, then use the textbook's subheadings to organise your summary: which should be in front of you on the desk. We all can read, can't we, Smith? No, don't answer that: let me live on in Fantasyland. Read *your* summary, Joanne. You appear to at least have your textbook (covered, too, unlike a couple I can see) ...

---

their learning. Students full of aggression, anger, fear or mischief, will not be in the right mood for academic involvement. How Theories X and Y are realised in teacher–student interaction and classroom climate are given in Boxes 11.5 and 11.6.

There are no prizes for guessing which classroom contained the more motivated students. But there is a further point, which these examples also imply. Theories X and Y are an expression of teachers' beliefs about human nature and are part of each teacher's personality. One prerequisite to becoming a good professional teacher thus means progressively growing into a particular philosophy of human nature, which some people with a different set of philosophical assumptions about human nature might find hard to accept.

Box 11.6   *Theory Y in a Year 11 history classroom*

Teacher:	This morning you'll need textbooks, notebooks and the results of your reading assignment examining the claim that 'Napoleon organised France'. You'll remember, too, that in one of his less restrained moments Tony suggested that Napoleon was a megalomaniac. Perhaps your reading might have provided some insight into this claim. Just to start things moving—did it appear to you that Napoleon's motives were personal or national?
Tony:	I still think I'm right.
Joanne:	But how do you know … and how do we know … that you are? Those reforms of the Consulate were France's gain, not Napoleon's.
Tony:	But how much power did Napoleon give the other Consuls? Hardly any. He made sure he stayed on top.
Teacher:	Well, some evidence each way. Let's look at these reforms and the so-called organisation of France. What were the reforms?
Several students:	There were those Codes … What about the Concordat with the Pope …? Local Government was reorganised too … There was a whole range of reforms …
Teacher:	We're not going to make much progress that way. Let's get organised in our approach. If there was a wide range of reforms, can't we make our approach more systematic by grouping the reforms? As a matter of fact, isn't this the way Lambert approaches the topic in your textbook? (Pause) I didn't exactly expect a roar of confirmation, but could someone provide one or more of the categories we could use to group the reforms?
Julie:	Oh, you mean legal reforms and, ah, religious reforms and so on.
Teacher:	That's it. Now what else do we need? Don't use your notes. Let's see if we can work out a classification. We have two groups of reforms: legal and religious. What other groups will be needed?

Setting the right atmosphere

Setting the right 'feel' of the classroom, however, goes beyond the general value system the teacher works from. There are particular things teachers can do and not do, in order to achieve the atmosphere they want.

Getting to like the squeak

A task, or a context, becomes pleasant (and is therefore approached) or unpleasant (and is therefore avoided) by association with pleasant or unpleasant stimuli. Technically, this process is called *classical conditioning:* its general outline may be seen in *A Clockwork Orange* (see Box 11.7).

This form of conditioning was first studied systematically by the Russian physiologist, Pavlov. He noted that when his laboratory dogs were being fed, one of the doors leading to the lab squeaked and that the dogs salivated soon after hearing the squeak of

> ## Box 11.7   *Classical conditioning in 'A Clockwork Orange'*
>
> Alex, the young anti-hero of Anthony Burgess' novel and film is deeply committed to three things: violence, sex and classical music. After a particularly nasty escapade involving the first two of his commitments, he is arrested and sent to a reformatory. It is decided he will be used as a guinea pig in an experiment on behavioural reform. He is forced to watch films of Nazi atrocities while he is being shudderingly ill as a result of the prior injection of a particularly effective emetic. His behaviour thereafter is gentle and considerate: even thinking about violence or sex makes him ill. Unfortunately, the same is true of the music: the experimenters had overlooked the fact that Beethoven's *Ninth Symphony* was used as background music to the film.

the door, before they saw the food itself. Rather unremarkable, one might think, but that basic observation led to a paradigm of learning that Watson (1924) and Guthrie (1952) thought remarkable enough to explain the whole of human learning. They were of course wildly wrong. Classical conditioning simply explains how certain responses, particularly emotional responses as it happens, can be transferred from an original eliciting stimulus (food, in this case) to a previously neutral stimulus (the squeaking door). Those dogs got to like the squeak when it occurred. Which is precisely what teachers need to do; see that students get to like the squeak.

There is a converse, which parents use when they train children to avoid dangerous objects. When a mother stiffens and shows great fear herself at the sight of a spider or snake, her fear evokes the child's fear through modelling, which becomes associated with, or conditioned to, the source of the parent's fear (the snake). Such an unconscious mechanism for 'teaching' the child what to be afraid of is biologically and culturally very useful, but it can also mean that irrational fears are transferred to the child as well.

Some forms of behaviour therapy use the same process; for example, the treatment for alcoholism using antabuse, which elicits violent, shuddering nausea when mixed with alcohol. After very few trials, an intense aversion to alcohol in general is produced. In *A Clockwork Orange*, Alex was the subject of aversive conditioning to violence but, as the music of Beethoven was also present, a subplot developed.

The application of these principles to education is clear. We need to make sure that a particular stimulus is associated with an appropriate emotion. Punishing a student with extra maths, for instance, is terrible psychology; associating maths with punishment can only result in an intensified dislike of mathematics. Associating a particular task with feelings of self-efficacy, a very pleasant feeling, makes one like the task. It is not really surprising that some children dislike school (or particular teachers, or the subjects that particular teachers have taught) if schoolwork has been associated with sarcasm, shame, discomfort, written impositions and physical pain. The classroom scene in Box 11.5 is unlikely to lead to a positive valuing of the task, context or teacher, while that in Box 11.6 might. No guarantees, but it's a positive start.

Management skills

Another prerequisite to academic motivation which teachers can do something positive about is management skills. A disorganised, chaotic classroom is not the right atmosphere for learning; the logistics and the emotional feelings will just be wrong.

A well-organised classroom, on the other hand, is no guarantee that students *will* be motivated. It simply creates the right stage setting; the play can still be acted terribly or very well. Then of course an overly well-managed classroom could be a sterile and a boring place; in that case, the stage setting has become the play.

The point about optimal class management is that it makes it possible to target the major tasks the teacher has in creating positive academic motivation:

- presenting the task so that it may be valued;
- leading the student to expect success in the task;
- creating the appropriate classroom climate;
- managing the classroom so that the task is clear.

The last two of these teacher tasks focus on students' non-task behaviour. Both really speak to the first two. A poor classroom climate makes it much more difficult to value classroom activities; likewise, a disorganised classroom says that the teacher either isn't prepared to take the time and trouble to prepare work properly, or is incapable of doing so. The last is awfully unfortunate for all concerned, but the first point again communicates the message that the teacher doesn't think the task, or the students, or both, are worth the time and trouble. A very demotivating message.

A disorganised classroom also stands in the way of the students obtaining realistic estimates of their likelihood of success. Included in the 'stage setting' is clearly acquainting the students with what is required of them and giving them feedback as to how well they are doing. Without such clarity of goals, or formative feedback, the students are fumbling in the dark; they don't know either where they're going or how far they have gone in any direction. All they can expect under those circumstances is to bump into the wall, which almost certainly isn't the point of their activities.

Motivating learning: An overview

In this and the previous chapter, several points have been made about teaching in a way to maximise student motivation. Box 11.8 brings the major points together in a checklist.

Academic motivation is enhanced by conditions suggesting competence and control, depressed by attributions suggesting powerlessness. That statement should provide the framework for everything the teacher says or does. Possibly the major motivational lesson is to create the appropriate expectations. Students, like most people, will go with the flow.

Box 11.8   *A motivational checklist*

Academic motivation is promoted by:

- meaningful tasks;
- clear expectations;
- positive associations of pleasure;
- social reinforcement (praise); the example of admired figures (modelling);
- ownership, anything to suggest: 'this is mine';
- indexes of competence, anything to suggest: 'you are good at this';
- the right mix of familiar and unfamiliar: the cognitive bottom line of intrinsic motivation.

And academic motivation is depressed by:

- meaningless tasks;
- confusing expectations;
- negative reinforcement (threats of punishment);
- surveillance, suggesting: 'you are about to make a mistake; I'll make sure you don't'; or 'you are untrustworthy; you won't do this if I don't watch'; or 'I call the shots, not you';
- unpleasant associations;
- reward, when unrelated to the task, at a rate set by an outsider;
- work that is either too easy or too difficult.

Plan and deliver your lessons around these points and your classroom will be a happier, more productive place.

Summary

When the task is valued

In real life, the context puts a value on the task. The obvious place for the teacher to start is from that point; utilising whatever interest already exists. By creating the right level of conflict or surprise and by creating teachable moments, it is possible to build on the motivational capital that is around. One can't always rely on that however.

From disinterest to interest

More often, it's a matter of trying to create interest from scratch: a much more difficult task. It's then a matter of getting things moving, by whatever means, until the point of involvement comes when (fingers crossed) many students do become intrinsically interested. Not any old extrinsic motivation will do, however.

From interest to disinterest

Even generous rewards can kill any interest that might have existed. It depends how they are handled. The crux is what message they deliver: do they increase ownership, or put the student on piece rates? Praise is a useful wrapping around a reward; it creates a present as a token of esteem. People like receiving presents; receiving wages is no big deal.

Social motivation

Other people, both authority figures and peers, are powerful motivators. Authority figures can use praise as an effective device for conveying both good feelings and useful feedback, if used properly. Peers can motivate in both cooperative and competitive contexts. Competition has been much used, yet it is for many students counter-productive. Cooperative learning has all the ingredients for high motivation: active involvement, immediate feedback, even pacing and a felt need to participate on the basis of peer expectations. Why isn't it used more often?

Creating appropriate expectancies

Students need to expect a reasonable chance of success; not too easily, or not too remotely, but reasonable for the student in context. Task selection and presentation is crucial; the appropriate level of difficulty, presented so that what is expected and what constitutes success are made clear. The students' expectations are built on past performance and messages as to why they have succeeded and why they failed. Those messages are built into the whole structure of teacher–student interaction.

The learning context

Positive motivation depends also on the context of learning. It should be seen as pleasant and supportive, built on Theory Y assumptions that the learner is OK and can be trusted. A classroom, or institutional, climate built on Theory X is terribly daunting and to be daunted is to throw in the motivational towel. The right classroom climate builds on positive feelings, some knowledge of classical conditioning (so they get to like the squeak) and management skills; the classroom needs to be well organised, the tasks clear and the rules simple and self-evident.

Learning activities

1. 'The good, the bad and the ugly (of praise)'

This activity is designed to bring out the principles that underlie the use of praise in the classroom. We have seen in this chapter how Brophy (1981) categorised six principles of praise (e.g., should be given after selected performances, not randomly). The task is to take those principles and produce a short video-taped documentary which shows the good and bad (and ugly!) effects of praise. This is a task for the creatively minded!

2. Cooperative learning

This activity can be approached from two perspectives: from your reflections on cooperative learning that you have experienced as a learner, or from your observations of cooperative learning taking place in a classroom. Perhaps the latter could be the focus of an in-school experience day.

We noted earlier in this chapter that optimal processing in small group contexts involved:

- a high level of activity;
- the provision of readily encoded feedback from each other;
- an even pacing of respective processing capabilities;
- a felt need to respond due to group expectations.

In your reflections or observations do you find these factors? What really happens when a group of students goes about solving some problem? Does the size of the group make any difference? What about the effects of different tasks?

An extension of this activity would be to suggest ways in which cooperative group work could be organised to encourage the optimal processing mentioned above.

3. Maximising student motivation

Box 11.8 provides the focus for this activity. We suggest you use it during the planning, implementation and evaluation of lessons that you teach. Using it to monitor your lessons by translating our points to questions: 'Are the tasks meaningful to the students?',

'Are there clear expectations of what is to be learned' etc. Of course, your answers may be 'Yes' at the planning stage but the evaluation may show that you overestimated yourself, or underestimated the students.

Another way to approach this activity (in class) would be to have groups prepare lesson notes that highlight factors that depress academic motivation. The lesson plans could then be presented to the class for discussion as to how the 'defect' could be remedied.

4. Classroom/school climate

Below we present a scenario that we suggest be role-played, acted out in the class.

You are in a school that serves an area in which there is a general feeling by parents that competition is vital for school learning. The staff at the school, however, want to balance this perspective by having a cooperative outlook on school learning. The staff meet on a number of occasions to put together a policy on cooperative learning and, aware of the community's feelings, decide to produce a newsletter for distribution to parents. The letter is distributed but the next day two parents confront you in the playground, arguing: 'Competition is what it's all about. Why do you want to bother with cooperation? After all, the world lives on competition ...' They say they know of other parents who will be coming to the school to complain about the cooperative learning policy.

How would you respond to such comments? What action would you take? What would you have included in the newsletter?

5. Quality of school life

The intent of this activity is for you to get a feel for some recent Australian research into students' views on the quality of their school experiences, particularly as it relates to motivation. The work by Ainley and Bourke (1988) considers primary students' perspectives, while Ainley, Reed and Miller's (1986) research comprehensively examines secondary students' views. It is the latter work that provides the focus for this activity; if you can get a copy of this research you will see that they used a 40-item questionnaire that tapped seven areas of school life (see p. 98): positive affect ('I like learning ... I get enjoyment from being there'); negative affect ('I feel depressed'); opportunity ('The things I learn are important to me'); achievement ('I really get involved in my school work'); teachers ('Teachers help me to do my best'); status ('People look up to me'); and identity ('I get on well with other students in the class'). Of these seven, the first four are clearly related to motivation. Look at the results (p. 104) from their sample of Years 7, 8, 9, 10, 11 and 12 students. Here you will see decreasing achievement and opportunity scores from Year 7 to Year 12 and increasing negative affect scores from Year 7 to Year 12. This suggests that the older students were less motivated in the two curriculum related areas and that they felt more depressed and anxious about school life. On the other hand, positive affect scores are high at Year 7, decline to Years 9, 10 and 11 but increase at Year 12. Consider these results (and others, say to do with ethnicity) in the context of Theory X and Theory Y.

An extension of this activity could be to devise your own scale or use the ACER scale to sample a few high school students to see how they perceive the quality of their school life.

6. Achievement goals in the classroom

There is a good article on achievement and motivation by Carol Ames and Jennifer Archer in the *Journal of Educational Psychology*, 1988, **80**, 260–7. They examine high school students' motivational processes as they relate to mastery and performance goals in actual classroom settings. Climate dimensions (e.g., reasons for effort) were related to mastery goals (e.g., learning something new) and performance goals (e.g., perform better than others). They found that students who perceived an emphasis on mastery goals in the classroom reported using more effective strategies, had a more positive attitude to class and had a stronger belief that their success was attributable to effort. What did Ames and Archer find for the performance goal students? Can you make any predictions on the basis of your knowledge gained from this chapter? A useful activity would be to summarise the paper, using schematic or concept maps.

Further reading

Because of the nature of motivation as discussed in this and the previous chapter, we repeat the further readings from Chapter 10 and then add several more readings.

On academic motivation
Deci, E. L. & Ryan, R. M. (1985). *Intrinsic Motivation and Self-determination in Human Behaviour.* New York: Plenum Press.
Dibley, J. (1986). *Let's Get Motivated.* Sydney: Corporate Publishing.
Weiner, B. (1986). *An Attributional Theory of Motivation and Emotion.* New York: Springer-Verlag.

Deci and Ryan, and Weiner, expound the declarative knowledge to do with the 'tender' (intrinsic motivation) and the 'tough' (achievement motivation) ways of being academically motivated. Dibley's book on achievement motivation is for the layperson; full of sound procedural advice.

Ainley, J., Reed, R. & Miller, H. (1986). *School Organization and The Quality of Schooling.* Hawthorn: ACER.

This work provides the focus for one of the learning activities in this chapter. It details a range of motivationally related factors and their changes over the years of secondary schooling. Challenging stuff.
Good, T. & Brophy, J. (1991). *Educational psychology.* New York: Longmans.
Hidi, S. (1990). Interest as a mental resource. *Review of Educational Research*, **60**, 549-71.
Schiefele, U. (1991). Interest, learning and motivation. *Educational Psychologist.*, **26**, 299-323.

We don't often recommend the opposition, but Good and Brophy's text is excellent on the 'how-tos' and more frequently the 'how-not-tos', of creating a good motivational climate. They are particularly strong on the use of classroom management, praise and common sense in providing a pleasant and purposeful context for handling tasks. Hidi's article is more technical, as is Schiefele's, but there are important practical points: good learning arises from interest, but the insertion of 'seductive details' into your lesson is a two-edged sword.

Weiner, B. (1991). Metaphors in motivation and attribution. *American Psychologist*, 46, 921–30.

A paper worthy of deeper examination. Weiner looks at research from an historical perspective using metaphors to reflect changes in our understanding of motivation. He uses two basic metaphors: Person as machine and person as Godlike.

PART 4

METACOGNITIVE PROCESSES

CHAPTER 12

HOW STUDENTS APPROACH THEIR LEARNING

How students approach their learning

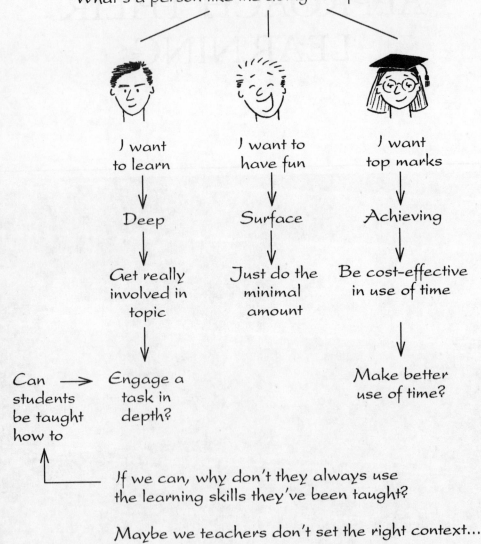

School learning

What's a person like me doing in a place like this?

I want to learn	I want to have fun	I want top marks
↓	↓	↓
Deep	Surface	Achieving
↓	↓	↓
Get really involved in topic	Just do the minimal amount	Be cost-effective in use of time
↓		↓

Can → students be taught how to

Engage a task in depth?

Make better use of time?

↑ If we can, why don't they always use the learning skills they've been taught?

Maybe we teachers don't set the right context...

HOW STUDENTS APPROACH THEIR LEARNING

In this chapter, you will find out:

- that people can be made aware of how they learn and solve problems, and regulate their own learning processes;
- how students typically see school and how that affects the way they approach learning;
- what approaches to learning are commonly found and how they affect the learning outcomes;
- what school and other factors encourage different approaches;
- that aspects of the more effective approaches can be taught as learning/study skills;
- that teaching study skills isn't always effective and why it isn't.

Watchers over our learning

One of the interesting characteristics of people is that they not only behave, but can watch themselves behaving and believe that they can exert a certain amount of control over how they behave. People are … active agents who can be aware that things are or are not going as intended, who can deliberately optimize their performance and who can learn from having become aware of their mistakes. (Robinson 1983: 106)

The picture given so far of the learner in school might suggest an information cruncher who precodes, encodes, recodes, dismembers and remembers on cue. That picture, which is valid as far as it goes, does not recognise that learners become aware of, and exert control over, their learning processes. That is not a new idea. The ancient Greeks saw it as educationally important to 'know thyself'. At the beginning of this century, Dewey (1910) talked of 'reflective self-awareness'. Flavell (1976) revived recent interest in reflective self-awareness, calling it the less informative 'metacognition', or: 'one's knowledge concerning one's cognitive processes and products … [and] refers to the active monitoring and consequential regulation of those processes' (Flavell 1976: 232).

What processes are we talking about? Metacognitive processes are those that imply self-determination, or autonomy, in learning and problem solving:

- *planning*, deciding what my goals are and what *strategies* to use to get there;
- deciding what further *knowledge* or resources I need;
- *monitoring* progress along the way; am I going in the right direction?
- *evaluating* when I have arrived; and
- *terminating* when the goals have been met.

Whereas cognition refers to the 'what' of learning, metacognition refers to controlling the 'how' and the 'when, where and why', or in other words, the *procedural* and *conditional knowledge* of learning. Such knowledge is particularly important in carrying out complex cognitive activities.

Attribution theory is essentially a metacognitive theory, because it refers to the student's awareness of success or failure and the causes attributed to each. The attributions are the conditional knowledge surrounding success and failure. Knowledge of these causes is important for controlling future learning; to make sure the successes continue and the failures turn into success. In particular, effective metacognition would attribute causes to something over which I have control, such as increased effort, or acquiring the right strategy. To say: 'Now, that failure was just bad luck; things are sure to be OK next time' is ducking the responsibility of turning that failure to success. But to say: 'I got it wrong that time; I misjudged what I needed to know' is allowing me to do something adaptive about the failed situation. The everyday word 'reflection' describes metacognition very well; reflection transforms error from a disaster into a positive learning experience.

There is now a great deal of research on how children and adults make use of their reflections on their own thought processes, and how teachers may make use of that knowledge to facilitate learning in their students (see Nickerson 1988 for a general review; Evans 1991a; Lawrence 1991; Lawson 1991; Moore 1991; White & Baird 1991 for examples of Australian studies on applications to teaching). The present text is guided by this metacognitive framework for construing learning and teaching. In this chapter we talk about how metacognition underlies students' approaches to learning in the classroom, and in the next chapter on the relationship between metacognition and how students read, take notes and write. The implications for teaching infuse several chapters, particularly Chapter 16, which deals with teaching methods specifically intended to encourage student metacognition.

In sum, metacognition simply means that we *reflect*, critically and realistically, on what we are doing; it helps us cope with new and complex situations of all kinds. It is therefore an important *educational aim*, as is recognised in systemic statements of the aims of education, as we saw in Chapter 1. 'Responsible self-direction' is how the NSW Education Department put it.

Metalearning

Yet schools discourage the very things they should be fostering; they are very other-directive as far as students are concerned. It is not entirely the schools' fault. The goals are already decided: that is the curriculum. The strategies for reaching those goals are taken over by someone else: they are the teaching method. Monitoring progress along the way is done too by someone else: that is the weekly test. Deciding when they have been reached adequately is the accreditation process itself. Students have to learn responsible self-direction by being responsibly directed by other people.

We are not saying that curriculum, teachers and the methods of teaching and assessing learning are all counter-productive. They are necessary for other reasons, dealt with in Chapter 1; students are required to learn things that they would not otherwise learn in their everyday lives. School learning thus necessarily deals with information that is second-hand, not directly experienced in a context that is personally significant. So somebody else has to decide the curriculum, to teach it and to ensure that some kind of learning has taken place. Thus, while schools tend to preclude the exercise of the metacognitive skills of planning, goal-setting, designing strategies, monitoring and the like, they nevertheless have to *value* these skills, if they are to prepare students for coping with everyday living outside of school.

The learning context in the school module

There is, then, a little bit of a contradiction between what schools actually do and what they *aim* to do. In 'situated' learning contexts, people's interest in their learning naturally deploys their metacognitive skills. In school learning contexts, we have to recognise that the metacognitive skills of most students do not tend naturally to be focused on the set school tasks, instead they focus on rationalising their place in the school environment: 'What's a girl like me doing in a place like this?' The main aim of many students when presented with a task in school is to get it out of the way, rather than to understand what it is intended to teach (Brophy 1986). The aims of students do not always coincide with their teachers' professed aims, giving rise to the issue of different approaches to learning tasks. How you approach the task depends on your original aim.

So teaching involves more than simply cranking up the coding machine. That machine has got to have a context in which to work, and a cranker-upper who knows what the whole thing is about and why. Bereiter (1990) sees learning as taking place in contextual *modules*; that is, any learning experience is situated in a particular context. When learning something, anything—Bereiter uses the example of making after-dinner speeches—you have to take a whole complex of things into account: the declarative knowledge of what to say; the procedural knowledge of the rhetorical skills telling you how to say it; your goals and purposes in devoting time and energy; how you feel about it (if the very idea simply makes you constantly nervous, with no ego rewards, then forget it); and perhaps overriding all this your self-concept as an after-dinner speaker.

School is such a contextual module. There is the institutional superstructure: the curriculum, the classroom, all those things that Marton (1981) refers to as the 'first order perspective', the official or outside description of what goes on in schools. There is also the 'second order perspective', which is what goes on in each student's mind; and *that* is what is going to determine students' intentions and their approaches to learning.

Many students see academic tasks as things to be got out of the way, rather than as activities that are supposed to teach them something and which they are to understand. Other students see a task as a means of showing the world how brilliant they are; others again see the task as what was intended from the first order perspective, an item to be understood, linked with cognate knowledge and used with flair.

Thus, many students do not even think of themselves primarily as *learners*; their metacognitive processes are directed at working out a comfortable or at least acceptable way of coming to terms with the school module. Those students who on the other hand do see themselves primarily as learners, enter an *intentional learning* module, where the intention is precisely to construct new knowledge, to monitor one's understanding of it; all those metacognitive things that go into what we later call a 'deep approach' to learning. Often a moral aspect, such as a commitment to truth and contempt for superficiality and pretence, is included in the intentional learning module (Bereiter 1990).

The module of school learning is thus very complex and means different things to different students, not to mention different teachers. The effect of these perspectives on learning-related activities in the school module is called *metalearning* (Biggs 1985; Novak & Gowin 1984). As a result of metalearning, students derive their ways of handling the problem of learning in institutions like schools and universities. Taylor (1984) refers to a *personal study contract* that students (in her case, university students) make with themselves: 'This is what I want. In order to obtain it, I shall have to do this, that or the other. If I don't, I would be breaking my contract with myself and I lose.' For example: 'I want a good time and a piece of paper at the end. That means doing just enough to pass'; or 'I want to really see if mathematics is for me. I'd like that, as I'm really interested in it, so I've got to be prepared to work on problems and assignments to the best of my ability.' Priorities may change, as students find out more about themselves and the task, but such a 'contract' is, with varying degrees of explicitness, in the minds of most students, whether primary, secondary or tertiary.

At its simplest, this contract breaks down into two questions, the will and the skill (Pintrich & DeGroot 1990):

• What do I want out of this? What are my *motives?*
• How do I propose going about getting there? What are to be my *strategies* of achieving what I want?

Motives tend to determine strategies; what I want determines what I do. Motive and strategy tend to be compatible, together forming an *approach* to learning (Biggs 1985; Marton & Saljo 1976a, 1976b). Approaches to learning derive from the need to handle the school learning module; they describe typical ways in which students' metacognitions come to terms with that situation.

What approaches to learning are there?

Approaches to learning were originally conceptualised by Marton (1975) in the context of students reading a text. He found that students approached the task with one of two intentions: to remember the *words used,* or to try to discover the author's *meaning.* Depending on their original intention, they would use a strategy to suit; if to remember the words, they would rote learn, using rehearsal strategies, and if to discover meaning, to try to understand the semantic content. The first was called a 'surface' approach, the second a 'deep' approach, after the levels-of-processing model of Craik and Lockhart (1972) that was briefly mentioned in Chapter 5. Marton and Saljo (1976a, 1976b) subsequently developed the deep and surface notions, and related approaches of learning to the quality and complexity of the outcomes: surface leading to the reproduction of words and detail, deep to structured arguments that reflected the author's meaning.

The importance of this concept of approach to learning has since been realised. It is powerful. Teachers need to realise that there is no one way in which students go about their learning; that some ways are more effective than others; and that, most important, there are things they as teachers can do to optimise the chances that students will go about learning in the most desirable ways.

Marton's original idea of intention is similar to that of motive, and as soon as you say that, then four broad categories of approach suggest themselves, based on extrinsic, social, achievement and intrinsic motivation, following the four ways of valuing learning described in Chapter 10. A great deal of research, using questionnaires completed by students in several countries and at all levels of schooling, has consistently produced three approaches to learning, labelled *surface, deep* and *achieving* (Biggs 1987a; Entwistle & Ramsden 1983; Watkins 1983a). A 'social' approach—the one missing category of motivation—loses focus, as the ensuing strategies for learning could vary, depending on who formed the motive (parents, peers or teacher) and the nature of the process (modelling, conformity or cooperation). The other three motives lead directly to clear-cut strategies, as we see below, and the approaches so defined have important implications for the understanding of learning and for the improvement of teaching.

Students have fairly stable sets of motives for school learning and each set determines a generic strategy for handling a range of learning tasks. Thus, the surface motive and surface strategy together comprise the surface approach, the deep motive and deep strategy the deep approach and so on. Each can be recognised as an attempt by students, involving varying degrees of metalearning, to handle the 'second hand' nature of many school tasks; in only one approach, deep, do students enter an intentional learning module and become directly engaged with the content of the task itself. In the other two, the institutionalisation of the task, and particularly its assessment with the inevitable consequences of passing or failing, determine the nature of the student's engagement, either in maximising the marks gained (which isn't always the same as engaging the task on its own terms), or in settling for an acceptable minimum.

The surface approach

The motive here is extrinsic; it is to carry out the task because of either positively or negatively reinforcing consequences. The student is willing to engage the task and pass minimally either because life will be even more unpleasant if he does not, or because she wishes to gain a paper qualification with minimal trouble or effort. Learning thus involves steering a middle course between two horrible fates: working too hard or failing.

The strategy usually adopted is based on rote learning. Surface motivated students focus on what appear to be the most important topics or elements and try to reproduce them accurately. Because of this focus, they do not see interconnections between elements, or the meanings and implications of what is learned. Sometimes accurate reproduction is important—for example when formulae need to be reproduced with accuracy whether or not they are understood—but the surface approach is too restricted to lead to the sort of learning required by many important school tasks. Students holding a quantitative conception of learning (see Chapter 1) believe that the reproduction of detail is the appropriate way to go and the more that is reproduced, the better the learning.

Students using the surface approach may well show metacognitive skill. For example, a student might deliberately rote-learn aspects of a solution that she cannot understand, confident that she can work the rest around that. Or he may know the teacher will be impressed if the Shakespeare paper is littered with copious quotations from the set play, the displays of erudition calculated to mask the fact that he doesn't understand the play, or even the question.

More commonly, the surface approach is used with less evidence of metacognition, as when Brophy (1986) says the main aim is get the task out of the way; this can often be done quite plausibly by rote-learning key details, whatever is actually required. Such a strategy pre-empts detailed resource and strategy planning, monitoring and in-depth involvement with the task, but it is likely to meet the teacher's minimal requirements, as the student appears to expend some effort in the general direction of the task, getting enough bits right.

The surface approach then does not mean simply that the student is prone to rote-learn details; that is one symptom of the surface pathology, when rote-learning is *not* appropriate. The essential nature of the surface approach is that it is corner-cutting; it is a learning pathology that does not engage the task in the way it should be engaged. That applies to any context when corners are cut; the surface way of handling it is to use a low-level strategy that gets you off the hook but doesn't solve the problem itself. Such an approach is only sensible from the second order perspective, for example when you are forced into a situation not of your own choosing and you couldn't care less as to the outcome. Unfortunately, that is how some students see the school module.

The deep approach

The deep motive is based on intrinsic motivation or more particularly, interest (Hidi 1990; Schiefele 1991); the strategy flowing from interest is to seek meaning. Curiosity and its more specific counterpart. interest, are only satisfied when the stimulus is understood; the only way to solve a problem that genuinely means something to you is to tackle it honestly. Intrinsic or deep motivation corresponds to the 'felt need' experienced in everyday problem solving in personally significant contexts, as discussed in Chapters 10 and 11. There is a personal commitment to learning, which means that the student relates the content to personally meaningful contexts or to existing prior knowledge, depending on the subject concerned. This is Bereiter's intentional learning module.

Literature, for example, is not learned as a chore. Whereas a surface learner would learn 'the story' of *Hamlet: Prince of Denmark,* embellished with a few speeches and two-liners, the deep learner would speculate about the possible meanings of the play, from a personal to a universal perspective; would relate the language used to the audience effects intended; or whimsically rewrite (but not for the HSC) *Hawkelet: PM of Ozmark.* In physics, the conceptual frameworks that may be used for encompassing the data are more constrained than in literature, but involve elaborative processing just the same: searching for analogies, relating to previous knowledge, theorising about what is learned, deriving extensions and exceptions; both convergent and divergent processes are involved. In order to derive such elaborative schemata, study behaviour is usually marked by wide reading, discussion with teachers and other students, playing with the task, thinking about it while jogging; playing with it, never letting it alone.

Unlike the surface approach, the deep approach is entirely plugged into the content of the task. It is thus not possible to say what 'the' deep approach is, in the way that one can say that the surface approach usually involves reproduction of concrete detail, beyond saying that in a deep approach, the student will:

- possess a great deal of relevant content knowledge;
- operate at a high, or abstract, level of conceptualisation;
- reflect metacognitively on what is to be done, using optimal strategies for handling the task;
- *enjoy* the process;
- be prepared to invest time and effort.

The particular optimal strategies will be determined by what the task is. Schiefele (1991) noted the strategies students used when reading high or low interest text, and found strongest positive relationships with willingness to put in much time and effort, in particular in such demanding strategies as relating new material to what is known, searching for main ideas, posing questions, seeking new information: all demanding and time-consuming activities. Rehearsal was actively avoided.

As we shall see in the next chapter, optimal writing strategies include reviewing and revising text; for note-taking, summarising at an abstract level and so on. In all cases, the student operates abstractly, using a conceptual framework that subsumes the relevant detail. The conception that drives the deep approach is Level 3: the view that learning is the construction of meaning. Deep learning changes the way the world appears and is understood.

A deep approach to learning involves a personal commitment and metacognitive reflection.

The deep approach is ideally what school learning should involve. That is not always the case. As we see later, students using a deep approach do perform at a higher qualitative level than those who do not, but do not necessarily obtain higher marks (Trigwell & Prosser 1991); these depend of course on what the marker gives credit for and some markers do value detail. Further, a 'pure' deep engages deeply only those tasks in which he or she is intrinsically interested, which can be fairly disastrous for performance across the curriculum. A little bit of achieving approach helps.

The achieving approach

The achieving approach is like the surface approach in that it is focused on the product. In this case, the focus is the ego trip that comes from obtaining high grades and winning prizes.

The achieving motive we have also met in the previous chapter. The achieving strategy is to maximise the chances of obtaining high marks and while this (hopefully) involves optimal engagement in the task (like the deep strategy), such engagement is the means, not the end (unlike the deep strategy); it really depends on what earns the most marks. If the teacher rewards accurate recall of detail, then that is what the achieving student will give. In one study of Year 11 history essays (Biggs 1987d), the students were asked: 'In what ways was the reign of Tutankhamen different from that of Akhenaton?' One student, Maria, a high achiever, wrote by far the longest essay and was gently rebuked for exceeding the word limit, but was then commended for her 'coverage and thoroughness' and given the highest grade in that class. Maria's essay did not in fact answer the question; she didn't compare Tutankhamen with Akhenaton, but gave the life histories of each. This is a familiar story; teachers feel obliged to reward students who have clearly expended much effort, particularly if they also write well. Metacognitively astute students make use of that.

The achieving strategy concentrates on cost-effective use of time and effort, a rather cold-blooded calculation, involving organisational behaviours that characterise the model student, such as keeping clear notes, planning optimal use of time and all those planning and organisational activities referred to as 'study skills'. If you want to pig out on marks, it pays to be self-disciplined, neat, systematic, always planning ahead, allocating time to tasks in proportion to their 'importance'. The element of competition may also prompt such grossness as racing to the library immediately the assignment is announced, taking out as many of the important books as can be handled cost-effectively, and hiding the rest randomly around the shelves.

Like the deep approach, then, the achieving approach involves a high degree of metalearning, relating both to context (awareness of self, task and context, with deliberate planning of time and resource allocation) and to content (optimal task engagement). While deep and surface are mutually exclusive at any given moment, an achieving approach may be linked to either: one can rote-learn in an organised or an unorganised way, or seek meaning in an organised or unorganised way. Surface-achieving is the approach adopted by students who want to obtain high grades and think that the way to do so is by using the surface strategy. (The evidence is that they usually are wrong; surface-achievers usually do not do well in school, unless like Maria they are very clever in their use of the strategy.) Deep-achieving, a planned and cost-effective search for meaning, is however characteristic of many of the better students (Biggs 1987a).

Approach to learning and learning style

The meaning of approach as a relatively stable predisposition towards learning suggests that 'approach to learning' and 'learning style' (see p. 189) are closely related concepts. There are, however, important differences. A learning style is like a cognitive style (see Chapter 7) in that it is a permanent personality characteristic or trait that is displayed over a range of tasks and situations and develops independently of schooling. An approach to learning, on the other hand, reflects the interaction between a student's current motivation and the teaching context and is modifiable. Further, an approach has an affective component in the form of motivation, whereas a style is purely cognitive.

How general are students' approaches to learning?

Consider these two senior high school girls, both with 'superior' IQs but with fundamentally different approaches to learning (Ogilvie & Steinbach 1988):

SA: socially and sports rather than academically oriented and scored low on deep and achieving strategy items from the Learning Process Questionnaire (see below).
JP: academically oriented and a perfectionist in whatever she undertook and she scored very high on deep and achieving strategy items.

Both girls were taught an 'academic' task (a computer chess program) and a 'sporty' task (juggling). Well: did *SA* beat *JP* at learning juggling and *JP* beat *SA* at learning chess?

Wrong. *JP* was significantly more effective at learning both. She used what Ogilvie and Steinbach called the problem solving approach of an intentional learner (what we would call a deep approach): involving self-monitoring, self-evaluation, analysis and diagnosis of a problem, and assessing consequences in order to build a knowledge base. On dropping balls:

> *JP:* 'Now, what did I do wrong then? How can I avoid that? Must remember to ...'
> *SA:* 'Just keep these little old balls movin' along here ... keep at it ... dropped one. Oh shoot! Win some, lose some.'

The question is: Could *SA* learn to take on board a deep approach? Despite her IQ, is she doomed to surface learn forever?

We don't know about *SA*, but we do know that approaches may be considerably modified either way by the teaching context or by special training (Biggs 1988a). Context can induce surface learning or deep, but unfortunately it is easier to make students surface than deep learners, and the context of school is such that the former is more likely than the latter. These points are taken up below.

An approach to learning can thus be described as:

1. an *orientation* or predilection for learning in a certain way, illustrated by *SA*'s and *JP*'s inclinations to go about learning.
2. how a student handles a *particular* task at a particular time, illustrated by how *SA* and *JP* actually handled the particular tasks of chess and juggling.

SA's and *JP*'s inclinations and processes coincided; each was deep or surface by inclination and behaved accordingly, at least in the two tasks examined here. Now take the case of a student at university to please his parents; he is inclined to a surface approach and intends simply to coast through with passing grades. But let us say that he is given an essay assignment on a topic in which he is passionately interested; for a while and on that task, his approach may well be deep. Or a girl who is by inclination a deep-achiever who has to take an extraneous subject to make up her course units; the result is unimportant as long as she passes. We'll bet she uses a surface approach.

The aim of teaching should be to get all students, whatever their inclinations, to process deeply. Chapter 16 processes that very deeply. For the moment, we ask: how do they get these inclinations?

How do students develop their approaches to learning?

Several factors appear to relate to the consistency with which students use particular approaches. But first, it is necessary to have an idea of how students' characteristic approaches are assessed.

Assessing students' approaches to learning

The usual method of assessing preferred approaches to learning is by questionnaire. There are two major ones: the *Approaches to Study Inventory*, developed by Entwistle and Ramsden (1983) for British tertiary students and the *Learning Process Questionnaire*

(LPQ) and the *Study Process Questionnaire* (SPQ) (Biggs 1987b, 1987c), developed and normed for Australian students. The latter are designed to assess the extent to which students endorse the more important approaches to learning and the motives and strategies comprising these approaches.

The LPQ has 36 items and is designed for secondary students, and the SPQ has 42 items and is designed for tertiary students. Students rate themselves on a five-point scale for each item (see Table 12.1).

Table 12.1   *Three prototypical approaches to learning*

	Approach	
	Motive	*Strategy*
Surface	Extrinsic: avoid failure but don't work too hard; e.g., 'In most subjects I try to work things so that I do only enough to make sure I pass and no more.'	Focus on selected details and reproduce accurately; e.g., 'I tend to study only what's set; I usually don't do anything extra.'
Deep	Intrinsic: satisfy curiosity about topic; e.g., 'I find that many subjects become very interesting once you get into them.'	Maximise understanding: read widely, discuss, reflect; e.g., 'I try to relate what I have learned in one subject to what I already know in other subjects.'
Achieving	Achievement: compete for highest grades; e.g., 'I see doing well in school as a sort of game and I play to win.'	Optimise organisation of time and effort ('study skills'); e.g., 'I regularly take notes from suggested readings and put them with my class notes on a topic.'

LPQ: 6 items in each cell comprise each subscale.   SPQ: 7 items in each cell comprise each subscale.

Approach scale score = motive subscale items + strategy subscale items.

There are several ways in which teachers, counsellors and researchers can use the data derived from these instruments. Teachers might obtain data on their own classes and consider the following kinds of questions:

1. Where do my own classes stand compared to other similar classes?
2. How does my teaching relate to the different approaches to learning?
3. How can I change my teaching to bring about better approaches?

Personal and background factors

Several personal and background factors have been found to be related to students' approaches to learning (measured mostly by self-report questionnaire):

Conceptions of learning

The link between a person's beliefs about what learning is, and how that person will engage a task, is a strong one. Van Rossum and Schenk (1984), for instance, found that surface learners overwhelmingly held a quantitative conception of learning (Level 1), while deep learners held the qualitative conception (Level 3). This link is perfectly reasonable: to see learning as the accurate retention of detail obliges the student to concentrate on the details of a task rather than on the structure. To change a student's approach it is thus necessary to induce an appreciation of higher conceptions of learning through the teaching environment (Ramsden, Beswick & Bowden 1986).

Abilities

Students of lower intelligence tend to use the surface approach, but use of the deep approach is not particularly associated with either high or low verbal ability (Biggs 1987a). The deep approach is not then the prerogative of only the brighter students, which is important as it means it is possible to encourage a deep approach across all except the very lowest ability levels. It has also been found (op. cit.) that by Year 11 it is the average and below student, rather than the above average, who uses the achieving approach: being systematic and organised, without any particular link to the deep approach, is what the ambitious but less than brilliant do in order to get on. Ability, then, has some bearing on the use of different approaches, but it is not the most important personal characteristic relating to approach.

Locus of control

Assuming control over oneself—an origin, with an internal locus of control, rather than a pawn—is a prerequisite to metalearning activity. Thus, numerous studies of locus of control indicate that internals (origins) participate more in class, are more reflective and attentive, seek and use information in problem solving, remain aware of information that might affect their behaviour in the immediate future and, not surprisingly, achieve more effectively than externals (Wang 1983); all of which is another way of describing metalearning. Not surprisingly, approach to learning is affected probably more by locus of control than by other variables (Biggs 1987a).

Experiential background

1. *Parental education.* Children's approaches to learning are related to the extent of education received by their parents; deep and achieving being associated with post-secondary education of the wage-earning parent, surface with little post-primary education (Biggs 1987a).
2. *Everyday adult experience.* Volet, Lawrence and Dodds (1986) found that a group of highly intelligent Year 12 scholarship girls performed much worse at a planning task, running errands within given time and distance constraints, which involved a high degree of metacognitive activity, than a group of mature-age mothers of average ability.
3. *Bilingual experiences.* Another group of students who show signs of high metalearning activity are students for whom English is a second language (Biggs 1987a). Continually monitoring the meaning of what others are saying, and being very careful about how one expresses oneself and checking others for signs of misunderstanding, is an extremely metacognitive thing to have to do. Thus, these students, at both secondary and tertiary levels and independently of country of origin, show more metacognitive aware-

ness of their approaches to learning than do native English speakers, although their actual performance is likely to be inferior (if tested in English).

4. *Experience in learning institutions.* Typically and terrifyingly, this appears counter-productive. In a national survey of Australian high school students, it was found that on average the use of a surface approach, decreased from Year 8 to Year 11, but so, too, did use of a deep-achieving approach and in boys far more than in girls. The same occurs at tertiary level. Several writers have found that, except for academically oriented students intent on pursuing a research degree, ordinary undergraduates drop deep and achieving approaches alarmingly, in science more than in arts, and in the then colleges of advanced education more than in universities (Biggs 1982; Gow & Kember 1990; Newble & Clarke 1986; Stokes, Balla & Stafford 1989; Watkins & Hattie 1985). The quotation in Box 12.1 may help explain why:

Box 12.1   *What an institution may do to a deep approach*

Most of all I write what 'they' like me to ... when I get the piece of paper with BA (Hons) then I will write the way I want using MY ideas ...

Source: An Arts undergraduate (Watkins & Hattie 1985, p. 137).

Fortunately, there is another side to this. While Watkins and Hattie (1990) replicated the usual finding that deep and (in boys) achieving approach declined from Year 7 to Year 11, both deep and achieving correlated positively with their perceptions of the quality of school life. Deep and achieving scores were highest when students said that they enjoyed school, saw school as useful and their teachers as fair. Also, Newble and Clark (1986) found deep and achieving to plummet over the years in a traditional medical school, where there was a heavy emphasis on lecturing but, in a highly innovative medical school using problem-based learning, surface was low and deep and achieving high, and got progressively higher over the year levels. So you *can* beat the institutionalising effects if you create a good affective and cognitive climate for learning.

In general, mature-age students report increasing use of achieving and especially deep, approaches the older they are when they enter university or college, suggesting that they have learned something about themselves and their learning that school-leavers have not yet learned. As noted earlier, the context of everyday learning requires the metacognitive skills of goal-setting, strategy selection, monitoring and termination; skills that are unnecessary in the high structure context of formal teaching and that may even be discouraged.

Reflective experiences seem to be richer outside the classroom than inside and it is easy to see why: the outside world is *much more important* to most students. It is easier to be metacognitive about activities that have an immediate and comprehensible bearing on our lives, with a high cost for not being metacognitive, than in a classroom in which the activities involve little choice and the outcomes of those activities are arbitrarily quantified. The challenge is to make the classroom a place where, if they are to survive, students must learn to reflect and to come to understand what being 'metacognitive' means.

In sum, then, approaches to learning are related to factors in the home and develop according to children's school experiences and their preferred way of making their in-school choices. These developments continue throughout life. Living with and solving real-life problems forces people:

- to approach the problem systematically, to plan ahead and to organise their time and workspace accordingly (attributes of the achieving approach);
- to build up interests and expertise in particular areas, learn to interrelate with cognate knowledge, diagnose and remedy one's errors, and build up a knowledge base for dealing with the task (attributes of the deep approach).

Relationships with outcome

In asking the extent to which approaches to learning affect performance, we have to remember that approaches reflect students' predilections, not necessarily the process actually adopted. Second, approaches refer to the *way* the task is handled, not *how well*. It is easy to imagine a brilliant surface learner getting higher marks than a plodding deep; or an involved deep burrowing into something irrelevant to what is being assessed. Nevertheless, approaches have consistent relationships with different aspects of performance.

Examination grades

LPQ scale scores obtained in Year 11 correlate 14 months later with HSC results at −.20 for surface and +.30 for achieving: low, but statistically significant (Biggs 1987a). Correlations between exam performance and deep were significant only in the student's favourite subject, in keeping with the theory that the deep strategy is used only when the student is intrinsically interested in the material. This is why deep-achieving is a good combination: the achieving component keeps you deep across the board, as was *JP.*

These comparatively low correlations do not take into account how particular subgroups of students behave. In one case, the achieving strategy was associated in one lower ability subgroup (but 'lower' within HSC candidature) with an improvement of 22 HSC marks in mathematics, and a decrement of 27 marks in the same exam in a high ability subgroup; cost-effective organising worked in the first group, but actually was cost-ineffective in the second group. Possibly the latter were using a deep approach very well already and stopping to organise was counter-productive. In another case, the deep approach was associated with a rise of 52 HSC aggregate points in lower ability internally controlled students, but had no effect with externally controlled of the same ability level; the latter possibly not having the metacognitive skill needed to use the strategy properly.

Results such as these illustrate the complexity and idiosyncracy of relationships between approaches to study and performance; no simple generalisations that apply to all students, naturally enough, when each is operating from his or her second order perspective. Metacognition is by definition personal and individual. Low overall correlations between approaches and performance do not preclude considerable effects with particular students.

An interesting sidelight on approach to learning and examinations is that students scoring high on deep suffered less stress while preparing for and during examinations, and less suppression to the immune system brought about by examination stress, than other students (Spinks, Chan, Lai & Jones 1990). A deep approach is good for you! For one thing, deep students are more able to handle heavy time demands; part-time evening students with family and full-time jobs who were predisposed to a deep approach saw the time demands as challenging and thought about their studies while doing these other things, while surface-prone students were simply overwhelmed and panicked under time pressure (Lee 1991).

Quality of performance

When we look at *kind* of performance, we see much clearer evidence that different approaches lead to different outcomes. Students endorsing a deep approach produce learning outcomes that are *structurally complex* (as indicated by high SOLO levels: see Chapter 3) at both secondary level (Kirby & Biggs 1981) and tertiary (Biggs 1979; Watkins 1983b). High surface approach scores are however associated positively with efficient reproduction of facts and details, but negatively with qualitative complexity of performance (Biggs 1979). In the last study, students scoring high on surface approach and instructed to learn for detail, obtained very high scores on a factual recall test, but when asked to write about the purpose of the experiment in the text they had read they did so at a very low level; most had missed the point. The opposite results were obtained for students using a deep approach; they recalled fewer details, but understood what the experiment was about. There seems to be a pay-off between understanding and attending to detail; people focus on what they believe to be important.

More recently, Hegarty-Hazel and Prosser (in press a, in press b) showed that growth in the complexity of university students' understanding of physics and biology concepts (assessed with concept maps as described in Chapter 5) was closely associated with their using a deep strategy. A surface strategy was reported among those who had little knowledge of the topic before the course unit began. The last finding emphasises that the surface approach is the fall-back position when you don't have a good knowledge base for your learning.

Secondary and tertiary students who endorse a surface approach see themselves as performing poorly, as compared with others in their class, and express a high degree of dissatisfaction with their performance. The opposite is true of both deep and achieving: students scoring high on these rate themselves as good performers and they are satisfied with that. They also plan to continue their education; school students to go on to tertiary level, and undergraduates to do postgraduate work. High-deep students prefer academic subjects, especially arts/humanities, high-achieving more science oriented, and high surface technical subjects and, in tertiary, business studies (Biggs 1987a).

These results come from several studies, summarised in Table 12.2:

Table 12.2   *Effects of approaches to learning*

Surface approach	*Performance*: Poor examination performance, including external examinations, but good for recalling unrelated detail.
	Educational: Intentions to terminate formal education as early as possible; poor academic self-concept; dissatisfied with academic progress; preference for technical rather than science or humanities subjects.
	Personal: An external locus of control (believes that other people and luck determine what happens to you), low verbal IQ, low parental education. Characteristic of younger rather than mature-age students.
Deep approach	*Performance*: Good performance in external examinations, but only in subjects of interest; learns concepts and principles of high structural complexity with which to interpret detail.

Educational: Intention to continue formal education to tertiary level; good academic self-concept, sees oneself as good performer and satisfied with progress. Often a preference for humanities, then science subjects.

Personal: Internal locus of control (believes one controls one's own destiny), but unrelated to IQ (allowing for higher performance in particular subjects), students with a bilingual background tend to have a deep orientation, as do mature-age students and adults.

Achieving approach

Performance: Tends to do well in examinations and generally 'cue seeks' to maximise on what is required for high grades.

Educational: Intends to stay in formal education to seek the highest qualifications. Sees oneself as a good performer relative to others, but tends to be dissatisfied unless performing at the very top. Preference for science subjects.

Personal: Internal locus of control, over-achieving (performs beyond what intelligence level would predict—bright, but not the brightest); like deep, related to experience and bilingual background.

In sum, then, the surface approach is generally associated with negative factors: poor performance, ill-structured learning, drop-out, poor academic self-concept. The deep approach is associated with positive factors: an 'academic' approach as long as the focus is on personally valued subjects, qualitatively rich learning and a good academic self-concept. The achieving approach is also positive academically, but more externally driven by the need to excel.

Approaches to handling tasks in context

Let us now turn to how students handle particular tasks in context. The key to how students will behave in particular situations is provided, once again, by working memory capacity. Metacognitive activity, like the awareness of anything (compare the discussion of anxiety in Chapter 9), requires working memory space. Deep and achieving approaches need more time and space within working memory for reflective activity than surface. Factors which 'crowd' working memory will thus increase the likelihood of a surface approach. Task complexity, and time or other stress, are obvious candidates that would affect the approach used in a particular case.

Task complexity

We use the same definition of task complexity as before: a simple task requires little working memory, a complex task a lot. While simple tasks allow plenty of space for metacognitive activity, little is required, precisely because the task is simple. One does not need to plan a simple activity in much detail, or to monitor progress.

A highly complex task, on the other hand, demands all the working memory space it can get; yet it is the difficult tasks that need analysing closely to see best how to proceed and to monitor as we go. The strategy that emerges then is rather like stress management (which is itself a metacognitive activity) as outlined in Chapter 9: define and clarify the nature of the problem, assemble and over-learn strategies for handling it. Precisely what strategies one might use we discuss in the next section.

Stress

Stress relates negatively with metalearning or any other metacognitive activity. In time stress, there is insufficient time to think and reflect metacognitively, which is often a slow process. Time stress possibly more than any other factor makes institutional life unfriendly to metacognition. Busy institutional routines—timetables, lesson changes, deadlines to be met, assignments to be done, assignments to be marked (it gets to teachers too)—tell one loud and clear to routinise: Don't think about different strategies, just get it done. The simplest approach, then, is of course surface: reproduce what you think will do the trick and run off the other routines without thinking too much about why.

Other forms of stress, such as high anxiety, simply dominate consciousness to the exclusion of metacognitive luxuries. On the other hand, an established metacognitive approach is a good antidote to anxiety, as we saw in the practice teaching example and as Spinks et al. (1990) found with Hong Kong students.

Approaches to particular tasks

What a deep approach to a particular task specifically involves depends on the task in question. There are three dimensions pertinent to deriving a deep approach: content knowledge, an abstract framework, and processes specific to the task in question.

1. Content knowledge

The whole notion of deep engagement is based on cumulative knowledge. As explained in Chapter 8, meaningful learning is precisely learning that links up with existing knowledge. You can't reach a stage where optimal mismatch occurs if there's nothing there to mismatch. A knowledge base is the fundamental starting point of deep learning. Where students have inadequate prior knowledge to commence a course, they *have* to rely on surface strategies, as Hegarty-Hazel and Prosser (in press a, in press b) showed.

This needs emphasising because, while metacognitive processes are very important (otherwise we wouldn't have wasted time writing this chapter), you can't have all process and no content. Planning means planning content; knowing how to say something clearly and well means knowing about good writing; composing is deciding *what* to say—content again. Knowledge, both declarative and procedural, is important; strategic skill arises out of a good content foundation (McCutchen 1986). So don't get too carried away with all this emphasis on metacognitive processes. Important though they are, knowing your stuff is the first prerequisite to deep engagement in the task. Being aware and controlling—all good metacognitive stuff—presuppose that you know what it is you are being aware of; the *how* presupposes the *what*. Process is a transitive verb; something is always being processed, so you need to get both content and process right.

2. Level of abstraction

Deep processing involves operating at a higher level of abstraction than the bare data of the problem. As we shall see in Chapter 13 in the case of writing, surface approaches involve working within the level of ideas contained in words and sentences, no higher.

Deep writers think also in terms of the theme; constantly in the back of their minds there is awareness of the big picture, what the message is.

The same applies whatever the task. Take medical diagnosis (Ramsden, Whelan & Cooper 1989). Medical students adopting a surface approach take symptoms at face value and ask what a particular symptom suggests on past experience. And in fact, the 'zebra' diagnosis is not a bad strategy: the medical maxim that 'when you hear hoofbeats, think of horses, not zebras' (Cook 1988: 52). If there's a measles epidemic and the patient has a rash, don't ignore the rash and look for stripes. At least not at first. But if horses are then counter-indicated, a higher level strategy is required. Medical students using a deep strategy formed hypotheses and tested them systematically against the presented symptoms before concluding their diagnosis. In short, they had a theory to work from.

Thus, not only does deep processing require more content knowledge, that knowledge needs to be structured hierarchically into generic codes. Whatever the content area, students need to attack higher order levels of content knowledge.

3. Task-specific activities

We now turn to the procedural knowledge of the area or topic. Each task has activities that need doing at the right time and focused at the right level. In the case of writing expository essays, subtasks include planning, composing, reviewing and revising. Surface writers employ fewer subtasks, which are focused on low order textual units (semantically no more than is contained in a sentence), whereas deep writers plan, compose and review up to the level of the main theme (Biggs 1987b). Summarising and writing are considered in more detail in Chapter 13, but similar task analyses can be carried out for virtually any academic task, as Ramsden, Whelan and Cooper (1989) have for clinical problem solving, but alas few such task analyses have been reported.

When approaches to such particular tasks are related to outcome, relationships are very much stronger than when general approaches are related to overall performance. Studies in history, computer studies and reading show that a surface approach, almost without exception, leads to a quantitative outcome of unstructured detail and a deep approach to a well-structured outcome (Marton & Saljo 1976a; Van Rossum & Schenk 1984; Watkins 1983b).

Such findings make a convincing case for deriving deep/surface descriptions for important academic tasks, by using the *knowledge* × *level* × *process* model (p. 352) to crystallise the procedural knowledge for that task. This would tell us what you need to know and what you need do, at what level of abstraction, in order to interact deeply with that task.

Increasing students' metacognitive effectiveness

The burden of this chapter is that metacognition is a very good thing and students ought to do more of it. Quite right too, but metacognition is rather like intelligence; you don't teach students to be more intelligent, but you may teach them to behave more intelligently in particular contexts. So our concern is to teach students to behave more metacognitively in particular situations: how to use deep and achieving strategies when handling academic tasks.

There are three main ways in which students acquire appropriate learning strategies:

1. *Spontaneously, through wit and experience.* This is the way most novelists acquire their skill. Few novelists are taught their craft; they just get on and write. Through self-

conscious monitoring, they improve with experience and rejection slips. The classroom equivalent incorporates a Level 1 conception. The teacher loudly transmits and if the student doesn't receive, then tough; it's not the teacher's responsibility. It's up to the student to acquire the skills of learning.

2. *Implicitly through teaching.* The teacher creates the situation, the scaffolding and the task; in order to engage the task effectively, good students evolve the appropriate strategies. This is the position in most enlightened teaching.

3. *Explicitly through teaching.* The teacher or counsellor explicitly teaches learning and study strategies outside the normal curriculum.

For teachers, the first position is irresponsible, the second admirable and the last controversial. The second position is implicit in many sections of this book, particularly Chapter 16. We deal with some examples here, however, as the distinction between helping students develop strategies in a particular context and across several contexts is sometimes difficult to maintain clearly. However, our main focus here is on the third position, most clearly expounded by McKeachie, Pintrich, Lin and Smith (1986: 30):

> Although some students seem to be able to acquire and use these strategies on their own, most students do not ... Accordingly, there is a need to teach students how to use learning strategies.

In discussing strategy training, however, we need to be clear about what it is we are trying to do. Are we:

- trying to improve learning *within* the context in which we are training the strategies?
- aiming to get students to *transfer* the strategies learned in one context to another context?

The first is easier to do than the second, but it is the second that is usually attempted in study skill training: the skills are taught in special classes, without reference to a particular subject, except that students are encouraged to think of examples within their own subjects and to make the transfer themselves. Let us take that case first.

Teaching study skills for transfer

The underlying assumption is that strategies are 'detachable' from task performance and generalise across tasks. This is clearly true for some memorisation strategies, for example, mnemonics, and for a variety of other metacognitive strategies for planning, monitoring and regulating work, and self and time management (Nickerson 1988; Weinstein & Mayer 1984). Such teaching has traditionally focused on study skills. What is the evidence for the effectiveness of such teaching?

First, what are some study skills? Examples include making sure that:

- notes once taken are kept neatly and systematically so that they can be found when needed;
- the key word in each sentence is underlined;
- one has a suitable place for study, with adequate light and furniture, such as filing cabinet, good desk, etc.;
- one's time is suitably apportioned so that all subjects or topics are given adequate time, in proportion to their importance;
- maximum use of time and prompts is used in preparing for examinations and in how to answer examination questions.

Some of these skills are directly concerned with handling text, such as underlining/highlighting, summarising, studying from text and note-taking. These are all matters best dealt with in the next chapter, which is on text processing, but of course they are also directly involved with strategies for learning from text. Here, our major concern is with more 'general' study skills that do not involve detailed knowledge of the processes of reading and writing.

It has long been assumed that training in study skills will improve students' performance, but the evidence is equivocal. It depends on the extent to which the training:

1. meshes with the existing teaching context; and
2. encourages metacognition rather than 'blind' skill use.

On the first point, consider a study by Ramsden, Beswick and Bowden (1986), who gave a course in study skills to first year undergraduates in a variety of faculties, focusing on such topics as managing study time efficiently, reading and note-taking, examination preparation and writing skills. The only discernible effects of the program, compared to a control group, were that the students increased their use of *surface* strategies, the opposite of course of what was intended. Subsequent interviews indicated that the students believed that effective first-year study comprised accurate retention of a great deal of content, so they took from the study skills course what they believed they needed. The various messages from their teaching—the focus in lectures, in particular the tasks set for assessment purposes—should have told them they needed deep-achieving strategies; they didn't get those messages and so continued their search for more effective surface learning. Clearly, the teaching context in which learning takes place must also be a target of intervention. Had these skills been taught *in context* by the teachers, then the students would have been more likely to have made the transfer.

There is a need to teach students how to use learning strategies.

The second point, on metacognitive rather than algorithmic strategy teaching, involves a distinction between training that is 'blind', in the sense that the students are not brought to see *why* it is important to carry out the skill, and metacognitive training proper (Brown et al. 1983). Blind training works where the students have major learning disabilities, or where certain algorithms are taught simply to provide the answer. Both come down to: 'This is the routine. Do it and you won't go wrong.' That is fine as far as it goes, but for normal educational tasks that is not far enough, we want students to operate on a wider front than routine. We also want students to have the conditional knowledge in which the strategies should be embedded, so that they are aware of what they are doing and why. Using study skills appropriately requires planning a strategy, with monitoring and check-ing to see if the strategy is working. The difference is between strategies and tactics (Snowman 1984). Tactics are short-term manoeuvres during learning: orders to be fol-lowed whether or not they are understood. Strategies involve long-term planning prior to learning and need to be monitored constantly.

However, it is not even as simple as this. Self-regulated learning involves more than the metacognitive strategies of planning and monitoring. Much *energy* is involved; as well as the skill, one needs the will (Pintrich & DeGroot 1990). The skill is in:

1. knowing what to do: the declarative knowledge of appropriate cognitive strategies;
2. knowing how to carry them out: the procedural knowledge involved;
3. knowing when to carry them out: the conditional knowledge that makes using those strategies the appropriate thing to do;

and the will is:

4. maintaining effort on the task.

The conditional and procedural knowledge components must go together: know-ing-when-to presupposes that you know-how-to. Knowhow on its own correlates *neg-atively* with performance; possessing merely a repertoire of skills can be counter-productive if you don't know how to use them properly (Pintrich & DeGroot 1990). Knowing all sorts of 'correct' study skills—keeping beautifully clear and accessible notes, for exam-ple—is a waste of time if you don't know when and how to use those notes. The pho-tocopier is the enemy of wide reading. You copy the article and, glowing with righteousness, file it away for future reading; always in the future. It never gets read.

Thus, study skills taught blind, as tactics, instruct students to underline key words, say, when they have no idea why they should. Teaching study skills in this way may ini-tially lower anxiety, but performance rarely changes and usually the tactics are rejected (Tabberer 1984).

Study skills taught metacognitively may result in change and improved performance. Edwards (1986) conducted a study with two Hunter Valley Year 11 classes, using the Study Habits Evaluation and Instruction Kit (SHEIK) (Jackson, Reid & Croft 1980) and a con-trol class who continued with normal lessons. The experimental students were each given feedback on their approaches to study; they then individually discussed the possible need for change. There were then seven weekly sessions presenting students with the possible ways of changing their approach in the following areas: place of study, planning times of study, organisation of study, reading skills, taking notes, studying for examinations and examina-tion technique. The SHEIK groups both improved their deep and achieving approaches to learning, while the surface approach remained unchanged, and their HSC performance was an average of 35 aggregate marks higher, in comparison to the control group.

Similar results were obtained by Biggs and Rihn (1984), with very highly achievement-motivated university students who were reporting difficulties in study. They took part in a course involving metacognitive processes through self-monitoring, peer tutoring and encounter groups; an ordinary study skills text (Pauk 1974) was provided as one source of activities to be metacognitive about. Deep approach and achieving strategy significantly increased; GPA significantly increased from between C and D average before the course, to between A and B up to two terms afterwards.

Both these studies involved the best case; highly motivated and intelligent students, with clear-cut goals. The infrastructure was there; what was needed was some procedural and conditional knowledge.

Strategy training within the context taught

In this kind of strategy training students are taught the content of their study together with the more relevant metacognitive skills for handling that content; a challenging collaboration between psychologist and teacher, that has strong empirical support for its success (Perkins & Salomon 1989).

A study by Martin and Ramsden (1986) makes the distinction between this category and the previous one of teaching outside the curriculum. They gave classes in effective study to first-year history students at a British university; one group was given a traditional series of lectures and exercises on study skills, the other group was taught in a metacognitive framework developed by Gibbs (1981), in which students in pairs and larger groups compared their work, deriving insights from each other about how they went about their assignments, their strategies being taught in the context of their set history work. The traditional study skills class reacted much more enthusiastically at first, but by the end of the second term most had rejected the skills taught them. The metacognitively taught class started slowly but by the end of the term, compared to the tactical class, they had deepened their approaches to learning, performed better in their assignments and had raised their conceptions of learning from quantitative to qualitative.

Kratzing (1990) compared three different ways of improving the learning strategies of first-year biology students:

1. *Student-centred*, where students discussed how they handled lecture notes, prepared for exams and what they found useful in what they had been taught. Group leaders did not contribute ideas or evaluate; only students' ideas were discussed.
2. *Strategy*, where students were told about different strategies, including deep, which they were encouraged to try out. They then discussed the strategies that worked and monitored their comprehension of the biology text with questions such as: 'What was it that the passage actually taught you?', 'Could you explain that another way?'
3. *Metalearning*, similar to (2) but with a wider discussion of personal and situational influences. They monitored with additional and more individual questions than (2): 'How did you try to go about understanding the passage?', 'How do you feel about this topic?'

All groups were oriented to biology content, but Group (1) less than the others as students talked about their strategies more than about the content itself. Groups (2) and (3) were more focused, both on specific passages of text and problems, and their attention was explicitly drawn to particular strategies for handling content. The last two groups both obtained significantly better outcomes than (1), in terms both of approach to learning and of quality of learning outcomes; (2), however, was better for reducing surface strategy, (3) for improving deep strategy. Student-initiated discussion, in the absence of any direction about what might be useful strategies, did not appear to be effective.

An interesting variant on the present theme is given by McKeachie, Pintrich and Lin (1984), who used the content being taught (learning theory, conveniently enough) to help psychology students be metacognitive about their own learning and to derive proper study strategies for themselves. Their approaches to learning improved and, in the case of bright and highly anxious students, so did their grade point average.

Finally, we might mention a very elaborate study by Volet (1991) who combined strategy training with modelling and coaching and a collaborative support network among the students. The course was on computer programming and the strategies were specifically adapted for the content of programming. The results strongly favoured the strategy training group: but only in some aspects of the course. On straight declarative knowledge there was no difference, but in *applied* aspects the experimental group were much better; and 50% more enrolled in an advanced course and survived much more readily. Their enjoyment, and their account of the learning processes adopted, indicated that qualitatively different things were going on in the traditional and metacognitive classes.

Why do students not use learning strategies they have been taught?

We've been looking at cases where strategy teaching works. Why does it not work? Garner (1990) gives five major reasons why people don't use strategies they have been taught:

1. *Poor cognitive monitoring.* If children don't know they are off track, they're not going to use strategies to get back on track.
2. *Use of low level routines* that get by, such as surface strategies. Why present a well-argued essay when a list of points will notch up a pass?
3. *Inadequate knowledge of what's required.* Having a good repertoire of study strategies is not much help if you don't know what is to be examined, or how (multiple-choice or essay).
4. *Matching attributions with strategies.* If you believe success is a matter of ability (and you believe yourself to be incompetent), why bother with strategic learning? What strategies do you use if you think success is just a matter of luck?
5. The *strategy becomes 'stuck' to the context* in which it is taught. Students in class may use the study skills taught in the classroom, but not when doing their homework, or sitting examinations.

Underlying all of these is the question of motivation and, more specifically, of motive–strategy congruence. You need both the skill and the will (Pintrich & De Groot 1990). If you're not motivated to achieve high grades, you'll not easily go to the bother of using study skills; if you're not intrinsically motivated, you'll not process deeply. So underlying any attempt to teach strategy use, the following appear to be essential conditions:

- high and appropriate motivation, including high self-efficacy and appropriate attributions;
- the contextual knowledge necessary for doing the task and feedback to support ongoing self-monitoring;
- a supportive learning–teaching context that reinforces the strategies being taught. Teaching deep strategies when testing for rote recall will not do.

Given these conditions, strategy training will work, in the contexts in which they have been taught, or even in the more difficult but not impossible case of teaching study skills across contexts.

Heuristics: Self-questioning

A particular case of strategy training involves heuristics, which can be like study skills taught in context or across contexts. Changing students' general approaches to learning is training them to be metacognitive on a broad front: 'What do I really want out of this? What will I settle for? Given my resources, what's my best way of proceeding?' Such self-questions are *heuristics*: set questions that learners may use to give themselves a nudge at crucial points, helping them to structure their approach to particular tasks.

The classic heuristic is Polya's *How to Solve It* (see Box 12.2), which was meant to apply to mathematical problems in the first instance but, as he says, the general steps he recommends apply to a wide range of problems.

Box 12.2   *How to solve it: A heuristic for problem solving*

Understanding the problem

First
You have to understand the problem

What is the unknown? What are the data? What is the condition? Is the condition sufficient to determine the unknown? Or is it insufficient? Or redundant? Or contradictory? Draw a figure. Introduce suitable notation. Separate the various parts of the condition. Can you write them down?

Devising a plan

Second
Find the connection between the data and the unknown. You may be obliged to consider auxiliary problems if an immediate connection cannot be found. You should obtain eventually a plan of the solution

Have you seen it before? Or have you seen the same problem in a slightly different form? Do you know a theorem that could be useful? Look at the unknown! And try to think of a familiar problem having the same or a similar unknown. Here is a problem related to yours and solved before. Could you use it? Could you restate the problem? Go back to definitions.

If you cannot solve the proposed problem try to solve first some related problem. Could you imagine a more accessible related problem? A more general problem? A more special problem? An analogous problem? Could you solve a part of the problem? Keep only a part of the condition, drop the other

---

part; how far is the unknown then determined, how can it vary? Could you derive something useful from the data? Could you think of other data appropriate to determine the unknown? Did you use all the data? Did you use the whole condition? Have you taken into account all essential notions involved in the problem?

Carrying out the plan

Third
Carry out your plan

Carrying out your plan of the solution, check each step. Can you see clearly that the step is correct? Can you prove that it is correct?

Looking back

Fourth
Examine the solution obtained

Can you check the result? Can you check the argument? Can you use the result, or the method, or some other problem?

Kurzeja (1986) adapted the *How to Solve It* paradigm for use with teaching library skills to 52 Year 3 children in a Western Australian inner-city primary school. She devised a 'Copy Cat' game whereby she thought aloud at each step of the heuristic about what she might do and the children imitated her. She then gradually withdrew, leaving the children verbalising the steps to themselves with each new problem. The children modelling the steps were able to use the library more successfully than non-metacognitively taught children: they were able to solve more difficult transfer problems and were (naturally enough) more able to talk about the steps in solving library problems.

Another classic heuristic is what its author Robinson (1946), when it was first published, modestly called 'the Australian Crawl' of study methods: Study, Question, Read, Recite, Review, or SQ3R for short (the Australian Crawl was a freestyle method of swimming which devastated the competition when it was first introduced to international swimming events). Thomas and Robinson (1982) later pumped it up to SQ4R, by the addition of 'reflect' (see Box 12.3).

SQ4R does appear to work, particularly if, as Robinson recommends, it is tailored to the student and the content; and if there is sufficient dedication by the student to carry out all the operations. If we look at it in terms of the *knowledge* × *level* × *process* model (p. 346), we can see that while it takes in knowledge and process (the processes being 'survey, question, …' etc.), it does not control for level. A danger, then, is that the questions may be pitched at too factual a level; a problem we will come across again shortly in the case of summarising and writing discussed in the next chapter.

Box 12.3   *The SQ4R method of studying*

SQ4R is a systematic method of reminding students how to learn from text with maximum effectiveness (Thomas & Robinson 1972). SQ4R involves:

1. *Survey* the text to see what it's about, what the headings and subheadings are, what the tables and figures say, so that you have a clear idea of what you are about to become involved in (see also overviews, p. 212).
2. *Question*: set yourself questions to answer from the text. Use the 'wh' questions to prompt: who? where? what? why?
3. *Read* the text, with a view to answering your questions.
4. *Reflect* on what you are reading: how does it relate to what you already know? how do the subtopics relate to the theme? how can you use this to solve related problems? can You think of anything that should have been covered to suit your needs?
5. *Recite* important information, facts, details, quotes, that you'll need to remember until you can readily recall it (see, rote-learning isn't all bad—it needs to be in context).
6. *Review* the material, particularly in light of your questions. Can you be confident that you'll be able to answer them in future?

Another general problem solver is Bransford and Stein's (1984) IDEAL:

I — Identify the problem.
D — Define what it is by representing it in some way.
E — Explore possible strategies for solving it.
A — Act on selected strategies.
L — Look back over solution and evaluate it.

Such strategies do not describe any *particular* actions and are in no sense a substitute for content knowledge. What they do, like SQ4R only on a broader scale, is help people put what content knowledge they have to better use, by nudging them at the crucial parts of any problem to stop and take stock of what they are doing and why. Not to do so is like a motorist who is unsure of the way, but continues to the end of the road to find out if it is the right one or not. Some learners similarly learn algorithmically: they automatically run through the procedure before checking that it is the right one.

The heuristic procedure can be generalised; probably most tasks that students will eventually need to carry out by themselves could be taught in this way. The teacher needs to work out at what point nudges would be most helpful and, according to the task, what form they should take. Public modelling is strongly advised, as that way students will themselves discuss the points at which they have difficulty. An adult thinking aloud in private is likely to miss aspects that novices might need to be nudged about.

Wong (1985) reviewed some 27 studies using self-questioning techniques in reading comprehension, with subjects ranging from learning-disabled primary school students to college and university level students, and uniform success: the only failure of the technique has been through inadequate time or training in question generation.

Finally, we should mention the Project for the Enhancement of Effective Learning (PEEL), which makes quite a different use of heuristics. PEEL, which has been established on a school-wide basis in a Melbourne high school, has as its first objective: 'Increased knowledge of the elements of metacognition' (Baird & Mitchell 1986; White & Baird 1991). It provides a comprehensive application of heuristic-like questions, posed in a question-asking checklist, that students systematically ask themselves and then evaluate themselves on an evaluation card.

The study was an action research case study; students were closely monitored by observation, their self-evaluations and notebooks, interviews with students and the teacher, video and audio recordings of lessons in progress and so forth. Its success was judged on the change in the way students went about their learning. Students were initially dependent and receptive, with the teacher dominant, but over the 23 weeks of the intervention, students came to exert greater control over their learning, although the teacher was still dominant ('he still talks a lot … doesn't allow students to battle with the work and generate their own questions …'). Nevertheless, evaluation cards showed that the students made more decisions and understood more often, and at higher levels, why they did particular things.

Although originally used to teach science, the geography teacher was impressed that 'the students now asked, unprompted, many questions of an insightful nature'. The work is ongoing and is an interesting example of how a metacognitive approach can be built into a traditional curriculum. The problems and difficulties arise mainly in the way in which the teacher's role shifts in ways that some teachers find hard to adapt to.

Summary

Watchers over our learning

'Metacognition', sometimes seen as the 'new look' in cognitive psychology, dates back to the ancient Greeks. It is the recognition that self-knowledge, and self-control on the basis of that knowledge, are fundamental goals in learning. It also recognises the constructivist view that learners actively and self-consciously construct their own knowledge, rather than have it piped into their skulls by teachers. Complex learning and problem solving can be improved markedly by helping students become more metacognitive in their approach.

Metalearning

Metacognitive processes applied to learning are referred to as 'metalearning', a process schools encourage in large print and discourage in the fine print. The institutional and compulsory nature of schools creates a 'learning module' that causes motivational problems which, in turn, lead to metalearning of varying adaptiveness.

What approaches to learning are there?

Typically, three approaches to learning have been distinguished, on the basis of extrinsic, intrinsic and achieving motivation, each involving characteristic strategies for approaching learning, which we call surface, deep and achieving respectively. The surface approach is a tired, impersonal reaction to an uninspiring work demand, with rote-learning usually playing a major part. The deep approach is an energetic involvement to maximise meaning. The achieving approach is a calculated attempt to maximise marks cost-effectively. Good students typically have elements of both deep and achieving approaches. People have stable predilections or inclinations for these approaches but, when actually engaging the task, what each approach actually involves, performance-wise, depends on the task.

How do students develop their approaches to learning?

Approaches to learning (usually measured by questionnaire) are associated with several personal, out-of-school, characteristics: locus of control, conceptions of learning, ability, maturity (post-school experience) and linguistic background. Some learning environments favour deep approaches, but a frequent finding is that schooling apparently encourages students to veer towards surface and away from deep approaches, although deep and achieving approaches favour academic achievement, surface approaches low achievement, unless retention of detail is specifically earmarked. All the academic 'positives' (wanting to continue on in school, having a good academic self-concept, preferring academic subjects) are associated with predilections for deep and achieving, the 'negatives' with surface.

Approaches to handling tasks in context

Students' predilections play some part in determining the actual approach used in processing a task, but so do other factors: whether or not working memory space is available, and whether or not the learner has the procedural knowledge for handling the task in question. Metalearning takes time and space. People with little time or who are overwhelmed by the complexity of the task or by the situation will not process at a meta level; they'll just charge ahead. Space handling strategies here are very similar to those useful for handling anxiety. They also have to know what to do: a *knowledge* x *level* x *process* model, expanded in Chapter 13 *vis-à-vis* text processing, may be applied to almost any task.

Increasing students' metacognitive effectiveness

Learners need to acquire strategies for self-direction and autonomy in learning. Two main approaches to teaching strategies are in use: teaching strategies within the context in which they are to be applied and teaching strategies so that they transfer across contexts. Teaching study skills is an example of the latter, which can be effective if done strategically rather than as blind tactics. Teaching strategies in context gives, however, rather more satisfactory results, but it requires tailoring strategy training programs into normal teaching. Heuristics, or self-questioning, can also be taught, either as general problem solving strategies or again as keyed into ongoing content teaching. There's also evidence that teaching students about the psychology of learning can help them learn better. Have you found that?

Learning activities

1. Approaches to learning

Table 12.1, which shows the three basic approaches to learning, is the nucleus for this activity. You'll remember that each approach (deep, surface, achieving) has both a motive and strategy component. The task is to develop a prototypical case for each of the approaches to show how such an individual would go about learning. To get you started a short case study is developed for the surface approach.

'Gina is a Year 9 student in a typical middle-class urban secondary school. She says she is not really interested in any of the work she does at school and sees her results as a way to getting a job later. Her preference, if she really has any, is for learning material that is very factual and easily rote-learned. She never studies beyond the information given by the teacher and tends to be quite anxious about her test results. She says that she has little confidence in her own knowledge and rarely challenges what the teachers say.'

Of course, in the development of your own cases, you can have the deep, surface and achieving as well as the deep-achieving and surface-achieving approaches. An extension of this activity would be to suggest remediation strategies for 'inappropriate' motives and strategies.

2. Analysis of your own learning

The task here is for you to analyse the processes and products of the class in which you feel or have felt most 'deeply' involved. So this could be your current classes or classes from your institutional learning career. Take the metalearning principles we have expanded upon in this chapter to guide you. (Is this using learning theory?) Issues you might want to address include: teacher characteristics, teacher style, methods of presentation and assessment, modes of evaluation, opportunities for individualised learning, the role of your own interest in the material.

3. Heuristics

In this chapter we looked at several heuristics: self-questions, 'How to solve it' and IDEAL. In this activity you are to take a topic and draw up a teaching plan in terms of one or other of these heuristics. Try it out on someone and keep notes on how going through it made (a) you and (b) your 'student' understand more deeply the topic in question.

An additional challenge in this activity is to locate research showing the effects of training in such heuristics. Wong's (1985) article is a good starting point.

4. SQ4R

Box 12.4 showed us a process approach to systematic reading comprehension and studying. While we deal with reading in the next chapter, we think it appropriate here to have an activity that extends activity 3 above by having you reflect upon the use of the Survey, Question, Read, Reflect, Recite, Review, approach to comprehension. We want you to try it. Perhaps you could use it in working from *The Process of Learning*. Bring your reactions back to class. Was there a problem in focus (details, main ideas, themes)? Are all texts suitable to be 'attacked' in this SQ4R manner?

5. Students' reflection on their own learning

This activity stems from the Project for the Enhancement of Effective Learning (PEEL) conducted in a Melbourne secondary school (Baird & Mitchell 1986; White & Baird 1991). As we saw in this chapter, the project aimed to increase student metacognitive awareness and monitoring of their own learning. The students completed learning checklists covering the following areas (see Baird & Mitchell p. 77 for details): Topic and Content ('What is the information about?'); Detail ('What are the important parts?

Does it make sense?'); Task ('What is the task? What do I have to do?'); Progress and Completion ('Am I going O.K.?'); Change in Views ('Does this knowledge affect other things I know?'); Increase Understanding ('Can I increase my understanding by questioning?'); Review of Understanding ('How well do I understand this?'); and Independent Learning ('How active was my learning?').

If you can get a copy of the PEEL book from a library, you can use the full checklist.

Use such a checklist with students in your class or during practice teaching. How much knowledge do students have about their own learning? Can that knowledge be increased by your teaching and what effects might that have on processes and products of learning? You could use the checklist with students as a discussion point for learning about learning (metalearning).

6. Investigating approaches to learning

The purpose of this activity is to examine either your own or high school students' approaches to learning and to give you some feel for two Australian instruments used to assess approaches to learning.

If done in your university class, the *Study Processes Questionnaire* (Biggs 1987c) could be completed and individual profiles generated. A worthy activity is to discuss individual items in the questionnaire as well as the overall picture for deep, surface, achieving, deep-achieving and surface-achieving approaches for you and your colleagues. If the focus is on secondary school students, collect some data using the *Learning Processes Questionnaire* (Biggs 1987b). You could do this perhaps during practice teaching. (Ensure that you have the permission of the school executive before you collect any information and ensure that anonymity is maintained.) If you analyse profiles as suggested by Biggs, then you should be able to provide guidance as to how remediation could be conducted if required. As a class activity the individual profiles could be presented and remediation suggested and discussed.

Further reading

On metacognition and learning
Biggs, J. B. (ed.) (1991). *Teaching for Better Learning: The View from Cognitive Psychology*. Hawthorn, Vic: Australian Council for Educational Research.
Review of Educational Research, **60**, 4. Special Issue: *Toward a Unified Approach to Learning as a Multisource Phenomenon*.

The ACER collection reports (mostly) Australian work on metacognitive approaches to teaching and learning: Evans on self-management, Lawson on problem solving, Lawrence on planning, White and Baird (see also Baird & Mitchell 1986) on the PEEL project, Moore on reciprocal teaching of study strategies and Mulcahy on SPELT, a Canadian strategy teaching program. Sweller emphasises that the knowledge base is all-important for deep learning (he doubts this metacognitive stuff); Kirby's work on reading and studying belongs in the next chapter; Goodnow's in Chapter 4; and Biggs says nothing more than has been said here, only a little differently.

The *RER* number is devoted to what learning psychologists have to say about 'the soft, slimy swamp of real-life problems' (p. 509). Swamps are situated and hot, and those who study them look at such things as why people don't use strategies they've been taught to use (Garner), how they learn in phases (Shuell), how interest makes a difference (Hidi), how learning doesn't flow through conduits neatly but spills every which way (Iran-Nejad) and how learning is encapsulated (Bereiter). We have referred to each of these authors already, but if you want a detailed state-of-the-swamp account, here it is.

On ways of learning
Biggs, J. B. (1987). *Student Approaches to Learning and Studying.* Hawthorn, Vic: Australian Council for Educational Research.
Marton, F., Hounsell, D. & Entwistle, N. (eds) (1984). *The Experience of Learning.* Edinburgh: Scottish Universities Press.
Schmeck, R. R. (ed.) (1988). *Learning Strategies and Learning Styles.* New York: Plenum Press.

The first book describes the research backing up the LPQ and SPQ, and the relations between various aspects of schooling in Australia and the three main approaches to learning. The second is based on a quite different methodology and is mainly based on tertiary students. However the chapters by Entwistle, Marton and Saljo, and Ramsden generalise to school contexts.

Schmeck's collection is another useful source of work on student learning by Entwistle, Marton, Ramsden, Schmeck and Weinstein.

On heuristics and study skills
Bransford, J. D. & Stein, B. S. (1984). *The Ideal Problem Solver.* New York: W. H. Freeman.
Gibbs, G. (1981). *Teaching Students to Learn: A Student-centred Approach.* Milton Keynes: The Open University Press.
Jackson, P., Reid N. & Croft, A. (1980). Study habits evaluation and instruction kit (SHEIK). Hawthorn, Vic: Australian Council for Educational Research.
Polya, G. (1945). *How to Solve It.* Princeton, NJ: Princeton University Press.
Bransford and Stein's IDEAL problem solver is based on Polya's and much easier to use. Gibbs uses group techniques to get students to reflect on their own learning; SHEIK is a conventional study skills kit which has been shown to work with Year 11 students (Edwards 1986).

CHAPTER 13

LEARNING AND HANDLING TEXT

Learning and handling text

Knowledge for the having!

Reading-to-learn

Summarising, note-taking,
reflecting on what's been read

Comprehending!

Cracking the code

Learning-to-read

Text

Mastering
the code

Learning-to-write

What do I say?
How do I say it?
Will grammar help?
Will word processing help?
Planning?
Reflecting on what I've written
Revising/replanning again …

Writing-to-learn

Knowledge for the making!

LEARNING AND HANDLING TEXT

In this chapter, you will find out:

- how reading and writing are involved in learning;
- how children can be taught to read for maximal understanding;
- how phonic and whole-word methods interrelate;
- what relationship decoding skills have to comprehension;
- how to study from text;
- how to summarise the gist of a passage;
- how skilled and unskilled writers differ from each other;
- how writing competence develops;
- how surface and deep approaches to writing essays differ;
- what effect word processors have on writing quality;
- what teachers can do to improve the quality of their students' writing.

Strategies for text processing

Handling text, or 'text processing' in the current buzz phrase, covers both learning *to* handle text (to read and to write) and learning *from* handling text (reading, studying and writing). In short, this chapter is about the major tasks of schooling. Successful learning relies heavily on students' ability both to comprehend the meaning of already written text and to create new texts containing their own meaning. The first few years of schooling are occupied with learning to read; the rest of one's life with reading to learn (Kirby 1991). Likewise, we learn to write and thereafter use writing as a tool for further learning. Writing is not simply a means for recording existing knowledge, but of transforming and creating existing knowledge.

The processes of learning to read and reading to learn, and learning to write and writing to learn, are closely interlinked, not least because they are heavily metacognitive activities. The following comments about teaching children how to read, for example, strongly recall the issue raised in the last chapter about blind and informed strategy training:

> The central tenet of our approach is that reading strategies can be explained directly to children. If they perceive the strategies as sensible and useful courses of action, we would expect children to use them appropriately and spontaneously in their subsequent reading. Our emphasis is thus upon how children's awareness about reading, or metacognition, can facilitate intentional use of particular strategies ... Strategic readers combine knowledge about the task with motivation to act accordingly. Their plans are self-generated and their actions self-directed. (Paris 1984: 2–3)

Thus, in teaching students to read, we ought also to be teaching them how to approach text so that they retain its meaning for future use; reading becomes then a tool for future learning. As we explore in this chapter, writing, in the forms of summarising, note-taking and composing from several sources, amplifies the power of reading to learn. In so doing, we develop further several points about learning and study strategies that were raised in the last chapter.

The complementary process is to communicate one's learning through the creation of text. The traditional and current layperson's view about writing is that competent writers know what they are going to say before they put pen to paper; writing to them is an output process, all the learning having already gone on beforehand (Hairston 1982). The view of professional writers, and now writing educators is quite different, which is that the act of writing is an act of learning (Applebee 1984; Bereiter & Scardamalia 1987). E. M. Forster, the famous novelist, commented: 'How can I know what I think until I see what I say?'

These two views are illustrated in Box 13.1.

Box 13.1   *Two views on writing*

'With writing, you've got to think before you print it on paper. But if you speak it out, you sort of don't have to think about what you're going to say.'—A Year 10 boy explaining his view of the writing process (Stelzer 1975: 39).

Writing can in fact be learning in the sense of discovery. But if we are to allow this to happen, we must give more credit than we often do to the process of shaping at the point of utterance and not inhibit the kind of discovery that can take place by insisting that children know exactly what they are going to say before they say it. (Britton 1982: 110)

In short, then, reading and writing are complex, interrelated acts which greatly enhance most higher order learning. They are both metacognitive processes from the outset. The child, in learning both to read and to write, needs not only to be able to use language, but to be aware that language is a tool to be used for one's own purposes and to be aware of so using it (Pramling 1983). And having learned these skills, the child thereafter needs to be aware of metacognitive strategies for enhancing the creation of meaning in either reading text or making text. In this chapter, then, we look at these interlocking processes: learning to read, reading to learn, learning to write and writing to learn.

Learning to read

First, some distinctions between various processes in reading:

* *decoding*, which is translating orthographics, or marks on paper, into words;
* *comprehension*, which is translating words into meanings simultaneously with the act of reading;
* *studying*, which is the extraction of meaning for future use;

and acts required by the reader:

* *skills*, which are existing cognitive routines often carried out automatically;
* *strategies*, which are metacognitive processes carried out with conscious deliberation (Kirby 1988).

These processes are deployed, either cognitively or metacognitively as the case may be, over eight different levels of text (see Figure 13.1) (Kirby 1988):

1. *features*, such as the loops, lines and curves that make up letters;
2. *letters* themselves;
3. *sounds*, which are associated with letters and letter combinations;
4. *words*, encoded both visually and phonemically (not one or the other);
5. *chunks*, or combinations of words in meaningful phrases which give a unit of sense. A sentence may comprise eleven words, say, but only three chunks: '/The three men // entered the room // and gaped in astonishment /';
6. *ideas*, a statement of meaning at the sentence level. For the first time, the meaning is not a direct association of what is on the page, but an *abstract synthesis* forming *micropropositions*;
7. *main ideas*, statements usually at the paragraph level, which as *micropropositions* comprise the gist, which is constructed out of all the ideas in the passage;
8. *the theme*, which is inferred, going beyond the main ideas, and which is often not stated explicitly.

The processes of decoding and comprehending focus on different levels.

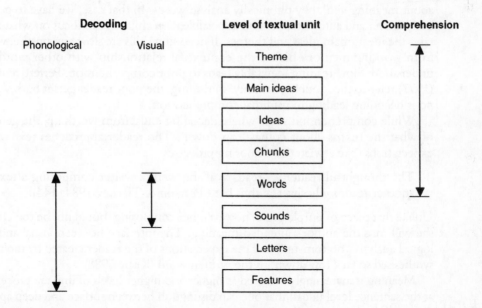

Figure 13.1 *Decoding and comprehension, and levels of textual unit processed*

Decoding may be done phonologically or visually. Phonological decoding links features to letters and letters to sound; visual decoding uses a whole word approach, each word being recognised in context. One or other of these phonic and look-and-say methods have been espoused by teachers with something like religious fervour: progressives favouring look-and-say, traditionalists, phonic.

Taking sides on this issue is unhelpful, because both are important. While skilled readers recognise whole words instantly, unskilled do not, and unless they do learn how to analysis phonic components in words, they will be unable to get any further. Pflaum et al. (1980) analysed over 90 studies of reading and found that sound–symbol blending (/b/, /a/, /d/ forms /bad/) consistently turned up in the superior methods and was the only aspect of teaching that did. On the other hand, sole use of phonological analysis can lead to 'the most fundamental paradox in reading disabilities ... that some children can pronounce words but show little understanding of what they read' (Paris & Lindauer 1982: 338). Reading, to such children, is to bark correctly at print, not to understand what the print means. They need to move from sound to word to the higher levels of idea and main idea. Yet current practice seems to equate 'reading' with training in decoding skills; 90% of reading instruction in United States classrooms is on skill mastery rather than on comprehension (Paris, Wixson & Palincsar 1986). There is no reason to suspect that the situation is greatly different in Australian classrooms.

This is not to say that decoding should be de-emphasised. Visual (whole word) decoding helps to make this shift to higher levels of text because words are immediately recognised and their meaning is then the sole matter of concern. On its own, however, whole word decoding cannot cope with new words. Clearly care is needed to provide strategies of sound/word recognition, because these can cope with the problem of handling new words. The trap is working memory, as ever. Novice readers can't think about meaning while they are busy phonically analysing words; neither can they think about meaning *until* they phonically analyse words. In that case, we have to get phonic analysis over and automated as soon as possible, *then* children can focus on what is important: the ideas, main ideas and themes. If decoding skills are slow and unsure, words slip from working memory before the contextual relationship with other words can be understood. Slow reading inevitably leads to poor comprehension. Perfetti and Lesgold (1977) refer to the 'double whammy' in reading: the poor reader gets it both ways, their poor decoding leading to minimal comprehension.

While comprehension starts where decoding ends, from words up, the general idea of what the text is about comes 'top-down'. The reader approaches text with clear expectations, like a writer's composing processes:

> The thoughtful reader ... reads as if she were a writer composing a text for yet another reader who lives within her. (Pearson & Tierney 1984: 144)

Unlike that piece of purple prose, however, her composing should not be too creative, or she will miss the author's intended meaning. The interface between visual and phonological analysis ('bottom-up') and the expectations of the reader created by the meanings synthesised so far ('top-down') is the written word (Kirby 1988).

Meaning is increasingly involved as higher and higher levels of unit are processed. It is at the sentence level (ideas) that one can distinguish between surface and deep approaches to reading and studying. Readers who focus on the words, phrases, and sentences used by the author, thus processing in the words–chunks–ideas range, adopt a surface approach to text and are likely miss the main ideas and theme. Readers who are interested in what the author means focus on larger and more abstract units. It must be emphasised, however, that even deep readers need to *range widely:* if they are too concerned with abstract themes, they might well miss significant lower order inputs that in fact signal a different or a changing theme.

The development of metacognition in reading

How early in their reading careers do children become aware that different features of the text, or of their knowledge of the topic, can affect their understanding? When do they make use of this knowledge to enhance their comprehension?

Children in Year 2 tend to be aware that their knowledge of a topic and their interest in it affects their comprehension when reading about it. Thus, reading about a place they have visited is much more interesting and better understood than reading about a strange place. By Year 4, children are aware that the context may be used in finding the meaning of a word, as for example in the 'cloze' procedure in which a gap in a sentence is filled with a word generated by the meaning of the passage (Myers & Paris 1978). On the other hand, such knowledge appears to be counter-productive in Year 4, because children's performance actually *worsens* when they try to use context, yet by Year 6 reading performance is greatly enhanced by using context (Moore & Kirby 1981). Kirby (1984a) explains this apparent contradiction by suggesting that working memory limitations prevent concentration on *both* decoding skills and meaning; but once the former are in place, by Year 6, students may bring their full attention to bear on meaning.

Findings such as this prompt a three-stage model of comprehension (Kirby & Moore 1988): (1) letter decoding, (2) comprehending semantic meaning, (3) metacognitive 'amplification' of (2). In other words, as students develop their knowledge of word meanings and the ideas of a context and main idea, *then* they may develop metacognitive comprehension strategies that become entirely focused on the real purpose of reading: to extract maximum meaning from the text. This last stage, however, does not appear to develop spontaneously until Year 6.

In essence, moving upwards in Figure 13.1 requires readers to be *strategic*. As working memory is limited, the processes lower than the level at which one is focusing need to be automatic. Ideally, then, the reader focuses on one transformation at a time (from words to chunks, from ideas to the main idea) and that is the immediate task, to be handled metacognitively with the best strategies available. All tasks *below* that level should be automatic skills: for example, you cannot think about meaning if you are busy working out how the word sounds.

Skilled readers, aiming high up the scale, do not consciously pay attention to lower level units. Are *you* aware of the particular words used when you are reading this? Probably not. If you are you will not be relating to the main ideas being expressed. Proof-readers tune themselves to letters, features and words, not higher order meanings. By the same token, students should tune themselves to meanings, not to the targets of proof-readers; they read to learn. Writers, on the other hand, when reviewing and revising their text, have a more difficult task; they have to concentrate on words, precisely to decide whether a particular word is 'the prop'rest word in the prop'rest place', as Coleridge put it. But the theme determines 'the prop'rest place'.

In a recent review of metacognitive approaches to the teaching of reading based on a meta-analysis of 20 studies, Haller, Child and Walberg (1988) showed that metacognitive approaches to the teaching of comprehension produced very strong effects, which were greatest in seventh and eighth grades. Making readers aware of their cognitions and monitoring their learning does have a powerful impact upon comprehension.

Maximising reading comprehension: Informed strategies for learning

Can students be encouraged to be more metacognitive about their reading comprehension strategies earlier than Year 6, which is typically when students seem to use these strategies effectively for themselves?

Paris, at the University of Michigan, with the help of 40 grade-three and grade-five teachers and over 800 students in local schools, showed that students can, gaining as much as two years on some comprehension tests (Paris 1987; Paris, Cross & Lipson

1984). His program, Informed Strategies for Learning (ISL), begins with the assumption that reading strategies can be explained directly to children and, if that is done effectively, they will then use them correctly and spontaneously in subsequent reading. There are several aspects of ISL:

1. Informed teaching

If teachers are to tell students *what* a strategy is, *how* it operates, and *when* and *why* it should be used, the teachers had better know themselves. Although this knowledge is simple enough, it does not appear in any teachers' manuals. Many people do not really understand what 'skimming' is, or what it is best used for. For their part, students have various notions of what they think skimming is: reading the first and last words of sentences, reading very fast, or missing out the long words. Worse, it is commonly believed to be something that only poor readers do. They do not realise that it is a quick way of finding out what a story is about, that it helps you to understand the story. Teachers do not realise that instruction in how to skim is very simple.

2. Use of metaphors

In order to cue students to use these strategies, vivid, concrete directions are needed. Paris uses various metaphors and analogies to do this, pasting each in bright colours on a bulletin board:

- *Prereading*—'Plan your reading trip.' (See Box 13.2)
- *Summarising*—'Round up your ideas.'
- *Identifying the main idea*—'Be a sleuth. Track down the main idea.'

3. Group discussion

Students need the opportunity to express their confusion, distress—or pride. Discussion enables students to share with others ways they have developed that seem to work for them; this works in a way very similar to the discussion groups used by Johnson Abercrombie (see Chapter 16). Paris notes that teachers are often surprised both at the naivety and at the understanding manifested by some young readers in their approach to text.

4. Guided practice

Each lesson requires students to read and apply the strategy they are currently learning and then they discuss again immediately afterwards: Did it work? How did it work?

5. Bridging to content area

One of the problems of teaching students to read with a prepared text is that students may learn to do the appropriate thing in that context, but not see it as something you do outside 'reading class' (Garner 1990). Science, history and all normal class content is used with each strategy to show that they should be applied to all their class work.

Paris has developed 20 modules, five grouped around each theme:

- planning for reading;
- identifying meaning;
- reasoning while reading;
- maintaining comprehension.

> **Box 13.2**   *Plan your reading trip: Instructions for ISL teachers (a sample)*
>
> On the analogy of taking a trip away for a holiday, children discuss questions such as the following:
>
> - How do you prepare for your holidays? What sorts of things do you have to think about?
> - How is planning to read like planning a trip?
> - Would you read in a different way if you wanted to learn lots of details or just the general idea?
>
> Construct a worksheet around a short passage that puts up road signs throughout. The students must obey these signs:
>
> - STOP!   Say the meaning in your own words.
> - DEAD END   Go back and reread the parts you didn't understand.
> - SLOW   Lower your reading speed.
>
> *Source:* Adapted and abbreviated from Paris (1987)

Reading to learn

There are several processes and activities which play a part in learning from text. The distinction between these processes and what we referred to in Chapter 12 as 'study skills' is that our present concern is specifically with addressing *text*, whereas study skills refer to the whole context of study, which may also include learning from text. But it is difficult to compartmentalise, and the following section and the corresponding sections 'Teaching study skills' and 'Self-questioning' in Chapter 12 complement each other.

Underlining and highlighting

Underlining and highlighting are activities designed to focus attention on important information in a text, usually the main ideas. The act of identifying the main idea and 'tagging' it takes more mental effort than passively reading and, as long as that effort is directed at the higher textual levels, learning is facilitated. There is no purpose served in indiscriminate highlighting and underlining texts without such higher level processing. Inbuilt into effective highlighting and underlining, then, is reader sensitivity to importance: poorer readers are less sensitive to main ideas than their more competent peers.

When readers are instructed to highlight structurally important information there are positive direct effects on learning, but if readers are instructed to highlight the *less* important information the effects on main idea learning is negative (Rickards & August 1975). The knowledge of *what* to highlight is therefore crucial. Chan and Cole (1986) focused on learning-disabled readers, 11 year olds three years behind in reading. They were trained for four 30 minute sessions to highlight two interesting words in each paragraph with a green fluorescent pen. A toy robot showed students how to highlight important information and explained aloud how such a process occurred. The students, in turn, had to explain to the robot their reasons for highlighting the words they chose and why they were important. The highlighting students outperformed a read–reread control group on comprehension measures and reported using the highlighting strategy on a different (transfer) task. For teachers, the message is clear: appropriate training in highlighting and underlining can make a positive impact upon student learning.

Advance organisers

An advance organiser is another form of overview (Ausubel 1968). Whereas we have seen in Chapter 8 that overviews simply let the student know in advance what particular topics in a text are important, an advance organiser is a preview that is written at a *higher* level of abstraction than the main text; it is intended to prime the student into organising the forthcoming information into the appropriate schemata.

They seem to be partially successful in this, depending on the kind of material used and how high 'higher level' it is (Hartley & Davies 1976). Kirby and Cantwell (1985) used various levels of advanced organiser with high school students and showed that high level organisers decreased the recall of detail for all students, and increased recall of main ideas and themes, but in the case of good readers only. Low level organisers helped poorer readers recall detail (note: a 'low level' organiser is not an advance organiser in Ausubel's sense, but an overview (see p. 212)). Kirby and Cantwell conclude that good readers are helped by abstract schemata because they can use them to orchestrate their interaction with the text, whereas poor readers need support at the level of detail. The real challenge is to turn the poor readers into good readers. Then all would benefit from advance organisers.

Summarising and note-taking

Taking notes from a text and writing a summary are means of helping readers clarify the meaning of a text and to help remember its main contents. Summaries help us read to learn and involve the production of a written text. Note-taking and summarising are, however, unlike most other writing tasks in that both are usually written for the *writer* to read, not someone else.

Do note-taking and summarising aid learning? They certainly may, but it all depends on what is being noted and summarised (Hidi & Anderson 1986; Kirby 1990; Penrose 1988). Take notes of facts and you'll retain facts; summarise main ideas and you'll remember main ideas. Let us look at the activity of summarising more analytically; properly used, it can help students adopt a deep approach to learning from text.

Let us use the *knowledge × levels × process* framework:

Knowledge is essential for meaningful processing of the text; we need to know something about the text, its content and context, and where it fits with our existing knowledge.

Levels. As with reading itself, we can categorise the levels of text into the eight described by Kirby (see Figure 13.1) and marry those levels with the processes involved. In the case of summarising, eight levels are too many; two levels will suffice, *micropropositions* (up to and including sentence level) and *macropropositions* (main ideas and theme).

Processes of summarising include (see Figure 13.2):

- *comprehension* of both micro- but particularly macro-propositions;
- *selection* of the more important propositions, especially macro and their *prioritisation;*
- *transformation* of material into macropropositions.

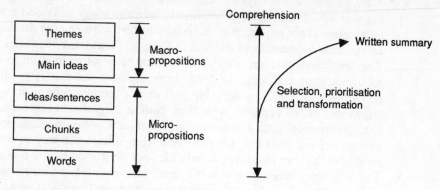

Figure 13.2 *Summarisation processes and level of textual unit processed*

Each process rests on prior relevant knowledge. Comprehension involves subsuming the new message under already known schemata; selection involves making judgements about what propositions are more important than others, which in turn involves a background of wider knowledge than that contained in the propositions; and transformation involves rephrasing and extending the presented knowledge, which again depends on knowledge that is beyond the given text.

You will note that there is continual emphasis on higher order knowledge; in order to summarise properly you have to understand the text in more abstract terms than the text itself expresses. But it also has to be based on the details in the text. Summarising may thus be expressed as a resolution between *depth* (the level processed) and *content* (the amount of detail included) (Kirby 1990). High content–low depth gives a poor summary, such as when the student copies out some sentences and omits others (the 'copy-delete' strategy); high depth–low content gives the rather vacuous writing sometimes observed in second language students (Cantwell & Biggs 1988; Kirby 1990); low depth–low content is no good for anybody. Good summaries need both depth and content.

In a deep approach to summarising, the student reads carefully for comprehension of all levels, not just at the sentence level. A selection has then to be made of the more important content or topics: What is central to the theme? What is merely illustrative? Trivial and redundant information should be dropped at this stage. One of the greatest differences between good and poor summary writers lies in the inability to distinguish what is important from what is less important (Hidi & Anderson 1986). Good summary writers are able to extract the *theme* of the text. This content has then to be transformed into a set of statements at macropropositonal level, conveying the content of the text; one topic sentence might replace a paragraph, for example. The final summary is thus written at a *higher*, more abstract, level than the original. If the text is processed at the level of micropropositions only, it will not be possible to judge what is more or less important.

There are three stages in the development of summarising skill (Hidi & Anderson 1986).

1. The 'deficiency' stage, which is found particularly in young children, indicates no sense of relative importance. Learners at this stage see what is important as what is interesting to them, not what is more or less relevant in terms of the text itself.

Thus, poor readers in eighth grade rated sentences that had high imagery (those dealing with rats, fires, gangs) as important, whereas adults and good readers saw such information as not important at all. In fact, the text was about the development of cities and referred incidentally to the fires in Chicago (Winograd 1984) (see also Box 8.2).

2. The 'inefficiency' stage, which shows some sense of relative importance, but the focus is still on the sentence level. Learners here use the 'copy-delete' strategy (Brown & Day 1983), observable well into secondary school, in which students copy more or less verbatim what they think is a significant sentence, omitting following sentences until the next 'significant' one is found. Students using such a strategy see the trees but not the wood; they ignore the way in which sentences modify each other to convey a main idea not contained in any one sentence.

3. The 'efficiency' stage, in which the significant sentences are restructured and transformed into new, higher order generative sentences that effectively subsume all the important information in the text, thus giving high depth and high content. The ability to write good topic sentences is, however, a problem even at tertiary level and may not be within the repertoire of young children prior to adolescence (Hidi & Anderson 1986).

Can students be taught summarisation?

The encouraging news is that they can (Baumann 1984), even remedial readers in secondary school benefit from strategy training at the first stage of locating main ideas (Stevens 1988). In the last study, training in identifying the topic of paragraphs was given through an interactive computer-assisted learning program; students read paragraphs and then selected main ideas from a list of alternatives and received feedback on their choices. Sixth graders also improved in identifying both explicit and implicit main ideas after training (Baumann 1984).

What though of the more complex levels of summarisation? Rinehart, Stahl and Erickson (1986) directly taught sixth grade students 4 summarisation rule operations at the level of macropropositions: locating main ideas, deleting trivial information, deleting redundant information, relating main and supporting information. The training program was based on:

- explicit explanation (each of the to-be-mastered skills was taught explicitly);
- modelling (the teacher modelled the procedures using a talk-aloud method with student talk-alouds encouraged);
- practice with feedback (ample opportunity was given for practice with immediate feedback);
- breaking down complex skills (summarisation began with short paragraphs and moved to the taking of effective notes from a chapter in a text book).

After 45 minutes each day for 5 consecutive days, the effects were substantial, the trained group being superior in recall of main ideas and in the quality of their summaries.

Presence of text during summarisation

Should texts be present or absent when they are being summarised? Are better, more abstract, summaries produced after reading the text and summarising it from memory? This would seem quite likely, because one is then forced to think of the higher level meanings, as they have been reprocessed and organised into memory by the reader, rather than being tempted to copy-delete from present detail.

With the text present, readers tend to scan inefficiently, rather than search actively for the structure of the text. Much depends, however, on the difficulty of the text and the approach to learning of the reader. Sophisticated readers, with a deep approach to learning (as measured by the SPQ), produced much better summaries from memory, but less knowledgeable readers and those who typically adopt a surface approach did better with the text present (Kirby & Pedwell 1989). This study raises the possibility that a good way of training people to adopt a deep approach to text might be to get them to summarise from memory because it forces them to read actively first, organising detail into appropriate schemata.

Learning to write

Writing is much more complex than reading. The ability to decode written text with speed, accuracy and comprehension develops earlier and, typically, reaches maximum efficiency much more quickly than its counterpart, the *creation* of written text. It involves a large number of what are called *rhetorical* skills: handwriting, spelling, punctuation, word choice, syntax, textual connections, purpose, organisation, clarity and reader characteristics (Scardamalia 1980). Given the limited capacity of working memory, we cannot devote conscious attention to all of these features simultaneously. Beginning writers, which includes most students well into high school, are so weighed down by the technicalities that their thinking is diminished; they explain things orally much better than they can put them into writing. Yet skilled writers find that expressing their thoughts in writing not only clarifies but significantly enhances their thinking.

Development of writing skill

What, then, are the main ways in which unskilled writers differ from skilled? Certainly, coping with the technical demands of writing is a major problem to be overcome. Let us now compare writing with that other verbal production skill, speaking. Why don't you 'have to think about what you are going to say' when speaking (see Box 13.1)? Actually, there is one occasion when you certainly do: making a speech, an act which is very similar to writing in one key respect. You are on your own. Normally, conversation is interactive: you say something, she replies, that prompts you to comment. Even a puzzled expression is a good prompt: 'tell me more' is what it says. A piece of paper doesn't do that. Neither does a sea of faces, politely blank.

So a second major difficulty in writing is that memory isn't cued; skilled writers need to set up a support structure that helps to prompt and to organise relevant information for the text, that acts just like a conversational partner (Bereiter & Scardamalia 1987). Such a structure, or general *plan* for writing, usually does not develop until late adolescence, under present conditions in school. When such an interactive structure is supplied, as it is when the teacher 'conferences' with young writers in the primary 'process writing' classroom (Graves 1983; see also below), there are much fewer production problems; little writers then write like much bigger writers.

Thus, there are two kinds of skill that need to be developed:

1. *production skills*: generating text content ('What do I say?')
2. *rhetorical skills*: transcribing that content into readable form using the rules of text generation ('How do I say it?')

Until these skills are well developed so that they can be used in concert, unskilled writing has these characteristics:

> Texts produced by younger children often seem choppy and ill-structured, as if sentences go down on the page in the exact form and in the same order they come to the child's mind, with little transition between one and the next. They focus on what they know *they* mean, rather than on what the *reader* will think they mean. (McCutchen 1985: 12)

Young writers write prose that is 'writer-based', not 'reader-based'.

Unskilled writers write prose that is 'writer-based' not 'reader-based' (Flower 1981). This is a form of egocentrism, not taking the perspective of the other person in the communication act into account. A well-developed writing plan becomes an 'alternative other', allowing 'conversation' with the writer, but that doesn't happen usually until senior high school (Burtis, Bereiter, Scardamalia & Tetroe 1984).

Growth in writing skill thus involves a shift in the writer's concerns, from saying what *I* want to say, to creating text that *others* will understand. Such a sense of audience requires a high degree of metacognition, in the form of a close examination of your own thoughts and, by reshaping what you see, writing becomes the 'learning in the sense of discovery' referred to in Box 13.1.

Skilled writers have several tasks to orchestrate. They need to:

- *Generate text without a respondent.* They therefore need a prompt system to help them find what they want to say at the right time. Just having the knowledge isn't good enough. It will probably surprise you to learn that bright Year 6 students do *not* write better essays on subjects they know a lot about compared to subjects about which they only know a little (Bereiter & Scardamalia 1987). What mattered was whether they could *access* that knowledge when they needed it.
- *Form abstract and flexible plans* to continually guide ongoing composition and subsequent revision. Such plans enable the writer to shift regularly from local concerns (this sentence I'm writing now) to whole text concerns (the theme) and to integrate them. The plans of unskilled writers simply foreshadow the words of the final text (Burtis, Bereiter, Scardamalia & Tetroe 1984).
- *Generate sentences* by integrating production skills (intended *meanings*) and rhetorical skills (*mechanics*). Given working memory limitations, the two processes interfere with each other if not separated or handled strategically.
- *Review and revise* before, during and after, text production. Exactly as in summaries, one has to 'see' *more* than the text as it is and at a more abstract level, otherwise any changes will be trivial. This 'text as it might be' is a formal and metacognitive operation. Skilled writers also know when, as well as how, to revise, in ways that least disrupt their composing (Fitzgerald 1987).

Unskilled writers have problems with each of these competencies. The difference is captured in two forms of writing, knowledge telling and reflective writing (Scardamalia & Bereiter 1982).

Knowledge telling

Knowledge telling results from a strategy that consists of reducing the essay to a list of topics and then simply telling what one knows about each: Maria's Tutankhamen essay (p. 314) is a skilled example of this. The concerns of the writer are simply what to say next, in suitable language.

Knowledge telling is a sentence-by-sentence routine that 'does' for most of the writing tasks that are demanded in high school, even in senior years (as the example of Maria makes clear). The problem lies not in lack of skill of the writer, but in the failure of the school to require other, reflective, writing strategies. Applebee (1984) points out that most writing in United States high schools takes place in two contexts:

1. in copying, making notes, filling in blank spaces: none of which require thinking higher than the level of idea that can be conveyed in one sentence; and

2. in conveying already organised content to an audience better informed than the writer.

In Tasmanian high schools not so many years ago, a Year 7 student on average produced just 1.7 pages a day, most of it in note form or copied; this figure rose to 2.5

pages in Year 10. On any one day, 40% of all high school students did no continuous writing at all (Annells et al. 1975). Would that figure be different today?

Several aspects of the classroom writing environment encourage knowledge telling, even some that in other contexts are desirable (Bereiter & Scardamalia 1987):

- testing only what is taught;
- testing items of knowledge in the order in which they were taught;
- using notes;
- using 'topics that turn students on'. Yes, that's one to think about! Don't such topics just haul out strings of personal reminiscence rather than require structure and argument?
- allowing students to pass 'if they can show they know at least something about the topic'.

What do these situations encourage? Writer-based prose: either an egocentric monologue in print, or a shopping list to jog the memory. What is lacking? Communicating with the reader, in reader-based prose. Reflective writing fulfils that function.

Reflective writing

Reflective writing requires the writer to consider the audience in relation to the way the content is expressed. The question is not 'What do I know?' but 'How can I say what I know in a way that my reader, who doesn't know what I know, will understand?' In reflecting on that, you find out what you really know. Whereas knowledge telling is unidirectional, reflective writing is a circular process, involving *knowledge-transforming,* as Bereiter and Scardamalia (1987) later called reflective writing.

Reflective writing sets out to solve a problem. While knowledge telling is initially part of that process, defining what I know, that knowledge then becomes the subject of further reflection, through the metacognitive activities of planning, reviewing, rearranging and recomposing. Let us look at these activities inherent in reflective writing in more detail.

Writing reflectively

Let us deal with reflective writing processes in the context of writing an essay. As with reading and summarising, we can use the *knowledge* X *level* X *process* approach to conceptualise writing.

Knowledge

In considering what goes into writing skill, it is easy to focus on 'process' at the expense of knowledge (Stein 1986). The knowledge required is of two main kinds: content or topic knowledge (knowledge of what to say) and rhetorical knowledge (procedural knowledge of how to say it).

Content or topic knowledge is always involved, especially in planning (see below). The food and restaurant review writer of *The Australian* is unlikely to be called on to write the political column. Professional writers often freelance, but they must know what they are talking about if they are to have any impact. Nevertheless, topic knowledge in itself doesn't make good writers out of poor writers; children do not write better essays on subjects on which they are more knowledgeable (Bereiter & Scardamalia 1987).

Likewise, subject matter experts, such as programmers and computer scientists have been 'notoriously ineffective' in writing computer documentation (Hayes & Flower 1986: 1108).

Rhetorical knowledge, which is used throughout the actual writing and reviewing processes, is what professional writers have in plenty, but experts in content areas may not. Such knowledge addresses the questions: How should this be said? What are the rules and conventions for maximum impact?

Rhetorical knowledge breaks down into several specific forms:

1. *The goals of composing.* Who am I writing this for and what is the best form in which to say it?
2. *Knowledge of the various forms of discourse.* Given a clear realisation of the goals, what options are there: report, dialogue, essay ... and if essay, what form: causal, description, compare-and-contrast ...?
3. *Syntactical knowledge.* There is a huge debate among English teachers as to the extent to which students need to know 'grammar'. Does it help to know *what* is wrong, when we can see that 'something's wrong with this!'? Yes, it does (Stein 1986). Recognising that the sentence hasn't got a main clause tells you to give it one.
4. *Knowledge about audiences.* Being quite clear about the beliefs, values and expectations of the target audience is very important to ensure that one's prose is in fact reader-based. You have to be clear to yourself who you are writing for.

Rhetorical knowledge thus covers a great deal, but several writers have collected the more common procedural 'how-tos' that may make life easier for beginning writers in particular genres. Such books are available for all fiction genres, often published by professional writers' associations, and for expository writing in various topic areas (see Further Reading at the end of this chapter). In actual fact, this kind of knowledge is more helpful to experienced than to unskilled writers, as the following may illustrate, from Strunk and White's (1972) *The Elements of Style* (see Box 13.3).

Box 13.3 *How to improve your writing style*

Under the heading 'Elementary Principles of Composition', Strunk and White (1972) list such points as the following:

- choose a suitable design and hold to it;
- use the active voice;
- put statements in a positive form;
- use definite, concrete language;
- omit needless words;
- express coordinate ideas in similar form;
- place the emphatic words of a sentence at the end.

For example, under 'Use the active voice' they say:

The active voice is always more direct and vigorous than the passive:

> I shall always remember my first visit to Boston.

This is much better than:

> My first trip to Boston will always be remembered by me.

The latter sentence is less direct, less bold and less concise. If the writer tries to make it more concise by omitting 'by me,'

My first visit to Boston will always be remembered,

it becomes indefinite; is it the writer or some person undisclosed or the world at large that will always remember this visit?

This rule does not, of course, mean that the writer should entirely discard the passive voice, which is frequently convenient and sometimes necessary.

The dramatists of the Restoration are little esteemed today.

Modern readers have little esteem for the dramatists of the Restoration.

The first would be the preferred form in a paragraph on the dramatists of the Restoration, the second in a paragraph on the tastes of modern readers. The need of making a particular word the subject of the sentence will often, as in these examples, determine which voice is to be used …

(Strunk and White 1972: 18)

But wait a minute! Shouldn't that last sentence before Box 13.3 read: 'In actual fact experienced writers will find Strunk and White's advice more helpful than will unskilled writers'? What do you think? Are you experienced enough to tell?

Levels

While writers will at some stage pay attention to all eight levels, from features and letters through to main ideas and themes, a useful working distinction, as we found with summarising, is between *micropropositions* (sentence level and below) and *macropropositions* (main idea level and above) (see Figure 13.2). In knowledge telling, the main focus is on micropropositions—sentences and their elaboration—while in reflective writing the focus switches from macro- to micropropositions.

These levels are the targets at which the various writing processes are aimed at the appropriate times.

Processes

Three major processes are distinguished as far as the expository essay is concerned: planning, composing and sentence generation, and reviewing and revising (Hayes & Flower 1986).

Planning

1. *Forming global intentions.* The essay question is read and interpreted and two major kinds of intention are formed: content, what to say; and rhetorical, how to say it. The student decides the broad way to go: 'I intend to make the general point that … meantime, I don't know enough about X, Y and Z … and had better find out …' At this early stage, and increasingly after, knowledge is represented in the planning process in various ways: images, or diagrams, specific words and phrases and a string of subgoals, which become closely interconnected in expert writers (Hayes & Flower 1986).

2. *Knowledge update and discourse synthesis.* Students may then turn to several sources to update their knowledge: books, other people, audiovisual resources, etc. This stage is

common to both knowledge telling and reflective writing; it is how the knowledge is *structured* afterwards that differs. *Discourse synthesis* involves selecting, organising and connecting content from different sources to compose a new, hybrid, text comprising the sources read (Spivey & King 1989). This process involves selecting the most important information from a source on the grounds of its contribution to the theme. Spivey and King found that Year 8 and younger students thought that frequency of mention determined importance, a finding similar to what we have already found with summarising. Discourse synthesis requires a thematic focus and is vital for knowledge-transformation rather than knowledge telling.

3. *Forming a structure.* In Box 13.4, Emma claims she 'doesn't plan anything ... just go around thinking about it all the time'. Her ideas just spring to mind. Jim, more disciplined, also finds 'a structure emerges'. Both are using their writing as a means of transforming their knowledge. Bill and Anne, on the other hand, use other people to help them decide what bits of knowledge to tell and in what order.

Box 13.4   *There's planning and planning ...*

... enthusiasm

Emma: As soon as I get the assignment I read what I can find. Race down to the library the minute the lecture finishes and get there first to get all the stuff and then read it and then I just think about it while I'm going about whatever I'm going about. And then I leave it as long as I can before I write anything except for the odd thought that I have ... so you see, I don't plan anything. I just go around thinking about it all the time when I'm driving my car and in the garden and thoughts just spring to mind ... you know, the light bulb flashes and I think, ah yes, that's great. I keep these little exercise books and I write down thoughts that may be useful when I come to the essay.

... a personal focus

Jim: Obviously notes and books are important. Then there are the critics in the various journals. That gives a broad outline and you can always agree with them or disagree; it gives a starting point from where to work ... I always try to include at least one reference I've dug out for myself; it's nice to have that as a focus. It's more 'mine'. Then I mull it all over until a structure emerges.

... class-based

Bill: The lecturer tells us the basic points are in the lecture notes. Then it's a matter of matching those up with selections from one or two of the recommended critiques. I go on from there.

... my old English teacher

Anne: I try to plan but I usually go straight into it. As soon as I think of an idea I write it down. I write bits and pieces ... just sit there grabbing ideas here and there, trying to see what I can do with them ... If I have a lot of trouble I go to my old English teacher. She helps me get my ideas together.

Source: From interviews with first year English students. Biggs 1988c.

McLaren and Hidi (1988) distinguish the following kinds of structure that occur in expository essays:

- description, comprising associatively linked sentences around a topic;
- collection, comprising linked topic descriptions;
- causal-explanation, comprising causal relations between units;
- problem/solution, comprising a problem stated and a solution provided;
- compare and contrast.

Description and collection are the simplest, being made up of collections of facts and descriptions of a multistructural kind, whereas the last three are relational in nature. McLaren and Hidi found that in regular classes, over 90% of both Year 4 and Year 6 students used description or collection units only, while gifted students used higher structures, 44% doing so in Year 6. These authors note that by Year 6 students are very familiar with higher order structures from their reading, but find it difficult to apply them to their writing, although by Year 6 they may be taught to do so (Raphael & Kirschner 1985). The structure of the final essay is also closely related to the approach used (see next section).

4. *Opportunistic planning* refers to the willingness of the student to tolerate deviation, to go in hitherto unplanned directions, or even to replan from square one. Unskilled writers are usually unwilling to allow this to happen: 'No, I ignore sudden inspirations. That'd make things too messy. I'd get right off the track' (Biggs 1988c: 201). Opportunistic planning is often significant in producing knowledge-transformation and is a likely byproduct of the recursive nature of writing.

5. *Monitoring.* During planning, sentence generation and again during reviewing, writers monitor their activity. The criteria they use vary according to the phase; during planning, monitoring is mainly in terms of the theme: sticking to the set question, or to its emerging redefinition (see 'Criteria for revision', below).

Composing and sentence generation

Somewhere around 'forming a structure' (Number 3, above), planning takes on a specific edge that makes the word 'composing' more appropriate. This process is at its most intense as inner thoughts become frozen as marks on paper (transcribing). Sentence generation, forming what to say, or 'shaping at the point of utterance' (see Box 13.1), is very difficult for writers to describe. Saul Bellow, the famous novelist, said of this:

Well I don't know exactly how it's done. I let it alone a good deal. (Salgado 1980: 70)

The working memory load during composition is heavy, writers having to remember:

- *content,* what they are saying, what they intend to say and what they have said already;
- *mechanics,* the rules and conventions governing text production.

As they can focus on only one domain at a time, they can handle the load on working memory in two main ways:

1. As in reading, automate the lower order rhetorical (mechanical) aspects of writing as far as possible, thereby freeing working memory for focusing on the main ideas and on the relationship each sentence (and word) has to the idea or argument.

2.   Separate the 'what' and the 'how' questions as far as possible: for example, keep the words rolling out even if misspelled, and review text separately for substance (revising) and for mechanics (editing). One of the major sources of writer's block in student writers is caused by frequent review while writing (Rose 1984). It's much more important to get it down while it's there. A wrong word can be picked up later, but a rush of ideas can be lost forever.

Reviewing and revising

Revision, once seen as any alteration at the sentence level in the written text, now means 'any changes at any point in the writing process' (Fitzgerald 1987: 484), including changes in written text, intended text, or to the plan. Three kinds of revision may be distinguished:

1.   *Editing,* the proof-reader's level, where only mechanical and syntactical features of the text are changed. Here the focus is low level, being on features of words, words and sentences. The most basic sense of audience requires that the text is at least legible. Badly formed letters are rewritten; blots are rubbed out. Primitive redrafting, then, sees to it that the text looks neat. After that, the focus is on words, chunks and sentences for spelling, punctuation, word selection, within-sentence grammar: the 'mechanics'.
2.   *Additive revision,* which involves adding more information on a point, but not deleting text. Semantically, the writer goes no further than single ideas; this is knowledge telling, trotting out one idea after another, with little view of their interconnections, beyond a linear sequence. Revision at this level therefore consists of *adding* new sentences, but not deleting sentences or cut-and-paste (moving sentences from one place in the text to another). Why adding and not deleting? Because adding does not require you to think higher than sentence length ('Ah yes, more of that'), whereas deleting requires an overview spanning more than a sentence ('This is not contributing to the main idea: out'). To see that something is superfluous presupposes a clear vision of the big picture, but you can just keep adding from wherever you are.
3.   *Interactive revision,* which involves deleting text, changing the order of paragraphs, or rewriting text. Alterations such as these affect the meaning of the whole text and can only be carried out when the writer is thinking at the highest levels of main ideas and theme. Deletion and cut-and-paste interact with the main idea and theme.

Skilled writers distinguish meaning-related change, (2) and (3), and surface-related change (1), while beginning college students focus predominantly on mechanical changes (Faigley & Witte 1984); skilled writers also realise that text is most efficiently reviewed in *large units* (Fitzgerald 1987). Younger writers do less revision than older, although in all writers a lot of covert revision occurs (e.g., deciding to use a different word before writing the first one down) (Fitzgerald 1987). Many students view revision as 'correction', even as a punishment for not getting the text right first time, as they think do 'good' writers. It comes as a real eye-opener when these students learn that 'good' writers revise more heavily than poor writers, not less (see Mr Boomer's modelling of writing, pp. 466–7). Such an attitude derives from an absolutist theory of knowledge; things are either right or wrong, not relatively more or less appropriate, and that it's only sensible to have a couple of goes at making the less appropriate more so. Learning to write reflectively may thus have far-reaching consequences on children's more general conceptions of learning.

Criteria for revision

What criteria do writers use when revising? Two sets of review-and-revise are recommended: for meaning and for mechanics.

Revision for meaning

1. *Compatibility with global intentions.* One goes through the text with a fine-tooth comb to see that each unit of meaning, individually and collectively, contributes to the global plan finally decided on.

2. *Genre* is the conventionally agreed structure for this kind of text, which the writer has to honour. Only highly skilled and innovative writers can deliberately break the genre rules. A compare-and-contrast essay, for instance, has a *different* structure from a causal-explanation; a thriller from a romance. Actually, if students concentrate on the substance of what is being written and see that the question is answered appropriately, genre takes care of itself. Professional writers have to be more self-consciously concerned with genre.

3. *Coherence.* The coherence of a text refers to its logical integrity, reflected by *cohesive devices* or connectives that link adjacent and remote sentences. All such devices should link inevitably to the theme and reflect the genre. Multistructural writing such as knowledge telling makes much use of conjunctions such as 'and', 'so', 'then', whereas relational writing uses cohesive devices that reflect the logical coherence of the main idea ('therefore', 'an interesting exception ...'). Cunning students turn this on its head by sprinkling cohesive markers throughout their multistructural text ('In contrast to this general trend ...', 'Accordingly, this writer would opine ...') making it a relational look-alike to a busy marker. Careful reading of the substance should flush these con-writers out.

4. *Sense of audience.* Most important, the text should be monitored, composing and reviewing from the point of view of the likely reader: attending to what Britton refers to as 'the face beneath the page'. Who are you writing for? Yourself, an abstract 'community of scholars', the individual you happen to know will be marking it? Some answers are given in Box 13.5. The ability to write for an abstract audience (such as the scholarly community) does not normally come about until senior high school (Bracewell, Scardamalia & Bereiter 1978). Nevertheless, younger writers can modify their work to suit particular audiences, as Cohen and Riel (1989) showed. Year 7 students writing on the same topic, (a) to an email penfriend and (b) for an end-of-term assignment, wrote superior essays to their electronic audience in terms of content, organisation, vocabulary and even language use and mechanics. The audience seemed to make the difference (or it could have been the email). Certainly the audience provided by a set assignment wasn't stimulating their best effort. Many professional writers, recalling their school days, would back that up.

Box 13.5 *Who is the audience?*

Emma: Funny, I've never thought of an audience. The whole process of writing seems to me to be such a strangely personal one that it's not as if it's for an audience. Now philosophy essays are much more for an audience because with them I have to keep telling myself, well, this is what he wants ... it's an important way of being able to even write the wretched thing.

> *Margaret:* I'm my own audience. I write it as if it's making sense to me to reread to myself. It's different to writing speeches because they are for a specific audience but you don't know who you are writing for in essays.
>
> *Anne:* I've got to look at it from the lecturer's point of view because it seems that what the lecturer thinks is the most important thing rather than what you think ... You really try to make it really sophisticated and complicated because you think you will be impressing the lecturer. It's what the lecturer thinks is what matters. I've found that if you don't give back what you've been given it's not accepted.
>
> *Source:* From interviews with first year English students. Biggs 1988c.

5. *Style.* Writers should master the appropriate 'grapholect', the written equivalent of dialect (Hausen 1968). Each discipline has its grapholect that students need to master, for example, conventions, vocabulary, usages, etc. that mark literary criticism from historical analysis or sociological description. Usually these are acquired tacitly rather than through formal instruction. Some student views on style are given in Box 13.6.

Box 13.6 *What two English students think about style*

Emma: Another thing I don't like about philosophy essays is that there isn't any joy in creating a lovely essay. They don't really care if it's a clumsy sentence as long as the point you are making comes across. So the crafting of an essay for itself alone doesn't have the enjoyment that I get from English ones. I am not able to look at a beautiful sentence and find some lovely words to go into it that are really expressive of the right feeling and exactly the right sort of emotion ... I think philosophy is so boring having to do away with things like beauty, joy and pleasure.

Bill: No, I don't worry about style. I write to say what I think is wanted, what they're looking for. I'm not a poet (laughs).

Source: From interviews with first year English students. Biggs 1988c.

---

6. *Lexicon.* Is this exactly the word I want? Let near-enough words remain during composing, rather than derail one's train of thought. During review, one can afford to spend time thinking up a better one, using a thesaurus or dictionary. (Only use the thesaurus and spelling check on your word processer *after* you've finished the main text, if you don't mind.)

Revision for mechanics

1. *Grammar.* Attention to sense often fixes grammatical problems but not always. After a generation in the wilderness, it is now being recognised again that knowledge of formal grammar is definitely helpful in working out which clauses are dependent or which verbs agree with what subjects (Stein 1986). Teaching such knowledge should however be regarded as a means, not an end.

2. *Orthographics and presentation.* Spelling (word level) and punctuation (chunk and sentence level) are matters for editing. Legibility of writing, typeface, margins and all matters of presentation are for final one-off concern.

Approaches to writing

Surface and deep approaches to the various phases of writing are defined in terms of the level of textual unit focused on and the phase of writing engaged in. They are similar to knowledge telling and reflective writing, but whereas these terms refer to functions of writing, surface and deep approaches specify the processes involved. Figure 13.3 shows the *level* X *process* aspects:

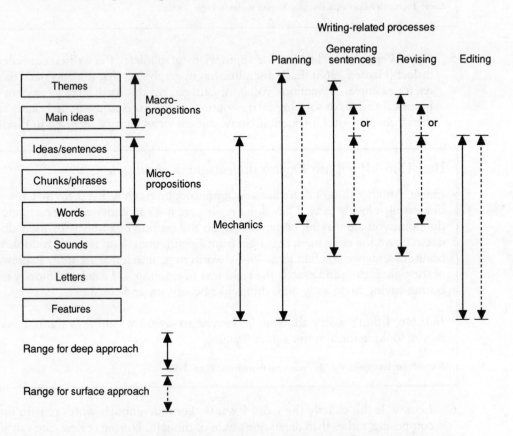

Figure 13.3   *Deep and surface approaches to writing and level of textual unit processed*

The solid line represents the range of levels traversed in a deep approach for each of the three processes: planning, sentence generation and review-and-revise: the dashed line the range of a surface approach.

At *planning*, a student using a deep approach covers all levels at various stages, but mainly would concentrate on the macropropositional end. Images of words and phrases could be collected, but their use structured. A student using a surface approach thinks in terms of what particular points to make and would gather particular facts and micropropositional quotes under, at most, paragraph headings.

At *sentence generation*, a deep approach generates sentences, with some tuning of words and phrases, perhaps even sounds, within the existing macro level plan. A surface approach unwinds sentences according to a simple linear structure.

At *review-and-revise*, a deep approach would pass (at least) twice: for meaning, with interactive revision; and for editing. A surface approach would probably review once, editing for mechanics only, or possibly combining some additive revision, adding in sentence level quanta of information.

Relations between process and outcome

How do these approaches affect the structure of the final essay? Twenty-four Year 11 and university student writers were interviewed about the way they were approaching a current assignment; three groups were distinguished: nine 'deep', whose focus was consistently high throughout planning, sentence generation, and revising; eight 'surface', who had a consistently low focus throughout all three processes, and seven 'mixed', whose focus varied (Biggs 1987; 1988b). When the structure of their essays was examined, it was found that all the deep writers had a relational or genre-appropriate structure (i.e., 'higher order' in McLaren and Hidi's (1988) terms), while all the surface writers achieved no higher than a multistructural structure ('collection' and below), which was not appropriate to the question. The mixed approach group had mixed outcomes. This is not to say, however, that the deep writers always got higher marks than the surface; our little friend Maria was a surface knowledge-teller and you will remember that she got very high marks.

Writing to learn

What do we learn from writing? It is commonly assumed, with the current emphasis on process writing, that writing facilitates learning in all subject areas. Let us be careful.

What you learn is what you focus on and what you focus on depends on what you want to learn, as we saw in summarising. Because reflective writing leads to a more complex understanding of selected information, whereas knowledge telling leads to retention of facts. These:

> teachers need to consider what kinds of learning they wish to encourage in students and then select the appropriate writing tasks. (Durst & Newell 1989: 386).

Consider the following. Penrose (1986; 1988) compared writing and studying parallel texts and found that studying led to superior learning. This applied to writing on recall of unrelated facts, related facts, main ideas, but not to application of the material to new contexts. Underlining was counter-productive; students who underlined micropropositions (words, phrases, sentences) as they studied were *less* likely to remember the main ideas of the text; Rickards and August (1975) found the same with highlighting. Note-taking before writing helped students remember related facts. Let us look at two case studies.

Jack, in taking notes for his essay, used a copy/delete strategy to the extent that when he wrote his essay, it looked as if it were plagiarised, yet he was completely unaware of this. A surface learner, we think you would agree. Ruth, on the other hand, worked much more quickly and took notes in schematic form, with heavy inferencing of her own, linking key words. Her essay developed her own inferences, not the original data; definitely a deep learner. On testing, Jack and Ruth scored about equally on factual recall and application, but Jack beat Ruth hands down on learning main ideas, while Ruth beat Jack equally dramatically on recall of related facts! Jack's methodical plodding through the text helped him recall the main points, but it prevented him from seeing that facts here were related to facts there.

Whose approach, Penrose asks, is the 'right' one? It depends what you want; each approach accomplished a different goal. The processes of knowledge-transformation, such as planning and audience awareness, seemed to *prevent* students from grasping the structure and factual infrastructure of the given passages; creating one's own structure (good—yes?) seemed to get in the way of apprehending the original writer's structure. So what do you want students to do: get it right, or create something new? While knowledge-transformation involves higher level cognitive processes, it may not result in as good a grasp of what's actually *given* as straightforward studying. It gets right back to the teacher and what she's after.

Penfold's study helps us see writing in its place. Writing as knowledge telling does not help students retain facts as well as ordinary study techniques, such as note-taking and summarising. The place of writing is therefore to facilitate *higher* level learning. Applebee (1984) argues that reflective writing enhances a person's reasoning ability: by 'freezing' thought out there, the writer may have second thoughts, or experiment with new combinations of ideas. Writing also forces the writer to try to be clear and precise in thinking a topic through; the reader's puzzled frown will not elicit any clarification from the page.

The problem is that the school environment overwhelmingly favours knowledge telling rather than knowledge-transformation. What can be done about that?

Teaching better writing

Even if you don't teach English: stay tuned!

All teachers should be concerned with the improvement of their students' writing; writing is *not* just the concern of the English department. Writing is a tool that spans disciplines; reflective writing is a *content* learning experience.

Eliminate cues for knowledge telling

We could turn Bereiter and Scardamalia's (1987) list on its head and sugggest that those features that elicit knowledge telling strategies should be eliminated:

* Do not test only what is taught, but surprise them by requiring some transfer.
* If you insist on testing what is taught, make sure the test items are not in the order of teaching.
* If you insist in using notes (and why not), make sure the *students'* notes are transformations of yours and that you do not test your own notes directly.
* Do not use 'topics that turn students on' except in creative or expressive writing. Sounds hard, we know, but if you want structure and argument in their essays you are unlikely to get it unless you are very clear and straight about your requirements.
* Do not allow students to pass 'if they can show they know at least something about the topic'. Probably too hard to follow through. Perhaps positive reinforcement is the way: richly reward those who show a detailed and structured knowledge.

Then there are positive things one can do to encourage reflective writing.

Direct instruction

As we now know many of the things that good writers do and poor writers do not do, an obvious strategy is to teach poor writers what good writers do. However, the evidence is that while teaching expert strategies works for students who have the knowledge to use them appropriately, for unskilled students:

> the procedure might be ineffective or harmful. Pushing students to use expert strategies too early might be like encouraging acrobats to start with the high wire. (Hayes & Flower 1986: 1112)

Some interventions, however, do work. At least at high school age, but possibly not before (Bracewell, Scardamalia & Bereiter 1978), feedback on what needs revising leads to better revision; and peer feedback is better than teacher feedback is better than self-feedback (Fitzgerald 1987). In other words, leave it to the average high school student to work out the problem on his own and little effective revision will take place, but give his work to his peers and they'll constructively rip it to shreds. The sexism here is intentional; females revise more effectively than males, so it's the boys who most need the peer treatment (op. cit.). It is interesting that peers are more effective than teachers in this role; again, more evidence of that much under-used resource, peer collaboration.

Even professional writers find self-criticism ineffective. Kipling used to place his just-completed manuscript in a drawer, 'to let it drain for a year' he said, after which time he'd revise it. Unfortunately we can't spare that sort of time, in these frenzied days, but the point is well taken; one is simply too close to gain an allocentric perspective on one's own work while it is still hot. If the codes that generated that text are still glowing, they will regenerate the same text. You need a planning structure that helps you rise above and see beyond your own text. One way of doing that is peer criticism.

Direct instruction on desired narrative structure also seems effective. Fitzgerald and Teasley (1986) instructed children in what makes a good story using Mandler and Johnson's (1977) story-grammars: setting——precipitating event——protagonist sets goal——tries to reach goal——setback (maybe)——new attempt——success?——long-term consequences (the happy ending) (see Box 13.7). As a result, the children write better stories. Raphael and Kirschner (1985) also found that direct instruction on compare-and-contrast essay structure was effective.

So direct instruction can help, but more research is needed when an idealogical issue makes it difficult to obtain research. Direct instruction in something as expressive as writing seems to some a return to the bad old days, where writing was product oriented and process wasn't even considered (Hairston 1982). Holistic approaches to the improvement of writing are more acceptable, that provide procedural support rather than direct instruction (Fitzgerald 1987). We examine three: conferencing, the word processor, and the total writing environment provided by the school.

Conferencing

Conferencing is the term used to describe the process approach to writing developed by Graves (1983) in the United States and in wide use in Australian schools (Turbill 1982). This approach gives the child, rather than the teacher, ownership over the what, when, and how of writing. The teacher's role is to assist the child in these decisions in a one-to-one 'conference' in which the activities of selecting a topic, updating knowledge, working out a structure, monitoring, attending to mechanics, redrafting,

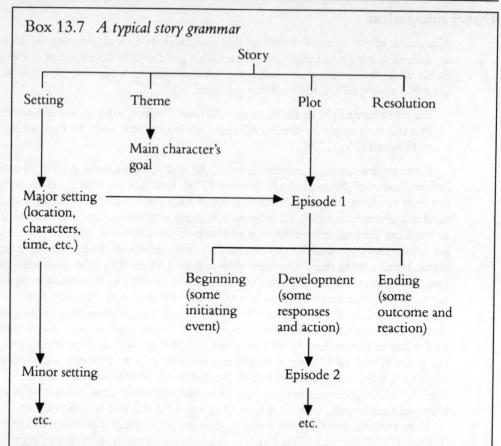

Box 13.7   *A typical story grammar*

Typical stories in Western cultures have four major 'rules' defining them: a setting, a theme, a plot and a resolution. More complex stories may involve multiple settings that lead to separate episodes until the main character's goal is achieved (or not); the resolution.

etc., are discussed as the need arises. In a class of 25 or so children, all writing at once, this seems a tall order, but according to Graves a single conference can last as little as 12 seconds; and with peer conferencing with older children, it is, he says, easy to arrange. In conferencing:

- the program is completely individualised;
- the child decides what to write;
- there is daily time to 'learn to write by writing';
- the child can discover his or her unique way of writing;
- there is time to conference individually with the teacher; and
- the conference focuses on improving the writing.

There are no teacher-assigned tasks beyond providing at least half an hour a day for writing. The teacher is encouraged to keep a list of each child's interests and any significant events that may have happened, so that the child may be helped towards a topic during early conferences. The provisional nature of writing is constantly emphasised: each piece of writing is introduced as a draft and some run up to six or more drafts before all agree that it is 'finished'.

All finished works go into each child's 'writing folder', from which each child is encouraged to select one or more 'books' for 'publication'. Each class has its library of books made by students within the class and they are read by the others just as eagerly as are trade books. Children *want* to make sure that presentation, spelling, etc., are correct.

Emphasis throughout the drafting stages is on 'flow'. Writing is seen as one of many forms of communication: talking, drawing, drama, role play. These activities are their topics and their drafts. Graves points out that as children have yet to internalise their thoughts (they cannot talk to themselves as adults do when they compose), *talking* is an important part of planning, composing and revising. Conferencing provides a scaffolding in the form of a prompt system, so that students can access their topic knowledge in an organised and appropriate way, with 'flow' uninterrupted. *Invented spelling* is therefore encouraged:

> John began composing when he wrote: 'SSTK (This is a truck)'. Fifteen minutes later John couldn't read the message. There were too few cues. Nevertheless he had the idea that the letters written had to correspond to sounds ... he is learning to write the way he learned to speak. (Graves 1983: 183)

Children spontaneously stabilise with the standard spellings (they want to get published). For example, Toni in grade one spelt 'and' in the following ways, from October to December: D D ND AD ND LA ANE AND ND AND AND AND. From 8 December, 'and' remained constant (op. cit). Graves claims that *all* mechanics can be taught in the conference as the need arises and that when learned in this way they are retained and used accurately.

Other educators, however, disagree with this position and argue for more explicit instruction in spelling. For example, Ehri and Wilce (1987) found that kindergarten children who were explicitly taught phonetic spellings improved their spelling performance and also their ability to read words. Exposure to misspellings concern other educators. They argue that constant exposure to incorrect spellings of words may be detrimental to subsequent spelling performance. Indeed, recent studies by Brown (1988) highlight this problem. Over exposure to incorrect spellings may not be beneficial to student learning of spelling patterns, rules, etc..

Writing and the word processor

Microcomputers seem to make revising and redrafting—the very features that distinguish reflective writing from knowledge telling—so much easier. Several factors have hitherto strongly discouraged students from redrafting:

- the belief that redrafting is what has to be done as a 'punishment' for not planning properly first time round;
- the high cost in terms of effort in rephrasing a section, or inserting material. One small alteration to a six-page paper means the whole lot has to be rewritten; and
- a reluctance to change what is already fixed in print.

Word processors (WPs), on the other hand, allow alterations to be made at a very *low* cost. The words on the screen can be changed instantly. The cut-and-paste functions enable one to move large, or small, slabs of text to any point in the document.

Initial expectations would therefore be that the use of WP would greatly improve the quality of both the planning and revision processes, and thus of the written product. It would also be expected that attitudes to writing might change, as the initial emphasis on 'getting it right first time' is removed. There is now a massive amount of research to guide us (Cochran-Smith 1991). What does it say?

Yes, students do revise *more* when using the WP than pencil-and-paper (Piolat 1991), but not necessarily better: less than 40% of studies show improvements in writing after revision (Hawisher & Fortune 1988). In other words, the WP encourages more revision, but often of a trivial kind, which does not result in improved text. Whether or not it does improve the quality of writing depends on the expertise of the writer in two areas:

- writing skill itself;
- knowledge of and skill in the WP functions.

Students do revise more when using the word processor than pencil and paper, but not necessarily better.

WPs increase the differences between novices and experts (Piolat 1991). Good writers, at home with their WPs, revise more effectively and produce much better quality text. Students who don't know how to use the machines, or who are not reflective writers anyway, aren't made so by endless revisions on the WP that are in fact trivial.

Part of the problem is the monitor and its limited capacity. The writer can only view a few sentences at a time, which may not be enough to keep the main idea in focus. The writer should therefore revise on the basis of the *complete text* before the final printout (that's what draft mode is for). Another problem is the matter of not being fluent in all the WP functions. On average, 13 year olds have been found to have a typing speed of 8 words per minute (Piolat 1991).

Daiute's (1986) study found that the major revision made by junior high school students was the addition of more information at the end of the text. Not being able to see the whole text, they moved quickly to the end of the text and then added the new information. The WP was actually encouraging knowledge telling, not reflective writing. The problem of inadequate mechanical/operational knowledge is illustrated by Dalton, Morocco and Neale (1988), who looked at the time that teachers spend in helping students in a writing/word processing laboratory; 45 to 55% of the teachers' time was taken up in trouble-shooting and individual mechanical problems, leaving substantially less time for the teacher to interact with the students on the processes and content of writing. Student confidence needs to be developed early, complex operations being introduced gradually. These operations should be practised and feedback provided, showing how they affect the quality of the final written product.

A qualitative change introduced by word processing is that the setting is public, allowing collaborative writing, or conferencing with peers or with the teacher (Cochran-Smith 1991). Software itself can be used in 'conferencing' to provide the prompting that young writers cannot provide for themselves, so that they actively think about rhetorical and content related issues. Daiute's (1986) students could call up a set of questions at any time while writing and they were encouraged to do so at the end of writing each paragraph. The prompting questions related to clarity, completeness, organisation, coherence, sentence structure and punctuation (e.g., 'Does this paragraph make a clear point?'). Students who undertook the prompting program revised their drafts more closely and extensively than those who had used only a WP program.

More sophisticated forms of interaction use software designed to address higher level, organisational and rhetorical issues during the development of a text. This would seem to be helpful to less experienced writers who have difficulties in planning, organising, integrating and analysing topical information (Kozma, in press). Kozma cites an array of software designed to allow the writer to organise and construct relationships among ideas which can be subsequently displayed on a split screen for reference and revision purposes. For example, 'Learning Tool' (Kozma & Van Roekel 1986) allows writers to enter and organise ideas in either of two coordinated 'spaces' in the computer. One of the spaces ('Masterlist') allows writers to outline their ideas and arrange them in sequence and levels of subordination so that the relationships among ideas become more apparent. In the other space ('Concept map') writers can make sets of 'cards' which contain relevant information about aspects of their writing and they can move these cards around on the screen to help plan and develop their texts. Both 'spaces' can be displayed on the screen at the same time via the spilt screen so that the writer can see their ideas and the relationships among their ideas before they actually write and also during composing.

Both types of software increased conceptual planning for novice and advanced writers at the college level. The effects of such planning on the final product, however, varied with the novice writers benefitting most from one package and the advanced writers gaining more from the other. Further, Kozma's analysis of the 'think-aloud' protocols produced during writing demonstrated quite convincingly that the novice writers did use the packages to create a representation of the text that was used to guide their writing.

So where do we stand? The mere provision of WPs may have very little impact upon the quality of the processes and products of student writing. But the careful classroom use of the WP has enormous potential to encourage writers to be more reflective and to use language in a way that more closely reflects and reshapes their thinking.

The total writing context

Undoubtedly, the most important way of improving writing lies not in any particular technique or method, although some techniques are certainly helpful, but in providing a context that *demands* reflective writing. Writing should be widely used across the curriculum in schools in order to sharpen thinking, whatever the content area.

Apart from the special case of the English class, which tends to emphasise creative writing, other subject areas tend to disclaim responsibility. Writing is used either as a means of storing and prompting knowledge that is already in existence, for example note-taking, which all too often only captures ideas at the sentence level, or for testing purposes, where the writer communicates second-hand content to someone who always knows more about the topic than does the writer. In neither case does writing involve knowledge-transformation: the knowledge is never shaped by the writer, simply reported back.

Further, the testing function of the essay or short answer introduces all the pressures and challenges that promote cynicism and anxiety, and which in turn promote a surface approach to learning. There seems to be something about the context of 'the assignment' that discourages high level processing. Recall Cohen and Riel's (1989) study where an essay written for a penfriend was superior in all ways to an essay on the same topic written as a final assignment.

General how-to-write courses are not the answer, as they are usually taught for all writers irrespective of content. Thus, writing has then to be taught in a generalised, content-free way, which means focusing on spelling, grammar, orthographics and vague all-purpose structures. Certainly, general hints and tips can be helpful (see Box 13.4), but they are really only the icing on the cake.

As we have seen, planning and sentence generation at least draw on a great deal of relevant content knowledge; certainly each subject not only has its gratholect, but its genres. Writing a history essay requires specialised rhetorical knowledge that is simply different from the rhetorical knowledge required to write a lab report; the science teacher is the best person to teach the latter, not the English teacher. To teach 'content-free' writing techniques inevitably draws attention away from main ideas and themes, focusing it on mechanics. Mechanics are obviously important, but their importance derives from the fact that they help to convey meaning efficiently.

When teachers themselves teach across the curriculum it is easier to tune reading and writing to a range of learning content. The Scottish Foundations of Writing Project concentrated on the first three primary years with group-based talking and writing activities that resulted in teachers perceiving their students in a new light: 'writing gave a depth to all the work of the classroom that had not existed before' (Jackson 1988: 14). The teachers realised they had under-estimated the potential of their children, Jackson reports.

To close, we might give some practical tips for non-English teachers to improve essay writing in their subject areas. First, the main points arising from this chapter in summary:

- Writing should be used for much more than testing and jogging the memory.
- Writing should be dealt with in the content areas in which it is used, requiring the writer to focus on main ideas and themes, rather than on disjointed ideas, facts and points.
- Markers of essays and exams should therefore focus on the main ideas and themes, rather than on mechanics. When mechanics are singled out for attention, it should be pointed out that the misspelling (or the sentence construction or the placement of the comma) interferes with the *meaning*.
- Emphasis should be placed on the cyclical, reflective, nature of writing rather than on the one-way transcription of preformed thoughts.

When setting essays, students should be made absolutely clear about what's expected of them and what constitutes a 'good' (and a 'poor') essay. They should be given clear, detailed, feedback quickly. Perhaps what emerges most clearly from this chapter is not how to teach students how to write, but to teach teachers what good writing is and what to do in order to obtain it. Clanchy (1985) prepared the following list of pointers for tertiary teachers, but they apply at all levels:

1. *Make expectations explicit.* If you want focus on the topic, wide and critical reading, a reasoned argument, competent presentation, or whatever else you may want: say so.
2. *Make expectations concrete.* Make it clear what you mean by your expectations: what a 'good' essay is. Clanchy recommends keeping a bank of poor, medium and good essays (duly rendered anonymous), so that students can see for themselves what you mean.
3. *The topic should be unambiguous.* Any teacher would agree to this, but often the ambiguity is only perceptible to someone else. Showing your proposed essay questions to a colleague is a useful check.
4. *The first essays should be 'redeemable'.* Actually, to follow through the points made about reflective writing, all essays should be redeemable, but that could take up huge amounts of time for both teacher and student. Certainly at the beginning of a course, inadequate essays should be handed back for revision and resubmission.
5. *Feedback should be swift, detailed and individual.* A vague comment and a letter grade ('An interesting point of view. B+') tells the student nothing about how the essay could be improved.

The coincidence between these points and those made about motivation in Chapters 10 and 11 is evident. Knowing where you are going not only feels good, it makes it much more likely that you'll get there.

Summary

Strategies for text processing

Learning how to handle text is the major task that schools undertake. Strategies of learning how to read and to write, and of reading to learn and of writing to learn, involve metacognition of a high order. The child has two kinds of task: to learn the technicalities of handling text and then to make text for higher order learning.

Learning to read

Reading involves two major processes: decoding print, so that we can see what the words are, and comprehending what those words mean. Text is structured into many levels; we considered eight, ranging from features of letters, through words and sentences, to main ideas and themes. Decoding skills include phonic analysis of letters and whole-word recognition. These skills need to be mastered solely so they needn't occupy working memory and students can concentrate on the game itself: comprehending the message.

Reading to learn

Underlining, highlighting, advance organisers, summarising and note-taking, are all ways of facilitating learning from text, but they need specifically to address the question of *level* of comprehension. The two crucial levels are: micropropositions (sentence level and below) and macropropositions (main ideas and theme). Summarisation involves comprehension, selection and transformation into thematic units; it is a particularly important, learnable, skill that is essential for both studying from existing texts and for writing one's own.

Learning to write

Writing expository text is very complex. Students frequently rely on a knowledge telling strategy that gets them through most or all school demands. Reflective writing, however, is the mode that addresses higher cognitive processes; it is recursive, transforming and constructing knowledge as much as transmitting it. Writing involves three major processes: planning, sentence generation and revision. While there is a developmental sequence in the accumulation of writing skills, it is not clear to what extent they are age-related or relate to teaching or to practice.

Writing an essay

The quality of text produced depends on: (1) topic or content knowledge and rhetorical knowledge of text structure, audience and syntax; (2) the level focused on; and (3) the processes of planning, sentence generation and revision. The processes are recursive and interactive; once writing is in progress, each may affect the other in any order. Planning involves developing the theme, the topic knowledge, the structure, and some illustrative images. Sentence generation requires two concerns: meaning (what to say) and rhetorical (how to say it), two domains that may cause a bottleneck in working memory if not strategically handled. Revision may involve three kinds of change: editing, which focuses on mechanical changes; additive, focusing on micropropositional additions of meaning at the sentence level; and interactive, involving deletion and cut-and-paste at a macropropositional level.

In a surface approach, the writer rarely focuses higher than the micropropositional level at planning (which may be rudimentary), sentence generation, or revision (which may also be rudimentary and often restricted to editing). In a deep approach, the writer plans from a thematic level downwards, generates sentences in a range extending from word to theme, and revises separately for meaning and for mechanics.

Writing to learn

Writing *per se* does not necessarily lead to better learning. It depends what is to be learned. Even knowledge telling does not lead to knowledge-gathering as well as good summarising and note-taking does. Reflective writing, from a deep approach, leads to a holistic understanding of the sources, but may even inhibit a focused understanding of any particular source. It depends whether you want synthesis and new constructions of knowledge, or a good grounding in what's already there. Probably both.

Teaching better writing

Reflective writing is not sought in school and is accordingly offered only by those few naturally inclined to do so. Approaches may be deepened up to a point by direct instruction in the processes of planning and revision, or by teaching 'process writing', as in conferencing. The word processor is also a promising tool but research confirms the obvious; it's not the tool, but how it is used. When used properly, the signs are encouraging. The ultimate answer to better writing across the curriculum has got to be in the hands of the teacher who sets the writing context.

Learning activities

1. The knowledge × level × process approach to conceptualising writing

A substantial part of this chapter has attempted to provide you with an understanding of the interactive nature of writing by using the *knowledge* × *level* × *process* concept. What do you understand by each of the components and their interaction? Generate, say, five questions (at least at the main idea level) for *knowledge*, for *level* and for *processes*. An example for knowledge is: 'Which is the more important in writing, content or rhetorical knowledge?' (The answer, we hope, will be at a main idea/thematic level.) The questions could form the basis of a seminar/discussion in class.

2. Level of abstraction in reading

The purpose of this activity is to test your understanding of Kirby's eight-level model of reading which is illustrated in Figure 13.1. Questions to be addressed include: What are the characteristics of each of the levels in the model? Why is comprehension essentially from the word level upwards? What are the different levels that are appropriate for decoding? What is automation and what levels need to be automated for competent reading? How do top-down and bottom-up processes operate and influence reading? Why is the word level often referred to as the 'bottleneck' in comprehension?

3. Maximising comprehension

When we looked at maximising comprehension, we drew upon the work of Paris and his colleagues and their Informed Strategies for Learning (ISL) program. This activity is group or class oriented and its purpose is for you to get an understanding of the complex nature of reading by generating posters for *each* of the modules from the ISL program. You will find the modules and their metaphors listed in Paris et al. (1984). For instance, one of the modules in comprehension and meaning is 'abstracting critical information'. In generating a poster for this you would use the metaphor 'tracking down the main ideas'. You could imagine a poster with a track on it with signs along the way such as 'delete trivial information', 'wrong way—not important information', 'locate important information', 'delete redundant information', 'relate main ideas to supporting ideas' and so on. You will undoubtedly recognise these signs as those discussed in the section on summarising and note-taking in this chapter. An alternative poster could use a detective on the trail of a main idea thief.

When all module posters are completed they can be presented to the class or group and discussed. Once you see the set of posters displayed, we guarantee that you will have a better understanding of comprehension, reading strategies and metacognition.

4. knowledge telling and reflective writing

The aim of this activity is to informally examine the types and amount of writing done in classrooms in which you teach. This activity could be done during practice teaching sessions. A good starting point are our references to Applebee (1984) and Annells et al. (1975) earlier in the chapter. You'll remember Applebee's comments about the preponderance of copying, note-taking, filling in blanks and the lack of continuous, more reflective writing in high schools in the United States.

Observe the writing done in a classroom for a period (say a day) and categorise it (e.g., copying or transcribing from the board, notes from texts, own notes during lesson, original composition, revision/redrafting of texts, planning of texts, etc.) and then quantify each category by the amount of time spent on each.

An interesting extension of this activity would be to compare types of writing and their frequency, in infant, primary and secondary schools. For a look at infants' writing read T. Newkirk, 'The non-narrative writing of young children' (*Research in the Teaching of English*, **21**, 1987, 121–44).

5. Learning from text: User-friendliness

Do you realise how much we rely upon textbooks to impart knowledge in our schools? Well, we haven't any information from Australia but data from the United States certainly show the magnitude of the textbook business: about 328 million textbooks were produced in 1986 at a retail cost of US$3.3 billion (cited in Britton, Van Dusen, Gulgoz & Glynn 1989). Have you had a good look at school texts to see how 'considerate' they are? Can the information be readily 'digested'? Are they conducive to effective learning?

The purpose of this activity is to examine several widely used high school texts to determine how user-friendly they are. Sample pages can be used rather than a total analysis of the book. Questions that could guide such an analysis include: Is the reading level too high (long words, difficult words)? Are the main points lost in the details? Are there signals such as sub-headings, 'first, second', etc. and introductions and conclusions? Is the text too wordy with lots of redundant or irrelevant information? Is there appropriate sequencing of information? Are there alternative modes of presenting important information (e.g., graphs, diagrams, tables, illustrations)? Is this information presented well? Is the setting out helpful?

The activity also could include discussion of the characteristics of text that facilitate learning. This could lead to the development of a checklist. If you are interested in looking at the effects of changes to texts on learning you can refer to the research by Britton et al. (1989).

6. Revision in writing

We have seen in this chapter that revision in writing is an important area of teaching and learning. In this activity you are to analyse Jill Fitzgerald's paper, 'Research on revision in writing' (*Review of Educational Research*, **57**, 1987, 481–506). You will notice that the paper is divided into four sections: Perspectives on Revision; Measuring and Revealing Revisions; Findings; and Conclusions, Limitations and Recommendations. As a class activity, groups could be responsible for summarising sections and then presenting their findings to the remainder of the group. On an individual basis, you might want to examine more closely a section that interests you. Think about the *knowledge* × *level* × *process* concept that we have been stressing throughout the chapter. How are you going about the task?

Further reading

On reading and learning from reading
Bryant, P. & Bradley, L. (1985). *Children's Reading Problems*. Oxford: Blackw[...]
Just, M. A. & Carpenter, P. A. (1987). *The Psychology of Reading and [...] Comprehension*. Boston: Allyn & Bacon.
Kirby, J. R. (1988). Style, strategy and skill in reading. In R. R. Schmeck (ed.) (1988). *Learning Strategies and Learning Styles*. New York: Plenum Press.
Kirby, J. R. (1991). Reading to learn. In J. B. Biggs (ed.), *Teaching for Better Learning: The View from Cognitive Psychology*. Hawthorn, Vic: Australian Council for Educational Research.
Rayner, K. & Pollatsek, A. (1989). *The Psychology of Reading*. London: Prentice Hall International.

Much has been written about learning to read and reading to learn. We have selected a few chapters and books that we feel will provide you with a good grasp of the field (after you've read our book and done the activities!).

All of the above books examine the complexities of learning to read. Bryant and Bradley show the vital role that phonemic awareness plays in early success in reading, as does Kirby's (1988) chapter, but within the framework of processing different levels of text. Just and Carpenter, and Rayner and Pollatsek all come from eye-movement research but they have a great deal to offer in understanding the reading process. Just and Carpenter's chapter on learning from texts should delight you. Kirby's (1991) chapter is about using the skill of reading once it is acquired.

On writing
(a) *Declarative*

Bereiter, C. & Scardamalia, M. (1987). *The Psychology of Written Composition*. Hillsdale, NJ: Lawrence Erlbaum.
Biggs, J. B. (1988c). Approaches to learning and to essay writing. In R. R. Schmeck (ed.), *Learning Styles and Learning Strategies*. New York: Plenum Press.
Hounsell, D. in Marton, Hounsell and Entwistle (1984): see reading for previous chapter.

(b) *Procedural*

Clanchy, J. & Ballard, B. (1981). *Essay Writing for Students: A Practical Guide*. Melbourne: Longman Cheshire.
Strunk, W. & White, E. (1972) *The Elements of Style*. New York: Macmillan.

There are many books about writing, but Bereiter and Scardamalia have written one that probably best integrates the psychology of writing. The Biggs chapter describes deep and surface approaches to writing illustrated by two detailed case studies of 'Syd' and 'Geoff'. Hounsell develops his own model of student essay writing, based on psychology and history students.

There are also many how-to-write books. We recommend an excellent home-grown one for the basics in expository writing for students; and for quite a different purpose and for a more sophisticated audience, the classic Strunk and White, which has been the benchmark for writing style for half a century (periodically updated); the flavour you will know from this chapter.

On teaching writing

Graves, D. (1983). *Writing: Teachers and Children at Work*. Exeter, New Hampshire: Heinemann Educational.

Turbill, J. (ed.) (1982). *No Better Way to Teach Writing*. Rozelle, NSW: Primary English Teaching Association.

Zinsser, W. (1988). *Writing to learn*. New York: Harper & Row.

The first two are all about conferencing. Graves' original work, highly detailed and practical. Turbill's describes how it was implemented in New South Wales. Zinsser's book is an excellant guide to teaching and learning writing post primary.

PART 5

THE OUTCOMES OF LEARNING

CHAPTER 14

LEARNING AND
ITS EVALUATION

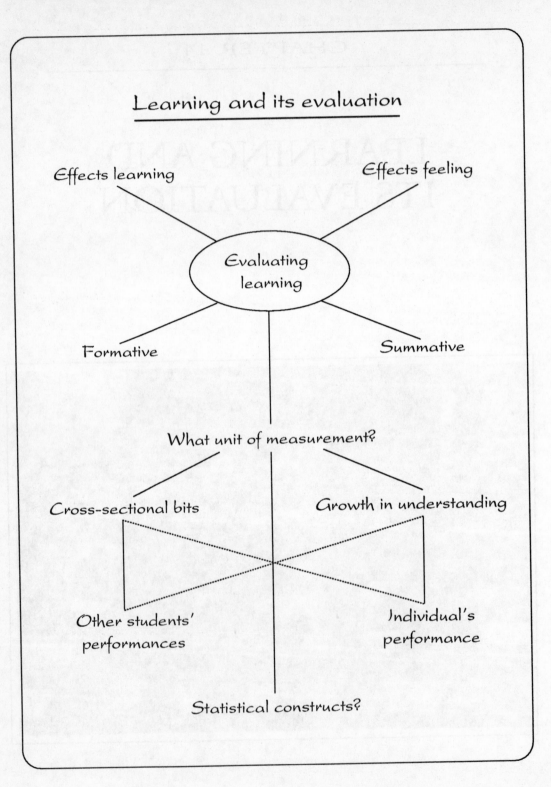

LEARNING AND ITS EVALUATION

In this chapter, you will find out:

- how 'evaluation' differs from 'assessment';
- that we usually evaluate learning in ways that are contrary to the way we learn;
- what the quantitative and qualitative traditions in evaluation are;
- what normative and summative evaluation are;
- what norm-referenced and criterion-referenced measurement mean;
- what mastery learning is and when it is best used;
- what 'item response theory' is; how it relates to the Rasch model; and what they have to offer to classroom testing;
- what the 'backwash' effects of testing on learning and teaching are, and how they m be made to work positively;
- how to define and measure learning 'quality'; and
- what aspects of learning should be assessed.

Learning, evaluation and assessment

Evaluation is the area where experienced educational researchers see the most interesting and important developments taking place over the next few years (Finn 1988). Quite simply, our knowledge of the processes of learning and of instruction have developed considerably in the past few years, and the techniques and models we use for testing learning have not (Shepard 1991). In an age of electronic learning, our tests and examinations are driven by steam.

First, let us clarify some basic concepts in educational evaluation that need to be understood before we can get our bearings on the question of the relation between testing and learning. Let us first look at two words: 'evaluation', which is in the title to this chapter, and 'assessment', which is in the title to the next.

Evaluation

Evaluation requires making a *judgment*, in terms of criteria, as to what constitutes good or poor learning. We first need to derive the criteria; these are or should be contained in the curricular goals. We must have some idea as to what we are teaching and to what level. Second, we need to make judgments about whether the student is approaching the task appropriately, or not. Finally, we need to judge whether the outcomes are satisfactory, or not; do they meet the initial objectives?

Almost every autonomous act of creation—writing a letter to the editor, designing a fernery, publishing a novel—involves the same three stages:

- setting up goals or intentions—and *judging* them to be realistic and appropriate;

- deciding how to go about achieving those goals—and *judging* what procedure is likely to be successful;
- deciding when the task is finished—and *judging* that the product is satisfactory.

Evaluation thus involves judgment at all stages of learning, with the intention of making substantive changes in the quality of the learning, and hence in our relationship with the world. This sequence and focus of activities is the same as that in metacognition, discussed in Chapter 12. Initially, it is the teacher who evaluates at these three levels, but if we are going to take seriously the notion that students are to become autonomous in their own learning, then clearly the *student* should increasingly take over these kinds of evaluations. Self-evaluation is in fact the core process in metacognitive acts, but a rarely cultivated process in the classroom.

Formative and summative evaluation

> Testing and learning cannot, as they do now, rely on separate communities of test developers and designers of curriculum and instruction ... Testing and learning should be integral events, guiding the growth of competence. (Glaser 1990: 480)

What tends to happen now is that we teach, then some time later we test. We then grade the test results on how they compare with each other, not on the basis of our original objectives in teaching. The purpose of most testing is either to label, or to select from a pool of applicants (for a job, for further study, or for some prize or scholarship), not to guide the growth of competence.

The distinction here is between *formative* and *summative* evaluation, first formalised by Scriven (1967). Formative evaluation provides feedback to both teacher and learner, and is used *during* the teaching process; summative evaluation indicates how well material has been learned *after* teaching is completed. Grading, or awarding marks, at the end of learning is a major procedure in summative evaluation. Every professional certificate, diploma or degree is a summative statement: This person has successfully completed certain requirements.

While summative evaluation tells the student, teacher and potential customer how well the course has been completed, formative evaluation tells the student and teacher how well the course is being learned at any given stage in the learner's development. Formative evaluation and the feedback it provides are intended simply to give information about the progress of learning to the participants: not to punish, grade, inform the public or award scholarships. Thus, formative evaluation is continuous, diagnostic and remedial; while summative is terminal, finite and descriptive.

What to evaluate?

Normally, we think of evaluation as applying only to learning outcomes, but as indicated above, we need to evaluate at other stages in educational learning.

Curriculum evaluation

When state departments set the curricula, they in effect tell teachers what should be tested—and until fairly recently, those departments themselves did the testing at the end of Years 10 and 12, inevitably along very quantitatively based lines. Now in many states it is the teachers' turn to decide what to teach and hence what to evaluate. This undoubtedly throws a larger responsibility onto teachers, but it also greatly frees up the instructional process, putting learning and its monitoring side by side with decisions as to what to learn, how to go about it, and how to decide when it has been learned sufficiently well. Such a holistic conception of education is much more appropriate than the traditional model, externally imposed, with artificial distinctions between curriculum and testing, resulting in over-emphasis on testing and grading. Further, bringing the whole process in-house enables the *student* to participate in ways that were simply not possible under the external model.

The specific question of what to put into the curriculum is a matter for curriculum development. Once it is there, however, the teacher needs to judge how best students' learning of each objective or aspect may be evaluated. This chapter will provide some concepts that will be helpful in achieving that.

Process evaluation

Evaluation usually focuses on *content*, and does not consider how the *student* has been changed by the learning experience. Evaluation of content learning outcomes and of process are both important, but relatively little attention has been focused on the latter.

There are many examples of process evaluation. The misnamed British 'public' school, for instance, insisted on the classics as part of the basic curriculum, not because the upper classes *needed* Latin in their future lives (except for upper class conversation), but because rigorous study of such formal disciplines as Latin and Greek was thought to be 'character building': not a content but a process outcome. The outcome of a study skills course, for example, is hopefully that the students are more strategic and more skilful about the way they go about studying in future (see Chapter 12). Paris' Informed Strategies for Learning (ISL) program, described in Chapter 13, aims to change the way young readers approach text. Writers become better writers by doing different things, for example, by reviewing in larger units than they did before.

Hand in hand with curriculum development, then, goes another task for the teacher: to specify how the students are to approach the task in question and then to evaluate how well they do so. This will involve a task analysis of the kind carried out in reading comprehension, summarising and writing (Chapter 13): to see what it is that good readers do and what good writers do. The same can be said of good mathematicians and scientists; many of the process science courses, like Nuffield, or *The Web of Life*, aim to get students to do what chemists, physicists and biologists do.

Assessment

Satterly (1981) points out that 'assessment' comes from the Latin, *assidere*, to sit beside. A cosy picture, of teacher and student cooperatively determining the extent and quality of the one's teaching, the other's learning. Unfortunately, the reality is not like this. The word assessment tends to be a cold prickly out of Theory X, not a warm fuzzy out of Theory Y. And it is usually not conducted in this formative sense, but summatively, at the end of the learning, when it is all over and we need to classify the product. And because the categories are graded, and the best and more desirable categories are rationed, the majority of students will receive less desirable labels. They feel threatened by this; the majority of students don't like assessment at all. Assessment, then, is one small aspect of evaluation: when the product is evaluated in terms of an instrument called a 'test', usually summatively, for grading purposes.

Progressive vs. terminal assessment

In progressive assessment, teachers give tests quite frequently—once a week, say—in order to take the heat off the big event of the final examination, given that test anxious students in particular suffer unduly under exam stress (Gaudry & Bradshaw 1970) (see also Chapter 9, p. 246). Progressive assessment is thus summative. But because it happens frequently and it's not the end of the year yet, teachers feel that they had better remediate what hasn't yet been learned properly, and that's a formative use. Thus, in practice, formative and summative evaluations are often fused, the weekly test result providing feedback and being included in the progressive assessment. This is not the good idea it seems to be.

The problem is that in summative evaluation, whether by progressive or terminal assessment, the students are being *graded* on what is being tested; their test-taking strategies are to be defensive, to hide what they don't know, and teachers set highly focused, even trick, questions to breach the defences. In formative evaluation, on the other hand, the teacher openly searches for faulty learning with broad questions (no trick questions here) so that learners' strategies should be revelatory, to reveal what they don't know or can't do. The best way to improve is to be frank about what one cannot do, but that is not a good idea when one is penalised with low grades for such frankness.

It is perhaps confusing to use the term 'evaluation' in both formative and summative senses. 'Assessment' best catches the summative meaning of evaluation and is accordingly used here in that sense. As techniques of formative and summative evaluation are quite different, teachers must be clear as to what they are trying to do when administering a test. Is it to find out how well students are taking to the material? Is it to find out if there are any misunderstandings so far; if the teaching is aimed at the right level? Or is it to gain information for grading purposes? Will the test data appear on final reports? The answers to these questions point to the different tests needed. They ought not to be confused.

We cannot honestly do without assessment, but it needs to be placed in context: as a device for making one kind of evaluation, not as an end in itself. Undoubtedly emphasis on assessment *per se* has led to damaging results. In this and the following chapter we shall try to put tests and testing into perspective.

Quantitative and qualitative traditions in evaluation

As we saw in Chapter 1, quantitative and qualitative conceptions of the nature of learning underlie all decisions to do with teaching, including, of course, assessment. The role of these conceptions in so far as they have affected decisions regarding assessment is explored by Cole (1990):

The quantitative tradition sees curriculum content in terms of basic skills and facts to be mastered; behaviourism is the psychological parent, and learning is seen as an assimilation process. Instructional processes are convergent or closed, involving the transfer and assimilation of facts and skills, either in expository teaching en masse or in individualised modules, such as mastery learning, which has an inbuilt system of checking that standards have been met (see below).

The qualitative tradition focuses on content expressed as higher order skills and advanced knowledge, the learning of which is seen as constructive, involving such processes as understanding and interpretation. Teaching takes place in experiential, discovery and open-ended contexts.

Cole argues that each tradition has different implications for assessment and that each has its place. So they do, but many of those who make major decisions about testing and examinations on a state and national basis (called 'testing directors' in the United States) do not recognise the qualitative tradition. Shepard (1991) was interested in the implicit theories of learning and teaching held by 50 nationally representative testing directors. She found that half believed learning to be linear and atomistic, quantitatively conceived and, that as tests comprise the essential data to be learned, teaching should be 'for the test'. She asks:

> But what if learning is not linear and is not acquired by assembling bits of simpler learnings? What if the process of learning is more a Faulknerian novel where one has glimpses and a vague outline of ideas before each of the concrete elements of a story fit in place? (Shepard 1991: 7)

In that case, we had better construct different kinds of tests and use them in a different way. That way is the way of 'authentic assessment' (McLean 1990; Wiggins 1989), in which assessment tasks are devised which require higher order thinking, not recognition or recall, in situated contexts designed to replicate those used in everyday use of the knowledge in question (the ACER-designed CATs are an example and these are discussed in the next chapter; see also Masters & Hill 1988). It follows that attempts to 'teach to the test' result in genuinely improved student learning and thinking, not as at present degraded teaching and learning (Frederiksen & Collins 1989).

School learning involves both quantitative and qualitative aspects of learning, depending on what is being learned at the time (Cole 1990); a framework is required, she says, that links both. As we saw in Chapter 2, the quantitative aspects are paramount in the early stages of learning within a mode, in the shifts from uni- to multistructural, in the *accretion* of knowledge; and the qualitative later, as relational and extended abstract levels become addressed, in qualitative shifts in *understanding*.

Quantitative evaluation, then, focuses on the accretion of knowledge and is comparatively easy to carry out. The teacher wants to know how many points the student can recall, the number of words spelt, the number of problems solved correctly, the number of grammatical rules applied and so on. The technology that can help the teacher to evaluate quantitatively in these terms has been built up over the years and is now sophisticated.

Quantitative assumptions clearly underlie the use of multiple-choice tests; the options presented are scored strictly in terms of correct/incorrect and the score that indicates good learning is the simple sum of all the correct answers (the technology is further explained in Chapter 15). Even essay marking has a quantitative bias in practice; the most common procedure in marking open-ended essay responses is to award a mark for each relevant point made and convert the ratio of actual marks to possible marks into some kind of number. The teacher then adjusts the final mark for overall quality, so that a final grade (A, B or D, or Pass, Fail, Distinction) is arrived at.

When we turn to tests that specifically address 'understanding', most teachers measure understanding in terms of problem solving, but as quantitatively conceived: the more problems addressing a topic the student can solve, the more that student 'understands' the topic (White 1984). But as White points out, concepts, whole disciplines, single elements of knowledge, extensive communications, situations and people, are all 'understood' differently; entirely different methods of seeing that we do 'understand' the domain in question are used. For example, understanding the situations set-up in the alternative frameworks research is often done by interview: asking the students to predict, observe and explain the demonstration. Understanding in mathematics may often be little more than being able to apply an algorithm to a stereotypical word-problem. Thus, teachers need to decide what is to be understood and to be creative about designing the most appropriate methods of evaluation understanding in each context.

Qualitative evaluation, then, needs to be much better understood and implemented more effectively. In practice it must be more subject-specific and focus on what we might mean when we say that this learning outcome is 'better' than that one, in this problem or learning context. What we *do* mean by 'better' depends on our theory of what constitutes good learning (Messick 1984). So Shepard is right; teachers and evaluators need to create an espoused theory that approximates more closely to what we now know about learning and, with luck, that will become the theory-in-use.

Calibrating tests

What is a test?

A 'test' is simply an instrument or a situation that provides information about the learner's progress (personality and attitude testing is not relevant to the present discussion). A test may consist of one or several items and it may be in one of several forms (e.g., multiple-choice, essay, practicum and so on). A test may yield a numerical score or a qualitative category, and the teacher has then to make a reasonable decision on the basis of this information.

Tests can be either instruction-dependent or instruction-free. Instruction-free tests are so called because they measure performances that are relatively free from the effects of instruction: they are ability tests that characterise the *person* and include measures of general abilities such as IQ, spatial ability, verbal reasoning or divergent ability. Instruction-dependent tests evaluate how well students have learned particular bodies of knowledge or skills which have been the subject of instruction. These are called *attainment* or *achievement* tests and are usually constructed by the teacher, although several commercial tests are available. The issue of whether—or rather, when—teacher-made or commercial tests should be used is discussed in Chapter 15. Our present concern is how we use tests to 'measure' learning.

In the days when the quantitative tradition reigned supreme, the information obtained from a test was quantified in a precise currency. These currency units, like those used for buying German herrings, had an exact value and even had the same name; they were called 'marks'. A test mark was something out of a hundred called a 'per cent' and a pass was 50 of them. This common currency enabled one, in those high and far off times, to compare student with student and subject with subject; determining grades was simplicity itself. In this currency, 50% was a pass, 49% was a fail; 74% was a credit but 75% was a distinction. A credit in English literature was as good as a credit in history (but oddly enough not *quite* as good as a credit in physics). Alas, all those valuable and self-evident qualities were in the eye of the beholder; they did not inhere in the test.

There are, however, ways of calibrating tests that do correspond to reality. The most suitable way for any particular occasion will depend on how the score is to be used.

Norm-referenced testing (NRT)

Norm-referenced measures are interpreted according to the performance of an individual in relation to others. The meaning of the score used, such as a rank, a standard score, or a percentile, depends on this relationship. 'Caitie was top of the class this year' is a norm-referenced statement of Caitie's ability, expressed in terms of how she compares to her population of classmates. Note, however, that it tells us nothing about what Caitie actually did, only that whatever it was, she was better at it than anyone else in her class. You cannot tell how she compares with James, who was top of a different class.

The simplest method of norm-referencing is thus ranking. Many commercial tests that compare students to some general population are also norm-referenced. IQ tests, for example, usually are designed to give an average of 100: the average score of the population is in fact set at 100 and other scores are expressed as a deviation from that average. In this case, the scores are made to fit a normal curve, so that most cluster around the mean or average, with progressively fewer and fewer people at either extreme (see Figure 14.1). In the case of intelligence, that is not a bad assumption to make.

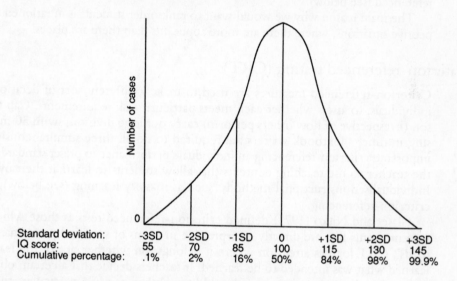

Standard deviation:	-3SD	-2SD	-1SD	0	+1SD	+2SD	+3SD
IQ score:	55	70	85	100	115	130	145
Cumulative percentage:	.1%	2%	16%	50%	84%	98%	99.9%

Figure 14.1   *The normal curve, IQ and percentage of population*
(where IQ = 100 and SD = 15)

The normal curve is not, however, the only distribution in frequent use: nor is it always the most suitable in attainment testing. HSC scores are frequently fitted to a rectangular distribution and expressed in deciles. That is, the bottom 9.9% of scores are collectively given the score '1'; the next 10% (10% to 19.9%) are given a score '2' and so on, with the top 10% (i.e., the best in the state) getting a score '10'.

All these scores, like ranks themselves, simply provide a way of discriminating between performances given by a population of students. You can't strictly compare across populations, but when large numbers of students are involved, selected according to similar criteria, it may be assumed that standards remain constant. Thus, over a whole state's HSC results, a decile of 9 in maths may, without too much problem, be thought to reflect the same level of competence as a 9 in science, and that a score of 5 in English this year will reflect the same standard as a 5 in English last year. But these are assumptions only and when NRT scores are derived from small groups of students, such as a class, cross-class comparisons *cannot* be made. All teachers know how drastically one class of the same grade and year level can differ from one year to another.

Norm-referenced measures are useful when we wish to select a few from a larger pool of people: for a job, or to enter university. In that case we need to produce a test with 'good discrimination', as it is called. Until quite recently, the elaborate technology of testing was designed precisely to do this. Likewise, if we wish to compare students against some reference group, NRT may be used. Diagnostic testing for a long time used the notion of stating a student's ability in age norms: a reading age of 10 years 5 months, meaning that this student is reading at a level of skill typical of a student of 10:5. In vocational guidance, a given student's profile of test scores may be compared with that of a particular occupational group. If student and group profile match, the counsellor might agree that the student's abilities are in keeping with those needed for the occupation; if they mismatched, the student would probably be advised against joining that occupation. Diagnostic testing or vocational guidance can, however, also be criterion-referenced (see below).

The main reason why we would want to rank order students is in rationed or competitive situations, where there are more applicants than there are places.

Criterion-referenced testing (CRT)

Criterion-referenced measures are used to make a different sort of decision about individuals: to assess whether each meets particular task requirements. Can this person (irrespective of how others perform) carry out long division, swim 50 metres, or sing in tune? (Textbook writers are required to do all three simultaneously.) Most important, criterion-referencing an individual's performance to preset standards enables the teacher to use teaching contexts that allow students to learn at their own pace. Individualised instructional methods, such as mastery learning (see below), rely on criterion-referencing.

Glaser and Nitko (1971) defined criterion-referenced tests as those which 'yield measurements that are directly interpretable in terms of specified performance standards'. CRT focuses attention where it belongs: on whether or not the learner has learned what was intended to be learned. If teachers decide that a certain objective is important, their major concern should be whether or not a particular student has achieved it, rather than how much of it was achieved relative to others in the class (Airasian & Madaus 1972; Popham & Husek 1969).

A common example of CRT is a driving test. In order to pass the test, one has typically to demonstrate:

* verbal knowledge of the traffic rules (usually around 80% accuracy); and
* pass–fail prowess in driving around a set route.

The purpose here is to ensure that all drivers have a minimal level of competence; setting that level is a matter of judgment independent of the testing event. If everyone, or nobody, passed the test on the first go, then no doubt questions might be asked about the suitability of the standards. But say the roads became very crowded and it was necessary to restrict the numbers passing the test. The CRT way of handling that would of course be to raise the standards, but you can't then predict accurately how many will pass. If it is important that only a definite, fixed number pass the test, then NRT is the answer; such a test would be designed to separate the required number of better drivers from the rest; the requirements and conditions of giving such a driving test would then be quite different from those which currently exist.

In instruction based on CRT, then, the objectives are the important thing. One school of thought advocated that all objectives should be *behavioural*: the student's behaviour had to be clearly and specifiably different after instruction from what it was before (Mager 1961). Such objectives would state, for instance:

The student will be able to correctly select, in at least 9 choices out of 10, which poem had been written by Milton and which by a lesser contemporary.

Instead of:

The student will be able to appreciate Milton's style.

The second version is vague; it does not say what the student has to do in order to show what 'to appreciate' means, nor does it specify a criterion saying that learning is sufficient. Thus behavioural objectives contain a *verb* and a *criterion*; Gronlund (1970) lists hundreds of them for different subjects. The problem with behavioural objectives, as you might have seen already, is that even something so uplifting as 'appreciating Milton' is tied down to earth in a way that oversimplifies, possibly even trivialises (McDonald-Ross 1973). And, of course, behavioural objectives are founded in a highly quantitative tradition that reduces all to numbers.

We should consider the relationship between NRT and CRT and formative and summative evaluation. Formative evaluation only makes sense when it is criterion-referenced. CRT can tell us that the student:

- gets 17 words correct out of 20;
- regularly makes errors in a particular mathematical operation; and
- keeps referring to 12 year olds as 'being at a certain SOLO level'.

In the first case, the feedback probably leads to no further action, but in the second (and the third), something is clearly wrong (particularly if you don't see what is wrong with the last one, in which case turn to p. 396). What errors in particular? Why was each made? How can they be remediated? Pointing out that a student is better or worse than others in the class at doing these things is unhelpful from the formative point of view.

Summative evaluation, on the other hand, may quite logically be based on either NRT or CRT. There are two stages to summative evaluation. First, we must derive the standard for awarding a mark or grade; second, we may then determine how each student is to be awarded that grade. In NRT, both stages are amalgamated: the group characteristics (e.g., how far above or below the mean) determine simultaneously what the standard is and where the student stands in relation to that standard. In CRT, however, the standard is determined first, which may quite reasonably be based on a norm-determined standard (e.g., the quality of work of the previous year's top 20% of students). Or it may be done *a priori*: by deciding that, given the nature of the task, such-and-such a standard is 'reasonable'. Then, once the standard has been fixed, the final grade or statement as to any student's performance is determined by its relation to that standard, *independently* of the grade or statement made about any other student in the group. It is the last step that makes the test criterion-referenced, not the first. Both students and teachers often confuse a norm-determined *standard* with norm-referenced *testing*.

As far back as 1918, Thorndike distinguished what we today call NRT and CRT and predicted that 'the latter seems to represent the type which will prevail if education follows the course of development of the physical Sciences' (quoted in Airasian and Madaus

1972). But education did not follow that course of development, but instead used a model of evaluation that *maximised differences between individuals,* not one that assessed the differences between an individual's performance and some absolute standard.

Mastery learning strategy

Mastery learning is a teaching strategy that is based on CRT and presupposes the closest links between learning and evaluation (Block 1971; Bloom, Hastings & Madaus 1971). It is used in areas such as core skills which all or most students may reasonably be expected to master. Testing is criterion-referenced; 'mastery' is defined in advance, usually to a '90:90' criterion, that is, 90% of the students pass 90% of the items in the test (which is, of course, a highly quantitative view of success in learning).

Where core skills can be defined fairly exactly—for example, spelling or calculation is correct or incorrect; facts are known or they are not known—mastery learning becomes a very logical way of approaching the task (see Box 14.1).

Box 14.1   *The place for mastery learning*

A level of performance is specified for mastery of the tasks set. If a student reaches this level, the instructional sequence is considered to have been successful for that student. If a student does not reach the mastery level, then additional teaching or alternative approaches will need to be used until he has mastered the objectives of the program. There is no place in this process for comparisons between one student and another. It is not helpful to demonstrate that Bill Smith is not as good as Mary Jones at long division, but just that he is not yet good enough to perform this operation confidently and needs further tuition. This approach to assessment would seem to be essential in the core area of the basic skills if all students are to reach a predefined standard of competence.

Source: Keeves, Matthews & Bourke, 1978, p. 59.

If the student fails the first test, one does not award an 'F' and then move on to the next topic; the teacher uses the formative feedback provided by the test. What items were failed? What appears to be the difficulty? The topic is then retaught and tested again. This procedure is repeated until the test is passed at the criterion level of mastery. Then the next topic in the sequence is taken.

The theory behind mastery learning is that performance is a function of two main factors: time on task and ability. Simply, bright students need to take less time to learn something to the same level of competence as do dull students. Thus—conversely—dull students can be brought up to the level of competence displayed by brighter students *if they spend more time on the task.* But the task must be a 'reasonable' one for that person, otherwise the time needed for some people may be too long. In fact, it has been demonstrated that if only the slowest 5% are omitted, the slowest learners will take about six times longer to 'master' a basic topic in the primary school than the fastest (Glaser 1968). Is that too long? Remember: the longer the time and the more the repeats, the more bored and alienated the student may become.

Mastery learning is therefore reserved for basic skills, such as literacy and numeracy, on which it *is* reasonable to expect mastery from most students. Second, while one would not prescribe too much time on task, for both logistic and motivational reasons, when we look at what happens in school we see a very odd thing. Time is held constant for all students, regardless of ability—and yet we expect most to achieve mastery! Of course, most do not. This is why IQ correlates with school performance: teach every student a topic for 40 minutes and then test them and the distribution of scores will follow the normal curve on which the IQ test is based (a few do well, most so-so, a few badly). If we decide to teach each person for as long as it took to reach mastery, we would then find that *time on task* correlated with IQ and followed the normal curve, while performance scores would all be at or above 90%. So what is important: to arrange the school day so that teachers can conveniently move around in 40-minute time slots, or that students should learn what they are supposed to learn?

But of course you don't get something for nothing, not even under mastery learning. While the slower learners are achieving mastery on basics, the faster learners, having reached their basic attainment targets long since, will be learning other, more interesting, non-core material. So differences between students will remain. The question is: Do we want all to know the core facts and skills, but slow learners will get little beyond that (a lot about a little), or slow learners to know little adequately but on a broad front (a little about a lot)?

Part of the answer to that not quite rhetorical question is provided by Bloom (in Block 1971) when he emphasises the affective consequences of mastery learning: that students in a mastery model have a better self-concept. He argues that it is better for the slower students to know a few things competently than to fail at most things; and he is probably right, particularly in those areas where society expects competence, such as literacy and numeracy.

Mastery learning, then, is not a method of teaching so much as a logistic; a decision not to teach an individual more until mastery in the preceding material is displayed. It is therefore best suited for content that is sequential and that permits clear-cut decisions as to learning progress. And that is seen as another problem.

Critics of mastery learning and of CRT say that it is only suitable for testing low level outcomes. Satterly (1980) says the most 'fundamental' objection to CRT 'concerns its psychological parentage' (p. 52): Behaviourism. CRT, in other words, is seen in Cole's first group of quantitative conceptions, along with behavioural objectives (see above and Cole 1990). There is something to be said for this view. P. Lai (1991) taught Year 10 biology conventionally and in four mastery learning units; students were classified as 'deep-bias' or 'surface-bias' on the basis of their responses to the *Learning Process Questionnaire*. Deep-bias students initially preferred mastery learning and did well in the first unit, but they subsequently found it boring and did progressively worse. Surface-bias students, on the other hand, started poorly, but by the fourth unit performed significantly better than the deep-bias students. Mastery learning thus appears to be the teaching strategy to use for surface-oriented students, as one would expect from the nature of that teaching strategy as it is usually applied, which is to teach and test in cumulative bits.

However, CRT need not necessarily target low cognitive levels, nor need it follow the 90:90 mastery model. If the attainment targets are set on *qualitative* rather than quantitative grounds, the backwash effect from focusing on high level outcomes would probably benefit both teaching and learning. When tests and exams are perceived to require accurate reproduction of detail, both teacher and learner will focus on that content and use teaching and learning strategies to enhance retention. But when testing is seen to require higher order thinking, both teacher and learner adapt to bring higher order strategies to bear.

Item response theory (IRT)

One of the troubles with NRT is that the unit of measurement is completely bland: a statistical deviation unit, with little logical relation to what has been taught and, unless the samples are large and random, the unit is elastic. One of the troubles with CRT, on the other hand, is that its emphasis on precision undoubtedly encourages the use of low cognitive level items. Further, NRT is tied to particular conditions of testing, CRT to particular items; one is context-specific, the other instrument-specific. It is as if you had to measure the temperature of the oven with one kind of thermometer and the weather outside with another, each calibrated in different units that were not mutually convertible (Choppin 1982).

In the last 30 years a new model of measurement has arisen that claims to meet these difficulties: *item response theory* (IRT), of which the best known example is the Rasch Model (Andrich 1982; Crocker & Algina 1986; Wright & Stone 1979). In this model it is assumed that the chances of a student getting an item correct depend on:

- the difficulty of the item; and
- the ability of the student in that content area;

and do *not* depend on:

- how other students perform (as NRT assumes); or
- the particular items making up the test (as CRT assumes).

The ability referred to is a 'latent trait', or personal characteristic, that is assumed to account for performance. This does not mean an innate ability, but *any* trainable competency, in the sense meant in Chapter 4 (such as bridge-playing, adding involving carrying), that can be accessed by performance items of some kind and where items vary in difficulty, but not too widely. Knowing the difficulty of the items, it is possible to estimate the ability of the students with respect to the trait underlying the items; that trait is expressed in units of difficulty called 'logits' or 'brytes', depending on the mathematics used. That same trait can then be accessed by a different set of items, which makes testing and retesting on a competency independent of any *particular* set of items (this may be used in practically important ways, as we see below in the example of the RAPT mathematics tests). There are several ways of doing this; the Rasch model is the simplest and the one most widely used. The mathematics need not concern us here, but the principle is an important one.

There are several *advantages* of the Rasch model:

- Student performance on different tests can be calibrated on what may be assumed to be the same scale, which combines the advantages of both NRT and CRT.
- Maximum information is squeezed out of a small number of items, so tests can be quite short and still yield reliable and valid information.
- Items can be calibrated and placed in an *item bank*, so that completely parallel or equivalent tests can be constructed very quickly. For example, teachers could give a short test before instruction and again afterwards, using completely different items, but remaining sure that they are measuring the same underlying competency (e.g., adding with carrying).

- Item banking could be used to overcome the clumsiness of present moderation procedures, where whole schools are tested and an individual student's score depends on the 'ration' of top decile scores allocated to that school.
- Instruction may be completely individualised, as in CRT.
- Microcomputers can be used at all stages: calibrating items, testing individuals, drawing on items from an item bank that are novel for that student, and providing scaled scores on the competencies in question; and (a separate issue) for maintaining complete and highly accessible records of student progress.

The main *disadvantages* of the Rasch model:

- The obvious one: it seems complicated and mystifying. Even though micros can do all the dirty work, and professional organisations such as ACER all the development and banking of items, the public's likely understanding of a student's score as so many brytes on a latent trait (or anything that doesn't range from 0 to 100) is likely to be minimal (Spearitt 1982).
- The experts disagree (surprisingly violently) on the mathematics and the assumptions (Goldstein 1979). But as Choppin (1982) points out, using a flat, two-dimensional, road map to help find your way in a bumpy 3-D world also violates some very basic assumptions, yet road maps work. So too, Choppin says, does the Rasch model.

From a practitioner's point of view, existing Rasch-based tests are encouraging. In ACER's *review* and *progress* tests (RAPT) in mathematics, for example, the review test (only 10 or so items) covers the competency needed for completing a set of objectives, while the progress tests address each objective (and are even shorter). The review tests can be used as a pre-test to determine the level of each student before teaching a particular topic: students can then be taken individually (or in small groups according to competency) in a mastery format until the particular objectives identified in the progress tests have been mastered. A review test can also be given after a period of teaching to determine where the students stand with respect to the topic. All this is possible because review and progress scores are expressed in units that may be directly compared with each other (Izard & White 1982).

Effects of testing on learning and teaching

Academic work is mainly directed towards earning points for a grade and preparing for tests and examinations which require recall of factual information and application of procedures. Thus examinations and tests have a strong effect on how students engage in classrooms. (Tobin & Fraser 1988: 76)

It is well known that the assessment tail wags the educational dog; tests 'drive instruction to concentrate only on what these tests seem to measure' (Snow 1990: 455; see also Frederiksen & Collins 1989; Hoffman 1962; Nickerson 1989). This effect is referred to as *backwash,* which, like the outcomes of learning themselves, may be cognitive or affective, with each influencing both teaching and learning.

You can't beat backwash, but you can minimise it or, better still, make it work for improved learning, not for worse. The trouble is, it usually is for worse, as Box 14.2 clearly states:

Box 14.2   *How to pass in psychology*

I hate to say it, but what you have got to do is to have a list of 'facts'; you write down the important points and memorise those, then you'll do all right in the test—if you can give a bit of factual information—so and so did that and concluded that—for two sides of writing, then you'll get a good mark.

(Ramsden 1984: 144)

Now how did this student get *that* idea?

When it is perceived that grades in tests and exams can be maximised by accurately reproducing detail (whatever the tester's intentions in setting the test), both teacher and learner will focus on that content and use teaching and learning strategies to enhance retention. But when testing is seen to require higher order thinking, the challenge for both teacher and learner is accordingly different and will require higher order strategies from each.

Take yourself back to your schooldays. The teacher has just announced that she is going to deal with a topic you are particularly interested in. Imagine three possibilities:

1. At the end of the week, she is going to test you on your knowledge of the topic by a *multiple choice* test.
2. At the end of the week, she is going to test you on your knowledge of the topic by an *essay*.
3. You are not going to be tested at all.

Think about how you will go about learning in each of the three cases: what sort of things you will pay attention to, what you would *do* (take notes, self-test, etc.), what *feelings* you are likely to have about the learning and the testing.

Cognitive backwash

The cognitive effects describe your strategies for learning for the test and then your strategies for approaching the test itself. For example, if you thought that the multiple choice test was going to focus on the facts and details, then those are what you would focus your attention on, and would probably note them down and periodically recite them to yourself, to make sure you could remember them correctly.

If you thought you were going to write an essay, then you would probably try to outguess the teacher: what things is she/he likely to be looking for? Facts and details (essay markers can focus on these just as much as can objective tests); an application of the topic to a new area; your own personal views? According to what you expect, so shall you prepare for the essay. In preparing for an end-of-term test, Tang (1991) showed that physiotherapy students chose test-taking strategies that accurately reproduced professionally relevant data and avoided deep strategies; in preparing for an assignment mode of assessing the same course, students switched to assignment-writing strategies that were deep-related but restricted to the topics dealt with. Further, these strategy preferences correlated with the performance in the appropriate assessment format; the students were wise to have been test-wise.

In learning complex subject matter, it is often difficult to pre-set the criteria of good learning in terms of high level outcomes, but not impossible. There are ways of indexing high level outcomes, and then the backwash effect from focusing on these high level outcomes can benefit both teaching and learning.

Cognitive backwash does not, of course, only affect the students' learning, but also the teachers' teaching. Where external examinations are important, teachers see it as their responsibility to package content that is likely to be tested and teach it in an expository fashion, requiring detailed note-taking by students and accurate reproduction of the content so taught (Morris 1985).

The problem is more subtle than it seems. Except for quite specific cases, such as a spelling test, responsible teachers do not *deliberately* set tests requiring low level processes. Tests usually assess low level teaching and learning processes *indirectly*. In indirect tests, what purports to be a high level cognitive skill is measured by more directly observable features of performance that relate to the skill (Frederiksen & Collins 1989); for instance, because calculating skill relates to problem solving, a student can appear to get a high score on 'problem solving' just by getting a bunch of sums right. In *direct* (or 'authentic') tests, the skill in question can only be solved by doing what is required; for example, getting a high score in practice teaching, although you *could* beat that by paying the students to be very very good when the supervisor drops in.

Affective backwash

The backwash effects of testing are different in NRT as in CRT. A common affective reaction to the prospect of testing is test anxiety, which as we have seen in Chapter 9 is based on the fear of failure, a common reaction of low need-achievers (see Chapter 10) and which is almost always deleterious to performance. The complementary reaction, experienced by high need-achievers, is to use the testing situation in order to demonstrate their brilliance, relative to others in the class. The affective backwash is thus entirely different, depending on the students' motivational orientation. It also depends on where they are studying (Box 14.3):

Affective backwash from NRT versus CRT

NRT necessarily involves competition and the affective backwash will vary according to the achievement orientation of the student: whether it is seen as an exhilarating challenge, or an ominous threat. The coping strategies that are then adopted vary enormously according to individual motivation: whether to maximise the public signs of learning by striving for the highest marks possible, or to minimise the threat to self, by deliberately not trying.

CRT may of course produce unpleasant affective outcomes too, but the focus here logically is on demonstrating the level of skill or knowledge required. Knowing that the outcome of what is to be tested will not vary according to who else happens to be taking the test makes it possible to work towards the requisite level.

The link between affective backwash from NRT and CRT and the subsequent effect on cognitive strategies is clearly brought out in the study by Ames and Archer (1988), already seen as the basis of a task in Chapter 11. They distinguish *performance* goals, which emphasise success in a norm-referenced context (where success is seen as competing with and beating others) and *mastery* goals, which emphasise success in a criterion-referenced context (where success is seen as acquiring new skills or knowledge).

Box 14.3   *To what extent do undergraduates worry about assessment? It depends where they are studying.*

Worries at:

A Metropolitan CAE	*A Rural CAE*	*A Coastal Resort CAE*
★ Number of assignments	Particular subjects	? Size of workload
★ Sitting examinations	? Size of workload	★ Exams
★ Size of assignments	Particular lecturers	Particular subjects
★ Low assessment results	Money	Particular lecturers
★ Assessment deadlines	Study motivation	Study motivation
? Class presentations	★ Exams	Money
? Course workload	? Poor study skills	Computers
Own expectations	Career prospects	Library
★ Spacing of exams	Lecturers unavailable	Following lectures
? Class assignments	Computers	? Poor study skills
★ Number of exams	Following lectures	Career prospects
Unclear instructions	? Essay writing	? Essay writing

★ Definitely assessment-related   ? Possibly assessment-related

It's easy to see where assessment exerts the pressure and where the problems are about learning or earning.

Adapted from: Sarros & Densten (1989); Bradley, McLachlan, & Sparks (1990).

Students in classrooms with a mastery goal orientation not only liked their schoolwork more, but preferred challenging tasks, believed that success was dependent on the effort they put in rather than their ability, and were more likely to use effective learning strategies, than students in classrooms with performance goal orientations.

The backwash effect of testing is thus not only a matter of the test itself, but the context and framework within which it is carried out.

Evaluation and the growth of competence

Chapters 2 and 3 looked at the development of cognitive competence both within and across modes, Chapter 8 at information processing, and Chapter 12 at metacognitive processes in learning. A complex picture emerges, telling us what constitutes the kind of learning that schools might be intended to foster and what, therefore, needs monitoring and evaluating. We are not only talking about the acquisition and reproduction of declarative knowledge in the form of isolated facts, or procedural knowledge in the form of reproducible skills, but about higher order knowledge and skills, ways of interpreting the world, and feelings we have about our competence in interacting with the world (Shepard 1991).

Learners' comprehension of taught content is gradual and cumulative, with qualitative changes taking place in the nature both of what is learned and how it is structured. To take a cross-section of isolated aspects of learning at any one point in the learning sequence, and counting to see which ones are 'correct' and which 'incorrect', is simply missing the point. It is rather like evaluating a movie by snipping out every hundredth frame, blowing up each into a large photograph and putting them in sequence. You might get some excellent shots, but you'll miss the plot. If the prospect of winning an Oscar is in the offing, then the director will work on producing the maximum number of beautiful stills, not on crafting an integral work of art.

That, when you think about it, is what conventional assessment philosophy and techniques have been doing and, like the director working on the stills, the learning process has been distorted; some pretty little snaps, maybe, but the surge and drama of learning is missed. Most current models of attainment testing assume learning proceeds in discrete quanta, in units described as correct/incorrect, which may be summed to give an aggregate or total score. In most objective tests, what is important is the total sum of items correct, any one item being 'worth' the same as any other. In standard methods of test construction and item analysis, items are selected on the extent to which they correlate with the total test score, as explained in Chapter 15, not in terms of their intrinsic content.

These procedures indicate a highly quantitative view of the nature of knowledge, which is quite adequate for items that are *intended* to be learned at a low cognitive level, such as spellings and formulae. It is not, however, adequate when dealing with more complex, developing concepts, when these assumptions break down at every point. Is a 5 year old's understanding of subtraction as adding-on *wrong*? Can you count the quanta of understandings displayed when a child describes why metal feels colder than plastic? Is an understanding of gravity worth the same in this standard currency as an understanding of mechanics, or of the principle of diminishing returns? When we add up exam marks, thereby treating responses to different questions as equivalent, we are violating what we know about the learning process.

Instead of marking children's evolving and partially correct ideas as 'incorrect', we should give credit for what they do know and see how far they are along the road towards the position we currently hold, thus integrating students' progressive interpretations of their experience with assessment technology (Masters 1987; Messick 1984). Attainment testing should reflect where students stand in relation to this orderly development of competence, rather than where they stand in relation to each other. Teachers would then be able to see how far along the path towards expertise given students, or a whole class, may be with respect to particular concepts, skills, or other curriculum content. In such a model, the attainment targets are defined in terms of the natural growth in the development of a concept.

You will of course have recognised that, as far as evaluation is concerned, we are talking about CRT, when the performance criteria are defined not in quantitative but in qualitative terms and about 'authentic' assessment that is grounded in the context in which it is learned and taught (Maguire 1990). It may even be possible to go from there to a mastery approach; *test*, to see if the qualitatively defined performance target is reached and if not, *reteach* until it is. CRT does not have to belong to the quantitative conception. Conceived in this way, 'criterion-referencing is a powerful aid to efficient and effective learning' (Commonwealth Schools Commission 1987: 75).

Frameworks for defining the quality of learning

There are several conceptual systems that could be used to define 'good' learning. A major distinction can be made between those that are generalised across different content areas, those that are content-specific and those which generalise from a content-specific foundation. Models that generalise across content areas focus on task structure (Biggs & Collis 1982a; Harvey, Hunt & Schroder 1961), judgments as to learning level (Bloom et al. 1956), or the originality or elegance of the problem solutions (Guilford 1967). Some frameworks use both general and specific aspects; the novice–expert framework focuses on the use made of abstract principles resulting from specific experience (Chi, Glaser & Farr 1988). Other models, such as those of the alternative frameworks researchers, focus entirely on the specific topic being learned (Marton 1981; Driver 1985). The topic-specific models address learning outcomes directly, but make it difficult to generalise about competence across topics. The general models require translation if they are to apply to particular topics, but make a techology of evaluation somewhat easier to construct. Let us start with the most general.

Bloom taxonomy

The Bloom taxonomy (Bloom et al. 1956) was derived by analysing the opinions of some 2000 educators concerning good learning. When these opinions were classified, Bloom and his colleagues constructed a hierarchy comprising six levels of response, ordered in increasingly levels of quality:

1. *Knowledge:* rote reproduction of the correct responses.
2. *Comprehension:* explaining the response in the student's words.
3. *Application:* applying the knowledge to a practical situation.
4. *Analysis:* to be able to isolate the crucial components of the knowledge.
5. *Synthesis:* recombining elements to yield new knowledge.
6. *Evaluation:* applying higher order principles to test the worth of the new knowledge.

The Bloom taxonomy has been influential. Possibly because it is not an empirical model of the way students learn, but reflects the opinions of what teachers think about student learning, it has mainly been used as a guide for selecting test questions or items (the teacher's contribution), rather than for analysing and evaluating the quality of responses (the student's contribution). In practice, however, it is often difficult to devise items that draw out levels of response quality much above comprehension, so that the taxonomy has been under-used at the higher levels (Anderson 1972).

The SOLO taxonomy

The SOLO taxonomy, already met in Chapter 3 and elsewhere, is used to classify the outcome, the student's response, not the item that is to elicit the response. SOLO is based on the empirical study of students' responses in several content areas, not educators' opinions, so that direct comparisons between the Bloom and SOLO taxonomies are inappropriate. Each is based on different data, to do different jobs.

The SOLO taxonomy may be used in two main ways. First, it can be used as a means of assessment, either by classifying responses to open questions, or by classifying questions to elicit specified levels of response. Second, and more comprehensively, it can be used as a broad framework for structuring curriculum objectives across primary, secondary and, to an extent, the tertiary sectors. How this may be done in secondary school science is outlined in Collis and Biggs (1989). Measurement of those objectives is discussed in Chapter 15. The framework itself was described in Chapter 3.

Novice–expert

In studying the development of expertise across a wide variety of areas, Glaser (1990) points out that the knowledge base becomes increasingly:

1. *Coherent*. It does not comprise isolated bits and pieces (multistructural), but increasingly well-organised and restructured chunks (relational). An expert can tell you how this piece relates to that: a novice cannot.
2. *Principled*. The restructuring of knowledge isn't only weak, but radical, in the sense meant by Vosniadou and Brewer (1987) (see also Chapter 2, p. 53). Experts identify principles to work from, while novices stick with surface features. In SOLO terms, the expert's knowledge base is organised at both relational and extended abstract levels.
3. *Useful*. A novice and an expert might score equally on a multiple-choice test of knowledge of a domain, but the expert would be able to put that knowledge to use. It is not simply declarative, but also conditional, knowledge; the expert has learned the conditions under which the knowledge may work.
4. *Goal-oriented*. The expert has the knowledge lined up in a context, which makes one able to monitor progress, predict outcomes, judge the difficulty of the task, manage time effectively, assess the relevance of knowledge. These self-regulatory, or metacognitive, skills are additional to domain knowledge, but the domain-specific foundation is essential for effective strategy use (Alexander & Judy 1988).

Glaser's points bring together the need for both specificity and generality in the creation of knowledge, but testing for expertise requires that we assess the general: high level of abstraction, transfer to new fields, and ability to stand aside and monitor oneself. Each one of these areas is a candidate for assessment of both outcome and process levels.

Bloom, SOLO, and Glaser address the schooled, non-spontaneous, route of knowledge construction and its expression in the concrete-symbolic mode. Topic-specific models allow for expressions of meaning in other modes, particularly the ikonic, and for the acquisition of knowledge through extracurricular, spontaneous experience.

Topic-specific models of increasing competence

The research by Driver and others into the frameworks children use to construe scientific phenomena has already been described in Chapter 3. Another approach that similarly focuses on the development of understanding of particular aspects of reality has been independently formalised by Marton and his coworkers in Gothenburg, Sweden, in what is called *phenomenography* (Marton 1981, 1988; Ramsden 1988). It is based on the two perspectives, first-order and second-order, that are present during a learning situation. The first-order perspective, the objective description of the event, such as might be given by a researcher or a teacher, would describe whether the student met the criteria of learning, as defined by the outsider; Marton calls this 'comprehension', not learning. That is, the learner may 'comprehend' or 'take on board' the first-order perspective, more or less, but actually *learns* what is constructed from the second-order perspective.

'Learning' is therefore not what *should* have been learned but what *has* been learned; what sense the student has found in the text, or learning episode. It is this aspect of learning that is described as an alternative framework in exactly the same sense as we have met in Chapter 3, while the first-order perspective describes the accepted framework.

As with the study of alternative frameworks, Marton and his colleagues have found that:

A discovery of decisive importance was that for each phenomenon, principle, or aspect of reality, the understanding of which we studied, there seemed to exist a limited number of qualitatively different conceptions of that phenomenon, principle, or aspect of reality. (Johansson, Marton & Svensson 1985: 235–6)

Alternative frameworks tend to stop at naive theories, which construct the complex with simple attempts. Phenomenographic work takes this a little further in that these naive conceptions form a hierarchy, often following that in the history of science, from vague, through increasingly precise, to scientifically acceptable, conceptions. We have actually come across one such hierarchical ordering of conceptions of learning itself (pp. 20–1). Another example is the phenomenography of the mole concept in high school chemistry (Lybeck, Marton, Stromdahl & Tullberg 1988), which has five conceptions of ascending complexity. Such conceptual hierarchies are remarkably stable, being found in student interviews in different educational systems, in different countries, and as has been said in different eras in the history of science. Each such conception is said to be 'relational' (Marton 1988); this has nothing to do with SOLO relational, but refers to the relation the individual has to the world. What conception I have of a topic describes my 'relation' to the world, as far as that topic is concerned. All of this suggests that the hierarchies describe a natural progression in the learning of the concept, rather like a SOLO learning cycle. A major difference is that the number of levels is different for different concepts, but those levels can be used in the same way as SOLO levels for defining the assessment targets in CRT.

A simple example involves only two levels. Marton (1988) refers to three different situations all of which are common in a senior secondary context: reading and drawing conclusions from a text. In one such, the text was about the welfare system, the message being to advocate a 'systems approach' to family problems (a 'systems approach' to the classroom is described in Chapter 16). The example was one Erik Jansson, married with three children, alcoholic, his wife has a stomach ulcer, the oldest boy steals cars. The text then gives lurid details of the hapless Janssons. The systems approach is to work with the whole family to explore solutions with them, instead of imposing expensive ones against their will and which don't work, such as committing Jansson to an institution for alcoholics and the oldest boy to a community home.

The respondents in this study were Swedish adults who had been interviewed about the welfare system. After reading the text, they were simply asked: 'Could you tell me what this text is about?' (Marton 1988: 56). Two groups of responses were found. Typical of the first:

A. 'It's about a low-wage family, three children, where the father has an alcohol problem ...'

And of the second:

B. 'Above all, it's about social welfare and how to master it. Here, they take up an example of a family—do you want me to tell you the whole story?'

A saw the text as about the Janssons (*and* about social welfare—in some vague sense) (Marton 1988:58), while *B* saw the text as about the welfare system, with the Jansson saga as only illustrative of a general point. One focused on the details, the other on the theme, as constructed from the details.

Marton talks about 'figure' and 'ground' becoming confused. The figure here should be the welfare system, seen against the background of the Janssons of this world; another way of putting the same point is to talk of the level of abstraction. The figure is the more abstract, the ground more concrete. Early in the learning process, one focuses on the ground but some never get beyond.

What has this to do with assessment? Some techniques, by testing for detail, focus attention on the ground, thereby creating the backwash that may actually prevent the proper message—the figure—from being perceived. How difficult it may be to detach from the ground to perceive the figure may be gauged from the perceptual example in Figure 14.2. If you focus on the white, the black becomes the ground and you see a pedestal. If, however, you focus on the black, the white becomes the ground and you see two faces.

Figure 14.2 *The figure-ground problem*

Let us translate this figure–ground situation to learning. If the details become the figure, then the higher, thematic level information may be lost. Imagine the message, or mental set, that is created when we set tests requiring detailed recall:

- 'How many children did the Janssons have?'
- 'Mrs Jansson stole cars. True or false?'

Setting such questions, and thereby creating in students the expectation that being able to supply such answers constitutes the point of reading the text, is really a very peculiar thing to do, when the message we want the students to get from the text is that it is about the welfare system!

Targets for assessment

Given these different models, what may we conclude should be the targets when assessing learning? There is a range of targets:

- domain-specific, declarative knowledge as displayed in learning outcomes;
- procedural and conditional knowledge that would indicate how well the learner can make that declarative knowledge work;
- self-management and metacognitive skills within and across content areas.

Snow (1989) has a similar list, but he adds in motivational orientation and, in particular, effort investment. He also suggests that the growth of competence in a particular task or topic should be assessed:

1. at the initial state of learning;
2. during the period of transformation during instruction; and
3 at the desired end-state.

Transitions from 1 through to 3 should then be monitored immediately on-task, daily, weekly and monthly. Fortunately, he insists that any such emerging testing technology should be easily accessible to and used by teachers; a daunting array here of what to test and when to test it.

To summarise and to bring the matter down to size, we can define several domains of learning that assessment might reasonably address.

At the level of *outcomes*:

- *what* has been taught as domain-specific declarative knowledge in particular subject areas (the traditional target of assessment). We need to know:

  (a) *how much* of what has been taught has been assimilated in some way. This is usually what we mean by 'coverage', which (let's face it) is a quantitative concept and is assessed by tests of recall, comprehension item by item (Bloom: knowledge, comprehension; SOLO uni-, multistructural).

  (b) *how well* what has been taught has been learned. This requires qualitative assessment: open-ended questions accessing structure, level of abstraction (facts, concepts, principles; higher SOLO and Bloom levels), elegance, originality (as appropriate to area).

- *how far* students can operate from the base and context in which they have originally been taught. That is, the ability to transfer procedural knowledge acquired in one domain to another domain (extended abstract responding) and knowing when and under what conditions transfer is possible.

And at the level of *process:*

- *task-related*: knowing how to operate key tasks in literacy, maths, science. Included would be: writing and note-taking skills, how to observe and summarise obervations, collating data.
- *self-related*: knowing one's limitations and capabilities, how to schedule time, self-management, study skills.

The question of how to test these targets is the subject of the next chapter.

Summary

Learning, evaluation and assessment

The terms 'evaluation', 'assessment', 'testing' and 'examinations' have come progressively to connote something from the bad to the downright horrible. Yet testing and learning should be 'integral events', as Glaser puts it. Evaluation is a matter of *making judgments* about learning, at any level: curriculum, teaching and learning processes, and teaching and learning outcomes. Our focus here is on process and outcome. Evaluation can be formative or summative. Assessment has come to mean summative evaluation: grading.

Quantitative and qualitative traditions in evaluation

All evaluation to date has been conducted either from a quantitative or a qualitative tradition. Both traditions have their place, but in practice, and until very recently, the quantitative tradition has been the most prevalent, giving rise to the current technology of objective test and item selection. Methods of 'authentic' assessment, based on qualitative theories of learning and in which contexts are devised to assess student learning at the cognitive levels applying in everyday life, are currently being developed.

Calibrating tests

A test provides information about the learner's progress and may take many forms. That information is usually quantified, a process that can distort as well as inform. Two ways of 'calibrating' tests to yield information are norm-referenced testing (NRT) and criterion-referenced testing (CRT). NRT derives its scores from the extent to which students' performances differ from each other; CRT from the extent to which students' performances differ from a predetermined standard. NRT is especially useful for selection purposes; CRT for finding out what is actually accomplished. Mastery learning is a teaching strategy based on CRT. Each testing model has problems of generality: NRT is restricted to its norming population, CRT to the test items used. Item response theory (IRT) is an attempt to meet both problems, but has yet to make a general impact on educational practice.

Effects of testing on learning and teaching

Tests follow instruction in time, but their anticipation determines how teachers teach and how learners learn; this effect is called backwash. Backwash occurs cognitively when students focus on the level and the content anticipated (in practice, this usually results in increased rote learning), and affectively when feelings induced by tests affect how students perform (in practice, this usually involves anxiety-induced and maladaptive learning strategies). Backwash is what has given testing its bad press, but this need not necessarily be so. Backwash from a suitably structured testing environment could lead to enhanced learning.

Evaluation and the growth of competence

The nature of learning should help us see what is most helpfully evaluated (and what, therefore, might signal positive backwash). Most testing to date has been founded on the quantitative tradition: that has signalled that learning comprises the accretion of items of knowledge. Learning, however, grows over time, changing qualitatively with increasing expertise; we should wish to signal to students that this is what learning is about. It enhances their maturity in coping with the world. There are several frameworks which, each in its own way, tell how far the learner has come and how far there is to go.

Frameworks for defining the quality of learning

Such frameworks include: the Bloom taxonomy, the SOLO taxonomy, expert–novice studies and, with particular reference to specific topics, phenomenography and studies of students' alternative frameworks. The first three focus on the ways of construing good learning that are general across subject matters and the last to content-specific topics.

Targets for assessment

Assessment should proceed:

(a) at the level of outcomes.

- What has been taught as domain-specific declarative knowledge, (i) quantitatively to see how much has been learned ('coverage') and (ii) qualitatively, to see how well it has been learned?
- Can students successfully transfer what has been taught in one context to a new context? Do they know when and under what conditions transfer is possible?

And (b) at the level of process.

- Do students know how to operate key tasks in literacy, maths, science, etc.?
- Do students know their limitations and capabilities, how to schedule time, how to plan, to use self-management and study skills?

The following chapter deals with the practical questions of how to test these targets.

Learning activities

1. Norm-referenced and criterion-referenced tests

We devoted a fair section of this chapter to the differences between norm referencing and criterion referencing and the associated benefits and problems of each. The purpose of this task is to summarise that information and present it in some condensed form such as a concept map, tree diagram or matrix. Your information should encompass similarities, differences, advantages and disadvantages of CRT and NRT.

As an extension of this activity you could examine a range of commonly used tests (say in reading), categorising them as NRT or CRT. What do you think you will find? Does it depend upon the subject area you examine? If you choose teacher designed tests rather than published 'standardised' tests, would there be differences in the proportion of NRT to CRT tests?

2. State-wide testing

In many educational systems there have been movements for state-wide testing in the basic skills. For instance, since the late 1980s all Year 6 and selected Year 3 students in New South Wales state schools have been tested on the basic skills of literacy and numeracy. What are the advantages and disadvantages of state-wide testing? What type of 'backwash' might there be to state-wide testing? Develop two cases for presentation to your colleagues: the case for state-wide assessment and the case against such testing.

3. Item response theory

We saw in this chapter that item response theory and one particular rendition (the Rasch model) were attempts to meet the difficulties inherent in CRT and NRT. This activity addresses your understanding of the details as well as the principles of Rasch modelling by having you generate a set of questions about Rasch, using either the Bloom or SOLO taxonomies to guide your questions. If, for instance, you took the Bloom perspective, you would generate questions that would tap increasing levels of quality (from knowledge, through comprehension, application, analysis, synthesis and evaluation). These questions about Rasch and item response theory could then provide the basis for self-testing or class discussion (exchanging questions—and answers).

4. Effects of testing on learning

The purpose of this activity is to explore cognitive and affective reactions to different forms of testing by interviewing a number of students. Take the scenario about multiple-choice, essay or no testing (p. 392) and develop it for use in an interview. You might interview primary, secondary, and university students to see if there are differences across the school ages. During the interview you would present the scenario and seek information about the types of information the student would attend to (e.g., details, themes), the ways in which that information would be learned (e.g., rote, elaboratively), and the affective outcomes (e.g., feelings towards testing and learning). What are the implications of your findings for teaching (and learning!)?

If done as a class activity, separate groups could be formed to examine primary, secondary and tertiary students and the results could be brought back for class presentation and discussion.

5. Mastery learning effects

In the *Review of Educational Research*, (1987, **57**, 175–213) Slavin reconsiders the reported effects of mastery learning on performance. The article is comprehensive and detailed so that sections can be used for individual, group or whole class activities. For instance, it describes the three basic forms of mastery learning and the link between theory and practice in mastery learning (our link with CRT). Of interest might be the 'Robin Hood' phenomenon: Do the poor gain while the good lose out?

Because of the comprehensive nature of the paper, we will not suggest any particular activities here but leave it to you to decide which sections interest you. (There will be no multiple-choice questions to be completed after you've read the article!)

Further reading

On the relation between learning and assessment
Cole, N. S. (1990). Conceptions of educational achievement. *Educational Researcher*, **19**(3), 2–7.
Nickerson, R. S. (1989). New directions in educational assessment. *Educational Researcher*, **18**(9), 3–7.

Snow, R. E. (1989). Toward assessment of cognitive and conative structures in learning. *Educational Researcher*, **18**(9), 8–14.

The fact that these articles are suddenly appearing in the American Educational Research Association's bulletin shows what's worrying people these days: assessment and how we seem to have been up a gum tree for so long. Cole's article is an excellent examination of the assumptions we make when we test; both Nickerson and Snow give their views on possible ways to go.

On calibrating tests
Crocker, L. M. & Algina, J. (1986). *Introduction to Classical and Modern Test Theory*. New York: CBS College Publishing.
Satterly, D. (1981). *Assessment in Schools*. Oxford: Basil Blackwell.
Spearrit, D. (ed.) (1982). *The Improvement of Measurement in Education and Psychology*. Hawthorn, Vic: Australian Council for Educational Research.

Satterly deals in an easy way with the norm-/criterion-referenced issues; Crocker and Algina with these and other test-related concepts, including item-response theory (Rasch model). Spearrit's book develops IRT in the Australian context.

On mastery learning
Block, J. H. (1971). *Mastery Learning*. New York: Holt, Rinehart & Winston.
Bloom, B. S., Hastings, J. T. & Madaus, G.F. (1971). *Handbook of Formative and Summative Education of Student Learning*. New York: McGraw-Hill.

Block's little book (if it is still available) is very easy to read and authoritative, but if you want the big guns then it's Bloom's handbook.

On the effects of testing
Crooks, T. J. (1988). The impact of classroom evaluation practices on students. *Review of Educational Research*, **58**, 438–81.

A comprehensive review and a good source for further references.

TECHNIQUES OF ASSESSING LEARNING

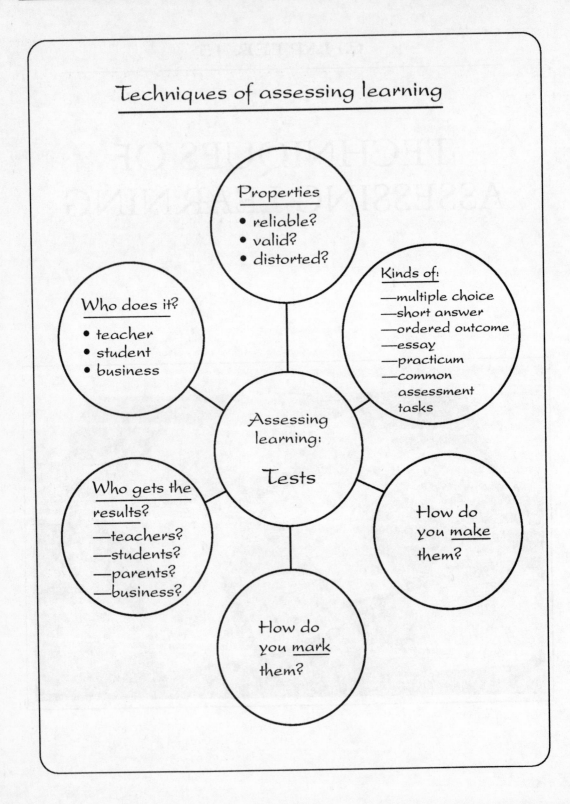

Techniques of assessing learning

Properties
- reliable?
- valid?
- distorted?

Kinds of:
—multiple choice
—short answer
—ordered outcome
—essay
—practicum
—common assessment tasks

Who does it?
- teacher
- student
- business

Assessing learning:

Tests

Who gets the results?
—teachers?
—students?
—parents?
—business?

How do you make them?

How do you mark them?

TECHNIQUES OF ASSESSING LEARNING

In this chapter, you will find out:

- how you know when a test is reliable;
- how you can find out if a test measures what it is supposed to measure;
- whether you should use teacher-made or commercial, standardised tests;
- what techniques can be used to assess the outcomes of learning;
- what are the advantages and disadvantages of: multiple-choice objective tests, short answer tests, ordered-outcome test items, the essay, the practicum and common assessment tasks (CATs);
- how to construct, use and interpret these forms of test;
- how realistic student self-assessment is;
- how to convert test results to a final grade; and
- what 'moderation' is; and if there is any better way of equalising school differences.

Some properties of tests

What, how and when to test

The targets of assessment defined in Chapter 14 tell us what to test; in this chapter the question of how to test is addressed. Inevitably, we concentrate on the assessment of outcomes, with particular reference to the techniques used for assessing declarative knowledge taught in specific subject areas, but we shall also look at broader questions of assessing conditional and procedural knowledge relating to transfer across domains, and at the assessment of process.

As to *when* to test, we shall not be as diligent as Snow, who you will recall from last chapter prescribed testing: immediately on task, daily, weekly and monthly. We leave that to the individual judgment of teachers, balancing purpose, pay-off and practicalities. Teachers can easily obtain some immediate formative feedback simply by sitting beside a student, as in the original meaning of assessment: *assidere*.

First, some properties of tests.

Reliability

An important property of a test is its stability or *reliability*. The test, like any measuring instrument, should perform identically from day to day, irrespective of who is administering it. A clock that is unpredictably fast or slow, or an elastic tape-measure, are unreliable. We need to assume that when we repeatedly administer a test, variation in the test score can be attributed to genuine change, rather than to errors of measurement. Some error of measurement is inevitable, however, and stems from the following sources:

1. *The testing environment.* If the test is administered in a noisy room, with many distractions, students' performance is likely to be erratic, due to misinterpreting questions, skipping items and the like. Then there is the way the test is presented. Are instructions given clearly? Is student anxiety likely to be aroused or reduced? If the test is timed, is it timed accurately? Standardised administration is particularly important in NRT (e.g., IQ tests), because the basis of norm-referencing is comparison (of individual with group norms). In both IRT (Rasch) and CRT, however, the test conditions should be optimal for each student, so that the *best* performance is extracted; some students might need a longer time than others, some will do well under pressure, others under relaxed conditions. NRT requires standard, CRT optimal, conditions.

2. *The learner.* The reliability of the test will also be affected by learner factors: tiredness or illness on the day of the test, anxiety, poor reading skills so that test items are capriciously misread or misunderstood.

3. *The test.* If items are poorly or ambiguously worded, they may be interpreted differently by different people, or differently by the same person on different occasions. The scoring of the test must be free of bias, so that the same scores are obtained by different markers. Short tests are more unreliable than long tests; a careless mistake on one item will create a larger error of measurement in a 3-item than in a 20-item test.

Unreliability thus has several sources; but how do we know whether a test gives a reliable score or not?

Methods of assessing reliability

Test–retest

If a person achieves the same score on the same test on two separate occasions, the test is a reliable one. But there are problems. First, the practice effect: having done the test once, the student will find it easier to do next time and hence will get a higher score. Second, if the student has learned or forgotten something that affects the score, the test may reflect these changes accurately, but will appear to be unstable.

Internal consistency

Another approach to reliability is to show that all items on the test are interrelated. *Split-half* is one method, where the test is divided into two halves: odd and even items are scored separately and then correlated. If the correlation is high (e.g., +.80 or above is a rule of thumb), the two half-tests are yielding compatible scores. The second method uses Cronbach's alpha coefficient, which is based on the number of items and the extent of their intercorrelation: when the coefficient is high (also about +.80 and above) all items are contributing to the total score, making it consistent and robust, but not necessarily *valid*, see below. Internal consistency is maximised by the process of *item analysis* (described later in this chapter), by means of which items that do not contribute to the total score are discarded.

Inter-judge agreement

A reliable test must be marker-proof. Two teachers marking an exam must be able to agree substantially about the marks awarded to a student's responses; equally, the same person must be able to make the same judgment about a response on two different occasions.

Validity

The validity of a test is its ability to measure what it is supposed to measure; a test of mathematical ability should not be composed of items that focus simply on how to calculate. Validity is, then, what a test is about and is its most important property. There are several kinds of validity.

Face validity

Competent judges should agree that the test *appears* to be measuring what it is intended to measure. This form of validity is a good start, but it is not in itself sufficient to establish validity.

Content validity

Tests scores should relate to other measures, the validity of which is known or assumed. IQ items were originally validated, for example, by comparing responses to teachers' ratings of students' intelligence. In a science test, scores could be correlated with laboratory performance, or some problem solving task.

Predictive validity

The test should be able to predict future related performances; a maths term test should correlate with the finals. Predictive validity is particularly important when the test is used for selection purposes; it must be demonstrable that those selected actually do perform better than those rejected.

Factorial validity

Factor analysis reduces the number of tests to a fewer number of factors, without significant loss of information. If the test 'loads on' (correlates with) the relevant factor, it is taken as valid. There are, however, many ways of using factor analysis: the issue is too complex to deal with any further in the present context.

Construct validity

How well do test scores relate to the construct being measured? Do children who score high on a test of metacognitive reading strategies really use those strategies? Such questions can usually only be established by research.

The proper determination of most kinds of validity and reliability requires experimental work, statistical knowhow and facilities that the classroom teacher will not usually have. The only kind of validity check realistically available to most teachers is that of face validity, where a teacher uses his or her own judgment and preferably also that of a colleague. Nevertheless, it is important that teachers understand these points if they are to use tests wisely.

Test distortion

Test distortion is a consistent tendency for scores to be influenced (positively or negatively) by characteristics of the learner that are independent of the content measured (Andrews 1968). It relates positively to reliability, negatively to validity, and applies to all forms of testing.

The objective test, for example, requires that the learner focus on the one correct answer, a characteristic of the high converger. Thus, students who do better on objective tests than on essays use the convergent strategy of focusing on and rote-learning essential detail in the course (Biggs 1973). Essays, on the other hand, do not necessarily show distortion in favour of divergers; it depends upon how the essays are marked and what characteristics the marker (consciously or unconsciously) favours (op. cit.).

It is important to recognise the presence of test distortion. It is not all bad. It is sensible to use oral tests in the assessment of teacher education students because their career requires them to be competent orally. Similarly, you would not test trainee journalists' knowledge of current affairs by objective test but by essay. General estimates of achievement, however, such as school leaving grades, should not favour any particular format of testing, but be *distortion-free*. As such a test is an impossibility, when you think about it, a *variety* of tests should be used, as is recommended in the Year 12 common assessment tasks (CATS) (Masters & Hill 1988), which we discuss later in this chapter.

Teachers and tests

We had better address one matter immediately. Check the correct answer to the following:

1. Teaching, learning and testing are interrelated and should be carried out by the teacher.

On the other hand;

2. Testing is a fearfully complex business, requiring expertise and resources frequently unavailable to the ordinary classroom teacher.

Which is correct:

(a)   (1)
(b)   (2)
(c)   both (1) and (2)
(d)   neither (1) nor (2)

The correct answer is (c). Yes, you are asked to do the almost impossible. But take heart; we did not say the completely impossible. As we have already emphasised, the field of evaluation is changing importantly and the technology hasn't yet caught up, but the ideas themselves are fairly simple. Our present task is consciousness-raising.

Commercial or teacher-made tests?

Given the technological haze that surrounds testing, why should teachers try to construct their own tests? Why not rely instead on what the experts purvey? Let those with the resources, such as Educational Testing Service, Psychological Corporation and here, the Australian Council for Educational Research, get on with the technical difficulties of test construction. Commercially produced tests are based on huge norming samples, are very valid and reliable, and they cover many important aspects of the curriculum; teachers can buy these excellent tests and validly and reliably assess their students.

Well, there are several reasons why not. The backwash from such tests is enormous and frequently harmful (Hoffman 1962). Even when such tests do address high cognitive levels and the backwash is positive, they cannot be integral with day-to-day learning; is your

Christmas dinner integral with your day-to-day nutritional schedule? Teacher-made tests can—and should—be designed to match everyday teaching activities, providing immediate feedback to what is still hot from teaching. Assessment needs to be grounded into a teaching context and authentic about what it assesses (McLean 1990; Wiggins 1989). Commercial tests, or externally constructed tests from whatever source, are usually neither grounded nor authentic and, in a rapid turn around, come to replace the curriculum, determining not only what is taught but how it is taught.

Nevertheless, there are times when tests need to be commercially developed. This is particularly the case when *across school* determinations need to be made, for example comparing this student from Macksville High with that from Turramurra High, when anchoring tests and special techniques based on IRT might need to be used (Masters 1988a). But in the day-to-month classroom round, teachers know what they have taught and they want to know what their students know of what they have taught. They need to build in their own assessment procedures to their teaching; this is the problem we address in this chapter.

How do teachers fare in the construction and use of their own tests? First, a survey of over 500 Wyoming teachers (Box 15.1):

Box 15.1   *How widespread is the use of tests in schools?*

In a survey of 555 Wyoming teachers, covering Grades 1 to 12, it was found that:

- six hours a week were spent on testing in schools;
- 55% of the tests were made by the teachers themselves;
- 40% of student grades were based on tests;
- 82% of teachers had at least one complete course on measurement;
- male teachers used more tests than female teachers;
- criterion-referenced tests were preferred to norm-referenced tests;
- micros were used infrequently for testing purposes.

What would a similar survey in Australia show?

Source: Green & Stager   1985.

Do Australian schools devote six hours a week over all years to testing? Do 82% of all Australian teachers seek courses (pre-service or in-service) in measurement and evaluation? We do not have figures, but ... probably not. It is, however, certain that teachers will in future need to understand evaluation and how it links with learning more thoroughly than previously.

How then do teachers handle teacher-made tests? Again, we have to turn to the United States for data. Marso and Pigge (1991) surveyed 326 Ohio teachers, asking each for a copy of a recently administered teacher-made test (in other than spelling or primary maths) and classified them in terms of item-type, cognitive levels addressed, and the number of 'violations' of the rules of test construction.

Multiple-choice, matching and then short-answer (over 1000 items received), were by far the most common item-types, followed by true–false and then problems. Essay questions (64 items) were the least common. Matching tests scored the most violations (unclear or missing directions), multiple-choice relatively few. As for cognitive level, 72% of all test items addressed the knowledge level of Bloom's taxonomy (straight recall), 11% for comprehension and 15% for application: 2% of items were spread over the three higher levels. Matching items consistently addressed the lowest level (knowledge), multiple-choice addressed knowledge, comprehension and some application, and essay questions occasionally went higher than application, but most commonly addressed the lowest two levels. Experienced teachers were no better than inexperienced at constructing tests or at setting items that addressed higher cognitive levels.

Marso's study is discouraging; Ohio teachers are not likely to be different from other teachers, so it seems that teachers in general are:

- not ambitious enough about the *level* of test; they test low-level outcomes;
- too ambitious about the *type* of test; they construct complex objective-type instruments and get them wrong.

Perhaps we can try to improve matters in the next generation of teachers. It is no answer to go back to commercially made tests for general classroom use; rather we need to think a little more carefully about *why* and *what* we are doing.

Methods of assessing outcomes

Assessments done in school are mainly of students' declarative knowledge of particular subjects and topics. Assessments address the lower cognitive levels, to check the extent to which the student has accurate knowledge, recall or recognition, of a range of topics taught ('coverage'), or higher cognitive levels, such as the knowledge structure, elegance and originality of thinking, ability to synthesise data, to apply to new situations and the like. Further, assessments may address transfer: how far the student can competently move from the content and context originally taught, and have the procedural and conditional knowledge to know when and under what conditions transfer is possible. These last kinds of knowledge are assessed infrequently at the school level.

Coverage is assessed by closed, forced choice, quantitative techniques such as the objective test and its variants: multiple-choice, matching, true-false. However, one form of objective test, the ordered-outcome format, is a special case of a qualitative assessment mode, addressing the structural aspects of topic knowledge. Otherwise, the higher cognitive levels are addressed by open-end techniques such as the essay, cognitive mapping, various situational devices involving interview and/or observation and, to an extent, the short answer (which looks like an open format test and is usually treated by teacher and student as closed).

Let us review these instruments, starting with the conventional measures of coverage, then extending to the higher cognitive levels.

The objective test

A very widely used technique that relies heavily on quantitative assumptions about learning and testing is the objective test, which is 'objective' only in that the scoring and collation of marks is independent of the prejudices and judgment of the scorer (but the latter show themselves in the items chosen and in the alternatives designated as correct). Three forms of the objective test are in common use:

- where two alternatives are provided (the *true-false* test);
- where several, usually four or five, alternatives are provided (the *multiple-choice* test);
- where items are placed in two lists and an item from list A (e.g., states) has to be matched with an item from list B (e.g., capital cities) (the *matching* test).

Other versions involve filling in blank diagrams, completing sentences and so on. The *ordered-outcome* test format (Masters 1987) is entirely different but is not (yet) in common use and will be dealt with later.

Of all these techniques, the multiple-choice format is the most acceptable. True–false is open to the obvious objection that a score of 50% could be obtained by guessing, although it is possible to offset this by penalising wrong replies. Matching is open to the obvious objections that (a) it relies on recall alone, (b) allows the possibility of obtaining correct answers by elimination (even more than the multiple-choice) and, as we now know from Marso and Pigge (1991), (c) it is most prone to error in its construction.

Objective testing has been developed in a quantitative framework in both NRT and CRT contexts. The test comprises items of knowledge that sample the population of items that have been taught in a subject, and performance is assessed on the proportion of items correct. Particularly in large tests, it is difficult to devise consistently good items that tap high cognitive levels, while the format itself requires that the response has to be unequivocally correct or incorrect; thus, the objective test tends overwhelmingly to assess recall, recognition and comprehension, as Marso and Pigge found. The quantitative foundation couldn't be clearer, but if you wish to assess whether the student has stayed awake through a series of classes, or has read the set texts with at least some comprehension, the objective test is ideal. Just as long as you know what you are doing.

Constructing norm-referenced tests

Say we are to construct a 50-item test, with four choices per stem. First one defines the item types and then collects examples of possible items. These should be checked for wording, etc., preferably with a colleague's help, and then roughly 150 items administered to a few classes. The test papers are then scored and placed in rank order, with the highest scorer on top, the next second and so on, with the poorest last (Table 15.1).

Let us say 21 students take the test. We mark the test, divide the students into thirds on the basis of total score, and compare the top-scoring third of seven students and the bottom-scoring third of seven students, with a checklist classifying each student's responses by each item. If we look down the column for item 1, we see that six of the top students got this right, but so did six of the bottom students. Obviously this item is too easy; it is not discriminating between good and poor students. Item 2 is worse than useless: only one top student got it, but six of the bottom students did. Items 3 and 4 are both very good, especially 4 which all the good students got correct and none of the poor students did. Item 5 is difficult, answered correctly by only five out of the 14 students and discriminates moderately well: four of the five were in the top group. Item 6 is very difficult and could be answered by only the best student.

Thus, a 'good' item is one that is answered correctly by all the top scoring and incorrectly by all lowest scoring students and is of middling difficulty; if an item is either too easy or too difficult, it cannot discriminate clearly between good and poor students. On this ground, we would have to scrap item 6, although it could well be a very searching item in terms of content. Few items survive such an analysis, hence the threefold increase in the numbers required for pre-testing. To obtain the final score, then, the

Table 15.1   *A typical item-analysis chart (simplified)*

Students	Items								
	1	2	3	4	5	6	7	8	9
Top third									
1	X	0	X	X	X	X			
2	X	0	X	X	X	0			
3	X	0	X	X	X	0			
4	0	0	X	X	0	0	etc.		
5	X	0	X	X	0	0			
6	X	0	X	X	0	0			
7	X	X	X	X	X	0			
Number correct	6	1	7	7	4	1			
Bottom third									
15	X	X	X	0	X	0			
16	0	X	0	0	0	0			
17	X	X	0	0	0	0			
18	X	X	0	0	0	0	etc.		
19	X	X	0	0	0	0			
20	X	X	0	0	0	0			
21	X	0	0	0	0	0			
Number correct	6	6	1	0	1	0			

X = item correctly answered
0 = item incorrectly answered

students' responses on the surviving 50 items are added up, *not* their responses on the original 150; and in future administrations, only the remaining 50 items would be used.

Constructing tests of this nature clearly requires a lot of work, although most of that would now be done by a microcomputer. Item analysis programs are readily available and they do all the sorting and correlating and also produce a reliability coefficient for the test. Important things to note are:

- selection of items is based on their statistical properties, not on their content;
- any item is considered as good as any other item in terms of content, in that a total score may be made up from any set of items responded to correctly;
- items are either right or wrong; there is no credit for getting them partially right;
- a test is as good as its ability to discriminate between students.

Tests constructed along these lines are robust; they are reliable and predict well. Like intelligence tests, they do the job because the technology has enabled them to, but also like intelligence tests until recently, they lack an adequate theoretical foundation.

Constructing criterion-referenced tests

The statistics used in constructing NRTs are inapplicable to CRTs; in CRT you want to select the item because it validly addresses some aspect of knowledge, irrespective of how other items behave.

Logically, there are three steps in the development of CRTs:

1. *Specify the target of assessment.* In CRT, one has to be clear about what is being measured and it has to be stated in terms that allow assessment. In mastery learning, it has been the practice to rely on behavioural types of objectives for each learning episode, where as we saw in the last chapter, each objective contains an operational verb, such as 'list', 'calculate', 'compare and contrast', which says in measurable terms what the learner has to do, whereas verbs such as 'appreciate' or 'glow inwardly' are out. The essence of CRT is in demonstrating that the student can, or cannot, meet *whatever* criteria have been prescribed.

2. *Decide what defines adequate knowledge or performance.* The logical criterion is perfection; the assessment target has been met, or not. But humans make errors, so realistically one would ask *how much* error is permitted and, in qualitative terms, *what kind* of error. Having decided that, we then come to the issue of item analysis. A good item reflects that instruction has taken place. If before instruction only 10% of students could pass the item, but after instruction the figure is 90%, this indicates both that instruction and the item measuring it are sound. If 50% passed the item before instruction and 60% after, you would have to look at both the item and the efficacy of the instruction. So whereas in item analysis in NRT we selected items on the basis of whether or not each internally discriminates between students scoring high and low on the total score, in CRT we select items on the basis of how each discriminates between instructed and naive students.

3. *Devising testing situations.* The final step is committing the objectives to some form of test format. A test format may involve pencil-and-paper items (as in the usual objective test), or where instructional objectives are behavioural, use of a practical context, in which student behaviours are evaluated (see the list of illustrative verbs supplied by Gronlund 1970).

Constructing tests on the Rasch model

IRT models provide 'an excellent underpinning for a theory and practice of criterion-referenced testing' (Hambleton & Cook 1977: 92). As the RAPT tests mentioned in Chapter 14 are designed to do, a test prior to instruction can assess students on the 'ability' concerned and a different set of items assesses the same 'ability' after instruction, which is of course the whole point of CRT. It all depends on the ability of the Rasch model to pinpoint the dimension relevant to instruction.

We shall not elaborate further on the IRT technique of test construction. While the tests themselves clearly have some classroom use, their construction and development will take place in institutions such as the Australian Council for Educational Research rather than in classrooms. The breakthrough here would probably depend on the extent to which teachers become sufficiently knowledgeable to use IRT on an everyday basis.

The short-answer test

In the short-answer technique, essay-type questions are set and the student is asked to answer in note form, using abbreviations and avoiding elaboration. This format is useful for getting at factual material—addressing or interpreting diagrams, charts and tables for example—but is limited in addressing main ideas and themes (see Chapter 13).

The usual presupposition behind the short-answer test is that the examiner is after something quite specific (i.e., it too is a one-correct-answer format), so the use of the model-answer technique is more justifiable here than in the essay proper (see below). The short answer is thus well suited to CRT where the answer cannot easily be put into a standard multiple-choice format. Another advantage of the short answer is that it is less susceptible to test-taking strategies than the ordinary multiple choice (you can't work out the answer by elimination). Whereas the multiple choice depends on a process of *recognition*, the short answer depends on *recall*, and it is much easier to recognise something than it is to recall it. Finally, you can of course set many more short-answer questions than essay questions: hence its value in probing coverage in a more flexible and deeper way than the objective test itself usually does, without the technical complexity of the latter.

We now turn to techniques aiming more deliberately at qualitative assessment of declarative knowledge.

Ordered-outcome items

Ordered-outcome tests are designed to:

- allow for *partial* credit, rather than a stark right or wrong, in responding to a test item;
- assess responses according to a theory of how those responses are learned.

The ordered-outcome test format looks like a multiple-choice item, but instead of opting for the one correct alternative out of the four or so provided, the student is required to attempt all sub-items, which are ordered into a hierarchy of complexity that reflects successive stages of learning that concept or skill. Students respond to the sequence as far as they can go.

In constructing such items, the aim is to ask a series of questions about a stem in such a way that satisfactory responses require a more and more sophisticated use of the information in the stem. The first question is to decide how to select the sub-items; this is where one's theory of learning comes in. Masters (1987) first suggested using a phenomenographic analysis of each topic tested, which assumes that the topic has in fact been researched in this way. A more general approach, which can be applied 'top-down' to any topic, subject to subsequent item-analysis, is to use the SOLO taxonomy.

The following criteria are used to design sub-items addressing the stem topic at each SOLO level:

1. Unistructural: Contains one obvious piece of information coming directly from the stem.

2. Multistructural: Requires using two or more discrete and separate pieces of information contained in the stem.

3. Relational: Uses two or more pieces of information each directly related to an integrated understanding of the information in the stem.

4. Extended abstract: Requires use of an abstract general principle or hypothesis which can be derived from, or suggested by, the information in the stem.

The unstructured accumulation of knowledge, of which rote learning would be one (but not the only) example, is emphasised in responding up to multistructural level; structuring knowledge with increasingly abstract frameworks is emphasised through relational to extended abstract responding.

To illustrate, an ordered-outcome mathematics test was given to several hundred Year 7 students in each of two Hong Kong schools (Biggs, Lam, Balla & Ki 1988); responses to one item are as in Figure 15.1:

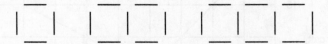

Toothpicks are used to make the above patterns. Four are used to make one box, seven to make two boxes, etc.

| | | Form 1 | |
		School A	School B
Unistructural	(a) How many toothpicks are used to make three boxes?	96%	99%
Multistructural	(b) How many more toothpicks are used to make 5 boxes than used to make 3 boxes?	74%	76%
Relational	(c) How many boxes can be made with 31 toothpicks?	57%	70%
Extended abstract	(d) If I have made y boxes, how many tooth-picks have I used?	6%	48%

Figure 15.1 *An ordered-outcome mathematics item*
(from Biggs, Lam, Balla & Ki 1988)

It can be seen that the two schools perform almost identically up to multistructural level, but they diverge sharply thereafter, School B performing at eight times the level of School A in the extended abstract subitem: 48% correct compared to 6%. In other words, differences between the students in Schools A and B are reflected only in the most complex cognitive processes. A conventional test, comprising an aggregate of mixed items scored correct or incorrect (which at this level would probably not exceed multistructural), would be unlikely to pick up this probably important qualitative difference in the students' mathematical thinking.

An illustration from an economics item is given in Figure 15.2.

The item addresses supply and demand; the *U*, *M* and *R* responses target increasing skill in dealing with the graphical expression of the concept in a concrete situation. The *E* response is open-ended and elicits students' thinking about the concept: some students incorrectly use a 'components' conception of value: that the value of a commodity depends on the sum of the value of its parts and, since those parts are now worn and older, the flat is worth less. This is a common misconception, which may co-exist with ability to handle textbook problems in supply and demand quite correctly (Pong,

The diagram below shows the market demand for and supply of vegetables in a local market. The law of demand suggests that the higher price, the lower will be the quantity of vegetables demanded; the law of supply suggests that at higher prices, more vegetables will be supplied to the market. The market will finally stay at the equilibrium price where the quantity demanded equals the quantity supplied.

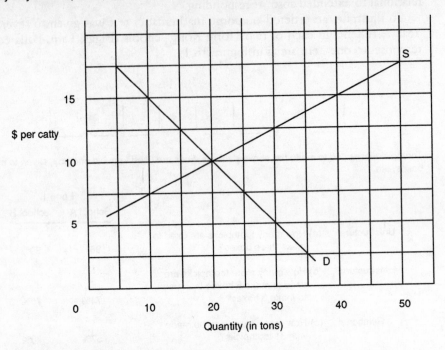

U.   According to the graph, what is the equilibrium price?

M.   If the price is fixed at $15 a catty, by how much will the quantity supplied be greater than the quantity demanded?

R.   If consumers are willing to buy 5 more tons of vegetables at every possible price, what will be the *new* equilibrium price?

E.   A flat-owner bought his flat at HK$1 million last year. He now wants to sell it and the best price he can find in the market is only HK$750 000. Using demand and supply, discuss several reasons how this may have happened. Draw graphs to illustrate your discussion.

* A 'catty' is a unit of weight (= 1.33lbs).

Figure 15.2   *An economics ordered-outcome item*
          (Pong, in Biggs, Holbrook, Ki, Lam, Li, Pong & Stimpson 1989)

in Biggs, Holbrook, Ki, Lam, Li, Pong & Stimpson 1989). That last point raises the issue—noted many times in other contexts—that conventional modes of assessment (handling textbook problems) may give little clue as to the level of understanding the students really have.

The backwash from this kind of test sends the message that what is important is to think in increasingly complex ways about a topic, not to obtain a certain number of correct items. Moreover, the gap between a student's best response and the highest response in the hierarchy tells both teacher and student what still remains to be learned.

Item-analysing ordered-outcome items

Item analysis of ordered-outcome tests is carried out by a 'staircase' approach, which assumes simply that unistructural items are easier than multi-, and multi- than relational, and relational than extended abstract, which is a basic assumption of the SOLO model. Such an analysis can be done either by a Rasch-type analysis called the 'partial credit model' (PCM) (Masters 1988b), or more directly by calculating the Guttman coefficient of reproducibility *(rep)*, which is far more practical for classroom use.

Guttman's (1941) 'scalogram' analysis is used to fine-tune items that don't quite fit the model and reject those that are clearly wrong. Students who respond correctly at one level are assumed to have responded correctly on all previous levels, so that if a person got the extended abstract sub-item correct and all the previous sub-items incorrect (see Student No. 9, Table 15.2), the indications are that something is badly wrong and the item should probably be discarded.

Table 15.2   *Analysing ordered-outcome items*

Item 1

	SOLO level of Sub-item*					
Student No.	U	M	R	EA	Item**	No. of errors
1.	1	0	0	0	U	0
2.	1	1	0	0	M	0
3.	1	1	1	0	R	0
4.	1	0	1	0	(R)	1
5.	1	1	1	1	EA	0
6.	0	0	1	0	(P)	1
7.	0	0	1	1	(EA)	2
8.	1	1	0	0	M	0
9.	0	0	0	1	(P)	1
10.	0	1	0	0	(M)	1
					Total	6

*1 = sub-item correct, 0 = sub-item incorrect

** P = prestructural, U = unistructural, M = multistructural,
R = relational, EA = extended abstract. The SOLO level is given by the *highest* level passed. ( ) = provisional SOLO level only as the responses to this item contain an error.

An 'error' is the number of alterations needed to make the item internally consistent with the hierarchical assumption of SOLO (see text).

Table 15.2 gives an example of an item and the responses of ten students to it. The first three are straightforward, showing that the highest level each can reach is unistructural *(U)*, multistructural *(M)*, and relational *(R)*, respectively. The next student (4) displays an 'error': an inconsistency with the 'staircase' model, having got the R level correct and the M incorrect. The simplest assumption to make is that the error (either due to the wording of the item or to the student) is at the M level, as it is more likely that the student got an easier sub-item wrong by chance than a more difficult sub-item correct, suggesting that more attention be given to the M sub-item. Student 6 managed to get U and M wrong, but R correct: were there two errors (at U and M), or one (at R). The simplest assumption this time is that there is one error, so provisionally this student is performing at the P level. Students 7, 9 and 10 point up more problems. Student 7 has two errors: you can't make his response pattern consistent without altering either U and M, or R and EA. There are clearly problems with this item: Student 9 was clever enough to get EA correct, but nothing else.

There will always be some errors of this type, but how many is too many? Guttman's coefficient of reproducibility (*rep*) gives us the answer. This is calculated from Table 15.2, as 1 - (no. of errors)/(total number of responses). There are 40 responses in all, each student having to respond four times to each item, and 6 errors. Thus:

$$rep = 1 - 6/40 = 1 - .15 = .85$$

The rule of thumb is that *rep* must be greater than .90, so that .85 is not good enough. This is what we suspected by looking at individual student responses. So what we would have to do is to reword the items—the U and M sub-items seem to be causing trouble consistently—and try again.

The scoring of ordered-outcome items is best done categorically, so that in a battery of tests a person could receive either an item-by-item profile—U on item 1, M on items 2 and 3, etc.—or an average, counting 1 = U, 2 = M, 3 = R and 4 = EA, so that 2.4 would mean that on average, on this test, the student scored roughly midway between multistructural and relational over all items. Alternatively, the PCM gives a score in logits (units of difficulty), either item by item, or a weighted average over all items.

Combined or average scores do not however give the best information, as the SOLO model makes most sense in terms of how a person responds to a *particular* topic or concept. Giving an item by item profile is thus the most acceptable and is certainly the most useful in formative terms, although clumsy when trying to deal with it summatively.

The essay

The essay is the most common method of assessing higher cognitive levels (not that it always does—that's up to the person who sets the question and marks it). It is a continuous piece of prose written in response to a question or problem. There are many variants:

- the timed examination, students having no prior knowledge of the question;
- the open-book examination, where students usually have some prior knowledge and are allowed to bring reference material into the exam room;
- the untimed exam, where students can take as long as they like, within reason;
- the take-home, where students are given notice of the questions and several days to prepare their answers in their own time;
- the assignment, which is an extended version of the take-home and which comprises the most common of all methods of evaluating by essay;
- the dissertation, which is an extended report of independent research.

We have of course looked at the essay in some detail in Chapter 13, and many of the points made there about appropriate discourse structure, answering the question, the dangers of knowledge telling and the like, apply here. We are concerned in this section with the criteria for marking essays and the reliability of essays. The two issues interact.

Years ago, when the essay was almost the exclusive method of formal evaluation, Starch and Elliott (1912; 1913a, 1913b) originated a devastating series of investigations into the reliability of essay-marking. They sent copies of two student papers in each of English, geometry and history to 180 teachers and asked that they grade the papers on a 100-point scale, with 75 as a pass mark. The range in marks in one English paper was 47 points (50% to 97%); and was even greater in geometry—some teachers marking for neatness, showing calculations, etc., while others did not.

In another classic study, Diederich (1974) looked at the marking of 300 English essays by 53 judges (including academics from different disciplines, professional writers and business executives) all of whom were concerned about the quality of students' writing. They were told they were free to grade as they liked, on a nine-point scale (1-9). The average correlation out of the 3000 possibilities was only +.31; in other words, less than 10% of the papers would have received the same grade from any two judges. Of the 300 papers, 101 received *every grade* from 1 to 9! Different markers were using different criteria, thereby shooting reliability to little pieces.

Using factor-analysis, Diederich found that there were five quite distinct characteristics that were emphasised by different markers:

- *ideas:* logical coherence, relevance to topic, originality and wit;
- *skills:* correct usage of words, sentence structure, punctuation and spelling;
- *organisation:* correct format, presentation, structure;
- *style:* individual expression and style.

Thus, a person keen on organisation would mark a well-organised but dull essay higher than a disorganised but highly original one.

The personal characteristics of the marker can influence judgment. For example, markers who are untidy writers mark neat and untidy essays equally; neat writers, however, tend to downgrade untidy essays heavily (Huck & Bound 1970). Either insist that all essays are typewritten, or only permit teachers with untidy writing to mark them! The marker's mood, however, does not appear to have a strong effect. Townsend, Lee and Tuck (1989) got markers to see a film that induced a particular mood before letting them loose on a pile of essays. While the first one of the batch showed some effect of the film on the marking (generosity with a happy mood; hard marking with an angry mood), the marking set thereafter was determined by the essays themselves.

Rather, it is the markers' intrinsic prejudices re the topic that are likely to sway their marking. Students tend to get higher grades than they deserve if they second-guess what the marker wants to read (Biggs 1973). Not only may different markers vary, the same marker can also vary from script to script. Apart from momentary lapses, fatigue and so on, one systematic source of unreliability is the *order* effect. When a marker sits down to a batch of thirty or so essays (the more there are, the worse the effect), the first half-dozen tend to set the standard for the next half-dozen, which in turn reset the standard for the next. A moderately good essay following a run of poor ones tends to be marked higher than it deserves; if it follows a run of very good ones, it would be marked down (Hales & Tokar 1975). The marker's standards thus tend to slide up or down according to the quality of the essays he or she happens to be marking at the time.

Improving the reliability of marking essays

From these and other findings, the following precautions can be recommended to help increase reliability:

- *All marking should be blind,* the marker being unaware of the identity of the student. This matters; attractive female students tend to receive higher grades than unattractive ones (Hore, 1971). Blind marking makes it less possible for teacher biases to influence the results.
- *All rechecking should be blind,* with the original mark concealed.
- *Grade generally at first,* say into 'Excellent', 'Pass' and 'Fail', and later try to discriminate more finely within these categories. All borderline cases should be reviewed.
- *Spot-check,* particularly borderline cases, using an independent marker. Gross disagreements should be resolved between the markers or by recourse to a third marker.
- *The wording of the original questions should be checked* for ambiguities by an independent marker.
- *Guard against bias due to handwriting,* by first quickly scanning all papers and deciding whether there are any particular ones that need to be rewritten.
- *Each question should be marked across students,* if several questions per student are involved, not each student across questions. Focus on the question not the student, to set a standard for each question, thus minimising 'halo effects' (a high mark on one question spreads to the student's answer to another question). Between questions, the papers should be shuffled to prevent systematic order effects.

These are all sensible things to do when marking essays and they are all procedural. Now let us turn to the major issue in essay marking.

The criteria of good quality

An essay is an attempt to convey meaning; that is its strength. A theory and a technology of writing assessment is only just beginning; that is its weakness. Approaches to assessment basically fall into two kinds: analytic and holistic (Huot 1990). When reading an essay, do you rate separately for particular qualities and then combine the ratings in some kind of weighted fashion? Or do you read and rate the essay as a whole and give an overall rating? The analytic method is more reliable; the mark is stable and judges agree more readily, but it is slow and it does not easily address the essay-as-a-whole. The holistic method is faster, less easy to obtain interjudge agreement, but seems to address the real point of an essay, which is to construct an integrated argument.

Why do we use the essay as a medium of assessment? Surely, it is to see if the student can think at as high a cognitive level as possible in the content area. To do that is to think at a superordinate level: at least relational, in SOLO terms. Using analytic dimensions is useful for assessing

- side-issues such as spelling, punctuation, style (but should *content* teachers be interested in the *mechanics?*—see Chapter 13);
- content-relevant issues such as originality, elegance, use of the appropriate conventions (such as how to acknowledge others' ideas), the extent to which the literature is 'covered'.

These points, especially the second, are usefully assessed by teachers, depending on their purposes, but analytic marking cannot help one appraise the *discourse structure*: the quality of the argument and how it is structured (see Chapter 13).

Using model answers to assist markers, with marks awarded for each congruence between the model and the student's essay, is useful particularly where essays are sectioned off to different markers and where analytic marking is used: the dimensions can be specified and defined. On the other hand, model answers presume a convergent learning outcome which may not only penalise highly original students, but focus attention away from the theme and the structured argument to the facts and details reported at the sentence level.

Writing research thus suggests a major distinction between essays (i) as devices for knowledge telling, where the focus is generally on reporting items at the sentence level (and which can as well be assessed by short-answer or even objective testing); and (ii) as devices for eliciting an elaborate structured argument. Two Finnish researchers were concerned that examination marks seemed to correlate highly with the length of the essay assessed. Were quantitative considerations swaying the markers; did they perceive that long essays must be good essays? Fortunately no; on separating out 'reproductive' (knowledge telling) from 'elaborative' (knowledge-transforming) essays, it was found that the latter were longer than the former, and it was the structure that accounted for the high marks, not the length (Lonka & Mikkonen 1989).

Markers thus need to be alerted to:

- the aspects of the essay that can be rated quantitatively on isolated scales; and
- the overall structure of the essay.

These two aspects of essay marking need to be assessed separately and combined in some way that would be adjusted to suit the teacher's purposes. First, then, it is necessary to decide what are important dimensions to look for and to let students know that you are looking for. Such would include the sorts of things Diederich found markers saw as important, although they will vary from subject to subject, if not topic to topic:

- *ideas*: originality, wit, relevance, 'logic' (but see below);
- *skills*: the mechanics;
- *organisation*: format, presentation, literature review;
- *style*: personal flair.

These dimensions (and others, as seen fit) could be rated and weighted according to one's *a priori* judgments, and combined with the holistic rating of the structure of the essay. As you look at them, however, it becomes apparent that some are quite interdependent; the 'logic' of ideas, and the quality of those ideas, is not something separate from, but is intrinsic to, the way those ideas are presented and to the case they make. Overriding any analytic judgments, then, must be assessment of the discourse structure itself.

The appropriate structure for the essay—its *genre*—is determined by the question and is very much a content matter. It does help considerably, however, if teachers can be alerted to structural aspects by a scheme such as SOLO. While not dictating the 'marking scheme', it helps the marker take on the reader on her own terms. Do the points listed make *a* coherent structure (not necessarily the one the question-setter had in mind)? If yes, the essay is at least relational. Is the structure the writer uses appropriate or not? If yes, then the question has been properly addressed and *that* part of the assessment is over. If no, then one will have to decide how far short of satisfactory it is. Does the writer's structure open out new ways of looking at the issue? If yes, the essay is extended abstract. If the answer is consistently 'no' to all of the above, the essay is multistructural or less. It should not be given good marks, because that is not the point of the essay proper. If one does want students to list points in a knowledge telling way, the short answer is more appropriate and easier for student to complete and teacher to mark.

Classifying an essay as multistructural, relational or whatever, does not of course answer the $64 000 question: How many marks do I give it? This raises the whole question of quantifying the unquantifiable: the issue of grading. We return to that one later.

The essay is not frequently used for assessing higher level processes in the sciences; there, other techniques are useful, many of which are summarised by White (1988: see especially Chapter 5). We consider some of these now.

Concept mapping

Concept mapping was introduced by Novak and Gowin (1984) and is as much a planning and learning procedure as an assessment procedure. Concept mapping can be used for planning an essay, for example by discovering ways in which one might see the interrelations between the topic components, for organising one's thinking for study purposes, or, as suggested here, for revealing to a teacher how students conceive a topic. Simply, a topic is chosen (say 'evaluation') and key terms or concepts relating to that concept are written, one to a card, and the student lays the cards out on a large sheet of paper in a way that makes sense to him or her and fixes them in place; the cards are then linked with lines and arrows, with brief notes of the kind of relationship making up each link. Each chapter of this book is preceded by a brief concept map.

The students can work singly or in groups; the terms or concepts can be supplied by the teacher or made up by the student. What emerges is the way the student sees the relationships between the important components or aspects of a topic; a view that can of course be greatly elaborated in a one-to-one interview. The interrelations may be correct, as taught; they may not be as taught but quite legitimate or even, importantly, original; or they may simply be misguided. Moreover, the richness of the connections can be assessed; it is easy to tell at a glance if a student has an intellectually impoverished knowledge structure relating to the topic, or a rich one. But how you convert that intellectual wealth into the currency of marks is, as we are continually finding, a difficult question. Concept maps are more easily used formatively than summatively.

Venn diagrams

Venn diagrams are a simple form of concept map, where the 'territory' of a concept is expressed in a circle or ellipse and interrelations between concepts expressed by the intersection or overlap of the circles. Figure 15.3 illustrates a commonly used Venn diagram to show the relationships among the three basic cueing systems in reading: the grapho-phonic (the symbol-sound relationship); the syntactic (the way in which the language flows, grammar, etc.); and the semantic (the meanings). The diagram shows that the intersection of all of these is meaning, comprehension.

Venn diagrams, like concept maps, are very economical ways of expressing relationships, both for teaching purposes, in conveying relationships to learners, and for assessment purposes, when learners convey their ways of seeing them to teachers.

Prediction, observation, explanation

A good way of assessing how students use their knowledge is by placing them in situations and questioning them. This can be quite unstructured, as for example asking why the plastic handgrips of a bicycle feel warmer than the handlebars (Clough & Driver 1984).

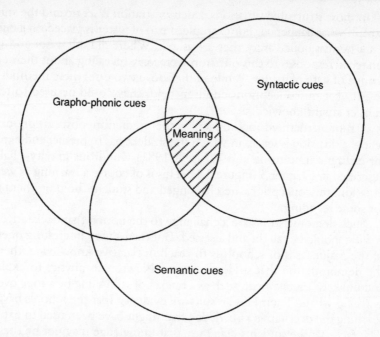

Figure 15.3   *Venn diagram of cues used in reading for meaning*

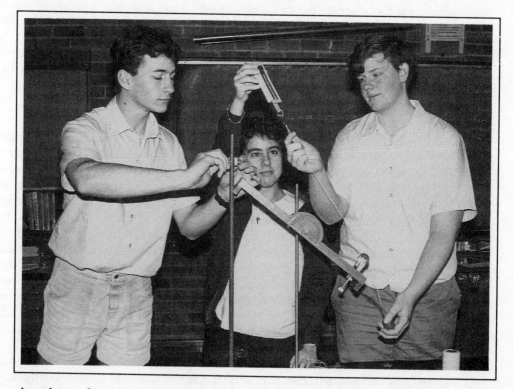

A good way of assessing how students use their knowledge is by setting up a demonstration and getting students to explain what happened.

In more structured situations, a demonstration is set up and the students are asked to explain what happened. For example, a pan of water is placed on a burner and when all the water has boiled away, they are asked: 'Where did the water go?' (Beveridge 1985). Students' responses to this question were very revealing about their conceptions of the change of state of matter. While in the above two cases these methods were used to discover what misconceptions children held, they could be used to test their ability to transfer taught knowledge.

A more structured method still is the prediction–observation–explanation model, where a situation is set up in which the student has to predict and explain the outcome, for example, Gunstone and White's (1981) wondrous gravity-challenging machine described in Chapter 3 (Figure 3.1). This is of course a learning as well as an assessment situation; misconceptions are challenged and students holding them perceive the need for some recoding.

Such demonstrations are a challenge to the notion that declarative knowledge alone is what should be taught and assessed. But then a very interesting question arises. If one of the major tasks of schools is to teach declarative knowledge, then one could greet the demonstration that students use pre-Newtonian physics to explain a complicated and unlikely arrangement, such as a bucket of sand slung by a rope over a bicycle wheel, with 'So what?' Their HSC results are evidence that the schools have done their bit in teaching the declarative knowledge that might have been used to explain that situation. The fact that the students *didn't* use that knowledge may not be the schools' problem, or even the students', but Gunstone and White's; the students' misconceptions tell us something about the nature or conditions of human learning, a datum of theoretical value to experimenters interested in testing the limits of the transfer of knowledge, rather than about a failure in schooling. What do you think? How wide does the gap between taught declarative knowledge and its application have to be before schools and students are let off the hook? That is a very important question for this chapter, because its answer will determine what you test.

The practicum

Now let us turn to assessing a much more specific kind of procedural knowledge: that used in practical situations. Here the student is put in a practical situation requiring the same procedural knowledge or behaviour as that required when instruction has ceased. In teacher-education courses, for example, student teachers are required to demonstrate at some point that they have acquired teaching skills, as opposed to passing a written examination in teaching method. Examples are manifold: students in woodworking should have to demonstrate that they can actually operate a power tool, or make a rubbed-glue joint; chemistry students, that they can set up the apparatus and carry out a quantitative analysis in the laboratory. Of course it may be necessary to supplement such evaluation with pencil-and-paper tests on relevant content, but the *critical* evaluations are in practical contexts.

CRT is most appropriate for evaluating the practicum. The objectives should be quite clear-cut: the student has to perform certain behaviours to a specified standard. It should then be simple to specify what these behaviours are, whether the learner can perform them and, if not, why not. An example is shown in Table 15.3.

Students should be well aware in advance of what such a list might contain and be given fairly immediate feedback, perhaps in conjunction with a video-taping (in which case, students would find it valuable to rate their own performance before discussing the supervisor's rating).

Table 15.3 *Evaluating the practicum*

PERFORMANCE RATING KEY

For each of the eight areas, supervisors are required to enter the appropriate code (below) in the column headed 'Performance Rating' and a comment in the next column.

O	=	Outstanding
HC	=	Highly competent
C	=	Competent
CI	=	Can improve (further attention needed)
U	=	Unsatisfactory

OUTLINE OF CRITERIA FOR ASSESSMENT OF PRACTICE TEACHING
(see also Section 7 of the Practice Teaching Handbook)

1. *Lesson preparation and evaluation of lessons taught:*
   Thorough lesson planning, preparation of teaching materials and lesson evaluation using systematic and intelligible procedures.

2. *Implementation of lesson plans:*
   Lesson preparation effectively translated into practice with flexibility and adaptability, clarity of presentation, effective use of teaching materials and good placing and timing: established links between lessons.

3. *Use of appropriate language in the classroom:*
   Appropriate vocabulary, clarity and fluency of expression and good voice control in keeping with lesson demands: purposeful movement about the classroom, effective eye contact and appropriate use of body language.

4. *Classroom management and control:*
   Appropriate positive techniques used to gain attention, give clear instruction, communicate expectations, anticipate potential problems and control classroom organisation and dynamics: awareness of peer dynamics and need for good interpersonal communication.

5. *Range of teaching strategies and learning activities:*
   Effective use made of the board and other teaching aids and materials when available and necessary: guidance of discussion, heightening pupil awareness through questioning and variety in teaching strategies to promote class involvement.

6. *Level and quality of pupil involvement:*
   Pupils involved constructively in the process of learning, gaps in pupil knowledge identified and individual needs are catered for, where necessary, during each lesson.

7. *Interpersonal empathy and sensitivity:*
   Develops a rapport with the pupils, consistency of personal presence, degree of approachability, thoughtfulness and humour.

8. *Familiarity with school organisation/personal adaptation and involvement:*
   Acquaintance with timetabling and school schedules, knowledge of available teaching resources, involvement in extra-curricular activities, cooperation with staff and colleagues, dependability, punctuality and general professionalism

Source: Department of Education, University of Newcastle.

The diagnostic value of such a checklist is considerable, far more so than an NRT version:

A: Definitely superior, among the best in the year
B: Above average
C: Average
D: Below average, but meets minimal standards
E: Not up to standard.

One general advantage of the practicum is its apparent face validity: the student is being assessed in a situation that models reality. The closer the practicum is to the real thing, the greater its validity. But how close do we really get in, say, practice teaching? The presence of the evaluator (either in person or by one-way screens or recording devices) distorts the situation so that nervous students in particular may behave differently from the way they would if they were not being observed, or if they had established a familiar working relationship with the students in the class. Still, it's obviously more valid than assessing practice teaching by written examination.

Oral tests: Presentations and interviews

A common oral test is the class presentation, which is evaluated in terms of the content conveyed and the effectiveness of presenting that content. Unlike the practicum, the class presentation is not necessarily meant to reproduce a situation in which students will later find themselves.

The class presentation can be evaluated in terms of the content conveyed and the effectiveness of presenting that content.

Another oral form of evaluation is the interview, where the teacher questions the student on a one-to-one basis. The great advantage is that this is a two-way process. Skilful examiners can plumb the depths of the student's knowledge and abilities in ways that they may not be able to prescribe in advance. They can also provide feedback to the student and thus serve a valuable formative function. On the other hand, the success of the technique depends to a large extent on the mental chemistry of the participants: some interviews are both enjoyable and stimulating, others painful. Unstructured interviews are very unreliable as assessment devices, but structured interviews conducted with a criterion-referenced checklist may be quite reliable.

Common assessment tasks (CATs)

We have canvassed quite an array of assessment methods and, depending on your aims, each has something to offer. Common assessment tasks, or CATs (Masters & Hill 1988), are designed on principles of authentic assessment and are being pursued in several states. CATs are tasks that are keyed to the curriculum of each Year 12 subject, designed to give a comprehensive coverage of students' competencies in that subject, not just the declarative knowledge and the correct handling of algorithms. The tasks are practically oriented and large enough to be engaged by all levels of student taking the course; there is no pass or fail, as such. For example, Box 15.2 gives a CAT in mathematics.

It can be seen that there could be a number of correct ways of going about the problem and probably all students in Year 12 could engage the task at some level of acceptability. In order to begin at all, the student will need to make some assumptions: not only those set out in the 'Information' column, but others such as the size of a bulb in an 'average' house, the hours of use and so on. The specification for the best (*A*) and the lowest (*E*) levels of assessment are:

A. Elaborated the problem effectively. Demonstrated understanding of the complexity of the problem. Formulated the problem mathematically at each stage of elaboration. Applied appropriate mathematical knowledge and problem solving techniques to find solutions. Justified solutions obtained and explained relevance to the problem.

E. Explored initial stages of problem. Applied some relevant mathematical knowledge and problem solving techniques to work towards solutions.

Students not demonstrating these qualities are assessed as ungraded (*UG*) (Ashenden 1990: 28).

The types of tasks that might be used for CATs include the following (Masters & Hill 1988):

- *Research projects:* designing an investigation, implementing a research plan, designing and colecting data, writing up report.
- *Folio* of student work carried out during the year and assessed for range and consistency of work, processes of developing and refining.
- *Practical work:* facility with apparatus, laboratory skills.
- *Oral production:* speaking and listening skills.
- *Essay, short-answer* tests of declarative knowledge.
- ...and many more.

Obviously, different tasks would be used in different subjects, but the attempt is made to grade them in ways such that it is possible to tell what kinds of abilities and skills

Box 15.2   *A CAT in mathematics*

3. Light bulbs

Several manufacturers of light bulbs are advertising new low-energy bulbs. These bulbs cost a lot more than conventional light bulbs, but they use much less electricity and they last much longer.

One company claims their bulbs

- last as long as eight conventional bulbs
- use 20% of the electricity used by conventional bulbs.

It is claimed that because of the savings possible through use of the low-energy bulbs, spending the money to change over the lights in an average house from conventional bulbs to the new bulbs would be a very good investment.

Use the information provided, and any other information you think relevant, to investigate this claim. Express the savings as an annual rate of return on the investment in the change over from conventional bulbs to low-energy bulbs.

Information

Electricity costs (domestic rate, as at January 1990)

kWh	cents/kWh
first 120/quarter	24.35★
next 900/quarter	9.79
balance	10.79

(★this means using one kilowatt, or 1000 watts, for one hour costs 24.35 cents)
Note: prices are indexed on 1 July each year, using the CPI (approximately 8%)

Electricity usage
An average household would use 1000–1500 kWh in three months.

Comparison of bulbs

	New bulbs	Conventional bulbs
Cost per bulb	$24	$1
Expected life of bulb	8000 hrs	1000 hrs
Equivalent light strength	7 watts	40 watts
	11 watts	60 watts
	15 watts	75 watts
	20 watts	100 watts

(From Ashenden 1990)

were displayed by students who received a common grade on a task. In many tasks, it is recommended that teachers form panels of judges for grading or verifying a grade. Reporting of student performance would usually be in the form of a profile.

What is new about the use of CATs is 'not so much the type of tasks used … as the proposal to systematise and integrate these tasks into a coherent assessment system in the secondary school … (so that) … assessment and reporting procedures reflect, rather than define, curricular priorities' (Masters & Hill: 284).

Assessing process

The ability to evaluate, and particularly to evaluate oneself, is part of 'responsible self-direction', which you will recall is that very metacognitive aim of schooling. Development of that ability must involve practice in evaluation: particularly must it mean that students should be given the opportunity to assess their own work.

Self-assessment

Assessing one's own work is a learning experience that is rarely encountered prior to entry into the real world where it is an immediate and natural expectation of the professional person. It seems reasonable that students be given the chance of that experience before entering that world. Boud (1985b) reports a survey of nearly 2000 graduates of the University of New South Wales, who ranked 'evaluating one's own work' as second (to 'solving problems') in a list of nine skills in importance to them in their work; only 20% felt that the university had contributed 'considerably' towards acquiring that skill. Boud argues that self-assessment (not necessarily involving self-grading) 'is an important skill which all graduates should possess and which universities do insufficient towards acquiring' (op. cit.: 1).

That is all very well when talking about graduates. The question is: Does self-assessment have a legitimate place in the school curriculum? Another question is: Why not? There are good reasons why it should.

Assessment of any kind involves two stages:

* *setting the criteria* for assessing the work;
* *making a judgment* about the extent to which these criteria have been met.

Students may be involved in setting the criteria, then in judging in accordance with them; or they may be involved only in judging, using the teacher's criteria. The last case is the most conservative. Let us take that first.

Self-assessment on teacher's criteria

Boud reports a conventional case of a mid-session examination, where students (in an electrical engineering course and after the examination) were provided with a paper of an unnamed fellow student and a detailed model answer. They were asked to mark their colleague's paper in line with the model answer, indicating exactly where the student had deviated from the model. They then applied the same procedure to their own paper, without knowing what marks someone else might have given it. The self- and other-marks were then compared: if the mark was within 10% of what the other student had awarded, the self-mark was given. If the discrepancy was greater than 10%, the lecturer in charge of the course remarked the script. Boud reports that the saving in staff time was considerable, especially in large classes.

There were also considerable improvements in content: the students not only learned the curriculum content to the extent usual for sitting exams, they then studied a model paper, another student's paper, and then their own paper. They had studied the specific exam content several times, from different perspectives in order to assess another student's paper, as well as their own. This technique works only where it is possible to write a model answer; the method could not work in a more open or divergent area, where a great deal of judgment is necessary. To deal with this latter kind of situation, students are involved in setting the criteria.

Self-assessment on student-generated criteria

The class is brainstormed for points that should be included in the assignment, which may be an essay, a project, a lab report, whatever. A large number of criteria are obtained: these are written up on a board and regrouped into smaller categories. It is important that the teacher keep out of the business of suggesting criteria, so that the students feel a genuine 'ownership' about what constitutes a good essay/project/ etc. In fact, Boud reports that no group he has attended has ever omitted a significant feature such as clarity of expression, coverage of literature, proper structure giving aims, method, conclusions, etc. The class then decides which categories to use and with what emphasis. A marking sheet is then drawn and distributed to the class.

The students then go and do the assignment, mark their own work in terms of the criteria and place that marking and its justification in a sealed envelope, which is returned to the teacher, with the assignment itself. It is up to the teacher what happens next. Whether the teacher uses the mark summatively or formatively, in either case the students have gone through an important learning experience:

- they have *decided* the important features of the assignment;
- they have *evaluated* their own work in terms of those features.

The end-product is greatly enhanced in quality as a result.

There are many variations of self-assessment. One is to mix group and individual aims, whereby some of the course content and agreed activities can be decided by the majority, with other aspects negotiated with each individual. In the latter case, a *learning portfolio* can be maintained by the student: a record of everything to do with the course is kept, including a diary on feelings about the course, interactions with individuals in and out of the class, and evidence of learning from these activities. A variation would include a partnership between two members of the class with similar aims towards the course. In such a course, students would state their aims in undertaking the course and then decide whether or not their aims had been met and the evidence they had in their portfolios for coming to that conclusion. Such activities are of course highly compatible with CATs.

Harris and Bell (1986) distinguish collaborative assessment (involving student and teacher, as in Boud's first case) from assessments by peers and self-assessment. All have their uses and, as we have seen in Boud's examples, can be used in conjunction with each other. The important thing is that the locus of evaluational judgment does not reside exclusively in the teacher, as that restricts the opportunities for learning that assessment provides.

Evaluation of process in specific tasks

The second aspect to process evaluation is evaluating the processes used in a specific task. In Chapter 13, we referred to deep processes in essay writing, where students undertake the activities of planning, composing and reviewing with units of a high semantic level, main ideas and especially the theme. The extent to which students actually undertake these activities, and at what level, may be established by interview, or interactive observation (if done sensitively) during the processes of writing. In fact, good teaching would necessarily involve this kind of teacher–student interaction.

In the case of reading, Paris in his ISL program assessed children's metacognitive knowledge of reading strategies, and the questionnaires developed in that work have been useful in identifying strengths and weaknesses in children's understanding of the processes of reading (e.g., Kirby & Moore 1988; Moore 1983). There are, however, really two different perspectives on this process evaluation. On the one hand, we want to know if students are aware of the range of successful strategies that can be employed to solve a reading (or other subject area) problem. That is in fact what has been tapped in the questionnaires used by Paris, and Kirby and Moore. On the other hand is the issue of how frequently students use such strategies when dealing with reading tasks. To have the metacognitive knowledge but not use it may indicate that the strategy knowledge has not reached the threshold level for it to be used readily in contexts where the strategy is required. In other words, the strategy knowledge is at an 'acquainted' rather than 'established' level. Clearly our aim is to ensure the establishment of strategies and the use of process-oriented questionnaires and observations should facilitate that in reading and other tasks.

In Chapter 7 it was suggested that process be assessed in terms of divergence, but within specific content areas. Thus, in social studies, teachers could address the ability to test hypotheses (e.g., that family structure is related to social stability). Divergence could be addressed with test items like 'What would happen if ...' (e.g., Western Australia seceded from the Commonwealth); 'Think of as many different ways as you can of slowing the drift from rural areas to the cities'. This kind of process testing is, in effect, using the psychological process variables as a *structure* for constructing the test items.

Grading

Implementing the results of evaluation involves that aspect of summative evaluation that causes most worries: grading. By grading, most people mean the award of labels (e.g., distinction, credit, pass, fail, or a numerical equivalent). Two particular aspects of the usual grading systems cause concern among teachers, students, parents, employers and the general public: grading is a system of *discriminating* between people—*publicly*.

Grading uses data that are to be made available to employers or educational institutions and, on that basis, decisions will be made that seriously affect the student's life.

Forms of grading

Written evaluations

These are qualitative statements made about each student for each subject: a criterion checklist, simple statements about each student's strengths and weaknesses, and so on. Such statements, if they are to be meaningful, need to be criterion-referenced, which also helps to avoid the subjectivity and unreliability of overall ratings. Such evaluations, however, take a long time to prepare and a lot of space to report. Further, they hardly meet the requirements of public evaluation: their main value is for the student, future teachers, parents, etc. Really, of course, they should be provided *whatever* other forms of grading are used.

Self-grading

In self-grading students evaluate their own work qualitatively (either in writing or in conference) in line with their own and their teachers' criteria. Then there are two options: The teacher may simply consider these evaluations when arriving at the final grade, or the students may set their own grade, which may or may not then be averaged with the teacher's grade. Both self-grading and self-evaluation are important learning experiences, given the obvious cautions: credibility and whether students have the content expertise to make appropriate judgments.

The contract system

Contracts between student and teacher can be devised either on an individual basis, whereby each student negotiates his or her own contract, or on a class basis, where the terms of the contract apply to everyone in the class. In either case, it is agreed between students and teacher that so much work is worth an 'A' (or whatever labels are used), so much a 'B' and so on. Where a student fails to meet the terms of the contract, a new one can be negotiated, or the outcome left to the teacher's judgment. A variation is the point-accumulation system: *A* may be worth 10-12 points; *B*, 7–9; *C*, 4–6; *D*, 2–4; and *F*, zero or 1 point. There is no need for students actually to sign a contract; they know the rules (and may well have a hand in deciding them) and each works until sufficient credit is gained towards a grade that satisfies. Under this kind of system, a student should be permitted to re-submit a poor paper.

Mastery learning

Already discussed at some length, mastery learning can be used in connection with a letter-grade system: 'A' if all tasks are complete, 'B' if most are, etc. *Pass/fail* is where the only statement on a student's report or transcript is whether the course is passed or failed. This used to be popular 20 years ago, but in the 1980s and 1990s, students want the option of high grades. Nevertheless, pass/fail still has a place; it results in a more pleasant classroom atmosphere, which is important where a high degree of participation and discussion is desired. *Credit/no credit* is a version of pass/fail, strongly endorsed by Glasser (1977). The student receives credit for *passing* a course, but there is no permanent record of *failing*.

From test marks to final grade

Whatever grading system is used, the teacher is faced with another of those 'almost impossible' tasks: to reduce a year's performance in one or several subjects to a single symbol. In quantitative terms it is fairly easy, in that we have to move from the student's performance expressed in marks, percentages or number correct, to the grading category (i.e., B, credit, pass). In principle, it is a very different problem when we assess performance qualitatively and end up with a profile (on CATs, or SOLO categories, or phenomenographic levels), which we have then to convert to a grading category. There are two violations in the last case: qualitative categories are best used formatively rather than summatively; and there is a blip in logic in trying to combine qualitatively different categories (a) with each other and then (b) converting them into a numerical system. Still, it has to be done and the simplest approach is best: replace ordered categories by numbers ($U = 1$, $M = 2$, etc.) and then combine them additively. It is not even worth trying to weight them differentially: 'there is probably little point in not giving all CATs within a study the same weight in an aggregate' (Masters & Hill 1988: 283). What applies to CATs should then apply to other categorical ratings.

There are two different issues: moving from a mark to a grading category and combining several marks or grades to form a final grade.

Determining grade from a distribution of marks

The first problem arises where marking is along a continuous scale, such as where points are awarded for various aspects of a paper (e.g., 5 marks for organisation, 1 mark for title, 15 marks for evidence of wide background reading, 10 marks for originality of approach, etc.) or where the marks of several raters are to be added in.

A typical score distribution (where 50 students have been given a 20-item objective test, with each correct response gaining one mark) and some suggested grading schemes are outlined in Table 15.4 (the figures are taken from an actual class list).

Table 15.4 *Some alternative grading schemes*

Final score distribution	Number of students	Norm-referenced compromises 1	2	3
20 (max.)	1			
19	2	6 As		
18	3	(nearest 10%)	7 As	Excellent
17	1			
16	0			
15	2	8 Bs	2 Bs	
14	0	(nearest 20%)		
13	2			
12	3			Satisfactory
11	6			
10	8	19 Cs	29 Cs	
9	5	(nearest 40%)		
8	5			
7	0			
6	0	10 Ds		Doubtful
5	2	(nearest 20%)		(borderline)
4	3		9Ds	
3	4			
2	0	7 Fs		
1	2	(nearest 10%)	3 Fs	Unsatisfactory
0	1			
TOTAL	50			

Scores on the test ranged from 0 to 20: one student got all 20 correct; two got 19 correct; three 18, one 17 and so on. The test is of moderate difficulty, with most scores around the halfway mark, so the problem is to allocate As, Bs., etc. Logically there are two alternatives, norm- or criterion-referenced, but there is in fact a compromise. Let us say the agreed 'ration' is: approximately 10% of the class to get As, 20% Bs, 40% Cs, 20% Ds and 10% Fs (a nice symmetrical near-enough-to-normal curve).

We count down the list and mark off the appropriate percentages (column 1). We cannot get exactly 10% As: if we allow 20 and 19 items correct, we have three students (6%); and if 18 items correct is also allowed, six students (12%). 12% is nearer, so we will give As to students scoring 18 and above. And so on down the distribution, leaving seven students as Fs, with 3 or fewer items correct.

This is hardly good sense; look at the gaps in the distribution. Let the shape of the distribution, together with the teacher's sense of what is or is not a good score, decide the cut-off points (column 2). We now see that the top seven students form a group: let us call them all As. The two who scored 15 correct would be Bs. There is now a run of students, from 13 to 8 items correct, that cluster around the halfway mark: these could all be Cs (column 2) or a division could be made between a score of 11 and 12, giving 5Cs and 24 Ds (column 3). A cluster of nine students with 3, 4 and 5 correct could become Es, leaving three clear Fs (column 2), or they could be classified as unsatisfactory (column 3). The teacher's judgment would have to decide on what provided the best grading solution, given the nature of the items and the quality of the students. In this case, the results on the basis of column 3 say that something utterly horrible has happened.

The main advantage of the method in columns 2 and 3 is that it is non-competitive: the grades are not rationed, they just follow the natural fall-out of marks. If 40 students scored 18 and above, then all 40 would receive As. Nevertheless, it is still the distribution determining the result, as in NRT proper, the content of the items only secondary.

The CRT way of determining the grades would be to decide in advance what the categories 'A', 'B', 'C', etc. stood for in relation to the items: for example, obtaining at least 80% correct, including the key items 1, 3, 6, 19 and 20, for an 'A'; 80% of any items for a 'B' and so on.

The teacher would have to decide what is most appropriate.

Combining grades

The second problem to be considered is that of combining grades to form a final grade. To illustrate, say the following have to be taken into account:

- a term paper;
- a research project;
- an objective examination;
- an essay examination.

There are two logical alternatives.

1. *Combine them all.* The most common procedure is to make each set of marks count, the assumption being that they all assess something different and are all important. Either one takes the average as the final grade, or requires a pass in each, so that a good student has to do a good term paper *and* a good project *and* good exams: the final grade is then composed of the sum (*union*) of the several sets of marks, as suggested in the case of CATs.

If the marks are to be combined additively, they have to be converted into the same scale (e.g., percentages, but strictly speaking one should convert them statistically into standard scores) and then one has to decide what weight to give each mark (e.g., is the project to count equally with the final objective?). The cleanest solution is that suggested by Masters and Hill (1988) for CATs: all receive equal weight. But maybe the students could decide in a class discussion.

2. *Grade the best result only.* The second alternative allows for both individual differences and the fact that test distortion might penalise students in areas that are actually irrelevant educationally. Here the assumption is that individuals do differ: students can arrive at different goals by different routes and still be competent. Hence, to pass this course, a student must show progress by writing a good term paper *or* do a good research project *or* pass a final exam in either essay *or* in objective format.

It is obviously a matter of educational philosophy as to which of the two models is considered more appropriate. Students who do best by using all tests and papers have been found to be surface-achievers (teacher-dependent, organised in their approach and rote learn a great deal). Those who do best when their best paper is selected tend to have a deep approach, putting all their efforts into what they were most interested in (Biggs & Braun 1972).

It does matter, therefore, how tests and assignment results are combined: it looks like the familiar dichotomy between quantity and quality of work. Clearly, teachers will have to do what they see as best given their own objectives.

The award at the end of schooling

After years of external examinations at Year 12, most Australian states moved towards school-based assessments, with Queensland starting the process after some horrifying results in the senior physics examination in 1976, when 75% failed. The reason was not that students were degenerating academically, intellectually and morally, as the chief examiners tended to believe (Campbell & Campbell 1978), but that tertiary requirements were out of kilter with what the schools were teaching and what students were learning in Year 12. It's our familiar problem: testing and learning should be integral events and frequently aren't.

One of the major problems of school-based curriculum development and student assessment, however, is that some judgments, for example awarding HSC results or selecting for tertiary entrance, require that students are compared on the same scale. With a single external assessment, there is little problem, but if there is no external exam and different schools are giving their students different tests, what do you do?

The way followed by many states involved using 'moderation' or 'reference' tests. In Victoria and previously in New South Wales, the reference tests were tests given in the middle of the year and the *school* (not the student) was awarded a grading, which determined the number of '9s', '8s' and so on that would be available for allocation between students at the end of the year. That then left the school free to allocate those grades in any way it saw fit, such as in-house tests, teachers' ratings, etc. There are considerable problems about this essentially norm-referenced procedure; competition for those 'rationed' higher grades will be fierce and the procedure itself can be unfair, if schools are naughty enough, for example, to program an excursion for the slower students on the day of the reference tests.

Using IRT, in-house assessments (teachers' ratings and other tests that each school has decided to give, such as CATs) can be rescaled against an 'anchor' test, which could be the original reference test, and direct comparisons across schools and populations can then be made (Masters 1988). This procedure avoids the possible shifts in population between the reference and the final assessment, and the competitive jostling for the high grades nominated by standard moderation testing procedures.

Summary

Some properties of tests

Three major properties are considered: how stable the scores are from occasion to occasion (reliability); whether the test measures what it is meant to measure, however stable it may be (validity); the extent to which it is reliable but not valid because it is measuring personality characteristics of the student (distortion).

Teachers and tests

Should teachers construct their own tests or use those constructed by commercial agencies, with vastly greater resources for norming and validating than teachers have? Commercial tests have their value, but for everyday use teachers should construct their own, because teaching, learning and assessment are integral events. But what about the evidence (from United States studies) that mostly teachers don't do a very good job at test construction? They favour objective tests that focus on the lowest cognitive levels, they make mistakes (like unclear instructions) in constructing the tests, and they do not seem to get better at it with experience. In fact they need to read *Process of Learning*.

Methods of assessing outcomes

Outcomes refer to: declarative knowledge of taught content, which includes both coverage (a quantitative outcome) and structure of knowledge, originality and transfer to new situations (qualitative outcomes). Various testing formats have been devised for each kind of outcome: objective test, especially multiple choice and the short answer (for quantitative outcomes), and ordered-outcome, essays, concept mapping, Venn diagrams, prediction–observation–explanation, the practicum, oral tests such as presentations and interviews and common assessment tasks (CATs) (for qualitative assessment). Each format has its own advantages and limitations.

Assessing process

One of the most important aspects of metacognitive learning—and of competence in professional and everyday life—is the process of monitoring one's own learning. Students should have the chance of assessing their own learning: of having a hand in determining the criteria of good learning and in assessing their products in terms of those criteria. There are many variations on self-assessment, peer-assessment and collaboration with the teacher in different aspects of assessment.

Another aspect of process assessment is when the processes used in producing an outcome in a particular task are defined and assessed. These range from the 'elegance' of a solution, to a fine-grained analysis of performance on key activities in producing an outcome. Such key activities of course vary between subjects: we have seen examples in reading and writing in Chapter 13.

Grading

Grading is the ultimate summative evaluational act. It involves reducing all the information pertaining to a learner's performance in a subject or course to a single, life-changing, symbol. There are systems of grading which may involve the student's collaboration, although mostly they don't. Qualitative and quantitative data involve different problems in determining grades, as do data derived from NRT and CRT. The quantitative case is a matter of combining different test scores and then determining the cut-off points for defining the grades; the qualitative, of deciding on logical grounds what link there should be between a level of performance and a category saying 'Distinction', 'Pass', or 'Fail'. The question of reporting grades (and supporting information) to other educators, parents, other interested parties such as prospective employers, means reconciling public relations with evaluational sense: not an easy task.

Learning activities

1. Test reliability and validity

The purpose of this activity is to demonstrate your understanding of the basic principles of test reliability and validity. As a group activity, present on chart paper or overhead transparencies the various types of reliability and validity that teachers need to be aware of in their testing. The presentation should stress the importance of knowing such data about tests before they are used in making inferences about student abilities and performance.

An extension of this activity would be to examine test manuals for commercially available, standardised tests to see what reliability and validity data are provided for users.

2. The objective test

In this chapter we dealt with four types of objective test formats: true-false, multiple-choice, matching, and ordered-outcome. In this activity you are to prepare a 5–10 minute paper for presentation at a school staff meeting. (The presentation could be part of a class simulation activity.) The paper should address the advantages and disadvantages of each format and you should provide examples which tap lower as well as higher cognitive levels of understanding.

3. The essay

The research we presented in this chapter about the reliability of essay marking should certainly make you aware of the problems of assessing continuous prose responses. In this activity, that research and the ways of increasing marking reliability are combined into the one presentation. Again we think that a presentation to a simulated staff meeting is an appropriate way of presenting the material. The presentation (perhaps as group presentations to a whole class) should use the research (e.g., Diederich 1974) to demonstrate the problems and also indicate ways in which reliability can be improved.

An alternative mode of presentation could be the development of a video-tape for presentation to the simulated staff meeting. In this context, various 'teachers' could be interviewed and asked about how they mark and assess essays. You could imagine a range of different perspectives being presented with these being drawn together to illustrate the nature of the problem.

4. Learning portfolios

One of the variations of self-assessment is the learning portfolio in which the student keeps records of any aspect of a course (e.g., feelings about the course, amount of learning and challenge, amount of interaction with teacher and peers). In this activity the focus is on YOU as we are suggesting you put together your own learning portfolio for any particular course and use it for your own purposes to see how things are going for you. You might decide to complete it each day after that class and then reflect upon your learning as you make new entries and also at the conclusion of the unit.

The learning portfolio could also be used as a class activity where individual portfolios are completed during class (using *Process of Learning*). As part of class activities, entries could be discussed. Do you think this type of activity would enhance your understanding of yourself, your own learning and the learning of others? (Your portfolio might show this.)

5. Teacher-made tests

Marso and Pigge's (1991) study of teachers in the United Sates suggested to us that teachers are not ambitious enough about the level they test (a focus on lower level outcomes) and they are too ambitious about the type of test they set (complex objective types of tests that they get wrong). In this activity you are to gather tests from teachers and analyse them along the lines detailed in our discussions of Marso. As a class activity, groups could be formed to examine teacher tests in different curriculum areas (e.g., maths, science, literature) and report the findings back to the whole class. It might prove fruitful to extend this activity by addressing reliability and validity problems as well.

6. Reporting to parents

Here is your chance to design the 'ultimate' report card for reporting student progress to parents. Several activities could be combined into one here. First, collect examples of school report cards and analyse them in terms of the information presented in Chapters 14 and 15. For instance, is there grading? How is it determined and presented? Are the tests of the NRT or CRT type? Is there information on the report card about how scores are obtained? Next you could rank the report cards in terms of their acceptability on the criteria explicitly and implicitly presented in these chapters, and finally you can produce your idea of the 'best-fit' report card that parents will understand.

This activity would probably be best done as a group activity and the results presented in a seminar.

Further reading

On assessing along traditional lines
Crocker, L. M. & Algina, J. (1986). *Introduction to Classical and Modern Test Theory*. New York: CBS College Publishing.
Linn, R.L. (ed.). (1988). *Educational Measurement*. New York: Macmillan/American Council of Education.
    Either of these two texts is excellent for detailed treatments of modern test theory, test construction and discussion of measurement issues.

On assessing in new formats

Boud, D. (1985). *Studies in Self-assessment* (Occasional Publication, no. 26, UNSW). Kensington: Tertiary Education Research Centre.
Harris, D. & Bell, C. (1986). *Evaluating and Assessing for Learning.* London: Kogan Page.
Masters, G. N. & Hill, P. W. (1988). Reforming the assessment of student achievement in the senior secondary school. *Australian Journal of Education,* **32**, 274–86.

Harris and Bell is a very useful book which emphasises why we are assesssing learning: it's not to distort the processes of teaching or of learning. They suggest inventive evaluation-type situations that evaluate higher order and creative aspects of learning without scaring students into hiding the very thing we're looking for. Boud give more detailed illustration of his self-assessing techniques. Masters and Hill explain what CATs are all about and why.

PART 6

TEACHING AND LEARNING

TEACHING FOR BETTER LEARNING

Teaching for better learning

Question

Question

What makes the difference to the outcome of learning?

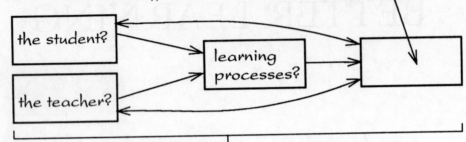

Answer   All of the above, acting together, but the student's learning processes are central

Question

What contexts encourage deep learning processes?

Answer

- Where the knowledge base is sound
- Where the learner is motivated
- Where the learner interacts with others
- Where the learner is actively involved

and • The more of each, the better

and • where

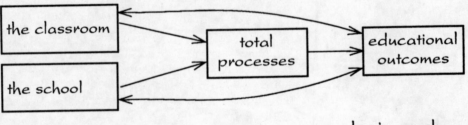

are also in synch.

TEACHING FOR BETTER LEARNING

In this chapter, you will find out:

- what the properties of a 'system' are;
- how the classroom shares the properties of a system;
- how the 3P model of the classroom can help you think about effective teaching and learning;
- how to improve student learning without placing the sole responsibility on students or on the teacher;
- what factors encourage a surface approach to learning and how they can be identified and minimised;
- what factors in the learning context favour deep-achieving approaches to learning;
- how to sharpen up the relevant knowledge base;
- how to set up a Theory Y environment;
- how to use peer interaction in learning;
- how to keep learners productively active;
- how the classroom system is part of, and the extent to which it is affected by, the larger school system

A systems approach to learning and teaching

What makes the difference?

> The best answer to the question, 'What is the most effective method of teaching?', is that it depends on the goal, the student, the content and the teacher ... Large and small classes, lectures and discussions, and other comparisons of teaching show few consistent and significant differences. The conclusion that teaching doesn't make a difference is, however, erroneous. (McKeachie, Pintrich, Lin & Smith 1986: 63).

Yes, schools do make a difference. It is necessary to say this because some well-publicised research is often quoted as saying that they do not. In the 1960s, Coleman (1966) found that the effects due to quality of teaching were small, compared to the huge differences in student achievement that could be attributed to the wealth of the district in which the school was situated. The lesson? Don't waste money on public sector schooling!

It would be very unfortunate if people (particularly teachers and students and, more particularly, politicians) believed that. And neither they should. There were several things wrong with Coleman's research design and with his statistical methods (Raudenbush & Bryk 1988–89). Husen and Tuijnman (1991) summarise the most recent work on this, including a re-analysis of longitudinal studies of attainment from primary school into adulthood and conclude that:

- home background affects attainment in school, but *not* adult cognitive ability (IQ);
- adult IQ is, however, directly affected both by childhood IQ and by educational attainment in school.

So home background has no direct effect on adult cognitive ability, but school does. Thus, schools and teaching *do* make a substantial difference, both to student achievement and to later functioning as an adult (Hattie, 1992). In this chapter we look at what makes learners learn more effectively. In the next chapter we look at what makes teachers teach more effectively.

The 3P model of learning and teaching

If students are to learn desired outcomes in a reasonably effective manner, then the teacher's fundamental task is to get students to engage in learning activities that are likely to result in their achieving those outcomes ... It is helpful to remember that what the student does is actually more important in determining what is learned than what the teacher does. (Shuell 1986: 429)

Shuell's statement is a simple, commonsense statement of constructivism and its translation into a Level 3 conception of teaching. Our next task is to structure the major components that make up what teaching in this sense involves, so that teachers may have a working description to guide their thinking.

What happens in classrooms is well captured by adapting Dunkin and Biddle's (1974) model of teaching:

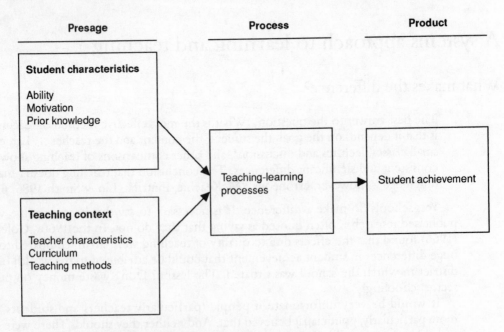

Figure 16.1 *Presage, process and product in the classroom*
(Adapted from Dunkin & Biddle 1974)

1. *presage* factors comprise the first stage; these are aspects of students' and teaching contexts that existed prior to the immediate action in the classroom. These feed into:
2. *process* factors, which refer to the teaching-learning mix that goes on during classroom interaction and which in turn produce the:
3. *product,* usually quantified in terms of student achievement (Figure 16.1):

This presage–process–product (3P for short) model has been adapted to suit the perspective of the learner in the previous edition of this book (Biggs & Telfer 1987). However, it is now clear that we are not dealing with a one-way situation, from presage-to-process-to-product, but with interaction between all the components, which form an integrated *system* (Von Bertalanffy 1968). The systems property adds considerably to our understanding of teaching and learning, as you shall see.

But what is a system?

The systems model

A system is a working whole made up of a set of component parts, which interact with each other to form an equilibrium; this state of equilibrium is the system. Introduce a new part, or change one of the existing parts, and one of two things happens. If the existing system is stable, it will be resistant to change; then the new part will die, or change to merge imperceptibly with the existing system. Alternatively, if the system is fragile, the new component will change the old equilibrium, forming a new system. Things will work differently in future.

Systems theory can apply to almost any complex situation. The prime example of course is an ecological system. Divert the waters of the Murray for irrigation purposes and things change drastically and mostly unforeseeably; among other things, in this case the watertable rises bringing salt with it. Once the swamplands could leach the salt, but now that they have died the salt level rises in the Murray itself. The Murray-Darling system of today is very different, saltier and nastier, than what it was even 20 years ago.

Anything you do to one part will affect the rest. In these days of environmental awareness that now seems obvious, but it is amazing how modern the idea is, at least to the educated public. And of course, like any constructivist idea, it is 'subversive' (Candy, 1991); it is a model of continuing change and questioning.

The alternative to the systemic model is the more primitive additive (including subtractive) one; that if you add something, or take something away, then all that has changed is what you have added or taken away. It is a multistructural deficit model, whereas a system proper is relational. Much depends on what and how much is added or subtracted. Sometimes taking away one tree from a forest will not affect the life of the system. But what system? If that tree contained the last colony of pigmy possums in the region it would be disastrous for the possums' system.

In the quantitative conception, learning does not form a system; it is additive or multistructural. When more knowledge is acquired in the quantitative conception, you know more. The end. In the qualitative conception, learning does form a system; when more knowledge is acquired your viewpoint changes. The result is different from the sum of the parts. Sometimes the simpler additive model works well enough with low level content, like facts and skills. With high level content and with other complex events, such as managing a classroom, the additive model does not do at all.

An excellent example of a system at work is given by Frederiksen and Collins (1989) when teachers and students succumb to pressures to maximise test scores:

The test scores, rather than playing the role of passive indicator variables for the state of the system, become the currency of feedback within an adapting educational system. (op. cit.: 27)

The old problem of backwash, in other words. A test that drives the system backwards (and downhill) is not a good test or a valid one. The testing tail wags the learning dog almost everywhere, but most damagingly in educational systems that rely heavily on external examinations or performance indicators (a likely development in Australia). Simply, as Frederiksen and Collins say, what should be variables indicating the state of the system becomes the currency that drives it.

Systems in educational contexts operate at several levels:

The individual task

When writing an essay, you can see it either as a system or additively. We saw in Chapter 13 that unsophisticated revision to text simply involves correcting spelling and adding in more sentences to 'say more'. Deleting sentences, or changing the order of paragraphs, as more sophisticated writers do when they revise, presupposes a systematic view of the whole essay.

The classroom

At the classroom level, we have interaction between the presage factors, *students*, and their characteristics individually or collectively, and *teaching context,* comprising the teacher and the school-determined constraints (curriculum, rules of interaction between teacher and students, etc.), which together focus on the central *process* issue of how students go about learning and what the *product* or outcome of learning is. The equilibrium built up here determines how all the parts interact; the students, the teacher, curriculum, discipline, methods of teaching and assessment, and so on. We expand this below.

The school

The classroom system is nested in the school system; it has a certain life of its own, but at some point the school takes over. In the film *Dead Poets' Society*, Mr Keating ran a wonderful classroom; his theme was not to settle for the established order but, at the right time, to step beyond: *'Carpe diem!* Seize the day!' Alas, Mr Keating was not a systems theorist (it may be something to do with the name). Having seized his day, the school system, which had established a very stable equilibrium, seized Mr Keating. The plot unfolded with ecological inevitability. Goodbye Mr Keating.

The state department

The school is in turn nested in the state system. Let us decentralise decision-making from the capital city to the regions, so that the regions respond directly on relatively minor matters that are to be decided within the region. Sound like a good idea? What would systems theory predict, do you think? Depending on how entrenched were the old methods, one might predict that the regions would still refer matters back to the capital city, 'for confirmation'. You would then have the old system, but working even less efficiently, as there would now be two levels of decision-making where previously there was one. Sound familiar? Yes, precisely this happened recently in one state on the matter of researchers attempting to gain access to schools.

The classroom system

There are four major components in the classroom system: two presage components, relating to the students and to the teaching context, one relating to learning processes and one relating to the product or outcomes of learning, whatever they be. In addition, there are interconnections between components. The elaborated model is given in Figure 16.2. The heavy arrows indicate the main directional thrust, from presage through processs to product; the lighter arrows the interactions between all components, which indicate the systemic nature of the whole.

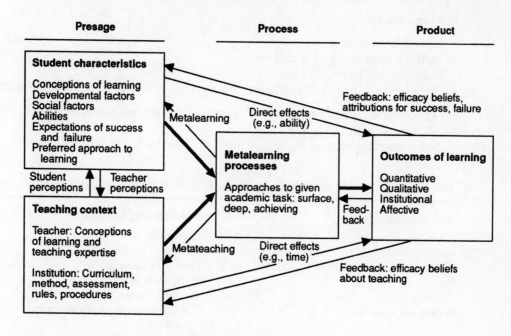

Figure 16.2   *The 3P model as a classroom system*

Presage

Student presage factors include relatively stable, learning-related, characteristics, all of which have been dealt with in this book:

- existing conception of learning (Chapter 1);
- developmental stage and how students typically bring age-related characteristics to their learning (Chapters 2, 3);
- social factors: social class, ethnicity, gender and moral development, values (Chapters 4, 5);
- abilities, such as intelligence, creativity (Chapters 6, 7);
- expectations and motivations for learning, typical attributions for success and failure (Chapter 10, 11);
- preferred approach to learning (Chapter 12)

To illustrate the systems point: If your students were of mixed ability, would you teach all in the same way, so that the bright would come out best and the not so bright worst? In the old days of the additive model you would; the system then was only interested in separating out the bright anyway. These days that will not do. We adapt our curriculum, methods and assessment to suit all students, which implies a higher order, more all-embracing system.

Teaching presage factors include the teachers' personal characteristics:

- their own conceptions of learning and teaching (Chapter 1);
- their expertise (Chapter 17);

and institutionally,

- curriculum content;
- methods of teaching (this chapter);
- assessment (Chapter 14, 15);
- the superstructure of rules and procedures within which all must work (Chapter 17).

This context, apart from its cognitive aspects, also generates a cold or warm climate for learning (Chapters 11, 17).

Some common presage factors are listed in Table 16.1.

TABLE 16.1:   *Some common presage factors (a) student-based, (b) classroom-based*

(a) *Student-based factors*	(b) *Classroom-based factors*
Developmental stage	Curriculum
Ability	Method of Teaching
Socioeconomic status	Method of assessing
Sex	Teacher 'personality'
Ethnicity	Teacher expertise
Conception of learning	Teacher's conceptions of learning and teaching
Typical attributions for success/failure	Compulsory/optional unit
Typical approach to learning	Classroom climate
Specific knowledge base for task	Other students in class
Interest in task	Nature of task
	Skill in task requirements

Process

Whatever balance is struck between teacher and student, and whatever the institutional givens, students interpret this teaching context in the light of their own preconceptions and motivations, and derive their learning processes through metalearning (Chapter 12). A learning process is the system's answer to the interaction between student and teaching presage factors. Depending on the students' predilections for a surface, deep, or achieving approach to learning, and depending on how they see the demands made by the teaching context, students clarify their intentions about handling the immediate task before them (e.g., to do it well, to get it out of the way as painlessly as possible) and so derive their particular way of approaching the task in question.

However, part of the metacognitive process is to monitor, evaluate, and change as you go, giving rise to further metalearning, in the students' case, and to metateaching (see below) in the teacher's case (note the reversed lines from process to presage).

Product

Outcomes are in large part determined by approaches, so that an important part of teaching is to optimise the chances that the most adaptive approaches to learning are utilised. The learning outcome may be described quantitatively (how much is learned), qualitatively (how well it is learned) and institutionally, which draws variously on both qualitative and quantitative aspects in deriving the marks and grades awarded for learning.

Again, the systems character is revelant to the outcome. Although process factors are very important, they are not the only ones. There are direct presage–product links. From the student side, IQ has a direct effect on the outcome: the brighter the student, the better the performance (other things being equal). On the teaching side, the more time on task, the better the outcome. Yet each of these factors is also mediated by process: brighter students are more likely to use more adaptive processes, and more time on task also affects the process used. Affective outcomes of learning refer to how students feel about their learning once it is over; but as it never really is over, they carry those feelings around with them in ways that affect future learnings for a long time.

Then, perceptions of outcome affect both student and teacher. The students' perceptions of outcome will determine *inter alia* their beliefs about their own efficacy, which are crucial in determining the quality and extent of their future involvement in learning (Chapter 10). The same could be said for teachers. Outcome measures could affect their own beliefs about how well they are teaching; as they should, as this is the most direct information teachers get about their teaching methods (Guskey 1986).

Thus, all levels interact with each other. At presage, students' conceptions of learning and teaching can be directly changed by what they see of the teaching context, while teachers' perceptions of students' abilities or interests will, or should, affect their decision-making.

The 3P model thus describes a cycle of events, in which student characteristics, the teaching context and students' learning processes are related to learning outcomes. There are several important implications for practice when you conceive your classroom as a steady state achieved by various components in balance, as we explore in this and the next chapter. And in case you hadn't realised it, 3P also provides a framework for structuring this book (see the part and chapter headings in the table of contents).

Who is responsible for learning?

The student? The teacher? The system?

The blame-the-student model

In the old days of educational psychology, ability or IQ was seen as the single most important factor determining the outcome of learning. Bright students learned well, dim ones didn't. All the teacher had to do was to provide, organise and present the content and keep the dim ones quiet; what determined the outcome, given a constant and non-interactive teaching environment, was IQ. This is a version of the deficit model called blame-the-student (Figure 16.3); it downplays the role of the teacher. When things aren't going too well, it's not the teacher's fault. While that might be a comforting thought, it's no help in providing solutions.

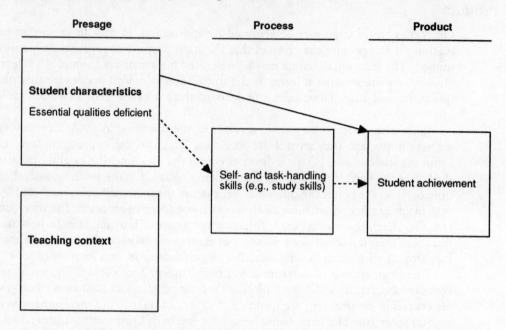

Problem: Low achievement is due to a deficit in the student. The students lack: diligence/ability/
           fortitude/interest/character/study skills/prefrontal lobes … (take your pick)

Solution: Make good the deficit if possible. If not, baby-sit them. You don't have to do anything
           about the teaching.

Figure 16.3   *The blame-the-student model*

This model is based on a Level 1 conception of teaching and is relatively common. Have you ever heard staffroom comments such as these?

- 'Next period is that shower (sic) from the Housing Commission. Hand me my cattle prod.'
- 'Anne shouldn't have been doing tech. drawing in the first place.'
- 'They're the bottom stream … what do you expect?'
- 'Study skills! That's what they need for the HSC.'

All these statements have in common the notion that something is missing from the student and that everything would be all right if you could only make good the deficiency. If they're dim, then you can't do much about that except baby-sit. If they're behavioural problems, then you'll just have to sit on them, hard; after all, you're not a psychologist. Even direct study skills training derives from a deficit model. The attribution to lack of study skills ignores the teaching context and as we have seen such training may even be counter-productive (Ramsden, Beswick & Bowden, 1986).

The blame-the-student model is too simple by half because it deflects attention from an important part of the action: teaching. It gives rise to a now discredited model of schooling as a screening device for sorting out those who have got it and will go far from those who haven't and who will become the early leavers.

The blame-the-teacher model

He wants to teach, doesn't he? That's what he's trained for. If we don't learn he might stop and take a look at what he's doing. (Adrienne, a Year 6 girl, quoted in Davies 1982: 128)

The corresponding deficit model on the teaching side is illustrated in Figure 16.4:

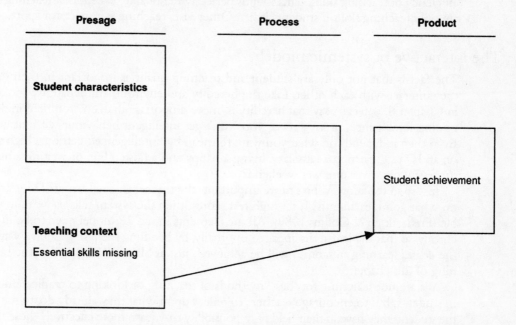

Presage	Process	Product

Student characteristics

Teaching context
Essential skills missing

Student achievement

Problem: Low achievement is due to a deficit in the teaching. The teaching context is spoiled by: poor resources/unskilled teachers/large classes/inappropriate curriculum/poor policy making ...

Solution: Make good the deficit with: staff development, political lobbying, calling in the Teachers' Federation ... Do nothing about student learning

Figure 16.4 *The blame-the-teacher model*

This is based on a Level 2 conception of teaching. The grossest form of this model was based on payment-by-results; in the last century, the teacher's salary depended on the students' examination results. The modern version is the accountability movement, much more prominent in the United States than it is ever likely to be in Australia.

Basically, the blame-the-teacher model sees the teacher as the prime actor in the classroom, the virtuoso who can dazzle with a fine display of mastery of teaching skills:

forward planning, two minutes introduction, a video here, a taped excerpt there, some rapid-fire questions, a perfectly timed squelch for that little Jones creep, funny story time, a couple of exercises, briefing on the homework ... There! Had 'em in the palm of my hand.

One teacher we visited had a multi—audiovisual—sensory overkill display, comprising one tape recorder, two automatic slide-projectors with twin screen simultaneous pictures (timed asynchronously), an overhead projector, and a record player. The aim was to use multimedia to project two simultaneous strands of content in as many modes as possible (visual, auditory, concrete-symbolic, ikonic). A very impressive orchestration but it was an entertainment, not a learning experience. Many staff development workshops are based on the assumption that their function is solely to increase the range and efficiency of teaching skills. This sounds perfectly reasonable, except that teaching skills are only teaching skills if students learn. Otherwise, teaching is a spectator sport.

The interactive or systemic model

The fact is that not only are student and teaching qualities important in themselves, they interact with each other. Like the heredity and environment debate we looked at in Chapter 6, you can't say that heredity is 'more' important than environment in determining intelligence, or vice versa; you won't get intelligent behaviour without either. Even then it depends on what you want to mean by 'intelligence': getting a high score on an IQ test, earning a fat salary, living a happy and adjusted life, or writing a hugely successful play over one wet weekend?

Just so in teaching. Who's more important, the teacher or the learner? Do we agree on what good learning is? If it's high test scores, then the system tells us we're in trouble (Frederiksen & Collins 1989). All the elements in the 3P model need to be in synchrony, so that the learner is engaged optimally, by handling the task in such a way that the *desired* learning outcomes will be achieved, just as Shuell (1986) said at the beginning of this chapter.

We are not searching for 'best' methods of teaching or looking to eradicate defects in students, but to encourage teachers to reflect upon what they already do, to see how the students they have in their field of responsibility may learn more effectively those things they are required to learn. When we become that specific, we will see that while there is no single 'best' method for all seasons, there are many things that some flexible reflection, or metateaching activity, will tell you should probably be done and many others you should certainly not do.

Metateaching

Are you as a teacher getting students to engage the tasks in the way that produces desired outcomes, as indicated in Figure 16.2? Are you in your teaching doing the equivalent of metalearning? If teachers are to help students become more metacognitive about their learning, they should themselves be metacognitive about their teaching. Metateaching gets teachers to think about the *way* they teach, as well as what they teach.

Every decision a teacher makes has its *functional* side (what's obvious to you) and its *impact* side (what's obvious to your students). For example, you set a deadline for assignments, then everyone knows where they stand and can plan around it. You then have to set sanctions for late submission, otherwise it won't work. Careful!

Students will hand in work they know to be incorrect, if your system punishes late submission more than it punishes error (Stipek 1986).

We deal with managerial aspects of the classroom in the next chapter. Here we are concerned with instructional issues. Basically, our aim is to encourage high level metalearning. We have two broad strategies:

- to remove or ease factors that *discourage* metalearning;
- to create or emphasise situations that *encourage* metalearning.

Specifically, this means identifying, then removing or diminishing, those factors that encourage a surface approach, and building into the classroom those factors that encourage deep and achieving approaches. Overriding all such changes is their systematic interrelations; it is these that determine their feasibility.

Discouraging surface approaches

Extrinsic motivation

Extrinsic motivation is the source of the surface strategy. Some form of extrinsic motivation is inevitable, as students need warm-up time before they become intrinsically motivated (if they ever do), but as little as possible, please, and of the right kind. Positive reinforcement (reward) can lead either to enhanced or diminished intrinsic motivation; it is helpful if it leads to ownership, but not if it is seen as a bribe. Negative reinforcement in the form of threats of punishment seems uniformly counter-productive, because it leads to a *cold classroom climate*.

A Theory X classroom (see Box 11.5) involves anxiety, threats, scolding, cynicism and poor interpersonal relations generally, all of which lead to surface motivation and from there to surface strategies. Neither an over-regimented classroom, based on mistrust, nor a chaotic one, can provide a basis for appropriate motivation.

These are some of the things that mark a cold classroom:

- 'dragginess', or insisting on trivia: 'Come on now! Sit up straight! Pencils pointing over your shoulder!' (Kounin 1970);
- sarcasm and intimidation;
- closed government, where students are kept in the dark about decisions that affect them;
- messages that teachers themselves feel negatively: about the subject, the students, or both. Cynicism devalues.

Two key emotions that mark the cold classroom are *anxiety* and *cynicism*. Anxiety almost always has a detrimental effect on learning (Chapter 9). Cynicism degrades learning because it invites students to beat the system; they bargain for the lowest rates they can get away with. Complicated rules and routines, pedantic insistence on trivia, hypocrisy, defensiveness and pretence of any kind on matters affecting students, send messages that invite replies at surface rates.

Time/workload stress

Insufficient time leads inevitably to surface learning. Some high achievers claim to 'work best under pressure': most people don't. While too low a workload leads to little being done, most classrooms probably err on the side of expecting too much, in terms of sheer quantity.

A common time pressure is caused by uncoordinated setting of assignments. Ironically, many individual teachers, in a genuine bid to relieve pressure, may allow students extensions to assignments to the point when there is a monumental build-up towards the end of the term. Teachers can ease that sort of pressure by planning more effectively in consultation with each other.

Routines

Routines that make the classroom an efficient workplace are one thing; routines that take the novelty and creativity out of learning tasks are another. Reducing problem solving to set procedures to be followed, or lab report writing to predetermined statements of what the teacher wants to be observed, forestall deep processing. Such routines say that the outcome is what matters, not the process of how you got there. An interesting comment on routines, or 'scripts', is given in Box 16.1.

Box 16.1   *Classroom scripts*

Classrooms have scripts; tacit rules that if challenged create problems. In secondary schools they are very difficult to change. The main script in most secondary classes has the teacher out in front doing most of the talking ... and asking a lot of questions. The answers to the questions are not to inform the teacher, for it is recognized that the teacher knows them already ... Their (students') role is to respond to the demands of the teacher. They are not there to initiate activities of any kind. This script is astonishingly pervasive ... For many subjects it is the only script most teachers have.

White (1988: 113–14)

The most common script calls for an active teacher and an inactive student; a prescription for surface learning. Teacher questions are frequently rituals; 'wait time' (the duration of the pause between utterances by either teacher or student) is usually less than one second, as found in several countries and at all levels of schooling (Tobin 1987). When teachers deliberately allow at least three seconds for students to respond, or for themselves to formulate a new question or response, the cognitive level of the discourse is higher and so is student achievement. Routines make for passivity; passivity makes for surface learning.

Assessment

Tests and examinations have two main effects: affectively, they create challenge for some students but anxiety in others; and cognitively, the backwash from tests tells students (and teachers) what is required and what is rewarded. Challenge leads to achieving strategies only in those challenged; 'challenge' means anxiety to others, where the game is to avoid failure, not to demonstrate competence. Failure can often be avoided by producing slabs of rote-learned material, which is not demonstrating the right kind of competence.

Test constructors therefore have to be very careful to test for higher cognitive processes. However, studies over many institutions and years have drawn attention to the wide gap between the rhetoric describing the qualities teachers say they want in their students' responses and the tasks they set, which frequently just elicit question-spotting and rote memorisation of facts and theories considered important by the teachers (e.g., Bowden 1988; Entwistle 1984; Ramsden 1985; Snyder 1971).

As Elton and Laurillard (1979: 100) pithily put it: 'The quickest way to change student learning is to change the assessment system.'

A wealth of evidence thus exists on what practices encourage surface approaches to learning (see also Crooks 1988; Marton, Hounsell & Entwistle 1984; Ramsden 1985, 1987):

- overwork;
- assessment practices emphasising recall of detail (of which there is a vast range and which probably more than anything accounts for surface learning);
- stress, both in the sense of time pressure and interpersonal friction between teacher and student;
- the cynical messages to be got from rewarding form rather than content in evaluating assignments, devaluing the topic, hoop-jumping;
- and so forth.

All these factors contribute their own two bob's worth towards a cold classroom climate, which sums up what we don't want. Box 16.2 brings in just about all of these features: dragginess, cold climate, assessment, routines ...

Box 16.2   *Blame the student? Blame the teacher!*

Student (S):   I can't do the last two sums ... $3\overline{)54}$, $4\overline{)64}$.

Teacher (T):   What's the problem? Others in the class can do them!!! You've obviously forgotten what I told you last lesson. You should listen. So, will three go into five?

S: Yes
T: So what do we do?
S: One?
T: Now what do we do?
S: Dunno
T: Think, think ...
S: Threes into five is ...
T: What about the two left over?
S: Dunno
T: Don't we put it somewhere?
S: Yes ... I think ...
T: Near the five?
S: Yes
T: (Teacher points between the 5 and the 4). Now what do we say?
S: Threes into ... er ... two.
T: No, no, no! You never listen do you? and your pencil is blunt too. Get on with it. Threes into twenty-four go ... how many times?
S: Six?
T: No

S: Seven?
T: NO !!
S: Eight?
T: At last! If you'd listen more often you'd know how to do them. Now get on
    with the next one ... Go and sharpen your pencil first ...

Source: Observed by one of the authors in a primary classroom.

Has the student the faintest idea of what she is doing? Does she care? *Should* she care, after that? Yet how common is this little scenario.

Cleaning up the act

Many of these surface-inducing features could fairly easily be pinpointed by a well designed questionnaire eliciting students' and colleagues' perceptions (Ramsden & Dodds 1989). Others are part of one's personality and not easily changed, such as habits of sarcasm. Others again are quite subtle. In one study involving an educational psychology class, one topic of instruction was the distinction between rote and meaningful learning. To bring home the message that rote recall was not evidence of understanding, the lecturer said that he would penalise reproductive material appearing in the final assessment. The class also completed a questionnaire on approach to learning, to familiarise them with meaningful and rote approaches (this was before the days of 'deep' and 'surface'). It was found that one subgroup of students with a rote-reproductive approach scored relatively higher in one essay assignment than they did in related objectively scored multiple-choice questions. You've got it; the marker unconsciously marked up those who replayed the lectures, despite what he'd said (regrettably, Biggs 1973).

Other factors that lead to surface learning are almost ineradicable given the way most institutions are run. To become aware of all these inhibitors of good learning in one's teaching involves a personal and an institutional self-searching that might be painful and, while it may not be very practical to eliminate them all, this is an act of metateaching that all teachers should undertake, perhaps using students' ratings and checklists of the kinds of factors.

Identifying and eliminating undesirable features of one's teaching is one thing. Another is to teach positively so that students acquire appropriate approaches and strategies for learning.

Teaching for metalearning and rich learning outcomes

In the research reviewed in this book so far, several teaching/learning contexts have been associated with deep approaches to learning and rich learning outcomes. They have one or more of the following characteristics:

1. A well-structured knowledge base.
2. An appropriate motivational context.
3. Interaction with others.
4. Learner activity.

Given (1), the knowledge base, which underlies all learning, the quality of learning processes and outcomes is likely to improve as each of the above characteristics adds to the others. We might portray the situation as a series of overlapping circles, the more overlaps the better (Figure 16.5):

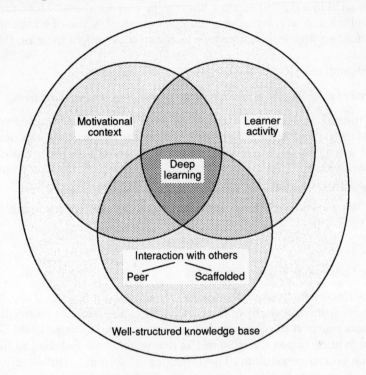

Figure 16.5   *Some characteristics of good learning contexts*

Figure 16.5 could be used to classify teaching methods into those that emphasise peer interaction, or motivation, or learner activity. Each such segment actually optimises different aspects of learning, so it can be used to choose the kinds of methods most likely to achieve desired outcomes.

We now review these four characteristics of good learning contexts and ask what each is best at achieving.

The knowledge base

A well-structured and accessible knowledge base is embedded in all good learning situations. As we saw in Chapter 8, learning is cumulative; the more relevant knowledge one has, the more are the opportunities for rich, generic codes to which new content can be related. Many psychologists would see the knowledge base, both declarative and procedural, as the single most important condition of expert performance (Chi, Glaser & Farr 1988; Sweller 1991). Intrinsic motivation, interaction with others and learner activity all presuppose a focus on content; otherwise they are empty.

What we mean by establishing a good knowledge base is simple. The more one knows about a topic, and the better organised and more accessible that knowledge is, the easier, deeper and more enjoyable will further learning about that topic become. But if good learners are the ones with the adequate knowledge base, what about the ones without? How do you create a knowledge base for them? This issue was addressed in Chapter 8 and several teaching strategies emerged, some of which are reviewed under 'scaffolding' and 'learner activity'. In addition, we might mention the following.

1. Alignment

• *Start by defining the curriculum goals appropriately: and enacting them!*

'Instructional alignment' means no more than our old friend 3P: curriculum intentions should match teaching processes should match learning outcomes (Cohen 1987). And when they do, the results are amazingly good: four times those achieved in non-aligned systems. Lack of excellence, Cohen thinks, is not due to poor teaching, but 'misaligned teaching':

'What's worth teaching' is the same question as 'What's worth assessing.' (Cohen 1987: 19)

So:

• *test for structure, not just lists of facts.*

Whatever curriculum statements might say about high level cognitive outcomes, in an overwhelming majority of cases teachers' logs and interviews show that at least in mathematics numbers of topics are 'taught for exposure' (Porter 1989). That is to say, the topic is brushed past the student and that is somehow intended to fulfil the intentions of the official curriculum. This tendency is of course reinforced by using multiple-choice test items based on recognition, which confirm that, yes, students can recognise that the topic swum vaguely into their ken, but beyond that … well, er…. uh … duuh.

Porter (op. cit.) also found, in a review of many studies of elementary (US) mathematics classrooms, that skills received ten times the attention given to conceptual understanding and problem solving. One teacher spent 93% of her time on computation and only 1% on problem solving. But these figures fluctuated according to absenteeism and circumstance, usually for the worse. It's likely to be no different in Australia. Teachers simply do not teach what the curriculum contains; knowledge bases are not being well structured.

2. Build on the known

• *Introduce the new material by drawing upon what is already known.*

Teaching techniques that make use of the relationship between establishing the knowledge base and motivation would include Ashton-Warner's (1980) 'organic reading', which used for reading material the child's own supplied words, relating to important personal events, thus clearly building on past experience and establishing ownership in a powerful way. In a different way, the use of surprise and variability (Berlyne 1966; Suchman 1961) deliberately conflict the new material with existing knowledge, to generate curiosity and a need-to-explain. Very little content is *completely* new. Analogies and metaphors can always be established, linking what is known to what is being taught.

3. Maximise structure

- *Present material in ways that facilitate structuring the content, using schemata that allow such structuring.*

New information should not be just 'dumped' on the learner, in rambling lessons, or poorly constructed texts. Good teaching always contains a *structure*: both conceptual, such as an advance organiser to structure content, a concept map, or even just a sequence of presentation, with cross-references; and physical, such as a visual layout, bold-faced headings and the like. Even the humble supermarket shopping list is more easily learned when organised into subheads.

You shouldn't do the work for the students, however (see 'Learner activity' below). Lessons that are too well structured can encourage low level processing and wherever possible students should be encouraged to develop their own structures. Inquiry methods properly presented help the students develop their own structure, the new learning fitting the initial question. In a meta-analysis of 39 studies, Lott (1983) found that, compared to traditional expository teaching, inquiry methods lead to better performance on higher level outcomes and equal performance on low level.

There is an optimal balance between presenting students with chaos and with cut-and-dried conclusions to learning. That balance varies between subject matters and between students.

4. Use error constructively

- *Focusing on students' errors is essential in correcting misconceptions*

Many teachers are extraordinarily shy of drawing attention to students' errors. Roth and Anderson (1988) describe two elementary science teachers. Ms Lane seemed an exemplary and humane teacher; she carefully planned her lessons, ensuring that all the material in the text would be covered, was highly interactive with her students, and sought to find something to praise in their verbal responses in class wherever possible: including responses that revealed misconceptions. Ms Ramsey, on the other hand, refused to accept incorrect responses and, on receiving one, would invite the rest of the class to build progressively on the wrong response until the correct understanding was publicly constructed:

> Ms Ramsey focused on the key issues that seemed to represent critical barriers to student learning. Her content coverage could be described as narrow and deep compared to Ms Lane's. This focus conveyed to students that science was about understanding and making sense of a few ideas, rather than a process of collecting and memorizing facts and words. (Roth & Anderson 1988: 127–8)

There are cultural differences in this alertness to the value of error. Japanese teachers typically deal with few problems per lesson, but analyse in great depth and with public discussion the errors made by a few students, so that the reasons why they are errors, and why they were made, become clear to everyone; this 'sticky probing', as Hess and Azuma (1991) call it, can last for two hours with the teacher adjudicating a group consensus compatible with a correct interpretation. We might think such treatment to be pretty tough on the erring individuals, but the Japanese do not see it as punishment; they see it as a learning experience for the benefit of the whole class. No wonder the performance of Japanese children in mathematics is much higher than Westerners' (Stevenson, Lee & Stigler 1986).

Bruner, as usual, has something extremely wise to say about the instructiveness of error and the role of the teacher:

> The existence of the teacher makes possible the commission of error without irreversible harm occurring. (Bruner 1971: 148)

It is in other words a specific responsibility of the teacher to capitalise on the potential for learning that errors create; accordingly, the classroom must be a safe place in which to err. Sadly, most students are not led to believe other than that error means failure and failure means disaster. Logic and psycho-logic pull in opposite directions. Logically, the fact that error occurs and that errors are not often due to random carelessness, enables one to learn both about the content itself and about the way people learn. Not to confront error constructively in the classroom is to waste valuable opportunities for teaching understanding.

> The educated person should be one who has internalized a sense of the instructiveness of error. (op. cit.: 154)

Now that is something to consider well.

5. Maximise metacogniton

• *Increase students' metacognitive awareness of their own knowledge construction.*

Establishing a knowledge base is done, not by the teacher as master builder on a public construction site, but by students constructing the edifice of their content knowledge with the materials supplied both by their teacher and by their life experience, in the context of the classroom. That is the essence of constructivism. And that being so, the students had better be actively involved in the task of construction, aware of what they are doing and checking how well they are doing it. Peterson (1988) specifically tried to get elementary school low ability students to think metacognitively, teaching them procedural skills for doing so. She then asked them to work aloud the following problem (Peterson 1988: 10):

> Twenty-nine students went on a field trip. Each van could hold 8 students. How many vans were needed?
> *Alex*: You have to multiply 8 by 9, um um, then 9 by 7 …
> *Alyssa*: I'm thinking I'm timesing it and I'm seeing which one is closest to 29, like 8 times what is closest to 29 …

After establishing the general strategy and what might be a reasonable number, Alyssa then draws little vans, putting marks in each. The concrete-symbolic method pure and simple was too much for her to handle, but switching between that and her ikonic 'commonsense' method, she got the answer. No prizes for picking the student who had been taught metacognitive thinking skills.

Things seem little better higher up the school. In a Year 12 maths class, ostensibly teaching students to be autonomous in their maths problem solving, teachers initiate more activities than do students, undercutting the higher order procedures and knowledge necessary for effective self-direction (Evans 1991a). There is plenty of room in normal teaching to help students see what they are doing, in particular by giving them the tools and experiences that will enable them to do so. Again, this is subject specific: the tools in maths will be different from the tools in science or in history. But such tools belong to the procedural knowledge of the content area.

The motivational context

A well-structured knowledge base is itself a condition for intrinsic motivation, which is associated with recoding known information in new and more generative ways. Further, good motivation requires that: (a) the task should be *valued*; and (b) the learner may reasonably *expect success*. Chapters 10 and 11 teased out the ways in which students value a task. Ownership emerged as one of the most important factors, and diminishing ownership by alienating students from the task as having the most damaging effect on motivation. Extrinsic rewards do not encourage ownership unless they are used as a demonstration of competence; otherwise they tend to distance the learner from the task. Negative reinforcement, involving the use of threats, is more damaging still because then the threats face the learner more insistently than does the task itself. A cold classroom climate, with its Theory X ecosystem, precipitates threats that alienate learners. A warm classroom climate, basking in Theory Y, radiates ownership and trust. These climates are however just that: necessary but not sufficient conditions for the cultivation of positive motivation. The teacher must further demonstrate that the task is intrinsically worthwhile and valued by the teacher.

Expectations of success and failure depend critically on what the students are most likely to attribute their success and failure to. How these attributions are built up is partly cultural, partly upbringing and partly what goes on in the classroom. Communicating that failure is due to factors that aren't going to go away, and that aren't controllable (such as low ability), is to instil an expectation of future failure. Attributing failure to lack of the appropriate skills, that can be taught, or to insufficient effort, that can be increased in future, help remove the crippling incapacity that failure may induce. Likewise, attributions of success to a special interest, or competence, is likely to increase feelings of ownership and hence positive motivation. Attributing success to luck or to help from someone is likely to decrease feelings of ownership.

Finally, an organised setting, with clear goals and instructions, discipline, a friendly atmosphere but with teacher control, are important prerequisites to motivating students and to the development of deep and achieving approaches (Entwistle, Kozeki & Tait 1989; Hattie & Watkins 1988). Only weirdos are highly motivated in a chaos and then it has to be a chaos of our very own making. The rest of you need order, organisation and some degree of predictability; the goals need to be clear, the requirements well structured, the feedback swift. Otherwise students lose interest.

Interaction with others

Learning is essentially a social activity. Such interactivity can be 'vertical', as in teacher–student interaction, or 'horizontal', as in student–student interaction. Each kind of interactivity has its own effects on learning, with the former emphasising deep integration of detail, the latter, elaboration and metacognitive awareness.

Teacher–student interactivity

Scaffolding

'Scaffolding' is a term used by Wood, Bruner and Ross (1976) to describe the close interactive relationship between the adult and child in language learning. There are many examples of such interactions of 'embedded teaching' (Fischer & Bullock 1984), from the earliest mother–infant relationships, to the one-to-one tutor–student relationship in certain British universities (alas, impossibly expensive as a general method elsewhere).

The essence of this process is that the tutor responds sensitively to the learner's last response, in such a way as to raise the game; a chain reaction is set up that is highly motivating. Scaffolded instruction is logically the beginning point of all instruction, but is not the end. As described originally by Vygotsky (1962, 1978), children's development requires such scaffolding so that they can enter the next higher level of development, but like the scaffolding on a construction site, it needs to be progressively removed until the new structure can stand on its own.

And isn't that what the process of instruction itself is about? Instruction can be seen as a conversation conducted from the standpoint of expert/mentor and tyro/novice, in which the former structures the responses of each to the other in a framework arising from superior knowledge and also conducted within a context of caring (Cazden 1988; Langer & Applebee 1986). It is a powerful method, much under-used, and it achieves quite specific, content related, goals. The student is led into handling a difficult topic or skill that would otherwise be too difficult to engage unaided. It is essentially a means of gaining depth in content.

Elements of scaffolded instruction are clearly appropriate at many points. Graves' (1983) use of conferencing in writing is an example of scaffolding, even though a particular exchange in class may be quite short, like a minute or so. From quite a different angle, and much more tightly structured, is the instruction derived from the expert–novice paradigm (Glaser 1984; Taylor 1991), where the steps used by the expert are prescribed as those to be followed by the novice. Unfortunately, some computer games with scurrilous software also do this extremely well and the motivation induced can become addictive.

Think-aloud modelling

Think-aloud modelling is related to scaffolding without the individual interaction. The technique simply starts with the teacher thinking out loud while doing the task the students are to learn. The teacher is doing the self-analysis and reflection publicly, letting the students know how to do it, so that eventually they do so themselves. In a writing workshop, for example, a writer can think out loud while planning, composing and revising, thus demonstrating the purposes of the various techniques that professional writers use. Students are brought face to face with processes and possibilities that they themselves would not think of.

Let us look at an example. Garth Boomer, a language expert at a writing conference, was asked to give a talk to a large group of Year 12 students and teachers on essay composition. The scenario, freely adapted, went something like this:

Mr Boomer enters the assembly hall of a large city school, where he finds 250 Year 12 students and the teachers from several city schools.

'Well, I'll let you have the bad news first. We're here for a talk on essay writing …' (groans from audience) … 'The good news is that we're going to change places. I'm going to do the writing and you're going to give me the topic …' (instant reaction of pleased surprise).

'OK, then, what's the topic? You tell me'

Mr Boomer stands in front of overhead projector, a large blank area behind him, felt pen poised in hand. Suggestions for essay topics, mostly facetious, are shouted.

The first one mentioned is chosen because 'you students don't always get to choose your topic so neither do I'. *Why is a banana bent?* is written on the transparency.

'Good. We've got the topic. Now I go into what I call "incubation". Let's all do it. For the next five minutes you write down all the things that occur to you that you think might—don't have to, just *might*—go into the final essay and I'll do the same. Then we'll swap notes.'

Mr Boomer switches off the overhead projector and in the next five minutes jots down some thoughts on the bentness of bananas. He then confers with the group, discussing what might go in and what might go out. A structure for the essay begins to emerge.

'Right. Don't know about you, but I'm ready to have a go at the first paragraph ...' and thinking aloud, he writes down the first few sentences, with some misspellings (deliberate). 'Must get something down first. We'll clean it up later.' He then goes back and edits out loud, slashing here, adding there, changing the tense of one sentence, leaving spelling corrections and punctuation until last because 'we don't want to derail our train of thought with mechanical stuff like that'. All redrafting, editing and correcting is done aloud, explaining the thinking behind each change.

After the first paragraph is done, the students are asked to predict each sentence by writing down their own. They find as they go through the essay, that their predictions begin to foreshadow Mr Boomer's composed sentences more closely ... they are beginning to model their writing on what 'real' writers do.

Afterwards, several students told him that was the first time they had realised how writers write. They thought text had to come out in finished form the first time; if it didn't it couldn't be any good. The idea of writing to examine their thinking, to see what they really *did* think about the topic, had never occurred to them.

Afterwards, too, some wryly amused (and a few not-so-amused) teachers came up to him: 'What *have* you let us in for!!?'

Think-aloud can be used in almost any pencil-and-paper task, such as writing essays, solving maths problems, drawing maps, taking notes: in fact, most of the tasks set in school. The advantage of overhead projectors is that every move, including every mistake, can be seen by a large class simultaneously, with the teacher maintaining eye contact and interaction meanwhile. Many teachers think aloud for their students automatically, but many do not. Some because they have not thought of it, some because they do not see the point ('after all, the students have got to learn to do these things for themselves'), but some because they see, as did Mr Boomer's not-so-amused teachers, that it could be a very threatening thing for them to have to do ('What if I got a block! ...').

Peer interactivity

The most common resource in the classroom is students; there are 20 or 30 of them for every one teacher. Teachers should use them more often. There is much evidence that student–student interaction, both formally structured and spontaneous, can enrich learning outcomes. Cognitive outcomes, apart from motivational and social outcomes, are twofold:

- *elaboration* of known content, with a heightened critical awareness of relevance;
- metacognitive awareness of *how* one arrives at a given position.

There are very many ways in which student–student interaction can be utilised.

Peer groups

We have already met peer group interaction in the classroom in Chapter 4, where we discussed role-play, values clarification and the 'bullring'. This use of groups is more in the affective than in the cognitive domain. But groups have of course been widely used for cognitive enrichment in higher education for many years. Tutorials are regularly used to supplement lectures, theoretically in order to develop in students higher level and especially critical thinking skills. That has been the aim, but tutorials typically do not do what they are intended to do. Students 'are often silent and often ill-prepared and the tutor often finds himself giving a lecture' (Collier 1985: 7). An ancient problem, which Johnson Abercrombie (1969) and Collier (1983), among others, have endeavoured to overcome.

Johnson Abercrombie (1969), working with medical students, started with the following theory:

> My hypothesis is that we may learn to make better judgments if we can become aware of some of the factors that influence their formation ... the student learns by comparing his observations with ten or so of his peers. He compares not only the results, but how the results were arrived at ... What the student learns, it is hoped, is not only how we make a more correct response when he is confronted with a similar problem, but more generally to gain firmer control of his behaviour by understanding better his own ways of working. (op.cit.: 18–19)

Her groups consisted of 10 or so students and the task was diagnosis, mostly using X-ray plates as content. That is a highly specialised content area, but the principle is applicable to any situation where students are learning to make judgments and where there is likely to be a strong difference of opinion. Students have to construct a hypothesis, where the data are insufficient to reach an unambiguous conclusion. Different individuals typically seize on different aspects of the data, or use the same data to draw different conclusions, so that astonished students find themselves at loggerheads with others equally convinced of the correctness of their own interpretations. The shock of that discovery can be powerful, forcing students to examine closely the basis of how they arrive at their conclusions. Students taught in this way made better diagnoses, based more firmly on evidence and they were less dogmatic, being more open to consider alternative possibilities.

In Collier's method, syndicate groups are formed out of a large class of 30 or so into four to eight students each. Each group has an assigned task. The heart of the technique is the intensive debate that is meant to go on in the syndicates. The assignments are designed to draw on selected sources as well as on students' first-hand experiences, so that everyone has something to say. The syndicates then report back to plenary sessions led by the teacher to help formulate and to consolidate the conceptual structures that have emerged from each group. Collier reports that student motivation is very high and that the higher level skills are enhanced. However, he does point out that unless assessment is *obviously* directed towards these higher skills, the method fails; students simply discuss and focus on what they think will assist them best in passing the assessment. The system has to be aligned.

In all group work, the students must have sufficient background to contribute, either because they have read or otherwise studied enough to have an informed discussion, or because the topic is directly relatable to personal experience. Above all, the group leader needs to be able to create the right sort of atmosphere so that students can discuss uninhibitedly. Some teachers find it hard to do this. The teacher must not correct a student, or be seen as the expert to arbitrate in disputes, because that kills the point of the exercise. Students cannot then evolve their own views, so they tend to sit back and wait for the teacher to tell them what to think.

Peer teaching

It's often said that you don't really know something until you have taught it to somebody else. One can see why. One asks very metacognitive questions of oneself. How did I come to learn this myself? How can I put it more simply? If teaching induces people to reflect on their own thinking, then it's obvious: get the students to teach other. Let us return to the question asked by McKeachie et al. at the very beginning of this chapter: 'What is the most effective method of teaching?' Let us now see the rest of their answer:

> Students teaching other students. There is a wealth of evidence that peer teaching is extremely effective for a wide range of goals, content and students of different levels and personalities. (McKeachie et al. 1986: 63)

Peer teaching as a formal method of instruction dates back to 1791, when Andrew Bell devised a system for coping with a very difficult school for soldiers' children in Madras. He arranged that an older child taught younger ones, both on a one-to-one basis and in large classes, with the help of younger assistants. Not only did this system provide successful instruction, it also brought about a marked improvement in the students' behaviour. As Bell commented: 'For months together it has not been found necessary to inflict a single punishment' (quoted in Allen 1976: 15).

What became known as the Bell–Lancaster system was widespread in Britain in the early nineteenth century. Paradoxically it died out with the growth of professionalism among teachers: 'A self-conscious teaching profession is likely to look with disdain upon the idea that untrained young children can perform the skilled functions of a teacher' (Allen 1976: 17).

Peer teaching was also widely used in one-teacher schools in rural Australia, where the same classroom might contain 30 or so children ranging anywhere from Years 1 to 6. Under those circumstances, it was natural that older children would take some sort of responsibility for the younger ones and teach them what they had learned, while the teacher was busy with another group.

Peer teaching has been much researched (Allen 1976; Devin-Sheehan, Feldman & Allen 1976; Johnson, Maruyama, Johnson, Nelson & Skon, 1981; Winter 1987). Usually, an older student (the tutor) is paired with a younger student (the tutee); the tutor is thus likely to know the subject more effectively and the tutee is less likely to resent the tutor. In the case of teaching English to L2 students, however, Tavener and Glynn (1989) found it better to pair an L2 tutee with an L1 tutor of the same age, but who also had some learning difficulties. Tutors are given prior training and are often selected when they are disadvantaged in some way, or a discipline problem; they are as much the target of intervention as the tutee. The most common finding is that both tutor and tutee benefit academically, the tutor more than the tutee; the tutor is also likely to have increased social skills and attitudes to school and self. Gains have been reported in reading and writing skills, mathematics and grade point average. One researcher, working with disadvantaged New York adolescents, offered a metacognitive explanation for the greater tutor effect:

> The findings from the Mobilization study indicated that the tutor was the major beneficiary of the tutorial experience. In attempting to help his low-achieving

elementary school pupil, the tutor greatly improved his own reading ability. The reason for this is not entirely clear, but the result deserves our serious attention. It may be an example of what every beginning teacher discovers: that one must relearn one's subject in order to teach it, that one has to reanalyze what he knows and how he learns in order to promote similar knowledge and learning in others. (Cloward 1976: 227)

Learning something by reanalysing what we know and how we learn it is a very powerful thing to do. The process of learning is *different* when one learns material in order to teach it rather than for, say, being tested on it (Benware & Deci 1984). In the first case, there is a heavy ego investment; you are owning the material, publicly taking responsibility for it and being subject to challenge for its validity. There is a heavy loss of face if you get it wrong. Learning for testing is ego challenging on other grounds (see Chapter 14). Learning for teaching is done in a context that is likely to be associated with *deep* processing, learning for testing with *surface*. Teaching enhances learning because it induces students to become deep learners and to be metacognitive about their learning.

Reciprocal teaching is a variant of peer teaching devised by Palincsar and Brown (1984) to improve the reading skills of grade 7 students; it has since been used in a variety of contents, including teaching study skills (Moore 1991). Reciprocal teaching is based on a dialogue between teacher and students around four important reading strategies:

1. summarising, or identifying the gist of a passage;
2. formulating test questions on the content;
3. clarifying the meaning in unclear passages;
4. predicting what is going to come up next in the text.

The procedure then follows from the teacher's think-aloud. The teacher first summarises the text and then generates a question to which the group responds and summarises their response for the group to elaborate. The teacher then discusses the responses to suggest where the content is unclear, finally predicting what the text might then say. The students take up the teacher's role as they became familiar with the task. Thus the skills were learned in context and the teacher prompted the students' metacognising by acting as model and then withdrawing. The results in Palincsar and Brown's original study showed that students' reading comprehension scores were greatly increased as they took on the role of teaching each other.

Reciprocal teaching even works for 'reluctant' learners. High school students with low motivation who were involved in an intensive study skills program showed substantial increases in their abilities to take notes, summarise and generate main idea questions about the texts they were reading. There was a transfer to essay writing as well, especially for the females (Moore 1991).

Reciprocal questioning (King 1990) is a variant of reciprocal teaching, where students are trained to ask questions of each other after a piece of content has been taught by the teacher. King compared the performance of tertiary students who use reciprocal questioning with students who simply 'discussed' the taught material in undirected ways for the same period of time in class. The reciprocal questioning group of students were trained to ask 'generic' questions:

*   What is the *main idea* in …?
*   How would you compare this with …?
*   But how is that different from …?

- What is a new example of ...?
- How does ... affect ...?

On testing, the discussion groups often gave more elaborations to a question, but they were almost entirely low level. On critical thinking and on high level elaborations, the questioning group was far superior.

Reciprocal questioning has also been found to impact upon learner's feelings about themselves. Undergraduate students showed (in addition to increased academic performance) significant reductions in depression, social avoidance and fear of negative evaluation after completing a semester of reciprocal questioning in small group contexts (Fantuzzo, Riggio, Connelly & Dimeff, 1989).

There is thus very strong evidence that placing students in the role of teacher improves their performance, almost certainly because it forces them to be more metacognitive about their own learning. The new role suddenly shifts the responsibility, so that the student is now in a situation where publicly accountable decision-making and action is required. The classroom is no longer a place where students can sit back passively to allow adults to go through their rituals, saving their involvement for the world of childhood. Given its many advantages, including its low cost, it is astonishing that peer teaching is not used more widely.

Cooperative and collaborative learning

Cooperative learning is where students work in small groups towards a common goal, say an assignment or project, the group being rewarded according to how well all group members have learned (Slavin 1983; Johnson & Johnson 1990). Reward could be awarded on the basis of the group average, so that students are motivated to help each other lift the average rather than to compete. The outcomes are as much affective and social as academic. This technique of rewarding cooperative effort can be used over an enormous variety of teaching/learning situations.

Whereas cooperative learning, and the group methods used by Collier and Abercrombie Johnson are formally structured by the teacher, even if during the group interaction the teacher takes a low profile, collaborative learning is spontaneously set up by students (Tang 1991). Thus, a formal task such as an assignment might be set by the teacher for individual submission in the normal way, but students then form their own groups, deciding who'll check out what set of references, what ideas might be included and so on. The collaborative effort extends variously through the planning phase of the assignment or project, but the final detailed plan and write-up is conducted individually.

Tang found that in a class of physiotherapist trainees in Hong Kong, the majority collaborated to some extent and, while not obtaining higher marks than those who did not collaborate, they did show greater structural complexity in their assignments as measured by SOLO. This is probably an example at the tertiary level of the collaborative network mentioned by Davies (1982); the business of existing peer groups being called into play for the business of the classroom. It is also likely that there are cultural factors at work, as this level of collaboration (87% in one tertiary class) would be unlikely in an Australian classroom, although it may be deliberately fostered, as Goodnow (1991) did at Macquarie University.

Both formally and informally, then, peer interactivity can be brought into play to enhance learning.

Learner activity

Learner activity is of course implied in establishing a knowledge base, ownership and interaction with others, but there are additional ways in which a learner can be made relevantly active: the more so, the better the learning. Examples of this proposition can be found throughout this book, especially in Chapter 8.

Learning in multiple modalities is particularly powerful, that is where relevant activities are designed that call on sensori-motor, ikonic and concrete-symbolic modes. Learning mathematics by multiple embodiment, using the multibase arithmetic blocks (Bruner 1964b; Dienes 1963), is a very good example. The concepts to be learned and their symbolisation are translated into things you do to blocks of wood, and only after that are they written down in symbolic form. Another example of quite a different kind is MacKenzie and White's (1982) geography excursion, where the concrete-symbolic lesson objectives were translated into doing active, unusual and sometimes scary things around the seashore. The notion of 'reconstructive elaboration' (Scruggs & Mastropieri 1989), using mental pictures, symbols and sounds as representations of the content to be learned, makes a similar point.

The place of activities in the curriculum has been strangely overlooked and lacked any kind of rationale (Brophy & Alleman 1991): indeed strange in view of the evidence we have seen of the importance of activity. Accordingly, Brophy and Alleman attempt to meet the gap, with particular reference to primary school social studies. The key to the effectiveness of the activity, they say, is its 'cognitive engagement potential' (op.cit.: 14), which is a posh way of saying that it should get students thinking actively about the task and applying the knowledge so gained.

Their view of activities is rather teacher-directed, involving four phases:

1. each activity needs to be introduced in context;
2. scaffolded by the teacher with adequate instructions and supports;
3. students allowed to work independently at it;
4. concluded, with a debriefing, reflection and assessment of its worth and what it has taught.

The activities themselves have certain essential characteristics:

*   They must be relevant to intended curriculum content and, in particular, be built around 'powerful ideas' or generic codes.
*   The activities need to represent those ideas accurately, in simple formats that don't confuse.
*   They must be at the appropriate level of difficulty. Often the students already know what is to be taught; on the other hand, the activities can be so complex the idea is missed.
*   Activities need to be 'authentic', that is belong to interesting, real life and not artificial contexts. Dienes' blocks are not 'authentic' in this sense, but are mathematically speaking.
*   Then, as is self-evident, activities need to be feasible, cost-effective in terms of time and trouble in setting them up, and the value of what it is they are intended to teach.

Brophy and Alleman's concept of activities is thus quite formal, with a deliberate structured place in the curriculum. The principle of increased activity is however far more general than they put it. The principle is simplicity itself:

Don't you, the teacher, do it. *Get them to.*

We have already seen this at work with teaching itself. Don't you teach; get them to. What about evaluation? Certainly; get them to. Boud (1985b) did just that, as we saw in Chapter 15.

The ways in which increased learner activity can be capitalised upon by the teacher are almost endless. Any facet of teaching or learning can be expanded by requiring, where there is a choice, students to be more rather than less active:

- In learning from text, underlining is better than passively sitting there reading, taking notes is better still, SQ4R better yet again.
- The old ploy of not telling students the meaning or spelling of a word: make them look it up in the dictionary for themselves.
- Make them role play rather than tell them. You name it, role play can be used for anything from historical scenes, court or parliamentary procedures, explaining fine differences of meaning, to any procedural knowledge (how to conduct interviews, how to differentiate equations ... back now to peer teaching, which is of course a perfect example of learning through activity).

But there is one important warning: the activities have to be both relevant and nontrivial. Requiring students to be active just for the sake of jumping around is time-wasting, trivialising, and demeaning; this is an area where some critical metateaching is required. Which is, of course, true of all teaching techniques.

Problem-based learning

One of the most effective contexts for learning is when it is problem-based (Boud 1985a; Newble & Clarke 1986). Problem-based learning (PBL) requires all the four characteristics we have been discussing; the motivational context is pressing so that the students 'own' the problem, there is interactivity both peer and scaffolded, learners are active, the knowledge base is ever-present. PBL is mostly used in professional education, having started out in McMaster Medical School and is now used in agricultural, medical, paramedical, business and architectural contexts. It could and should also be used in schools, one example using computer-assisted instruction (CAI) being the Cognition and Technology Group at Vanderbilt (1990), which used a sophisticated interactive videodisc system to teach writing to primary school children.

PBL, as it has been used in educating for the professions, has the following phases:

1. *A problem is defined.* When a medical student is faced with (and with a group of others is responsible for,) a patient with a broken leg, an immediate need-to-know is created: in particular, a need to know some anatomy.
2. *Knowledge is sought.* Students are variously guided towards resource materials, including films, videos, the library, and lecture room.
3. *Knowledge is elaborated.* Students meet with a tutor and discuss the case in relation to the knowledge they have obtained.
4. *Knowledge is applied.* The case is treated.
5. *Knowledge is organised and consolidated.* At some stage, the knowledge gained through treatment of various, carefully chosen, cases is organised and consolidated so that it meets the requirements of the source disciplines. By the end of a PBL course of study, students are expected to have a similar knowledge base, in terms of declarative knowledge of disciplines, as students trained in the conventional method of mastering the declarative knowledge first.

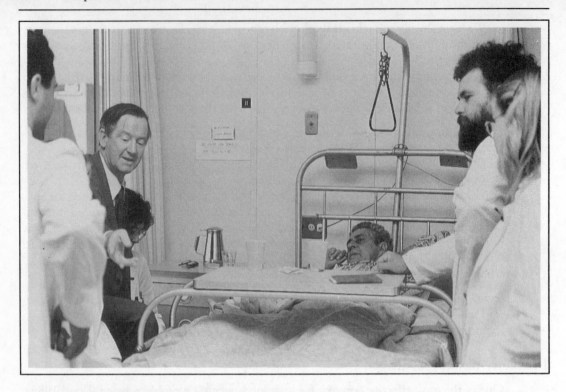

Problem based learning: to understand the case, it is necessary to find out and analyze a lot of information.

A medical example has been given here, but PBL can be used in many different contexts. The reasons why PBL is not more widely used are not educational, they are individual and organisational; it is fairly radical and therefore requires acceptance by teachers, and it also requires considerable institutional flexibility to make it work. It is much easier for experts to give lectures on their speciality, with motivation and application being left as the students' problems.

Conclusions

The preceding techniques are not really teaching methods, with the exception of problem-based learning, which requires its own redesigned delivery system. They are ways of approaching teaching that can be built into a teacher's general approach, depending on one's aims. Once it is clear what it is that is to be achieved—mastery of a skill, conceptual understanding in depth, an elaborated knowledge structure, metacognitive awareness—then, following 3P the principles of 'instructional alignment' (Cohen 1987), the teacher should use methods of instruction and of assessment that will achieve the aim or set of aims.

All the approaches discussed here are content-oriented—peer teaching, scaffolded instruction, learner activity—are all focused on a target: for mastery in depth, elaboration, application. Even ownership is of a task, or of a skill. Then there are the spin-offs; peer interaction, whether in syndicate groups or peer teaching, has affective and social consequences, which in certain circumstances may be as significant as the cognitive outcomes themselves.

The thing all these approaches have in common is the students' approaches to learning. They are focused on the student constructing knowledge and skill. Many of these points are quite old; as we saw, peer teaching was established and used as an effective teaching method back in 1791. Inquiry methods have been vindicated since the 1960s. Official curriculum statements are inspirational in their emphasis on high level outcomes. Yet even today, many teachers use expository methods that merely 'touch on' key topics, at the lowest of cognitive levels; a situation unchanged for much of this century. It may be that they don't know any better. But an important factor in this conservatism in the classroom is institutional, not individual.

Teaching within the system

Effective teaching means working within the system. We have discussed at length the classroom system; let us now look at the school. Just as there is an equilibrium in the classroom, so the classes and their teachers form a larger coherent system within the school as a whole. Then you can go further if you like and look at the system formed by the community itself: a system that country teachers particularly ignore at their peril. Each of these levels forms its own system, with its own components in equilibrium. This enveloping superstructure often prevents individual teachers from teaching the way they would like to do.

The school as a system

A school version of 3P is given in Figure 16.6.

The teacher-based factors are the same as in Figure 16.2 (see also Figure 16.1). The school-based factors include the aims, resources, traditions and social structure of the institution. Institutions form an equilibrium between: (a) the aims of the institution;

Presage	Process	Product

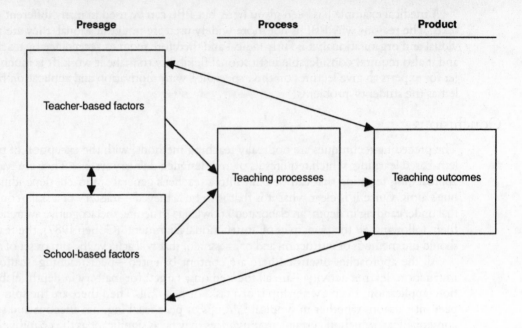

Figure 16.6 *The school as a system*

(b) the social structure surrounding the individuals within it; and (c) the technology that makes it function (Reid 1987). We need to balance what is officially wanted, what is technically possible in the circumstances of that institution, and what has evolved so far through consensus among colleagues. It is important to understand this if we are to operate within the system as an autonomous professional, rather than as an unimaginative hack.

We have already met one manifestation of the social system of the institution in Chapter 4, in the form of the hidden curriculum. The system includes the hidden curriculum but is wider than it, comprising such things as resource allocation, rules and routines, administrative structures, industrial stipulations, and the expectations and norms of fellow teachers and students, to which teachers are expected to conform. Often this social system has a greater effect on classroom practice than the aims of the official system. Often such sociocentric pressures hinder enlightened change. Twenty years ago, it was policy in many British universities not to reveal grades to students, obviously not for educational reasons, but because it made life easier for lecturers. For it to work, all had to agree. If one lecturer told students what their grades were, life it was feared would become hell for the rest; teachers have their collaborative networks too.

Caning is a very good example. Officially 'the last resort', the cane was by (male) consensus the macho thing to flourish at the first sign of trouble and woe betide any male teacher who overtly campaigned against its use. Not many years ago at all, one New South Wales high school went on strike until a teacher, who had made a public bonfire of his colleagues' canes in the playground, was removed to another school. The remedy for such conflict between social, official and individual norms is ultimately honest reflection on an institutional basis, but because of institutional lethargy, such soul-searching probably needs to be sparked off by the more sociopathic of the dissenters from the self-serving consensus.

If we take the systems model too far it would seem too pessimistic; if all must conform to 'the system' how then can some individual teachers be better than others? Such teachers certainly exist. Tobin and Fraser (1988) studied secondary science and maths teachers nominated as 'exemplary' by inspectors, principals and tertiary educators; these teachers achieved results in the classroom, in terms of learning outcomes, that their colleagues did not. They operated differently, but how?

> These exemplary teachers operated in the same schools as the contrast teachers and their implemented curricula were exposed to the same powerful driving forces as those teachers ... Yet the exemplary teachers were able to create a positive learning environment and the comparison teachers generally could not. (Tobin & Fraser 1988: 91)

These highly effective teachers were all found to operate from a Level 3 conception of teaching; they had excellent content knowledge and held high expectations of their students; they used a repertoire of different teaching strategies and were themselves open to possible changes in their teaching. They were sensitive to learning outcomes and to the learning processes students used to produce those outcomes. What makes an expert teacher is a matter we consider at more length in the next chapter. Our present question is: If the system determines outcomes, how could these teachers do well and their colleagues not?

As we know, systems operate at several levels: classroom, school, departmental, community, national ... Each has its own integrity, but depends to some extent on the next one of which it is part. There's enough slip between systems to allow some degree of freedom. If you really want to change things then the focus should be the whole school rather than the classroom (White & Baird 1991, on the implementation of PEEL). White and Baird originally operated through workshops, attended by individual teachers. One very enthusiastic teacher, 'Mr Atkin', attempted to introduce the program into his own classroom. He achieved some positive outcomes, but not as readily as hoped for; students could not relate what he was doing to what other teachers were doing, and other teachers brought their own pressures to bear. The classroom system had hit the interface with the school system. So White and Baird then made their target an entire school, not just individual teachers; and across the curriculum, not just science. They didn't quite win them all, but PEEL was used in a majority of classrooms and in subjects other than science and maths, with a considerable degree of success, in terms of student achievement and student and teacher attitudes.

Summary

A systems approach to learning and teaching

Schools make a difference to people's learning and thinking. Complex interacting systems, like the classroom, school, or state department, work on systemic principles, rather than additively. This means the component parts of the system affect each other and achieve a functional and ongoing equilibrium. When you change one of these parts significantly, a new equilibrium, a new system, is established.

The classroom system

The Presage–Process–Product (3P) model of classroom learning and teaching is just such a system. Presage factors relate to students, teachers, and teaching context; process to the way students approach the particular academic task in question; product to the outcome of learning. All these components interrelate, so that decisions about any one affect all the others. The 3P model helps to define the components in that total context, and metateaching is what keeps them in focus, enabling on the spot judgments about what is currently creating surface learning and what needs to be done to encourage conditions appropriate for deep-achieving approaches to learning. The alternative to this holistic approach is a deficit model, which lays the blame either at the student's door or at the teacher's.

Who is responsible for learning?

When learning fails it is very easy to blame the student: lazy, low ability, unmotivated, a behaviour problem. Anything that the teacher is unable to remedy or be held responsible for. Or the student blames the teacher. The systems approach allows neither to blame the other: all are responsible, although at any given time one might be more responsible than the other. The bottom line must however be the teacher's professionalism, seeing that where the teacher has some leverage, the component parts of the system are to be aligned.

Discouraging surface approaches

Several factors can be nominated as encouraging surface learning and which need to be minimised: extrinsic motivation, particularly using negative reinforcement, a cold classroom climate, an excessive workload, particularly of 'busywork' and needless routines, and excessive and inappropriate assessment. Many of these factors, particularly perhaps those that belong to one's personality (such as a sarcastic sense of humour), cannot easily be monitored by oneself, let alone improved. Others, however, certainly can be. Certainly the collective act can be cleaned up at staff meetings, such as rationalising the workload, routines, reward/punishment systems and the like.

Research has nominated several features as contributing to deep and achieving approaches to learning and to rich outcomes. These include: a well-structured knowledge base, an appropriate motivational context, interaction with others, and learner activity. Many of these do not comprise teaching methods as such, but are aspects that can be incorporated into one's own teaching, whatever particular methods are used.

The knowledge base

Good learning, deep learning, proper outcomes, all start with a well-structured knowledge base. How can it be established? We can start by defining the curriculum goals appropriately and enacting them. Much instruction is 'misaligned'. We say one thing, teach another, and test something else again. In following through from our high intentions, we can introduce new material by drawing upon what is already known; we can present material in ways that both facilitate structuring the content, using schemata that allow such structuring; we can use error constructively to fine-tune the knowledge base; we can increase students' metacognitive awareness of their own knowledge construction.

The motivational context

Establishing a positive, Theory Y, motivational environment is one prerequisite. Essential features of that environment establish that the task is valued, that it is really worth doing and that one has a good chance of success in carrying it out. An enabling feature of this environment is that it is ordered: well-planned and resourced, with the directions for action clearly established.

Interaction with others

So much learning is based on interaction with others. Scaffolded interaction, or embedded teaching, involves hierarchical interaction: child with parent, student with teacher, novice with expert, hacker with software. Such interaction is one-to-one, often intense, particularly good for supporting the learner in hitherto too-difficult tasks (hence the term scaffolding), and for constructing the learner's knowledge in depth. Peer interaction is more broadening; elaborating knowledge, challenging misconceptions, applying to new or unthought of areas. There are also social and affective outcomes particularly associated with peer teaching.

Learner activity

All the above require much activity from the learner, but to emphasise the point it is worth mentioning in its own right; the more task-oriented activity required of the learner, the better will the learning be. The difference between this and busywork, already established as a no-no, lies in the phrase 'task-oriented' and in common sense. Wherever activity can be stretched with relevance across different modes, sensori-motor, ikonic and concrete-symbolic, learning is enriched; the learner can inject input from sense experience into otherwise uninspiring words and symbols, and see more readily where they might touch upon experience again.

Teaching within the system

If only we could teach, sitting on a log, one-to-one with the student. But we can't—and get paid for it—so we have to settle for institutions and the limits they undoubtedly impose on our teaching creativity. But some, perhaps many, teachers within the system do teach creatively. While recognising the limitations we have to face, particularly at the whole school level, we must also recognise the opportunities for creating a learning environment in our own classrooms. It is important, then, to recognise what freedoms one has at the classroom level and what at the school level. In this chapter, the main focus has been the-student-in-the-classroom constructing knowledge; our intention to acquaint teachers with situations, contexts and activities that we have evidence to believe are particularly effective in creating learning-rich situations. But as became clear in the last section, that is not the whole story. There are other systems at work, which affect and often inhibit, both teacher and learner.

Finally, then, we need to focus on the teacher; how one manages in the classroom, what makes a good teacher and what good teachers do that is so different from the rest of us. Chapter 17 picks up these threads.

Learning activities

1. The 3P model

The 3P (presage, process, product) model underlies the whole of this book and in that sense this task may prove to be a real challenge at this early stage of your learning. We have represented the model in Figures 16.1 (in the classroom) and 16.2 (as a classroom system). The task is to take each of the components of the model and explain it to your colleagues. Of course, it will be important to demonstrate the interactive nature of the model, each 'bit' influences the other. One way of doing this would be to use overhead transparencies in an 'overlay' manner. The first overhead would contain only the presage factor of student characteristics (and that could be described in detail). The first overlay (or another transparency placed on top of the first) would then be the presage factor of teaching context, etc. In this way the model is built up from its pieces and the picture should become clearer. (You may have to check your understanding by making reference to relevant sections in later chapters.) As we have said above, this task may not be easy but we guarantee that you will have a better understanding of learning and teaching if you successfully complete the task.

2. Diminishing surface approaches to learning

We have argued in this chapter that one of the important aspects of metateaching is to know about reducing the likelihood that teaching will encourage surface approaches to learning. We discussed motivation, classroom climate, time/workload stress, routines and assessment as candidates for your attention. This activity should be a challenge, for your task (in a group?) is to prepare, say a 10 minute video-presentation of a teacher (simulated we would hope) who is encouraging surface level learning. For the really creative, the content of this chapter dealing with reducing surface approaches to learning could be the content that is taught! Clearly the presentation would want to conclude by drawing out the ways in which these problems might be overcome. If done in groups, then class presentations of the videos could be the basis for discussion.

3. Encouraging deep approaches to learning

Obviously this activity and the one above are interrelated so you may have to use some of the information in the first learning activity to complete this one. The task here is a simulation and goes something like this: You have been allocated to a new school and the principal is keen for you to tell the staff about the material you have recently been reading on encouraging deep approaches to learning. The principal informs you that most of the staff know nothing about approaches to learning but they would be interested in seeing the practicalities of it all; they would undoubtedly ask the question 'Well, how can I do anything about it in my classroom?' You have been allocated 15 minutes for your presentation.

The task could be completed at several levels. The presentation could be written out by you (is that encouraging surface approaches?). Would it not be better to actually make the presentation to a group of your colleagues who could simulate different teacher interest in your topic?

4. Characteristics of good learning contexts

This activity focuses upon Figure 16.5, the characteristics of good learning contexts. (You have probably realised that the figure summarises much of the chapter.) This task can be completed individually or in class groups. If done in a class, five groups could be formed with four each taking a section of the figure (Knowledge base; Motivational context: Interaction with others; Learner activity) and the fifth group showing how the pieces all fit together for effective learning. In other words the task asks you to 'decompose' the model and then build it back up again. Group presentations to the class could be done using overhead transparencies, charts, etc. Poster presentations could also be done.

5. Reciprocal teaching

In this activity you are to try some reciprocal teaching with one student. This could be done during practicum or on an informal basis with a child who is a relative, etc. To make it a little easier, rather than focus on the four strategies that Palincsar and Brown (1984) taught we will use only one, questioning during reading. You will need a piece of text that both of you will read. You inform the child that you are both going to be involved in reading but you will be asking questions of each other, questions that teachers would ask, as you read through (usually at the end of each paragraph). After silently reading the first paragraph you ask a *main idea* level question of the child. You provide feedback to the child on the correctness of that response. Next the child asks you a question at the end of the next paragraph. (Our experience tells us that it will probably be a *detail* level question.) After answering, you show the child how you got the answer (perhaps by pointing to the part of the text from which you got the answer). You continue through moving the child to main idea questions by using your own examples. Encourage the child to show how he got the answer, again through modelling. If you wanted you could move onto summarising, predicting and clarifying (the other strategies used by Palincsar and Brown) when you felt the child was able to cope.

6. Think-aloud modelling

If you have not spent much of your time thinking out aloud you might find this activity a little peculiar to begin with for its purpose is to get you to do some modelling in front of a small group of students. This would probably be best done during practicum sessions if you are in a teacher education program.

In this chapter we used Garth Boomer's writing presentation at a conference to give you some idea of how think-alouds go. The activity will vary dependent upon the subjects that you teach, but give yourself say 10 minutes of modelling strategy use in front of the group. Note your reactions to the think-aloud procedure and any reactions of the students. Bring those reactions back to class for discussion.

7. Institutional effects

The purpose of this activity is to summarise the data presented in Biggs' (1987a) national study of Australian high school students' approaches to learning. Biggs showed that from middle to upper levels of secondary schools, the reported use of deep and achieving approaches to learning declined, more in boys than girls. What factors may be responsible for those declines and, to link with one of the earlier activities, what could schools do to change that trend? Discuss your analyses with your colleagues. Perhaps, if you worked in pairs or small groups, reciprocal questioning could be part of the study activities you undertake. (Remember the research by Fantuzzo et al.?)

Further reading

On systems
Emery, F. E. (ed.) (1969). *Systems Thinking*. Harmondsworth, Middlesex: Penguin Books.
    Systems theory is itself not new, as this book and von Bertalanffy (1968) (the classic) attest, but its applications have been slow in arriving. The focus is on management, but if you are interested in systems thinking, it is worth reading the selections selectively.

On improving student learning through teaching

Baird, J. & Mitchell, I. (eds) (1986). *Improving the Quality of Teaching and Learning: An Australian Case Study—The PEEL Project.* Melbourne: Monash University.

Biggs, J. B. (ed.) (1991). *Teaching for Better Learning: The View from Cognitive Psychology.* Hawthorn, Vic: Australian Council for Educational Research.

Ramsden, P. (ed) (1988). *Improving Learning: New Perspectives.* London: Kogan Page.

Ramsden, P. & Dodds, A. (1989). *Improving Teaching and Courses: A Guide to Evaluation.* University of Melbourne: Centre for the Study of Higher Education.

The first book describes the PEEL project in great detail, with illustrative interviews with teachers and students. The ACER book has already been described. Ramsden's book mainly draws on phenomenography and the illustrations largely from science education. Roth and Anderson are particularly good on poor and good teaching. Bowden uses a workshop method, in which teachers are confronted with the misconceptions their students hold, to convince them that something has to change.

Ramsden and Dodds are in a different category. Although their book is addressed to tertiary teachers, there is plenty here to help all teachers, at whatever level, to improve their teaching. It is particularly useful on how to make use of student evaluation of teaching (one needs to be very careful).

On using groups

Collier, K. G. (1983). *The Management of Peer-group Learning: Syndicate Methods in Higher Education.* Guildford: Society for Research in Higher Education.

Johnson Abercrombie (1969) *The Anatomy of Judgment.* Harmdondsworth, Middlesex: Penguin Books.

Johnson, D. W. & Johnson, R. T. (1990). *Learning Together and Alone: Co-operation, Competition and Individualisation.* Englewood Cliffs, NJ: Prentice Hall.

The first two books assume that one is working with tertiary students, but that doesn't detract from their value in seocndary school. The first is general in the use of groups, the second a very easy-to-read account of the writer's work with medical students. Johnson & Johnson is the latest edition of a classic on setting up cooperative learning groups in the classroom.

On problem-based learning

Boud, D. (1985). *Problem-based Learning in Education for the Professions.* Sydney: Higher Education Research and Development Society of Australasia.

It really is amazing that nothing is available on problem-based learning (PBL) in pre-tertiary schooling. The evidence (at tertiary level) is overwhelming that this is the way to go; and Boud's is the only general book available at even this level (which is not to say that this book is not very good indeed). PBL combines all the attributes of a good learning context, provided of course that it is handled properly. Learning through vibrant problems slices through the in-school/out-of-school dichotomy that was so worrying in Chapter 1 of this book.

CHAPTER 17

LEARNING ABOUT BETTER TEACHING

Learning about better teaching

Is teaching: a management exercise?
              a spontaneous conversation?

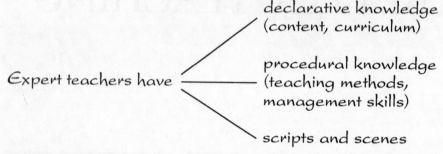

Expert teachers have
- declarative knowledge (content, curriculum)
- procedural knowledge (teaching methods, management skills)
- scripts and scenes

So that they:

- plan ahead
- fill gaps
- have momentum, smoothness, 'with-it-ness'
- handle an unscripted crisis per 2 mins
- negotiate a management deal for each class
- reward and punish authentically

all of which maintain a working environment based on skill, not fear.

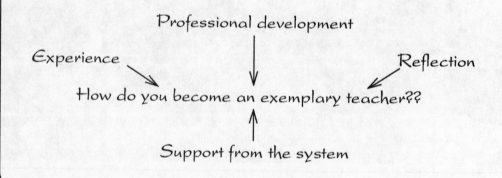

Professional development

Experience

Reflection

How do you become an exemplary teacher??

Support from the system

LEARNING ABOUT BETTER TEACHING

In this chapter, you will find out:

- what some useful metaphors for teaching are;
- how expert teachers differ from novice teachers;
- what relationship theories of teaching have to competent teaching;
- how to manage the classroom through negotiation;
- how to decide on a high structure or a low structure management style;
- what effect class size has on teaching quality;
- what role behaviour modification might have in the classroom;
- what role whole-school policies have on effective classroom discipline

Metaphors for teaching

Effective teaching has been described in terms of several different metaphors. Teaching has been referred to as:

- problem solving (Shuell 1988)
- clinical problem solving (diagnosis, remediation) (Kagan 1988)
- a cognitive skill (Leinhardt & Greeno 1986)
- work (Marshall 1988)
- management (Biggs & Telfer 1987)

and also as:

- conversation (Green & Weade 1988)
- improvised conversation (Yinger, in press).

You will notice two things. First, 1988 was a good year for metaphors. Second, the list breaks into two distinct kinds: metaphors that treat teaching as an ordered, sequential activity, requiring skills in which people can presumably be trained and in time become expert; and metaphors that see teaching as unpredictable, simultaneous, and interactive.

Our metaphors thus present two quite different slants on teaching. The first is based on what the teacher knows and does; the teacher is the key figure, the expert, on which the success of the teaching enterprise depends. The teacher-as-expert model has been built up from a considerable amount of research (e.g., Berliner 1986; Leinhardt & Putnam 1987; Swanson, O'Connor & Cooney 1990) and like much of the expert–novice research (Chi, Glaser, & Farr 1988; also see pp. 84–5) carries with it the implication that there are isolatable things that experts do that, with time and the right technique, can be taught to novices.

Some think that the teacher-as-expert implies a specific, exclusive and standardised view of what teaching is, and one that excludes the social and moral obligations that teachers might have other than teaching cognitive content; it implies a particular sort of classroom, where the teacher is the expert authority and locus of power (Welker 1991). Those who don't see the classroom that way prefer the second slant, which sees the classroom as a place where 'teachers and students collectively construct meaning' (Green & Weade 1988: 1). All participants are involved and there is no standard pattern, set by an expert; classroom processes and outcomes are interactive, are to an extent unpredictable and develop bottom-up. Yinger (in press) makes much of the 'improvisational' nature of teaching; that a teacher's actions are tuned from situation to situation, as each occurs, which discourages deliberation and planning. Have you yet had the experience yourself, or have heard other teachers say: 'Just taken my best lesson ever and I didn't plan a thing! It all started from a question asked out of the blue ...' Well, it does happen, but don't bet on it happening when you want it to. And who does it usually happen to? Experienced teachers, with a great deal of expertise under their belts.

Teaching is both of the above: a planned orchestration of learnable skills *and* a conversation that develops unpredictably. Teaching involves special kinds of knowledge and experience, and expertise in particular skills that can be developed; and it also involves improvising in an unpredictable environment, where the most significant things suddenly jump up at you all. But whether they enrich all your lives, or they escape out the door before you realise what's happening, is up to the teacher; the skill of seizing such moments derives from 'craft knowledge', or the wisdom of practice (Leinhardt 1990; Shulman 1986). Teaching is both planned and conversational; teachers who improvise effectively are those with well-developed knowledge structures concerning the content and processes of teaching (Borko & Livingston 1989).

Expertise is therefore important in both aspects of teaching. Sometimes the expert in teaching as planned management is expert in conversational teaching; sometimes expertise is more evident in one area than in the other. It is likely that there are personal and stylistic differences, as well as subject matter differences, that determine whether one teaches more planfully or conversationally.

In this chapter, then, we look at good teaching from several aspects. First, at the nature of expert teaching, with the focus on the teacher. But teaching takes place in classrooms and, as we now know, classrooms are systems. The teacher is but one component in that system, so good teaching depends on how one has come to terms with and manages, or is managed by, all those other horrible little components. The question of discipline or classroom control is addressed here, but within the context of *class* management rather than of control of deviant individuals. This systems approach to what was once regarded as 'the discipline problem' extends to the whole school, as is now being recognised in some states. Finally, then, we look briefly at the school as a whole, but only briefly, as this opens up new and different questions.

The expert teacher

Boag (1989), writing for *The Bulletin*, consulted academics, administrators, teachers, parents and students in an attempt to find out 'what makes the great teacher'. The result is summarised in Box 17.1.

The most important function, all agree, is the teacher-as-motivator: 'putting the light in the student's eye' (op. cit.: 47). Then the list emphasises the interpersonal, affective and social side of teaching: the big picture, of student, parents and teachers interacting together in a major life-affecting role. Less exciting, but fundamental, is the

Box 17.1 *What makes a great teacher?*

Great teachers:

1. *Enthuse students.* 'The big one, with near-unanimity among bureacrats, academics, teachers, parents and students'. (p.47)
2. *Treat them as individuals.* One administrator said: 'He treated all the kids in his grade as something special. The day my daughter turned 21, she got a letter from him congratulating her. He enclosed a letter she had written in Grade 6, saying what she wanted to be when she was 21. He had kept it all those years.' (p. 47)
3. *Know the subject.* 'Perhaps the surprise is that it's not No. 1. (but) ... Any Dumbo can amass knowledge: the trick is to impart it'. (p. 49)
4. *Are loving, warm.* 'Student Ian, 16, says of a good teacher: "She doesn't just teach. She's a friend." ' (p. 49)
5. *Teach to learn.* 'The good teacher gets her or his students to learn—to ask their own questions, seek out their own answers, with the teacher as guide.' (p.49)
6. *Empathise with students* ... and you get your stolen hubcaps back.
7. *Relate to others.* Not just students, not just parents, not just colleagues, but to the whole community.
8. *Are firm, fair, flexible.* 'Humans are not naturally firm, fair and flexible; when they are, they're as boring as porridge without the raisins ... (but) the Three F's are important. Students said of good teachers: "You know where you stand with them." ' (p. 50)
9. *Are organised.* ... 'means more than simply having lessons well prepared. It means organising in your mind an overall idea of what you're teaching in a given week, term or year and working through it as a naturally developing plan.' (p. 51)
10. *Prepare students for life.* 'A good teacher looks well beyond the four walls of the classroom.' (p. 51)
11. *Manage the classroom.* 'Once (management) meant ensuring the kids all sat in their rows ... Now it tends to relate to a far more relaxed environment, with much more and freer student involvement and questioning, although still without the spitballs.' (p. 51)
12. *Have high self-esteem.* ... 'for 50 years, teaching has not been regarded as one of the most important professions ... Good teachers are also necessarily altruistic ... respecting yourself and encouraging students to respect you.' (p. 51)
13. *Have a sense of humour* ... 'not to take themselves too seriously.' (p. 51)
14. *Need to be a complete person.* 'Teachers may want to work in a rock 'n' roll band after school. I tell them to go ahead and do it—and use it in their teaching.' (p. 52)
15. *Take risks.* 'This is a vital asset, if "risks" means daring to try something new.' (p. 52)

From Charles Boag, 'What makes a great teacher', *The Bulletin*, 18 July, 1989.

teacher-as-manager, emphasising the knowhow to control a complex and essentially difficult situation. How do researchers see the expert teacher?

Most research, following the expert–novice paradigm (Chi, Glaser & Farr 1988), focuses on the knowledge base that experts need to have, rather than on interpersonal skills. That direction of research is not so much a value judgment about what is important; the focus is on what good teachers do and need to know in making effective minute-to-minute decisions, rather than on what they are. What, then, do teachers need to know?

Following are some of the kinds of knowledge referred to by several writers (Berliner 1986; Borko & Livingston 1989; Leinhardt & Greeno 1986; Leinhardt 1990; Shulman 1986).

Content knowledge is of two main kinds:

- of *subject matter*. That teachers need to know what they are talking about is so obvious that it has distorted conceptions of teaching, leading direct to the Level 1 transmission model: The more you know about the subject the better you will be able to teach it and the more the students will know at the end. Not true, of course. Content knowledge is important because it becomes the framework for constructing other forms of declarative and procedural knowledge that are important for teaching.
- of *pedagogical content*, which concerns what forms and aspects of a topic are related to teachability. Some of this knowledge can be learned as declarative knowledge, but a lot is craft knowledge. Take the case of a student, Glen, trying to multiply two fractions: $6\frac{3}{4} \times 5\frac{1}{3}$ (Leinhardt 1990). Glen can do the class taught method but wants to know why 'his' method, multiply the whole numbers then the fractions and then add them, does not work. Adults may know the general case, $(a + b)(c + d) = (ac + ad + bc + bd)$, but does that tell you how to solve Glen's problem? The problem is not one of content knowledge but of pedagogical knowledge: what aspect of content is teachable and when and how to teach it.
- of *curriculum*. This knowledge is knowing what is to be taught and where to go to find out. Such knowledge may be 'lateral, that is knowing the relevance of the present topic to other topics in the curriculum; and 'vertical', that is knowing how the topic has been dealt with previously and how it is related to content subsequently to be taught.

Procedural knowledge of the classroom is likewise of several kinds:

- *knowing how to use various teaching methods:* how to run small groups, to interpose questions, to use 'wait time' (see below), to prepare O/H transparencies for maximum impact. These are all important skills that can be taught and usually are taught in methods classes. Such knowledge is usually fairly general, either applying across subjects, or broadly within a subject (how to run a group to discuss current affairs). The level of knowledge required to solve Glen's problem is much more specific.
- *pedagogic strategies*, that is knowing how to explain a particular topic in the most effective way; how to handle Glen's problem in other words. This kind of knowledge is topic-specific and first-hand experience is probably the most important way in which it is gained.
- *management knowledge* again follows the public and individual ways of acquisition; much can be taught, as we see in the next section there is a lot of knowledge about how to manage a classroom that beginning teachers should know. Additionally, however, as with teaching content, there is also an important micro level of functioning, the fine grain, which is acquired through the accumulation of experience.

- *scripts and scenes* are terms used to describe managing at this level of the fine grain. For example, Berliner (1986) mentions a script called 'grooving', which he found almost all experts did, without thinking. On entering a new class, they would set a task or tasks that had to be done a certain way. The task wasn't important, but it established who was boss without raving and shouting: that in future things had to be done the *new* way, not the way they had been done with their previous teacher. 'Grooved' students were much easier to manage thereafter than ungrooved. Scenes are schemata of a spatial kind, which teachers use to take a hold of their proposed and unfolding classroom arrangements; groupings, their placement and the students', where the essential furniture is. These scenes guide their decision-making.

Experienced teachers build up a complex network of schemata comprising these elements, which incorporate knowledge about: the subject matter, how it is to be taught, how to manage the classroom and, increasingly with experience, the deep knowledge base with which they learn to deal effectively with highly specific matters, such as explaining a particular learning difficulty in ways that best suit students at particular stages of their learning.

The *improvisational* nature of teaching takes place within the scripts and scenes. Just like an actor who improvises on stage, it is done successfully by drawing upon an extensive repertoire of routines and knowledge of audiences, rather than from a detailed script. The successful teacher thus needs powerful schemata, founded both upon formal knowledge and upon a rich experiential background. Often this allows that deliberate planning for a lesson is minimal in the case of expert teachers. As Scott, an expert teacher, describes his planning: 'A lot of times I just put the objective in my book and I play off the kids' (Borko & Livingstone 1989: 483). But that was definitely for the experts. Their student teacher novices, Borko and Livingston found, indulged in a great deal of short-term, detailed planning; were unable to predict where their students would have difficulties with the problems they doing; and were unable to maintain the direction of the lesson, or to relate across topics. They did *not* improvise, but would plough on with their too well-prepared lesson, almost whatever the feedback from the class. We describe an extreme example of this in the next section.

On the question of content knowledge, Sabers, Cushing and Berliner (1991) studied how three groups of teachers—experts, complete novices to teaching but who had content expertise, and teacher trainees, who had some knowledge of teaching and of content but little experience—managed to cope with three dimensions that characterise classrooms: *simultaneity* (with several things happening at once); *multidimensionality* (the sheer number of things needing attention); and *immediacy* (the rapid pace of classroom events). These authors estimate that together, these factors require non-trivial decisions about once every two minutes; something that air traffic controllers and expert teachers can handle but the others cannot. The major feature differentiating expert teachers was in deciding on what to focus attention. Experts focused on the salient points of effective teaching, novices on discipline issues, and while novices expressed much more disapproval about difficult or deviant behaviour, they had fewer ways of dealing with it. When experts thought about discipline, it was in terms of evaluating the results of a discipline strategy, while novices were intent on finding 'the' correct way of handling the present problem, rather than on analysing and clarifying the problem itself (Swanson, O'Connor & Cooney 1990).

In general, the study of expert teachers shows that they have a deep knowledge base, with detailed schemata that can be pulled out to handle situations, yet their thinking and planning is long-term and abstract. Teaching is both a 'situated' skill (Borko & Livingstone 1989; Brown, Collins & Duguid 1989), requiring that the knowledge underpinning good teaching is learned on the spot, in context and first hand, but on the other hand is generalisable; each scenario, unique as it may seem to the novice, fits into a basic and familiar plot.

What does this say about the preparation of teachers?

The preparation of teachers

If the greatest difference between experts and beginning teachers lies in their integrated schemata, in which formal knowledge is empowered by experiential knowledge, then the important thing is to structure the experiences, knowledge base and reflective activity of student teachers so that they build these schemata more quickly.

An obvious area for concern is how the experience gained in practice teaching relates to other knowledge structures. This issue has been variously addressed by several writers (Borko & Livingstone 1989; Evans 1991b; Feiman-Nemser & Buchmann 1987; Hollingsworth 1989). The following generalisations emerge.

1. The usual practice of making school experience full-time seems mistaken; it should comprise just a few lessons, to allow reflection and absorption of the experiences. The multidimensionality of the classroom cannot be handled all at once, given the limitations of working memory, and so skills and points should be routinised and mastered piecemeal.
2. Following from this, teachers need time to be *reflective*. They should be encouraged to constantly monitor their actions and interpret what is happening in their teaching environment: to be constantly involved in metateaching.
3. Management skills, as the major concern of beginning teachers anyway, should be addressed and mastered to the point of automaticity, so that they do not dominate teachers' thinking. As we elaborate below, teachers need to master the techniques necessary to enable them to be automatically 'with-it', 'smooth', able to maintain their momentum and to implement routines.
4. Beginning teachers should teach where they already have strong content knowledge: not only to relieve working memory, but specifically to derive *pedagogical* content knowledge from that knowledge base and from experience.
5. The same lessons should be taught several times over, to give multiple opportunities to teach the same content, so that student teachers may more readily reach automaticity and derive their own pedagogical content knowledge.
6. Scaffolding should be provided, in their respectively different ways, by the cooperating classroom teacher and by the university-based supervisor. The classroom teacher can point out the expert-grounded cues as they occur—for example, by think-aloud—to interpret signs of poor understanding, of impending trouble, and of the consequences of an action. The supervisor's role is to help relate the specifics of practice to the various knowledge bases: of pedagogical content, of curriculum and of the psychology of learning.

From the students' viewpoint, on the other hand, the biggest problem perceived by student teachers is the matter of managing a class full of kids, not of instructing effectively (Telfer 1979a, 1981; Veenman 1984). That perception stands in the way of the beginning teacher and the looming expert. Picking up the signs of faulty understanding, or reflecting on one's own communicative skill, play second fiddle to keeping 3C remotely cooperative for the rest of the period.

Classroom management is clearly the place to begin exploring the road towards teaching expertise. Good management depends firstly on establishing a working relationship with the class.

Teacher–student collaboration: Negotiating the contract

Even the most unilateral business deals (to pick up the work–management metaphor) require the cooperation of the customers. The students in the classroom are in effect the other negotiating party to the contract offered by the teacher-manager. Teachers and pupils *cooperatively construct* the-order-that-is-to-be (or not-to-be) in the classroom (Davies 1983).

Consider what happens when that cooperation is withdrawn: 'never in my most anxiety-ridden professional nightmares had I imagined that a school room could be like this one' (Wax 1971: 253). The students were not violent, or even slightly aggressive towards their teacher, Mrs Walker; they totally ignored her. Wax describes how Mrs Walker went on with the lesson, addressing the whole class, writing on the board, issuing materials, calling on individuals ... as if the pupils were attending, writing, responding. Instead, they were walking around the room, not once glancing at her (but as Wax notes 'two boys grin at me knowingly'), children queuing at the noisy pencil sharpener to maintain a continual background of noise. When relative quiet descends 'it is because the pupils grow tired of their game'. It was not because these students were particularly evil. Simply, there was no mutuality, no contract, between teacher and students.

We saw in Chapter 4 that children attend to two agendas: their own, and to them the more important one, and the teacher's, in which they are required to participate and are willing to do so—up to a point. That point is negotiable. Even before the teacher enters the classroom for the first time, some of the basic ground rules are laid for the collaboration that is to be negotiated. The outlines are based on previous experience of both parties and school policy, but the details are negotiable between the parties.

The moment the teacher enters the room, the specifics begin to harden. The teacher's presence establishes remarkably quickly the negotiating positions. The following are some indices of presence:

- body language: does the teacher stride, slink, strut, slide, sweep or shuffle into the room?
- eye contact: does the teacher eye contact students while talking?
- tone of voice: is it abrasive, humorous, loud, wheedling?
- dress: is it trendy, formal, quiet, gaudy?
- the form of what is said. What dominates: commands, questions, factual statements?

Figure 17.1 illustrates the main features.

The student agenda is set at C, a relatively low level of dominance. Usually, the teacher's agenda is placed at a higher level, at B or, in the case of highly assertive teachers, at A. Occasionally, teachers attempt to enter and establish a contract as peers, at C. Very occasionally, the teacher deliberately allows the students to set the terms for negotiation, by coming in at D. After the initial negotiating skirmish, 'gravity' usually takes over and the teacher slides downwards, in the worst case from B to D, entering in the formally dominant position, but in the end becoming a functional doormat.

Sometimes the students can take over the teacher's agenda because it is being played so badly. One of the authors supervised a practice teaching student who was a kind of reverse Mrs Walker: *he* ignored the *class!* He became a caricature of the plan-dominated

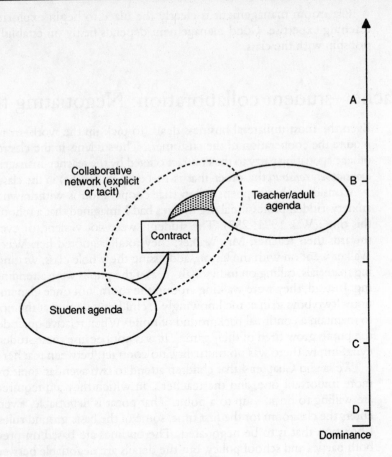

Figure 17.1 *The teacher-student collaborative network*

novice, standing at the side-front of the class, lecturing in a monotone, totally ignoring the students: no eye contact, no seeking for signs of incomprehension, no variation. Instead of 'absolutely murdering' him (see Box 4.4), however, the class, which consisted of senior girls in a religious school, remained silent, busily taking notes, pretending they understood (at least when the supervisor was in the room). They felt sorry for him and his obvious incompetence and took him into their 'network of caring' (Gilligan 1982). Other classes, however, were not so caring. Neither was the supervisor.

Usually, of course, the teacher is the first to state the terms, both overtly and implicitly, at the first encounter, from the position of dominance established then. The students can accept, reject outright (as perhaps they did with Mrs Walker, if she offered one in the first place), or counter-offer. Typically, they test the water to see what is allowable and what the consequences might be. Please note that this is their first move in a negotiation; ignore it at your peril!

In carrying out these negotiations, it must help if the teacher knows and understands the specific frameworks in the students' agenda (see Chapter 4), remembering that once a reciprocal network of agreements has been set up, it is usually in a sociocentric framework that is situation-specific and rigid to its application: one in, all in. Including you, the teacher.

The explicit rules—what is acceptable, what is unacceptable, and what the formal and stated consequences are to be in each case—can be set up fairly quickly. The tacit rules, lurking in the hidden curriculum, need to be discovered over a longer period of time—and as Mr Bell found with the children under the blanket—often with surprise and resentment.

The old schoolie's advice, 'Crack down hard at first, you can always ease up later', thus has a lot of truth, but it should not be taken too literally; a teacher must always operate from a personally authentic position. In most contexts, the teacher should enter at a point higher than C (the students' dominance level). It is also true that 'classroom gravity' will pull downwards not upwards: the teacher's position may settle lower, but it is unlikely to float higher. So one should start at a position higher than that position of dominance finally desired *vis à vis* the class: but not from a position so high that the teacher cannot maintain it authentically, or that will lock both parties into a set of negotiations neither wants. For instance, Dillon (1989), a white teacher in an elementary school of poor black students in the United States, negotiated with his class on their basis: 'not too different from the way I relate to kids when I'm not teaching ... it has differences ... (but) it's spontaneous ... it's communication more than anything' (Dillon 1989: 229). As Dillon's article shows, however, his experience is that of a skilled negotiator; the teaching profession has both its Kissingers and its Homer Simpsons.

This collaborative network builds up over a period of time around the initial contract and is different between each teacher and each class. It is obviously desirable that the teacher's management style should match the evolving collaborative network, and discipline problems will be worked out within that framework. In only a few weeks of practice teaching, one of our students, a mature-age woman, negotiated a contract based essentially on her 'network of caring': mothering the students (junior high school). It worked, although her classes tended to be noisy: the noise of naughty children with a caring mother. Twice, she spoke sharply to a boy who promptly swore back at her, loudly and violently. On the second occasion, his best friend sought her out afterwards and apologised on the boy's behalf. The other members of the class were disgusted and expressed their feelings too; the sociocentric network took over and isolated the deviate as he had violated the contract. You can be naughty with mums, but you do not tell them to 'f*** off'.

Classroom management

The teacher-as-manager metaphor springs from the changing nature of society, society's expectations of teachers (see Box 17.1) and the increasing complexity of the teaching task. Management in the good old days, such as it was, was top-down. Teaching involved two tasks: provide the instruction and keep them obediently on task. To be a 'good disciplinarian' only meant one thing. Passive obedience was society's expectation so society was happy if the teacher used strong measures in ensuring it (see Box 17.2). School policies and procedures were designed to assist the teacher in maintaining order; the criterion was student silence.

Today the task of teaching has become vastly more complicated, with expository methods only one of the wide range of techniques a teacher must master. To maintain student interest and participation in the lesson, the teacher now is forced to rely more on personal resources (see Box 17.1), as harsh methods of control are incompatible with the atmosphere and methods required to achieve our more complex educational goals.

Box 17.2 *How to maintain good discipline*

The following misdemeanours and their penalties were published by an American high school in 1848:

1. Playing cards at school:	10 lashes
2. Swearing at school:	8 lashes
3. Drinking liquor at school:	8 lashes
4. Telling lies:	7 lashes
5. Boys and girls playing together:	4 lashes
6. Quarrelling:	4 lashes
7. Wearing long fingernails:	2 lashes
8. Blotting one's copybook:	2 lashes
9. Neglecting to bow when going home:	2 lashes

(Quoted in Fontana 1986:7)

Yet there are peculiar blips; between the first and second editions of this book corporal punishment was abolished in nearly all state systems (two centuries after it was banned in Polish schools), but was reintroduced, as an option, in New South Wales after the second edition appeared. (We're holding our breath to see what effect the third edition will have.)

Thus, the Theory X line of thinking, which sees discipline as a matter between the teacher and a few twisted individuals, is alive and well. Unfortunately, it is a line that is self-defeating (see Box 17.3);

Thus we come to the position of the systems approach, that 'keeping order' through top-down discipline is not the issue. Rather, teaching is a matter of establishing a manageable relationship with the entire class, the context being mutually rewarding engagement in worthwhile tasks. This conception replaces that which saw discipline as a trial of strength between teacher and student. The focus now is managing the whole class, not 'deviant' individuals who need to be straightened out by individual counselling, punishment and, failing all else, removal from the scene (Slee 1988). While focusing treatment on a few individuals may be necessary in the very end, the blame-the-student model should not underpin our thinking about discipline. General management policy, including discipline, should be based on an equilibrium embracing the whole class and the whole school if at all possible:

> Disruption emanates from a distinction between the culture and interests of students and the curriculum content, the school organizational ethos, or school culture. Within this scenario, class, gender, race ethnicity and teacher and student expectations all become crucial variables in the genesis and maintenance of resistance and disruption in schools. (Slee 1988: x)

In this view, disruption is seen as a conflict between the students' culture(s) and the school culture, and its minimisation therefore a matter of integrating the two cultures. This may seem a fearsome task for the classroom teacher, but there are moves in state departments for schools to develop their own policies, which we look at later in this chapter.

Box 17.3 *The ultimate deterrent?*

As one gentleman, much-punished in his school days, wrote to the *Morning Post* in 1856 (concerning the right of the Headmaster of Eton College to flog a boy for smoking):

> Now, I can vouch that, from the earliest ages to the days of the immortal Keate*, and thence to those of the present headmaster, they have, one and all, appealed to the *very seat of honour.* 'Experientia docet.' And, mark me, flogging, used with sound judgment, is the only *fundamental* principle upon which our large schools can be properly conducted. I am all the better for it and am, therefore—
>
> ONE WHO HAS BEEN WELL SWISHED.

*Dr John Keate, a notorious flogger at Eton.

(Quoted in Pearsall 1983: 409)

And now we know why:

> … Although the heavy blows may not at first induce erotic pleasure, the inital pain soon gives way to a sensation of warmth which envelops the whole of the seat like a soft, warm blanket, producing a pleasurable sensation and this may easily connect up with the sexual area. Boys after a sound thrashing are often surprised by the subsequent pleasant sensation of warmth in the seat and for this reason they sometimes endeavour to obtain a repetition of the chastisement which may ultimately affect them sexually.

The psychologist, E. Wulffen, writing in 1913, quoted in Pearsall (1983: 405)

Our main concern here, however, is with the individual teacher at the classroom level. Basically, the teacher looks not to remedy disciplinary problems once they have occurred, but to manage events so that problems are less likely to arise in the first place (Doyle 1986). Order through obedience has been replaced by planning, management, routines and activities: by professionalism, in other words. Yesterday's teachers had only to know their subject and to be recognised as not an easy mark. Today's have not only to know their subject, but to be able to use a range of management skills beyond the Victorian simplicity of just being strict.

These management skills involve several categories of concern (Coulby 1988):

- setting up a smoothly running organisation, that minimises the likelihood of classroom disruption;
- reducing and controlling disruption when it does occur;
- planning, instructing, and evaluating effectively;
- teacher–student and other interpersonal relations.

Seeing things this way takes the heat off. Most of the points relate to skills that are learnable. A teacher with a disorderly class is not to be seen as an incurable wimp, but as someone who has a lot still to learn. As we have seen, teachers (most of them at least) do profit from experience and become expert. The nature of expertise is such that the process may be accelarated, hopefully by initial training, certainly by metacognitive reflection (Evans 1991b).

Management: High structure and low structure

The teacher's authority is the major issue underlying all issues of classroom management, so let's get that straight first. Five bases of authority over others have been identified (French & Raven 1959):

1. *Legitimate:* the perceived right, by virtue of status or position, of a person to control others.
2. *Reward:* the extent to which a person is seen as being able to provide rewards.
3. *Coercive:* the extent to which a person is seen to be able to punish others.
4. *Expert:* the extent of relevant knowledge and skills a person has.
5. *Referential:* the extent to which others identify with a person, as in modelling.

Teachers have access to all of these sources of power, but the last two provide the most effective bases for influence and are means for a teacher to cope with the changed societal context for classroom management. Reliance on being an expert and modelling espoused values, such as a belief in education and a love of learning, gives the teacher validity and authenticity. It also forces the teacher to make use of personal and professional resources, not by being a martinet, but in the ability to defuse situations through the use of humour, knowledge of subject, compromise and discussion.

Teachers need to derive workable models of management in order to cope with this complex situation. We cannot provide teachers with a finished set of prescriptions; it is intrinsic to the systems model that each individual teacher's way of resolving must derive a personal resolution through reflection on decisions about teaching. We can, however, help make that process of metateaching easier by drawing out some of the dimensions on which management decisions have to be made.

We may distinguish three major areas of management decisions (we are not concerned here with purely instructional decisions, which will be dealt with in other aspects of your course):

1. *Setting up operational structures.* What are the ground rules for your classroom? Who decides: you, the students, or you and they together? How do you go about that?
2. *Student–teacher interaction.* What underlies effective and efficient communication? Are you going to be assertive or empathetic? Do you know how to be either?
3. *Rewarding and punishing.* Should you always reward desirable behaviour? What are effective ways of punishing pupils? Should you punish students at all?

The teacher-as-manager does not transform the lovable, fallible, ineffable you into a faceless corporation type. There are styles of management decisions:

1. *high-structure* decisions emphasise the teacher's role in setting up the learning environment, allowing relatively few options, and hence require a reactive role from the students;
2. *low-structure* decisions provide the student with many options and maximum autonomy when in the learning experience (which is not to say that the teacher does not have to work very hard to provide a low-structure environment).

For each management decision, then, the possibilities fall between the highly structured decision emanating from the teacher and the low structure which effectively places students in a situation where they initiate their own decision. Teacher-centred methods emphasise the use of classroom routines (Yinger 1979) and methods which are presented with prescriptive detail and sequence (Berliner 1984). In contrast, low-structure management focuses on the motivation and personal growth of the individual (Gnagey 1975), student participation in decision-making, with logical rather than arbitrary consequences for rule infringement (Dreikurs & Cassel 1972; Glasser 1977) and clear, situationally based rather than personally based, communication (see below) (Ginott 1971).

Essentially, then, each management decision has a bias towards high structure (because it comes from the teacher) or low structure (because it comes from the student) (see Figure 17.2).

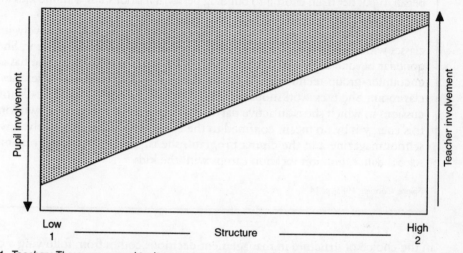

1. *Teacher*: There are several topics we can cover next and we should now decide which will be done, and how we are going to do it...

2. *Teacher*: I have decided on our next topic—explorers and exploration. I want you to make notes from the following references and have a 1000-word essay handed in by lunchtime Friday...

Figure 17.2 *Structure in pupil management decisions*

So what sort of manager of learning do you want to become? Remember the classroom is a system; you are part of that system. If you are operating in way that is not authentic you, things will not feel right. Take a look at Sheila and how she adapted her management style until it was authentic (Box 17.4).

It is important that teachers' choices made along this continuum are compatible both with their philosophies and with how they feel they can operate. Some teachers, like Sheila, are uncomfortable operating in a style that depends on a low degree of student self-direction, whereas others operate very well in such an environment. Such decisions must also be compatible with school policy in general; and perhaps most important of all, these decisions have to be compatible with each other. To make low-structure decisions on some aspects of a lesson, and high-structure decisions on others will lead to contradictions and to the likelihood that neither set of decisions will work. Consistency

Box 17.4   *Sheila: A teacher who adapted*

The school is not exceptionally rough, but it has problems of control. The kids walked all over her. In retrospect she is critical of her teacher training. It gave her lots of ideas for lessons, 'but I was never prepared for the discipline, at all. I think it was unreal'. Facing the classic shock of the idealistic young teacher dumped into her first classroom, she reacted in a classic way. She came down hard on the kids. She called in support from the school hierarchy, and insisted on silence and order. After a few months she got it.

But she soon came to see this as the wrong solution. She had control, all right; but the kids still were not learning anything. 'Learning doesn't necessarily happen in a dead quiet classroom with everyone jumping when you say "jump".' So she began to put her main effort into building personal relationships with the kids in which they *would* become involved.

This has led in two directions. On the one hand it has produced lively, informal classes with a great deal of student participation. Most of the kids love it. Sheila has gone far beyond the conventional devices of debates and projects. She has adapted encounter-group techniques, and uses them as 'self-exploration' exercises in the classroom. She uses workshops, self-directed group projects and free-floating discussions in which she is an active participant but not the source of all wisdom. And this energy is by no means confined to the classroom. She is also involved with the school magazine and the drama program, she supervises debating, organises the school dance, goes on vacation camps with the kids.

Source: Connell, 1985, p. 14.

in the choice of structure in management decisions comes from following a clear personal philosophy of teaching, something which the reflective teacher tries to develop from the very beginning and to modify with experience.

Classroom climate

The affective expression of these negotiations on management style is almost tangible as soon as you walk through the door of any classroom: what it *feels* like. A 'warm' climate is characterised by a caring, empathetic relationship between teacher and students and between student and student; a 'cold' climate by aggression, negative feelings, criticism and sarcastic exchanges between participants.

High-structure decisions may tend to elicit a cold climate, because they frequently assume Theory X; students are basically not to be trusted, so I shall have to make all the major decisions for them and ensure that they are properly enacted. Low-structure decisions tend to assume Theory Y; students can be trusted to make good decisions. Nevertheless, it is perfectly possible to set up a formal, high-structure classroom in an atmosphere of caring and good will. Equally, a low-structure classroom can be cold and uncaring, as it would be in a completely *laissez-faire* classroom; a teacher leaving students to live with poor decisions, or no decisions at all, is definitely uncaring.

The climate of a classroom is the affective side of professionalism. The teacher will necessarily create a climate of feeling in which the management decisions will play their part. The management decisions and climate together make the *total learning environment* in both cognitive and affective aspects.

To summarise, in arriving at a management policy, teachers are not strictly speaking dictating the terms; they are *offering* terms that are 'negotiable' in a very real sense. If the students can be open and genuine parties to the negotiations so much the better; the sense of ownership will be that much stronger and the contract more binding. Everyone knows where everyone stands.

Teachers need to be as metacognitive about this as possible. They should enter into negotiations knowing very clearly what sort of climate they want, what sort of policy they will settle for which will achieve their goals, and what sort of dominance they want and can sustain without violating their authenticity as a person.

Setting up operating procedures

Operating procedures seal the negotiations. When these are established both teacher and students know where they stand. There are two important principles in setting up a smoothly running classroom with minimal problems in keeping order. Ensure that there are:

1. no gaps;
2. no dead time, with things just hanging fire.

The basis of good management is to keep purposeful activity continuing through the lesson, either through good advanced planning or through expert improvisation.

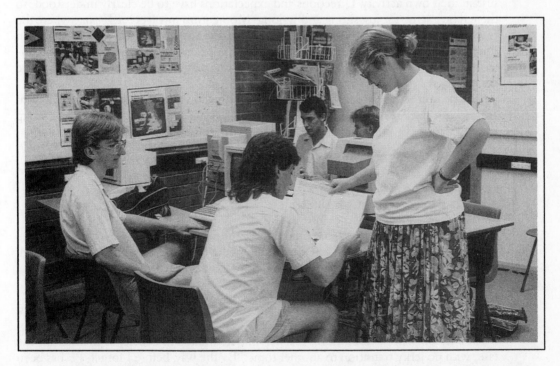

With the establishment of operating procedures, both the teacher and the pupils know where they stand.

Nothing is more conducive to misbehaviour than gaps in the execution of a lesson. However, as we have seen, the classroom is a complex environment at the best of times because it:

- is *multidimensional*, with numerous student–student and student–class interactions as well as the teacher–class and teacher–student interactions;
- is *unpredictable*; and
- *requires immediate teacher decisions*, which cannot be deliberated but have to made on the spot. If they are not, there will be gaps.

It was precisely at this point where expert teachers managed smoothly—they made swiftly flowing decisions, leaving no gaps and no opportunity for disruption. Students will not sit there and do nothing unless severe coercion is used. If, however, student activity can be aligned with the learning task, leading towards your objectives for the lesson, your job is done. Simply, the teacher ensures that what students do is relevant to the lesson by ensuring that appropriate activities are available. If the structured learning activities are not available, the students' efforts will be expended on something else, almost certainly disruptively. Several effective techniques have been reported in the literature, most notably in the work done by Kounin (1970).

Momentum and smoothness

Good teachers keep students productively busy (not just busy-busy). Instructions are clear, equipment is to hand and when students have finished one task they know what to do next. Students should know where books or equipment are kept, so that they can sustain their own activity. Directions and expectations have to be clearly understood, so there is no excuse for just sitting and waiting. Momentum involves *overlapping*, where the teacher handles more than one task or focus of attention at a time, so that the main thread can be continued while an individual seeks personal attention. Non-verbal communication is important to keep the momentum going; talking here but making eye contact there.

Momentum is destroyed by interruptions and slowdowns. Many of these interruptions are teacher-caused. Kounin quotes one example of a teacher who was trying to start a group reading session. Overlapping was beyond her. She constantly interrupted the activity:

'Let's wait until the people in Group Two are settled and working ...'
'Now, John, what did you do with your pencil?'
(John mutters inaudibly.)
'I'd like to know what you did with it.' ...
'Well, did you eat it?' ...
'What happened to it? What colour was it? You can't do your work without it.' ...
'I'll get you a pencil. Make sure the pencil is here tomorrow morning. And don't tell me you lost that one too. And make it a new one. And see that it's sharpened' ...
(Kounin 1970: 104)

Sound familiar? That took 1.4 minutes in lost time, causing even greater losses in effective classroom climate.

In a lesson with 'smoothness', teacher-initiated talk and activity is focused on the task, with no jerky transition to another topic: 'By the way, before I forget, PE has been cancelled this afternoon. I'll give you the details later. Now, where was I? ...'

Routines

Routines help groove students; they're useful to fall back upon when the planned part of the lesson has been played through or there has been some kind of disruption; they ease transitions from one activity to another; they give structure. They are also very boring and teach little; they provide for teaching what polystyrene provides for the Big Mac: no more than the wrapping but with less danger to the environment. Routines simplify management by reducing the need to fully plan around each activity. There are various kinds:

1. *Activity* routines control and coordinate where students go, what materials are needed and where they are kept, any special behaviour. For example, art is Wednesday afternoon: Who is to distribute paints and paper? When? What do students have to bring? Protective clothing? When do we start cleaning up? Who collects up the materials? Heady stuff, but all these questions have to be answered and it's better if they're routinised.
2. *Instructional* routines are worked out to suit each lesson. What do we want them to do at various points in each maths period; at the beginning, after seatwork on problems ... Each teacher will have their own preferences; the point is, once you have worked out what you want to do, make sure the students know and carry it out automatically. At such a transition, the teacher should give a signal, to which the students have been taught the response: 'When I say "Change" I want you to stop what you are doing, put your work away and take out the homework I gave you yesterday. OK? Change!'
3. *Management* routines cover other contingencies: wet weather cancellation of sport, when visitors enter the classroom ...

Such routinising of the classroom can be done top-down from the teacher or in consultation with students.

Withitness

'Withitness' is Kounin's term for the teacher's ability to monitor what is going on in the multidimensional classroom; having eyes in the back of the head. The important thing here is to be aware of what is going on before things brew into a larger confrontation. Frequently a teacher who isn't aware of the lead-up to a problem ends up blaming the wrong students and loses face. Tom pinches Bill who jumps and feints to pinch back; Mary nudges Stewart to let him know what is happening. Teacher sees Stewart turn: 'Stewart! See me after the lesson!' Stewart is outraged, Mary feels guilty, Tom and Bill can't believe their luck; all think the teacher 'is a dork'.

Often the teacher is 'withit', the misdemeanour *is* noticed, but judges that in the interests of smoothness and good relations, and in the hope that this is a minor one-off thing that is best ignored, pretends that nothing was seen. There is no right or wrong answer to this very common dilemma. In many cases, it can be handled in a low-key manner by overlapping—a warning look or a gesture, while talking to the rest of the class— so that a minor disciplinary problem can be handled without losing momentum. Much depends on the teacher's own personal management style and on the climate that one wishes to create. As we shall see when we discuss behaviour modification, ignoring unwanted behaviour may be the best way of extinguishing it.

Teacher–student communication

Just about all teaching is a matter of teacher–student communications. Here, we are concerned with the style we want to establish: teacher-centred or student-centred, assertive or sympathetic.

The assertive teacher uses communications that (a) remind students of the rules and (b) indicate what should be done (Canter & Canter 1979): 'We agreed that there would be no talking while some of the class were still completing the test. I want silence.' Rather than the non-assertive: 'Now, children, do please try to be a little quieter'. Or the hostile: 'Shut up!'

The Canters suggest that students' names should be used regularly in communications, maybe combined with the 'broken record' technique, making argument all but impossible:

Teacher: 'Now Julie, I want you to bring that work in by tomorrow morning.'
Julie mumbles an excuse.
Teacher: 'Julie! That does not matter. I want you to bring that work by tomorrow morning.'
Julie: 'Mmdhgts'
Teacher: 'That's as maybe, Julie, we'll see about that when you bring in that work tomorrow morning.'

By now Julie is quite sure where she, Julie, stands. She'd better bring that work in tomorrow.

Questions can be used assertively to convey limits: 'Shouldn't you be working on the set question on your own rather than chatting to Phil about it?' This technique, highly developed, conveys: I-am-in-charge-here-because-we-all-know-the-answer-don't-we? If you want to create a strong, assertive image, the Canters' technique is likely to be highly successful.

If, however, that is not the authentic you, you will want to create a sympathetic image. A different technique is required. Ginott (1971) talks about 'sane' messages, which communicate feelings about situations rather than about people. Teachers do not label students or lose their temper, feigned or otherwise. They acknowledge students' feelings, with the question: 'How can I help?': 'You appear upset over your results, Sylvester. How can I help?' Ginott suggests that praise should be linked to *acts*, not students. Not: 'Good girl, Elizabeth!' But: 'It was thoughtful of you to have collected up the art brushes before you went home yesterday, Elizabeth.' Such a comment focuses on what is praiseworthy; it is less phony, makes her feel better——and she is more likely to collect up the art brushes tomorrow.

Gordon (1974) similarly proposes that teachers avoid confrontation, which he sees as no-win as it can so easily escalate. If the teacher gains the upper hand, then that tells the student that it's power that counts, which in turn justifies revenge for the embarrassment of defeat. Or the failure could prompt a helpless withdrawal of the student who is now feeling inadequate. But if the student gains the upper hand it leaves the teacher feeling worse than inadequate.

To prevent confrontation Gordon suggests using 'I' messages instead of 'you' messages. This has the effect of avoiding pushing students into a corner:

'I can't continue to chair the debate if I can't hear the speaker.'

not

'If you keep talking the debate's off.'

Imagine the difference between 'you' and 'I' messages in the context of a staff meeting, or a marital dispute. The difference in effect will leap out at you. Try it (in either context).

These styles of communication may helpfully be analysed in terms of transactional analysis (TA), which originated in psychotherapy (Berne 1964). TA sees communication as coming from, and being addressed to, one of three ego states: parent, adult and child. These have nothing to do with age, but with the style of communication we want to set up. Thus, the teacher who adopts a strutting 'academic–expert' pose is setting up a parent-to-child pattern of communication, to which the students are being forced to communicate back as children. The 'democratic' approach has its dangers: that can force one into a child–child pattern, rather than the desired adult–adult, and the former is untenable for a teacher (Lett 1971). Likewise, adult-to-adult communication might be untenable for some students (Davies 1982).

Questioning

Questioning is a vital skill in teaching. It can be used for managerial or for cognitive/instructional purposes. As we have seen, questions can be used in straight managerial ways: 'We know we shouldn't be doing that, don't we Jill? What should we be doing? ... Working on Problem 18? Did I hear right? Well that's odd, Jill, isn't it? What were *you* doing?'

Seeming instructional questions, shot rapid fire round the class, are frequently not in fact used instructionally, to see who knows the answers to a barrel full of low level questions, but to groove; get the class settled, with the teacher in charge getting instant reactions to teacher-initiated activities, thus establishing without doubt who is calling the shots. Managerially, questions can also be used as a device for filling gaps in the proceedings.

We shall say something about the instructional use of questions here because the instructional and the managerial so closely interact in this case, often counter-productively. When using questions for instructional purposes, that is when the answers matter substantively, it is important to allow adequate *wait time*. Thinking takes time and high level thinking takes more time than low level thinking. Wait time can be divided into several kinds, two important ones being the length of time allowed for response after the *teacher* has ceased talking and the length of time allowed when the *student* has finished talking.

Studies over many years, grade levels and countries have shown that wait time is very rarely over 3 seconds and usually under one (Tobin 1987). One second is just not long enough to allow for anything beyond memory responses. What happens if teachers are requested to allow 3 to 5 seconds wait time; that is, they say nothing and ask students to say nothing, for at least 3 and up to 5 seconds? Tobin (1987) reviewed over 30 studies relating to this question and found that several things happened, both to students' and to teachers' behaviour (Table 17.1):

Even 5 seconds seems very short. How long do students take to answer if given unlimited time? Ellsworth, Duell and Velotta (1991) tried just that and found that tertiary students averaged 9 seconds to answer convergent (one correct answer) questions, to over 30 seconds to divergent questions. It looks like with even 5 seconds we're not giving students anywhere near long enough.

Tobin emphasises that increasing wait time in itself does not necessarily have all the marvellous effects in Table 17.1. These effects come about when increased wait time changes the discourse pattern of the classroom, when the game becomes perceptibly different. These questions are not for grooving; they are for real. Then the interaction pattern changes, with students contributing more, at a higher level, and the teacher in

Table 17.1   *What happens when you give students time to answer ?*

The effects of extending wait time to beyond three seconds:

On teachers' behaviour:	*On students' behaviour:*
Less teacher talk	Longer student responses
Fewer repeated verbal patterns	More student discourse, less failure to respond
Fewer questions asked	More alternative responses
Fewer 'chain' questions	More student–student interactions
More higher cognitive level questions	Increase in the complexity and cognitive level of student responses
More probing questions	Content (physics) perceived as less difficult
Less mimicry of student replies	Better classroom climate
Greater teacher anxiety	Higher achievement

turn coming back with higher level questions of substance, not rhetorical questions and mimicry of low level answers. It cuts both ways: Ask a silly question and you get a silly answer. Ask a complex question and you get a complex answer. The major negative effect of increasing wait time is to increase teacher anxiety; giving students more time is to relinquish power, which worries some teachers.

It was suggested that the managerial aspects of questions were in some conflict with the instructional. The reason of course is that the managerial use of questions is low level; waiting time is wasting time for the teacher-as-manager. We want snappy replies to show we're awake and on the ball, don't we? No slackers in this class. On the other hand, as teachers-as-co-constructors-of-knowledge, if we want students to take our questions seriously, then we have to allow them wait time; and even 5 seconds isn't long enough in real terms.

The answer is simple: make quite sure that we know what we're doing when we ask questions. High level instructional use of questions is a way of opening out the classroom discourse, with an adult-to-adult style of interaction. We have to make that use of questioning manifestly different from managerial questions.

Class size

Class size, from the teacher's point of view, is a crucial factor in effective classroom management. Oddly enough, the evidence—apart from opinion—has been unconvincing until recently. One Australian study found that while teachers' attitudes were more positive in smaller classes, student achievement was actually lower, only partly because better students are typically allocated to larger classes. Even after allowing for that, gains by students in larger classes were still superior, possibly because larger classes had 'a superior classroom climate' and presumably better teachers (Larkin & Keeves 1984). Nevertheless, Glass and Smith (1978), in an extensive meta-analysis, did find that small classes in general achieved better results, but most notably in the dreamy range of 5 to 15 students; over 25 students per class there was little effect.

More recent work involves classroom management as the crucial factor. Allowing for larger are brighter, Bourke (1986: 558) found that smaller is better, depending on *how teachers used* the smaller group size. In smaller classes, there were fewer teacher–student communications on management, more on instruction; in particular, more probing teacher questions with longer wait time, from which followed the positive results on wait time that Tobin reports: higher level responses and higher achievement.

In an elaborate study of 328 elementary classes drawn from across the state of Tennessee (with random allocation of students and teachers to classes over the first two years of schooling to avoid the problems of selectivity or of drop-out that so easily distort the picture), classes were defined as: small (13–17), regular (22–25), regular-plus-aide (22–25) (Finn & Achilles 1990). Attainment in arithmetic and reading was monitored. The results were clear:

- small classes did better in reading and in mathematics, confirmed in both cross-sectional and longitudinal analyses;
- the presence of a teacher's aide helped in the regular size classes but not sufficiently to allow them to catch up to the small classes;
- ethnic minority students benefited much more than white students, particularly on the tests based on the school curriculum, as opposed to standardised tests;
- motivation and self-concept measures were unaffected by class size;
- teachers much preferred the smaller classes (a common finding).

We conclude from all these studies, then, that it's not the fact of having small or large classes that matters, or asking slow- or rapid-fire questions, it's what you do with the space provided. The data reviewed here suggest that expert teaching requires monitoring and management skills that lose their effectiveness when spread too thinly. Only really expert experts can handle large classes *and* teach interactively at a high cognitive level. Beginning teachers in particular, if they are to teach at a high cognitive level, need small classes where they can develop the appropriate management skills.

Rewarding and punishing

After patterns of communication, the way we reward and punish students is the most important feature of classroom management that teachers need to consider. What do we do when students are doing just what we expect of them? Do we always comment favourably or otherwise reward them, or only sometimes? Or do we ignore 'good' behaviour on the grounds that that is what they *should* be doing? What sort of rewards should we give, if we are going to? How?

The same questions could be asked about misbehaviour. Do we always follow up with some form of punishment or only sometimes? Or should we avoid punishing at all times? If we do punish, what forms are effective? How and when should they be administered? Whether or not we punish, what do we do in a crisis? The teacher needs to develop strategies for crisis management.

One might decide that the desired classroom climate and style of interaction with students is more likely when desirable or appropriate behaviour is rewarded when it occurs, and misbehaviour ignored rather than punished. Alternatively, one might find it personally inauthentic to ignore misbehaviour, or out of keeping with the rest of the school; in that case, one needs to decide on what sorts of punishments one is going to consider. Whatever the answers to these questions, it is vital to be consistent. A teacher needs to derive a policy on rewarding and punishing.

The first issue to consider is punishment: whether to punish, how and for what.

Punishment

Punishment is widely used to stop undesirable behaviour, but it is in fact a very unreliable weapon. Sometimes it works; other times it actually increases the unwanted behaviour. Always, it has profound effects on classroom climate and on teacher–student relations. It is therefore a matter that needs to be considered carefully, in the light of what we know about it.

First, we define punishment as an unpleasant consequence to a particular behaviour, which is perceived as being administered by another person: sarcasm, a slap, a deprivation of some right. Glasser (1977) saw a difference between discipline and punishment. Discipline to Glasser (not how we have been using it in this chapter) involves pain as a natural and realistic consequence of a person's behaviour because that's the way things are; if you step barefoot on a sharp rock, it hurts. Punishment involves pain caused by someone else's disapproval and deliberate agency; if I disobey you, you hurt me. It-hurts leads to an internal attribution (silly me); you-hurt-me leads to an external attribution (nasty you).

Wherever possible, the sanctions for infringing classroom rules should be presented as a natural consequence, coolly and unemotionally, not as a personal matter: 'How dare you disobey me!' Future behaviour and future teacher–student relations are clearly going to differ radically depending on whether the student reads the situation as discipline ('my fault') or punishment ('teacher's spite'). Clearly, the distinction between discipline (in Glasser's sense) and punishment depends on how it is perceived. The best the teacher can do is to make unpleasant consequences appear as 'natural' as possible, not as a personally driven assault accompanied by anger. Involving students in setting up classroom rules and the sanctions for breaking them is clearly a good strategy for setting up a discipline-oriented rather than a punishment-oriented classroom (Glasser op. cit.; Dreikurs & Cassel 1972).

There have been many studies of punishment. The following points summarise the main conclusions (Johnston 1972):

1. The initial intensity of punishment should be as great as possible and this intensity should be maintained. This principle is almost always violated. The first offence is invariably punished more leniently than the second and following offences.
2. Punishment must be administered each time it is warranted. This principle follows from the first: the negative consequences must be seen as inevitable and as far outweighing the positive ones. Such conditions are not attainable in the classroom. Not only would the severity of the punishment be unacceptable, teachers simply cannot guarantee 100% effectiveness in policing deviant behaviour.
3. Punishment is more effective when it is combined with reward. This way there is an 'out'; the student could have made the choice marked by reward and did not. The attribution following punishment is in this case likely to be internal rather than external.
4. Punishment makes people become emotional and they then react to that emotion. They are more likely to become emotional if the punisher is obviously angry. Anger is highly contagious. A contract is sealed, with revenge a major clause.
5. Punishment makes people dislike the whole context of learning. We learn not to like the people and situations that cause us pain. If you punish by giving added schoolwork, you are committing educational treason. You are making students hate the very thing a teacher is paid to make them love.

6. Punishment is often used as a means of moral education, but only by those who have not read Chapter 4. Punishment encourages students to regard the pain caused as the price for doing what they want to do: 'I want to do what you don't want me to do. You have set the price of my doing it. I think your price is worth my pleasure, so I'll do it and pay your price. Then I'm free to do it again—especially if I think that I can get away with it.'

The problem is that the individual being punished can react in so many different ways; from deciding the behaviour is not worthwhile (the desired effect), to deciding that he or she has found an excellent way of controlling the punisher. There is no surer way of making a teacher angry than repeating the very behaviour that led to the punishment. In order to ensure that the effects of punishment are predictable and desirable, it is necessary to punish immediately, infallibly and with maximum severity. And that is not possible in most schools these days.

The Dettman Committee (1972), investigating punishment in Western Australian classrooms, found an interesting link between the frequency and perceived dislike of punishment, which illustrates these points (see Table 17.2).

Table 17.2   *Frequency and perceived dislike of punishment*

Punishment		Frequency of visits to deputy					
		None N = 4065	*One* 438	*Two* 200	*Three* 115	*Four* 53	*Five+* 101
		%	%	%	%	%	%
Physical punishment (e.g., with cane, ruler or hand)	It does not worry me	16	22	30	26	52	41
Suspended from school	It does not worry me	9	15	20	28	26	38
Sent out of the classroom	It does not worry me	39	49	63	69	71	66
Note from the teacher or principal to your parents	It does not worry me	8	10	16	15	16	25
Made fun of by the teacher with a sarcastic remark	It does not worry me	16	23	22	29	24	33

Source: Dettmann, 1972, pp. 143–4.

Those students who were punished most were worried least by the punishments. This was particularly true of corporal punishment.

A scale of punishments

Telfer and Rees (1975) listed the more common punishments used in school, with an analysis of advantages and disadvantages of each. The punishments are in ascending order of severity.

1. *Ignoring the behaviour.* The advantages of this are that if done in context (see below), the unwanted behaviour is likely to disappear. The disadvantages are that the teacher may not be the only one providing reinforcement for the behaviour. The student could conclude that the teacher is condoning the behaviour.

2. *Recognition.* If the teacher pauses 'significantly', or calls the pupil's name, the latter cannot but conclude that the bounds of what is acceptable have been exceeded. Except in the hands of an experienced teacher with charisma, and with whom the pause or naming is indeed 'significant', this tactic is likely to wear very thin.

3. *Rebuke.* This may range from mild comment to cutting sarcasm, perhaps in either event with a request to see the teacher after the lesson. The benefit of the comment alone will depend upon the nature of the sarcasm (if used) and the reaction of the student. The advantages of seeing the student later and in private are that interruption to the lesson is minimised; that neither teacher nor student has to play a role publicly; and that the class is kept guessing as to the severity of the penalty. Private reprimands are also more effective (Houghton, Wheldall, Jukes & Sharpe 1990).

4. *Mild punishment,* such as detention, isolation, loss of a privilege. Detention raises many difficulties: no states, for instance, permit detention during recess times. Restriction of favoured activities (e.g., sport) may involve an activity the student particularly benefits from.

5. *Send from the room.* If done naturistically (i.e., as a logical consequence of antisocial or other unacceptable behaviour), this is a sound procedure. It also leaves the class undistracted. One obvious problem is that students may refuse to go; another is where to send them if the school has made no special provision for this. Also, if used frequently, both students and school administrators might think that teachers are abdicating their responsibilities.

6. *Corporal punishment.* This is no longer a legal alternative in most public education systems, although it is an option in New South Wales schools. (The school and its community make the decision as to whether or not corporal punishment is part of the school's discipline code.) The problems of severity, unpredictability and revenge are most evident in this case (see also Table 17.2).

7. *Drastic consequences.* These range from arrangements for a parent interview to expulsion, which may perhaps be classified as natural consequences rather than punishments. If a child is consistently and seriously misbehaving, the problem reasonably requires consultation with parents and school counsellor.

That's the teacher's view. Students see the following as more severe than do teachers: shaming/personal insult, parent–principal conference and permanent suspension (Zeidner 1988). The first, public shaming, is one that teachers should note; frequently such comments spring too easily to the lips of teachers, with little idea of the negative effects they have. Suspension might be the end of a problem for the teacher, but it is the beginning of a larger problem for the student.

Related to this point of perspectives is the effect of praising and reprimanding *privately* rather than publicly. Private praise and reprimands are more effective with high school students than public praise (Houghton, Wheldall, Jukes & Sharpe 1990). Public praise is likely to embarrass rather than please, while public reprimands are public challenges to adolescents; challenges to save face and to get revenge, also publicly. Private reprimands are much more easily taken as well-meant feedback; also, the teacher may be perceived to have thoughtfully gone out of the way specifically to avoid humiliating the student. The point has been made with minimal interpersonal conflict.

Glasser (1969, 1977) advises teachers to focus on improving pupil self-esteem to develop responsible behaviour. Groups formed in the class can enable students to discuss concerns. Instead of being given an imposition, a misbehaving student would be asked to compose a plan which will result in improved behaviour and that plan becomes a contract: a formal agreement to behave accordingly in future. Glasser believes that in general students should be involved in formulating rules, which should focus on learning activities and be subject to regular review. The students thus have an input and a responsibility when the rules are broken:

Teacher (in an unthreatening manner): What are you doing?
Student: Nothing.
Teacher: Is that helping you or the class?
Student: I don't know.
Teacher: What could you do that would help?
Student: I don't know.
Teacher (gives alternatives): Let's see. You could get on with the set work and fix that book tonight at home. Or you could fix the book straight away and stay back after the lesson and finish the work. Or you may have to replace the book. What do you think?

The student's responses are now likely to be more constructive and the teacher uses whatever is suggested. If the student's response remains non-committal or negative, the teacher arranges a later private discussion to produce a plan stipulating exactly what the student has to do. Any infringements lead to isolation. The last alternative is for the principal to ask the parents to come to the school.

Behaviour modification

Behaviour modification, contingency management and applied behavioural analysis are all terms used to refer to the technology of changing the behaviour of another person by manipulating the consequences that follow their behaviour. The critical difference between behaviour modification (the most widely used term) and other kinds of management centres on the word 'contingency': something must clearly happen after the person has committed some overt act. The contingent links between desirable and undesirable acts and various pleasant, unpleasant or natural consequences are set out in Table 10.1. In a behaviour modification scheme, unlike any other schemes of classroom management, these relationships are applied as consistently as possible. The reasons *why* the student misbehaves are not the point and are not investigated, as they would be in other forms of management. Typically, behaviour modification involves rewarding desired behaviours and ignoring unwanted, although in some programs punishment, or rather discipline in Glasser's sense, is also used systematically.

Setting up a formal behaviour modification program
There are a few simple steps in making a formal program:

1. *Define the target behaviours.* This is exactly like defining behavioural objectives in instruction. It is not good enough to say 'I'll reward him when he's good'. What exactly does 'good' mean in this context? What do the students have to do? Talk? Not talk? Raise hands when asking a question? Sit at desks and at least look as if working? If so,

for how long? Ten seconds? Ten minutes? The unit of behaviour must be defined exactly, so that the teacher knows when to reinforce and the students know why.

2. *Record the baseline.* Once the target behaviour has been clearly defined, it is necessary to see what the pre-treatment or baseline rate of that behaviour is. Do the students sit at their desks for 5 minutes in total per lesson; 15 minutes; not at all? The importance of this step is that the rate of behaviour can be compared with the baseline during and after treatment. If this is not done, you might only have vague and subjective impressions about the success of the program.

3. *Decide the reinforcers.* What are to be the contingencies? What consequences are to follow the target behaviours? A token (later to be 'cashed' for an agreed privilege) could be awarded every time the target behaviour occurs. Are there to be any negative consequences for unwanted behaviours, such as a 'fine' of one token? Or are unwanted behaviours to be ignored?

4. *Reinforcement contingencies applied.* Now we come to the heart of the program: the contingencies are to be applied, so that when the target behaviours occur, the chosen consequences follow. The students themselves should be utterly clear as to what it is they are or are not supposed to be doing and what the consequences will be. The rules or contingencies should be applied without exception.

5. *Measure target behaviours.* Now the reinforcement schedule has been applied, what has happened to the rate of target behaviours? Is it higher? If not, there has been an error of judgment in the appropriate reinforcer and another one should be applied. Steps 3 and 4 should be reapplied until there is a marked variation in the appropriate direction.

6. *Reversal.* This step is a check: not always necessary, but recommended. Remove step 3, the reinforcement; within a few days, the target behaviours should revert close to the baseline rate.

7. *Reapply contingencies.* The rate of responding should now return to the level at Step 4, thus confirming that the program is having the desired effect on the students' behaviour.

The essence of the procedure is in the first five steps; if the program is working it will usually be pretty clear to the teacher that the students are a lot quieter or are attending more to their work. Nevertheless, it helps to have the data available. The really tricky parts are to decide on a suitable reinforcement schedule and to stick to it.

Figure 17.3 is a typical graph of a behaviour modification program.

The time on task (minutes per 40-minute lesson) is plotted for each day (based on observing a few target students for one lesson per day). Baseline is established on days 1–3: only 10–15 minutes are spent on task. Then the contingencies are applied: now 25–35 minutes are spent on task. Reversal for days 10–12 shows a typical drop: but when the contingencies are reapplied from day 13 onwards, on-task behaviour settles around 35+ minutes per lesson.

Behaviour modification at work

If the program is carried out properly, the results are usually striking and positive (Hanley 1970). A study by Packard (1970) of classroom attention is typical. In normal classes (ranging from 25 to 34 students in each), from kindergarten and Grades 3, 5 and 6, the teachers distributed tokens for 'attending' behaviours (e.g., writing in a book, watching the teacher when requested) and ignored inattention. The

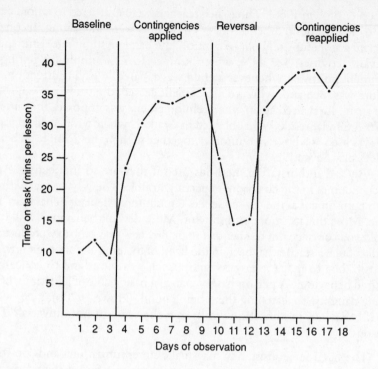

Figure 17.3 *A typical record of a behaviour modification program*

tokens could be exchanged for preferred activities that were discussed in advance and decided upon by each class on a contractual basis.

In Grades 5 and 6, the percentages of time that children devoted to 'attending' behaviours during class instruction were as follows:

Grade	Baseline	Reinforcement	Reversal	Reinforcement
6	24	78	43	76
5	58	78	58	80

Similar results were found in earlier grades. The effects of the reinforcement and the reversal are clear. When the reinforcement schedule was in place, time spent in attending was near 80%; when not in place (at baseline and reversal) attending times were much lower.

Two more studies will be discussed. The first shows how to make a good class bad (Thomas, Becker & Armstrong 1968). The teacher of a class of 28 well-behaved primary school children typically praised and encouraged rather than scolded. In the interests of science, she was asked to become more authoritarian: to decrease her praising and encouraging and to increase the threats, punishments, etc., for bad behaviour. Watch carefully: the bad behaviour *increased* under threats, from an initial 9% to 31% at the end of eight days. In the interests of education, she then resumed her usually positive approach—and the disruptive behaviours reverted to their initial rates.

Now to make a bad class good. Or how to make beginning teachers, whose only experience with controlling children has been unhappy, effective class managers (Hall, Panyan,

Rabon & Broden 1968). Three such teachers were instructed to ignore deviant behaviour and to reward desired behaviours. The results were life-saving. In one Grade 6 class, described as 'completely out of control', the baseline study rate (time spent attending to relevant activities) was 44%, which jumped to 72% simply by getting the teacher to comment positively whenever a child was apparently paying attention. A reversal procedure was used and, when reinforcement ceased, the study rate approached the baseline again. It reversed again when reinforcement was imposed, this time reaching a rate of 76%. Similar results were obtained in Grade 1, where a much-liked game called Seven Up was used as a positive reinforcer together with praise ('You're all being *very* good—so let's play Seven Up …').

Why are authoritarian methods used if they are so ineffective? An authoritarian teacher comes to the classroom expecting trouble. The way to deal with that? Threaten, with punishment as the consequence. Result: more deviant behaviour. Too soft the first time. More threats, more punishment. More deviant behaviour. Still too soft … How could you convince this teacher that such 'firmness' was probably producing the unwanted results? Such a teacher has been in the habit of focusing attention on unwanted behaviour for too long to make it easy to ignore such behaviour and to concentrate instead on desired behaviour. A person has to change a basic habit of a lifetime: of 'catching them being naughty' to 'catching them being good' (Howe 1970b).

If behaviour modification works so well, why is it not universal? There are several reasons:

1. The need for consistency may make superhuman demands on the teacher-reinforcer. A flash of anger or impatience can confound the whole system of reinforcement. Or take the situation when a child sidles up to the desk to ask a question, jumping the queue for the teacher's attention. The easiest thing to do is to forget psychology and attend to the student who is nearest. But is it a rule that the only way to get teacher's attention is for hands to be raised, or to queue at the desk and to obtain permission to speak? If so, a student patiently waiting with hand up should never be ignored because nuisance-at-the-desk is easier to attend to and get out of the way.
2. *Teachers* are not immune to reinforcement. The transition from chaos to a deathly stillness, following a sudden yell, is ecstatically reinforcing. Unfortunately, the desired effect is as temporary as it is immediate. Yells have to be progressively louder and more sustained to maintain the same shock value. Stop it, before you become hooked on an increasingly counter-productive strategy.
3. Ignoring deviant behaviour instead of punishing it is quite difficult for most teachers. Supervisors, colleagues and parents are likely to view teachers apparently letting the kids get away with murder as either weak or subversive. There is a moral conviction that wrong behaviour should be punished; the teacher may think so too. Obviously such views discourage the implementation of behaviour modification. A complication here is that ignoring deviant behaviour does indeed result in an increase in such behaviour; in the short term. It takes a few days for the program to take effect (Hanley 1970), by which time many would-be behaviour modifiers are wondering what on earth possessed them to even consider such a crazy idea.

Behaviour modification in the Australian scene: A footnote on local use

Behaviour modification methods have been used in Australia in the area of special education, but rarely in Australian classrooms with normal children. After a series of studies of the use of behaviour modification in open-plan primary schools in Sydney, Winkler

(1976) concluded that the methods and concepts of behaviour modification were inadequate to handle the diversity found in open-plan schools. The reason for the unpopularity of behaviour modification in Australia is, however, more deep-rooted than that; it is more a question of the basic values underlying behaviour modification and the social context. Here, we tend to see behaviour modification as involving 'bribery', as encouraging materialism and as poor moral training to ignore wrongdoing. In the United States, founded upon rugged individualism and the Puritan ethic, according to which effort receives its due reward, behaviour modification finds strong compatibility (Gardner 1976).

The exemplary school

However well set up and ordered we make our own classroom, the system of the classroom is nested in the broader system of the school. That of course sets limits to the class management system the teacher might like to establish. Indeed, the problem of installing a fully blown behaviour modification program in one's own classroom is that it may not only clash with the system of values operating in the school ('Jones lets his class do what they like! What a wanker!'), but also in the wider community. There is obvious value in having the different management systems operated by each teacher drawing on the same basic set of assumptions.

There is also the point mentioned by Slee (1988): that problems of management arise from a conflict between the school culture and the students' culture. Gifted individual teachers can often handle that (Dillon 1989), acting as a bridge between the two cultures, but teacher educators would be out of a job if policy were to rely on gifted individuals coming to the rescue. We saw in the last chapter how, in terms of an instructional innovation, the PEEL Project (Baird & Mitchell 1986) operated most effectively when it was on a whole-school basis. The same principle applies when dealing with management policy.

What would an 'exemplary school' look like? Pink (1988), involved in a program to identify outstanding schools in the United States, concluded:

1. While buildings themselves said nothing, he 'sensed an ambience of warmth, orderliness and purposefulness. Student work was prominently displayed, corridors were clean and freshly painted (by students) and work areas like the library were comfortably appointed ... It was evident that the school's activities were directed towards student learning.' (Pink 1988: 214–15)
2. Students enjoyed being at school and stressed fairness and honesty when talking of teachers and adminstrators. There were active student councils. Teachers were well-qualified, often with higher degrees, but were continually involved in staff development. Administrative priorities were on decentralised decision-making and instructional excellence.
3. The teaching was well coordinated. Each student was given detailed course syllabi and study guides. Subject teachers had two days free from teaching to visit classes and give teachers feedback. Other teachers and the principal regularly visit classes. Staff development programs are designed around such visits. Curriculum is school-based and teachers have time off to develop curriculum materials.
4. Discipline policy is developed and endorsed by: students, teachers, principal and community (through the P&C or equivalent). Staff development programs make the connection between instructional and management skills.

5. Extra-curricular programs are viewed as important and are indulged in by over 95% of students.

6. Relations between teacher–office–principal and principal–school board (read regional office–state department) are both characterised by the same philosophy: the delegation of decision-making to the locus most affected by the decision. Regional inspectors challenge 'each school to improve according to its own game plan' (op. cit.: 216).

Not many surprises here: a Theory Y operation from the state department downwards, creating a warm school climate, high morale, a focus on learning excellence with priorities set accordingly, openness to inspection and feedback at all levels.

The trouble with systems theory is that if you do not have, and are not likely to get, a Theory Y-driven Director-General, it is easy to conclude that a Theory Y-driven classroom or school is a lost cause. This would be erroneous; as we noted in the last chapter, there is more than one system and there is slippage between the systems operating at classroom, school and community levels. Thus, while integration between these systems makes each the more effective, you can control your own destiny up to an important point. But ideally, there should be as much coordination as possible between classrooms and school; specifically, in the development of a school-based management and curriculum policy.

Our present concern is with (4): the development of a school-based discipline policy. Gill, Trioli and Weymouth (1988) describe the implementation of code of behaviour at Princes Hill Primary School, Melbourne. This is an instructive case study of how a school management policy may be set up; their code was not simply a list of rules and sanctions, but a detailed discussion of the kind of working environment that principal, parents and students wished to create in their school. In this case they found Dreikurs' model (Dreikurs & Cassel 1972) a suitable conceptual base for considering management issues and instructional issues. A broader survey of student participation in the development of management policies is given by Holdsworth (1988).

Postcript

A school such as that described by Pink (1988) would be a marvellous place in which to teach. However, the cutting edge is in the classroom; the chief agent the individual teacher. As we saw at the beginning of this chapter, good teachers do make a difference.

There are many qualities that make up a good teacher. Some are undoubtedly matters of 'personality'. Some of the qualities mentioned in Box 17.1—loving, warm, a sense of humour, high self-esteem, ability to relate to others—are intrinsic ones that a teacher-education program can do little to change. Other qualities are however more in the cognitive domain and it is these that this book has been particularly concerned to address.

Our point of departure is a particular conception of good learning and teaching. The central process is learning: it involves the individual deeply and it changes that individual's life. But it is also a social process, carried out in a peculiar kind of institution that makes learning both easier and more restricted. Without a school, a teacher and other students, the lives of many would be considerably impoverished. Yet much of the learning that goes on in school is geared to the life of the school, not to the world outside school. The teacher's task is to work through the institution to help in the construction of the knowledge that transcends the institution.

No wonder so many deep qualities are needed for such a difficult task. Our contribution has been to spell out part of the knowledge for that task: the knowledge relating to learning. So far, it will be largely declarative; that young children learn in images, that we can only think of a limited number of things at a time, that we shall be less discouraged if we attribute failure to a lack of knowhow than to lack of ability. But we hope that experience will charge these dry propositional schemata with procedural energy. Then may you find, as we suggested in Chapter 1 that you would: 'Teaching well is a thrill.' (Connell 1985: 127)

Summary

Metaphors for teaching

Common metaphors for teaching emphasise the two-faced nature of the enterprise: the role of the expert, planning top-down, and the scintillating conversationalist, improvising an unscripted scene. Teaching is both of these and more. There are aspects that need careful planning, but the interaction with students takes us on unmapped routes. Both aspects take expertise.

The expert teacher

The expertise of teaching springs from knowledge of different kinds. Declarative knowledge of content, of content transformed to suit pedagogic needs, of curriculum; procedural knowledge of teaching method, of pedagogic strategies, of management skills, of scripts and scenes that derive from the fine grain of craft experience. A teacher needs to make a significant decision about once every two minutes in a busy environment with 30 or so craft coming in to land. The successful handling of this requires the development of complex schemata, founded in good theory and grounded in much practice. Beginning teachers can be helped in developing these schemata by appropriate integration of school experience.

Teacher–student collaboration: Negotiating the contract

The first step in a management exercise is to negotiate a contract with the consumer: the class, in this case. A degree, and hopefully a high degree, of collaboration has to be constructed. Negotiations in obtaining that agreed contract are usually tacit and commence from day one. The agreement has to be one that is workable and authentic to both teacher and students.

Classroom management

A policy is necessary to bring the contract to life and make the negotiations functional. Such a policy comprises instructional and management aspects and requires a coherent set of decisions about setting up operating procedures, maintaining a workable style of teacher–student communications, and of rewarding and punishing. Such decisions can be high structure, essentially top-down and teacher-dominated, or low structure, essentially bottom-up and student-centred.

Setting up operating procedures

The teacher needs to master a set of skills that leave no gaps in the pace of events and no dead time for students, collectively or individually. Several such skills have been identified: maintaining momentum and smoothness, overlapping of activities, setting up routines at critical points that the students know and can enact, being 'withit' through continual monitoring of the classroom and nipping potential problems in the bud.

Teacher–student communication

The style of teacher–student communication one wishes to establish needs to be decided and enacted; that will then interact with the operating procedures being set up. One might be an assertive broken record that brooks no argument; or sympathetic, allowing more two-way interaction. Questioning is an important skill; one needs to be clear whether one really wants to know the answers or one is using questions for managerial reasons. The issue of wait time is crucially different in each case. Class size is an important variable in setting up successful managerial skills; unless you are very, very expert, large classes restrict the effectiveness of a range of skills.

Rewarding and punishing

Rewarding and punishing are central to a management policy; one must decide if/when/how/what to reward and to punish. Such decisions should be such that (a) you can live with them, (b) the students can live with them and (c) the school can live with them. Research on the conditions under which reward and punishment are effective makes the decisions a little easier, if only you can get colleagues and parents to agree (they probably won't, if behaviour modification seems otherwise indicated).

The exemplary school

We started with the exemplary teacher, we finish with the exemplary school. As a satisfactory management policy is not aimed at fixing up the errant child, but with establishing a policy integral with instructional decisions, such a policy is the more effective if it can be implemented on a whole-school basis constructed by teachers, students and parents. It then becomes not you versus them but we-working-on-this-thing-together. Schools with warm climates, a focus on learning, and student-painted corridors are like this. May you be lucky enough to crack one.

Learning activities

1. What makes a good teacher?

Box 17.1 summarised the views of a wide range of people on what constitutes a good teacher. We saw there that there were at least 15 'factors' that could be identified. The purpose of this activity is to consider that list and rank order the factors. However, the way in which you consider the ordering may depend upon the experience of the teacher, so we are suggesting that the list be contemplated from several perspectives: a student teacher preparing for practice teaching; a teacher in their first year out of training; and an experienced teacher. For instance, for the teacher going out to practice teaching, would it be more important to stress organisation, knowing the subject and having a sense of humour? ...

This could be done as a whole class activity, in groups or individually. If you wanted to extend this activity, you could look at the expert/novice research we mentioned early in the chapter to see how it might fit with the rankings you have made from the list in Box 17.1. (That literature shows, for instance, that novices focus on discipline while experts focus on salient points of teaching.)

2. Questioning

Questioning can be used for both managerial and cognitive/instructional purposes. In the former context, questions tend to be fired rapidly around the room to keep students on task. As we have seen though, this machine gun approach may do very little for learning, particularly higher level learning. The intent of this learning activity is to demonstrate—no, exemplify—the differences between questions as managerial devices and questions as cognitive springboards. This can be done as a group activity. You will need a video camera and someone to be the 'teacher', perhaps some 'students' as well. Record two 5 minute teaching sessions, one managerial, the other cognitive in orientation. The tapes could then be presented to the class for discussion.

3. Management: Setting up operating procedures

This activity is designed to be carried out during a practicum session where you can observe an experienced teacher using operating procedures. As we noted, with the establishment of operating procedures both the teacher and the pupils know where they stand. Momentum and smoothness, routines and withitness were the factors we identified. Can you see them in operation in the class you are in? Keep a diary of the ways in which the teacher sets the parameters for classroom operation. Which factors work best for that teacher? Can you use the same operating procedures? What happens when you attempt to change the procedures? The results of your observations could be brought back to your university classes for comparison with other students' findings.

4. Scale of punishment

This activity uses Telfer and Rees' (1975) list of punishments in school as its basis. You will remember that they showed that punishments can vary from ignoring the behaviour (as the least severe) to 'drastic consequences' (obviously the most severe). For this task, you are to generate a set of, say, four discipline-based scenarios that could conceivably occur in classrooms. These scenarios can then be the basis for discussion on how that problem should be dealt with, given the context. To get you started, we present one.

'Kathy is in her first year of teaching at an inner-city high school. Her history classes are quite keen to learn but one of her classes, 8H5, has some rather unruly individuals in it. She puts a lot of effort into preparation and is "super" organised but she is a little anxious about the swearing that she hears in 8H5. She figures that her teacher educators were correct when they told her, "ignore such things, that's the best way to deal with it". To date she has ignored it but on the day in question she enters the room to find two students writing several swear words on the board. What is she to do?'

Which of Telfer and Rees' levels would be appropriate in this situation? Why?

An extension of this activity could be to examine school discipline policies. In many states, schools have responsibility for the development of their own discipline codes.

5. Class size

The effects of class size on learning seems to be a perennial issue, often used by politicians to dismiss the need for more teachers. We have shown in this chapter that it is important, but its importance is related to what actually occurs in the room. Bourke's (1986) research illustrates this point well, so we suggest that his paper be analysed more thoroughly. A good starting point (after quickly overviewing the paper) is to look at the discussion section (pp. 566–70). You will notice that Bourke discusses two aspects of his results: teaching variables (class grouping, teacher/student interactions, teacher questioning behaviour, homework practices and noise levels in rooms) and relationships in the causal model (student ability, school factors, teacher experience, class size and teaching practices). Do the models in Figures 1 and 2 make sense? (The first is looking at background factors, class size and achievement, while the second is the same model with the addition of the teaching practices variable.) Bourke's findings could be presented at a simulated staff meeting or as a simulated presentation to a parent group.

6. Analysing teacher education

Here is your chance to be reflective and creative. This activity is designed to those in teacher-education programs to reflect upon the type of teacher education they are receiving. We noted early in this chapter that six generalisations could be made from research on the preparation of teachers. Has your practicum program been consistent with these generalisations? If you could design a teacher-education program, how would you maximise the possibility that the teachers emerging from it had the integrated schema that seems to be required for effective (and enjoyable) teaching?

Further reading

On teacher expertise and staff development
Cole, P. G. & Chan, K. S. (1987). *Teaching Principles and Practice.* Sydney: Prentice Hall of Australia.
Comber, B. & Hancock, J. (eds) (1987). *Developing Teachers: A Celebration of Teachers' Learning in Australia.* North Ryde: Methuen Australia.
Good, T. L. & Brophy, J. E. (1987). *Looking in Classrooms* (4th edition). New York: Harper & Row.
Kounin, J. (1970). *Discipline and Group Management in Classrooms.* New York: Holt, Rinehart & Winston.
Review of Educational Research (1992) *62,* No2. (Summer)

Kounin's book is the classic on how to be competent as a traditional teacher. Cole and Chan, who focus on Australian classrooms, and Good and Brophy continue that tradition with the important material that has emerged since Kounin did his pioneering work.

Cole and Chan's methodical approach you'll find helpful. The checklists at the end of their chapters will allow you to assess yourself and others while teaching.

Comber and Hancock lay their lives down that it doesn't all end with your present program! As this chapter should have made clear, there is a lot to learn over and above soaking up experience once you're Out There. We're sure the subtitle of Comber and Hancock doesn't mean that such learning is so rare that it's a cause for celebration; certainly the contents are (written as they are mostly by teachers, for teachers, about teachers), with emphasis on the affective—a good antidote to the at times heavy cognising we've laid on you. Areas addressed include collaborating with colleagues, learning from students, working with parents, keeping journal to help improve teaching and attending inservice courses.

A very recent edition of *RER* gives an up-to-the-minute interchange about the management-versus-conversational views of teaching by Kagan and Grossman, respectively. For good measure, Solas, of QUT, tells us about the thinking of good constructivist teachers and students.

On classroom management

Balson, M. (1982). *Understanding Classroom Behaviour.* Hawthorn, Vic.: Australian Council for Educational Research.

Rogers, B. (1990). *You Know the Fair Rule*. Hawthorn, Vic.: Australian Council for Educational Research.

Fontana, D. (1985). *Classroom Control*. Leicester/London: British Psychological Society/Routledge.

Slee, R. (ed.). (1988). *Discipline and Schools: A Curriculum Perspective*. S. Melbourne: Macmillan.

Balson and Rogers are 'how-to' books addressed directly to teachers: the first based on behaviour modification, the second a cognitive-humanist approach. If Balson and Rogers deal with the procedural knowledge of discipline, Slee's collection deals with declarative. Fontana's falls in between, recounting different approaches to discipline, with advice on implementation. The flavour of Slee's book has been indicated in our preceding chapter: a sociological, whole-school approach whereby discipline policy and enactment are part of the 'curriculum', an approach which somehow makes psychology (= behaviourism) evil. But don't mind a psychologist; there are some excellent articles in addition to those by Slee, Coulby, Pink, Gill et al. and Holdsworth mentioned here.

On deriving whole school policies

Bassett, G. W. Cullen, P. & Logan, L. (1984). *Australian Primary Schools and Their Principals*. Sydney: Harcourt Brace Jovanovich.

Twenty case studies contributed by primary school principals showing how they constructed and implemented programs based on whole school participation, including parents. See also the chapter by Gill, Trioli and Weymouth in Slee's book listed in the preceding section.

GLOSSARY

Note: Cross-references appear in bold

ability A stable tendency to perform well on a *range* of tasks. Abilities are part-learned, part-inherited traits that underlie and 'explain' test performance. Abilities may be classified in terms of content (e.g., number ability) or process (e.g., divergent ability).

ability grouping Arranging students between-classes in terms of their general ability over all subjects (streaming), in subject-specific classes (setting), or within a class, according to their ability.

accommodation The term used by Piaget to describe the process whereby **cognitive structures (codes)** are made more complex by the modification wrought by new experiences. Equivalent to **recoding**.

accountability The view that teachers and schooling can be held responsible for the amount of learning that students evidence. A 19th-century version paid teachers according to the examination results of their students ('payment by results').

accreditation The role of schools and tertiary institutions in issuing certificates, diplomas, degrees, officially certifying that certain requirements have been met.

acculturation Refers to the mutual interaction between minority and majority groups in a **multicultural** society, resulting in a changed majority society.

achievement motivation Motivation for academic learning that is based on the ego-enhancement achieved by winning in a competitive situation; desire to achieve success, as opposed to desire to avoid failure.

achieving Applies to **motives, strategies** and **approaches to learning:** associated with institutionally desirable **learning outcomes** (high grades). Achieving strategy comprises typical study skills.

activation See **arousal**.

advance organiser Prefacing information to be learned with a brief statement that organises the concepts involved under an over-achieving, higher level, conceptual structure.

affective domain The domain that emphasises feelings, motivation and reactions to other people and oneself; to be distinguished from the **cognitive domain**, which is concerned with thought.

aggression Thought or action that wilfully inflicts psychological or physical hurt on another; to be contrasted with **assertion** and **altruism**.

allocentric Thought (and sometimes feeling) that is centred around respect for the rights of other people and what they think and feel; as opposed to **sociocentric** and **egocentric**.

alternative frameworks Explanations children create to explain phenomena for themselves, which fall short of the accepted frameworks of science

altruism Helping others without regard for the material consequences to oneself which will result from the action.

anxiety A feeling of threat, accompanied by high **arousal**. Trait anxiety is a predisposition for some individuals to react to a variety of situations with anxiety. State anxiety refers to the anxiety felt in a particular situation, such as **test anxiety**.

approach to learning A consistent way of going about a particular task, or learning/study in general, that derives from the student's **metacognition**, linking **motive** and **strategy**, with perceived task demands and desired type of **learning outcome**. Approaches, as may motives and strategies, can be referred to as **deep, surface** and **achieving**, with deep-achieving and surface-achieving as other possible combinations. Approaches can be used either in the **presage** sense of orientation or

521

predisposition to learn in a certain way, or in the **process** sense of handling an ongoing task.

arousal   Arousal or activation is a generalised motivation to behave, irrespective of the direction of behaviour. Low arousal is associated with low drive; high arousal with 'hyper' behaviour. The physiological source of arousal is the reticular arousal system (RAS), which is located in the brain stem.

assertion   Treating others firmly, but with no deliberate intention of harming them, in order to obtain one's own ends. High-structure teaching requires that teachers be assertive.

assessment   In general, the **summative evaluation** of student performance after a teaching episode, usually quantitatively conceived. In progressive assessment, the student's final grade is determined by performance throughout the course; in terminal assessment, the grade is determined by performance in a final examination at the end of the course. See also **self-assessment**.

assimilation   (a) The merging of minority groups so that they become indistinguishable from the majority group. (b) The term used by Piaget to describe the understanding and interpretation of experiences in terms of the individual's existing **cognitive structures**. Exactly equivalent to **encoding** (or coding).

associative interference   A theory of forgetting based on the similarity between items learned; may be retroactive (recall of previously learned material is inhibited by later material), or proactive (recently learned material inhibited by previously learned). This theory is mostly relevant for **rote** rather than **meaningful** learning.

attainment   Performance on a *particular* test, as opposed to **ability**, which refers to a range of tests.

attending   Selecting relevant from irrelevant material in the **sensory register** through a process of **precoding**; being aware of material in **working memory**.

attribution theory   A theory which bases motivation for performance of a particular task on previous performance of that task. Specifically, attribution theory emphasises the factors (such as ability, luck, effort or task difficulty) to which the subject attributes his or her performance.

autonomy (in moral development)   Acting out of principle, rather than out of **conformity** or self-interest. The highest level of moral development, ahead of **sociocentrism** and **egocentrism**.

backwash   In testing, the influence that knowledge of the nature and level of the test has on teaching and learning. Backwash may be cognitive or affective and useful or deleterious to learning: usually the latter.

baseline   The level of performance, in a **behaviour modification** program, that is obtained in the absence of any deliberate rewards or **contingencies**.

behaviour modification   A technique of changing the behaviour of individuals by deliberately altering the consequences of a particular behaviour in order to change the frequency of future occurrence of that behaviour, based on Skinner's principles of operant **conditioning**.

behavioural objective   An educational goal that specifies the learned behaviours a student is to exhibit after a learning episode (lesson or series of lessons). The objective should detail the conditions under which the learning is to occur and the level of performance expected. Instructional **objectives** in general are less stringent.

behaviourism   A school of psychology which is concerned only with the conditions associated with changes in behaviour. Internal ('mentalistic' or 'cognitive') events are regarded as irrelevant. Behaviourist psychologists rely on classical and operant **conditioning** as explanatory models of human behaviour.

bottom-up   A theory or procedure derived from the grass-roots, inductively (data-driven vs. theory-driven). Where the lower status determine policy (e.g., student-centred vs. teacher-centred). As opposed to **top-down**.

burnout   Various physical and psychological reactions to prolonged job stress, particularly noted in helping professions, including teaching, resulting in poor morale, irritability and depression.

common assessment tasks (CATs)   Attempts to ground assessment at HSC level in authentic tasks that de-**institutionalise** assessment and its **backwash**.

chunks   The units of information, grouped in **working memory**, that determine the amount of information a person can handle at any given time. A phrase-length unit of meaning.

classical conditioning   See **conditioning**.

climate, classroom. The 'feel' that is generated by teachers and students in a classroom; usually 'warm' or 'cold', depending on whether **theory Y** or **theory X** drives the participants.

codes (elaborated and restricted) Elaborated codes of communication are learned, according to Bernstein, by middle-class children and these emphasise public and formal rules of grammar. Restricted codes—where language is limited to personal reference, following instructions and particularly to context—are said to be learned by working-class children.

codes (in general) Codes are the part of **cognitive structure** which allow input to be incorporated with previous learnings. Generic codes have a high degree of access to cognitive structure; surface codes access to only a few, limited aspects of cognitive structure.

coding See **encoding**.

cognitive domain That aspect of human functioning that refers to thought; as opposed to the **affective domain**, which refers to feeling, emotion and motivation.

cognitive psychology A school of thought in psychology that refers to a model of human nature in which humans are represented as thinkers. As opposed to **humanist psychology** and **behaviourism**.

cognitive structure The internal organisation of **codes** or **schemata** that determine how information will be **encoded**. Cognitive structure generally grows more complex with development.

cognitive style A qualitatively distinct and consistent way of encoding, storing and performing that is mostly independent of **intelligence**.

collaborative learning Where the participants spontaneously work together for part or whole of a learning episode.

competitive learning Where the reward system of a learning episode is arranged so that gain for one student means loss to the others.

cooperative learning Where the reward system is arranged so that gain for one student means gain for the rest.

competence An enduring characteristic, based on learning, that enables one to put in a high performance on a specified task, unlike **ability** which refers to a wide range of tasks.

comprehension (in reading) The final phase, after **pre-reading** and **decoding**, where the reader synthesises meaning from the text, using 'top-down' and 'bottom-up' processes for clues. Comprehension can be enhanced by **metacognition**, using **heuristics** to self-check on understanding.

computer assisted instruction (CAI) The use of computers in actually instructing students. This may range from reactive, as in programmed instruction, to highly interactive, as in **embedded teaching**. CAI includes simulations, word processing and teaching writing, problem solving, etc.

computer managed instruction (CMI) The use of computers in administering instruction, for example establishing data bases, testing students and scoring their results, report writing, etc. CMI does not use computers in an instructional role.

concept map A very economical way of ordering data using words, symbols and diagrams that illustrate their interrelationships. Can be used for teaching or assessment.

conception of learning The view a person holds about what constitutes learning. Conceptions are basically quantitative ('a good learner knows a lot') or qualitative ('a good learner understands and constructs a viewpoint'); conceptions affect **approach to learning** and **learning outcome**.

concrete-symbolic The mode of development, typical of middle to late childhood, wherein children learn to use symbol systems to refer to their experienced world.

conditional knowledge Knowing when to apply procedural knowedge to a particular situation and how. Requires **metacognitive** knowledge relating to the situation and to self: planning, monitoring, adjusting, terminating.

conditioning A form of learning (and of motivation) that suggests that the performance of responses is conditional on the intervention of the external environment. In classical conditioning, responses are emitted as a function of the association between an unconditioned and a conditioned stimulus; operant (or instrumental) conditioning occurs when the responses are associated with rewarding or punishing consequences. Both forms of conditioning are examples of **behaviourism**.

conferencing (in writing) A technique of one-to-one interaction between the writer and (usually) the teacher, to assist primarily in parawriting and **revising** activities.

conformity Changing behaviour because of perceived pressure from others; in particular, from the peer group and from authority. Conformity to peers is the hallmark of **socio-centric** behaviour and thought.

conservation A concept, emphasised by Piaget, according to which properties of an object (e.g., length, weight, quantity) remain the same regardless of any changes that may be made to the object (e.g., pouring into a different container) which do not alter its constancy.

constructivism A viewpoint of the nature of learning, which emphasises the relativity of knowledge; that knowledge is constructed by the individual, not transferred; that individual constructions vary according to previous knowledge. Constructivism is obvious psychology, but profound pedagogy.

content learning Learning in which the main interest of both teacher and student is the subject matter to be learned, rather than on the **processes** involved, or on the impact on the learner.

contingency A result (rewarding or punishing) signalled prior to the elicitation of a response, in order to affect the frequency of that response.

conventional In Kohlberg's theory of moral development, the middle level **(sociocentric)**, where right and wrong are determined according to conformity with peer (Stage 3) or societal (Stage 4) norms. Preconventional judgments are **egocentric** and are based on avoidance of punishment (Stage 1) or maximisation of reward (Stage 2). Postconventional judgments rely on **formal** principles; societal (Stage 5) or universal (Stage 6).

convergence A type of thinking that emphasises arriving at the 'one correct answer' to a problem. Convergent thought can be measured, particularly, by IQ tests.

core (curriculum) Generally, the subjects that should be taught to all students, comprising basic skills, knowledge and concepts in all subject areas that are thought to be the minimum necessary for effective citizenship.

correlation coefficient A statistical technique that expresses the degree of relationship between two variables: +1.00 indicates a perfect positive relationship (rarely obtained); −1.00, a perfect negative relationship (also rare); and 0.00, no relationship at all.

creative writing Writing, in either prose or poetry, in which the writer's intention is to entertain or express emotion and/or ideas, rather than to pass on information.

creativity A type of thinking that emphasises flexible, original and productive ways of responding. Related to **divergence**.

credentialling Providing a **summative** formal statement of standards of attainment either with respect to an individual, or to the level of courses offered in an institution.

criterion-referenced evaluation Evaluation of student performance in terms of how well the student meets pre-set standards, as opposed to **norm-referenced evaluation**.

curriculum In general, the total process of instruction from setting **objectives**, through teaching method, to **evaluation**. In Australia, the term 'curriculum' has tended to become equated with 'syllabus', that is, the selection and arrangement of content to be taught in particular subjects to particular year groups. Curriculum development is becoming increasingly **school-based**.

declarative knowledge Knowing about a topic so that one may 'declare' that knowledge, often in concrete-symbolic statements so it is also called 'propositional knowledge', with no implications at all that the knowledge is usable. Espoused **theory** is declarative. Often contrasted with **procedural knowledge**.

decoding (a) Retrieving material from long-term memory (see also **dismembering**), (b) the second phase, after **pre-reading**, in which the particular association between visual symbols and sounds are handled and words are recognised. This should merge with **comprehension**.

deductive process Learning by moving from general concepts to more specific ones, according to logical principles: **top-down** process.

deep **Intrinsic** when applied to **motive**: meaning-oriented, to **strategy**. Deep **approach** leads to highly structured **learning outcomes**.

development (cognitive) The description of shifts in level of abstraction in **modes** within which **learning** takes place.

direct teaching A high-**structure** method teaching, where **objectives** are clear and student performance is systematically evaluated. Direct teaching is expository, competency-based and prescriptive.

discipline (a) Painful consequences that are natural or endemic, as opposed to **punishment**; (b) a mode of classroom control based on the implied authority of the teacher, as opposed to (a) above and to **management**; (c) a body of knowledge organised at the **relational** level of the **postformal** mode.

disembeddedness See **embeddedness**.

dismembering Based on the theory of memory, according to which individuals **code** the different aspects of an experience in semantic, temporal, logical or spatial codes and reassemble these components on recall.

divergence A type of thinking that generates many novel alternatives to a given situation; often equated with creativity (see **convergence**).

drive See **arousal**.

editing (one's own text) Changing and correcting text at the word and sentence levels for mechanics (grammar, spelling, etc.).

egocentricism In Piaget's theory, a viewpoint of the world and other people that takes into account only the perspective of the individual; a period of development covering early to middle childhood. This meaning must be distinguished from the non-technical one.

embeddedness (a) In cognitive development, to the young child when a problem is embedded in its context and its crucial aspects hidden. Complete disembedding occurs only in the **formal** mode. (b) Embedded teaching involves close one-to-one interaction between teacher and learner.

encoding (or coding) Reading in, interpreting and understanding input in terms of existing coded knowledge.

English-as-a-Second-Language (ESL),

English-as-a-Foreign-Language (EFL) The teaching of English to non-English speakers, for example, migrants in Australia, whose mother tongue (L1) is not English.

espoused theory. See **theory**

essay tests Tests or examination in which students structure their own responses in continuous prose.

evaluation Sampling student performance and making a judgment as to its adequacy. Evaluation may be **norm-referenced, criterion-referenced, formative** or **summative**.

exit levels Curriculum statements specifying the **target mode** and level in **learning cycle** when a particular topic may be judged to have been learned adequately and at which point the student's performance may be accredited with some **summative evaluation** statement.

exophoric reference When a pronoun is separated from its referent, with ambiguous results: 'Hebe, Emily and Georgette arrived in the empty room. She ...'

expectancy-value theory A family of motivational theories proposing that students will be 'motivated' to do a task only when it is perceived *both* as valuable in some way and that they have a reasonable chance of succeeding if they attempt it. Schools tend to screw up on both counts.

expert Someone with a great deal of experience, which they have been able to transform into an abstract and well-structured **knowledge base**, which is specific to a task or area and which they can deploy in that area with a consistently high level of **competence**. It is the specific knowledge base that distinguishes them from a **novice**.

extended abstract A sophisticated response that 'overshoots' the **target mode**. See also **SOLO taxonomy**.

external examination A system of assessment in which exams are set and marked outside the institution which teaches in the subject (as opposed to **school-based** assessment).

extinction The weakening and disappearance of a learned response through lack of reinforcement.

extrinsic motivation Where learning or performance takes place as a means of gaining some material reward or avoiding a punishment, it is extrinsically motivated; learning for the material consequences.

formal An abstract **mode** of thought developing in early adolescence, which does not mature at all in some people. A level of abstraction that transcends situation and specific detail.

formative evaluation Evaluation conducted during the performance of a task to provide feedback information on how well the task is being performed and how performance may be improved.

generativity Wittrock's term to emphasise the view in cognitive psychology that learning and recall are constructive processes, involving active participation by the learner.

heuristics Guided self-questioning whereby, in

the course of some task, the learner asks an open-ended question that prompts **meta–cognition** and hopefully improved performance.

humanist psychology   A philosophical position, as much as a scientific one, that emphasises human values, authentic relationships and feelings about oneself and others as being the proper concern of psychology.

ikonic   A mode of cognitive development in which information is processed in terms of unidimensional codes, often of a perceptual or emotional nature.

implicit (hidden) curriculum   Teaching particular values by requiring the student to do things that imply those values; such values are not examined consciously by the student.

improvisational nature of teaching   A view of teaching emphasising the unpredictable, interactive and 'conversational' nature of teaching, as opposed to the planned, management oriented view. Both are valid.

individualised instruction   Instruction designed to meet the needs of the individual student in terms both of content and method of teaching. In particular, individualised, or personalised, systems of instruction (PSI) often mean just that the student proceeds at his or her own pace until the instructional objectives are met, as in **mastery learning**.

inductive process   Learning general principles from specific concrete examples, as in discovery learning; a **bottom-up** process.

information processing theories   A form of the **cognitive** theory of learning in which human behaviour is described in terms of the individual selectively interpreting, storing and recalling the information in the environment, based on the metaphor of a self-programming computer.

instrumental motivation   See **extrinsic motivation**.

institutionalisation of learning   The view that learning in institutions is fundamentally different from everyday learning, in a way that makes it all the more difficult to foster.

intelligence   A hypothetical factor of wide generality that is presumed to underlie an individual's competence in performing cognitive tasks. A great deal of controversy surrounds the nature, generality and modifiability of intelligence.

intrinsic motivation   Where learning or performance takes place in the absence of any **extrinsic**, **social** or **achievement** motivation, it is positively intrinsically motivated; where learning is abruptly terminated for no evident reasons it is negatively intrinsically motivated. Positive intrinsic motivation usually signals high quality learning.

IQ   Intelligence quotient (IQ) is the score yielded by an intelligence test, which measures a person's general ability in relation to the population (see also **intelligence**).

item response theory (IRT)   A technique for determining, in units that are comparable across tests and samples of students, the 'latent trait' or **ability** of students in a category of performance.

knowledge base   What distinguishes the **expert** from the **novice** in a given area. Some argue that the knowledge base is all important; others that **metacognitive** or **conditional knowledge** is as important.

latent trait theory   See **Rasch model**.

learned helplessness   A state of depression and inability to cope brought about by the realisation that one has no control over one's environment.

learning   The acquisition of skills or information through interaction with the environment. See also **learning cycle**.

learning cycle   The levels of complexity achieved with respect to a **target mode**. Three major transitions are involved: from uni- to multistructural (the accretion of knowledge); from multistructural to relational (the structuring of knowledge); and from relational to extended abstract (the generalisation of knowledge).

learning outcome   The product of a learning experience; may be construed or evaluated quantitatively or qualitatively. Qualitative aspects can be assessed by the **SOLO taxonomy**.

literacy   Displayed competence in reading and writing.

locus of control   A concept introduced by Rotter describing how individuals perceive themselves in relation to the external world. Individuals with an external locus of control perceive themselves as being controlled by chance, other people or 'fate'; those with an internal locus of control perceive themselves as having control over their decisions and what happens to them.

long-term memory (LTM) Storage of previous learning to be reconstructed when appropriate in **working memory**.

look-and-say A method of teaching reading (also called 'whole word approach') which relies on recognising each word in its entirety, as opposed to breaking the word into letter–sound components.

macropropositions Units of text that go beyond the level of a sentence and that express integrated main ideas or themes rather than single ideas.

management A view of classroom control that is 'adult mode': a mutually acceptable 'contract' is negotiated to the mutual advantage of teacher and class. Teaching is characterised by planning, expertise and mutual regard. Contrasted to classroom control based on **discipline**.

mastery learning An **individualised** method of teaching and **criterion-referenced** evaluation, based on the assumption that virtually all students can learn basic **core** content, if given sufficient time and adequate instruction.

match–mismatch The state in which input is to be interpreted by cognitive structure. Match implies complete interpretation **(encoding)**; mismatch the need for **recoding**. According to the degree of mismatch, **intrinsic motivation** will be positive or negative.

mean The average of a distribution of scores, that is, the sum of the scores divided by the number of scores.

meaningful learning Learning verbal material by the method of coding **(encoding)** with the intention of understanding the message well enough to be able to express the sense of the message in different words.

median In a distribution of scores from lowest to highest, the median score is the one at the midpoint of the distribution. In a **normal curve** the median is the same as the mean.

memory The storage and retrieval of information. Three levels, based on period of retention, are postulated: ultra-short **(sensory register)**, short **(working memory)** and long **(long-term memory)**.

mental set A condition where the **plan** is consciously adjusted to attend to a particular task or train of information.

metacognition (a) Awareness of one's own cognitive processes rather than of the content of those processes. (b) Use of that self-awareness in controlling and improving cognitive processes such as study skills, reading comprehension, writing. All writers agree that (a) is metacognitive, some would not include (b), the control aspect, seeing that as a different issue. Metacognitive knowledge is vital in **conditional knowledge**, as one is the agent in applying knowledge.

metalearning **Metacognition** applied to student learning, whereby students derive **approaches to learning**.

metateaching **Metacognition** applied to one's teaching, with particular reference to the Level 3 conception: How is my teaching affecting student learning?

micropropositions The ideas/semantic content contained in a sentence or less of text.

mnemonic An artificial coding device to aid memory by linking new information to well-known material, for example, 'ROY G. BIV' for the colours of the spectrum.

modality A sensory channel of information, for example, verbal, visual, kinaesthetic (touch), etc. Cross-modal coding occurs when material is deliberately linked to more than one mode (e.g., writing down a new word, as well as listening to it).

mode A level of abstraction in which content may be encoded. Modes unfold developmentally, starting with the most concrete, **sensorimotor** through **ikonic**, **concrete-symbolic** and **formal**, to **post-formal**.

modelling Learning that takes place as a result of seeing someone else carry out the performance.

moderation A technique for equating schools by a pre-test and then 'rationing' final grades on the basis of the result.

monitoring A metacognitive activity in which one checks that one's processing and outcomes are in line with **plans**.

morality The rules that govern interpersonal behaviour. In Piaget's theory, moral absolutism results where the rules are perceived as unalterable and imposed by authority; moral relativism where they arise from group consensus **(sociocentrism)** or from a principled consideration of others **(allocentrism)**. (See also **conventional**.)

motivation The reasons for undertaking a task: a particular problem in **institutionalised**

learning. See **expectancy-value** theory.

motive   The reason(s) why a student approaches a task. In general, motives may be **instrumental**, **intrinsic**, **achieving** and **social**. In connection with **approaches to learning**, motives corresponding to the first three categories are referred to as **surface**, **deep** and **achieving**.

multiculturalism   A view of society that advocates maintaining and respecting the cultural diversity found in society. Biculturalism, in Australia, refers to Aboriginal education.

multiple-choice   A form of **objective** test in which the 'stem' of the item is presented and the student has to select the correct response to the stem from, usually, four or five alternatives.

multistructural   The middle point in the **learning cycle**; data-rich but inadequately structured. See also **SOLO taxonomy**.

myelin sheath   A coating around neurones that grows progressively at different stages of development, improving the efficiency of neuronal transmission. Progressive myelinisation could help account for our ability to think more abstractly as we grow older.

narrative   A way of knowing used to understand the world in terms of meaningful myth, parable and 'understanding'. Contrasted to **paradigmatic** way, narrative develops earlier but is also present in highly creative adult thought and feeling.

need-achievers   Individuals who are highly **achievement** motivated.

non-standard English   A form of dialect of English that is used by people to communicate in informal contexts and which differs in vocabulary, phonology and grammatical structure from **standard English**; 'This joker come up to me' instead of 'The man approached me'.

norm-referenced evaluation   Evaluation of student performance in terms of how well the student compares to some reference group such as class, age peers, etc.; as opposed to **criterion-referenced evaluation**.

normal curve   A bell-shaped curve that is assumed to correspond to the distribution of many ability test scores.

novice   A relative beginner at a task who, no matter how bright, has yet to build a specific **knowledge base** for the task in question.

numeracy   Displayed competence in calculating correctly and in understanding and applying the four rules of number to real-life situations.

objective (instructional)   A precise statement of the teacher's intentions when designing a learning episode; the **behavioural objective** is the most rigorous kind of objective.

objective test   A test format in which the student chooses from a limited number of alternatives to indicate the desired response, using recognition or elimination rather than recall. Subjective judgment is minimised in scoring, but not in setting the 'correct' alternatives.

open education   A process of educating that relies on discovery learning, student activity and carefully monitored experiences, usually in the physical context of open-plan architecture.

operant   See **conditioning**.

oracy   Displayed competence in speaking and listening.

ordered-outcome format   A form of **criterion-referenced objective** test that extends the student's ability to answer until a cut-off is reached for each item. Obviates the need for the correct/incorrect dichotomy, by showing levels of understanding, usually but not necessarily indexed by SOLO.

origin   Individuals with an internal **locus of control** who see their behaviour as being caused by their own decisions. De Charms links this belief with **intrinsic motivation**.

paradigmatic   The way of knowing used by scientists and encouraged by schooling. Contrasted to the **narrative** way of knowing.

pawn   Individuals with an external **locus of control** who see their behaviour as being directed from outside themselves.

percentiles   Rank ordering converted to a percentage basis; 99th percentile indicates a score at the top 1% of the population. The 50th percentile is the same as the median. A decile occurs every 10 percentiles and a quartile every 25 percentiles.

phenomenography   A research methodology, originated by Marton in Gothenburg, Sweden, in which learning is studied from the point of the view of the student, not the teacher or researcher. Typically, a fixed number of levels of understanding of (usually) science concepts can be discovered. An example of **constructivism**.

phoneme   A linguistic term referring to the smallest complete sounded unit in a word and written /th/.

phonics A method of teaching reading which relies on breaking a word into **phonemes** and relating each phoneme to a letter(s) (as opposed to **look-and-say**).

plan (a) The 'executive' system that controls and integrates cognitive processes from selective attention, coding and/or rehearsal and storage and retrieval. (b) An essential metacognitive activity based on relevant **conditional knowledge** that, for example, distinguishes a **strategy** from a **tactic**.

post-formal A **mode** of development that appears in some in late adolescence that goes beyond the **formal mode** in level of abstraction.

post-test In an experiment, a test conducted after the experimental treatment (as opposed to **pre-test**).

practicum An instructional situation that involves practising a role or learning a skill through active participation, for example, practice teaching in teacher education.

precoding The process, which takes place in the **sensory register**, of selecting a particular train of information for conscious attention on the basis of its current importance.

Premack principle A principle suggested by Premack to help the selection of suitable reinforcers in behaviour modification. It states that if behaviour A is more frequent than behaviour B, the frequency of behaviour B can be increased by making behaviour A contingent on behaviour B (see **contingency**).

preparedness A biologically based theory explaining why skills that were basic to survival early in the evolutionary history of humans (e.g., **oracy**) are acquired more easily than historically recent ones that are not basic to survival (e.g., **literacy**).

pre-reading An orientation phase, before **decoding** and **comprehension**, in which the child 'relates' to the text.

presage The first of the '3Ps'. Presage factors are those that exist prior to the actual ongoing learning situation; and derive from the *learner* (e.g., abilities, prior knowledge) and the *teaching situation* (e.g., curriculum, course demands, pressures, etc.).

prestructural A response that falls short of the required **target mode**. See also **SOLO taxonomy**.

pre-test In experiment, a test conducted prior to any experimental treatment (as opposed to **post-test**).

problem-based learning Learning **declarative** and **procedural** knowledge in a context that has defined a need for that knowledge.

procedural knowledge Knowing *how* to do something; **theory**-in-use. Often contrasted with **declarative knowledge**.

process The second 'P'; more generally, a way of going about a task that will determine the **product** or outcome. In process learning, the emphasis is more upon *how* something is learned than *what* is learned.

product The third 'P', which in our case refers to the learning outcome.

propositional knowledge See **declarative knowledge**

punishment An unpleasant event that follows a particular behaviour as a result of a deliberate decision by an authority figure, as opposed to a naturally occurring consequence (see **discipline**).

rank order Placing scores in order from lowest to highest.

Rasch model See **item response theory**

reader-based Text that has been written with the reader's concerns and knowledge base in mind. **Novice** writers' text is **writer-based**.

readiness The notion that a student has to be cognitively, socially and physically developed to a predetermined extent before a particular topic may be taught; for example, reading readiness. Piaget's stages were interpreted as providing that information but current belief is that no single set of tests have the generalising power for such a decision.

reciprocal teaching A method of peer teaching originally used to teach students the **procedural** and **conditional** knowledge associated with reading so that they could then teach each other; since used in many areas.

reciprocity Piaget's term for the idea of moral obligation: an **altruistic** act puts the person helped in a situation of obligation to the helper.

recoding Change in **codes** or **cognitive structure** brought about as a result of mismatch (see also **match**). With the optimal degree of mismatch, cognitive structures grow more complex and **intrinsic motivation** is experienced.

reconstruction A theory of memory which postulates that recall of previously learned material is not so much a matter of retrieving stored information as reconstructing the original event from stored 'clues' (see also **generativity**).

reflective   A **metacognitive** process: thinking about one's own thoughts and actions, as **reflective writing**.

reflective writing   Writing that clarifies the thinking of the writer on the topic in question; contrasted to 'knowledge-telling', or writing that simply conveys information.

rehearsal   Storing material by repeated practice rather than by linking to previously learned material **(encoding)**. In the case of verbal material, rehearsal produces **rote learning**.

reinforcement   The process whereby a (rewarding) consequence of a response results in the increased likelihood of that response occurring in future. A positive reinforcer refers to a pleasant consequence; a negative reinforcer to the avoidance of an unpleasant consequence. Reinforcements may be allocated according to various schedules, such as partial, interval, self-administered and so on.

relational   The highest point in the **learning cycle** within the **target mode**. See also **SOLO taxonomy**.

reliability (test)   A test is reliable if it is internally consistent (the items measure the same construct) and the scores are stable over time.

remediation   Reviewing prior learning where it has been incorrect or otherwise inadequate and taking steps to rectify the faults.

reticular arousal system   See **arousal**.

retrieval   The usual, if somewhat misleading, term for recalling previously learned information and material. See also **reconstruction**.

reversibility   A logical concept, emphasised by Piaget, which implies that a logical operation may be cancelled by its inverse.

revising (in writing)   Rewriting text, with a focus on the meaning of the theme and main ideas. Contrasted to **editing**.

rote learning   Learning verbal material by the method of **rehearsal** with the intention of exactly reproducing the original, with or without understanding it. A key element in the **surface approach** when higher level processes would be more appropriate for the task in question.

scaffolding   The assistance given by an older person/teacher to a beginner so that the latter may handle a task that is in their developmental sights, but is currently beyond them. Such assistance may be verbal, prompting, cueing, 'psychological', etc.

schema   A schema (pl. schemata) is similar to **code**; the units used by individuals to organise their experience, but with the emphasis more upon an organisational network.

school-based   In general, the location of a function in the individual school rather than externally (e.g., the State Department of Education). Curriculum development and assessment are two common functions that are becoming increasingly school-based in Australia and most recently, the development of school policies (e.g., on disipline/management issues).

selective attention   The process of attending to particular stimuli and not to others (see also **precoding**).

self-assessment   Requiring the student to contribute towards his or her own assessment, by (a) determining the criteria for assessment, (b) judging in accordance with those criteria, or both (a) and (b). Self-assessment may or may not be used in grading or **summative evaluation**.

self-efficacy   A person's expectation that he or she will perform a task at a particular level of effectiveness. Beliefs in self-efficacy have a strong effect on **intrinsic motivation**.

self-concept   The image or concept people have of themselves, particularly of their abilities (physical, mental and social) and the value (positive or negative) they place on these self-evaluations.

self-fulfilling prophecy   Occurs when believing or saying something is true actually causes it to happen; for example, not giving a student enough work in the belief that he or she is stupid and 'proving' the belief by the lack of output.

self-management   A **metacognitive** skill that has become an aim of education.

semantic   Refers to word meanings: semantic input or semantic coding thus refer to verbal messages and to storing information according to word meaning. Semantic processing is believed to occur mainly in the left hemisphere of the brain.

sensori-motor   In general, learning that involves linking perceptions with motor responses. In particular, the term describes the stage of development taking place during infancy.

sensory input Information supplied by the sense: vision, touch, hearing, taste, smell, etc.

sensory register The first stage in information processing; a brief (about $\frac{1}{4}$–1 sec.) period during which information is held and scanned **(precoding)**.

sexism Making discriminatory and prejudicial decisions or statements about individuals or groups because of one's beliefs about their gender.

situated cognition The currently very fashionable notion that cognitive processes are best learned in specific contexts and most easily applied back to those contexts. That much is unarguable; what is arguable is the conclusion that it is therefore wrong to teach for general applications.

social motivation Where learning or performance takes place because of the influence of one or more other people, as in **modelling**, or conforming to a group.

social learning The theory that much (particularly **moral**) behaviour is learned in particular situations, rather than being innate, or developmental, in nature.

socialisation Part of the role of the school: to pass on the culture and values of society. There is a balance between socialisation and **acculturation**, which tilts this or that in discussions of **multiculturalism**.

sociocentrism Piaget's middle stage of moral development, during which judgments of 'right' and 'wrong' are dictated by social norms.

socioeconomic status A term referring to the relative power or prestige of different groups of people in society.

SOLO taxonomy A classification system that may be used both for setting curriculum objectives and for evaluating the quality of learning outcomes. There are three levels of complexity within the **target mode (unistructural, multistructural** and **relational); prestructural** outcomes are inadequate, falling within a mode of a lower level of abstraction than the target; **extended abstract** outcomes fall within the next higher mode.

spatial Refers to information pertaining to the arrangement of objects in space, for example, a map. Spatial coding would refer to the storage of information in visual terms, for example, an image. Spatial processing is believed to occur mainly in the right hemisphere of the brain.

stage A period during the lifespan when, in some definable respect, individuals resemble their age peers more than they do themselves at young or older ages. This respect is frequently hierarchically ordered as in the Piagetian or Kohlbergian stages.

standard English The formal version of English used in official and public communications; standard English is minimally **embedded** and makes no assumptions about non-verbal support (gestures, etc.).

standardised tests Tests that have been previously trialled and revised and which yield reliable (usually **norm-referenced**) information. The conditions of testing and scoring must be carefully adhered to.

strategy A way of tackling a type of problem, or learning material, that may be applied to a whole class of learnings, not just to the particular problem in question. Strategies, unlike **tactics**, involve forethought and **metacognition**.

streaming Placing students of similar ability in one class for learning purposes (also called 'grading', 'ability grouping'). Streaming can be a basis for one, several, or all subjects in the curriculum.

stress Heavy psychological or physical pressure that results in strong increases in **arousal**. Mild stress may improve performance, but heavy stress usually impairs performance (see **Yerkes-Dodson law**).

structure (of individuals) See **cognitive structure**.

structure (of instructional settings) Usually refers to extent of student- or teacher-centredness: low structure being student-centred, with wide student choice in instructionally relevant decisions and high structure being very constrained, with the teacher making most decisions.

structure (of subject matter) The fundamental ideas and relationships or **generic codes** that make up a discipline.

summative evaluation Evaluation conducted after a task or learning episode has been completed in order to see how well it has been done; grading a task. Summative evaluation may be **norm-referenced** or **criterion-referenced**.

super-items See **ordered outcome**.

surface Instrumental when applied to motive; reproductive to **strategy**. Surface **approach** leads to low structure outcomes.

system A dynamic relationship between components so that an equilibrium is formed and a function is served thereby. A significant change in any of the components results in a new equilibrium and a new system, which may serve the original function better, or worse. The classroom is such a system, as expressed in the 3P model; it is also part of the large school system.

tactic An algorithm or set procedure for producing an answer. Requires little planning or monitoring; contrasts with **strategy**.

target behaviour The particular behaviour(s) in a behaviour modification program that are to be the subject of modification. They must be specified exactly and measures of their emission rate taken.

target mode The level of abstraction chosen for presenting a task or a curriculum objective. The quality of learning within the selected mode may be evaluated by the **SOLO taxonomy**. Target modes are selected from **sensori-motor, ikonic, concrete-symbolic, formal, post-formal** levels of abstraction.

tautology A statement that rephrases what is known and thus conveys no further information; for example, 'I couldn't sleep because I had insomnia'.

teacher anxiety A form of state **anxiety** experienced by classroom teachers. In beginner teachers, a common focus of teacher anxiety is discipline.

temporal Refers to the relationships between events in time. Temporal coding is using chronological order as a basis for storing and remembering information: for example, historical events.

test A task presented to the learner to assess performance; an important component in **assessment** and **evaluation**.

test anxiety A form of state **anxiety** that is focused on the **test** situation and specifically on the individual's fear that he or she will fail. Test anxiety usually impairs performance.

test distortion Occurs when a particular test format, for example, **essay** or **objective**, consistently inflates or depresses a person's performance because of a personal characteristic.

text processing Reading, summarising, writing ... using text as a means of handling information.

theory An integrated statement of principles that explain what is known about a particular area of study or practice. In professional practice, espoused theory is the 'official' statement to which lip-service is paid and theory-in-use is implicit in a person's actions; professionalism requires their integration.

theory X The assumption that individuals cannot be trusted to work or to learn unless it is made worth their while—usually by coercion. Contrasts to **theory Y**.

theory Y The assumption that individuals work and learn at their best when they are trusted, are not under surveillance and can feel 'ownership' in their product.

time-out A procedure used in some behaviour modification programs whereby a student is removed from the room as a consequence of inappropriate behaviour. Time-out is meant to relate more to **extinction** than to **punishment**.

token economy A behaviour modification program in which the reinforcers (see also **reinforcement**) are tokens (tallies or buttons) that may later be exchanged for material goods, privileges, etc.

top-down A theory or procedure imposed from first principles, deductively (theory-driven vs. data-driven). Where those with high status determine policy (e.g., teacher-centred vs. student-centred). As opposed to **bottom-up**.

traditional schools Schools which appear to have a strong **cognitive** emphasis, but the practices of which carry a strong **implicit curriculum**. For example, motivation is usually controlled by devices that emphasise reward, competition and punishment, and which tend to preclude intrinsic motivation. The basics of traditional schooling have changed little in the last 100 years.

transductive process A primitive form of reasoning which precedes **deductive** and **inductive** processes, in which a conclusion is drawn (usually incorrectly) on the basis of preference or coincidence, rather than of logic or fact.

unistructural The lowest point in the **learning cycle**; one relevant datum is learned. See also **SOLO taxonomy**.

validity The extent to which a test measures what it is designed to measure.

value A belief in the worth of a class of activities, people or objects and deriving from the **affective** rather than the **cognitive domain**.

values clarification Classroom experiences which encourage students to discover their own values, reflect on them and compare them to others, while avoiding teaching specific values to students.

variability (of teaching) Switching from one pattern of interaction teaching medium, style and content to another in order to maintain student interest.

variability (of test scores) The extent to which a set of test scores vary from the **mean** of the group; usually expressed as standard deviations (SD) or variance (SD2).

wait time The amount of time the teacher gives a student to respond to a question.

working memory The short-term memory system in which conscious thought takes place; roughly equivalent to 'span of attention'.

writer-based Text that has been written without considering the reader's concerns or knowledge, the writer being too concerned about 'what to say'. The result is immature and ambiguous text, which says little.

Yerkes–Dodson law A law of motivation formulated early this century stating that under increasing motivation **(arousal)**, performance in complex tasks will be impaired before that in simple tasks. In the latter, performance may show improvement before impairment.

REFERENCES

Ainley, J. & Bourke, S.F. (1988). Student views of primary schooling. Paper presented at the Australian Association for Research in Education Conference, Armidale, December.

Ainley, J., Reed, R. & Miller, H. (1986). *School Organization and the Quality of Schooling.* Hawthorn, Vic: Australian Council for Educational Research.

Airasian, P. & Madaus, G. (1972). Criterion-referenced testing in the classroom. *Measurement in Education* (Special reports of the National Council on Measurement in Education 3, No. 4, East Lansing, Mich.)

Alexander, P.A. & Judy, J.E. (1988). The interaction of domain-specific and strategic knowledge in academic performances. *Review of Educational Research*, **58**, 375–404.

Allen, V.L. (1976). The helping relationship and socialisation of children: Some perspectives on tutoring. In V. Allen (ed.), *Children as Teachers.* New York: Academic Press.

Ames, C. & Archer, J. (1988). Achievement goals in the classroom: Students' learning strategies and motivational processes. *Journal of Educational Psychology*, **80**, 260–7.

Anderson, C.C. & Cropley, A.J. (1966). Some correlates of originality. *Australian Journal of Psychology*, **18**, 218–27.

Anderson, J. & Yip, L. (1987). Are sex roles represented fairly in children's books? A content analysis of old and new readers. *Unicorn*, **13**, 155–61.

Anderson, J.R. (1985). *Cognitive Psychology and its Implications.* San Francisco: Freeman.

Anderson, R.C. (1972). How to construct achievement tests to assess comprehension. *Review of Educational Research*, **42**(2), 145–70.

Anderson, R.C. & Anderson, R.M. (1963). Transfer of originality training. *Journal of Educational Psychology*, **54**, 300–4.

Andrews, A.S. (1968). Multiple choice and essay tests. *Improving College and University Teaching*, **16**, 61–6.

Andrich, D. (1982). An extension of the Rasch model for ratings providing both location and dispersion parameters. *Psychometrika*, **47**, 105–13.

Angus, M.J. (1979). *The Australian Open Area Schools Project.* Perth: Western Australian Education Department.

Angus, M.J. (1981). Children's conceptions of the living world. *Australian Science Teachers Journal*, **29**(3), 65–8.

Annells, J.W. et al. (1975). *What Do Pupils Write?* Hobart: Curriculum Centre, Education Department of Tasmania.

Applebee, A.N. (1984). Writing and reasoning. *Review of Educational Research*, **54**, 577–96.

Argyris, C. (1976). Theories of action that inhibit individual learning. *American Psychologist*, **31**, 638–54.

Armbruster, B., Anderson, T. & Ostertag, J. (1987). Does text structure/summarization instruction facilitate learning from expository text? *Reading Research Quarterly*, **22**, 331–46.

Aronson, E. (1984). *The Social Animal* (4th edn). San Francisco, Calif: W.H. Freeman.

Asch, S. (1956). Studies of independence and conformity: A minority of one against a unanimous majority. *Psychological Monographs*, **70** (9), Whole No. 416.

Ashenden, D. (1989). Schooldays, bloody schooldays. *The Independent Monthly*, October, 21–22.

Ashenden, D. (1990). Secondary school hurdle. *The Independent Monthly*, October, 27–28.

Ashman, A.F. & Elkins, J. (1990). *Educating Children with Special Needs.* Sydney: Prentice Hall.

Ashton-Warner, S. (1980). *Teacher.* London: Virago Press.

Atkinson, J.W. (1964). *An Introduction to Motivation.* New York: Van Nostrand.

Atkinson, R.C. & Shiffrin, R.M. (1968). Human memory: A proposed system and its control processes. In J. Spence and K. Spence (eds),

The Psychology of Learning and Motivation, 2. New York: Academic Press.

Ausubel, D.P. (1968). *Educational Psychology: A Cognitive View.* New York: Holt, Rinehart & Winston.

Ausubel, D.P. (1978). Defence of advance organisers. *Review of Educational Research*, 48, 251–7.

Baddeley, A.D. (1976). *The Psychology of Memory.* New York: Basic Books.

Baird, J.R. (in press). Improving learning through enhanced metacognition: A classroom study. *European Journal of Science Education*, 8.

Baird, J. & Mitchell, I. (eds) (1986). *Improving the quality of teaching and learning: An Australian case study—The PEEL project.* Melbourne: Monash University.

Baird, J.R. & White, R.T. (1984). Improving learning through enhanced metacognition: A classroom study. Paper read to American Educational Research Association Annual Conference, New Orleans.

Baker, C. & Freebody, P. (1989). *Children's First School Books.* Oxford: Blackwell.

Baldwin, G. (1990a). Single sex schooling and subject choice: Pattern of enrolment at Monash University. *Australian Educational Researcher*, 17(3), 47–64.

Baldwin, G. (1990b). Gender roles in education: Who is missing out? *HERDSA News*, 12(2), 10–13.

Baltes, P.B. (1987). Theoretical propositions of life-span developmental psychology: On the dynamics of growth and decline. *Developmental Psychology*, 23, 611–26.

Baltes, P.B., Kliegl, R. & Dittman-Kohli, F. (1988). On the locus of training gains in research on plasticity of fluid intelligence in old age. *Journal of Educational Psychology*, 80, 392–400.

Bandura, A. (1969). *Principles of Behaviour Modification.* New York: Holt, Rinehart & Winston.

Bandura, A. (1977). Self-efficacy: Toward a unifying theory of behavioural change. *Psychological Review*, 84, 191–215.

Bandura, A. & Schunk, D. (1981). Cultivating competence, self-efficacy and intrinsic interest through proximal self-motivation. *Journal of Personality and Social Psychology*, 41, 586–98.

Barker-Lunn, J.B. (1970). *Streaming in the Primary School.* London: National Foundation for Educational Research.

Barrish, H.H., Saunders, M. & Wolf, M.M. (1969). Good behaviour games: Effects of individual contingencies for group consequences on disruptive behaviour in a classroom. *Journal of Applied Behaviour Analysis*, 2, 119–24.

Bar-Tal, D. (1978). Attributional analysis of achievement-related behaviour. *Review of Educational Research*, 48, 259–71.

Bartlett, F.C. (1932). *Remembering.* London: Cambridge University Press.

Bartlett, F.C. (1958). *Thinking.* Reading, Mass: Allen & Unwin.

Bassett, G.W., Cullen, P. & Logan, L. (1984). *Australian Primary Schools and their Principals.* Sydney: Harcourt Brace Jovanovich.

Baumann, J.F. (1984). The effectiveness of a direct instruction paradigm for teaching main idea comprehension. *Reading Research Quarterly*, 20, 93–115.

Beaty, E., Dall'Alba, G. & Marton, F. (in press). Conceptions of learning. *International Journal of Educational Research*, 13.

Beez, W.V. (1970). Influence of biased psychological reports on teacher behaviour and pupil performance. In M. Miles and W.W. Charters (eds), *Learning in Social Settings.* Boston, Mass: Allyn & Bacon.

Benbow, C.P. & Stanley, J.C. (1982). Consequences in high school and college of sex differences in mathematical reasoning ability: A longitudinal perspective. *American Educational Research Journal*, 19, 598–622.

Bennett, N. (1976). *Teaching Styles and Pupil Progress.* London: Open Books.

Benware, C.A. & Deci, F.C. (1984). Quality of learning with an active versus passive motivational set. *American Educational Research Journal*, 21, 755–65.

Bereiter, C. (1980). Development in Writing. In L. Gregg and E. Steinberg (eds), *Cognitive Processes in Writing.* Hillsdale, NJ: Lawrence Erlbaum.

Bereiter, C. (1990). Aspects of an educational learning theory. *Review of Educational Research*, 60, 603–24.

Bereiter, C. & Engelmann, S. (1966). *Teaching Disadvantaged Children in the Pre-school.* Englewood Cliffs, NJ: Prentice Hall.

Bereiter, C. & Scardamalia, M. (1987). *The Psychology of Written Composition.* Hillsdale, NJ: Lawrence Erlbaum.

Berliner, D. (1984). *Research and Teacher Effectiveness.* ERIC Microfiche, ED249584.

Berliner, D.C. (1986). In pursuit of the expert pedagogue. *Educational Researcher*, **15**(4), 5–13.

Berlyne, D.E. (1966). Curiosity and education. In J. Krumboltz (ed.), *Learning and the Educational Process.* Chicago, Ill: Rand McNally.

Bernard, J. & Delbridge, A. (1980). *Introduction to Linguistics: An Australian Perspective.* Sydney: Prentice Hall of Australia.

Berne, E. (1964). *Games People Play.* New York: Grove.

Bernstein, B. (1961). Social structure, language and learning. *Educational Research*, **3**, 163–76.

Bernstein, B. (1965). A sociolinguistic approach to social learning. In J. Gould (ed.), *Penguin Survey of Social Sciences.* Harmondsworth, Middlesex: Penguin.

Bernstein, B. (1970). A sociolinguistic approach to socialisation with some reference to educability. In F. Williams (ed.), *Language and Poverty: Perspectives on a Theme.* Chicago, Ill: Markham.

Bessant, B. & Spaull, A. (1976). *Politics of Schooling.* Carlton, Vic: Pitman Pacific.

Beveridge, M. (1985). The development of young children—understanding of the process of evaporation. *British Journal of Educational Psychology* **55**, 84–90.

Bidell, T. & Fischer, K. (1992). Cognitive development in context. In A. Demetriou, M. Shayer A. Efklides (eds), *Neo-Piagetian Theories of Cognitive Development Go to School.* London: Routledge & Kegan Paul.

Biggs, J.B. (1959). The teaching of mathematics Part I. The development of number concepts in children. *National Foundation for Educational Research*, **1**, 17–34.

Biggs, J.B. (1962). *Anxiety, Motivation and Primary School Mathematics* (Occasional Publication, No.7). London: National Foundation for Educational Research.

Biggs, J.B. (1966). *Mathematics and the Conditions of Learning.* London: National Foundation for Educational Research.

Biggs, J.B. (1968). *Information and Human Learning.* Melbourne: Cassell Australia.

Biggs, J.B. (1970). Personality correlates of some dimensions of study behaviour. *Australian Journal of Psychology*, **22**, 287–97.

Biggs, J.B. (1973). Study behaviour and performance in objective and essay formats. *Australian Journal of Education*, **17**, 157–67.

Biggs, J.B. (1979). Individual differences in study processes and the quality of learning outcomes. *Higher Education*, **8**, 381–94.

Biggs, J.B. (1982). Student motivation and study strategies in University and CAE populations. *Higher Education Research and Development*, **1**, 33–55.

Biggs, J.B. (1985). The role of metalearning in study processes. *British Journal of Educational Psychology*, **55**, 185–212.

Biggs, J.B. (1987a). *Student Approaches to Learning and Studying.* Hawthorn, Vic: Australian Council for Educational Research.

Biggs, J.B. (1987b). *The Study Process Questionnaire (SPQ) Users' Manual.* Hawthorn, Vic: Australian Council for Educational Research.

Biggs, J.B. (1987c). *The Learning Process Questionnaire (LPQ): Users' Manual.* Hawthorn, Vic: Australian Council for Educational Research.

Biggs, J.B. (1987d). Process and outcome in essay writing. *Research and Development in Higher Education*, **9**, 114–25.

Biggs, J.B. (1988a). The role of metacognition in enhancing learning. *Australian Journal of Education*, **32**, 127–38.

Biggs, J.B. (1988b). Students' approaches to essay-writing and the quality of the written product. Paper presented at the Annual Meeting, American Educational Research Association, New Orleans, April.

Biggs, J.B. (1988c). Approaches to learning and to essay writing. In R.R. Schmeck (ed.), *Learning Styles and Learning Strategies.* New York: Plenum Press.

Biggs, J.B. (1990). Asian students' approaches to learning: Implications for teaching overseas students. Keynote discussion paper, *Proceedings of the 8th Australasian Tertiary Learning Skills and Language Conference*, (pp. 1–51). Brisbane: Queensland University of Technology, Counselling Services.

Biggs, J.B. (1991a). Good learning: What is it? How can it be fostered? In J.B. Biggs (ed.), *Teaching for Learning: The View from Cognitive Psychology.* Hawthorn, Vic: Australian Council for Educational Research.

Biggs, J.B. (1992). The modality of learning and forms of competent behaviour. In A. Demetriou, M. Shayer A. Efklides (eds), *The Neo-Piagetian Theories of Cognitive Development Go to School.* London: Routledge and Kegan Paul.

Biggs, J.B. & Braun, P.H. (1972). Models of evaluation and student characteristics. *Journal of Educational Measurement*, **9**, 303–9.

Biggs, J.B. & Collis, K.F. (1982a). *Evaluating the Quality of Learning: The SOLO Taxonomy.* New York: Academic Press.

Biggs, J.B. & Collis, K.F. (1982b). The psychological structure of creative writing. *Australian Journal of Education*, **26**(1), 59–70.

Biggs, J.B. & Collis, K.F. (1989). Towards a model of school-based curriculum development and assessment: using the SOLO Taxonomy. *Australian Journal of Education*, **33**, 149–61.

Biggs, J.B., Fitzgerald, D. & Atkinson, S.M. (1971). Convergent and divergent abilities in children and teachers' ratings of competence and certain classroom behaviours. *British Journal of Educational Psychology*, **41**, 277–86.

Biggs, J.B., Holbrook, J.B., Ki, W.W., Lam, R.Y.H., Li, W.O., Pong, W.Y. & Stimpson, P.G. (1989). Curriculum objectives and criterion-referenced assessment in various secondary subjects. A symposium presented at the International Conference, *School-based Innovations: Looking forward to the 1990s*, Faculty of Education, University of Hong Kong, 13–16 December.

Biggs, J.B., Lam, R.Y.H., Balla, J.R. & Ki, W.W. (1988). Assessing learning over the long term: The 'Ordered Outcomes' Model. Conference, Hong Kong Educational Research Association, 26–27 November.

Biggs, J.B. & Rihn, B. (1984). The effects of intervention on deep and surface approaches to learning. In J. Kirby (ed.), *Cognitive Strategies and Educational Performance*. New York: Academic Press.

Biggs, J.B. & Telfer, R. (1987). *The Process of Learning.* (2nd edn.) Sydney: Prentice Hall of Australia.

Binet, A. & Simon, T. (1908). Le Developement de l'Intelligence Chez les Enfants. *Année Psychologique*, **14**, 1–94.

Blakeslee, T. (1980). *The Right Brain.* New York: Doubleday.

Blasi, A. (1980). Bridging word cognition and moral action: A critical review of the literature. *Psychological Bulletin*, **88**, 1–45.

Block, J.H. (1971). *Mastery Learning.* New York: Holt, Rinehart & Winston.

Bloom, B.S. (1971). The affective consequences of mastery learning. In J. Block (ed.), *Mastery Learning.* New York: Holt, Rinehart & Winston.

Bloom, B.S. (ed.), Engelhart, M.D., Furst, E.J., Hill, W.H. & Krathwohl, D.R. (1956). *Taxonomy of Educational Objectives I: Cognitive Domain.* New York: McKay.

Bloom, B.S., Hastings, J.T. & Madaus, G.F. (1971). *Handbook of Formative and Summative Education of Student Learning.* New York: McGraw-Hill.

Bloom, B.S., Krathwohl, D. & Masia, P. (1960). *Taxonomy of Educational Objectives II: Affective Domain.* New York: McKay.

Boag, C. (1989). What makes a great teacher? *The Bulletin*, 18 July.

Bond, G.L. & Dykstra, R. (1967). The co-operative research program in first grade reading instruction. *Reading Research Quarterly*, **2**(4), 5–142.

Borke, H. (1978). Piaget's view of social interaction and the theoretical construct of empathy. In L.S. Siegel and C.J. Brainerd (eds), *Alternatives to Piaget*. New York: Academic Press.

Borko, H. & Livingston, C. (1989). Cognition and improvisation: Differences in mathematics instruction by expert and novice teachers. *American Educational Research Journal*, **26**, 473–98.

Boud, D. (1985a). *Problem-based Learning in Education for the Professions.* Sydney: Higher Education Research and Development Society of Australasia.

Boud, D. (1985b). *Studies in Self-assessment* (Occasional Publication, No.26, UNSW). Kensington: Tertiary Education Research Centre.

Boulton-Lewis, G.M. & Halford, G.S. (1991). Processing capacity and school learning. In G.T.Evans (ed.), *Teaching and Learning Cognitive Skills*, (pp. 27–50). Hawthorn, Vic.: Australian Council for Educational Research.

Bourke, S. (1986). How smaller is better: Some relationships between class size, teaching practices, and student achievement. *American Educational Research Journal*, **23**, 558–71.

Bourke, S.F. & Keeves, J.P. (1977). *Australian Studies in School Performance, vol. 3, The Mastery of Literacy and Numeracy: final report* (Report No. 3, AGPS). Canberra: Educational Research and Development Committee.

Bourke, S.F. & Parkin, B. (1977). The performance of Aboriginal students. In S.F. Bourke and J.P.Keeves (eds), *The Mastery of Literacy and Numeracy.* Hawthorn, Vic.: Australian Council for Educational Research.

Bowden, J. (1988). Achieving change in teaching practices. In P. Ramsden (ed.), *Improving Learning: New Perspectives*. London: Kogan Page.

Bower, G.H. (1970). Analysis of a mnemonic device. *American Scientist*, **58**, 496-510.

Bracewell, R.J., Scardamalia, M. & Bereiter, C. (1978). The development of audience/awareness in writing. Paper presented at American Educational Research Association Annual Meeting, Toronto, March.

Bradley, G., McLachlan, A. & Sparks, B. (1990). Concerns of our students: A cross institutional study. *Higher Education Research and Development*, **9**, 111-22.

Brady, L. (1979). *Feel, Value, Act: Learning about Values, Theory and Practice*. Sydney: Prentice Hall of Australia.

Braggett, E.J. (1985). *Education of Gifted and Talented Children: Australian Provision*. Canberra: Commonwealth Schools Commission.

Brainerd, C.J. (1975). Structures-of-the-whole and elementary education. *American Educational Research Journal*, **12**, 369-78.

Bransford, J.D. & Stein, B.S. (1984). *The Ideal Problem Solver*. New York: W.H. Freeman.

Britton, B., Van Dusen, L., Gulgoz, S. & Glynn, S.M. (1989). Instructional texts rewritten by five expert teams: Revisions and retention improvements. *Journal of Educational Psychology*, **81**, 226-39.

Britton, J. (1982). *Prospect and Retrospect: Selected Essays*. Upper Mountclair, NJ: Boynton/Cook.

Britton, J., Burgess, T., Martin, N., McLeod, A. & Rosen, H. (1975). *The Development of Writing Abilities*, (pp. 11-18). London: Macmillan Educational.

Broom, L., Duncan-Jones, P., Lancaster-Jones, F. & McDonnell, P. (1977). *Investigating Social Mobility*. ANU, Department of Sociology, Department Monographs No.1.

Brophy, J. (1981). Teacher praise: A functional analysis. *Review of Educational Research*, **51**, 15-32.

Brophy, J. (1986). On motivating students. Occasional Paper No. 101. Institute for Research in Teaching, Michigan State University.

Brophy, J.E. & Alleman, J. (1991). Activities as instructional tools: A framework for analysis and evaluation. *Educational Researcher*, **20**(4), 9-23.

Brown, A., Bransford, S., Ferrara, R. & Campione, J. (1983). Learning, remembering and understanding. In P.H. Musson (ed.), *Handbook of Child Psychology*, vol.3, *Cognitive Development*. 4th edn. New York: Wiley.

Brown, A.L. & Day, J.D. (1983). Macrorules for summarizing texts: The development of expertise. *Journal of Verbal Learning and Verbal Behavior*, **22**, 1-14.

Brown, A.S. (1988). Encountering misspellings and spelling performance: Why wrong isn't right. *Journal of Educational Psychology*, **80**, 488-94.

Brown, J.S., Collins, A. & Duguid, P. (1989). Situated cognition and the culture of learning. *Educational Researcher*, **18**(1), 32-42.

Bruner, J.S. (1957). *On Going Beyond the Information Given*. In *Cognition: The Colorado Symposium*. Cambridge, Mass: Harvard University Press.

Bruner, J.S. (1960). *The Process of Education*. Cambridge, Mass: Harvard University Press.

Bruner, J.S. (1964a). The course of cognitive growth. *American Psychologist*, **19**, 1-15.

Bruner, J.S. (1964b). Some theorems on instruction illustrated with reference to mathematics. In E.R. Hilgard (ed.), *Theories of Learning and Instruction* (63rd Yearbook of the National Society for the Study of Education). Chicago, Ill: University of Chicago Press.

Bruner, J.S. (1966). *Towards a Psychology of Instruction*. Cambridge, Mass: University Press.

Bruner, J.S. (1971). The functions of teaching. In W. Morse and G. Wingo (eds), *Classroom psychology*. Glenview, Ill.: Scott Foresman.

Bruner, J.S. (1985). Narrative and paradigmatic modes of thought. In E. Eisner (ed.), *Learning and Teaching the Ways of Knowing* (86th Yearbook of the National Society for the Study of Education, Part II). Chicago, Ill: University of Chicago Press.

Budby, J. (December 1982). A blueprint for the future—Integrating Aboriginal studies into the curricula. *Education News*, **18**(2), 42-3.

Buggie, J. (18 November 1975). Reported in *The Australian*.

Bullivant, B.M. (1988). The ethnic success ethic challenges conventional wisdom about immigrant disadvantages in education. *Australian Journal of Education*, **32**, 223-43.

Burt, C. (1966). The genetic determination of differences in intelligence: A study of monozygotic twins reared together and apart. *British Journal of Psychology*, **57**, 137-53.

Burtis, P.J., Bereiter, C., Scardamalia, M. & Tetroe, J. (1984). The development of planning in writing. In B. Kroll and C.G. Wells (eds), *Exploration of Children's Development in Writing*. Chichester: Wiley.

Butler, S. (1990). *The Exceptional Child*. Sydney: Harcourt, Brace Jovanovich.

Calder, B.J. & Staw, B.M. (1975). Self-perception and intrinsic and extrinsic motivation. *Journal of Personality and Social Psychology*, **31**, 599–605.

Calf, B. (1990). Educational implications. In S. Butler (ed.), *The Exceptional Child*. Sydney: Harcourt, Brace Jovanovich.

Callan, V.J. (1986). *Australian minority groups*. Sydney: Harcourt Brace Jovanovich.

Campbell, W.J. (21 April 1980). What Australian society expects of its schools, teachers and teaching. *Education*, 156–7.

Campbell, W.J. & Campbell, E.M. (1978). *School-based Assessments: Aspirations and Achievements of the Radford Scheme in Queensland* (Report No.7A, AGPS). Canberra: Educational Research and Development Committee.

Candy, P.C. (1991). *Self-direction for Lifelong Learning: A Comprehensive Guide to Theory and Practice*. San Francisco: Jossey-Bass.

Canter, L. & Canter, M. (1979). *Assertive Discipline*. Los Angeles: Canter and Associates.

Cantwell, R.H. & Biggs, J.B. (1988). Effects of bilingualism and approach to learning on the writing and recall of expository text. In M.M. Gruneberg, P.H. Morris & R.N. Sykes, (eds.). *Practical Aspects of Memory: vol 2–Clinical and Educational Implications*. London: Wiley.

Carmi, G. (1981). The role of context in cognitive development. *The Quarterly Newsletter of the Laboratory of Comparative Human Cognition*, **3**(3), 46–54.

Carpenter, P. (March 1985). Does the school make a difference? *Education News*, **19**(2), 12–15.

Carpenter, P. & Western, J.S. (1984). Origins, aspirations and early career attainments. Report to the Department of Education and Youth Affairs, Canberra.

Case, R. (1985). *Cognitive Development*. New York: Academic Press.

Case, R. (ed.) (1991). *The Mind's Staircase: Exploring the Conceptual Underpinnings of Children's Thought and Knowledge*. Hillsdale, NJ: Lawrence Erlbaum.

Case, R. (1992). The role of central conceptual structures in the development of children's sci-entific and mathematical thought. In A Demetriou, M. Shayer & A. Efklides, (Eds). *The Modern Theories of Cognitive Development go to School*. London: Routledge & Kegan Paul.

Cattell, R.B. (1971). *Abilities: Their Structure, Growth and Action*. Boston, Mass: Houghton Mifflin.

Cazden, C. (1988). Social interaction as scaffold: The power and limits of a metaphor. In M. Lightfoot and N. Marton (eds), *The Word for Teaching is Learning*. London: Heinemann Educational.

Cazden, C. (1989). Richmond road: A multilin-gual/multicultural primary school in Auckland, New Zealand. *Language and Education*, **3**, 143–66.

Ceci, S.J. & Liker, J. (1986). Academic and nonaca-demic intelligence: An experimental separa-tion. In R.J. Sternberg and R.K. Wagner (eds), *Practical intelligence*. Cambridge: Cambridge University Press.

Chan, L.K.S. (1991). Metacognition and reme-dial education. *Australian Journal of Remedial Education*, **23**, 4–10.

Chan, L.K.S. & Cole, P.G. (1986). The effects of comprehension monitoring training on the reading competence of learning disabled and regular class students. *Remedial and Special Education*, **7**, 33–40.

Charles, C.M. (1985). *Building Classroom Discipline: From Models to Practice*. New York: Longman.

Chi, M. (1978). Knowledge structures and mem-ory development. In R. Siegler (ed.), *Children's Thinking: What Develops?*. Hillsdale, NJ: Lawrence Erlbaum.

Chi, M., Glaser, R. & Farr, M. (1988). *The Nature of Expertise*. Hillsdale, NJ: Lawrence Erlbaum.

Chipman, L. (1980). The menace of multicultur-alism. *Quadrant*, 3–6 October.

Chipman, S., Segal, J. & Glaser, R. (eds) (1984). *Thinking and Learning Skills*. Hillsdale, NJ: Lawrence Erlbaum.

Christensen, C. & Massey, D. (1989). Perpetuating gender inequity: Attitudes of teacher education students. *Australian Journal of Education*, **33**, 256–66.

Choppin, B. (1982). The use of latent trait mod-els in the measurement of cognitive abilities and skills. In D. Spearitt (ed.), *The Improvement of Measurement in Education and Psychology*. Hawthorn, Vic: Australian Council for Educational Research.

Clanchy, J. (1985). Improving student writing. *HERDSA News*, **7**(3), 3–5 November.

Clarke, V.A. (1990). Sex differences in computing participation: Concerns, extent, reasons and strategies. *Australian Journal of Education*, **34**, 52–66.

Clement, J.J. (1983). A conceptual model discussed by Galileo and used intuitively by physics students. In D. Gentner and A.L. Stevens (eds), *Mental models*, 325–39. Hillsdale, NJ: Erlbaum.

Clements, D.H. & Gullo, D.F. (1984). Effects of computer programming on young children's cognition. *Journal of Educational Psychology*, **76**, 1051–88.

Clendening, C.P. & Davies, R.A. (1980). *Creating Programs for the Gifted: A Guide for Teachers, Librarians and Students*. New York: Bowker.

Clifford, M.M. (1986a). The comparative effects of strategy and effort attributions. *British Journal of Educational Psychology*, **56**, 75–83.

Clifford, M.M. (1986b). The effects of ability, strategy and effort attributions for educational, business and athletic failure. *British Journal of Educational Psychology*, **56**, 169–79.

Clough, E. & Driver, R. (1984). A study of consistency of students' conceptual frameworks across different task contexts. Unpublished paper, Centre for Studies in Science and Mathematics Education, University of Leeds.

Clough, E. & Driver, R. (1985a). Secondary students' conceptions of the conduction of heat: Bringing together scientific and personal views. *Physics Education*, **20**, 176–82.

Clough, E. & Driver, R. (1985b). What do children understand about pressure in fluids? *Research in Science and Technology Education*, **3**(3), 210–20.

Cloward, R.D. (1976). Teenagers as tutors of academically low-achieving children. In V.L. Allen (ed.), *Children as teachers*. New York: Academic Press.

Coates, T.J. & Thoreson, C.E. (1976). Teacher anxiety: A review with recommendations. *Review of Educational Research*, **46**, 159–84.

Cochran-Smith, M. (1991). Word processing and writing in elementary classrooms: A critical review of related literature. *Review of Educational Research*, **61**, 107–55.

Cognition and Technology Group at Vanderbilt (1990). Anchored instruction and its relation to situated cognition. *Educational Researcher*, **19**(6), 2–10.

Cohen, M. & Riel, M. (1989). The effect of distant audiences on students' writing. *American Educational Research Journal*, **26**, 143–59.

Cohen, S.A. (1987). Instructional alignment: Searching for a magic bullet. *Educational Researcher*, **16**(8), 16–20.

Colangelo, N. & Kerr, B. (1990). Extreme academic talent: Profiles of perfect scorers. *Journal of Educational Psychology*, **82**, 404–09.

Cole, M. & Traupman, K. (1980). Comparative cognitive research: Learning from a learning disabled child. In W.A. Collins (ed.), *Aspects of the Development of Competence, Minnesota Symposia on Child Development* (Vol. 12). Minneapolis: University of Minnesota Press.

Cole, N.S. (1990). Conceptions of educational achievement. *Educational Researcher*, **19**(3), 2–7.

Cole, P.G. & Chan, L.K.S. (1987). *Teaching Principles and Practice*. Sydney: Prentice Hall of Australia.

Cole, P.G. & Chan, L.K.S. (1990). *Methods and Strategies for Special Education*. Sydney: Prentice Hall.

Coleman, J. (1966). *Equality of Educational Opportunity*. Washington, DC: United States Government Printing Office.

Collier, K.G. (1983). *The Management of Peer-group Learning: Syndicate Methods in Higher Education*. Guildford: Society for Research in Higher Education.

Collier, K.G. (1985). Teaching methods in higher education: The changing scene, with special reference to small-group work. *Higher Education Research and Development*, **4**(1), 3–26.

Collis, K.F. (1975). *A Study of Concrete and Formal Operations in School Mathematics: A Piagetian Viewpoint*. Melbourne: Australian Council for Educational Research.

Collis, K.F. & Biggs, J.B. (1983). Matriculation, degree requirements, and cognitive demands in university and CAEs. *Australian Journal of Education*, **27**, 41–51.

Collis, K.F. & Biggs, J.B. (1986). Using the SOLO taxonomy. SET, **1**(1), Item 3A.

Collis, K.F. & Biggs, J.B. (1989). A school-based approach to setting and evaluating science curriculum objectives: SOLO and school science. *Australian Journal of Science Teachers*, **35**(4), 15–25.

Collis, K.F. & Biggs, J.B. (1991). Developmental determinants of qualitative aspects of school learning. In G. Evans (ed.) *Learning and Teaching Cognitive Skills* (pp. 185–207). Hawthorn, Vic.: Australian Council for Educational Research.

Collis, K.F. & Davey, H.A. (1986). A technique for evaluating skills in high school science. *Journal of Research in Science Teaching*, **23**, 651–63.

Comber, B. & Hancock, J. (eds) (1987). *Developing Teachers*. N. Ryde: Methuen Australia.

Commons, M.C., Richards, F.A. & Kuhn, D. (1982). Systematic and metasystematic reasoning: A case for levels of reasoning beyond Piaget's stage of formal operations. *Child Development*, **53**, 1058–69.

Commonwealth Schools Commission (1987). *In the National Interest*. Canberra: Government Printing Office.

Condry, J. (1977). Enemies of exploration: Self-initiated versus other-initiated learning. *Journal of Personality and Social Psychology*, **35**, 459–77.

Connell, R.W. (1985). *Teachers' Work*. Sydney: George Allen & Unwin.

Connell, R.W., Ashenden, D., Kessler, S. & Dowsett, G.W. (1982). *Making the Difference: Schools, Families and Social Division*. Sydney: Allen & Unwin.

Conway, R. (1975). On mutual liberation: The need for a liberated female and a liberated male. *Education News*, **15**(4), 22–9.

Conway, R. (1990). Behaviour disorders. In A.F. Ashman & J. Elkins (eds), *Educating Children with Special Needs*. Sydney: Prentice Hall.

Cook, R. (1988). *Outbreak*. London: Pan/Macmillan.

Cooper, C.R. & Odell, L. (eds) (1978). *Research on Composing: Points of Departure*. Urbana, Ill: National Council of Teachers of English.

Corno, L. & Snow, R.E. (1986). Adapting teaching to individual differences among learners. In M.C. Wittrock (ed.), *Handbook of Research on Teaching*. New York: Macmillan.

Coulby, D. (1988). Classroom disruption, educational theory, and the beleaguered teacher. In R. Slee (ed.), *Discipline and Schools: A Curriculum Perspective*, (p.153–63). South Melbourne: Macmillan.

Covington, M. & Beery, R. (1976). *Self-worth and School Learning*. New York: Holt, Rinehart and Winston.

Craik, F.I.M. & Lockhart, R.S. (1972). Levels of processing: A framework for memory research. *Journal of Verbal Learning and Verbal Behaviour*, **11**, 671–84.

Craik, F.I.M. & Tulving, E. (1975). Depth of processing and the retention of words in episodic memory. *Journal of Experimental Psychology*, **104**, 268–94.

Creed, K. (ed.) (1984). *Free to be*. Camberwell: Talented and Gifted Children Curriculum Committee.

Crocker, L.M. & Algina, J. (1986). *Introduction to Classical and Modern Test Theory*. New York: CBS College Publishing.

Crooks, T.J. (1988). The impact of classroom evaluation practices on students. *Review of Educational Research*, **58**, 438–81.

Cropley, A.J. (1966). Creativity and intelligence. *British Journal of Educational Psychology*, **36**, 259–66.

Cropley, A.J. (1967). *Creativity*. London: Longmans Green.

Cropley, A.J. (1976). Some psychological reflections on lifelong education. In R. Davel (ed.), *Foundations of Lifelong Education*. Oxford: Pergamon Press.

Cropley, A.J. (1991). Improving intelligence by fostering creativity. In H. Rowe (ed.), *Intelligence: Reconceptualization and Measurement* (pp. 267–80). Hawthorn:ACER/Hillsdale: Lawrence Erlbaum.

Cropley, A.J. & Field, T.W. (1968). Intellectual style and high school science. *Nature*, **217**, 1211–12.

Cruickshank, D.R. (September 1985). Teacher clarity. *International Journal for Teacher Education*.

Cruickshank, D.R. (February 1986). A synopsis of school effectiveness research. *Illinois School Research and Development*.

Cummins, J. (1979). Linguistic interdependence and the educational development of bilingual childen. *Review of Educational Research*, **49**, 222–51.

Daiute, C. (1986). Physical and cognitive factors in revising: Insights from studies with computers. *Research in the Teaching of English*, **20**, 141–59.

Dale, R.R. (1974). *Mixed or Single Sex School?* vol. 3, *Attainment, Attitude and Overview*. London: Routledge & Kegan Paul.

Dalton, B.M., Morocco, C.C. & Neale, A.E. (1988). 'I've lost my story!' Mastering the machine skills for word processing. Paper presented at the Annual Meeting of the American Educational Research Association, New Orleans, April.

Das, J.P., Kirby, J. & Jarman, R.F. (1979). *Simultaneous and Successive Cognitive Processes.* New York: Academic Press.

Davey, C.P. (1973). Physical exertion and mental performance. *Ergonomics,* **16**, 595–9.

Davies, B. (1982). *Life in the Classroom and Playground: The Accounts of Primary School Children.* Henley: Routledge & Kegan Paul.

Davies, B. (1983). The role pupils play in the social construction of classroom order. *British Journal of Sociology of Education,* **4**, 55–69.

Davies, B. (1984a). Children through their own eyes. *Oxford Review of Education,* **10**, 225–92.

Davies, B. (1984b). Friends and pupils. In M. Hammersley and P. Woods (eds), *Life in Schools,* (p. 256). Milton Keynes: Open University Press.

Davies, B. (1990). Lived and imaginary narratives and their place in making oneself up as a gendered being. *Australian Psychologist,* **25**, 318–33.

Davis, G.A. & Rimm, S.B. (1985). *Education of the Gifted and Talented.* Englewood Cliffs, NJ: Prentice Hall.

de Charms, R. (1968). *Personal Causation: The Internal Affective Determinants of Behaviour.* New York: Academic Press.

de Charms, R. (1972). Personal causation training in the schools. *Journal of Applied Psychology,* **2**, 95–113.

de Charms, R. (1976). *Enhancing Motivation: Change in the Classroom.* New York: Irvington.

Deci, E.L. (1971). Effects of externally mediated rewards on intrinsic motivation. *Journal of Personality and Social Psychology,* **18**, 105–15.

Deci, E.L. (August 1972). Work—Who does not like it and why? *Psychology Today,* p. 57ff.

Deci, E.L. (1975). *Intrinsic Motivation.* New York: Plenum.

Deci, E.L. & Ryan, R.M. (1985). *Intrinsic Motivation and Self-determination in Human Behaviour.* New York: Plenum Press.

de Lacey, P. (1974). *So Many Lessons to Learn: Failure in Australian Education.* Ringwood, Vic: Penguin.

de Lacey, P. & Poole, M.E. (eds) (1979). *Mosaic or Melting Pot: Cultural Evolution in Australia.* Sydney: Harcourt Brace Jovanovich.

de Lemos, M. (1975). *Study of the Educational Achievement of Migrant Children* (final report). Melbourne: Australian Council for Educational Research.

Demetriou, A. (ed.) (1988). *The Neo-Piagetian Theories of Cognitive Development.* Amsterdam: North-Holland.

Demetriou, A. & Efklides, A. (1985). Structure and sequence of formal and postformal thought: General patterns and individual differences. *Child Development,* **56**, 1062–91.

Dempster, F.N. (1981). Memory span: Sources of individual and developmental differences. *Psychological Bulletin,* **89**, 63–100.

Dettman, H.W. (1972). *Discipline in Secondary Schools in Western Australia: Report of the Committee.* Education Department, Perth.

Deutsch, J.A. & Deutsch, D. (1963). Attention: Some theoretical considerations. *Psychological Review,* **70**, 80–90.

Devin-Sheehan, L., Feldman, R. & Allen, V. (1976). Research on children tutoring children: A critical review. *Review of Educational Research,* **46**, 355–85.

Dewey, J. (1910). *How We Think.* Boston: Heath.

Dibley, J. (1986). *Let's Get Motivated.* Sydney: Corporate Publishing.

Diederich, P.B. (1974). *Measuring Growth in English.* Urbana, Ill: National Council of Teachers of English.

Dienes, Z.P. (1963). *An Experimental Study of Mathematics Learning.* London: Hutchinson Educational.

Dillon, D. (1989). Showing them that I want them to learn and that I care about who they are: A microethnography of the social organisation of a secondary low-track English-reading classroom. *American Educational Research Journal,* **26**, 227–59.

Directorate of Special Programs (1985). *Towards Non-sexist Education—Curriculum Ideas: Visual Arts.* NSW Department of Education.

Disibio, M. (1982). Memory for connected discourse: A constructivist view. *Review of Educational Research,* **52**, 149–74.

di Vesta, F.J. & Palermo, D. (1974). Language development. In J. Carroll (ed.), *Review of Educational Research,* **2**. Itasca, Ill: Peacock.

Donaldson, M. (1978). *Children's Minds.* Glasgow: Fontana.

Doyle, W. (1986). Classroom organization and management. In M.C. Wittrock (ed.), *Handbook of Research on Teaching,* 3rd edn, (pp. 392–431). New York: Macmillan.

Dreikurs, R. & Cassel, P. (1972). *Discipline without Tears.* New York: Hawthorn.

Driver, R. (1981). Pupils' alternative frameworks

in science. *European Journal of Science Education*, **3**, 93–101.

Driver, R. (1983). *The Pupil as Scientist.* Milton Keynes: The Open University Press.

Driver, R. (1985). Cognitive psychology and pupils' frameworks in mechanics. In P. Lijnse (ed.), *The Many Faces of Teaching and Learning Mechanics.* Utrecht: WCC Publications.

Driver, R. & Bell, B. (1986). Students' thinking and the learning of science. *School Science Review*, 443–56.

Driver, R. & Easley, J. (1978). Pupils and paradigms: A review of literature related to concept development and adolescent science studies. *Studies in Science Education*, **5**, 61–84.

Driver, R. & Oldham, V. (1986). A constructionist approach to curriculum development in science. *Studies in Science Education*, **13**, 105–22.

Driver, R. & Warrington, L. (1985). Students use of the principle of energy conservation in problem situations. *Physics Education*, **20**, 171–5.

Duke, D.L. & Meckel, M.A. (1984). *Teachers' Guide to Classroom Management.* New York: Random House.

Dulay, H.C. & Burt, M.K. (1974). Errors and strategies in child second language acquisition. *TESOL Quarterly*, **8**, 129–36.

Dunkin, M.J. & Biddle, B.J. (1974). *The Study of Teaching.* New York: Holt, Rinehart & Winston.

Dupuis, M.M. & Snyder, S.L. (1983). Develop concepts through vocabulary: A strategy for reading specialists to use with content teachers. *Journal of Reading*, **26**, 297–305.

Durst, R.K. & Newell, G.E. (1989). The uses of function: James Britton's category system and research on writing. *Review of Educational Research*, **59**, 375–94.

Dweck, C.S. (1975). The role of expectations and attributions in the alleviation of learned helplessness. *Journal of Personality and Social Psycholoigy*, **31**, 674–85.

Easley, J. (August 1984). A teacher educator's perspective on students' and teachers' schemes. Paper presented to Conference on Thinking, Harvard Graduate School of Education, Boston.

Ebbinghaus, H. (1913). *Memory.* New York: Teacher College Press.

Education Commission of NSW (1986). *Multicultural Education* (Information Sheet No.6).

Edwards, A.D. (1976). *Language in Culture and Class.* London: Heinemann.

Edwards, J. (1986). The effects of metacognitive training in study skills on students' approaches to learning and examination performance. Unpublished Masters of Psychology (Educational) thesis, University of Newcastle.

Egan, K. (1984). *Educational Development.* New York: Oxford University Press.

Egan, K. (1988). *Teaching as Storytelling: An Alternative Approach to Teaching and the Curriculum.* London: Routledge.

Ehri, L. & Wilce, L. (1987). Does learning to spell help beginners learn to read words? *Reading Research Quarterly*, **22**, 47–65.

Elashoff, J. & Snow, R.E. (eds) (1971). *Pygmalion Revisited.* Worthington, Ohio: C.A. Jones.

Elkind, D. (1967). Egocentrism in adolescence. *Child Development*, **38**, 1025–34.

Elkind, D. (1968). Adolescent cognitive development. In J.F. Adams (ed.), *Understanding Adolescence.* Boston: Allyn & Bacon.

Ellsworth, R., Duell, O.K. & Velotta, C. (1991). Length of wait-times used by college students given unlimited wait-time intervals. *Contemporary Educational Psychology*, **16**, 265–71.

Elton, L.R.B. & Laurillard, D. (1979). Trends in student learning. *Studies in Higher Education*, **4**, 87–102.

Englert, C.S. & Hiebert, E. (1984). Children's developing awareness of text structures in expository materials. *Journal of Educational Psychology*, **76**, 65–74.

Entwistle, N. (1984). Contrasting perspectives on learning. In F. Marton, D. Hounsell N. Entwistle (eds), *The Experience of Learning.* Edinburgh: Scottish Academic Press.

Entwistle, N., Kozeki, B. & Tait, H. (1989). Pupils' perceptions of school and teachers—II: Relationships with motivation and approaches to learning. *British Journal of Educational Psychology*, **59**, 340–50.

Entwistle, N. & Ramsden, P. (1983). *Understanding Student Learning.* London: Croom Helm.

Epstein, H.T. (1978). Growth spurts during brain development: Implications for educational theory and practice. In J.S. Chall and A.F. Mirsky (eds), *Education and the Brain* (77th Yearbook of the National Society for the Study of

Education, Part II). Chicago, Ill: University of Chicago Press.

Erikson, E. (1959). *Identity and the Life Cycle*. New York: International Universities Press.

Evans, G.T. (1991a). Student control over learning. In J.B. Biggs (ed.), *Teaching for Learning: The View from Cognitive Psychology*. Hawthorn, Vic: Australian Council for Educational Research.

Evans, G.T. (1991b). Judging approaches to preservice teacher education by using models of knowledge and skill development. In Kam, H.W. (ed.), Improving the quality of the teaching profession. *International Yearbook of Teacher Education 1990*. Singapore: Institute of Education.

Evans, G., Georgeff, M. & Poole, M.E. (1980). Training in information selection for communication. *The Australian Journal of Education*, 24(2), 137–54.

Eysenck, H.J. (1957). *The Dynamics of Anxiety and Hysteria*. London: Routledge and Kegan Paul.

Eysenck, H.J. (1971). *Race, Intelligence and Education*. Melbourne: Sun Books.

Faigley, L. & Witte, S. (1984). Measuring the effects of revisions on text structure. In R. Beach & L.S. Bridwell (eds), *New Direction in Compositions Research*. New York: The Huntford Press.

Fantuzzo, J.W., Riggio, R.E., Connelly, S. & Dimeff, L.A. (1989). Effects of reciprocal peer tutoring on academic achievement and psychological adjustment: A component analysis. *Journal of Educational Psychology*, 81, 173–7.

Farber, J. (1970). *The Student as Nigger*. New York: Pocket Books.

Farkas, G., Sheehan, D. & Grobe, R. (1990). Coursework mastery and school success: Gender, ethnicity and poverty groups within an urban school district. *American Educational Research Journal*, 27, 807–27.

Faw, H.W. & Waller, T.G. (1976). Mathemagenic behaviours and efficiency in learning from prose materials: Review, critique and recommendtions. *Review of Educational Research*, 46, 691–720.

Feather, N. (ed.) (1982). *Expectations and Actions*. Hillsdale, NJ: Erlbaum.

Feigelson, N. (1970). *The Underground Revolution*. New York: Funk & Wagnalls.

Feiman-Nemser, S. & Buchmann, M. (1987). When is student teaching teacher education? *Teaching and Teacher Education*, 3, 255–73.

Fennema, E. (1983). Success in mathematics. In M. Marland (ed.), *Sex Differentiation and Schooling*. London: Heinemann Educational.

Fensham, P. (1980). A research base for new objectives of science teaching. *Research in Science Education*, 10, 23–33.

Fesl, E. (July 1983). The irrelevance of literacy. *Education News*, 18(5), 14–15.

Festinger, L. (1968). The psychological effects of insufficient rewards. In W.H. Bartz (ed.), *Readings in General Psychology*. Boston, Mass: Allyn & Bacon.

Field, T.W. & Poole, M. (1970). Intellectual style and achievement of arts and science undergraduates. *British Journal of Educational Psychology*, 40, 338–41.

Finn, C.E. (1988). What ails education research? *Educational Researcher*, 17(1), 5–8.

Finn, J.D. (1972). Expectations and the educational environment. *Review of Educational Research*, 42, 387–410.

Finn, J.D. & Achilles, C.M. (1990). Answers and questions about class size: A statewide experiment. *American Educational Research Journal*, 27, 557–77.

Fischer, K. (1980). A theory of cognitive development: The control and construction of hierarchies of skills. *Psychological Review*, 57, 477–531.

Fischer, K. & Bullock, D. (1984). Cognitive development in school-age children: Conclusions and new directions. In W. Collins (ed.), *Development During Middle Childhood: The Years from Six to Twelve*. Washington, DC: National Academy of Sciences Press.

Fischer, K. & Pipp, S. (1984). Process of cognitive development: Optional level and skill acquisition. In R. Sternberg (ed.), *Mechanics of Cognitive Development*. New York: W.H. Freeman.

Fischer, K. & Silvern, L. (1985). Stages and individual differences in cognitive development. *Annual Review of Psychology*, 36, 613–48.

Fitts, P. (1962). Factors in complex skill training. In R. Glaser (ed.), *Training Research and Education*. Pittsburgh: University of Pittsburgh Press.

Fitzgerald, J. (1987). Research on revision in writing. *Review of Educational Research*, 57, 481–506.

Fitzgerald, J. & Teasley, A. (1986). Effects of

instruction in narrative structure on children's writing. *Journal of Education Psychology*, **18**, 424–32.

Fixx, J. (1977). *The Complete Book of Running*. New York: Random House.

Flavell, J.H. (1976). Metacognition aspects of problem solving. In L.B. Resnick (ed.), *The Nature of Intelligence*. Hillsdale, NJ: Lawrence Erlbaum.

Flavell, J.H., Botkin P., Fry G., Wright J. & Jarvis P. (1968). *The Development of Role-taking and Communication Skills*. New York: John Wiley.

Flavell, J.H. & Wellman, H. (1977). Metamemory. In R.V. Kailn and J.W. Hagen (eds), *Perspectives on the Development of Memory and Cognition*. Hillsdale, NJ: Lawrence Erlbaum.

Flower, L. (1981). *Problem Solving Strategies for Writing*. New York: Harcourt Brace Jovanovich.

Fontana, D. (1987). *Classroom Control*. London: Methuen.

Foon, A.E. (1988). The relationship between school type and adolescent self-esteem, attribution styles and affiliation needs. *British Journal of Educational Psychology*, **58**, 44–54.

Foster, V. (ed.) (1981). *The Consultants' Role in Non-sexist Education: A Resource Book*. Sydney: Central Metropolitan Region, Department of Education.

Fransson, A. (1977). On qualitative differences in learning IV—Effects of intrinsic motivation and extrinsic test anxiety on process and outcome. *British Journal of Educational Psychology*, **47**, 244–55.

Fraser, B.J. (1981). *Learning Environment in Curriculum Evaluation: A Review*. London: Pergamon, Evaluation in Education Series.

Frederiksen, J.R. & Collins, A. (1989). A systems approach to educational testing. *Educational Researcher*, **18**(9), 27–32.

Freire, P. (1970). *Pedagogy of the Oppressed*. New York: Herder & Herder.

French, J.R.P. & Raven, B. (1959). The bases of social power. In D. Cartwright (ed.), *Studies in Social Power*. Ann Arbor, Mich: Institute for Social Research.

Freud, S. (1905). *The Basic Writings of Sigmund Freud*. Random House: New York.

Friedman, L. (1989). Mathematics and the gender gap: A meta-analysis of recent studies on sex differences in mathematical tasks. *Review of Educational Research*, **59**, 185–213.

Fryer, M. & Collings, J. (1991). Teachers' views about creativity. *British Journal of Educational Psychology*, **61**, 207–19.

Furth, H.G. (1970). *Piaget for Teachers*. Englewood Cliffs, NJ: Prentice Hall.

Gagne, E.D. (1978). Long-term retention of information following learning from prose. *Review of Educational Research*, **48**, 629–65.

Gagne, R.M. (1967). Curriculum research and the promotion of learning. In R. Tyler, R. Gagne and M. Scriven (eds), *Perspectives of Curriculum Evaluation*. Chicago, Ill: Rand McNally.

Gallagher, J.J. (1985). *Teaching the Gifted Child* (3rd edn). Boston: Allyn & Bacon.

Garbarino, J. (1975). The impact of anticipated rewards on cross-age tutoring. *Journal of Personality and Social Psychology*, **32**, 421–8.

Gardner, H. (1985). *Frames of Mind*. London: Paladin.

Gardner, H. & Hatch, T. (1989). Multiple intelligences go to school. *Educational Research*, **18**(8), 4–10, November.

Gardner, J.M. (1976). Cross-cultural diffusion of behaviour modification. In P.W. Sheehan and K.D. White (eds), *Behaviour modification in Australia* (Monograph Supplement No. 3, *Australian Psychologist*, p. 11).

Gardner, R.W., Holzman, P., Klein, G.S., Linton, H. & Spence, D. (1959). Cognitive control: A study of individual consistencies in cognitive behavior. *Psychological Issues*, **1**(4), Monograph 4.

Garner, R. (1990). When children and adults do not use learning strategies: Towards a theory of settings. *Review of Educational Research*, **60**, 517–29.

Gaudry, E. & Bradshaw, G. (1970). The differential effect of anxiety on performance in progressive and terminal school examinations. *Australian Journal of Psychology*, **22**, 1–4.

Gerencser, S. (1979). The Calasanctius experience. In A.H. Passow (ed.), *The Gifted and the Talented: Their Education and Development* (78th Yearbook of the National Society for the Study of Education, pp.127-37). Chicago, Ill: University of Chicago Press.

Getzels, J.W. & Jackson, P. (1962). *Creativity and Intelligence*. New York: Wiley.

Gibbs, G. (1977). Can students be taught to study? *Higher Education Bulletin*, **5**, 107–18.

Gibbs, G. (1981). *Teaching Students to Learn: A Student-Centred Approach*. Milton Keynes: The Open University Press.

Gilbert, J., Osborne, R. & Fensham, P. (1982). Children's science and its consequences for teaching. *Science Education*, **68**, 623–33.

Gilbert, J. & Watts, M. (1983). Concepts, misconceptions and alternative conceptions: Changing perspectives in science education. *Studies in Science Education*, **10**, 61–98.

Gilbert, J., Watts, M. & Osborne, R. (1982). Students' conceptions of ideas in mechanics. *Physics Education*, **17**, 62–6.

Gill, J. (1988). *Which Way to School? A Review of the Evidence on the Single Sex vs. Co-education Debate and an Annotated Bibliography of the Research.* Canberra: Commonwealth Schools Commission.

Gill, P., Trioli, C. & Weymouth, R. (1988). A disciplined partnership: Code of behaviour at Princes Hill Primary School. In R. Slee (ed.), *Discipline and Schools: A Curriculum Perspective*, (p. 246–67). South Melbourne: Macmillan.

Gilligan, C. (1982). *In a Different Voice: Psychological Theory and Women's Development.* Cambridge, Mass: Harvard University Press.

Gilligan, C., Ward, J., Taylor, J. & Bardige, B. (1988). *Mapping the Moral Domain.* Cambridge, Mass: Harvard University Press.

Ginott, H. (1971). *Teacher and Child.* New York: Macmillan.

Ginsburg, H. & Opper, S. (1987). *Piaget's Theory of Intellectual Development.* Englewood Cliffs, NJ: Prentice Hall.

Glaser, R. (1968). Adapting the elementary school curriculum to individual performance. *Proceedings of the 1967 Conference on Testing Problems.* Princeton: Educational Testing Service.

Glaser, R. (1981). The future of testing: A research agenda for cognitive psychology and psychometrics. *American Psychologist*, **36**, 923–36.

Glaser, R. (1984). Education and thinking: The role of knowledge. *American Psychologist*, **39**, 93–104.

Glaser, R. (1990). Toward new models for assessment. *International Journal of Educational Research*, **14**, 475–83.

Glaser, R. (1991). Intelligence as an expression of acquired knowledge. In H. Rowe (ed.), *Intelligence: Reconceptualization and Measurement* (pp. 47–56). Hawthorn:ACER/Hillsdale: Lawrence Erlbaum.

Glaser, R. & Nitko, A.J. (1971). Measurement in learning and instruction. In R.L. Thorndike (ed.), *Educational Measurement.* Washington, DC: American Council on Education.

Glass, G.V., McGaw, B. & Smith, M.L. (1981). *Meta-analysis in Social Research.* Beverly Hills: Sage.

Glass, G.V. & Smith, M.L. (1978). *Meta-analysis of Research on the Relationships of Class Size and Achievement.* San Francisco: Far West Laboratory for Educational Research and Development.

Glasser, W. (1977). 10 Steps to good discipline. *Today's Education*, November-December.

Gmelch, W.H. (1983). Stress for success—How to optimise your performance. *Theory into Practice*, **22**(1), 7–14.

Gnagey, W. (1975). *The Psychology of Discipline in the Classroom.* New York: Macmillan.

Goldstein, H. (1979). Consequences of using the Rasch model for educational assessment. *British Educational Research Journal*, **5**, 211-20.

Goleman, D. (1980). 1528 little geniuses and how they grew. *Psychology Today*, **13**(9).

Good, T. (1985). Goodbye, little red schoolhouse. *Creative Computing*, 64–76, April.

Good, T.L. & Brophy, J.E. (1987). *Looking in Classrooms* (4th edn). New York: Harper & Row.

Good, T.L. & Brophy, J.E. (1991). *Educational Psychology.* New York: Longmans

Good, T.L. & Marshall, S. (1984). Do students learn more in heterogeneous or homogeneous groups? In P. Peterson, L.C. Wickinson, and M. Hallinan (eds), *The Social Context of Instruction: Group Organization and Group Processes* (pp. 15–38). Orlando, Fla: Academic Press.

Goodlad, J.L. (1983). *A Place called School.* New York: McGraw Hill.

Goodnow, J.J. (1991). Cognitive values and educational practice. In J.B. Biggs (ed.), *Teaching for Learning: The View from Cognitive Psychology.* Hawthorn, Vic: Australian Council for Educational Research.

Gordon, D. (1980). The immorality of the hidden curriculum. *Journal of Moral Education*, **10**, 3–8.

Gordon, D. & Grouws, D. (1977). Teaching effects: A process—Product study in fourth-grade mathematics classrooms. *Journal of Teacher Education*, **28**, 49–54.

Gordon, T. (1974). *TET—Teacher Effectiveness Training.* New York: Wyden.

Gow, L. & Kember, D. (1990). Does higher education promote independent learning? *Higher Education*, *19*, 307–22.

Graham, D. (1972). *Moral Learning and Development*. Sydney: Angus & Robertson.

Grainger, A.J. (1970). *The Bullring: A Classroom Experiment in Moral Education*. Oxford: Pergamon Press.

Grassby, A.J. (1978). It's time for migrant education to go. In P.R. de Lacey and M.E. Poole (eds), *Mosaic or Melting Pot? Cultural Evolution in Australia*. Sydney: Harcourt Brace Jovanovich.

Graetz, B. (1990). Private schools and educational attainment: Cohort and generational effects. *Australian Journal of Education*, *34*, 174–91.

Graves, D. (1983). *Writing: Teachers and Children at Work*. Exeter, New Hampshire: Heinemann Educational.

Green, J. & Weade, R. (1988). Teaching as conversation and the construction of meaning in the classroom. Paper given to Annual Meeting, American Educational Research Association, New Orleans, April.

Green, K. & Stager, S. (1985). Improving performance assessment: A study of teachers' coursework in testing, attitude, towards testing and use of classroom tests. Paper presented to Higher Education Research and Development Society of Australasia, Annual Conference, Auckland, New Zealand, 22–4 August.

Gronert, R.R. (1970). Combining a behavioural approach with reality therapy. *Elementary School Evidence and Counselling*, *5*, 104–12.

Gronlund, N.E. (1970). *Stating Behavioural Objectives for Classroom Instruction*. New York: Macmillan.

Guilford, J.P. (1967). *The Nature of Human Intelligence*. New York: McGraw-Hill.

Gunstone, R., Champagne, A. & Klopfer, L. (1981). Instruction for understanding: A case study. *Australian Science Teachers Journal*, *27*(3), 27–32.

Gunstone, R. & White, R. (1981). Understanding of gravity. *Science Education*, *65*, 291–9.

Guskey, T.R. (1986). Staff development and the process of change. *Educational Researcher*, *15*(5), 5–12.

Guthrie, E.R. (1977). *Sexism in education—The Report of the Minister's Committee*. Sydney: AGPS.

Guthrie, E.S. (1952). *The Psychology of Learning*. New York: Harper & Row.

Guttman, L. (1941). The quantification of a class of attributes: A theory and a method of scale construction. In P. Horst (ed.), *The Prediction of Personal Adjustment*. New York: Social Science Research Council.

Hadamard, J. (1954). *The Psychology of Invention in the Mathematical Field*. Princeton, NJ: Princeton University Press.

Haddon, F.A. & Lytton, H. (1968). Teaching approach and the development of divergent thinking abilities in primary schools. *British Journal of Educational Psychology*, *38*, 171–80.

Haddon, F.A. & Lytton, H. (1971). Primary education and divergent thinking abilities—Four years on. *British Journal of Educational Psychology*, *41*, 136–47.

Hairston, M. (1982). The winds of change: Thomas Kuhn and the revolution in the teaching of writing. *College Composition and Communication*, *33*, 76–88.

Hales, L.W. & Tokar, E. (1975). The effects of quality of preceding responses on the grades assigned to subsequent responses to an essay question. *Journal of Educational Measurement*, *12*, 115–17.

Halford, G.S. (1982). *The Development of Thought*. Hillsdale, NJ: Lawrence Erlbaum.

Hall, R.V., Panyan, M., Rabon, D. & Broden, M. (1968). Instructing beginning teachers in reinforcement procedures which improve classroom control. *Journal of Applied Behaviour Analysis*, *1*, 315–22.

Haller, E.P., Child, D.A. & Walberg, H.J. (1988). Can comprehension be taught? A quantitative synthesis of 'metacognitive' studies. *Educational Researcher*, *17*(9), 5–8.

Halpin, A.W. (1966). *Theory and Research in Administration*. New York: Macmillan.

Hamaker, C. (1986). The effects of adjunct questions on prose learning. *Review of Educational Research*, *56*, 212–42.

Hambleton, R.K. (1972). Towards a theory of criterion-referenced tests. Paper presented to the National Council on Measurement in Education, Chicago, Ill.

Hambleton, R.K. & Cook, L.L. (1977). Latent trait models and their use in the use of educational test data. *Journal of Educational Measurement*, *14*, 75–96.

Hamilton, J. (1989). *Just Lovely*. J. McKenzie (ed.). Maryborough, Victoria: Australian Print Group.

Hanley, E.N. (1970). Review of research involving applied behaviour analysis in the classroom. *Review of Educational Research*, **40**, 597–625.

Haring, N.G. & Whelan, R.F. (1966). Modification and maintenance of behaviour through systematic appliation of consequences. *Exceptional Children*, **32**, 281–89.

Harlow, H.F. (1953). Mice, monkeys, man and motives. *Psychological Review*, **60**, 23–32.

Harris, D. & Bell, C. (1986). *Evaluating and Assessing for Learning*. London: Kogan Page.

Hart, N.W.M. (1976). *The Mt Gravatt Developmental Reading Programme*. Sydney: Addison-Wesley.

Hartley, J. & Davies, I.K. (1976). Preinstructional strategies: The role of pretests, behavioural objectives, overviews and advance organisers. *Review of Educational Research*, **46**, 239–65.

Hartshorne, H. & May, M. (1928). *Studies in the Nature of Character*, vol. 1, *Studies in deceit*. New York: Macmillan.

Harvey, O., Hunt, D. & Schroder, H. (1961). *Conceptual Systems and Personality Organisation*. New York: Wiley.

Hasan, P. & Butcher, H. (1966). Creativity and intelligence: A partial replication with Scottish children of Getzel's and Jackson's study. *British Journal of Psychology*, **57**, 129–35.

Hattie, J. (1992). Measuring the effects of schooling. *Australian Journal of Education*, **36**, 5–13.

Hattie, J. & Fitzgerald, D. (1987). Sex differences in attitudes, achievements, and use of computers. *Australian Journal of Education*, **31**, 3–26.

Hattie, J. & Watkins, D. (1988). Preferred classroom environment and approach to learning. *British Journal of Educational Psychology*, **58**, 345–9.

Hau, K.T. & Salili, F. (1990). Examination result attribution, expectancy and achievement goals amongst Chinese students in Hong Kong. *Educational Studies*, **16**, 17–31.

Hau, K.T. & Salili, F. (1991). Structure and semantic differential placement of specific causes: Academic causal attributions by Chinese students in Hong Kong. *International Journal of Psychology*, **26**, 175–93.

Hausen, E. (1968). Linguistics and language planning. In W. Bright (ed.), *Sociolinguistics*. The Hague: Mouton.

Hawisher, G.E. & Fortune, R. (1988). Research into word processing and the basic writer. Paper presented at the Annual Meeting of the American Educational Research Association, New Orleans, April.

Hayes, J. & Flower, L.S. (1986). Writing research and the writer. *American Psychologist*, **41**, 1106–13.

Healy, C.C. & Welchert, A.J. (1990). Mentoring relations: A definition to advance research and practice. *Educational Researcher*, **19**(9), 17–21.

Hearnshaw, L.S. (1979). *Cyril Burt, Psychologist.* London: Hodder & Stoughton.

Hebb, D.O. (1946). On the nature of fear. *Psychological Review*, **53**, 259–76.

Hebb, D.O. (1949). *The Organisation of Behaviour.* New York: Wiley.

Hebb, D.O. (1955). Drives and the CNS (Conceptual nervous system). *Psychological Review*, **67**, 243–54.

Heckhausen, H. (1975). Fear of failing as a self-reinforcing motive system. In I.G. Sarason and C. Spielberger (eds), *Stress and Anxiety*. Washington, DC: Hemisphere.

Hegarty-Hazel, E. & Prosser, M. (in press *a*). Relationship between students' conceptual knowledge and study strategies, Part I: Student learning in physics. *International Journal of Science Education*.

Hegarty-Hazel, E. & Prosser, M. (in press *b*). Relationship between students' conceptual knowledge and study strategies, Part II: Student learning in biology. *International Journal of Science Education*.

Hemming, J. (1980). Another prospect in moral education. *Journal of Moral Education*, **9**, 75–80.

Henry, J. (1963). *Culture against Man*. Harmondsworth, Middlesex: Penguin Books. (First published, Random House, New York, 1963.)

Hepworth, A.J. (1979). Vales education—Some New South Wales experiences. *Journal of Moral Education*, **8**, 193–202.

Hess, R.D. (1970). Social class and ethnic influences upon socialisation. In P. Mussen (ed.), *Carmichael's Manual of Child Psychology*. New York: Wiley.

Hess, R.D. & Azuma, H. (1991). Cultural support for schooling: Contrasts between Japan and the United States. *Educational Researcher*, **20**(19), 2–8.

Hickson, F. (1990). Terminology: the concept of difference. In Butler, S. (ed.), *The Exceptional Child*, Sydney: Harcourt, Brace Jovanovich.

Hidi, S. (1990). Interest and its contribution as a mental resource for learning. *Review of Educational Research*, **60**, 549–71.

Hidi, S. & Anderson, V. (1986). Producing written summaries: Task demands, cognitive operations and implications for instruction. *Review of Educational Research*, **56**, 473–93.

Hill, W.F. (1985). *Learning: A survey of psychological interpretations* (4th edn). New York: Harper & Row.

Hocking, H. (1984). Interpreting disruptive behaviour by high school students and its implications for curriculum and school management. Paper presented to the Australian Association for Research in Education National Conference, Perth.

Hoffman, B. (1962). *The Tyranny of Testing*. New York: Collier.

Hoggart, R. (1959). *The Uses of Literacy*. London: Chatto & Windus.

Holdsworth, R. (1988). Student participation projects in Australia: An anecdotal history. In R. Slee (ed.), *Discipline and Schools: A Curriculum Perspective*, (p.283–320). South Melbourne: Macmillan.

Holland, J.L. (1959). Some limitations of teacher ratings as predictors of creativity. *Journal of Educational Psychology*, **50**, 219–23.

Hollingsworth, S. (1989). Prior beliefs and cognitive change in learning to teach. *American Educational Research Journal*, **26**, 160–89.

Holloway, S.D. (1988). Concepts of ability and effort in Japan and the United States. *Review of Educational Research*, **58**, 327–43.

Holt, J. (1970). *How Children Fail*. New York: Dell.

Hore, T. (1971). Assessment of teaching practice: An 'attractive' hypothesis. *British Journal of Educational Psychology*, **41**, 327–28.

Horin, A. (1989). Myths about maths. *The Independent Monthly*, November, 12–14.

Horn, J.L. (1968). Organisation of abilities and development of intelligence. *Psychological Review*, **75**, 242–59.

Houghton, S., Wheldall, K., Jukes, R. & Sharpe, A. (1990). The effects of limited private reprimands and increased private praise on classroom behaviour in four British secondary school classes. *British Journal of Educational Psychology*, **60**, 255–65.

Hounsell, D. (1984). Learning and essay-writing. In F. Marton, D. Hounsell and N. Entwistle (eds), *The Experience of Learning*. Edinburgh: Scottish Universities Press.

Howard, R.W. (1987). *Concepts and Schemata: An Introduction*. London: Cassell.

Howe, M.J.A. (1970a). Repeated presentation and recall of meaningful prose. *Journal of Educational Psychology*, **61**, 214–19.

Howe, M.J.A. (1970b). Positive reinforcement: A humanising approach to teacher control in the classroom. *The National Elementary Principal*, **49**, 31–4.

Howe, M.J.A. (1972). *Understanding School Learning: A New Look at Educational Psychology*. New York: Harper & Row.

Huck, S.W. & Bound, W.G. (1972). Essay grades: An interaction between graders, handwriting clarity and the neatness of examination papers. *American Journal of Educational Research*, **9**, 279–83.

Hudson, L. (1966). *Contrary Imaginations*. London: Methuen.

Hudson, L. (1968). *Frames of Mind*. London: Methuen.

Huey, E.B. (1968). *The Psychology and Pedagogy of Reading*. Cambridge, Mass.: MIT Press.

Hull, C.L. (1943). *Principles of Behaviour*. New York: Appleton-Century.

Humphreys, M. & Revelle, W. (1984). Personality, motivation and performance: A theory of the relationship between individual differences and information processing. *Psychological Review*, **91**, 153–84.

Hunsley, J. (1987). Cognitive processes in mathematics anxiety and test anxiety: The role of appraisals, internal dialogue, and attributions. *Journal of Educational Psychology*, **79**, 388–92.

Hunt, D.E. (1971). *Matching Models in Education*. Toronto: Ontario Institute for Studies in Education, monograph series No. 10.

Hunt, E. (1978). Mechanics of verbal ability. *Psychological Review*, **85**, 109–30.

Huot, B. (1990). The literature of direct writing assessment: Major concerns and prevailing trends. *Review of Educational Research*, **60**, 237–63.

Husen, T. & Tuijnam, J. (1991). The contribution of formal schooling to the increase in intellectual capital. *Educational Researcher*, **20**, 17–25.

Illich, I. (1971). *Deschooling Society*. New York: Harper & Row.

Iran-Nejad, A. (1990). Active and dynamic self-regulation of learning processes. *Review of Educational Research*, **60**, 573–602.

Isaacs, E. (1979). Social control and ethnicity: The

socialisation and repression of a Greek child at school. In P. de Lacey and M. Poole (eds), *Mosaic or Melting Pot? Cultural Evolution in Australia*. Sydney: Harcourt Brace Jovanovich.

Izard, J. & White, J.D. (1982). The use of latent trait models in the development and analysis of classroom tests. In D. Spearritt (ed.), *The Improvement of Measurement in Education and Psychology*. Hawthorn, Vic: Australian Council for Educational Research.

Jackson, B. (1964). *Streaming: An Education System in Miniature*. London: Routledge & Kegan Paul.

Jackson, P., Reid N. & Croft, A. (1980). *Study habits evaluation and instruction kit* (SHEIK). Hawthorn, Vic: Australian Council for Educational Research.

Jackson, W. (1988). Talking through writing. *Language and Education*, 2, 1–14.

James, W. (1890). *The Principles of Psychology*, vol.I. New York: Henry Holt.

James, W. (1962). *Talks to Teachers on Psychology*. New York: Dover. (Original edition, Henry Holt, New York, 1899.)

Jensen, A.R. (1969). How much can we boost IQ and scholastic achievement?. *Harvard Educational Review*, 39, 1–123.

Jensen, A.R. (1970). A theory of primary and secondary familial mental retardation. In N. R. Ellis (ed.), *International Review of Research in Mental Retardation*, vol. 4. New York: Academic Press.

Johansson, B., Marton, F. & Svensson, L. (1985). An approach to describing learning as change between qualitatively different conceptions. In L.H. West and L.A. Pines (eds), *Cognitive Structure and Conceptional Change*. Orlando, Fla: Academic Press.

Johnson, D.W. (1980). Group processes: Influences on student-student interaction and school outcomes. In J. McMillan (ed.), *Social Psychology of School Learning*. New York: Academic Press.

Johnson, D.W. & Johnson, R.T. (1982). Co-operation—The key to success. *Education News*, 17(10), 17–19.

Johnson, D.W. & Johnson, R.T. (1990). *Learning Together and Alone: Co-operation, Competition and Individualisation*. Englewood Cliffs, NJ: Prentice Hall.

Johnson, D., Maruyama, G., Johnson, R., Nelson, D. & Skon, L. (1981). The effects of cooperative, competitive and individualistic goal struc-tures on achievement: A meta-analysis. *Psychological Bulletin*, 89, 47–62.

Johnson Abercrombie, M. (1969). *The Anatomy of Judgment*. Harmondsworth, Middlesex: Penguin Books.

Johnston, J.M. (1972). Punishment of human behaviour. *American Psychologist*, 27, 1033–54.

Jones, J. (1990). Outcomes of girls' schooling: Unravelling some social differences. *Australian Journal of Education*, 34, 153–67.

Jones, R.M. (1968). *Fantasy and Feeling in Education*. New York: New York University Press.

Jopson, D. (1990). Why Asian kids do better at school. *The Independent Monthly*, 1(7), February. 14–15.

Joyce, B. & Showers, B. (1988). *Student Achievement through Staff Development*. New York: Longman.

Joynson, R.B. (1989). *The Burt Affair*. London: Routledge & Kegan Paul.

Jung, C.G. (1956). *The Integration of the Personality*. Routledge & Kegan Paul: London.

Kagan, D. (1988). Teaching as clinical problem solving: A critical examination of the analogy and its implications. *Review of Educational Research*, 58, 482–505.

Kagan, J. (1965). Reflection–impulsivity and read-ing ability in primary grade children. *Child Development*, 36, 609–28.

Kagan, J. (1966). Reflection and impulsivity: The generality and dynamics of conceptual tempo. *Journal of Abnormal and Social Psychology*, 71, 17–24.

Kamin, L.J. (1974). *The Science and Politics of IQ*. Potomac, Ill: Lawrence Erlbaum.

Karmel, P.H. (1973). *Schools in Australia: Report of the Interim Committee for the Australian Schools Commission*. Canberra: AGPS.

Kassin, S.M. & Wrightsman, C.S. (eds) (1985). *The Psychology of Evidence in Final Procedure*. London: Sage.

Katz, M.B. (1968). *The Irony of Early School Reform*. Cambridge, Mass: Harvard University Press.

Kaufman, A.S. & Kaufman, N.L. (1983). *Kaufman Assessment Battery for Children*. Circle Pines: American Guidance Service.

Keavney, G. & Sinclair, K.E. (1978). Teacher con-cerns and teacher anxiety: A neglected topic of classroom research. *Review of Educational Research*, 48, 273–90.

Keeves, J.P. & Bourke, G.F. (1976). *Australian Studies in School Performance*, vol.1, *Literacy and Numeracy* in *Australian Schools: A First Report*. Educational Research and Development Committee (ERDC), report No. 8, Woden, ACT.

Keeves, J.P., Matthews, J.K. & Bourke, S.F. (1978). *Educating for Literacy and Numeracy in Australian Schools* (Australian Education Review No. 11). Hawthorn, Vic: Australian Council for Educational Research.

Kelly, G.A. (1955). *The Psychology of Personal Constructs*. New York: Norton.

Khoo, C. (1990). Multicultural education: Lost directions? *Education Australia*, **8**, 14.

Killen, L. (1983). Applications of the SOLO Taxonomy in Technical and Further Education. Extended essay (unpublished). Master of Educational Studies, Faculty of Education, University of Newcastle.

King, A. (1990). Enhancing peer interaction and learning in the classroom through reciprocal questioning. *American Educational Research Journal*, **27**, 664–87.

Kinman, J. & Henderson, D. (1985). An analysis of sexism in Newbery Medal Award books from 1977 to 1984. *The Reading Teacher*, **38**, 885–9.

Kirby, J.R. (1980). Individual differences and cognitive processes. In J.R. Kirby and J.B. Biggs (eds), *Cognition, Development and Instruction*. New York: Academic Press.

Kirby, J.R. (ed.) (1984a). *Cognitive Strategies and Educational Performance*. New York: Academic Press.

Kirby, J.R. (1984b). Educational roles of cognitive plans and strategies. In J.R. Kirby (ed.), *Cognitive Strategies and Educational Performance*. New York: Academic Press.

Kirby, J.R. (1984c). Strategies and processes. In J.R. Kirby (ed.), *Cognitive Strategies and Educational Performance*. New York: Academic Press.

Kirby, J.R. (1988). Style, strategy and skill in reading. In R.R. Schmeck (ed.), *Learning Style and Learning Strategies*. New York: Plenum Press.

Kirby, J.R. (1990). Cognitive processes in summarization (final report). Social Sciences and Humanities Research Council of Canada.

Kirby, J.R. (1991). Reading to learn: Toward an applied psychology of reading comprehension. In J.B. Biggs (ed.), *Teaching for Learning: The View from Cognitive Psychology*. Hawthorn, Vic: Australian Council for Educational Research.

Kirby, J.R. & Biggs, J.B. (1981). Learning styles, information processing abilities and academic achievement (final report). Australian Research Grants Committee, Belconnen, ACT.

Kirby, J.R. & Cantwell, R.H. (1985). Use of advance organizers to facilitate higher level text comprehension. *Human Learning*, **4**, 159–65.

Kirby, J.R. & Moore, P. (1988). Metacognitive knowledge and reading ability. *Journal of Psychoeducational Assessment*, **5**, 119–37.

Kirby, J.R., Moore, P.J. & Schofield, N.J. (1988). Verbal and visual learning styles. *Contemporary Educational Psychology*, **13**, 169–84.

Kirby, J.R. & Pedwell, D. (1988). Who benefits from text absence during summarization? Paper presented to American Educational Research Association Annual Conference, San Francisco.

Kirby, J. & Williams, N. (1991). *Learning Problems: A Cognitive Approach*. Toronto: Kagan & Woo.

Kirschenbaum, H., Napier, R. & Simon, S.B. (1971). *Wad-ja-get? The Grading Game in American Education*. New York: Hart.

Klich, L. & Davidson, G. (1984). Toward a recognition of Australian Aboriginal competence in cognitive functions. In J. Kirby (ed.), *Cognitive Strategies and Educational Performance*. New York: Academic Press.

Knowles, M. (1978). *The Adult Learner: A Neglected Species*. Houston: Gulf.

Knox, A.B. (1977). *Adult Development and Learning*. San Francisco: Jersey Bass.

Kogan, N. (1971). Educational implications of cognitive styles. In G. Lesser (ed.), *Psychology and Educational Practice*. Glenview, Ill: Scott, Foresman.

Kohlberg, L. (1969). Stage and sequence: The cognitive-developmental approach to socialisation. In D. Goslin (ed.), *Handbook of Socialisation Theory and Research*. Chicago: Rand McNally.

Kohlberg, L. (1970). Stages of moral development as a basis for moral education. In C. Beck E. Sullivan (eds), *Moral Education*. Toronto: University of Toronto.

Kohlberg, L. & Turiel, E. (1971). Moral development and moral education. In G.S. Lesser (ed.), *Psychology and Educational Practice*. Glenview, Ill: Scott, Foresman.

Kolb, D.A. (1976). *Learning Style Inventory: Self-scoring Test and Interpretation Booklet*. Boston: McBer and Company.

Kounin, J. (1970). *Discipline and Group Management in Classrooms*. New York: Holt, Rinehart & Winston.

Kounin, J. & Gump, P. (1961). The comparative influence of punitive and non-punitive teachers for children's concepts of school misconduct. *Journal of Educational Psychology*, **52**, 44–9.

Kozma, R.B. (in press). The impact of computer-based tools and embedded prompts on writing processes and products of novice and advanced college writers. *Cognition and Instruction*.

Kozma, R.B. & Van Roekel, J. (1986). *Learning Tool* (Computer program). Santa Barbara, C.A: Kinko's Courseware Exchange.

Kramer, J.J., Piersel, W.G. & Glover, J.A. (1988). Cognitive and social development of mildly retarded children. In M.C. Wang, M.C. Reynolds & H.J. Walberg (eds), *Handbook of Special Education: Research and Practice, Vol. 2, Mildly Handicapped Conditions* (pp.43–58). New York: Pergamon Press.

Kratzing, M. (1990). Metalearning and the facilitation of learning. In *Proceedings, Eighth Australasian Learning and Language Conference* (pp. 170–83). Brisbane: Queensland University of Technology Counselling Services.

Kruglanski, A., Riter, A., Amitai, A., Bath-Shevah, M., Shabtai, L. & Zaksh, D. (1975). Can money enhance intrinsic motivation: A test of the content-consequence hypothesis. *Journal of Personality and Social Psychology*, **31**, 744–50.

Krywaniuk, L. (1974). Patterns of Cognitive Abilities of High and Low Achieving School Children. Unpublished Ph.D. thesis. University of Alberta, Alberta.

Kuhn, T. (1962). *The Structure of Scientific Revolutions*. Chicago: University of Chicago Press.

Kulhavy, R.W., Dyer, J.W. & Silver, C. (1975). The effects of notetaking and text expectations on the learning of text material. *Journal of Educational Psychology*, **68**, 363–65.

Kurtines, W. & Greif, E. (1974). The development of moral thought: Review and evaluation of Kohlberg's approach. *Psychological Bulletin*, **81**, 453–70.

Kurzeja, D. (1986). An intervention using cognitive modelling and verbal mediation for the induction of a problem: Solving heuristic problems in primary school children. Unpublished Master of Education dissertation. School of Education, Murdoch Univeristy.

Labov, W. (1970). The logic of non-standard English. In F. Williams (ed.), *Language and Poverty*. Chicago, Ill: Markham.

Lai, K.T.P. (1991). Effects of mastery learning on students' approaches to learning and learning outcomes in S3 Biology. Unpublished M. Ed. Dissertation, University of Hong Kong.

Langer, J. & Applebee, A. (1986). Reading and writing instruction: Toward a theory of learning and teaching. In E.Z. Rothkopf (ed.), *Review of Research in Education*, (Vol. 13, pp.171–94). Washington, DC: American Educational Research Association.

Larkin, A.I. & Keeves, J.P. (1984). *The Class Size Question: A Study at Different Levels of Analysis*. Hawthorn, Vic: Australian Council for Educational Research.

Lashley, K.S. (1960). In search of the Engram (1950). In F.A. Beach, D.O. Hebb, C.T. Morgan & N.W. Nissen (eds), *The Neuropsychology of Lashley*. New York: McGraw-Hill.

Lawrence, J. (1991). The importance of planning for education. In J.B. Biggs (ed.), *Teaching for Learning: The View from Cognitive Psychology*. Hawthorn, Vic: Australian Council for Educational Research.

Lawson, M. (1984). On being executive about metacognition. In J.R. Kirby (ed.), *Cognitive Strategies and Educational Performance*. New York: Academic Press.

Lawson, M.J. (1991). Managing problem solving. In J.B. Biggs (ed.), *Teaching for Learning: The View from Cognitive Psychology*. Hawthorn, Vic: Australian Council for Educational Research.

Leach, D.J. (1989). Teachers' perceptions of the work of psychologists in schools. *Australian Psychologist*, **24**, 357–76.

Leder, G. (1987). Teacher–student interactions: A case study. *Educational Studies in Mathematics*, **18**, 255–71.

Lee, N.Y.A. (1991). The impact of the time factor on student approaches to learning in continuing education. Unpublished M. Ed. Dissertation, University of Hong Kong.

Leinhardt, G. (1990). Capturing craft knowledge in teaching. *Educational Researcher*, **19**(2), 18–25.

Leinhardt, G. & Greeno, J. (1986). The cognitive skill of teaching. *Journal of Educational Psychology*, **78**, 75–95.

Leinhardt, G. & Putnam, R. (1987). The skill of learning from classroom lessons. *American Educational Research Journal*, **24**, 557–88.

Lepper, M. & Greene, D. (1975). Turning play into work: Effects of adult surveillance and extrinsic rewards on childen's intrinsic motivation. *Journal of Personality and Social Psychology*, **31**, 479–86.

Lepper, M., Green, D. & Nisbett, R.I. (1973). Undermining children's intrinsic interest with extrinsic reward: A test of the 'Overjustification' hypothesis. *Journal of Personality and Social Psychology*, **28**, 129–37.

Lett, W.R. (1971). Teacher games and the problems of control. In S. d'Urso (ed.), *Counterpoints: Critical Writings on Australian Education*. Sydney: Wiley.

Levinson, D., Darrow, C., Klein, E., Levinson, H. & McKee, B. (1978). *The Seasons of a Man's Life*. New York: Knopf

Liebert, R.M. & Caron, R.A. (1972). Some immediate effects of televised violence on children's behaviour. *Developmental Psychology*, **6**, 469–75.

Linn, M.C. & Hyde, J.S. (1989). Gender, mathematics and science. *Educational Researcher*, **18**(8), November, 17–27.

Linn, R.L. (ed.). (1988). *Educational Measurement*. New York: Macmillan/American Council of Education.

Lippman, L. (1977). *The Aim is Understanding: Educational Techniques for a Multicultural Society*. Sydney: Australian and New Zealand Book Company.

Lloyd, P. (1970). *Our Wide Wonderful World: Compass Series*, **1A**, 49. Australia: Thomas Nelson.

Lonka, K. & Mikkonen, V. (1989). Why does the length of an essay-type answer contribute to examination marks? *British Journal of Educational Psychology*, **59**, 220–31.

Lott, G.W. (1983). The effects of inquiry teaching and advance organizers upon student outcomes in science education. *Journal of Research in Science Teaching*, **20**, 437–52.

Lovell, K. (1961). *The Growth of Understanding in Mathematics: Kindergarten through Grade 3*. New York: Holt, Rinehart & Winston.

Lovibond, S.H., Mithiran, T. & Adams, W.G. (1979). The effects of three experimental prison environments on the behaviour of non-convict volunteer subjects. *Australian Psychologist*, **14**, 273–87.

Luria, A.R. (1966). *Human Brain and Psychological Processes*. New York: Harper & Row.

Lowenbraun, S. & Thompson, M. (1989). Environments and strategies for learning and teaching. In M.C. Wang, M.C. Reynolds & H.J. Walberg (eds), *Handbook of Special Education*, vol 3, *Low Incidence Conditions*. New York: Pergamon Press.

Lybeck, L., Marton, F., Stromdahl, H. & Tullberg, A. (1988). The phenomenography of the mole concept in chemistry. In P. Ramsden (ed.), *Improving Learning* (pp. 81–108). London: Kogan Page.

McClelland, D.C., Atkinson, J.W., Clark, R.W. & Lowell, E.L. (1953). *The Achievement Motive*. New York: Appleton-Century-Crofts.

McCutchen, D. (1985). Sources of developmental differences in children's writing: Knowledge of topic and knowledge of discourse and linguistic form. Unpublished Ph.D dissertation. University of Pittsburgh.

McCutchen, D. (1986). Domain knowledge and linguistic knowledge in the development of writing ability. *Journal of Memory and Language*, **25**, 431–44.

McDiarmid, G. & Pratt, D. (1971). *Teaching Prejudice*. Ontario Institute for Studies in Education, curriculum series No. 12, Toronto.

McDonald-Ross, R.M. (1973). Behavioural objectives: A critical review. *Instructional Science*, **2**, 1–52.

McGeoch, J.A. & Irion, A.L. (1952). *The Psychology of Human Learning*. New York: Longmans Green.

McGregor, D. (1960). *The Human Side of Enterprise*. New York: McGraw-Hill.

McInerney, D. (1987). Teacher attitudes to multicultural curriculum development. *Australian Journal of Education*, **31**, 129–44.

McKeachie, W., Pintrich, P. & Lin, Y.G. (September 1984). *Learning to learn*. Paper given to 23rd International Congress of Psychology, Acapulco, Mexico.

McKeachie, W.J., Pintrich, P., Lin, Y.G. & Smith, D. (1986). *Teaching and Learning in the College Classroom*. University of Michigan: NCRIPTAL.

MacKenzie, A. & White, R. (1982). Fieldwork in geography and long-term memory structures. *American Educational Research Journal*, **19**(4), 623–32.

McKenzie, B. (1980). Review of Vernon's intelligence: Heredity and environment. *Australian Journal of Psychology*, **32**, 155–61.

McKinney, J.D. (1988). Research on conceptually and empirically derived sub-types of specific learning disabilities. In M.C. Wang, M.C. Reynolds & H.J. Walberg (eds), *Handbook of Special Education*, vol 2, *Mildly handicapped conditions*. New York: Pergamon Press.

McLaren, J. & Hidi, S. (1988). The development of text structures in children's written expositions. Paper presented at Annual Meeting, American Educational Research Association, New Orleans, April 5.

McLean, L.D. (1990). Time to replace the classroom test with authentic measurement. *Alberta Journal of Educational Research*, **36**, 79–85.

MacMillan, D. (1982). *Mental Retardation in School and Society*. Boston: Little, Brown.

McNally, D.W. (1975). *Piaget: Education and Training*. Sydney: Hodder & Stoughton.

Maccoby, E.E. & Jacklin, C.N. (1974). *The Psychology of Sex Differences*. Stanford, Calif: Stanford University Press.

Mackay, C.K. & Cameron, M. (1968). Cognitive bias in Scottish first year science and arts undergraduates. *British Journal of Psychology*, **38**, 315–18.

Mackay, D. (1971). *Schools Council Program in Linguistics and English Teaching*. London: Longman.

Madsen, C.H. & Madsen, L.K. (1970). *Teaching/Discipline*. Boston: Allyn & Bacon.

Mager, R. (1961). *Preparing Instructional Objectives*. San Francisco: Fearon.

Maguire, T.O. (1990). Grounded authentic assessment and teacher education. Paper presented to the Second Conference on Classroom Assessment, Vancouver, BC, May 31–June 1.

Malin, M. (1990). The visibility and invisibility of Aboriginal students in an urban classroom. *Australian Journal of Education*, **34**, 312–29.

Mandaglio, S. (1984). The helping professional and teacher burnout. *The South Pacific Journal of Teacher Education*, **12**(1).

Mandler, J.M. (1984). *Stories, Scripts, and Scenes: Aspects of Schema Theory*. Hillsdale, NJ: Erlbaum.

Mandler, J. & Johnson, N. (1977). Remembrance of things parsed: Story structure and recall. *Cognitive Psychology*, **9**, 111–15.

Manzo, A.V. (1985). Expansion modules for the ReQuest, CAT, GRP and REAP reading/study procedures. *Journal of Reading*, **28**, 498–503.

Marsh, H.W. (1988). *The Self Description Questionnaire (SDQ): A Theoretical and Empirical Basis for the Measurement of Multiple Discussions of Preadolescent Self-concept: A Test Manual and Research Monograph*. San Antonio, Tx: The Psychological Corporation.

Marsh, H.W. (1989a). Effects of attending single-sex and co-educational high schools on achievement attitudes, behaviors, and sex differences. *Journal of Educational Psychology*, **81**, 70–85.

Marsh, H.W. (1989b). Sex differences in the development of verbal and mathematical constructs: The high school and beyond study. *American Educational Research Journal*, **26**, 191–225.

Marsh, H.W., Cairns, L., Relich, J., Barnes, J. & Debus, R. (1984). The relationship between dimensions of self-attribution and dimensions of self-concept. *Journal of Educational Psychology*, **76**, 3–32.

Marsh, H.W., Owens, L., Myers, M. & Smith, I. (1989). The transition from single-sex to co-educational high schools: Teacher perceptions, academic achievement and self-concept. *British Journal of Educational Psychology*, **59**, 155–73.

Marsh, H.W., Smith, I.D., Marsh, M.R. & Owens, L. (1988). The transition from single sex to co-educational high schools: Effects on multiple dimensions of self concept and on academic achievement. *American Educational Research Journal*, **25**, 237–69.

Marsh, R. (1985). Phrenoblysis: Real or chimera? *Child Developmental*, **56**, 1059–61.

Marshall, H.H. (1988). Work or learning: Implications of classroom metaphors. *Educational Researcher*, **17**(9), 9–16.

Marso, R.N. & Pigge, F.L. (1991). An analysis of teacher-made tests: Item-types, cognitive demands, and item construction errors. *Contemporary Educational Psychology*, **16**, 279–86.

Martin, E. & Ramsden, P. (1986). Learning skills or skill in learning? In J.A. Bowden (ed.), *Student Learning: Research into Practice*. University of Melbourne: Centre for the Study of Higher Education.

Marton, F. (1975). On non-verbatim learning—I: Level of processing and level of outcome. *Scandinavian Journal of Psychology*, **16**, 273–79.

Marton, F. (1981). Phenomenography—Describing conceptions of the world around us. *Instructional Science*, **10**, 177–200.

Marton, F. (1988). Describing and improving learning. In R.R. Schmeck (ed.), *Learning Strategies and Learning Styles* (pp. 53–82). New York: Plenum.

Marton, F., Hounsell, D. & Entwistle, N. (eds) (1984). *The Experience of Learning*. Edinburgh: Scottish Academic Press.

Marton, F. & Saljo, R. (1976a). On qualitative differences in learning—I: Outcome and process. *British Journal of Educational Psychology*, **46**, 4–11.

Marton, F. & Saljo, R. (1976b). On qualitative differences in learning—II: Outcome as a function of the learner's conception of the task. *British Journal of Educational Psychology*, **46**, 115–27.

Marton, F. & Saljo, R. (1984). Approaches to learning. In F. Marton, D. Hounsell and N. Entwistle (eds), *The Experience of Learning*. Edinburgh: Scottish Academic Press.

Maslach, C. (1976). Burned-out. *Human Behavior*, **5**(9), 16–22.

Mason, J.M. & Allen, J.B. (1986). A review of emergent literacy with implications for research and practice in reading. In E.Z. Rothkopf (ed.), *Review of Research in Education* (pp. 3–48). Washington, DC: American Educational Research Association.

Masters, G. (1987). New views of student learning: Implications for educational measurement. Research working paper 87.11. University of Melbourne: Centre for the Study of Higher Education.

Masters, G.N. (1988a). Anchor tests, score equating and sex bias. *Australian Journal of Education*, **32**, 25–43.

Masters, G.N. (1988b). Partial credit model. In J.P. Keeves (ed.), *Handbook of Educational Research Methodology, Measurement and Evaluation*. London: Pergamon Press.

Masters, G.N. & Hill, P.W. (1988). Reforming the assessment of student achievement in the senior secondary school. *Australian Journal of Education*, **32**, 274–86.

Meacham, M.L. & Wiesen, A.E. (1974). *Changing Classroom Behaviour*, 2nd edn. New York: International Textbook Co.

Mehrabian, A. (1970). *Tactics of Social Influence*. Prentice Hall: Englewood Cliffs, N.J.

Mehrens, W.A. & Lehmann, I.J. (1978). *Measurement and Evaluation in Education and Psychology*. New York: Holt, Rinehart & Winston.

Meichenbaum, D., Bowers, K. & Ross, R. (1969). A behavioral analysis of the teacher expectancy effect. *Journal of Personality and Social Psychology*, **13**, 306–16.

Messick, S. (1984). The psychology of educational measurement. *Journal of Educational Measurement*, **21**, 215–37.

Meyer, P. (1970). If Hitler asked you to electrocute a stranger, would you? Probably. *Esquire*, February.

Meyer, W.U., Bachmann, M., Biermann, M., Hempelmann, M., Ploger, F. & Spiller, H. (1979). The informational value of evaluative behavior: Influence of praise and blame on perception of ability. *Journal of Educational Psychology*, **71**, 259–68.

Milgram, S. (1964). Group pressure and action against a person. *Journal of Abnormal and Social Psychology*, **69**, 137–43.

Miller, G.A. (1956). The magical number seven, plus or minus two. *Psychological Review*, **63**, 81–97.

Miller, G.A., Galanter, E. & Pribram, K. (1960). *Plans and the Structure of Behaviour*. New York: Holt.

Miller, I.W. & Norman, W.H. (1979). Learned helplessness in humans: A review and attribution-theory model. *Psychological Bulletin*, **86**, 93–118.

Miller, J.S. (1979). What science teaching needs. *The Primary Journal*, **1**, 51.

Miller, L.R. (August 1985). Teacher absenteeism—What are the realities? *Australian Educational Research*, 29–41.

Molloy, G.N., Browne, A.C., Pierce, C.M.B. & King, N. (1990). Cognitive effects of aerobic exercise. *Patient Management*, **14**, 63–71.

Molloy, G.N. & Pierce, C. (1980). Do token rewards lead to token learning—A note on the use of extrinsic incentives. *Australian Behaviour Therapist*, **7**, 33–42.

Moore, P.J. (1983). Aspects of metacognitive knowledge about reading. *Journal of Research in Reading*, **6**, 87–102.

Moore, P.J. & Kirby, J. (1981). Metacognition and reading: A replication and extension of Myers and Paris in an Australian context. *Inquiry*, **4**(1), 18–29.

Moore, P.J. (1991). Reciprocal teaching of study skills. In J.B. Biggs (ed.), *Teaching for Learning: The View from Cognitive Psychology*. Hawthorn, Vic: Australian Council for Educational Research.

Morgan, M. (1984). Reward-induced decrements and increments in intrinsic motivation. *Devices of Educational Research*, **54**, 5–30.

Morris, P. (1985). Teachers' perceptions of the barriers to the implementation of a pedagogic innovation: A South East Asian case study. *International Review of Education*, **31**, 3–18.

Mosston, M. (1972). *Teaching: From Command to Discovery*. Belmont, Calif: Wadsworth.

Moulton, R.W. (1969). Effects of success and failure on level of aspiration as related to achievement motives. *Journal of Personality and Social Psychology*, **1**, 339–406.

Munn, P. & Stephenson, J. (1990). The developmental example of Aboriginal bridging education in the '80s. *HERDSA News*, **12**(2), 12–13.

Myers, M. & Paris, S. (1978). Children's metacognitive knowledge about reading. *Journal of Educational Psychology*, **70**, 680–90.

Narrett, C.M. (1984). Test review: Kaufman assessment battery for children (K-ABC). *The Reading Teacher*, **37**, 626–31.

Naylor, F. (1972). *Personality and Educational Achievement*. Sydney: Wiley Australia.

Neill, A.S. (1960). *Summerhill*. Hart: New York.

Neisser, U. (1967). *Cognitive psychology*. New York: Appleton-Century-Crofts.

Newble, D. & Clarke, R.M. (1986). The approaches to learning of students in a traditional and in an innovative problem-based medical school. *Medical Education*, **20**, 267–73.

Newkirk, T. (1987). The non-narrative writing of young children. *Research in the Teaching of English*, **21**, 121–44.

Newman, D. (1985). So you want to leave teaching. *The Australian Teacher*, **11**, 11–12.

Newman, H.H., Freeman, F.N. & Holzinger, K.J. (1937). *Twins: A Study of Heredity and Environment*. Chicago, Ill: University of Chicago Press.

New South Wales Department of Education (1983). *Multicultural Education Policy Statement*. Sydney: Government Printer.

New South Wales Department of Education (1985). *Towards Non-sexist Education Curriculum Ideas*. Sydney: Directorate of Studies.

Nickerson, R.S. (1988). An improving thinking through instruction. In E.Z. Rothkopf (ed.), *Review of Research in Education* (pp. 3–58). Washington, DC: American Educational Research Association.

Nickerson, R.S. (1989). New directions in educational assessment. *Educational Researcher*, **18**(9), 3–7.

Nix, P. (1986). Assessment and reporting practices for girls in mathematics. Melbourne: Ministry of Education (Schools Division).

Norman, D.A. (1990). *Memory and Attention*. New York: Wiley.

Novak, J.D. & Gowin, D.B. (1984). *Learning How to Learn*. Cambridge, United Kingdom: Cambridge University Press.

Nuthall, G. & Lee, A.A. (1982). *Measuring and Understanding the Way Children Learn in Class*. Technical Report: Teaching Research Project, Education Department, University of Canterbury, Christchurch, New Zealand.

Oakes, J. (1990). Opportunities, achievement, and choice: Women and minority students in Science and Mathematics. In C.B. Cazden (ed.), *Review of Research in Education* vol. 16, (pp. 153–222). Washington, DC: American Educational Research Association.

O'Connor, P. & Clarke, V. (1990). Determinants of teacher skills. *American Journal of Education*, **34**, 41–51.

Office of the Commissioner for Community Relations (1979). *Let's End the Slander*. Canberra: Union.

Ogilvie, M. & Steinbach, R. (1988). Learning across domains: The role of generalized strategies. Paper presented at Annual Meeting of American Educational Research Association, New Orleans, April 5-9.

O'Neill, A., Speilberger, C. & Hansen, D. (1969). Effects of state-anxiety and task difficulty on computer-assisted learning. *Journal of Educational Psychology*, **60**, 343–50.

O'Neill, M. & Reid, J.A. (1985). *Educational and Psychological Characteristics of Students Gifted in English*. Canberra: Commonwealth Schools Commission.

Otto, R. (1986). *Teachers Under Stress*. Melbourne: Hill of Content.

Packard, R.G. (1970). The control of 'Classroom Attention': A group contingency for complex behaviour. *Journal of Applied Behaviour*, Analysis 3, 13-28.

Paivio, A. (1986). *Mental Representations: A Dual Coding Approach*. New York: Oxford University Press.

Palincsar, A.S. & Brown, A.L. (1984). Reciprocal teaching of comprehension—Monitoring activities. *Cognition and Instruction*, **1**(2), 117–75.

Pallas, A.M. & Alexander, K.L. (1983). Sex differences in qualitative SAT performance: New evidence on the differential coursework hypothesis. *American Educational Research Journal*, **20**, 165–82.

Pallett, R. (1985). *SOLO Taxonomy in Teaching Science*. Hobart: Education Department Bulletin.

Paris, S. (1984). Improving children's metacognition and reading comprehension with classroom instruction. Paper read to Annual Conference, American Educational Research Association, New Orleans, April.

Paris, S. (1985). Teaching children to guide their reading and learning. In T.E. Raphael and L. Reynolds (eds), *Contexts of Literacy*. New York: Longman.

Paris, S.G. (1987). *Reading and Thinking Strategies*. Lexington, Mass: D.C. Heath and Company.

Paris, S. (in press). Using classroom dialogues and guided practice to teach comprehension strategies. In E. Cooke and T. Harris (eds), *Reading, Thinking and Concept Development: Tuteractive Strategies for the Classroom*. New York: The College Brand.

Paris, S., Cross, D.R. & Lipson, M. (1984). Informed strategies for learning: A program to improve children's reading awareness and comprehension. *Journal of Educational Psychology*, **76**, 1239–52.

Paris, S. & Lindauer, B. (1982). The development of cognitive skills during childhood. In B. Wolman (ed.), *Handbook of Developmental Psychology*, Englewood Cliffs, NJ: Prentice Hall.

Paris, S.G., Lipson, M.Y. & Wixson, K.K. (1983). Becoming a strategic reader. *Contemporary Educational Psychology*, **8**, 293–316.

Paris, S. & Oka, E.R. (1986). Children's reading strategies, metacognition and motivation. *Developmental Review*, **6**, 25–56.

Paris, S.G., Wixson, K. & Palincsar, A.M.S. (1986). Instructional approaches to reading comprehension. In E.Z. Rothkopf (ed.), *Review of Research in Education*, Vol. 13 (pp. 91–128). Washington, DC: American Educational Research Association.

Parliament of New South Wales (1981). *Report from the Select Committee of the Legislative Assembly upon the School Certificate* (the McGowan Report). Sydney: Government Printer.

Pauk, W. (1974). *How to Study in College*. Boston: Houghton.

Pearsall, R. (1983). *The Worm in the Bud: The World of Victorian Sexuality*. Harmondsworth, Middlesex: Penguin Books.

Pearson, P.D. & Tierney, R.J. (1984). On becoming a thoughtful reader: Learning to read like a writer. In A. Purves and O. Niles (eds), *Becoming Readers in a Complex Society* (83rd Yearbook of the National Society for the Study of Education, Part 1). Chicago: University of Chicago Press.

Penny, H.H. (March 1980). *The Training of Aborigines for Teaching in Aboriginal Schools of the Northern Territory*. Report to the Education Department of the Northern Territory, the National Aboriginal Education Committee, and the Education Research and Development Committee.

Penrose, A. (1986). Individual differences in composing effect or learning through writing. Unpublished Ph.D. Dissertation, Carnegie–Mellon University.

Penrose, A. (1988). Strategic differences in composing: Consequences for learning through writing. Paper presented AERA Annual Conference, New Orleans.

Perfetti, C.A. & Lesgold, A.M. (1977). Discourse comprehension and sources of individual differences. In M. Just & P. Carpenter (eds), *Cognitive Process in Comprehension*. Hillsdale, NJ: Lawrence Erlbaum.

Perkins, D.N. & Salomon, G. (1989). Are cognitive skills context-bound? *Educational Researcher*, **18**(1), 16–25.

Perry, W.G. (1970). *Forms of Intellectual and Ethical Development in the College Years: A Scheme*. New York: Holt, Rinehart & Winston.

Peters, W. (1971). *A Class Divided*. New York: Doubleday.

Peterson, C. (1984). *Looking Forward through the Lifespan*. Sydney: Prentice Hall of Australia.

Peterson, P.L. (1988). Teachers' and students' cognitional knowledge for classroom teaching and learning. *Educational Research*, **17**(5), 5–14.

Pezzullo, T.R., Thorsen, E. & Madaus, G. (1972). The heritability of Jensen's level 1 and level 2 and divergent thinking. *American Educational Research Journal*, **9**, 539–46.

Pflaum, S.W., Walberg, H., Karegianes, M. & Rasher, R. (1980). Reading instruction: A quantitative analysis. *Educational Researcher*, **9**(7), 12–18.

Phillips, D.C. & Nicolayev, J. (1978). Kohlbergian

moral development: A progressing or degenerating research program? *Educational Theory*, **28**, 286–301.

Phillips, S. (1979). *Young Australians: The Attitudes of Our Children*. Sydney: Harper & Row, Sydney.

Piaget, J. (1926). *The Language and Thought of the Child*. London: Routledge & Kegan Paul.

Piaget, J. (1932). *The Moral Judgment of the Child*. London: Routledge & Kegan Paul.

Piaget, J. (1950). *The Psychology of Intelligence*. London: Routledge & Kegan Paul.

Piaget, J. & Inhelder, B. (1958). *The Growth of Logical Thinking from Childhood to Adolescence*. New York: Basic Books.

Pickens, K.A. (1980). Recent research on open education. *SET: Research Information for Teachers* (special issue No. 1). Australian Council for Educational Research.

Pierce, C. & Molloy, G. (1990a). Relations between school type, occupational stress, role perceptions and social support. *Australian Journal of Education*, **34**, 330–8.

Pierce, C. & Molloy, G. (1990b). Psychological and biographical differences between secondary school teachers experiencing high and low levels of burnout. *British Journal of Educational Psychology*, **60**, 37–51.

Pines, A.L. & West, L.H.T. (1986). Conceptual understanding and science learning: An interpretation of research within a sources-of-knowledge framework. *Science Education*, **70**, 583–604.

Pines, M. (1979). Good samaritans at age two. *Psychology Today*, **13**(1), 66–77.

Pines, M., Aronsen, E.A. & Kafry, D. (1981). *Burnout—From Tedium to Personal Growth*. New York: Free Press.

Pink, W. (1988). School climate and effective school programmes in America. In R. Slee (ed.), *Discipline and Schools: A Curriculum Perspective*, (pp. 199–224). South Melbourne: Macmillan.

Pintrich, P. & DeGroot, E. (1990). Motivational and self-regulated learning components of classroom academic performance. *Journal of Educational Psychology*, **82**, 33–40.

Piolat, A. (1991). Effects of word processing on text revision. *Language in Education*, **5**, 255–72.

Polya, G. (1945). *How to solve it*. Princeton, NJ: Princeton University Press.

Poole, M.E. (1971). Social class differences in code elaboration: A study of oral communication at the tertiary level. *Australian Journal of Education*, **15**, 152–60.

Poole, M.E., de Lacey, P.R. & Randhawa, B.S. (1985). *Australia in Transition*. Sydney: Harcourt Brace Jovanovich.

Popham, W.J. (1975). *Educational Evaluation*. Englewood Cliffs, NJ: Prentice Hall.

Popham, W.J. & Husek, T.R. (1969). Implications of criterion-referenced measurement. *Journal of Educational Measurement*, **6**, 1–9.

Porter, A. (1989). A curriculum out of balance: The case of elementary school mathematics. *Educational Researcher*, **18**(5), 9–15.

Power, C. (1986). Criterion-based assessment, grading and reporting at Year 12 level. *Australian Journal of Education*, **30**, 266–84.

Pramling, I. (1983). *The Child's Conception of Learning*. Gothenburg: Acta Universitatis Gothoburgensis.

Premack, D. (1959). Toward empirical behaviour laws: I. Positive reinforcement. *Psychological Review*, **66**, 219–33.

Pribram, K.H. (1969). The amnestic syndromes: Disturbances in coding? In G. Talland and N. Waugh (eds), *The Pathology of Memory*. New York: Academic Press.

Purkey, W.W. (1970). *Self-concept and School Achievement*. Englewood Cliffs, NJ: Prentice Hall.

Quay, H.C. (1979). Classification. In H.C. Quay & J.S. Werny (eds), *Psychopathological Disorders of Childhood* (2nd edn). New York: Wiley.

Quigley, S.P. & Paul, P.V. (1989). English language development. In M.C. Wang, M.C. Reynolds & H.J. Walberg (eds), *Handbook of Special Education*, vol 3, *Low Incidence Conditions*. New York: Pergamon Press.

Ramsden, P. (1984). The context of learning. In F. Marton, D. Homsell & N. Entwistle (eds), *The Experience of Learning*. Edinburgh: Scottish Universities Press.

Ramsden, P. (1985). Student learning research: Retrospect and prospect. *Higher Education Research and Development*, **5**(1), 51–70.

Ramsden, P. (1987). Improving teaching and learning in higher education: The case for a relational perspective. *Studies in Higher Education*, **12**, 275–86.

Ramsden, P. (ed.) (1988). *Improving Learning: New Perspectives*. London: Kogan Page.

Ramsden, P., Beswick, D. & Bowden, J. (1986).

Effects of learning skills interventions on first year university students' learning. *Human Learning*, **5**, 151–64.

Ramsden, P. & Dodds, A. (1989). *Improving Teaching and Courses: A Guide to Evaluation.* University of Melbourne: Centre for the Study of Higher Education.

Ramsden, P., Whelan, G. & Cooper, D. (1989). Some phenomena of medical students' diagnostic problem solving. *Medical Education*, **23**, 108–17.

Raphael, T. & Kirschner, B. (1985). The effects of instruction in compare/contrast text structure on sixth grade students' reading comprehension and writing productions. Paper, AERA, Chicago.

Raucher, H. (1970). *Watermelon Man*. New York: Ace.

Raudenbush, S.W. & Bryk, A.S. (1988-89). Methodological advances in analyzing the effects of schools and classrooms on student learning. In E.Z. Rothkopf (ed.), *Review of Research in Education* (Vol.15), (pp. 423–76). Washington, DC: American Educational Research Association.

Reavis, G.H. (1968). The animal school. In E.C. Short & G.D. Marconnit (eds), *Contemporary Thought on Public School Curriculum.* Dubuque, Iowa: Borwn.

Reid, W.A. (1987). Institutions and practices: Professional education reports and the language of reform. *Educational Researcher*, **16**(8), 10–15.

Renzulli, J.S. (November 1978). What makes giftedness? Re-examining a definition. *Phi Delta Kappan*, **60**, 180–84.

Renzulli, J.S. (1986). The three-ring conception of giftedness: A developmental model for creative productivity. In R.J. Sternberg & J.E. Davidson (eds), *Conceptions of Giftedness.* New York: Cambridge University Press.

Resnick, L.B. (1987). Learning in school and out. *Educational Researcher*, **16**(9), 13–20.

Resnick, L., Bill, V. & Lesgold, S. (1992). Developing thinking abilities in arithmetic class. In A. Demetriou, M. Shayer & A. Efklides (eds), *The Neo-Piagetian Theories of Cognitive Development Go to School.* London: Routledge and Kegan Paul.

Rest, J. (1974). Developmental psychology as a guide to value education: A review of 'Kohlbergian' programs. *Review of Educational Research*, **44**, 214–59.

Rest, J., Turiel, E. & Kohlberg, L. (1969). Relations between level of moral judgment and preference, and comprehension of the moral judgment of othes. *Journal of Personality*, **37**, 225–52.

Reynolds, M.C. (1976). New alternatives through a new cascade. Paper presented at the Sixth Invitational Conference on Leadership in Special Education.

Rickards, J.P. & August, G.J. (1975). Generative underlining strategies in prose recall. *Journal of Educational Psychology*, **67**, 860–65.

Rikys, P. (1990). Multicultural educational issues and biculturalism in Aotearoa (New Zealand) and Australia. *HERDSA News*, **12**(2), 5–7.

Rinehart, S., Stahl, S. & Erickson, L. (1986). Some effects of summarization training on reading and studying. *Reading Research Quarterly*, **21**, 422–37.

Robinson, E. (1983). Metacognitive development. In S. Meadows (ed.), *Developing Thinking Approaches to Children's Cognitive Development.* London: Methuen.

Robinson, F.P. (1946). *Effective Study.* New York: Harper & Row.

Robinson, G.W. & Kirby, J.R. (1987). Information integration in reading. *Australian Journal of Reading*, **10**, 32–44.

Rogers, C.R. (1951). *Client-centred Therapy.* Boston, Mass: Houghton Mifflin.

Rogers, C.R. (1969). *Freedom to Learn.* Columbia, Ohio: Merrill.

Rogers, C.R. (1983). *Freedom to Learn in the 80s.* Columbia: Charles E. Merrill.

Rose, M. (1984). *Writer's Block: The Cognitive Dimension.* Carbondale, Ill: Universities Press.

Rosenbaum, J.E. (1976). Making inequality: The hidden curriculum of high school tracking. *Review of Research in Education.* New York: Wiley.

Rosenbaum, J.E. (1980). Social implications of educational grouping. *Review of Research in Education*, **8**, 361–401.

Rosenthal, R. (1971). Teacher expectations and their effects upon children. In G. Lesser (ed.), *Psychology and Educational Practice.* Glenview, Ill: Scott, Foresman.

Rosenthal, R. & Jacobson, L. (1968). *Pygmalion in the Classroom.* New York: Holt, Rinehart & Winston.

Roth, K. & Anderson, C. (1988). Promoting conceptual change learning from science textbooks. In P. Ramsden (ed.), *Improving Learning: New Perspectives.* London: Kogan Page.

Rotter, J.B. (1966). Generalised expectancies for internal versus external control of reinforcement. *Psychological Monograph*, **80**.

Roussey, J.Y., Piolat, A. & Guercin, F. (1990). Revising strategies for different text types. *Language and Education, 4*, 51–66.

Rowe, K.J. (1988). Single-sex and mixed-sex classes: The effects of class type on student achievement, confidence and participation in mathematics. *Australian Journal of Education*, **32**, 180–202.

Rushton, J. & Littlefield, C. (1979). The effects of age, amount of modelling and a success experience on seven-to-eleven-year-old children's generosity. *Journal of Moral Education*, **9**, 55–6.

Russell, T. & Johnson, P. (1988). Teachers learning from experiences of teaching: Analyses based on metaphor and reflection. Paper presented to Annual Conference, American Educational Research Association, New Orleans, April 5-9.

Ryba, A.K. & Chapman, J.W. (August 1983). Toward improving learning strategies and personal adjustment with computers. *The Computing Teacher* (pp. 48–53).

Ryle, G. (1949). *The Concept of Mind.* London: Hutchinson.

Sabers, D., Cushing, K. & Berliner, D. (1991). Differences among teachers in a task characterised by simultaneity, multidimensionality and immediacy. *American Educational Research Journal*, **28**, 63–88.

Salgado, G. (1980). The novelist at work. In M. Seymour-Smith (ed.), *Novels and Novelists.* New York: St Martin's Press.

Samuelowicz, K. (1987). Learning problems of overseas students: Two sides of a story. *Higher Education Research and Development*, **6**, 121–34.

Sarason, S.B. (1971). *The Culture of the School and the Problem of Change.* Boston: Allyn & Bacon.

Sarason, S.B. et al. (1960). *Anxiety in Elementary School Children.* New York: Wiley.

Sarros, A. & Sarros, J. (1990). How burned out are teachers? A cross-cultural study. *Australian Journal of Education*, **34**, 145–52.

Sarros, J. & Densten, I. (1989). Undergraduate student stress and coping strategies. *Higher Education Research and Development*, **9**, 47–5.

Satterly, D. (1981). *Assessment in Schools.* Oxford: Basil Blackwell.

Scardamalia, M. (1980). How childen cope with the cognitive demands of writing. In C.H. Frederiksen, M.R. Whiteman & J.P. Dominic (eds), *Writing: The Nature, Development and Teaching of Written Communication.* Hillsdale, NJ: Lawrence Erlbaum.

Scardamalia, M. & Bereiter, C. (1982). Assimilative processes in composition planning. *Educational Psychologist*, **17**, 165–71.

Schaie, K.W. (1979). The primary mental abilities in adulthood: An exploration in the development of psychometric intelligence. In B. Baltes & O. Brim (eds), *Life Span Development and Behaviour.* New York: Academic Press.

Schatzman, O.L. & Strauss, A. (1955). Social class and modes of communication. *American Journal of Sociology, 60*, 329–38.

Schiefele, U. (1991). Interest, learning, and motivation. *Educational Psychologist*, **26**, 299–323.

Schlaefli, A., Rest, J. & Thoma, S. (1985). Does moral education improve moral judgment? A meta-analysis of intervention studies using the defining issues test. *Review of Educational Research*, **55**, 319–52.

Schofield, M. & Kafer, N. (1985). Children's understanding of friendship issues: Developmental by stage or sequence? *Journal of Social and Personal Relationships*, **2**, 151–65.

Scribner, S. (1986). Thinking in action: Some characteristics of practical thought. In R.J. Sternberg & R.K. Wagner (eds), *Practical Intelligence.* Cambridge: Cambridge University Press.

Scriven, M. (1967). The methodology of evaluation. In R. Tyler, R. Gagne & M. Scriven (eds), *Perspectives of Curriculum Evaluation.* Chicago, Ill: Rand McNally.

Scruggs, T. & Mastropieri, M. (1989). Reconstructive elaboration: A model for content area learning. *American Education Research Journal*, **26**, 311–27.

Seligman, M.E.P. (1970). On the generality of the laws of learning. *Psychological Review*, **77**, 406–18.

Seligman, M.E.P. (1975). *Helplessness: On Depression, Development and Death.* San Francisco: W.H. Freeman.

Selye, H. (1974). *Stress without Distress.* Philadelphia: Lippincott.

Shaughnessy, M.F. (1990). Cognitive structures of the gifted: theoretical perspectives, factor analysis, triarchic theories of intelligence, and insight issues. *Gifted Education International*, **6**, 149–51.

Shavelson, R. & Stern, P. (1981). Research on teachers pedagogical thoughts, judgments, divisions and behaviour. *Review of Educational Research*, **51**(4), 455–98.

Shayer, M. & Adey, P. (1981). *Towards a Science of Science Teaching*. London: Heinemark Educational.

Shepard, L.A. (1991). Psychometricians' beliefs about learning. *Educational Researcher*, **20** (6), 2–16.

Shuell, T.J. (1986). Cognitive conceptions of learning. *Review of Educational Research*, **56**, 411–36.

Shuell, T.J. (1988). Teaching and learning as problem solving. Paper presented in *Metaphors of Classroom Research*, symposium at the Meeting of the American Educational Research Association, New Orleans, April.

Shuell, T.J. (1990). Phases of meaningful learning. *Review of Educational Research*, **60**, 531–47.

Shulman, L. (1986). Those who understand: Knowledge growth in teaching. *Educational Researcher*, **15**(2), 4–21.

Shuy, R. (1973). The language that the child brings with him to school. In *The teaching of English*. Proceedings of the National Seminar on the Teaching of English, AGPS, Sydney.

Siegler, R. S. (1986). Unities across domains in children's strategy choices. In M. Perlmutter (ed.), *Perspectives on Intellectual Development: The Minnesota Symposia on Child Psychology* (Vol 19). Hillsdale, NJ: Lawrence Erlbaum.

Silberman, C.E. (1970). *Crisis in the Classroom*. New York: Random House.

Silberman, M.L. (ed.) (1971). *The Experience of Schooling*. New York: Holt, Rinehart & Winston.

Skinner, B.F. (1965). *Science and Human Behaviour*. New York: Free Press.

Skinner, B.F. (1968). *The Technology of Teaching*. New York: Appleton-Century-Crofts.

Slavin, R. (1983). *Cooperative Learning*. New York: Longman.

Slavin, R.E. (1987a). Ability grouping and student achievement in elementary schools: A best-evidence synthesis. *Review of Educational Research*, **57**, 293–336.

Slavin, R.E. (1987b). Mastery learning reconsidered. *Review of Educational Research*, **57**, 175–213.

Slee, R. (ed.) (1988). *Discipline and Schools: A Curriculum Perspective*. South Melbourne: Macmillan.

Smith, F. (1971). *Understanding Reading*. New York: Holt, Rinehart & Winston.

Smith, F. (1982). *Writing and the Writer*. New York: Holt, Rinehart & Winston.

Snow, R.E. (1976). Research on aptitude for learning: A progress report. In L.S. Shulman (ed.), *Review of Educational Research*, **4**. Itasca, Ill: Peacock.

Snow, R.E. (1977). What do we know about ATI? What should we learn? In L. Cronbach and R.E. Snow (eds), *Aptitude–treatment Interaction*. New York: Wiley.

Snow, R.E. (1989). Toward assessment of cognitive and conative structures in learning. *Educational Researcher*, **18**(9), 8–14.

Snow, R.E. (1990). New approaches to cognitive and conative assessment in education. *International Journal of Education Research*, **14**, 455–74.

Snowman, J. (1984). Learning tactics and strategies. In G.D. Phye & T. Andre (eds), *Cognitive Instructional Psychology: Components of Classroom Learning*. New York: Academic Press.

Snyder, B.R. (1971). *The Hidden Curriculum*. New York: Knopf.

Solomon, J. (1984). The social construction of children's knowledge and the epistemology of Jean Piaget. Paper presented to British Educational Research Association, University of Lancaster.

Solomon, J. (1985). Children's explanations. Paper read to American Educational Research Association Annual Conference, Chicago, Ill.

Spalding, I. (1974). Race bias in social studies. *The Aboriginal Child at School*, **2**(1), 20–30.

Sparkes, R. et al. (1970). *Australia's Heritage*. Brisbane: Jacaranda.

Spearman, C. (1927). *The Abilities of Man*. New York: Macmillan.

Spearrit, D. (ed.) (1982). *The Improvement of Measurement in Education and Psychology*. Hawthorn, Vic: The Australian Council for Educational Research.

Spinks, J., Chan, C., Lai, J. & Jones, B. (1990). Examination anxiety in Hong Kong students: Gender and psychological influences on longitudinal changes in salivary immunoglobulin A. Paper presented at the 30th Annual Meeting, Society for Psychophysiological Research, Boston.

Spivey, N. & King, J.R. (1989). Readers as writers composing from sources. *Reading Research Quarterly*, **24**, 7–26.

Starch, D. & Elliott, E.C. (1912). Reliability of the grading of high school work in English. *School Review*, **20**, 442–57.

Starch, D. (1913a). Reliability of grading work in Mathematics. *School Review*, **21**, 254–59.

Starch, D. (1913b). Reliability of grading work in history. *School Review*, **21**, 676–81.

Stein, N. (1986). Knowledge and process in the acquisition of writing skills. In E.Z. Rothkopf (ed.), *Review of Research in Education*, Vol. 13 (pp. 225–58). Washington, DC: American Educational Research Association.

Steinberg, E.R. (1984). *Teaching Computers to Teach*. Hillsdale, NJ: Lawrence Erlbaum.

Steinkamp, M. & Maehr, M. (1984). Gender differences in motivational eventuations towards achievement in school science: A quantitative synthesis. *American Educational Research Journal*, **21**, 39–59.

Stelzer, E. (1975). Writing about writing. *Language in Education*, **1**, Tasmanian Department of Education, 37–42.

Sternberg, R.J. (1980). Towards a unified componential theory of human intelligence. In M. Friedman, J.P. Das & N. O'Connor (eds), *Intelligence and Learning*. New York: Plenum.

Sternberg, R.J. (1985). *Beyond IQ*. New York: Cambridge University Press.

Sternberg, R.J. (ed.) (1988). *Handbook of Human Intelligence*. New York: Cambridge University Press.

Sternberg, R.J. (1991). Theory-based testing of intellectual abilities: Rationale for the triarchic abilities test. In H. Rowe (ed.), *Intelligence: Reconceptualization and measurement* (pp. 183–202). Hawthorn:ACER/Hillsdale: Lawrence Erlbaum.

Sternberg, R.J. & Rifkin, B. (1979). The development of analogical reasoning processes. *Journal of Experimental Child Psychology*, **27**, 195–232.

Sternberg, R.J. & Wagner, R. (eds) (1986). *Practical Intelligence*. Cambridge: Cambridge University Press.

Sternberg, R.J. & Weil, E.M. (1980). An aptitude-strategy interaction in linear syllogistic reasons. *Journal of Educational Psychology*, **72**, 226–34.

Stevens, R. (1988). Effects of strategy training on the identification of the main idea of expository passages. *Journal of Educational Psychology*, **80**, 21–6.

Stevenson, H., Lee, S.Y. & Stigler, J. (1986). Mathematics achievement of Chinese, Japanese, and American children. *Science*, **231**, 693–9.

Stipek, D. (1986). Children's motivation to learning. In T. Tomlinson & H. Walberg (eds), *Academic Work and Educational Excellence*. Berkeley, Cal.: McCutchan.

Stokes, M.J., Balla, J.R. & Stafford, K.J. (1989). How students in selected degree programmes at CPHK characterise their approaches to study. *Educational Research Journal*, **4**, 85–91.

Strauss, S. (ed.) (1988). *Ontogeny, Phylogeny, and Historical Development*. New York: Ablex.

Strunk, W. & White, E.B. (1972). *The Elements of Style*. New York: Macmillan.

Suchman, J.R. (1961). Inquiry training: Building skills for autonomous discovery. *Merrill-Palmer Quarterly Behaviour Development*, **7**, 148–69.

Suppes, P. (1974). The place of theory in educational research. *Educational Researcher*, **3**(6), 3–10.

Swanson, H.L., O'Connor, J. & Cooney, J. (1990). An information processing analysis of expert and novice teachers' problem solving. *American Educational Research Journal*, **27**, 533–56.

Sweller, J. (1991). Some modern myths of cognition and instruction. In J.B. Biggs (ed.), *Teaching for Learning: The View from Cognitive Psychology*. Hawthorn, Vic: Australian Council for Educational Research.

Sweller, J., Mawer, R. & Howe, W. (1982). Consequences of history-cued and means–end strategies in problem solving. *American Journal of Psychology*, **95**, 455–83.

Sylvester, R. (1983). The school as a stress reduction agency. *Theory into Practice*, **22**(1), 3–6.

Tabberer, R. (1984). Introducing study skills at 16–19. *Educational Research*, **26**, 1–6.

Tang, D.K.T. (1991). Restructuring the concepts of force and motion. Unpublished M. Ed. Dissertation, University of Hong Kong.

Tang, K.C.C. (1991). *Effects of Different Assessment Methods on Tertiary Students' Approaches to Studying*. University of Hong Kong: Ph.D. Dissertation.

Tavener, J. & Glynn, T. (1989). Peer tutoring as a context for children learning English as a second language. *Language and Education*, **3**, 45–56.

Taylor, B.M. & Beach, R.W. (1984). The effects of text structure on middle-grade students' comprehension and production of expository text. *Reading Research Quarterly*, **16**, 72–103.

Taylor, E. (1984). Orientation to Study: A Longitudinal Investigation. Unpublished Ph.D dissertation, University of Surrey.

Taylor, J.C. (1991). Designing instruction to generate expert cognitive skill performance: empirical evidence. In G.T. Evans (ed.), *Learning and Teaching Cognitive Skills*, (pp. 164–84). Hawthorn, Vic: Australian Council for Educational Research.

Telfer, R. (1979a). A teaching problem questionnaire. *The Forum of Education*, **38**(1), 27–32.

Telfer, R. (1979b). The use of behavioural objectives in flight instruction. Paper presented to the Flight Instructor Examiners' Conference, Department of Transport, Melbourne.

Telfer, R. (1981). Analysing parochial teaching problems: A nomothetic approach. *Journal of Teacher Education*, **32**(1), 39–45.

Telfer, R. (1982). Teaching problems of beginning teachers. *The Forum of Education*, **40**(1), 23–6.

Telfer, R. (1985). *Program Equity and Participation: A Report of an Evaluation Study of Gorokan High School*. Research Report, Department of Education, University of Newcastle.

Telfer, R. & Rees, J. (1975). *Teacher Tactics*. Sydney: Symes.

Terman, L.M. (1925). *Genetic Studies of Genius*, vol 1, *Mental and Physical Traits of a Thousand Gifted Children*. Stanford, Ca.: Stanford University Press.

Terman, L.M. (1954). The discovery and encouragement of exceptional talent. *American Psychologist*, **9**, 221–30.

Thomas, A. (1979). Learned helplessness and expectancy factors: Implications for research in learning disabilities. *Review of Educational Research*, **49**, 208–21.

Thomas, D.B. & McLaikn, D.H. (1983). Selecting microcomputers for the classroom: A rethinking after four years. *AEDS Journal*, **17**(1 and 2), 9–22.

Thomas, D.R., Becker, W.C. & Armstrong, M. (1968). Production and elimination of disruptive classroom behaviour by systematically varying teacher's behaviour. *Journal of Applied Behaviour Analysis*, **1**, 35–45.

Thomas, E.L. & Robinson, H.A. (1982). *Improving Reading in Every Class: A Source Book for Teachers*. Boston: Allyn & Bacon.

Thomas, P.R. & Bain, J.D. (1984). Contextual dependence of learning approaches: The effects of assessments. *Human Learning*, **3**, 227–40.

Thorndike, R.L. (1968). Review of Pygmalion in the classroom. *Educational Research Journal*, **5**, 709–11.

Thorndike, R.L. (ed.) (1971). *Educational Measurement*. Washington, DC: American Council on Education.

Thurstone, L.L. (1938). Primary mental abilities. *Psychometric Monographs*, No. 1. Chicago, Ill: University of Chicago Press.

Tibbetts, S.L. (November 1978). Wanted: Data to prove that sexist reading material has an impact on the reader. *The Reading Teacher*, **32**(2), 165–69.

Tierney, R.J., Readence, J.E. & Dishner, E.K. (1990). *Reading Strategies and Practices*. Boston: Allyn & Bacon.

Tobin, K. (1987). The role of wait time. *Review of Educational Research*, **57**, 69–95.

Tobin, K. & Fraser, B.J. (1988). Investigations of exemplary practice in high school science and mathematics. *Australian Journal of Education*, **32**, 75–94.

Tomporowski, P.D. & Ellis, N.R. (1986). Effects of exercise on cognitive processes: A review. *Psychological Bulletin*, **99**, 338–46.

Torrance, E.P. (1960). *Educational Achievement of the Highly Intelligent and the Highly Creative: Eight Partial Replications of the Getzels–Jackson study*. Bureau of Educational Research, University of Minnesota, Minneapolis.

Torrance, E.P. (1961). Primary creative thinking in the primary grades. *Elementary School Journal*, **62**, 34–41.

Torrance, E.P. (1963). *Education and the creative potential*. Minneapolis: University of Minnesota Press.

Torrance, E.P. (1965). *Guiding Creative Talent*. Englewood Cliffs, NJ: Prentice Hall.

Torrance, E.P. & Myers, R.E. (1970). *Creative Learning and Teaching*. New York: Harper & Row.

Tough, A. (1971). *The Adult's Learning Projects*. Toronto: Ontario Institute for Studies in Education.

Townsend, M., Lee, Y.K. & Tuck, B. (1989). The effect of mood on the reliability of essay assessment. *British Journal of Educational Psychology*, **59**, 232–40.

Trigwell, K. & Prosser, M. (1991). Relating approaches to study and quality of learning outcomes at the course level. *British Journal of Educational Psychology*, **61**, 265–75.

Tulving, E. (1985). How many memory systems are there? *American Psychologist*, **40**, 385–98.

Turbill, J. (ed.) (1982). *No Better Way to Teach Writing*. Rozelle, NSW: Primary English Teaching Association.

Turiel, E. (1966). An experimental test of the sequentiality of developmental stages in the child's moral judgments. *Journal of Personality and Social Psychology*, **3**, 611–18.

Turney, C. & Cairns, L.G. (1976). *Sydney Micro Skills: Series 3 Classroom Management and Discipline*. Sydney: Sydney University Press.

Turney, C., Eltis, K.J., Hatton, N., Owens, L.C., Towler, J. & Wright, R. (1983). *Sydney Microskills Redeveloped, Series 1 Handbook, Reinforcement Basic Questioning, Variability*. Sydney: Sydney University Press.

Turney, C. & Ryan, C. (1978). *Inner-city Teaching: Awareness and Simulation Materials*. Sydney: Sydney University Press.

Tyler, L.E. (1978). *Individuality*. San Francisco, Calif: Jossey-Bass.

Valsiner, J. (1992). Social organization of cognitive development. In A. Demetriou, M. Shayer & A. Efklides (eds), *The Neo-Piagetian Theories of Cognitive Development Go to School*. London: Routledge and Kegan Paul.

van Kraayenoord, C. & Elkins, J. (1990). Learning difficulties. In A. Ashman & J. Elkins (eds), *Educating Children with Special Needs*. Sydney: Prentice Hall.

Van Rossum, E.J. & Schenk, S.M. (1984). The relationship between learning conception, study strategy and learning outcome. *British Journal of Educational Psychology*, **54**, 73–83.

Vaughan, W.J.A. (1973). *Aims and Objectives of Secondary Education in NSW.* Sydney: Directorate of Studies, NSW Department of Education.

Veenman, S. (1984). Perceived problems of beginning teachers. *Review of Educational Research*, **54**(2), 143–78.

Vernon, P.E. (1950). *The Structure of Human Abilities*. London: Methuen.

Vernon, P.E. (1969). *Intelligence and Cultural Environment*. London: Methuen.

Vernon, P.E. (1979). *Intelligence: Heredity and Environment*. San Francisco, Calif: W.H. Freeman.

Victorian Education Gazette, 13 February 1980.

Viennot, L. (1979). Spontaneous reasoning in elementary dynamics. *European Journal of Science Education*, **1**, 205–21.

Viney, L. (1980). *Transitions*. Melbourne: Cassell.

Vivian, W. (1984). The twang factor. *Education News*, 36–9.

Volet, S. (1991). Modelling and coaching of relevant metacognitive strategies for enhancing university students' learning. *Learning and Instruction*, **1**, 319-36.

Volet, S., Lawrence, J.A. & Dodds, A.E. (1986). Adolescents' organizational strategies for planning errands. In C. Pratt, A. Garton, W.E. Tunmer & A.R. Nesdaile (eds), *Research in Child Development*. Sydney: Allen & Unwin.

Von Bertalanffy, L. (1968). *General Systems Theory*. New York: Braziller.

Vosniadou, S. & Brewer, W.F. (1987). Theories of knowledge restructuring in development. *Review of Educational Research*, **57**, 51–67.

Vygotsky, L.S. (1962). *Thought and Language*. New York: Wiley.

Vygotsky, L.S. (1978/1934). *Mind and Society*. Cambridge, Mass: Harvard University Press.

Wagner, R.K. & Sternberg, R.J. (1984). Alternative conceptions of intelligence and their implications for education. *Review of Educational Research*, **54**, 179–223.

Wall, M. (1989). The effects of exertion on the mental performance of fit, medium fit and unfit primary school children. Unpublished dissertation, Master of Psychology (Educational), University of Newcastle.

Wallace, I., Wallechinsky, D. & Wallace, A. (1984). *The Book of Lists—3*. London: Corgi Books.

Wallace, J.D. & Mintzes, J. (1990). The concept map as a research tool: Exploring conceptual change in biology. *Journal of Research in Science Teaching*, **27**, 1033–52.

Wallach, M. & Wing, C. (1969). *The Talented Student*. New York: Holt, Rinehart & Winston.

Wang, M.C. (1983). Development and consequences of students' sense of personal control. In J.M. Levine and M.C. Wang (eds), *Teacher and Student Perceptions: Implications for Learning* (pp. 213–47). Hillsdale, NJ: Erlbaum.

Warren, D.H. (1989). Implications of visual impairments for child development. In M.C. Wang, M.C. Reynolds & H.J. Walberg (eds), *Handbook of Special Education, vol 3, Low Incidence Conditions*. New York: Pergamon Press.

Watkins, D.A. (1983a). Assessing tertiary students' study processes. *Human Learning*, **2**, 29–37.

Watkins, D.A. (1983b). Depth of processing and the quality of learning outcomes. *Instructional Science*, **12**, 49–58.

Watkins, D.A. & Hattie, J. (1981). The learning processes of Australian University students: Investigations of contextual and physiological factors. *British Journal of Educational Psychology*, **51**, 384–93.

Watkins, D.A. & Hattie, J. (1985). A longitudinal study of the approach to learning of Australian tertiary students. *Human Learning*, **4**(2), 127–42.

Watkins, D.A. & Hattie, J. (1990). Individual and contextual differences in the approaches to learning of Australian secondary school students. *Educational Psychology*, **10**, 333–42.

Watson, H.J., Vallee, J.M. & Mulford, W.R. (1981). *Structured Experiences and Group Development*. Canberra: Curriculum Development Centre.

Watson, J.B. (1924). *Behaviourism*. New York: People's Institute.

Watt, D. (1984). Tools for writing. *Popular Computing*, **78**, 75–6.

Watts, D. & Zylbersztajn, A. (1981). A survey of some children's ideas about force. *Physics Education*, **16**, 360–65.

Watts, M.D. (1983). A study of school children's alternative frameworks of the concept of force. *European Journal of Science Education*, **5**, 217–30.

Watts, M.D. & Bentley, D. (1984). The personal parawriting of cognition: Two personal aims in science education. *Oxford Review of Education*, **10**(3), 309–17.

Watts, M.D. & Gilbert, J. (1983). Enigmas in school science students' conceptions for scientifically associated words. *Research in Science and Technological Education*, **1**, 161–71.

Wax, R. (1971). *Doing Fieldwork*. Chicago, Ill: University of Chicago Press.

Wechsler, D. (1949). *Wechsler Intelligence Scale for Children: Manual*. New York: Psychological Corporation.

Wechsler, D. (1955). *Wechsler Adult Intelligence Scale Manual*. New York: Psychological Corporation.

Weiner, B. (1967). Implications of the current theory of achievement motivation for research and performance in the classroom. *Psychology in the Schools*, **4**, 164–71.

Weiner, B. (1972). Attribution theory, achievement motivation and the educational process.

Review of Educational Research, **42**, 203–15.

Weiner, B. (1986). *An Attributional Theory of Motivation and Emotion*. New York: Springer-Verlag.

Weinstein, C. & Mayer, R. (1984). The teaching of learning strategies. In M.C. Wittrock (ed.), *Handbook of Research on Teaching*. New York: Macmillan.

Welker, R. (1991). Expertise and the teacher as expert: Rethinking a questionable metaphor. *American Educational Research Journal*, **28**, 19–35.

West, C.K., Farmer, J.A. & Wolff, P.M. (1991). *Instructional Design: Implications from Cognitive Science*. Englewood Cliffs, NJ: Prentice Hall.

White, R.T. (1984). Understanding and its measurement. Paper read to Australian Educational Research Association Annual Conference, Perth.

White, R.T. (1988). *Learning Science*. Oxford: Basil Blackwell.

White, R.T. & Baird, J. (1991). Learning to think and thinking to learn. In J.B. Biggs (ed.), *Teaching for Learning: The View from Cognitive Psychology*. Hawthorn, Vic: Australian Council for Educational Research.

White, R.T. & Tisher, R. (1983). Research on natural science. In M. Wittrock (ed.), 3rd Handbook of research on teaching. Chicago: Rand McNally.

White, R.W. (1959). Motivation reconsidered: The concept of competence. *Psychological Review*, **66**, 297–333.

Wiggins, G. (1989). Teaching to the (authentic) test. *Educational Leadership*, **46**, 41–7.

Williams, P. (1991). *The Special Education Handbook*. Milton Keynes: The Open University Press.

Williams, T. & Carpenter, P. (1990). Private schooling and public achievement. *Australian Journal of Education*, **34**, 3–24.

Willms, J.D. & Jacobsen, S. (1990). Growth in mathematics skills during the intermediate years: Sex differences and school effects. *International Journal of Educational Research*, **14**, 157–74.

Wilson, G. (1979). The sociobiology of sex differences. *Bulletin of the British Society*, **32**, 350–53.

Wilson, J. (1979). Moral education: Retrospect and prospect. *Journal of Moral Education*, **9**, 3–9.

Wilson, J. (1981). *Student Learning in Higher Education*. London: Croom Helm.

Winkler, R.L. (1976). New directions for

behaviour modification in homosexuality, open education and behavioural economics. In P.W. Sheehan & K.D. White (eds), *Behaviour Modification in Australia* (Monograph supplement No. 5), *Australian Psychologist*, **11**.

Winograd, P.N. (1984). Strategic difficulties in summarizing texts. *Reading Research Quarterly*, **19**, 404–25.

Winter, S.J. (1987). Parents and pupils as remedial tutors. *Bulletin of the Hong Kong Psychological Society*, **18**, 15–31.

Witkin, H., Moore, C.A., Goodenough, D.R. & Cox, P.W. (1977). Field-dependent and field-independent cognitive styles and their educational implications. *Review of Educational Research*, **47**, 1–64.

Wittrock, M.C. (1977). The generative processes of memory. In M.C. Wittrock (ed.), *The Human Brain*. Englewood Cliffs, NJ: Prentice Hall.

Wong, B. (1985). Self-questioning instructional research. *Review of Educational Research*, **55**, 227–68.

Wood, D., Bruner, J.S. & Ross, G. (1976). The role of tutoring and problem solving. *Journal of Child Psychology and Psychiatry*, **17**, 89–100.

World Health Organisation (1980). *International Classification of Impairments, Disabilities and Handicaps: A Manual of Classification Relating to the Consequences of Disease*. Geneva: WHO.

Wright, B.D. & Stone, M.H. (1979). *Best Test Design: Rasch Measurement*. Chicago: MESA Press.

Wrightsman, L.S. (1962). The effects of anxiety, achievement motivation and task importance upon performance on an intelligence test. *Journal of Educational Psychology*, **53**, 150–56.

Yamamoto, K. (1963). Relationships between creative-thinking abilities of teachers, and achievement and adjustment of pupils. *Journal of Experimental Education*, **32**, 3–25.

Yamamoto, K. (1965). Effects of restriction of range and test unreliability on correlation between measures of intelligence and creative thinking. *British Journal of Educational Psychology*, **35**, 300–5.

Yinger, R. (1979). Routines in teacher planning. *Theory into Practice*, **18**(3), 163–9.

Yinger, R.J. (in press). The conversation of practice. In R. Cliff, R. Houston, & M. Pugach (eds), *Encouraging Reflective Practice: An Examination of Issues and Exemplars*. New York: Teachers College Press.

Zeidner, M. (1988). The relative severity of common classroom management strategies: The student's perspective. *British Journal of Educational Psychology*, **58**, 69–77.

AUTHOR INDEX

Ainley, J. 301, 302
Airasian, P. 386, 387
Alder, M. 287
Alexander, P.A. 397
Allen, V.L. 469
Ames, C. 301, 393
Anderson, C.C. 180
Anderson, J. 135
Anderson, J.R. 8
Anderson, R.C. 186, 396
Andrews, A.S. 409
Andrich, D. 390
Angus, M.J. 40
Annells, J.W. 352, 372
Applebee, A.N. 340, 351, 362, 372
Argyris, C. 17
Aronson, E. 100, 101, 102, 114
Asch, S. 100
Ashenden, D. 257, 429, 430
Ashman, A.F. 189
Ashton-Warner, S. 211, 462
Atkinson, J.W. 265
Atkinson, R.C. 208
Ausubel, D.P. 215, 234, 346

Baddeley, A.D. 217
Baird, J.R. 332, 334, 482, 513
Baker, C. 135, 145
Baldwin, G. 109, 110, 113
Balson, M. 519
Baltes, P.B. 55, 155
Bandura, A. 263, 271
Bar-Tal, D. 272, 274
Bassett, G.W. 519
Baumann, J.F. 348
Beaty, E. 20
Beez, W.V. 159, 167
Benbow, C.P. 108

Benware, C.A. 470
Bereiter, C. 122, 206, 309, 340, 349, 351, 352, 362, 373
Berliner, D. 485, 488, 489, 497
Berlyne, D.E. 268, 283, 462
Bernard, J. 119, 121, 146
Berne, E. 503
Bernstein, B. 119, 120
Bessant, B. 132
Beveridge, M. 82, 426
Bidell, T. 54
Biggs, J.B. 35, 48, 50, 56, 68, 72, 87, 88, 126, 165, 178, 180, 183, 206, 228, 244, 293, 309, 310, 313, 314, 316, 317, 318, 319, 320, 323, 327, 335, 355, 356, 359, 361, 373, 396, 410, 417, 418, 421, 437, 448, 460, 481, 482, 485
Binet, A. 152
Blakeslee, T. 107, 108
Blasi, A. 100, 101
Block, J.H. 388, 389, 404
Bloom, B.S. 12, 388, 389, 396, 404
Boag, C. 486, 487
Borke, H. 39
Borko, H. 84, 486, 488, 489, 490
Boud, D. 431, 441, 473, 482
Boulton-Lewis, G.M. 130, 131, 228, 234
Bourke, S.F. 125, 130, 504, 518
Bowden, J. 459
Bower, G.H. 218
Bracewell, R.J. 358, 363
Bradley, G. 394
Brady, L. 139, 140, 146
Braggett, E.J. 191
Brainerd, C.J. 50
Bransford, J.D. 331, 336
Britton, B. 372
Britton, J. 340

Broom, L. 118
Borphy, J. 258, 282, 284, 289, 300, 309, 311, 472
Brown, A.L. 13, 326, 348
Brown, A.S. 365
Brown, J.S. 6, 13, 206, 490
Bruner, J.S. 21, 36, 37, 38, 48, 49, 51, 223, 226, 464, 472
Bryant, P. 373
Budby, J. 130
Buggie, J. 133
Bullivant, B.M. 125, 126, 274
Burt, C. 158
Burtis, P.J. 47, 350, 351
Butler, S. 189, 192, 193, 199

Calder, B.J. 286
Callan, V.J. 117, 123
Campbell, W.J. 15, 437
Candy, P.C. 22, 28, 58, 59, 64, 449
Canter, L. 502
Cantwell, R. 347
Carmi, G. 81
Case, R. 35, 36, 53, 213, 214, 234
Cattell, R.B. 56, 155
Cazden, C. 124, 466
Ceci, S.J. 150
Chan, L.K.S. 192, 345
Chi, M. 84, 88, 213, 217, 396, 461, 485, 488
Chipman, S. 84
Christensen, C. 111
Choppin, B. 390, 391
Clanchy, J. 369, 373
Clarke, V.A. 108, 244
Clement, J.J. 77, 83
Clifford, M.M. 273, 274
Clough, E. 78, 85, 86, 424
Cloward, R.D. 470
Coates, T.J. 248
Cochran-Smith, M. 366, 367
Cognition and Technology Group 473
Cohen, M. 358, 368
Cohen, S.A. 462, 475
Colangelo, N. 190
Cole, M. 11
Cole, N.S. 20, 382, 383, 389, 403
Cole, P.G. 189, 192, 194, 198, 518
Coleman, J. 447

Collier, K.G. 468, 482
Collis, K.F. 72, 73, 75, 76, 88, 397
Comber, B. 518
Commons, M.C. 48
Commonwealth Schools Commission 395
Condry, J. 285
Connell, R.W. 26, 78, 118, 498, 515
Conway, R. 137, 193
Cook, R. 323
Corno, L. 165
Coulby, D. 495
Covington, M. 270, 271
Craik, F.I.M. 223, 310
Crocker, L.M. 390, 404, 440
Crooks, T.J. 404, 459
Cropley, A.J. 180, 182, 185, 186, 187, 198, 199
Cummins, J. 127, 129

Daiute, C. 366, 367
Dalton, B.M. 367
Das, J.P. 151, 160
Davey, C.P. 241
Davies, B. 93, 99, 102, 103, 104, 105, 106, 114, 455, 471, 491, 503
Davis, G.A. 191
de Charms, R. 270, 277, 291
Deci, E.L. 263, 278, 286, 302
de Lacey, P. 122, 123
de Lemos, M. 125
Demetriou, A. 35, 48, 55, 63
Dempster, F.N. 213
Dettman, H.W. 507
Deutsch, J.A. 209
Devin-Sheehan, L. 469
Dewey, J. 307
Dibley, J. 278, 302
Diederich, P.B. 421, 439
Dienes, Z.P. 51, 226, 472
Dillon, D. 493, 513
Directorate of Special Programs 129
Disibio, M. 219
di Vesta, F.J. 121, 127
Donaldson, M. 8, 39, 41
Doyle, W. 495
Dreikurs, R. 497, 506, 514
Driver, R. 22, 77, 80, 81, 82, 85, 88, 396
Dulay, H.C. 127

Dunkin, M.J. 448
Dupuis, M.M. 225
Durst, R.K. 361
Dweck, C.S. 273, 275

Ebbinghaus, H. 217
Education Commission of NSW 124
Edwards, A.D. 120
Edwards, J. 336
Egan, K. 40, 41, 51
Ehri, L. 365
Elashoff, J. 167
Elkind, D. 45, 46
Ellsworth, R. 503
Elton, L.R.B. 459
Emery, F. 481
Entwistle, N. 25, 310, 315, 459, 465
Epstein, H.T. 52
Erikson, E. 55, 56
Evans, G.T. 63, 122, 308, 464, 490
Eysenck, H.J. 157, 171, 242

Faigley, L. 357
Fantuzzo, J.W. 199, 471
Farber, J. 134
Farkas, G. 108
Faw, H.W. 212
Feather, N. 258
Feigelson, N. 97
Feiman-Nemser, S. 490
Fennema, E. 107
Fensham, P. 82
Fesl, E. 129
Festinger, L. 286
Field, T.W. 182
Finn, C.E. 379
Finn, J.D. 137, 167, 505
Fischer, K. 35, 36, 40, 48, 52, 54, 466
Fitts, P. 51
Fitzgerald, J. 351, 357, 363, 372
Fixx, J. 240
Flavell, J.H. 40, 208, 307
Flower, L. 350
Fontana, D. 254, 494, 519
Foon, A.E. 110
Frederiksen, J.R. 383, 391, 393, 449, 456
Freire, P. 211
French, J.R.P. 496

Freud, S. 57
Friedman, L. 107
Fryer, M. 185
Furth, H.G. 35, 50

Gagne, E.D. 212
Gallagher, J.J. 191
Garbarino, J. 287
Gardner, H. 41, 48, 150, 171
Gardner, J.M. 513
Gardner, R.W. 188
Garner, R. 328, 344
Gaudry, E. 244, 382
Getzels, J.W. 180, 182, 183
Gibbs, G. 327, 336
Gilbert, J. 77, 82
Gill, J. 111
Gill, P. 514
Gilligan, C. 99, 114, 492
Ginott, H. 497, 502
Ginsburg, H. 9, 35, 63, 114
Glaser, R. 160, 380, 386, 388, 397, 466
Glass, G.V. 504
Glasser, W. 434, 506, 509
Gnagey, W. 497
Goldstein, H. 391
Goleman, D. 154
Good, T.L. 137, 165, 166, 167, 258, 302, 518
Goodnow, J.J. 11, 146, 471
Gordon, T. 502
Gow, L. 318
Graham, D. 114
Grainger, A.J. 142
Grassby, A.J. 123
Graetz, B. 118, 119
Graves, D. 349, 363, 365, 374, 466
Green, J. 485, 486
Green, K. 411
Gronlund, N.E. 387, 415
Guilford, J.P. 177, 179, 396
Gunstone, R. 16, 24, 79, 80, 82, 83, 426
Guskey, T.R. 453
Guthrie, E.R. 135
Guthrie, E.S. 297
Guttman, L. 419

Hadamard, J. 41
Haddon, F.A. 182, 186

Hairston, M. 340, 363
Hales, L.W. 421
Halford, G.S. 35, 36
Hall, R.V. 511
Haller, E.P. 343
Hamaker, C. 212, 233
Hambleton, R.K. 415
Hamilton, J. 6
Hanley, E.N. 512
Harris, D. 432, 441
Hart, N.W.M. 211
Hartley, J. 212, 346
Hartshorne, H. 100
Harvey, O. 188, 396
Hasan, P. 182, 183
Hattie, J. 108, 465
Hau, K.T. 126, 274
Hausen, E. 359
Hawisher, G.E. 366
Hayes, J. 353, 354, 363
Healy, C.C. 11
Hearnshaw, L.S. 158, 171
Hebb, D.O. 154, 237, 269
Heckhausen, H. 275
Hegarty-Hazel, E. 320, 322
Hemming, J. 142
Henry, J. 267
Hepworth, A.J. 139
Hess, R.D. 463
Hickson, F. 191
Hidi, S. 206, 285, 302, 312, 346, 347, 348
Hill, W.F. 206
Hoffman, B. 391, 410
Hoggart, R. 121
Holdsworth, R. 514
Holland, J.L. 149, 183
Hollingsworth, S. 490
Holloway, S.D. 126, 274
Holt, J. 209
Hore, T. 422
Horin, A. 109
Horn, J.L. 155
Houghton, S. 508
Howard, R.W. 225
Howe, M.J.A. 219, 512
Huck, S.W. 421
Hudson, L. 179, 182, 183, 186
Hull, C.L. 260

Humphreys, M. 239
Hunsley, J. 244
Hunt, D.E. 188
Hunt, E. 192
Huot, B. 422
Husen, T. 447

Illich, I 13
Iran-Nejad, A. 205
Isaacs, E. 137
Izard, J. 391

Jackson P. 133, 326
Jackson, W. 368
James, W. 17, 216
Jensen, A.R. 157, 158, 159
Johansson, B. 398
Johnson, D.W. 141, 289, 290, 469, 471, 482
Johnson Abercrombie, M. 468, 482
Johnston, J.M. 506
Jones, J. 107, 110
Jones, R.M. 183
Jopson, D. 125, 274
Joynson, R.B. 158, 171
Jung, C. 56
Just, M. 373

Kagan, D. 485
Kagan, J. 188
Kamin, L.J. 153, 154, 157, 159
Karmel, P.H. 25
Kassin, S.M. 219
Katz, M.B. 132
Kaufman, A.S. 192
Keavney, G. 248
Keeves, J.P. 152, 388
Kelly, G.A. 188
Khoo, C. 124
King, A. 470
Kinman, J. 135
Kirby, J.R. 161, 171, 189, 192, 199, 320,
        339, 340, 341, 342, 343, 346, 347,
        349, 371, 373, 433
Klich, L. 162
Knowles, M. 57, 64
Knox, A.B. 55, 56
Kogan, N. 188, 189
Kohlberg, L. 34, 95

Kolb, D.A. 189
Kounin, J. 264, 457, 500, 518
Kozma, R.B. 367
Kramer, J.J. 191, 192
Kratzing, M. 327
Kruglanski, A. 287
Krywaniuk, L. 162
Kuhn, T. 22
Kurtines, W. 98, 138
Kurzeja, D. 330

Labov, W. 121
Lai, K.T.P. 389
Langer, J. 466
Larkin, A.L. 504
Lashley, K.S. 224
Lawrence, J. 308
Lawson, M.J. 308
Leach, D.J. 250
Leder, G. 107
Lee, N.Y.A. 319
Leinhardt, G. 17, 84, 485, 486, 488
Lepper, M. 287, 288
Lett, W.R. 503
Levinson, D. 55, 56, 64
Liebert, R.M. 264
Linn, M.C. 107, 108
Linn, R.L. 440
Lloyd, P. 134
Lonka, K. 423
Lott, G.W. 463
Lovell, K. 35, 50
Lovibond, S.H. 292
Luria, A.R. 160
Lowenbraun, S. 193
Lybeck, L. 398

McClelland, D.C. 119, 265
McCutchen, D. 322, 350
McDiarmid, G. 134
McDonald-Ross, R.M. 387
McGeoch, J.A. 217
McGregor, D. 292
McInerney, D. 123
McKeachie, W.J. 324, 328, 447, 469
MacKenzie, A. 228, 233, 472
McKinney, J.D. 192
McLaren, J. 356, 361

McLean, L.D. 383, 411
MacMillan, D. 108
Maccoby, E.E. 106
Mackay, C.K. 182
Mackay, D. 211
Mager, R. 387
Maguire, T.O. 395
Malin, M. 131, 145
Mandaglio, S. 249
Mandler, J.M. 224, 363
Marsh, H.W. 107, 108, 110, 272
Marsh, R. 52
Marshall, H.H. 485
Marso, R.N. 411, 413, 440
Martin, E. 77, 327
Marton, F. 20, 28, 309, 310, 323, 336,
    396, 397, 398, 399, 459
Maslach, C. 249
Mason, J.M. 41
Masters, G.N. 383, 395, 410, 411, 413, 416,
    419, 429, 431, 435, 437, 438, 441
Mehrabian, A. 262
Meichenbaum, D. 167
Messick, S. 384, 395
Meyer, P. 102
Meyer, W.U. 273
Milgram, S. 101, 113
Miller, G.A. 206, 213
Miller, I.W. 275
Miller, J.S. 283
Molloy, G.N. 241, 287
Moore, P.J. 308, 343, 433, 470
Morgan, M. 287
Morris, P. 393
Mosston, M. 283
Moulton, R.W. 266
Munn, P. 131
Myers, M. 343

Naylor, F. 243
Neill, A.S. 286
Neisser, U. 219, 220
Newble, D. 318, 473
Newman, H.H. 158
New South Wales Department of Education
    14, 124, 135, 136, 190, 195, 253
Newkirk, T. 372
Nickerson, R.S. 308, 324, 391, 403

Nix, P. 107
Norman, D.A. 234
Novak, J.D. 225, 309, 424
Nuthall, G. 222

Oakes, J. 107
O'Connor, P. 249
Office of the Commissioner for Community
    Relations 134
Ogilvie, M. 314
O'Neill, A. 243
O'Neill, M. 185
Otto, R. 253, 254

Packard, R.G. 510
Paivio, A. 51
Palincsar, A.S. 470, 481
Pallas, A.M. 107
Pallett, R. 75
Paris, S.G. 8, 339, 342, 343, 345, 371
Pauk, W. 327
Pearsall, R. 495
Pearson, P.D. 342
Penrose, A. 346, 361
Perfetti, C.A. 342
Perkins, D.N. 84, 327
Perry, W.G. 21
Peters, W. 141
Peterson, C. 104
Peterson, P.L. 464
Pezzullo, T.R. 180
Pflaum, S.W. 341
Phillips, D.C. 98
Phillips, S. 109
Piaget, J. 34, 36, 37, 38, 39, 44, 46, 77, 91
Pierce, C. 123, 249, 253
Pines, M. 98, 250
Pink, W. 513, 514
Pintrich, P. 310, 326, 328
Piolat, A. 366
Polya, G. 336
Poole, M.E. 120
Popham, W.J. 386
Porter, A. 462
Pramling, I. 20, 340
Premack, D. 262
Pribram, K.H. 219
Purkey, W.W. 270

Quay, H.C. 193, 194
Quigley, S.P. 193

Ramsden, P. 24, 317, 323, 325, 392, 397,
    454, 459, 460, 482
Raphael, T. 356, 363
Raucher, H. 141
Raudenbush, S.W. 447
Rayner, K. 373
Reid, W.A. 12, 476
Renzulli, J.S. 189
Resnick, L.B. 10, 28, 52, 81
Rest, J. 138
Reynolds, M.C. 195
Rickards, J. 345, 361
Rikys, P. 129
Rinehart, S. 348
Robinson, F. 330
Robinson, G. 170, 192
Rogers, B. 519
Rose, M. 357
Rosenbaum, J. 165
Rosenthal, R. 137, 167
Roth, K. 463
Rotter, J.B. 270
Rowe, K.J. 111
Rushton, J. 98
Russell, T. 25
Ryle, G. 7

Sabers, D. 489
Salgado, G. 356
Samuelowicz, K. 126
Sarason, S. 244
Sarros, A. 249
Sarros, J. 394
Satterly, D. 381, 389, 404
Scardamalia, M. 349, 351
Schaie, K. 55, 56
Schatzman, O. 119
Schiefele, U. 302, 312
Schlaefli, A. 138
Schmeck, R. 336
Schofield, M. 103, 113
Scribner, S. 11, 150
Scriven, M. 380
Scruggs, T. 472
Seligman, M.E.P. 5, 274

Shaughnessy, M.F. 190
Shavelson, R. 16
Shayer, M. 74
Shepard, L.A. 379, 383, 394
Shuell, T.J. 448, 456, 485
Shulman, L. 486, 488
Shuy, R. 121
Siegler, R.S. 35
Silberman, C.E. 137
Skinner, B.F. 219, 260
Slavin, R.E. 166, 289, 290, 403, 471
Slee, R. 494, 513, 519
Snow, R.E. 391, 400, 404
Snowman, J. 326
Snyder, B.R. 459
Solomon, J. 77, 78
Spalding, I. 134
Sparkes, R. 134
Spearman, C. 154
Spearrit, D. 391, 404
Spinks, J. 319, 322
Spivey, N. 355
Starch, D. 421
Stein, N. 352, 353, 359
Steinkamp, M. 107, 108
Sternberg, R.J. 10, 28, 150, 151, 162, 163,
          169, 172, 189
Stevens, R. 348
Stevenson, H. 463
Stipek, D. 457
Stokes, M.J. 318
Strauss, S. 77, 83
Strunk, W. 353, 354, 373
Suchman, J.R. 283, 462
Suppes, P. 19
Swanson, H.L. 87, 485, 489
Sweller, J. 84, 461

Tabberer, R. 326
Tang, D.K.T. 82
Tang, K.C.C. 392, 471
Tavener, J. 469
Taylor, E. 309
Taylor, J.C. 85, 88, 466
Telfer, R. 17, 248, 293, 294, 490, 507, 517
Terman, L.M. 154, 189
Thomas, A. 275
Thomas, D.R. 511

Thomas, E.L. 330
Thorndike, R.L. 167
Thurstone, L.L. 155
Tibbetts, S.L. 135
Tobin, K. 20, 293, 391, 458, 477, 503
Tomporowski, P.D. 241
Torrance, E.P. 180, 182, 183, 184, 186,
          187, 197, 199
Tough, A. 58
Townsend, M. 421
Trigwell, K. 313
Tulving, E. 221
Turbill, J. 363, 374
Turiel, E. 138
Turney, C. 210, 232
Tyler, L.E. 151, 152

Valsiner, J. 54
van Kraayernoord, C. 192
Van Rossum, E.J. 317, 323
Vaughan, W.J.A. 14
Veenman, S. 490
Vernon, P.E. 154 158, 171
Victorian Education Gazett 14, 15
Viennot, L. 16
Volet, S. 55, 56, 317, 328
Von Bertalanffy, L. 448
Vosniadou, S. 53, 67, 397
Vygotsky, L.S. 54, 466

Wall, M. 241
Wallace, I. 94
Wallach, M. 182
Wang, M.C. 199, 317
Warren, D.H. 193
Watkins, D.A. 310, 318, 320, 323
Watson, H.J. 141
Watson, J.B. 297
Watts, M.D. 82
Wax, R. 491
Wechsler, D. 55, 153
Weiner, B. 166, 272, 278, 302
Weinstein, C. 324
Welker, R. 486
White, R.T. 88, 308, 332, 334, 383, 458,
          477
White, R.W. 268
Wiggins, G. 383, 411

Williams, P. 199
Williams, T. 118
Willms, J.D. 107
Winkler, R.L. 512
Winograd, P.N. 348
Winter, S.J. 469
Witkin, H. 188
Wittrock, M.C. 24, 223, 225, 226, 234
Wong, B. 331, 334
Wood, D. 465

World Health Organization 191
Wright, B.D. 390
Wrightsman, L.S. 243

Yamamoto, K. 180, 185
Yinger, R.J. 485, 486, 497

Zeidner, M. 508
Zinsser, W. 374

SUBJECT INDEX

Note: A **bold** entry refers to the Glossary where the term is defined.

Abilities 149–52, **521**
  convergent 177–8, **524**
  divergent 177–87, 433, **525**
  grouping by 164–6, 266, **521**
  Level 1, Level 2 157
  structure of 154–5
Aboriginal education 122, 129–32
  attainments of aboriginal students 122, 162
  bicultural education 129–32
acculturation 117–18, 132–3, **521**
achieving **521**
  approach 310, 312–15, 316–22
  motive 313–16
  strategy 313–16, 325
  see also 'study skills'
adolescents 46–7, 55, 94, 264
advanced organisers 212, 246, **521**
aggression 264, **521**
aims see 'schools, schooling'
allocentricity, allocentric thought 46, 92, 94–7, 100, **521**
alternative frameworks 76–84, **521**
  see also 'conceptions, misconceptions of natural phenomena'
altruism 98, **521**
anxiety 241–9, 457, **521**
  computer 108, 244
  number 244
  state 244
  teacher, burnout 123, 247–50, **522, 532**
  trait 242–4, 458
  test 244, 319, 322, 382
approaches to learning 310–23, **521**
  see also 'achieving', 'deep', 'surface' and 'teaching' 451–3, 457–75

arithmetic *see* 'mathematics'
arousal 208, 237–44, **522**
  and information processing 237–41
  exertion arousal 240–1
  personality differences in 241–4
  see also 'stress'
Asian students 125–6, 274
assessment 381–2, 458–9, **522**
  accreditation 12, 437–8, **521**
  'authentic' 353, 395
  and hidden curriculum 138
  common assessment tasks (CATs) 429–31, 432, 434–5, 436–7, 438, **522**
  divergent methods of 433
  progressive 382
  self-assessment 12, 380, 431–2, 473, **530**
  targets 400, 407, 415
  See also 'criterion-referenced testing', 'evaluation' 'norm-referenced testing'
attention 208–12
  see also 'sensory register'
attributions for success/failure 258, 272–5, 308, 465, **522**

behaviour modification 263, 275, 509–13, **522**
behaviourism 206, 382, 389, **522**
bicultural education *see* 'Aboriginal education'
Bloom taxonomy 396, 397, 400
burnout, *see* 'stress on teachers' **522**

classroom management 297–8, 485, 487, 488–513, 527
  discipline 493–6, **525**
  structure 496–8
  operating procedures 499–501

teacher-student collaboration 491–3
climate 318
    classroom 294–6, 457, 459, 498–9, 506, **522**
    school 292–4
coding (as in encoding) 213, 215–16, 217, 269, **525**
    generic codes 223–4
    surface codes 223–4
cognitive styles 187–9, 314, **523**
competencies 151–2, **523**
competition *see also* 'motivation, achievement' 266–7, 289–90
concept maps 225, 424, **523**
conceptions
    misconceptions of natural phenomena 16, 24, 395, 426, 463
    of evaluation 382–4, 389, 394–5
    of learning 20–7, 317, 382–3, 389–90, 412, **523**
    of teaching 24–7, 454, 455
conditioning **523**
    classical 260, 296–7
    operant (instrumental) 260–3
    see also 'behaviour modification'
conformity 100–2, **524**
conservation, in cognitive development 43–4, **524**
constructivism 22–4, 35, 80, 206, 449, 464, **524**
context, and
    conformity 100–2
    intelligent 160
    learning (situated learning/cognition) 6, 8, 11, 12, 13, 206, 309, **530**
    social development 91
    strategy training 327–9
    transfer 324
counselling and guidance 249–51
creativity 180–2, **524**
    and divergent ability 180–2
    and IQ 180
criterion-referenced testing (CRT) 266, 386–90, 391, 395, 398, 408, 427, 436, **524**
    test construction 415
culture, and education 117, 143
curriculum 12, 13–16, 85, **524**

and evaluation 379–80
evaluation of 380
knowledge 488
implicit/hidden 133–8
objectives 72–6, 386–90, 449, 451, 452, 462
see also 'schools, aims of'

decoding, *see* 'reading'
deep **524**
    achieving 313, 314, 325
    approach 310, 312–13, 314–15, 316–22, 460–75
    motive 312, 316
    strategy 312, 313, 316, 325
development **524**
    adult 46, 55–9
    affect in 40, 41
    and learning 36, 48–55, 69, 205
    cognitive 22, 32–59, **524**
    language 33, 37, 38–9, 340–3, 349–51
    moral 91–102
    neo-Piagetian theory 35–6, 48–9
    Piagetian stage theory 34–7, 38, 48–50
    stages 33–4, 36–7
    social 91–105
discipline, *see* 'classroom management' **525**
divergent thinking 117–87, 433, **525**
    and attainment 182–3, 185
    and creativity 180–2
    factors producing 180
    in the classroom 182–7
    measurement of 178–80
    see also 'creativity'

economics teaching 418
egocentricity, egocentric thought 39–40, 46–7, **525**
    and moral development 92–3, 95–6, 100
English
    as a second language (ESL) 123–9, **525**
    standard/non standard 119–22, **528**, **531**
essay **525**
    as a means of evaluation 392, 420–4
    writing 313–14, 322–3, 349–69, 450, 466–7
evaluation 379–99, **525**

and assessment 379–80
   formative and summative 380, 382,
      387, **525**, **531**
   curriculum 380
   process 381
   quantitative and qualitative conceptions
      of 382–4
   in relation to learning 379–84, 391–9
   see also 'criterion-referenced/norm-ref-
      erenced testing'
exceptionality 175–95
   giftedness 175–7, 189–91
expert-novice 84–5, 160, 397, 485, 487,
      488–90, 491–513, **525**
extinction 261, 262, **525**

forgetting 217–19
   associative interference 217
friendship 103–4

gender 105–11
   in moral development 99–100
   and conformity 101
   differences in school subjects 106–11
   and coed schools 109–11
   sexism in schools 135–7
generativity, in learning 225, **525**
geography teaching 69–70, 228–9
grading 433–8

heuristics 329–32, **525**, **526**
history teaching 76

information integration theory, *see* 'intelli-
      gence, theories of'
information-processing 206–22, **526**
intelligence 149–67, 317, **526**
   academic and everyday 150–1
   crystallised, flind 56, 155–7
   generality of 150–2
   IQ 152–9, 165–7, 182, 448, 453, **526**
   nature-nurture controversy 157–9
   theories of 150, 153–64
      information integration 160–2
      triarchic theory 162–4
introversion-extroversion 242–3
item response theory 390–1, 411, 415,
      419, 438, **526**

knowledge
   base; prior knowledge 53, 460, 461–4,
      526
   conditional 7–10, 205, 307, 400, **523**
   in teaching 17, 486, 488–90, 515
   intuitive 41
   metacognitive 8
   procedural 7–9, 11, 50, 205, 307, 309,
      400, 488, 515, **529**
   propositional (see 'declarative')
   rhetorical 353
   tacit 8, 205
   see also 'constructivism'

Language 8, 23
   and development 33, 37, 38–9
   second language learning 126–9,
      317–18
   standard/non-standard English 119–23
   see also 'reading', 'writing'
learned helplessness 270, 274–5, **526**
learning **526**
   activity in 226, 460, 461, 472–3
   and relation to evaluation 379–84,
      391–9
   and systems theory 447–57
   and teaching 447–77
   and writing 361–2
   approaches to, *see* 'achieving', 'deep',
      'surface' **521**
   collaborative, cooperative 289–90, 471,
      523
   conceptions of, *see* 'conceptions' 20–6
   constructivist theory of, *see* 'construc-
      tivism'
   cycles 70–2, **526**
   disabilities 11, 191-2, 251
   everyday 5–16
   from errors 308, 463–4
   from text 345–9
   information processing models of 206–8
   intentional 309, 314–15
   linear metaphors for 205–6
   mastery 388–90, **527**
   meaning of 215–16, 269, 322
   meaningful 215–16, 223–9, 527
   outcomes (*see also* 'SOLO taxonomy')
      319–21, 448, 453–5, 526

preparedness for 6–7, 9, 529
poblem-based 328, **529**
processes *see also* 'approaches' and
            'achieving', 'deep', and 'surface'
in acquiring and structuring knowledge
            53, 67–8
rote 215–16, **530**
school *see also* 'schools', 'schooling' 10–16
skills 51
social nature of 11, 23, 35, 54–5, 460,
            461, 465–73
style 189
see also particular content subjects
            ('mathematics', 'geography', etc.)
            'constructivism'
Learning Process Questionnaire (LPQ)
            314, 315–18, 389
locus of control 270–1, 317, **526**
long-term memory 217–22, **527**
    episodic memory 221–2
    mnemonics 218–19
    process in remembering 219–21
    procedural memory 221–2
    semantic memory 220–2

mastery learning 388–90, 391, 434, **527**
mathematics teaching 51–2, 75–6, 226–8,
            266, 417, 430, 462, 464
    see also 'gender differences'
memory, see 'working memory', 'long-
            term memory' **527**
mentor relations 11–12
metacognition 307–10, 316–32, 380, **527**
    and age 56
    and planning 56, 161, 307–8
    and text-processing 339–40, 433
    and approaches to learning 309–15
    in reading 339–40, 342–4
    in teaching 456–7
    in writing 352–61
    strategy training 323–32, 464
    see also 'metalearning', 'metateaching'
metalearning 308–10, 317, 327, 457, **527**
metateaching 456–7, 460, **527**
modelling 263–4, **527**
modes in cognitive development 36–55,
            71–6, 205, **527**
    concrete-symbolic 37, 41–4, 49, **523**

formal 37, 44–8, 49, **525**
ikonic 36, 38–41, 44, 49, 77, 221–2,
            526
in moral development 92–4
postformal 37, 47–8, 49, **529**
sensori-motor 36–8, 49, **530**, **531**
multimodal/intermodal processes 48,
            50–2
processes relating to change
            across modes 50–5
            within modes 67–76
moral education 133–43
motivation 257–75, 281–99, **527–8**
    achievement 258, 259, 264–68, **521**
    and context 258, 292–8, 369, 400, 461
    and expectations of success 258–9,
            270–5, 290–1
    and value of task 258–9, 259–70
    as felt need 10, 25, 257–8, 281, 312
    effects of reward on 286–8
    expectancy-value theory 258–9, 465,
            525
    extriosic (instrumental) 258–63, 285,
            457, **525**
    in approaches to learning (*see also*
            'achieving, motive', 'deep,
            motive', surface, motive') 310–16
    intrinsic 10, 182, 211, 216, 258,
            259–60, 264, 268–71, 281–8,
            461, 465, **526**
    social 258, 259, 263–4, 285, 288–90,
            531
multicultural education, multiculturalism
            123–6, **528**
multiple choice test, *see* 'objective test'

neuroticism-stability 242–4
norm-referenced testing (NRT) 266,
            384–6, 387, 390, 393, 408, 428,
            435–6, 437, **528**
    test construction 412–14
note-taking 312, 346–9
novice, *see* 'expert-novice'

objectives test, *see* 'test, objective'
overviews 212

phenomenography 397–9, **528**

physiology
  in cognitive development 52–3
  in preparedness for learning 9, **529**
  and brain deterioration 55–6
  physical handicap 193
  and arousal 237–8, **522**
planning 56, 161–2, 207, 307, **529**
  as metacognition 56, 161, 307–8
  in study 314, 326
  in teaching 486, 489–90
  in writing 349–51, 354–6, 365, 367
praise 262, 263, 285–6, 288–9
precoding 207–12, **529**
presage-process-product (3P) model **529**
  re classroom 448–56
  re school 475–7
problem-based learning 473–5, **529**
punishment 260, 261, 263, 264, 297, 457,
    476, 494–6, 505–9, **529**

questions, questioning 458, 503–4

racism 126, 134, 137
Rasch model, *see* 'item response theory'
reading 339–49
  comprehension 340–5
  decoding 340–3
  learning to read 339–45
  levels of textual unit 341–3
  'organic' 462
  reading to learn 345–9
recoding 216, 269–70, 465, **529**
rehearsal 215, **530**
  see also 'rote learning'
reinforcement 260–3, **530**
remembering, *see* 'long-term memory'

scaffolding, *see* 'learning, social nature of' **530**
scheme 216, 224, 312, **530**
schools, schooling
  aims of 9–10, 21
    of various state departments 10,
      13–15, 25, 133, 308
  as a system 450, 475–7, 513–14
  bureaucracy in 10, 12, 15, 16
  efficacy of 447–8
  school learning and everyday learning
    5–16, 308–10, 318

science teaching 16, 24, 73–5, 77–84, 424–6
  see also 'Conceptions, misconceptions of
    natural phenomena'
self-concept 270–2, 320, 389, **530**
self-direction
  in learning 58–9
  in assessment 400, 431–3, 473, **530**
  in educational aims 10, 13–14, 25, 308
self-efficacy 258, 271–2, 451, 453, **530**
sensory register 207–12, **531**
short-term memory, *see* 'working memory'
simultaneous/successive synthesis 160–2
situated learning, cognition 6, 8, 11, 12,
    206, 309, **531**
social class 118–23
  private/public schooling 118–19
  and teacher stress 249
sociocentric thought 92, 93–6, 99, 100, **531**
SOLO taxonomy 67, 68–76, 103, 320, **531**
  and curriculum objectives 72–6
  and assessment 396–7, 398, 400,
    416–20, 422, 423, 434–5, 471
  particular SOLO levels 68–76
  and modes 71–2
special education, schools 18–19
  catering for special needs 175, 189–95
    giftedness 189–91
  learning disabilities 191–2
  physical handicap 193
  behavior disorder 193
  mainstreaming 194–5
story grammar 224, 363–4
strategies **531**
  in medical diagnosis 323
  in intentional learning 314–15
  reading 340, 342–5, 433
  Study 310, 324–32
  vs. tactics 326
  see also 'approaches to learning', 'study skills'
streaming, *see* 'ability grouping' **531**
stress, nature of 208, 241, **531**
  exam 246, 382
  during practice teaching 247–8
  management of 244–8, 250
  on teachers, burnout 123, 248–50, **522**,
    532
  effects an approach to learning 322,
    457, 459

Study Process Questionnaire (SPQ) 316, 318
study skills 251, 314, 316
    teaching 324–32, 454
summarising 346–9
surface **532**
    -achieving 314
    approach 310–12, 314–15, 316–22, 457–60
    codes 223–4
    motive 311
    strategy 311, 325
symbol systems 7, 9, 13, 33, 43
    see also 'concrete-symbolic' in Modes in cognitive development
systems theory 447–53, 457, 494, **532**

teaching 447–77, 485–515
    and approaches to learning 457–77
    conceptions of 24–7, 454, 455
    contexts for good learning 460–75
    craft knowledge of 17, 486
    espoused theory 17–19
    expertise in 17, 486–90
    interaction with students 104–5, 183–6, 491–3, 502–5
    metaphors for 485–6, 491
    peer teaching 469–71
    professional nature of 16–19
    psychology's contribution to 17
    teacher expectations 131, 137–8, 166–7
    theory in-use 17–19
    see also 'classroom management'
tests, testing 334–400, 407–38, **532**
    'backwash' on learning 391–5, 418, 449–50, **522**
    criterion-referenced 386–90, **524**

distortion 409–10
intelligence 152–9
item response theory 390–1, **526**
norm-referenced 384–6, 490
objective (inc. multiple choice) 392, 410, 412–20, **528**
ordered outcome 416–20, **528**
reliability 407–8, 421–2, **530**
short answer 415–16
teacher-made tests 410–12
validity 409, **532**
text processing **339–69**
    see also 'note-taking', 'reading', 'writing'
Theory X, Theory Y 258, 292–3, 295–6, 457, 465, 494, **532**

variability 210, **533**

wait-time, *see* 'questions'
working memory 207, 208, 212–16, 321–2, **533**
    arousal and perferenced 239–41, 245–8
    in reading 342
    in writing 349
    optimising use of 213–14
    processes in 214–16
    see also 'coding', 'rehearsal'
writing 312, 339–40, 349–69
    and learning 361–2
    and word processors 365–9
    approaches to essay writing 313–14, 322–3, 360–1, 433, 450
    development of 349–51
    knowledge-telling 351–2, 423, 424
    reflective 352–62
    teaching 362–9, 466–7
    see also 'essay'